FIFTH EDITION

Transportation

FIFTH EDITION

Transportation

John J. Coyle

Edward J. Bardi

Robert A. Novack

South-Western College Publishing
Thomson Learning™

Australia • Canada • Denmark • Japan • Mexico • New Zealand • Philippines
Puerto Rico • Singapore • South Africa • Spain • United Kingdom • United States

Transportation 5e, by John J. Coyle, Edward J. Bardi, and Robert A. Novack

Acquisitions Editor: Steve Scoble
Developmental Editor: Mardell Toomey
Marketing Manager: Joseph A. Sabatino
Production Editor: Anne Chimenti
Manufacturing Coordinator: Sandee Mileweski
Internal Design: Jennifer Lambert
Cover Design: Jennifer Lambert
Cover Photographer: © Steve Uzzell
Production House: D&G Limited, LLC
Printer: R. R. Donnelley & Sons Company

Printed in the United States of America
2 3 4 5 02 01 00 99

For more information contact South-Western College Publishing, 5101 Madison Road, Cincinnati, Ohio, 45227 or find us on the Internet at http://www.swcollege.com

For permission to use material from this text or product, contact us by

- **telephone: 1-800-730-2214**
- **fax: 1-800-730-2215**
- **web: http://www.thomsonrights.com**

Library of Congress Cataloging-in-Publication Data

Coyle, John Joseph, [DATE]
Transportation / John J. Coyle, Edward J. Bardi, Robert A. Novack.
--5th ed.
p. cm.
Includes bibliographical references and index.
ISBN 0-538-88180-1
1. Transportation. I. Bardi, Edward J., [DATE] II. Novack, Robert A. III. Title
HE151.C88 1999
388--dc21 99-16907

This book is printed on acid-free paper.

To our wives, Barbara, Carol, and Judith for all their support and sacrifice.

Contents

Preface

Many trends that stem from the economic deregulation of transportation during the last two decades are intensifying as we enter the new millenium. The buying and selling of transportation services today occurs in a highly complex and rapidly changing environment. That the transportation marketplace has undergone volatile changes is evidenced in the evolution of third-party providers, partnerships between shippers and carriers, an increase in intermodal movements, and a decrease in logistics expense as a percent of GDP.

Since the last edition of our book, government regulation of the modes of transportation has continued to be eliminated. The ICC has been replaced by the Surface Transportation Board, whose major responsibility is economic regulation of the railroad industry and significant changes have taken place in international ocean regulation. All modes of transportation must now be compliant with antitrust regulations.

These changes in government intervention allow carriers and shippers to do business in a market that is ruled by the laws of supply and demand while outsourcing continues to grow. Third-party providers, both asset and non-asset based, are beginning to offer shippers more than just transportation services. Some third parties offer expanded services in warehousing, inventory management, order management information technology, financial services, and consulting that enable them to more completely manage the activities in the supply chain. With these expanded services, third parties and shippers are beginning to develop more sophisticated and complex relationships.

Technology used in the transportation industry has also expanded rapidly. Carriers and third parties find that many technologies no longer provide a competitive advantage and are needed simply as a basic requirement for doing business. Satellite technology, bar coding, global positioning systems, and locator systems for vehicles are now commonplace for many carriers.

Innovations in routing and asset utilization technology have allowed many carriers to eliminate operating costs from their fleets. The use of enterprise resource planning (ERP) and transportation requirements planning (TRP) systems by shippers has allowed them to share forecasts and timely shipment information with carriers to further improve asset productivity.

Another major change since the last edition of ***Transportation*** is the consolidation of carriers in several modal markets. Mergers and acquisitions in the rail industry include the joining of the Union Pacific and Southern Pacific into a single entity. Parts of Conrail were bought by the Norfolk Southern with the remainder being purchased by CSX, basically eliminating the once government-owned entity. Federal Express purchased RPS, Roberts, Express, and Caliber Logistics from Roadway creating a formidable competitor in the small package express industry with UPS and the U.S. Postal System.

Finally, deregulation has given carriers the incentive to understand their costs. The development and implementation of activity-based costing (ABC) systems by many carriers allows them to understand both market and customer profitability. This knowledge gives carriers the tools to more effectively price their services and manage their overall profitability.

With all of these changes, transportation still provides the basic service of moving people and freight. This movement creates time, place, and quantity utilities for the commodoties moved. With the explosion of supply chain management over the last several years, the utilities created by transportation have taken on heightened meaning. The management of product, information, and cash flows in the supply chain are all influenced by transportation cost and quality. Sophisticated carriers and shippers no longer evaluate the role of transportation in the supply chain by price alone. The new standard used is transportation value: the relationship between service and least total cost. Increased prices for better service are more than offset by reductions in inventory and loss and damage. Transportation has become a critical cost and service component in the supply chain.

Change in the transportation industry has been dramatic and revolutionary during the last two decades. ***Transportation*** is an important tool for understanding this dynamic field for both students and professionals alike. At the same time, this book provides readers with a solid background and history of transportation that emphasizes the fundamental role and importance the industry plays in our society. This is a text written for students at the undergraduate and graduate levels, but it is equally suitable as a reference for business practitioners in the transportation industry.

NEW TO THIS EDITION

- While continuing to use a managerial approach in the fifth edition, we pay special attention to both perspectives of the marketplace—that of carriers and of shippers. This increased emphasis is evident in three new chapters:

  "Relationship Management" (Chapter 12), explores managing relationships between carriers and shippers in today's logistics environment (especially significant given the growth of third-party providers). This chapter introduces the different types of relationships found in transportation/logistics as well as ways to manage these relationships.

  "Information Management and Technology" (Chapter 13), highlights the importance of managing information in successful supply chain implementation. Special attention is given to information and technology used to manage the transportation process. This chapter covers basic data gathering techniques for transportation management, data transmission technologies, and decision tools for optimizing the transportation process for both carriers and shippers.

  "Shipper/Carrier Network Strategies" (Chapter 14), focuses on the shipper/carrier transportation infrastructure and processes used to successfully complete the transportation transaction. An important topic examined in this chapter is how shippers can help carriers reduce their operating expenses in transporting freight. This follows in the spirit of supply chain management of eliminating costs, rather than shifting them to other supply chain partners. This chapter also discusses how shippers manage their transportation process and how carriers design and operate their transportation networks.

- **New organization** of the book. The fifth edition of ***Transportation*** is divided into four parts and includes a total of 14 chapters. **Part 1** features the role and importance of transportation. **Part 2** presents an overview of the five major modes of transportation as well as intermodal carriers and international transportation. **Part 3** focuses on carrier management and **Part 4** discusses topics pertinent to both shippers and carriers and technology.

• **Walter Weart**, new member of the writing team, has added more recent tables, examples and recommended readings, assuring that this edition is as up-to-date as possible.

• To support the instructor, Walter Weart has written a **new instructor's manual** with a test bank (ISBN 0-324-00752-3). This supplement includes Learning Objectives, key terms and a detailed chapter outline for each chapter. There are notes for the cases, Internet activities, and other additional teaching materials. The testing material is comprised mainly of multiple choice, short answer and essay questions.

• Also new to this edition is an **appendix with URL listings** for all companies and organizations related to transportation that we mention in the text.

While making changes to the new edition, we retained features of the book that made previous editions successful: "Stop Offs" that expand chapter material and deepen students' understanding with real life examples, thorough chapter outlines, and summaries along with suggested readings and cases.

ACKNOWLEDGEMENTS

We wish to thank the following reviewers for their contributions:

Richard Barsness	Lehigh University
Michael Demetsky	University of Virginia
Phil Evers	University of Maryland
Jerry Foster	University of Colorado
Lester A. Hoel	University of Virginia
Clyde Walter	Iowa State University

The authors and South-Western College Publishing also wish to acknowledge the exceptional contribution of Walter Weart. Walter's academic affiliations include the University of Northern Colorado, Oakton Community College, where he served as department chair, College of Du Page, and William Harper College. Having used various editions of ***Transportation*** in his teaching experience, Walter has stepped forward to offer his invaluable assistance based on knowledge garnered as both academician as well as an executive and specialist in transportation in the business community. He has tirelessly researched, updated, and reworked articles and tables, rewritten portions of the text that were outdated, and has coordinated the materials of all authors to ensure 2000 copyright publication. Mr. Weart has also written the instructor's manual with the test bank that accompanies this text. Thank you, Wally, for all of your help.

John J. Coyle
Edward J. Bardi
Robert A. Novack

PART 1

The Role and Importance of Transportation

CHAPTER 1

Transportation, the Supply Chain, and the Economy

The 1990s: A Decade of Change
The Logistics Concept
The Supply Chain Concept
Total Cost Analysis
Stop Off: "Supply Chain Black Holes"
Business Logistics Activities
Quality, Value, and Customer Satisfaction
- Dimensions of Logistics and Transportation Quality
- Logistics Value
- Customer Satisfaction and Attitude

Transportation and the Economy
Historical Significance
Economic Significance
- Value of Goods
- Utility of Goods
- Transportation Patterns
- Gross Domestic Product

Environmental Significance
- The Environment
- Safety
- Substance Abuse

Social Significance
Political Significance
- Government Responsibility

Overview of Modern Transportation
Overview of Transportation Trends
Stop Off: "Challenges and Opportunities"
Demand for Transportation
Demand Measurement Units
Level of Aggregation
Demand Elasticity
Freight Transportation

Transportation is a vital activity in moving both freight and passengers around the world. The management of transportation is concerned with the overall purchase and control of this movement service used by a firm in achieving the objectives of its logistics process. **Business logistics** is the process of planning, implementing, and controlling the efficient and effective flow and storage of goods, services, and related information from the point of origin to the point of consumption for the purpose of conforming to customer requirements.[1] This definition specifically includes the importance of transportation in business logistics. Recently, a new term is being used to describe this flow and movement in an organizational environment: supply chain management. **Supply chain management** is an expanded version of the logistics process. Whereas logistics has traditionally focused its attention on coordinating the product, the information movement, and the flow activities of an individual firm, supply chain management is concerned with coordinating the product, information, cash movement, and flow activities in a **logistics channel environment.** The effective and efficient management of transportation has a significant impact on all three types of inter-firm flows and is critical in achieving supply chain integration and objectives.[2]

The objective of this chapter is to place emphasis on the importance of transportation to the individual firm as well as to the economy. Attention is given to how transportation functions within the realm of supply chain management and business logistics. Finally, the nature of transportation demand is discussed.

The 1990s: A Decade of Change

During the 1990s, many businesses throughout the United States were compelled to reevaluate their approach to doing business and to focus their attention upon some fundamentals to successful business operations, such as customer service, quality, and the value added by service and/or productivity. The external factors that resulted in this reexamination of business practices included intensified global competition and increased involvement in international markets, deregulation of transportation, mergers and acquisitions, and shrinking profit margins.[3]

The focus of attention on basics, such as the **value added** by customer service, attracted increasing management attention to logistics as a source of potential contribution to revitalizing the organizations and making them more competitive again. Although logistics has been a growing area of responsibility in many companies since the 1960s, it is fair to say that the profile of logistics managers in corporate

America was not as high in most companies prior to 1980 as it is today. Logistics managers tended to be regarded as hard-working individuals who played primarily a supporting role to marketing and manufacturing. However, the "back-to-basics" movement helped to change the profile level of logistics in the 1980s, particularly because a growing number of companies recognized the role that logistics is capable of playing *at the margin* in their strategic efforts to gain or regain a sustainable competitive edge.[4] Efficient transportation systems support such logistics practices as "just-in-time" inventory and manufacturing or "effective consumer response" in retail manufacturers such as General Motors and retailers such as Wal-Mart have used such techniques to gain lower cost and competitive market advantage.

The 1990s actually began on a continuing, evolutionary basis for logistics from the decades following World War II but quickly changed because of the exogenous variables mentioned above:

1. Globalization of business
2. Deregulation of transportation and a changing governmental infrastructure
3. Organizational changes in businesses
4. Rapidly changing technology[5]

Because the influence of these factors will continue to be felt throughout the 1990s, a brief explanation is in order here.

The globalization of business has had a tremendous impact on the way companies operate today. The scope of **globalization** runs the gamut from foreign sourcing in the procurement area and/or selective sales in other countries to multifaceted international distribution, manufacturing, and marketing strategies that encompass international production sites, multiple staging of inventory, countertrading in the sale of products, and so on. Whatever the situation, the cost of logistics as a percentage of total cost is greater for international ventures, and the complexity of logistics operations usually increases at a geometric rate in the international arena. Often if procurement is included, logistics is the single most important factor for successful international ventures.[6] Transportation, in particular, has been affected because of the distances involved both inbound to manufacturing from foreign sourcing and outbound for additional manufacturing or delivery to customers. Transportation may account for as much as 50 percent of the total logistics costs.

The changes in the transportation marketplace were accelerated with the advent of **deregulation** of air, motor, and rail carriers in the 1980s. A virtual revolution has occurred in the U.S. transportation system that has resulted in many fundamental changes —some positive, some negative. Overall, it is probably fair to say that the cost and/or quality of transportation service have improved for many shippers with only minor exceptions. In fact, transportation costs on a relative basis declined during the 1990s and played a major role in helping to lower overall logistics costs on a relative basis.

However, changes in government infrastructure have been far more widespread than what occurred in the U.S. transportation system. These changes include the deregulation of banking and communications, the deregulation of motor carrier transportation in Canada, and changes in the European economic community, resulting in more open market structures in the 1990s. The opening up of Eastern Europe and the dissolution of the USSR were additional changes. The North American Free Trade Agreement (NAFTA) is yet another governmental change that will affect transportation and the globalization factor discussed above.

The restructuring of business organizations has also been a factor affecting logistics (mergers, acquisitions, leveraged buyouts [LBOs], employee stock ownership plans [ESOPs], spin-offs, etc.). In some instances, the logistics functions have been consolidated into one to streamline the organization and gain reduced costs and added efficiencies. The flattening of organizations has also led to other changes, particularly the outsourcing of supplies and/or services and the growth of third-party logistics organizations who supply all or part of the logistics services required. Outsourcing logistics activities has also been a manifestation of the focus upon core competencies.

Another factor is the rapidly changing **technology** and, in particular, the changes in computer hardware and software. The significant price reductions for powerful computer equipment have helped bring about better inventory control, better equipment scheduling, more efficient rating of transportation movements, and so on. The technological changes in communications (such as satellite global positioning systems to maintain contact with motor carrier fleets) have helped to improve service quality to the extent that motor carrier companies are now able to meet narrowly defined time windows for pickups and deliveries. The interface between communication technology and computers is another area that has tremendous potential for logistics. These items are just a tip of the iceberg; many other things could be included in this area, such as bar coding and robotics.[7]

In concluding this section, a few brief comments about the development of logistics prior to the 1980s should be provided. Logistics, as we know it today, began to develop after World War II in response to internal cost pressures associated with expanding product lines and increased product value, as well as external pressures from more competitive market conditions. All of these factors led to activities being revamped in companies on the physical distribution side of logistics. Essentially, what happened in many cases was an **integration** of outbound transportation and field warehousing to more systematically examine trade-offs that would result in overall lower costs (see Figure 1.1). Integration was a key element even during this

FIGURE 1.1 Typical Logistics Network—Physical Distribution

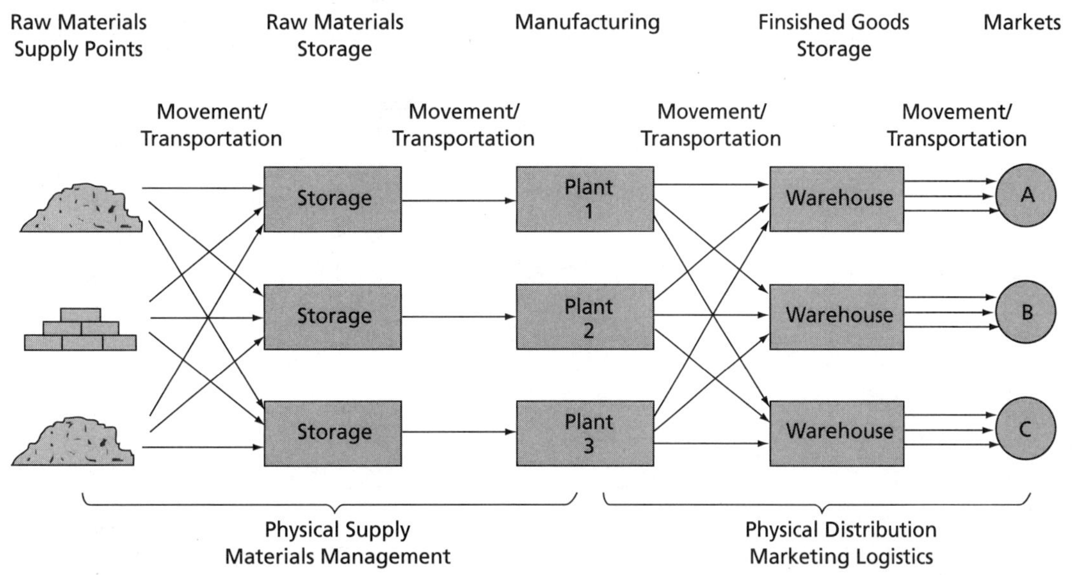

very early period of the development of logistics (i.e., an integration of outbound transportation and field warehousing and the application of a systems perspective that emphasized total cost).

The cost and market pressures continued to mount in the 1960s and 1970s with more global competition in U.S. domestic markets, rising labor costs, and shortages of some essential raw materials and supplies, which resulted in additional activities being added to the logistics function in many organizations (see Figure 1.2). These activities usually included **inbound** transportation, production scheduling, customer service, and packaging, which were integrated into the logistics function for additional cost control and evaluation of trade-offs. So, again, it could be stated that integration and the systems concept played a key role in the development of successful logistics organizations in the 1960s and 1970s. As noted, the 1980s were a period of rapid or revolutionary change with the addition of more activities, that is, further integration of the logistics function and a more comprehensive package of line and staff activities to manage (see Figure 1.3).

FIGURE 1.2 Typical Logistics Network—Materials Management

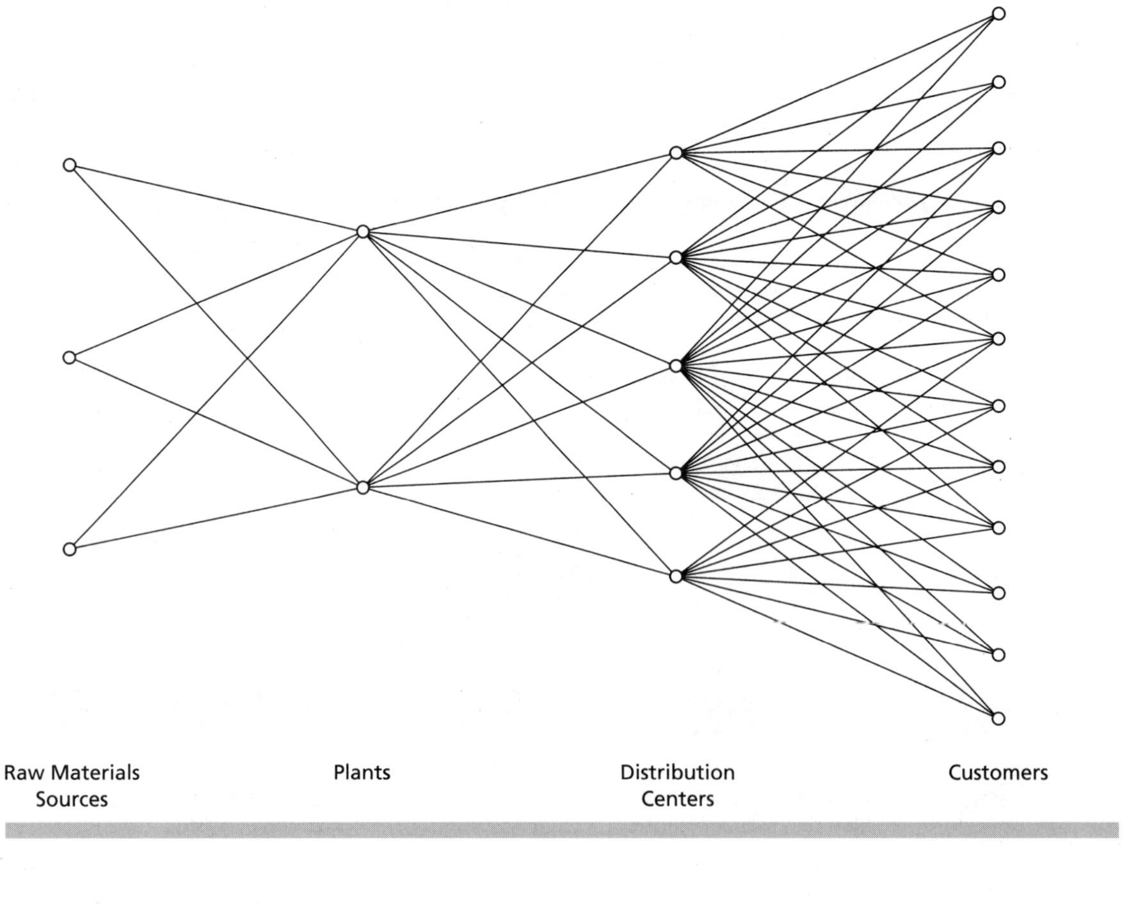

FIGURE 1.3 The Logistics Evolution

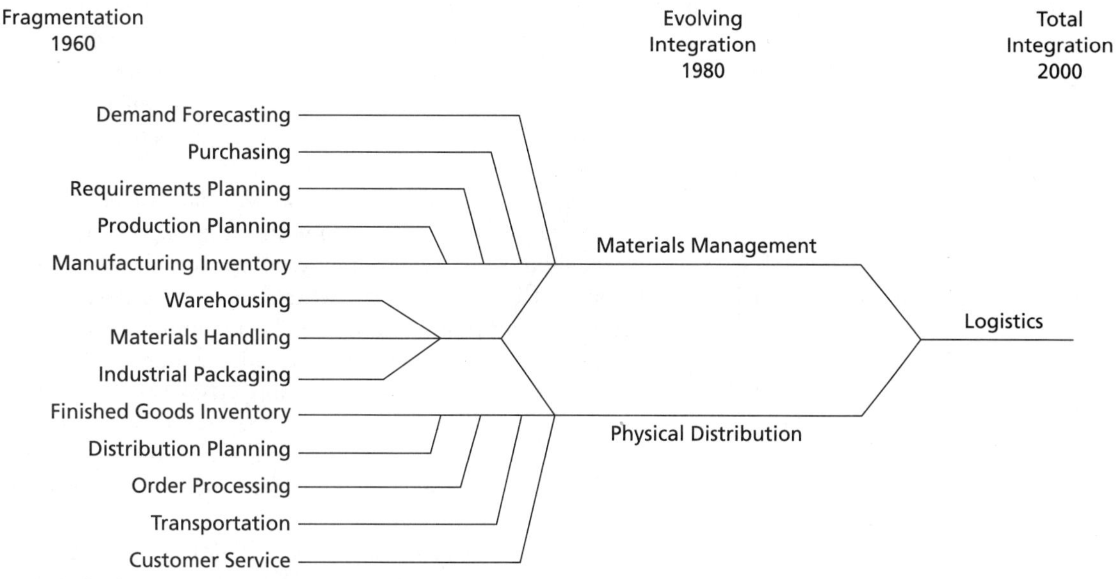

The Logistics Concept

As indicated previously, the origins of the modern logistics concept in businesses can be traced to developments in military logistics during World War II. The Persian Gulf War again demonstrated the importance of logistics to a successful military effort. In fact, the Persian Gulf effort has been referred to as the "logistics war," and the importance of the integrated logistics pipeline supporting the fighting effort was acknowledged repeatedly by the military and civilian leadership. The *integrated* logistics concept was obviously critical to the military's success in the Gulf War.

One of the most widely used and cited definitions of logistics is as follows:

> Logistics is the process of planning, implementing, and controlling the efficient, effective flow and storage of raw materials, in-process inventory, finished goods, services, and related information from point of origin to point of consumption (including inbound, outbound, internal, and external movements) for the purpose of conforming to customer requirements.[8]

Implied in the definition is that the logistics process *provides a systems framework for decision making* that integrates transportation, inventory levels, warehousing space, materials handling systems, packaging, and other related activities that encompass appropriate trade-offs involving cost and service. Another widely used definition states that logistics involves the efficient and effective management of inventory, whether in motion or at rest, to satisfy customer requirements and organizational objectives.[9] The important aspect of the latter definition is that transportation service is recognized as inventory in motion; therefore, the true cost is more than the actual rate charged by the transportation company.

In order to gain some additional perspective on the importance of the integrated logistics concept and how it has affected business organizations, let's use Dow Chemical Company as an illustrative example.[10] Dow Chemical Company is a diversified manufacturer of chemicals and plastics, and produces and sells more than 1,800 products that can be categorized into four major product groups: basic chemicals, basic plastics, industrial specialties, and consumer specialties. There are many different formulations of these products, which are packaged in many different containers at 28 manufacturing locations in the United States. These products can be distributed through any one or a combination of 350 stocking points.

Because Dow is highly integrated, the supplier for raw materials for one manufacturing process is often another Dow plant. Managing work-in-process inventories is not difficult, but managing finished goods inventories is complex and challenging. Many of the finished products must be in inventory when customer orders are received without incurring excess carrying costs. Just the size and complexity of the logistics network makes managing it extremely difficult, but other factors add to the problem as well. Traditionally, for example, the product supply chain of manufacturing, distribution, and suppliers worked independently of one another trying to anticipate demand, but without any real insight into the future demand from the other links in the chain. Inventory was used to buffer uncertainty at each step, which resulted in large inventories at plant and field warehouses.[11]

Computer systems are now being used to substitute information for inventory all along the supply chain. Each link works with the same demand information, properly offset by time and rounding qualities. The result is that each link in the supply chain provides a time-phased schedule of the demand it expects to place on the next link.

Demand forecasting is used to anticipate customer demand. Some customers may provide estimates of demand, leaving forecasting to anticipate the rest. Distribution Requirements Planning (DRP) considers inventory position and translates forecasts into realistic shipping quantities and schedules, and then consolidates that demand at each shipping point in the distribution network and, ultimately, to the plants. Master Production Scheduling (MPS) systems are used to translate schedules of DRP demand into feasible master schedules of when finished goods will be produced. The master schedule puts demand on raw materials, so MRP translates master schedules into a schedule of when raw materials need to arrive from the suppliers.[12]

Computer systems also support the flow of materials and products along the supply chain. Purchasing and transportation systems supported by electronic data interchange (EDI), and more recently the Internet, manage the flow of material from vendors. Numerous technologies, such as CAD/CAM and automatic materials handling systems, support the manufacturing process. Deployment planning, vehicle load management, and vehicle routing and scheduling systems plan the movement of products from plants to warehouses to customers. The benefits from using an integrated systems approach to supply and demand have allowed Dow to reduce its logistics costs on a relative basis and improve its customer service.

Much more could be included here in relation to integrated logistics at companies like Dow, but it is hoped that enough perspective has been provided to show that companies want to attain high levels of customer service while reducing inventory levels and transportation costs. The improvement of service and the reduction of cost would have been described as contradictory 10 years ago, but not today. Logistics and transportation systems in the leading organizations are achieving these seemingly contradictory goals by strategic management of their logistics systems.[13]

As indicated above, modal choice decisions are now made using a selection framework based on an integrated set of logistics-related factors. Decisions are no longer based simply on transportation cost (rates). Other logistics factors can significantly influence the decision.

The Supply Chain Concept

The concept of supply chain management is the newest thrust for many organizations attempting to integrate business processes between their channel partners. Many companies and authors are using the terms logistics and supply chain to mean the same thing. This is not appropriate. Supply chain management integrates **product, information,** and **cash flows** among organizations from the point of origin to the point of consumption with the goal of maximizing consumption satisfaction and minimizing organization costs.[14] Figure 1.4 is an attempt to depict this integration.

Logistics has traditionally been responsible for managing the physical flow of products among organizations. Activities such as transportation and warehousing were used to ensure that the movement of goods was continuous and reliable. Marketing and sales have been responsible for providing information to customers before and after the transaction. Information technology has allowed logistics to take on additional responsibility for also managing information flow among organizations. Bar coding and electronic data interchange (EDI, discussed in Chapter 13, "Information Management and Technology") have allowed logistics to provide information on product flows before they occur, during movement, and after delivery. Finally,

FIGURE 1.4 Logistics Evolution to Supply Chain Management

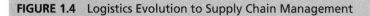

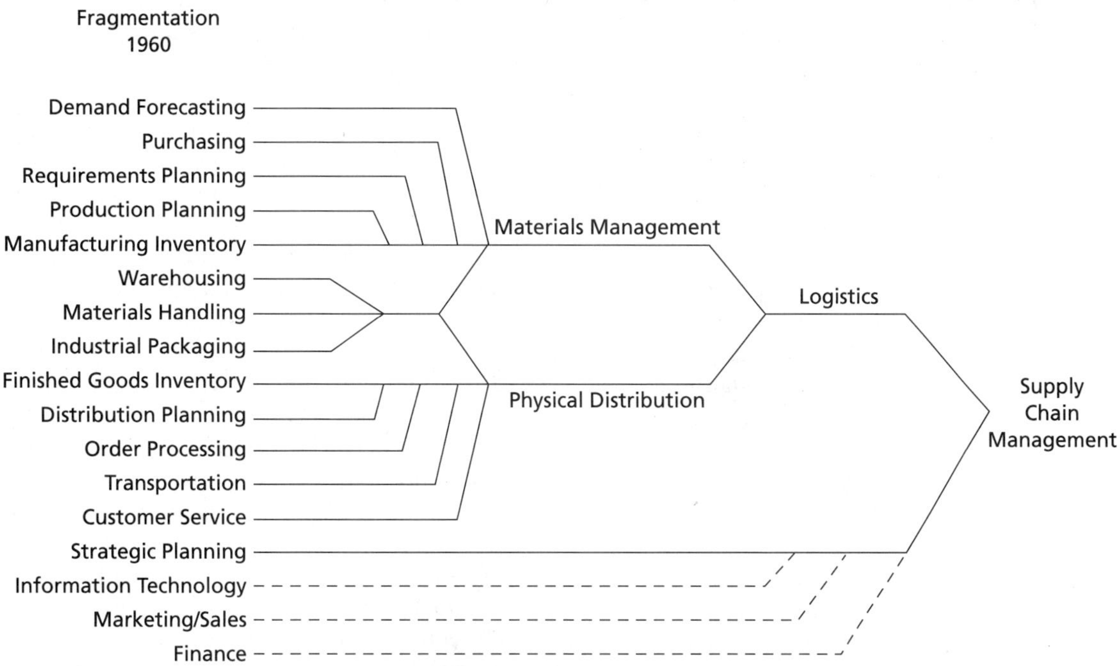

finance and accounting have been responsible for cash flows among organizations in a channel by controlling invoicing and collections. Some logistics organizations, like Welch's Foods, have taken on these additional cash-flow activities. Even if logistics does not have control over a firm's cash flow, it certainly has influence over it. For example, many firms will invoice a customer upon receipt of an order. The customer will not process payment until proof of delivery is received, so faster and more reliable transportation can begin this customer payment process sooner as well as offer the ability to generate a proof of delivery document through EDI. Thus, logistics management is part of supply chain management. In some organizations logistics controls all three flows: product, information, and cash. In other organizations logistics controls product flow, manages additional information flows, and influences cash flows. This integral involvement of logistics in supply chain management might be one explanation for the two terms that denote the same concept.

As is the case for logistics, transportation plays a significant role in integrating these flows among channel partners. The concept of flows has traditionally been a part of how transportation is managed, a continuous movement of product and its related information between suppliers and customers. Along with its impact on cash flows, it is easy to realize the importance of transportation to the supply chain. Satellite technology and EDI have allowed the transportation activity to reduce inventories, improve service, and generate positive financial results for supply chain partners. These technologies allow firms in the supply chain to "see" inventory while it is moving, thus improving the predictability of delivery time.

The concept of supply chain management is the next stage in logistics evolution. Logistics has proven to be an enabling process for firms in their attempts to integrate product, information, and cash flows into a true enterprise model. Many firms have found that logistics has provided the impetus for this integration.[15]

Total-Cost Analysis

An inherent characteristic of the business logistics approach is the **total-cost analysis.** The interrelationship between transportation, warehousing, inventory, and customer service suggests that a decision made in one area of logistics has a definite impact upon other areas of the firm. No one area of logistics operates independently. The decisions made in the transportation area, for example, have an impact upon the cost of warehousing and inventory, product marketability, and the cost of lost sales or productivity.

In the absence of a total-cost approach to the transportation decision, a company may use a mode of transportation that has a low transportation rate. The use of a low transportation cost method of movement may minimize transportation costs, but it does not guarantee the minimization of total movement and storage costs. Low-cost transportation usually is associated with slow service, which means higher warehousing and inventory costs and lower customer service.

The total-cost analysis requires the decision maker to consider **cost trade-offs** within the system. A decision to use air rather than motor carrier transportation would trade the higher costs of transportation for possible savings in warehousing, inventory, and increased sales. Cost trade-offs may result in lower overall logistics costs or higher total costs. The significance of the cost trade-off, and the total-cost analysis, is the recognition of the interrelationship of the logistics variables.

Without a business logistics approach within a company, the total-cost approach may pose some difficulties in implementation. For example, total costs may be low-

STOP OFF

Supply Chain Black Holes

One of the major reasons for using supply chain management is to gain visibility of material flows through the entire manufacturing and distribution process. With better visibility, manufacturing schedules are more tightly defined. Customer service improves and expensive inventory can be replaced with inexpensive information.

Although supply chain visibility has improved, inventory is still less visible than it should be. In fact, huge blind spots still exist in most companies' supply chains. Here are the four darkest and deepest black holes of supply chain information:

1. Inbound supply chains are usually not linked with outbound supply chains. At the plant level, this means trucks drop off components and leave empty when they could be used to carry outbound goods. On a global level, companies commonly export products to the same countries where they source other products and materials. As a result, they fail to take advantage of tremendous opportunities for lowering ocean shipping rates based on two-way movements.

2. Manufacturers do not have an efficient way to instantaneously compile material orders at their suppliers. Even at the best manufacturing facilities, component requirements often change during the day. Unfortunately, orders to suppliers are usually sent once with no ability to change them. A better way would be to electronically build orders as manufacturing schedules became concrete.

3. Many companies with multiple plants and the same suppliers fail to look at the total material requirements for all of the plants. Inbound shipments are never coordinated. Transportation costs spin out of control because separate trucks with small orders are dispatched to go to each plant.

4. Although most large companies are global in their production, stock location, and distribution, few have globally inventory visibility. Domestically, most companies are able to ship an order from the closest plant or warehouse to the customer because there is almost always a centralized order-processing system linked to a centralized inventory system. This usually is not the case with international orders. There often is no centralized order-processing system for international orders. If there is such an order system, there rarely is a centralized inventory system to determine where the order should be shipped from. As a result, international orders are slow in being filled, or inventories are kept unnecessarily high. Transportation costs are always higher than they should be.

All of these black holes are really just gaps in a company's information systems. In many cases, companies have the technology on hand, but no one has taken the trouble to apply it to the supply chain. In a few cases, such as with global order and inventory systems, the solution may require a substantial investment well into the six figures.

So is it worth making the investment in time and money to fill these gaps? Just start adding up the costs of lost sales, excess transportation charges, production downtime, and inventory investment. Before you get halfway down the list, you will be running down the hall to your information systems people with a very long calculator tape waving in your hand.

ered by the switch to higher-cost air transportation, because the higher transportation costs are traded for lower costs of warehousing and inventory. From the viewpoint of the total firm, such a decision would be desirable. However, from the transportation manager's viewpoint (performance is measured upon transportation costs incurred), the decision to use air carriage is not desirable. In the absence of an integrated, business logistics approach, the switch to air carriers probably would not be made.

The total-cost approach of business logistics emphasizes the interrelationship of logistics to other areas of the firm. The two functions most directly affected by logistics are marketing and production. Physical distribution activities are sometimes considered part of the marketing function, because the movement of the finished goods to the customer completes the sales transaction. The quality of the logistics service provided to the customer can be used as a marketing tool to enhance sales, or, if the service is unacceptable, logistics service can cause a loss in sales. Firms that are capable of offering logistics service levels that reduce a buyer's cost will have a competitive edge in the marketplace.

This logistics impact upon sales is considered in a total-cost context by examining decisions in terms of cost of lost sales (profits). The level of inventory, the number and location of warehouses, and the carrier used to deliver goods determines the level of service provided and the resultant impact upon sales and profits. When changes are considered in any of these areas, the total cost of the proposed change must reflect the benefit of increased profits as well as the added cost of lost profits due to the service level changes.

The relationship between production and logistics stems from the physical supply activities that support the production process. More specifically, the production department is the customer for the raw materials required for manufacturing. The movement and storage functions establish a quality of service that will impact the cost of production. If goods are late or not available for use, the production line may be forced to stop. Most firms recognize the cost of stopping the production line is extremely high and that the potential total cost associated with low supply levels is also very high. Accordingly, the logistics decisions are made in such a manner as to ensure high service levels and virtually no shortages.

Another total-cost impact of logistics and production deals with the length of the production run and the amount of inventory generated. Cost trade-offs exist between long production runs that result in low production costs and the corresponding high inventory and inventory carrying costs. The length of the production run is determined by examining the total cost of the average production costs and the inventory holding costs at various levels of production.

The total-cost concept of logistics provides an analytical framework for considering the impact of logistics decisions. Decisions in an area of logistics such as transportation have a cost trade-off effect with other areas of logistics and of the firm. The minimization of total logistics costs is the objective of logistics.

Business Logistics Activities

The business logistics function recognizes the movement-storage interaction in the provision of time and place utility in goods. That is, a positive and direct relationship exists between the movement and storage elements of the logistics system. This relationship enables the transportation or traffic manager to make decisions that are beneficial to the total logistics system and the company as a whole, rather than to the transportation area exclusively.

Transportation decisions have an impact on the functional costs of finance, production, and marketing. The decision regarding the mode of transportation used affects the level of **inventories** to be held, the size of raw material orders, and the quality of **service** provided to the customer. For example, water transportation is slow, requires large-sized shipments, and is discontinuous during the winter months, causing increased inventory levels and costs. The purchasing department must purchase in lot sizes approximating 1,000 to 1,500 tons, causing large inventories to be held. In addition, large inventories are required to prevent business stoppage during the winter months, a definite customer service disadvantage.

The above example illustrates how the transportation decision affects other functional areas in a company. Figure 1.5 shows the interrelationship of the logistics

FIGURE 1.5 Business Logistics Functions

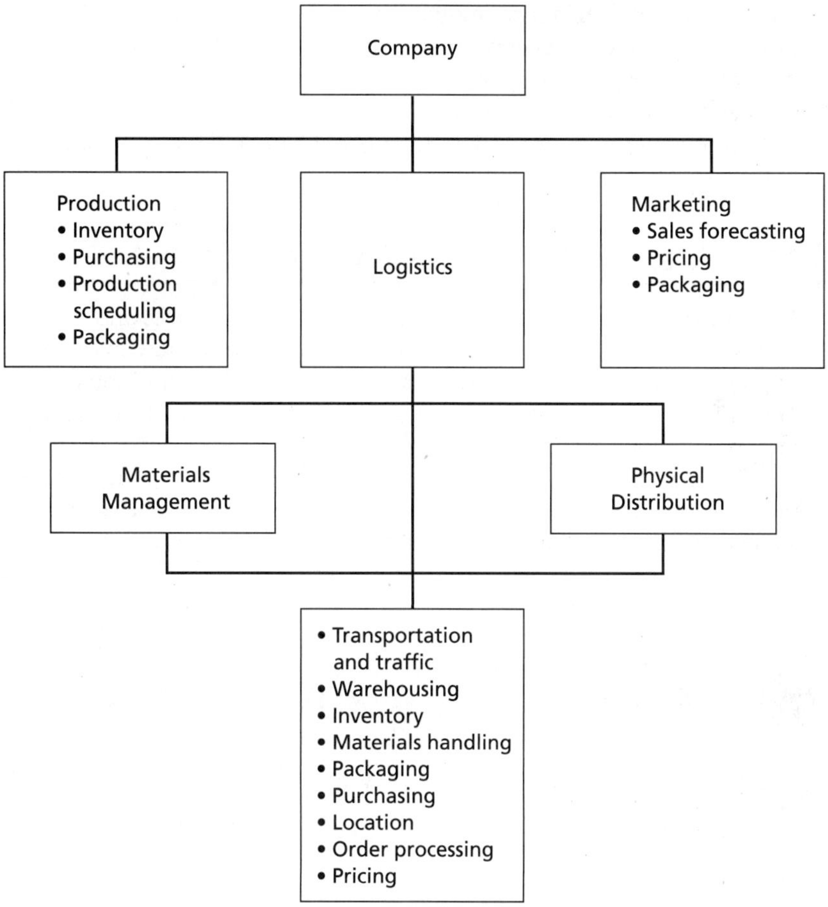

functional areas and of logistics and other functions of the firm. For simplicity, company functions in Figure 1.5 are based on **utility creation,** that is, form utility created by production, time, and place utility created by logistics, as well as possession utility created by marketing. Other functional areas are required for the viable operation of any business, but these three functions permit examination of the role of transportation in business logistics and in the operation of a company.

A number of functions included in logistics also are included under production and/or marketing. For example, purchasing is included under the auspices of production and the materials management portion of logistics, pricing is included in both marketing and logistics, and packaging is contained in all three functions. The reason for this duplication is the multifunctional consideration that must be given to these areas. Packaging decisions, for example, must consider the efficiency of the production process, consumer acceptance (marketing), and the need to protect the product while it is in storage and transit while making efficient use of the carrier's vehicles (logistics).

The conclusion to be drawn is that the logistics function does not operate in a vacuum; the decisions made in the logistics area impact other areas of the company.

In addition, a number of logistics functions also can be included in production or marketing because of the impact these functions have on all these areas.

Further examination of Figure 1.5 shows the dichotomy of the business logistics function into **materials management** and **physical distribution.** The materials management function is concerned with the inbound movement and storage of raw materials, while physical distribution is directed toward the outbound movement and storage of finished products. However, the activities performed are basically the same in both logistics areas; that is, transportation and traffic activities are conducted in both inbound and outbound product moves.

Quality, Value, and Customer Satisfaction

It is important to understand the role that quality in logistics and transportaton plays in customer satisfaction. Just because a firm achieves quality in the form of meeting requirements does not mean that value has been added and the customer satisfied. The creation of value means that the customer has perceived that the supplier has met expectations and achieved quality.

The perception of the **customer** acts as a **filter** for the output of logistics processes, which is customer service. This relationship can be seen in Figure 1.6. Assume that a United Airlines flight lands within 15 minutes after its scheduled landing

FIGURE 1.6 Logistics Value Creation

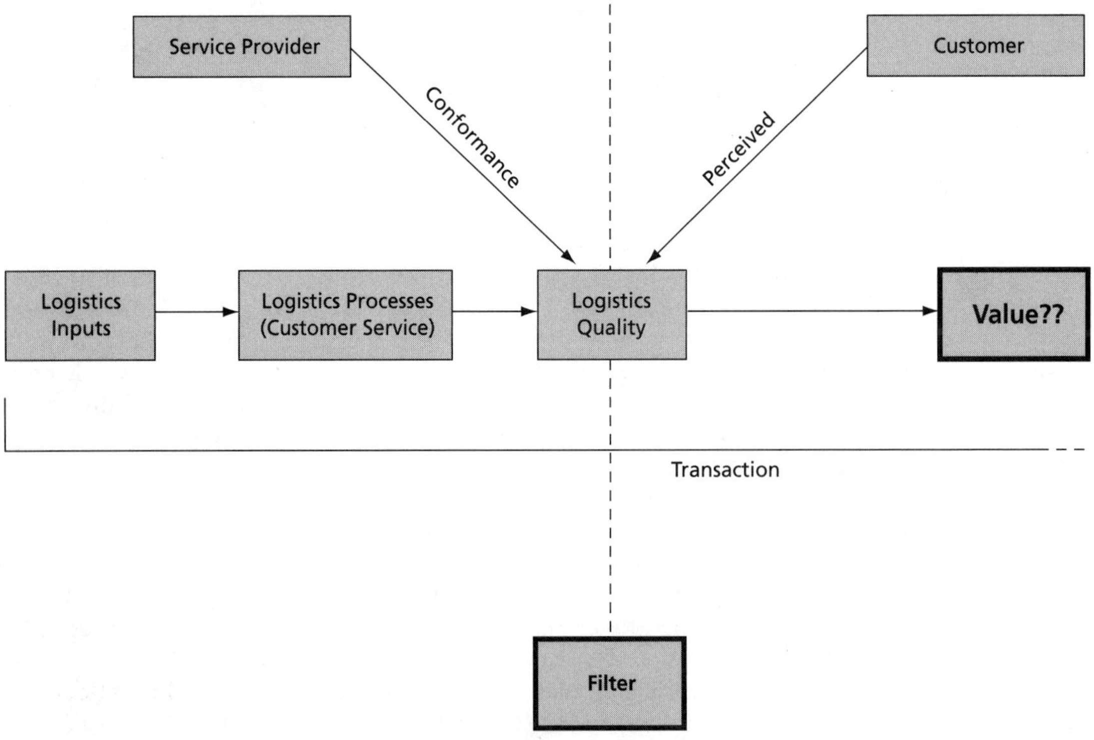

time, so it is considered on time. However, a passenger who just missed the last connection of the evening might not perceive this flight to be on time. In the customer's view, quality has not been achieved and value has not been created, so, for this transaction, the customer was not satisfied. Another important point to remember is that satisfaction is transaction-specific; that is, it is related to the last interaction between the supplier and the customer.

Many times the service that is delivered to the customer is affected by the perceptions of the service provider. Logistics managers will deliver those services at specific levels in agreement with what they think the customer wants. If the service provider's perception differs from that of the customer, a **"quality gap"** is created.[16] A difference between what the service provider actually delivers and what the customer perceives to be delivered creates another quality gap. So the logistics executive is faced with the challenge of managing logistics inputs to create services for the customer that do not create gaps, that meet the requirements of the customer, and that agree with the perceptions of the customer. If this occurs, quality is achieved and value is created.

Dimensions of Logistics and Transportation Quality

With the goal being the creation of value, logistics managers must identify those critical elements of quality that can be managed to help meet customer requirements. From the perspective of the customer and service provider, quality can take the forms of productivity improvements, logistics service peformance, and logistics service performance measurement.[17] In other words, customers require service providers to perform that service cheaper than competitors (productivity), better than competitors (service performance), and/or with the goal of providing information about the service in order to continuously improve (performance measurement system). In many cases, customers want service providers to deliver all of these quality dimensions. This would be the equivalent of a customer asking UPS to make an overnight delivery at second-day prices, to continuously monitor the shipment through UPS's system, and to guarantee future price reductions through productivity improvements. This type of request might be extremely difficult for a carrier to fulfill.

The logistics **service provider's perceptions** of what the customer wants will influence the dimensions of logistics quality offered and the potential for value creation. For example, if a carrier perceives that its customers want "no-frills" service, then it will provide low-cost transportation even if customers actually want improved service at a higher cost. This is an area that can benefit greatly from customer satisfaction surveys that ask the customer what is important. Research was performed by Novack, Rinehart, and Langley to determine the perceptions of logistics executives concerning how they feel logistics adds value to a firm's products.[18] These logistics executives were first asked to determine how important logistics inputs are to their firms' competitive advantage. The results of this ranking can be seen in Table 1.1. Not surprisingly, these executives said that outbound transportation was the most important logistics activity for its contributions to competitive advantage. Transportation is usually the single largest logistics cost component and the activity that can directly affect on-time delivery and product availability.

The second question asked the logistics executives to determine which logistics deliverable or logistics service output was most important to their firms' competitive advantage. Table 1.2 clearly shows that product availability is by far considered the most important logistics service output. Once again, transportation plays an important role in providing this service.

TABLE 1.1 Summary of Importance Scores for Logistics Inputs

		Importance Score*	
Measure	**Activities**	**Mean**	**S. D.**
Inbound Logistics			
	Sales Forecasting	5.09	1.756
	Production Planning	5.52	1.525
	Sourcing/Purchasing	4.98	1.611
	Inbound Transportation	4.39	1.539
Operations			
	Production	5.48	1.561
	Packaging	4.56	1.477
	Raw Materials/WIP Inventory Management	4.51	1.670
	Finished Goods Plant Warehousing	4.94	1.539
Outbound Logistics			
	Intracompany Transportation	4.75	1.492
	Finished Goods Field Warehousing	5.43	1.525
	Order Processing	5.55	1.558
	Outbound Transportation	5.78	1.285
Logistics Support			
	Logistics System Planning	5.61	1.300
	Logistics Engineering	4.63	1.484
	Logistics Control	5.41	1.191

*Seven-point scale with 1 equaling "not important," and 7 equaling "extremely important."

TABLE 1.2 Summary of Importance Scores for Logistics Deliverables

		Importance Score*	
Measure	**Deliverables**	**Mean**	**S. D.**
Logistics Service Performance			
	Product Availability	6.79	.541
	Order Cycle Time	5.98	1.102
	Logistics System Flexibility, Malfunction, and Recovery	5.58	.884
	Logistics System Information	5.76	1.039
	Postsale Product Support	3.89	1.806

*Seven-point scale with 1 equaling "not important," and 7 equaling "extremely important."

Finally, these executives were asked to express their level of agreement on several statements regarding how they perceive logistics and how they think their customers perceive logistics. The results from this question can be seen in Table 1.3.

Several conclusions can be drawn from this research. First, changes in logistics productivity do not result in reactions from customers. The logistics executives in the study agreed that productivity improvements do not result in more revenue from their customers, possibly because any productivity improvements or cost reductions generated by the firm might not get passed on to the customers in the form of lower prices. Productivity improvements in logistics are important to internal customers, however, namely upper management.

TABLE 1.3 Summary of Agreement Scores for Perception of Logistics Value

Measure	Deliverables	Agreement Scores* Mean	S. D.
Logistics Service			
Logistics Productivity			
	"Improving logistics productivity is a high priority in our firm"	5.91	1.298
	"We are constantly trying to reduce overall logistics costs"	6.11	1.069
	"We view achieving productivity through quality as critical to our success"	5.96	1.221
	"We are constantly trying to increase overall customer service levels"	6.23	1.134
Performance Measurement			
	"We are able to measure and identify elements of quality"	4.85	1.339
	"We are able to express the value of these quality measures in dollar terms"	3.89	1.637
	"Logistics adds value to our firm's output and provides a competitive advantage"	5.97	1.136
	Customer Reaction		
	"Our customers are not pleased with the levels of service we are giving them"	2.89	1.111
	"Our customers reduce their business with us when logistics service levels are below their expectations"	4.78	1.704
	"Our customers increase their business with our firm when logistics service levels meet or exceed their expectations"	5.0	1.458
	"Our customers notice when logistics service levels exceed their expectations"	4.63	1.833

*Seven-point scale with 1 equaling "not important," and 7 equaling "extremely important."

Second, logistics executives felt that customers will tend to increase their business with a supplier if logistics service to those customers meets or exceeds their expectations. So, although logistics does not add value through productivity improvements, it can add value in a service performance for the customers.

Finally, logistics executives agreed that logistics does add value to a firm's products, but this value cannot yet be quantified; that is, a dollar value cannot be connected with service improvements and quality achievements in logistics. If logistics executives feel that their customers value service performance, then they will make decisions to maximize this performance to meet or exceed their customers' expectations.

Logistics Value

Value in a firm's product can be measured using a simple formula: function ÷ cost. Adapting this formula to logistics makes it take this form: service ÷ cost. A customer will determine value based on expectations of cost versus service performance. For example, passengers are willing to pay a higher price to travel first class because they perceive that the extra service given is worth the higher ticket price. (This concept was covered in Chapter 11 under "Value of Service Pricing.") Likewise, shippers are willing to pay more for faster and more reliable transportation service because they feel the extra service is worth the extra cost. Value is created, then, when conformance quality meets or exceeds customer perceptions of the logistics service delivered; in other words, all quality gaps have been eliminated. Logistics service value can be measured by changes in customer revenues, changes in traffic lane revenues/volumes, and changes in the nature or volume of customer complaints. Invariably, **value creation** will elicit some type of response from customers. Failure to achieve value can negatively affect customer satisfaction and detract from a firm's revenues and/or volumes.

Customer Satisfaction and Attitude

Customer service and customer satisfaction are not necessarily the same. Satisfaction is linked to customer service through the achievement of quality and the creation of value. Customer satisfaction is also **transaction-specific;** that is, satisfaction, or dissatisfaction, occurs with every transaction between a supplier and customer.

For example, a railroad promises to make JIT deliveries to a manufacturing facility every morning between 8:00 A.M. and 8:30 A.M. If Monday's delivery is on time and the receiver perceives it to be on time, quality has been achieved, value has been created, and the customer is satisfied with that delivery. If Tuesday's delivery is late, the customer will not be satisfied. So, satisfaction with Monday's performance will not affect the customer's satisfaction level with Tuesday's late delivery. As such, satisfaction is transaction-specific. However, continuously satisfying a customer over time will positively influence the customer's perception of the service provider. Not satisfying the customer over several transactions will have the opposite effect.

The **customer's perception** of service quality is basically the same as the **customer's attitude.** These relationships can be seen in Figure 1.7. A customer's attitude is developed over time and is not necessarily changed by a single transaction. For example, assume that a motor carrier has had a long and successful relationship with a shipper, offering excellent on-time service to customers and damage-free product. As a result, the shipper has developed a positive attitude toward the carrier.

FIGURE 1.7 Creation of Customer Attitude

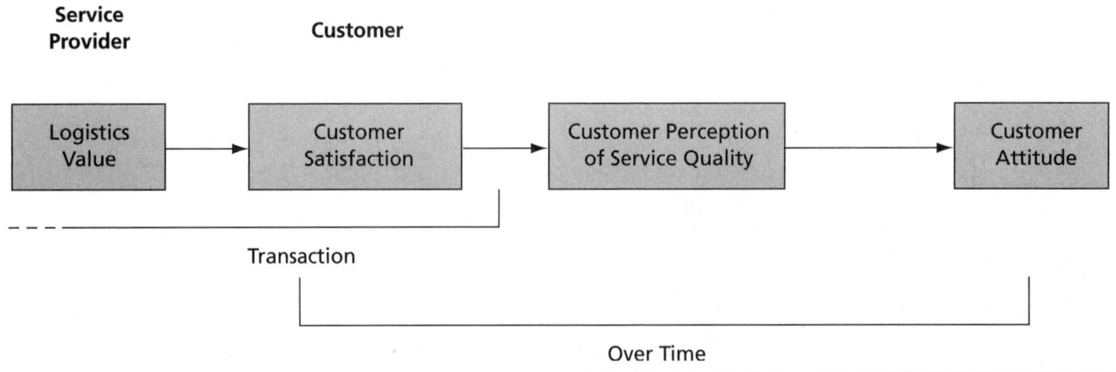

If the carrier fails on one shipment, the shipper's positive attitude toward the carrier will probably not change because of the previous good relationship. However, if the motor carrier continues to deliver inferior customer service, the shipper's attitude might become increasingly negative.

Attitude, then, is what logistics executives need to develop and manage among their customers because it is attitude that directs repurchase decisions. As seen in Figure 1.8, the customer's attitude toward the service provider is what determines the service provider's longevity and profitability. A good customer attitude will allow the service provider to grow and be profitable, while a negative attitude will dramatically slow growth and reduce profits. Thus, logistics executives need to be aware that continuously and reliably delivering quality to customers is the key to developing a positive attitude among their customers. Doing things right the first time is important, but what's more important is doing them right every time. Managing for the short term then does not put a firm on the road to quality and a positive customer attitude.

Transportation and the Economy

The previous discussion attempted to show the importance of transportation to the firm in its attempts to implement both the logistics and supply chain concepts. This portion of the chapter will present a discussion on the importance of transportation to the economy. Transportation is one of the tools that civilized societies need to bring order out of chaos. It reaches into every phase and facet of our existence. Viewed in historical, economic, environmental, social, and political terms, it is unquestionably the most important industry in the world. Without transportation, we could not operate a grocery store or win a war. The more complex life becomes, the more indispensable are the elements of transportation systems.[19]

Transportation systems are so well developed that most citizens rarely stop to think about their benefits. Americans, though, use transportation every day in one form or another. It provides the thoroughfare for the nation's products, it provides

FIGURE 1.8 Customer Attitude Impact on Service Provider Success

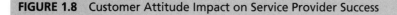

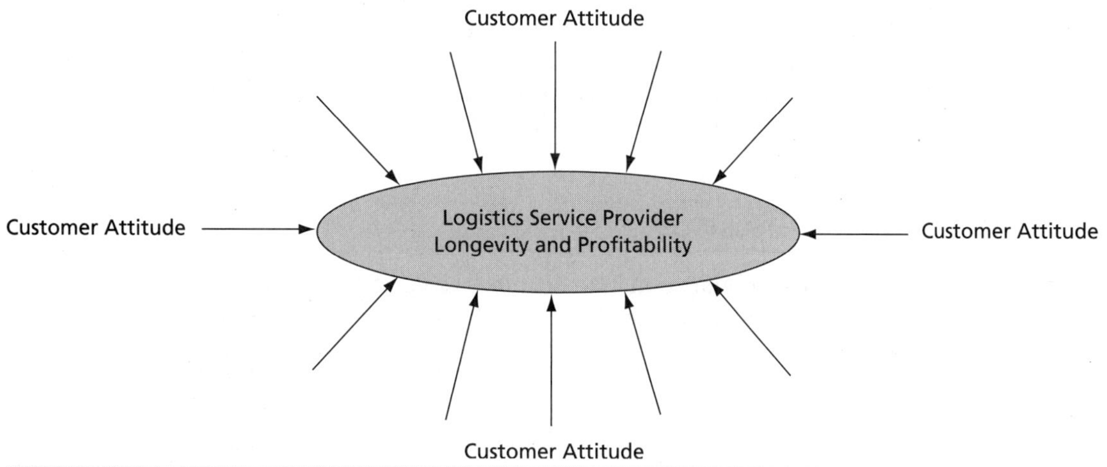

a means for traveling to and from work, and it supports our communication networks. Seldom do individuals stop and wonder how restricted their life-styles would be if the U.S. Post Office lost its right to use any of the common modes of transportation.

At this early stage, it may be helpful to define the transportation product. **Transportation** is the creation of place and time utility. When goods are moved to places where they have higher value than they had at the places from which they originated, they have place utility. Time utility means that this service occurs when it is needed. Time and place utility are provided to passengers when they are moved from where they don't want to be to places where they do want to be and at the demanded time.

Some individuals find it difficult to understand the nature of transportation because it is a service and not a physical, tangible product. Transportation is a service to the user, but it has basic characteristics that make purchasing this service similar to buying goods.

One aspect of transportation is the movement service. This includes speed (whether it is door-to-door or terminal-to-terminal), reliability, and the frequency of the service. Another factor is the equipment used, which is a major factor for both passengers and freight. For passengers, the equipment affects comfort and safety. For freight, equipment affects shipment preparation, the size of the shipment, and loading and unloading cost.

The third factor is the cost of the transportation service. Cost includes a charge or rate quoted by the primary carrier as well as any peripheral costs borne by the user. The latter may include pickup and delivery costs, packaging requirements, damage or detention charges, and special service charges such as refrigeration or heat.

Transportation should not be viewed as the simple movement of persons or things through space. The user is actually purchasing a **"bundle of services"** from a carrier at a certain cost. The "bundle of services" varies among carriers and modes of transportation with different prices frequently in effect from the different services. If the user focuses on the simplistic version of transportation, that is, movement through space, the lowest-priced service will be selected. However, the higher-priced carrier may be the best choice because of superior service, which will result in lower costs in other areas, such as inventory.

Transportation is also one of the economic factors in the production of goods and services. The basic function of transportation is to provide the market with access to the resultant products. Transportation plays a major role in the spatial relations between geographic points, and it also affects temporal relationships.

The following discussion will investigate the historical, economic, environmental, social, and political effects of a well-designed transportation system.

Historical Significance

The importance of transportation becomes more apparent when one understands its history-making role. The growth of civilizations is directly associated with the development of transportation systems. The strength of ancient Egypt demonstrated how one form of transportation, water, could become the foundation for a great society. The Nile River held Egypt together. It provided a means to transport Egyptian goods, a way to communicate, and a way in which Egyptian soldiers could move to defend the country. The Nile River, like all transportation systems, also affected the society's political and cultural development. The Roman Empire was successful due in part to the system of roads which linked distant areas and made communication, trade, and military conquest possible. This continues today in the United States with our interstate highway system.

A transportation system can also help create a social structure. People traveling or living within the bounds of a particular transportation network share ideas and experiences. Eventually a society develops with unified political opinions, cultural ideals, and educational methods.

Yet methods of transportation also can tear societies apart when people are alienated from the common systems. For example, America's secession from Great Britain can be partly attributed to the localized systems developing in the 13 colonies. Transportation to and from Great Britain was slow and inefficient, and Americans found that they could economically lead more efficient lives trading among themselves without having to pay dues to the government of King George III. As the colonies grew into a separate economic nation, political and cultural attitudes that were unique to America took hold.

The United States continued to grow in tandem with its transportation network. Few families thought to move west without first knowing that explorers had blazed trails or found rivers suitable for travel. The Erie Canal, steamboats, early turnpikes, and the rail system developed to meet the economic and social needs of the growing nation. See Table 1.4 for an overview of transport developments in the United States.

TABLE 1.4 U.S. Transport Developments

Year	Development	Year	Development
1774	Lancaster Turnpike: first toll road—Pennsylvania	1927	Lindberg solo flight—New York to Paris
1804	Fulton's steamboat—Hudson River—New York	1956	Congress passes bill inaugurating interstate system of highways
1825	Erie Canal: first canal—New York	1961	Manned space flights begin
1830	B&O Railroad—Maryland	1970	Amtrak established
1838	Steamship service—Atlantic Ocean	1976	Contrail established
1865	First successful pipeline—Pennsylvania	1978	Act to deregulate airlines passed
1866	Completion of transcontinental rail link	1980	Act to deregulate motor carriers and Staggers Rail Act passed
1869	Bicycles introduced—United States	1982	Surface Transportation Assistance Act
1887	First daily rail service coast to coast		
1887	Federal regulation of transportation begins	1983	Double Stack Rail container service initiated
1903	First successful airplane flight—Wright Brothers	1984	Act to loosen regulation over maritime industry passed
1904	Panama Canal opens	1986	Conrail profitable and sold by government
1916	Rail track mileage reaches peak		
1919	Transcontinental airmail service by U.S. Post Office begins	1986	Norfolk Southern initiates successful roadrailer service
1925	Kelly Act: airmail contract to private companies	1990	National Transportation Policy Statement
		1995	ICC Abolished

Transportation also plays a major role in national defense. This role has long been recognized by governments. The Roman Empire built its great system of roads primarily for military reasons. Sir Winston Churchill once wrote, "Victory is the beautiful, bright-colored flower. Transport is the stem without which it could never have blossomed."[20] In the United States, the requirements of national defense have been advanced as a major reason for the construction of a system of nationwide, interconnected superhighways. Similarly, the large expenditures on air transport are based more on military and political considerations than on economic ones.

Economic Significance

Transportation systems have a great impact on population patterns and economic development. Consider Table 1.5, which indicates that New York City needs more than 6,000 tons of foodstuffs per day.

The approximately 400 truckloads that this figure represents is not all inclusive of products that would be used. For example, it does not include all foods nor does it include newsprint, clothing, books, cigarettes, gasoline, cars, appliances, furniture, and so on. It does not take much imagination to understand why transportation is sometimes referred to as the lifeline of cities.

Value of Goods

Transportation systems help determine the economic value of products. A simple model will serve to illustrate this point. Consider a certain commodity that is desired in one location, provided it is offered below a certain price. In Figure 1.9, this commodity is produced at point A and costs OC at the point of production. The community desiring the commodity, located at point B, is the distance AB from A. The maximum price that people will pay for the commodity is shown on the vertical axis as OE, at community B.

TABLE 1.5 Foodstuffs Required Daily in New York City

Product	Quantity (in Lbs.)
Butter	53,600
Dry milk	60,032
Cheese	102,912
Fluid milk and cream	3,323,200
Eggs	125,000
Meat, poultry, or fish	2,200,000
Fruits and juices	1,340,000
Fats and oils	600,000
Flour and cereal products	1,407,000
Potatoes	1,072,000
Sugar and other sweeteners	1,072,000
Coffee, tee, and cocoa	168,000
Syrup, molasses, and honey	482,400
Rice and grain	75,040
Total	12,080,984 lbs. (6,040 tons)

Source: Based on U.S. Department of Agriculture estimates of daily average per capita consumption of these products for a metropolitan area population of 11.5 million.

If the original, inefficient transport system is used, moving the commodity from A to B will cost CH. The CD portion of the cost line is known as the fixed cost, and the DH portion of the line is the cost per mile of slope. With this inefficient system, the total cost at B is OH, a price greater than the maximum cost limit in the community B or OE.

Now assume the transport system is improved. The cost per mile or slope is reduced and the transportation variable cost line becomes DJ. The cost at the community now becomes OJ, well below the maximum cost of OE. The market for the commodity would be expanded to community B, while production continues at A.

Place Utility

The reduction in transportation costs between points A and B gives the commodity **"place utility."** In the less efficient system, the goods will have no value because they would not be sold at the market. The more efficient method of transportation creates utility; the goods now have value at point B.

Reductions in transportation costs will encourage market areas to purchase products from distant suppliers that might otherwise be produced locally. The reduction in transportation cost is actually much greater for long distances than for short ones because of the fixed charges alluded to in Figure 1.9. If a supplier can cover the transportation cost of a certain amount in his or her price, an increase in the distance over which this given amount will cover the transport of goods will increase the market area of the product in an even greater ratio.

Dionysius Lardner, an early transportation economist, referred to this phenomenon as the Law of Squares in Transportation and Trade (also known as **Lardner's Law**). As shown in Figure 1.10, a producer at A can afford to transport a product 100 miles and meet competitive laid-down costs. The boundary of the relevant market area is shown by the circumference of the smaller circle. If transportation cost is cut

FIGURE 1.9 Landed Cost with Old and New Transport Systems

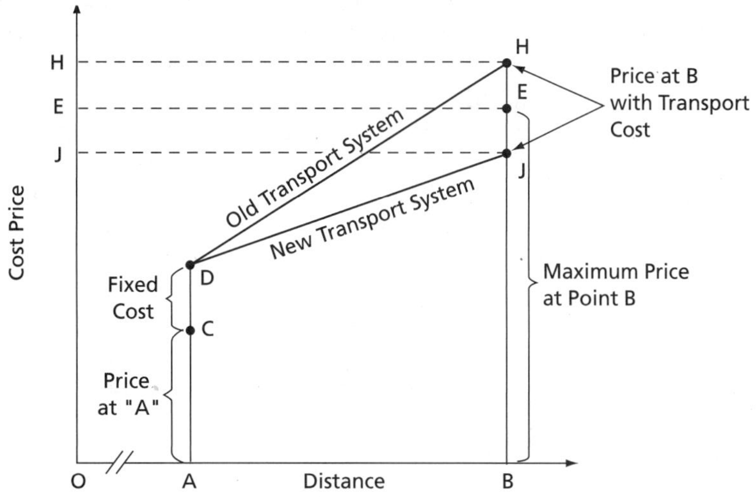

Source: Adapted from Morlok, Edward, *Introduction to Transportation, Engineering, and Planning* (New York: McGraw-Hill, 1978), p. 33.

FIGURE 1.10 Lardner's Relevant Areas

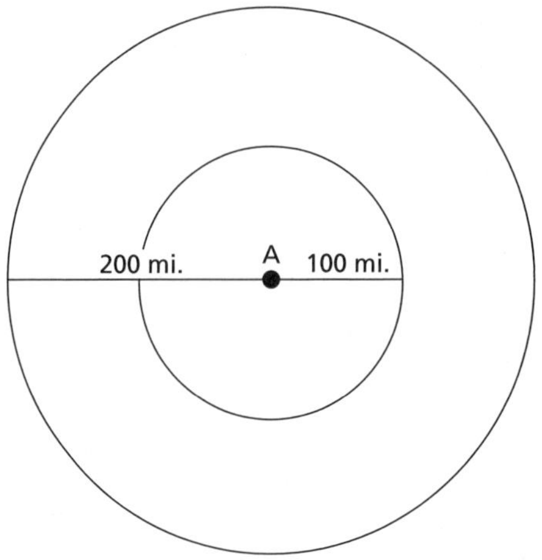

in half, the same sum will now transport the supplier goods for twice the distance, that is, 200 miles. Now the market boundary is shown by the circumference of the larger circle. The relevant market area increased four times in size when the radius doubled from 100 to 200 miles.

Time Utility

The concept of **"time utility"** is closely aligned to that of place utility. The demand for a particular commodity can only exist during certain periods of time. If a product is at a market in a time when there is no demand for it, then it possesses no value. For example, the demand for Halloween costumes only exists during a specific time of the year. After Halloween passes, these goods have little value to the holder. Efficient transportation creates time utility by ensuring that products are at the proper locations when needed. For example, raw materials for production, fruit, and Christmas toys all need to arrive at certain locations during specific times, or their value will be limited.

Lardner's Law can also be related to time utility. For example, the speed of transportation may be a governing factor for the transportation of certain perishable products that have a limited shelf life. Suppose the small circle in Figure 1.10 represents the current market area based on a specific transportation speed. If the speed were doubled, the potential service area would quadruple.

In addition, transportation gives goods utility through the assurance that the goods will arrive without damage. The form of the product can be altered, however, to ensure safe transportation. Mechanical products, glassware, and food all need special protection if they are to have any value at the time of arrival.

Utility of Goods

Transportation adds utility to goods. Efficient highway systems and modern modes of transportation allow geographic specialization, large-scale production, increased competition, and increased land values.

Geographic Specialization

The concept of geographic specialization assumes that each nation, state, or city produces products and services for which its capital, labor, and raw materials are best suited. Because any one area can't produce all needed goods, transportation is needed to send the goods that may be most efficiently produced at point A to point B in return for different goods efficiently produced at point B. The concept is closely aligned to the principle of **comparative advantage**. This principle assumes that an area will specialize in the production of goods for which it has the greatest advantage or the least comparative disadvantage. Gain from the specialization of goods will be mutually advantageous when the cost ratios of producing two commodities are different in different areas. Hence, Pennsylvania can concentrate on the production of steel, California on citrus fruit, and the Greek Islands on olives.

Large-scale Production

Geographic specialization is complemented by large-scale production, but without the use of effective and efficient transportation networks, the advantages of scale economies, production efficiencies, and cheaper manufacturing facilities would be destroyed. The raw materials for production need to be transported to the manufacturing facility, and the finished products must be transported out of an area at reasonable costs. Geographic specialization assumes that the large-scale production of efficiently produced goods is demanded at distances far from the production site. Obviously, one area cannot rely upon its comparative advantage and large-scale production without the use of systems to transport the goods efficiently to the distant areas requiring them.

Increased Competition

Efficient transportation also provides the consumer with the benefit of increased competition. Without transportation, local entrepreneurs are capable of producing inefficient goods and charging high prices for their consumption. Transportation increases the market area for a product; thus, goods must be produced in the most efficient fashion, or distant competitors will enter the market and legitimately capture its attention.

Land Values

Transportation improvements are also credited with enhancing an area's economy by increasing the value of land that is adjacent to or served by the improvements. Thus, the land becomes more accessible and more useful. Today the suburban centers provide excellent examples of land areas that have increased in value due to the accessibility that results from efficient transportation systems. Suburbanites can take advantage of nearby city life for work and pleasure and then retire to rural areas via public transportation networks to avoid crowded conditions. Commuters from Greenwich, Connecticut, to New York City and from Cherry Hill, New Jersey, to Philadelphia all reap both city and suburban benefits as the result of reliable train systems. Hence, the value of the land in these areas has increased to reflect the advantageous life-styles that the new or improved transportation systems have made possible.

However, transportation does not always have a positive effect on land values. Noise and air pollution accompanying some networks decrease adjacent land values. The homeowners who have to bear this pollution also suffer from overaccessibility.

Transportation Patterns

Transportation patterns reflect the flow of people and commerce. Transportation has a catalytic effect on a society in that it stimulates commerce and movement. The reverse is true also. That is, the demand for commerce and movement will cause transportation to be developed.

The world's major water routes for transporting merchandise are shown in Figure 1.11. The merchandise includes finished and semifinished goods but does not include heavy bulk goods such as ores and petroleum. These routes traditionally go to and from Europe, the United States, and the Far East (Japan, Korea, Hong Kong, and Taiwan). These routes have an east-west pattern between the developed nations and a north-south pattern between the developed and developing nations in Africa and South America. These routes closely resemble major air cargo and passenger routes of the world.

Major North American routes of commerce are shown in Figure 1.12. In the United States, these routes link the major metropolitan areas and represent the existing rail trunk line, interstate highway, and inland waterway patterns. The Canadian pattern links the major cities that are in a narrow population band along the border with the United States. This route connects Halifax, Montreal, Toronto, the industrial sectors of southern Ontario, Edmonton, Calgary, and Vancouver. Here the route follows Trans-Canada Highway as well as the mainlines of the Canadian Pacific and the Canadian National Railroads. The Great Lakes and St. Lawrence River water system is also important because it is an outlet for grain and other products from Canada to the rest of the world.

FIGURE 1.11 Major World Water Routes—Merchandise Traffic

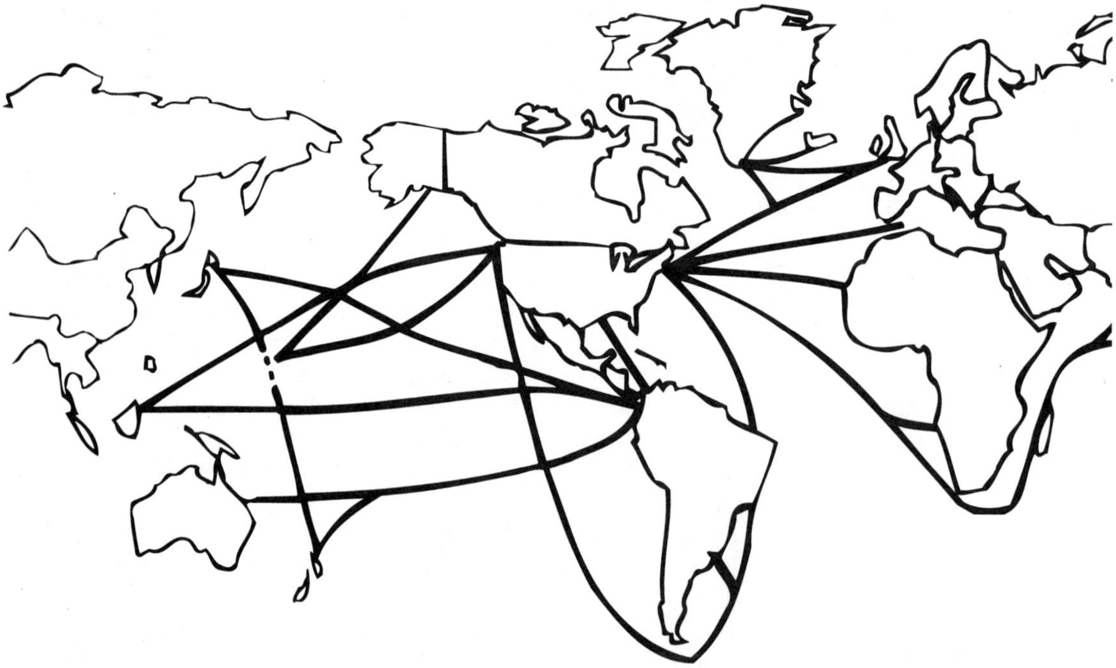

FIGURE 1.12 Major Commerce Routes of North America

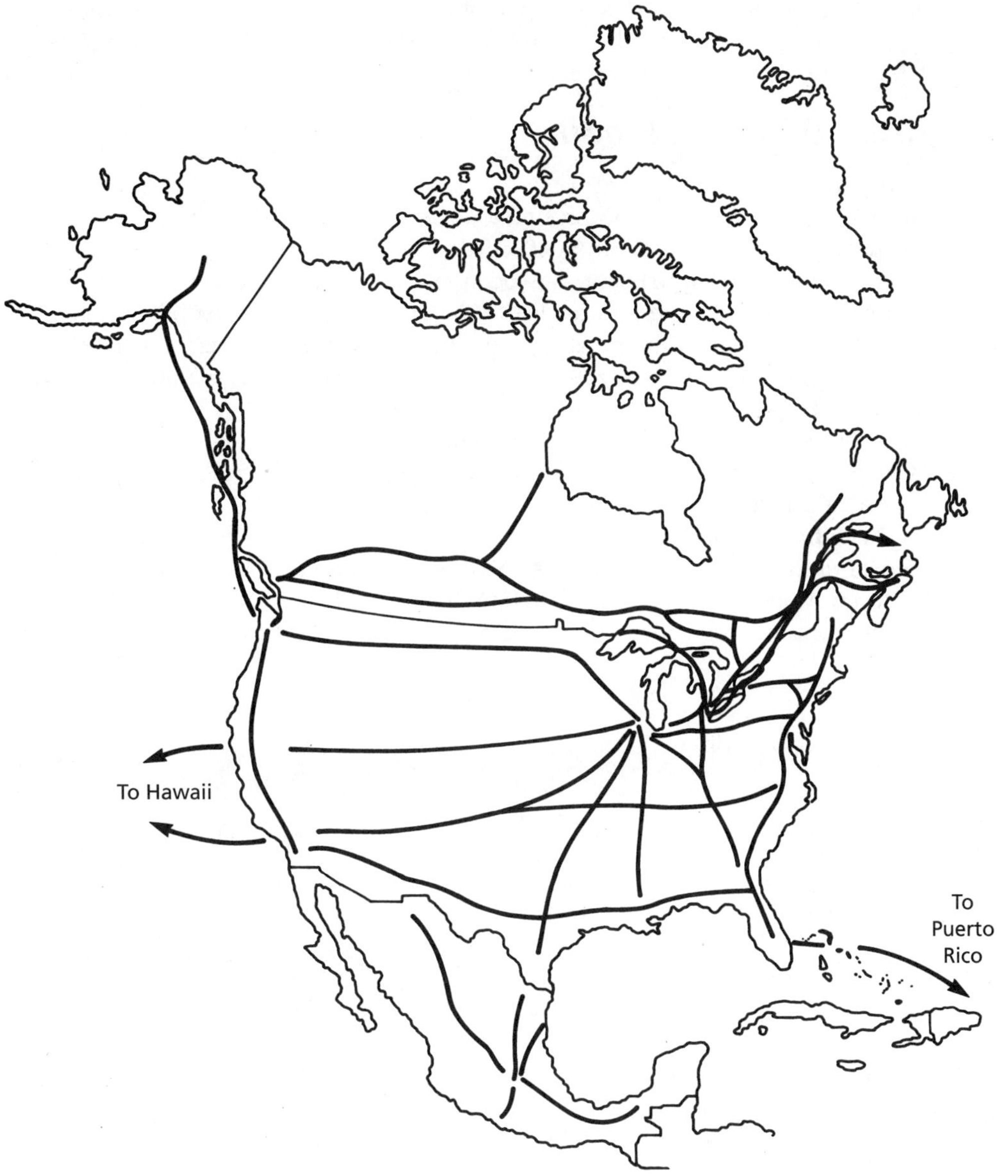

Mexico's major commerce routes are strongly tied to its economic center, represented by Mexico City. Here again the railroad mainlines and early highway development created an economic and social orientation in this pattern. The airline industry, however, does not require specific geographic routes to move persons or freight from origins to destinations. Unlike rail, highway, and water transportation, which must traverse specific routes, airlines only require the end points. In recent years, the creation of airline hub and spoke systems have created travel through cities that heretofore were not significant in that traffic. For example, in years past, a person traveling from New York to Roanoke, Virginia, would use a multistop airplane that would stop in Philadelphia, Baltimore, and Washington. Today that same person would probably travel on U.S. Airways to Pittsburgh and change to a commuter flight to Roanoke. This is an out-of-the-way route, but it is much faster than in the past. Major airline hubs in the United States and Canada are shown in Figure 1.13. These represent central connecting points for long-distance and feeder routes.

Gross Domestic Product

Transportation plays a major role in the overall economy of the United States (see Table 1.6). On the average, transportation now accounts for less than 20 percent of this nation's gross domestic product (GDP).

Passenger transportation has been growing in relation to the GDP until recently. Much of this increase was due to the greater use of automobiles and the energy costs associated with operating them. Air travel also accounts for a large part of the transportation expenditures in the economy. The U.S. Department of Transportation (DOT) reports that in 1980 airlines generated 204.4 billion passengers miles; by 1995, this had grown to more than 403 billion passenger miles, an increase of 97 percent in 15 years. Travel for business, personal, and vacation purposes is an important activity in the economy.

Freight transportation has traditionally accounted for between eight and nine percent of the GDP. In recent years, this has decreased to 6.1 percent, as shown in Table 1.6. Much of this decrease is due to the more efficient use of transportation resulting from less regulation. Although the economy is expanding, productivity in-

FIGURE 1.13 Major U.S. and Canadian Air Hub Points

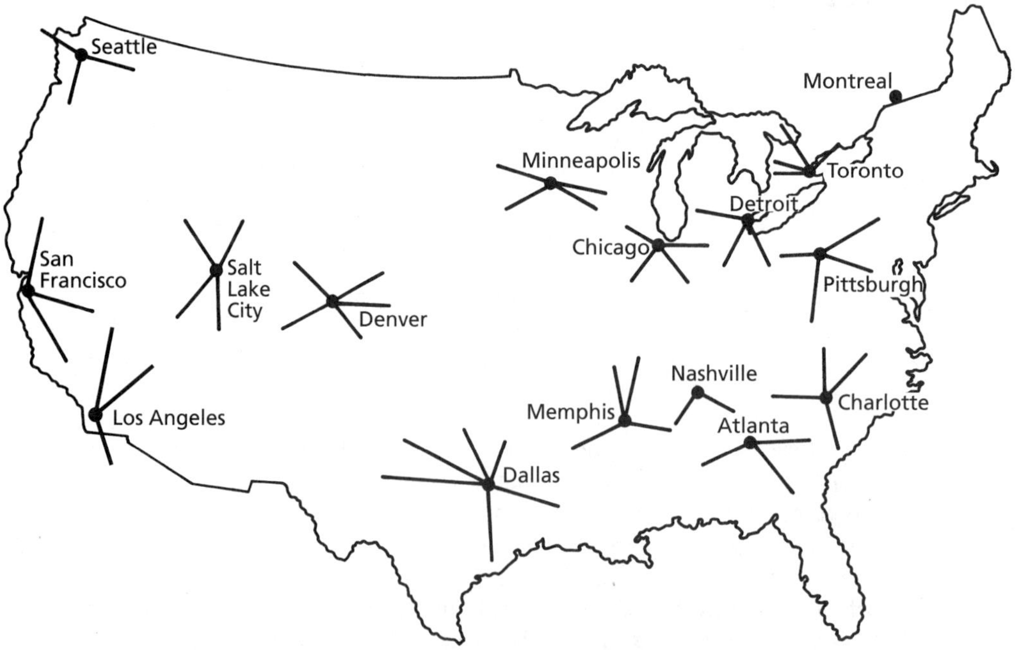

creases in and better use of existing transportation systems have enabled this growth to take place without proportionate increases in freight expenditures.

"Modal split" is a useful analytical tool in the study of transportation. This concept divides the entire transportation passenger or freight market according to the major modes of transportation. Table 1.7 shows the relative splits of intercity passenger travel. The two major categories are for-hire forms of transportation versus private automobile and private aircraft. The automobile dominates with more than 80 percent of this travel in the U.S. economy. The proportion has been decreasing slightly over the past two decades due to growth in airline travel. Deregulation of airline service in the 1980s has brought about a great increase in travel options and services for the traveling public. During this period, the relative level of air fares did not keep pace with the overall inflation level. As a result, air travel became more convenient and relatively cheaper for long-distance travel.

The freight intercity modal split is dominated by railroads with more than 35 percent of the ton-miles (see Table 1.8). Railroads have declined in relative share since World War II, with trucks, rivers, and oil pipelines increasing relative shares of the total ton-mile market in that time. Railroads typically move bulk, low-value commodities such as grain, coal, ore, and chemicals. In recent years, rail traffic by container, which transports relatively high-value finished goods, has increased. The air mode, while highly visible, still handles less than one percent of the total ton-miles in the United States.

The economy has expanded at a faster rate than the demand for freight transportation. The total ton-miles of all modes has increased between 1970 and 1990, as

TABLE 1.6 Transportation as a Part of the Gross Domestic Product (GDP)

	Percent of GDP			
	1965	1975	1985	1995
Freight Expenditures	9.2	7.1	6.5	6.1
Passenger Expenditures	11.4	11.5	11.8	10.0
Total Freight and Passenger Expenditures	20.6	18.6	18.3	16.1

Source: U.S. DOT Bureau of Transportation Statistics, *National Transportation Statistics,* Washington, D.C., 1997.

TABLE 1.7 Modal Split of Passenger Miles

For-Hire Passenger Modal Split

Year	Railroads	Buses	Air Carriers	For Hire Percentage of Total Passenger	Automobile Percentage of Total Passenger
1965	17.6	24.1	58.3	6.2	93.8
1975	4.7	14.0	81.3	8.4	91.6
1985	3.5	7.3	89.2	13.2	86.8
1995	N/A	6.5	93.5	13.5	86.5

Source: U.S. DOT Bureau of Transportation Statistics, *National Transportation Statistics,* Washington, D.C., 1997.

TABLE 1.8 Percent Volume of Intercity Freight Expressed as Percent of Total

Year	Railroads	Trucks	Great Lakes	Rivers and Coast	Oil Pipelines	Air	Total Ton-Miles (Millions–100%)
1965	37.6	19.4	4.1	22.3	16.5	.07	1,854,427
1975	33.0	19.9	3.0	21.8	22.2	.15	2,284,706
1985	29.7	20.7	1.6	28.6	19.1	.17	2,949,411
1995	35.8	25.3	1.6	20.5	16.4	.3	3,645,764

Source: U.S. DOT Bureau of Transportation Statistics, *National Transportation Statistics,* Washington, D.C., 1997.

shown in Table 1.8. One simple explanation gives some insight into this phenomenon. In the past, a domestic steel firm purchased transportation of raw materials (ore, lime, coal) and the movement of the outbound finished goods to the customer. At the very minimum, this involved four different movements. Today the steel might be imported, requiring one domestic movement between the port and the customer. Thus, steel is being used in the economy, but fewer transportation moves are involved in making it available to the customer.

Good transportation spurs economic development by giving mobility to production factors, which permits scale economies and increased efficiency. Good transportation enlarges the area that consumers and industries can draw on for resources and products. Good transportation expands the area to which a given plant may distribute its products economically, and the resulting specialization and scale economies provide a wider choice of products for consumers at a lower cost.

Environmental Significance

Although transportation provides the economy with numerous benefits, these positive aspects are not without associated costs. Transportation sometimes pollutes the environment and exploits natural resources, although most citizens feel that the benefits provided by transportation far exceed these costs. The environmental challenge of the future shall be to accurately assess the relationship between industrial benefits and their external societal costs.

The Environment

There has been growing concern over the impact of transportation on the environment with particular emphasis on air quality (pollution), noise, and water quality. The synergy between the transportation system and the environment is increasingly being investigated by both environmentalists and by transportation planners at all governmental levels. In fact, increasing pressure from the environmentalists has resulted in legal restrictions to help govern the balance between a sound and efficient transportation system and a safe and clean environment.

There will be a growing challenge into the twenty-first century to ensure efficient transportation facilities and mobility by maintaining our present system and developing new facilities to meet the growing needs of individuals and organizations. There will be even more trade-offs between competing objectives. Highway and air planners will be particularly challenged to develop innovative design solutions because of the 30+ federal statutes and executive orders governing the environment.

Air Quality

Pollution is an external side effect of transportation because of the widespread use of internal combustion engines. In fact, the internal combustion engine emissions are a concern not only for its effect on urban air quality (pollution), but also its involvement in acid rain and potential global climate changes.

Transportation is a major contributor to air pollution, accounting for about 67 percent of carbon monoxide, 30 percent of ozone-producing hydrocarbons, about 42 percent of nitrogen oxides, and 44 percent of suspended particles. Dramatic reductions have taken place in motor vehicle emission rates because of governmental requirements, but economic and population growth will result in persisting problems with pollution. Table 1.9 summarizes current motor vehicle emission standards.

Acid Rain

Essentially, acid rain is a pollution-related phenomenon whereby falling rain is much more acidic than normal rain. The addition of sulfur dioxide, nitrogen oxides, and volatile organic compounds to the atmosphere causes the acid rain. The pollutants result from industrial and commercial processes and combustion, as well as vehicle emissions. The acid deposits have an adverse impact on aquatic systems, crops, forests, human health, and visibility. It is difficult to reliably measure transportation's contribution to acid rain, but it is likely that this area will be a source of growing concern and increased regulation on transportation emissions in the future.

Global Climate Changes

An important issue facing the United States and the rest of the world is the so-called "greenhouse effect" and the related climate changes. Basically, the greenhouse effect is the physical process by which energy from the sun passes through the atmosphere relatively free, while heat radiating from the earth is partially blocked or absorbed by particular gases in the atmosphere released by human activities such as transportation.

TABLE 1.9 1995 Motor Vehicle Emission Standards

Autos (Light-Duty Vehicles)	(Grams per Mile)
Hydrocarbons	0.25
Carbon Monoxide	3.4
Oxides of Nitrogen (Gasoline)	0.4
Particulates	0.08
Light-Duty Trucks	(Grams per Mile)
Hydrocarbons	0.25
Carbon monoxide	3.4
Oxides of Nitrogen (Gasoline)	0.4
(Diesel)	1.0
Particulates	0.08
Heavy-Duty Trucks	(Grams per Brake Horsepower-Hour)
Hydrocarbons	1.9 (Gasoline-Powered) 1.3 (Diesel-Powered)
Carbon Monoxide	37.1 (Gasoline-Powered) 15.5 (Diesel-Powered)
Oxides of nitrogen	5.0 (Gasoline- and Diesel-Powered)
Particulates	0.10 (Diesel-Powered)

Source: U.S. DOT Bureau of Transportation Statistics, *National Transportation Statistics,* Washington, D.C., 1997.

A big concern is the ozone reduction in the stratosphere because it reduces the amount of ultraviolet radiation reaching the earth's surface from the sun. The hole in the ozone layer has been the focus of much concern and investigation because of the health-related problems and of increased risk of skin cancer. A particular concern in this area is the CFC compound used as the refrigerant for recharging and servicing air conditioning units in homes and vehicles. Again, we can expect worldwide concern and the development of protocols to reduce the risks in this area.

Maritime and Water Quality

The protection of the marine environment from the adverse effects of oil spills, garbage dumping from ships, hazardous material losses, and so on is a growing concern shared by many federal state agencies. One of the largest oil spills occurred in 1989 near Valdez, Alaska, from a tanker ship carrying crude oil from Alaska for the Exxon Oil Company. Almost 11 million gallons of crude oil were spilled; this environmental disaster raised the awareness for controls and better contingency preparedness to respond to such accidents.

In recent years, there has been a growing concern about the damage that plastic items and other ship-generated garbage can cause to the marine environment. Birds, marine mammals, and sea turtles are susceptible to this type of problem because they ingest the materials, which cause death. It is estimated that more than one million birds die each year from these causes.

Water quality, both for surface water and drinking water sources, is an area of risk and concern. Both surface water and drinking water sources are highly susceptible to many types of potential pollutants. Again, there will be continuing pressure to protect water quality by governmental controls and standards.

Noise

Another type of pollution is noise, which can emit from many sources, including transportation. There is an annoyance factor but also a health concern involved. Airplanes and motor vehicles are the major causes of noise. The U.S. DOT and the Federal Aviation Administration have been particularly active in this area, helping to guide land use planning for compatibility with transportation facilities and conducting research to help solve the problem. Noise emissions are governed by the Noise Control Act of 1972, which allows the setting of operational standards for aircraft and trucks and even rail equipment operated by interstate carriers.

Safety

One of the most disturbing by-products of transportation is injury and loss of life. In 1995, 44,229 persons lost their lives in the United States while engaged in transport. Approximately 94 percent of those fatalities occurred in highway vehicles. However, as Table 1.10 shows, the number of deaths has declined in relation to the ever-growing amount of transportation demand. This positive statistic is the result of increased licensing regulations and more reliable vehicle designs. Unfortunately, trends in the area of safety for freight transportation aren't as promising. Train accidents, oil spills, and the threat of gaseous explosions while in transit have increased. With the increasing variety of products being shipped and the increasing volume of transportation, these problems require greater attention. We can hope that safety in freight transportation will soon parallel the progress made in passenger transportation; however, much work remains to be done.

TABLE 1.10 Transportation Fatalities

	1975	1985	1995
Motor Vehicles	44,525	43,825	41,798
Auto Occupants	25,928	23,212	22,358
Truck Occupants	5,817	7,666	10,183
Motorcycle Riders	3,189	4,564	2,221
Pedestrians/Others	8,600	7,782	6,524
Railroad	575	454	567
Aircraft	1,473	1,594	961
Large-Scheduled	124	526	168
Commuter	28	37	9
Air Taxi	69	76	52
General Aviation	1,252	955	732
Water Vessels	1,709	1,247	882
Commercial	243	131	46
Recreational	1,466	1,116	836
Pipeline	15	33	21
Gas	8	28	18
Liquid	7	5	3
Total Transportation-Related Fatalities	48,297	47,153	44,229

Source: U.S. DOT Bureau of Transportation Statistics, *National Transportation Statistics,* Washington, D.C., 1997.

The nation's increasing demand for transportation services has imposed social costs in addition to monetary costs. Over the past 25 years, great strides have been made, particularly at the national level, in mitigating those negative social costs. Overall, the benefits far outweigh the costs to society, but vigilance is necessary. Table 1.11 indicates some of the actions taken to constrain the negative impacts of transportation.

Substance Abuse

Abuse of alcohol and drugs is an issue in transportation. Railroad, truck, and air crews are involved in public safety when they help move passengers or when they operate freight vehicles on the highways and through towns. Success has been achieved as recent studies have shown that less than one percent of drivers tested were positive for alcohol and less than two percent tested positive for drugs. Much has been achieved by joint industry-carrier partnership which changed attitudes from adversarial to cooperative. The federal government has also played a significant role by drafting regulations which focus not only on detection but assistance as well.

Social Significance

Transportation provides employment and enhances travel. Transportation employs approximately nine million persons (see Table 1.12). This has increased since the 1970s, which indicates the increasing service intensity of the industry.

A good transportation system also can enhance the health and welfare of a population. One of the major problems facing the famine relief efforts in the eastern

TABLE 1.11 Actions to Mitigate the Negative Impact of Transportation

Impact	Action
Noise	Vehicle and equipment standards; researching the impact of noise and developing solutions; improved aviation operating procedures; environmental impact statements.
Air pollution	Emission standards; transportation control plans; environmental impact statements.
Water pollution	Compulsory oil spill insurance, improved regulations concerning waste and hazardous materials handling; environmental impact statements.
Marred vision	Billboard standards in interstate system.
Safety	Increased safety regulations; safer design standards.
Petroleum dependence	Auto fuel consumption standards; more realistic petroleum fuel costs.
Alcohol and substance abuse	Tighter laws and greater enforcement.

region of Africa in the middle 1980s was the lack of sufficient and effective transportation networks to move needed food and farm supplies from the ports inland to the population centers. Insufficient railroads, roads, vehicles, storage, and related distribution facilities hampered effective delivery of the needed food and supplies. In addition, one of the problems facing the region in normal times is insufficient transportation, which hinders inbound and outbound product flows.[21]

Political Significance

The origin and maintenance of transportation systems are dependent on the government. Government intervention is needed to design feasible routes, cover the expense of building public highways, and develop harbors and waterways. Adequate transportation is needed to create national unity; the transportation network must permit the leaders of government to travel rapidly to and communicate with the people they govern.

Governmental Responsibility

The government is responsible for aiding all passenger and freight transportation systems in which the costs cannot be covered reasonably by a central group of users. The government has also created regulations that offer consumers the opportunity to transact in a competitive free market environment.

One outgrowth of regulation is the **common carrier.** The common carrier has a duty to render service without discrimination based upon set rates for specific commodities.

The government's role as a regulator of transportation services does mean certain drawbacks for the public. For example, the right of **eminent domain** often forces individuals to move and sell their land, even though they may not wish to do so. The government's power of eminent domain gives it the right to acquire land for

TABLE 1.12 U.S. Employment in Transportation and Related Industries

	Number of Persons Employed (In Thousands)		
	1975	**1985**	**1995**
Transportation Service			
Air Transport	363	522	788
Bus (Intercity and Rural)	40	35	24
Local Transport	69	92	203
Railroads	548	359	239
Liquid Pipeline	18	19	15
Taxi	85	38	32
Trucking and Warehousing	1,108	1,361	1,867
Water	194	185	174
Total	2,425	2,611	3,342
Transport Equipment and Manufacturing			
Aircraft and Parts	499	616	449
Motor Vehicles, Equipment, Tires	916	977	1,048
Railroad Equipment	57	33	37
Ship and Boat Building and Repair	194	187	159
Other Transportation Equipment	157	241	172
Total	1,823	2,054	1,865
Transport-Related Industries			
Automotive and Home Supply Stores	212	304	373
Automotive Wholesalers	382	454	492
Automotive Repair Services and Parking	439	730	1,020
Gasoline Service Stations	622	588	647
Highway and Street Construction	297	264	227
New and Used Car Dealers	731	856	996
Other Automotive Retail	112	140	174
Total	2,795	3,336	3,929
Government Transport Employees			
U.S. Department of Transportation	112	100	101
Highway Employees (State and Local)	604	549	NA
Total	716	649	101
Total Transportation Employment	7,759	8,650	9,237

Source: U.S. DOT Bureau of Transportation Statistics, *National Transportation Statistics,* Washington, D.C., 1997.

public use. Hence, the construction of many highways displaces families because governmental intervention has opened the right-of-way for certain transportation routes. Although families may be displaced, the government's role is to act in the best interest of the public by designing routes that help the citizens of the nation efficiently conduct their business.

Closely connected with transportation's political role is its function as a provider for national defense. Today our transportation system enhances our life-styles and protects us from outsiders. The ability to transport troops acts as both a weapon and a deterrent in this age of energy shortages and global conflicts. The conflicts in Central America and the Middle East place even greater emphasis on the importance of logistics in protecting our distant vital interests.

Although it is accurate to say that the American transportation system has been shaped by economic factors, political and military developments have also played important roles. Transportation policy incorporates more than economics—the expected benefits of the system extend beyond the economic realm.

Overview of Modern Transportation

The significance of our transportation system touches all aspects of life. For example, the location of transportation facilities has effects on the surrounding communities. Railroads and superhighways divide towns and neighborhoods, and the location of highway interchanges can determine the location of manufacturing, retailing, and distribution operations. The character of a neighborhood or a city is often determined by its ability to act as a transportation center. The port city of New Orleans, the rail city of Altoona, Pennsylvania, and St. Louis's role as the "Gateway to the West" are examples of towns that have become known for their ability to provide transportation services.

Factors can be identified correlating network changes to changes in neighborhood characteristics. However, transportation factors in connection with a whole series of other factors cause sociological change that extends beyond transportation factors alone. According to sociologists and urbanologists, the regional shopping centers, the higher-income commuter enclaves, and the resort, vacation, and amusement districts grow as the result of available transportation networks, as well as the relative expense of maintaining these areas.

The consumer makes decisions based on transportation services, availability, cost, and adequacy. Product decisions (what products or product to produce or distribute) are closely related to this availability of transportation and adequacy of the transporter to move the goods. Market area decisions are dominated by the ability of the transporter to get the product to market at a low cost. Decisions about whether to purchase parts, raw materials, supplies, or finished goods for resale must reflect transport costs. Location decisions, too, are influenced by many transportation factors. The decisions about where plants, warehouses, offices, and stores should be located all take transportation requirements into consideration. Last, pricing decisions are strongly affected by the transportation operation. The logistics area of the firm is often considered a cost center; therefore, changes in the price of transportation will often have a serious effect on the prices of products in general.

Overall, **transportation interacts** with three groups of our society: users, providers, and the government. Thus, transportation decisions are expected to consider all aspects of society in one form or another.

The role of the user is to make decisions that will maximize the relevant consumer-oriented goals. The power of the user lies in the ability to demand and pay (or not pay if the wrong service is offered) for certain forms of transportation.

The providers, both public and private, including agencies such as freight forwarders and brokers, must determine the demands of the system and services to be offered. These decisions are made in light of total modal use, the importance of each mode to the economy, profits, and the way in which each company views itself in relation to its competitors.

Overview of Transportation Trends

The transportation industry is in a constant state of flux. It is intertwined with the social, political, and economic forces in a society and economy. The industry as a whole has undergone a tremendous change from deregulation since the late 1970s.

STOP OFF

Challenges and Opportunities

The vitality of the United States has always been linked to mobility—from immigrants coming to our shores to wagons moving West, from rail lines spanning the continent to ships and planes fanning out across the oceans, and now vehicles racing into space. Transportation is an engine for economic growth, and a link between both the regions and the businesses and the people of the nation and the world. Americans have moved farther, gone faster, and made more progress as a nation than any other society in history. As we enter the twenty-first century, our transportation system, the symbol of that movement, will drive our growth, foster our freedom, and signal our success in forcing solutions to the social and economic challenges we face. America's success in building and developing transportation is a proud accomplishment. Through our combined talents and resources, imagination, and innovation, transportation will be tomorrow—as it has always been in the past—integral not only to the way we live but also to building a better America for the future.

What We Have Achieved

After more than 100 years of industrial and technological development, the United States has a mature transportation industry. The basic technologies for railroads, shipping, highway vehicles, and mass transit were developed decades ago, and those systems are well established today. The array of airports that began in the early days of commercial aviation in the 1930s served 90 million flights in 1988. In 1956, President Dwight D. Eisenhower initiated the National System of Interstate and Defense Highways—our **interstates**—for the first time creating a unified network of roadways designed for high-speed, efficient, safe motor vehicle travel across the country. Today that system is virtually complete.

Now the focus must shift from building the nation's basic transportation systems to adapting and modernizing transportation systems and services to support economic growth, meet the competitive demands of the international marketplace, contribute to our national security, and improve the quality of life for all Americans.

As we begin a new decade and prepare for the twenty-first century, the United States must renew its commitment to maintaining our transportation system as the finest in the world. We are entering an era in which our ability to compete internationally is critical to our economic vitality and quality of life. To meet the changing demands of the international marketplace, we must have safe, efficient transportation to carry people where they want to go and to move the vast quantities of goods we produce and consume. Projected transportation needs for the twenty-first century eclipse our present public and private sector programs. We must broaden the base of support or transportation, reinvigorate investment, and tap new sources of ideas and capital to meet growing demands.

Source: U.S. Department of Transportation, *Moving America* (Washington, D.C., February 1990), pp. 1, 13.

This has affected how carriers have organized, priced, sold their services, and managed operations. Table 1.13 presents many of the key forces in transportation during the 1990s and the impact they may have in the 2000s. These points set the stage for the remaining chapters of this book, which deal with individual modes of transportation, cost and rate making, the buying and selling of transportation service, government regulation and policies, carrier management, and directions for the future.

As we move into the twenty-first century, our transportation system faces significant challenges and problems because of global competition, governmental budget constraints, and increased demand from special interest groups such as senior citizens. The patterns of trade that help to drive transportation are changing more quickly and becoming more complex because of the dynamic global environment that we now have and the changing economic base in the United States.

Transportation touches the lives of all U.S. citizens and affects their economic well-being, their safety, their access to people and places, and the quality of their environment. When the transportation system does not function well, it is a source

TABLE 1.13 Transportation Trends

The Transportation Market
Tailoring of services and equipment for specific shipper/receiver needs
Freight transportation provided for just-in-time, sequenced movements
User cost for international transportation declining
International transactions easier
Sale of transportation service being done more by parties other than the sales and marketing group of the carriers
Shift from heavy industrial, production-oriented transportation to fast, service-demanding finished goods transportation
Users of transportation are seeing transportation less as a distinct operation and more in the context of total production, overhead, sourcing, labor, distribution, and marketing factors
Greater marketing orientation by carriers
More travel
More discretionary travel
More international transportation
Transportation Supply
Increased use of third-party services
Consolidation in air, rail, and motor modes
Integration of modes via joint ownership or special arrangements
Strength and health of feeder firms (commuters, regional motor carriers)
Continued technological advances in most modes
Less private carriage use for reasons of cost savings; still present where special services are involved
More international alliances of carrier
Operations and Management
Operations in closer link with marketing and sales of the carrier
Leasing of containers, aircraft, terminal facilities, and other assets on increase
Information-driven organization and structures
Decision making and accountability being pushed lower in the organization
More substitution of communication of transportation
Government Policies and Regulation
Deregulation spreading from the United States to Canada and Europe
Less economic regulation (rates, routes, services, finance)
Increased noneconomic regulation (environmental, substance abuse, safety)
Government funding not keeping up with the deterioration of transportation infrastructure

of great personal frustration and, perhaps, economic loss, but when the transportation system performs well, it provides opportunity and economic rewards for everyone.

Demand for Transportation

Transportation is an important and pervasive element in our society, affecting every person, either directly or indirectly. The goods we consume, our economic livelihood, our mobility, and our entertainment are in some way affected by transportation.

The growth of the U.S. economy, as well as the economy of most industrialized countries, is attributable in part to the benefits derived from mass production and the division of labor. This specialization of labor and production results in an oversupply of goods at one location and an undersupply, or demand, for these goods at another place. Transportation bridges the supply-and-demand gap inherent in mass production.

The interrelationship between transportation and mass production points out the dependency of our society on transportation. As each of us specializes in the production of a particular good or service, we are relying upon someone else to produce the goods and services that we need to survive. Also, we depend upon transportation to move these goods and services to our location in an efficient and economical manner. Like the citizens of most industrialized countries, U.S. citizens, as individuals, are not self-sufficient.

On a global scale, countries recognize international dependencies. The United States supplies many countries with manufactured goods, while other countries provide the United States with raw materials and agricultural products. For example, the United States is dependent on the Arab oil-producing nations for oil, and these countries rely on the United States to provide a vast array of manufactured goods such as aircraft, clothing, and computers. Again, transportation plays a key role in this international dependency, or trade, by permitting the equalization of supply and demand on a global basis.

Likewise, people must move from areas where they are currently situated to areas where they desire to be. Within the supply-demand context, the origin of a passenger is an area of oversupply and the destination is an area of undersupply. Transportation performs the bridging function between the supply-demand gap for people, such as the movement of people from their homes to their work locations.

As with freight, people depend on transportation for their **mobility.** The more mobile a society, the more critical and efficient an economical passenger transportation system is to its citizens. With today's technology, an executive in Chicago leaves home at 6:00 A.M. on Monday to catch an 8:00 A.M. flight to Los Angeles to attend a 1:00 P.M. meeting. At 5:00 P.M. (Pacific Coast time) that afternoon, the executive boards a flight to Australia with a continuation to London later in the week. This global workweek is possible because of the speed of air transportation.

Transportation has a definite and identifiable effect upon a person's life-style. An individual's decisions about where to work, live, and play are influenced by transportation. Cultural differences among geographic regions in the United States, as well as among countries and regions of the world, are lessened by the ability of residents to travel outside the confines of their region (country).

The automobile has been the form of transportation that most affects U.S. life-styles. The convenience, flexibility, and relatively low cost of automobile travel has permitted individuals to live in locations different from where they work. The growth of suburbs can be attributed to the automobile, because people can drive 20 to 60 miles or more one way to work. The automobile also enables people to seek medical, dental, and recreational services at varying locations throughout a region.

A prime ingredient in increased passenger travel is economical transportation. Unfortunately, the rising cost of automobile and air travel, a result of escalating energy, labor, and equipment costs, is beginning to cause a change in life-styles. Instead of traveling long distances for a vacation, many people now stay closer to home or do not travel at all. Areas of the country that are highly dependent on tourists have experienced economic difficulties.

Flight from the cities to the suburbs has been somewhat stalled by the rising costs of automobile travel. The 500- to 100-mile round trip per day is becoming quite expensive for many families. Some recent developments indicate that families are returning to the cities to live so that they can reduce travel-to-work expenses. This trend is not overwhelming yet, but the next few years may see a stronger growth in the demand for city rather than suburban dwellings.

In the remainder of this chapter, our focus is on the demand for freight and passenger transportation. Attention is directed to the economic characteristics of freight and passenger transportation demand as well as the traits unique to each. Initially, consideration is given to transportation demand measurement units and the level of aggregation.

Demand Measurement Units

Transportation demand is essentially a request to move a given amount of cargo or people a specific distance. Therefore, the demand for transportation is measured in weight/passenger-distance units. For freight, the demand unit is the ton-mile and for people, it is the passenger-mile.

The **ton-mile** is not a homogenous unit. The demand for 200 ton-miles of freight transportation could be for moving 200 tons one mile, 100 tons two miles, one ton 200 miles, or any other combination of weight and distance that equals 200 ton-miles. In addition, the unique transportation requirements for direction, equipment, and service will vary among customers with a 200 ton-mile demand. For example, the demand for 200 ton-miles of ice cream from Pittsburgh may require movement in all directions and a refrigerated vehicle with same-day delivery, whereas the demand for 200 ton-miles of gasoline from Philadelphia may be for movement north, south, and west in a tank vehicle with next-day delivery.

The above examples are aimed at delineating the heterogenous nature of the transportation demand unit. The same unit demand may have a different cost of producing and different user service requirements. However, no other measurement unit reflects the basic weight and distance components of freight transportation demand.

Similarly, the **passenger-mile** is a heterogenous unit. A 500 passenger-mile demand could be one passenger moving 500 miles or 500 passengers moving one mile. The demand of 500 passenger-miles could be via automobile, railroad, or airplane as well as first class or coach, luxury or basic, and quick or slow. The demand attributes of the passenger-mile vary from passenger to passenger.

Level of Aggregation

The demand for transportation can be examined at different levels of aggregation. **Aggregate demand** for transportation is the sum of the individual demands for freight and passenger transportation. In addition, aggregate demand is the sum of the demand for transportation via different modes, and the aggregate demand for a particular mode is the sum of the demand for specific carriers in that mode. Table 1.7 shows the allocation of aggregate passenger miles and Table 1.8 shows the allocation of aggregate ton-miles.

Demand Elasticity

Demand elasticity refers to the sensitivity of customers to changes in the price. If customers are sensitive to price, a price reduction will increase the demand for the item and total revenue received. If customers are insensitive to price, that is, demand is inelastic, a price reduction will result in a small relative change in quantity demanded and total revenue will fall.

In traditional terms, demand elasticity is the ratio of the percentage change in quantity demanded to percentage change in price, or,

$$\text{Elasticity} = \frac{\%\ \text{change in quantity}}{\%\ \text{change in price}}$$

If demand is elastic, the quantity demanded changes more than the change in price and the elasticity coefficient (E) is greater than one. Conversely, a product or service is said to be **price inelastic,** or insensitive to price change, if the quantity demanded changes less than the change in price (E is less than one).

In general, the demand for freight transportation is inelastic. Freight rate reductions will not dramatically increase the demand for freight transportation because transportation costs represent, in the aggregate, less than four percent of a product's landed cost. Substantial rate reductions would be required for a meaningful increase in the demand for the product and consequently demand for transportation of the product.

On a modal and specific carrier basis, demand is price-sensitive. The relative modal share of aggregate demand is in part determined by the rates charged. Reductions in rates charged by a particular mode will result in increases in volume of freight handled by that mode. This assumes that the mode that reduced the rate is physically capable of transporting the freight.

For example, the long-haul transportation of new automobiles was dominated by truck transportation in the 1960s. In the 1970s, the railroads developed a new railcar specifically designed to transport new automobiles. This new railcar enabled the railiroads to improve efficiency and reduce the rates charged for hauling new automobiles. The percentage of new automobiles hauled by railroads increased following the railroads' use of the new railcar, while lower rates and the share of intercity ton-miles of new automobiles transported by truck decreased. Today trucks are used primarily to transport new automobiles short distances, from rail yards to dealerships.

Modal and specific carrier demand is also **service elastic.** Assuming no price changes, the modal or specific carrier demand is much more sensitive to changes in service levels provided. Many air passengers monitor the "on-time" service levels of the various air carriers and, when possible, will select the air carrier that provides the best on-time service. For example, if two air carriers are available and one is on time 100 percent of the time and the other only 60 percent of the time, the air passenger is more likely to use the carrier that has a 100 percent on-time performance record.

Freight Transportation

The demand for freight transportation is based upon the demand for a product in a given location. Because of the specialization of labor and mass production, specific areas have an oversupply of product while other geographic areas face a deficit. This geographic imbalance in the supply of a product gives rise to the demand for freight transportation. In this section, attention is given to the characteristics of freight transportation demand.

Derived Demand

The demand to transport a product to a given location depends on the existence of a demand to consume (use) the product at that location. Freight is generally not transported to a location unless a need for the product exists at the location. Thus, the demand for freight transportation is derived from the customer demand for the product.

For example, Figure 1.14 illustrates the derived demand nature of freight transportation. The oversupply of widgets at the production site, City A, will not be transported to City C because no demand for widgets exists at City C. However, there is a demand for 100 widgets at City B and, consequently, a demand for the transportation of 100 widgets to City B. Because of the demand for 100 widgets at City B, there is a demand for the transportation of widgets from City A to City B.

The derived demand characteristics imply that freight transportation demand cannot be affected by freight carrier actions. As noted above, this assumption is true for the aggregate demand for transportation. For example, if a freight carrier lowers the rate to zero for moving high-tech personal computers from the United States to a developing nation, this "free" transportation will not materially change the demand for personal computers in the developing nation. The demand for personal computers is dependent on educational levels of the citizens, electrical power availability, and so on, not price alone.

However, at the disaggregate level, i.e., modal, carrier, or specific traffic lane, the rates charged or service level provided can influence the demand for the product and the demand to transport the product. This impact on product demand considers the value of the service provided to the user of the product and is discussed next.

Value of Service

Value of service considers the impact of the transportation cost and service on the demand for the product. Lower transportation cost will cause a shift in demand for transportation among the modes and specific carriers. It can also affect the demand to transport freight over a specific traffic lane.

The impact of transportation cost on the demand for a product at a given location focuses on the **landed cost** of the product. The landed cost of a product includes the cost of the product at the source plus the cost to transport the product to

FIGURE 1.14 Derived Demand for Freight Transportation

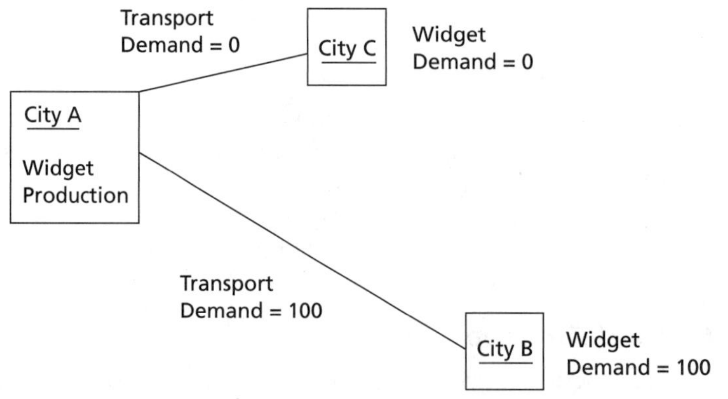

its destination. If the landed cost of a product is lower than that of other sources, there will be a demand for that product and for transportation of that product.

For example, in Figure 1.15, a manufacturer of bicycle tires located in Chicago is competing in the Boston market with local producers. For the Chicago bicycle tire manufacturer to be competitive, the landed cost of its tire must be lower than the cost of the local manufacturers' tires. The Boston manufacturers have a manufacturing cost of $4 per tire, while the Chicago manufacturer's cost is $3. As long as the transportation cost per tire from Chicago to Boston is less than $1, the Chicago tire will have a **landed cost advantage** and a demand for the Chicago tire will exist in Boston (assuming the quality is equal to that of the locally produced tires). Conversely, if the transportation cost exceeds $1 per tire, Boston consumers will purchase tires from local manufacturers and there will be no demand for, as well as no demand to transport, the Chicago tire.

The landed cost also determines the extent of the market for a business. The greater the distance the product is shipped, the greater the landed cost. At some distance from the product source, the landed cost becomes prohibitive to the buyer, and there is no demand for the product. Also, the landed cost can determine the **extent of the market** between two competing companies.

The works of Fetter and Losch[22] suggest that the extent of the market area for two competing firms is the point at which the lowest price (or landed cost) is equal for the products of the two firms. The market area for a seller will be the area where the seller has a landed cost advantage over its competitor because the buyer is assumed to select the seller that offers the lowest price.

To illustrate this concept, Figure 1.16 presents an example of two producers located 200 miles apart. Producer P has a production cost of $50 per unit and a transportation cost of $0.60 per unit per mile. Producer S has a production cost of $50 per unit and a transportation cost of $0.50 per unit per mile. The extent of the market between the two producers is the point at which the landed cost (LC) of P is equal to that of S, or where x is the distance from P's plant to the limit of the market area and $(200 - x)$ is the distance from S's plant to the market area.

$$
\begin{aligned}
\text{LC (P)} &= \text{LC (S)} \\
\text{Production (P)} + \text{Transportation (P)} &= \text{Production (S)} + \text{Transportation (S)} \\
\$50 + \$0.60\,(x) &= \$50 + \$0.50\,(200 - x) \\
\$0.60\,(x) + \$0.50\,(x) &= \$50 + \$100 - \$50 \\
\$1.1 &= \$100 \\
x &= 90.9 \text{ miles from P}
\end{aligned}
$$

Solving the equation for x shows that P has a market area that extends 90.9 miles from its plant and S has a market area that extends 109.1 miles from its facility. The

FIGURE 1.15 Demand and Landed Cost

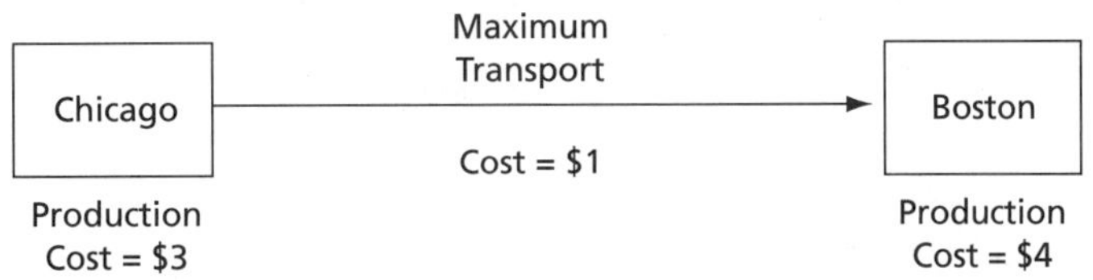

company with the lower transportation cost (S) has a greater market area than the firm with the higher transportation cost (P).

Service Components of Freight Demand

Shippers of freight have varying service requirements of transport providers. These service requirements range from specific pickup times to equipment and communication. The service demands are related to the cost implications of the transportation service provided. The transportation service characteristics of freight shippers include transit time, reliability, accessibility, capability, and security.[23]

Transit time affects the level of inventory held and the cost of holding inventory. The longer the transit time, the higher the inventory levels and inventory carrying cost. The longer the transit time, the more inventory must be held while awaiting the arrival of the shipment. Also, transit times impact the cost of inventory in the supply chain pipeline. For example, the supply of clothing produced in the Pacific Rim may require 45 days transit time from manufacturer to retail store. While the clothes are in transit for 45 days, someone, either buyer or seller, incurs the cost of financing the shipment for 45 days. If the transit time is reduced to 15 days by use of air transportation, this in-transit inventory financing cost would be reduced by 30 days.

The longer the transit time, the greater the potential cost of stockouts. Using the Pacific Rim example above, a stockout of clothing at the retail store could mean a maximum of 45 days, during which sales are lost and the profits from these potential sales are foregone. Shorter transit times reduce the potential stockout cost.

Reliability refers to the consistency of transit time. Meeting pickup and delivery schedules enables the shippers and receivers to optimize inventory levels and minimize stockout costs. Unreliable transit time requires the freight receiver to either increase inventory levels to guard against stockout conditions or incur stockouts. Reliable service directly affects the level of modal and specific carrier demand; that is, a shipper will shift from an unreliable carrier (mode) to one that is reliable. And the customer may switch from a supplier who provides unreliable delivery service to one that is reliable, thereby impacting the transportation demand for specific carriers on specific traffic lanes.

Accessibility is the ability of the transportation provider to move the freight between a specific origin-destination. The inability of a carrier to provide direct service between an origin-destination results in added costs and transit time for the shipper. For example, an air carrier does not move freight from Lansing, Michigan, directly to Angers, France. First, the freight is moved by truck from Lansing to Detroit; it is then flown to Paris, and last, it is moved from Paris to Angers by either truck or rail. The inability of the air carrier to provide direct service requires additional transportation by truck and rail and adds to the transit time. Similar conditions exist for rail and water carriers. Motor carriers have a distinct advantage in accessibility.

FIGURE 1.16 Extent of Market Area

200 Miles

P ———————————————— S

P	S
Production = $50/unit	Production = $50/unit
Transportation = $0.60/unit/mile	Transportation = $0.50/unit/mile

The ability of the carrier to provide such "special" service requirements is the essence of **capability.** Based on the physical and marketing characteristics of the freight, shippers have unique demands for equipment, facilities, and communication. Products requiring controlled temperature necessitate the use of refrigerated vehicles. Time-sensitive shipments demand state-of-the-art communication systems to monitor their exact location and arrival time. Marketing considerations may dictate the demand for carriers to provide freight consolidation and break-bulk facilities to lower total freight costs and transit times so as to maintain or increase the demand for the product. These are just a few of the many and varied demands placed on transportation service providers.

Finally, **security** is concerned with the safety of the goods in transit. Shipments that are damaged or lost in transit cause increased costs in the areas of inventory and/or stockouts. A damaged shipment cannot be used (sold), and the buyer faces the possibility of losing a sale or stopping the production process. Increasing inventory levels to guard against the stockout cost resulting from a damaged shipment causes increased inventory carrying costs. Table 1.14 provides a summary of the service components of freight demand.

Location of Economic Activity

Transportation has been a major determinant in the location of industrial facilities since the Industrial Revolution. The cost of transporting raw materials into a facility and the cost of transporting finished goods to markets directly affect the profitability of the plant or warehouse. In addition, the quality of the transport service, such as the time required to traverse the spatial gap between sources of supply, plants, warehouses, and markets, affects inventory, stockout, and other costs as identified above.

Water transportation has played an important role in the location of many major cities. The early settlers to the United States relied on water transportation to tie European markets and supply sources to the developing country. Thus, cities that are major population centers such as New York, Philadelphia, and Boston are port cities. As the U.S. frontier was settled, it became tied to these port cities that provided a source of supplies and markets for the western region. Other cities—Pittsburgh, Cincinnati, and St. Louis—developed along the internal waterways. As railroad transportation developed, however, cities and industrial facilities grew at locations that were not adjacent to waterways. Later, the automobile and truck enabled the development of cities and industrial facilities at virtually any location.

As the U.S. market grew, firms had to decide where new facilities should be located. Today many companies are faced with the question of where to locate plants and warehouses in light of changing markets, especially the exodus of people and

TABLE 1.14 Service Components of Freight Demand

Service Component	User Implication
Transit Time	Inventory, stockout costs
Reliability	Inventory, stockout costs
Accessibility	Transit time, transportation cost
Capability	Meets products' unique physical and marketing requirements
Security	Inventory, stockout costs

many industries to the Sun Belt states, as well as changing raw material supply locations. As markets and supply locations change and transit times become longer, firms experience higher costs for transportation, inventory, and warehousing.

As the location of economic activity changes, so does the demand for transportation. The aging of the U.S. population has seen a shifting of population to, for example, the southern states of Florida, North and South Carolina, and Arizona. This shift in population requires businesses supplying consumer products to demand more transportation services into these states, and some companies have responded to this population shift by locating production facilities in these states.

Passenger Transportation

Passenger transportation is the movement of people. Passenger movement accounts for about 10 percent of the annual GDP. In addition, there are many related industries, including hotels/motels, parks and recreation facilities, restaurants, and travel agencies. The study of passenger transportation demand requires an examination of people's motives for travel and movement. Attention is directed initially at long-distance, intercity passenger demand and finally urban, short-distance, travel demand.

Business Travel

Business travel is one of the major passenger markets. This is employment-related travel, and it is often travel in which the person is reimbursed or otherwise compensated in some way. This is a major market segment of the airline industry. Business travel is a much smaller part of the bus and water passenger markets.

The air-travel business market is highly sensitive to schedules rather than to price. The strength of a carrier's business is often based on this market segment. Airlines find that it is important to offer many flights throughout the day between two points in order to become a dominant carrier in a market. Further, it is a travel demand that usually consists of "out in the morning and back in the evening" scheduling. Traffic is typically heaviest Monday through Friday. Travel convenience, schedules, in-flight amenities, and special services are important to business travelers.

A low fare is generally not as important in this market as it is with personal or vacation travel. Business travel is derived from the need for a meeting at another location, and the cost of travel is usually not a major factor in the decision to go or not to go. For this reason, the airlines find that they can charge higher full coach fares, rather than resorting to discount fares in this market. Business travelers are the first-class passengers or the full-fare coach passengers.

Vacation Travel

Vacation travel, a pleasure travel, represents another major passenger market. These travelers often view transportation as a means of getting to a vacation destination point. In some cases, carriers have been able to include the transportation leg itself as part of the vacation experience; that is, the transportation leg can be both part of the derived demand for the trip to a destination as well as part of the vacation experience. This is the case with cruise ship travel and long-distance rail movement.

Vacation travel is typically **price-sensitive** and often concerned with the particular time of day or day of week schedules. Vacation travel has been heavily promoted by the airlines for Saturday and Sunday travel when their transport capacity is not heavily used by business travelers. Further, the vacation travel market is where

STOP OFF

Georgia-Pacific Unlocks Door to Doublestacks

Transportation executives at Georgia-Pacific felt as though they were missing out on something significant. Time and time again, they read or heard accounts of the recent dramatic advances in intermodalism, particularly in the area of double-stack train operations. But they themselves couldn't take advantage of these developments for one very simple reason: Their products were incompatible with the equipment. As the nation's largest producer of bulk forest products, they required flatbed transport. But until very recently, double-stack train operators offered only closed-van containers.

Today that's all changed. By leveraging the company's position as one of the nation's highest-volume shippers, the building products logistics division at Georgia-Pacific was able to bring about a revolutionary development in containers. That development was the creation of a new type of stackable intermodal container called the Flat-Tainer. A stackable, collapsible flatbed unit, the new piece of equipment is ideally suited for handling lumber, plywood, steel, and other building materials. When fully erected, it provides a full 48-foot deck with bulkheads at both ends.

Although the idea sounds simple enough, its realization was a long time coming. In fact, where the first Flat-Tainer was test-loaded in February, the event marked the culmination of a four-year effort. "We went to over five (railcar) manufacturers before we found someone who would do it," explains Michael Blackwell, Director of Logistics. "After that, we were getting a little discouraged, so we asked Union Pacific if they could identify a manufacturer that might be interested."

UP pointed Blackwell and his staff to Mid-American Intermodal Equipment Corporation. "As it turns out," the manager notes, "they had been working to develop the same sort of equipment, but they weren't sure there was a market for it!"

Apparently convinced that Georgia-Pacific's business alone represented a large enough market for the unit, Mid-America went ahead with production of the Flat-Tainer. As a result, Georgia-Pacific now is enjoying the advantages of double stack that had previously eluded the company. "It's the key that unlocks the door to the economies of double stack for Georgia-Pacific," says Thomas Carpenter, Assistant Group Manager/Motor Carriers.

Today Georgia-Pacific plans to expand its use of the equipment nationwide. This, of course, comes as good news to railroads like UP, which are excited about obtaining higher freight volumes. By the looks of things, the rails' hopes may well be realized. Georgia-Pacific, for one, expects to be able to divert more freight to rail than it has in many years. "Twenty years ago, we moved over 70 percent of our freight on rail," says Blackwell. "Last year, we moved just 28 percent by rail and 72 percent by truck. This may help turn that trend around a little bit."

Source: "Georgia-Pacific Unlocks Door to Doublestacks," *Traffic Management,* October 1992, p. 35. Reprinted with permission.

the airlines often offer lower fares. These tickets often have many restrictions designed to prevent regular business travelers from switching to the lower fares. For example, the super-saver fare requires the passenger to stay at the destination over a Saturday night. Such fares are not good during certain heavy holiday periods or Monday and Friday flights, or they constitute only a small number of seats on flights that normally would not be filled by full-fare business passengers.

The vacation market is an important one to Florida, the Caribbean, Colorado, and Vermont during the winter months for sun and ski vacations. The United States to Europe and the United States coast to coast are strong vacation markets in the summer. Travel agents and tour operators are heavily involved in the vacation market. Charter bus trips and tours are also major parts of the vacation market.

The vacation travel market is also splintering into "boutique" travel niches as well. These are specialty vacations in which recreation and/or rest at a hotel or on a cruise ship are not the major elements of the trip. Trips in this category that have become increasingly popular in recent years include viewing rare animal life at the Galápagos Islands, whale watching in Baja California, hiking in Nepal, photographic expeditions in the wilds of Alaska or the Northwest Territories, safaris in Africa, and nature cruises up the Amazon River. These trips typically are educational; they often employ naturalists who give speeches and show films relating to the site on the trip.

Personal Travel

Personal travel is the other major long-distance passenger market; this is travel that is motivated by visits to home, travel to school, and emergency trips. People in this market segment might be attracted to the fastest possible means of travel, but low price can also be a significant demand characteristic.

The dominant demand characteristic for emergency trips, such as visiting an ill relative, is speed. The traveler is interested in arriving at the destination as quickly as possible, and, depending on the type of emergency, without regard to the cost. Alternatively, the college student traveling between home and college is more concerned with the cost of the trip and will wait hours or days to get a "free" ride with a friend or relative. The traveler going home to visit family is usually concerned with the departure and arrival times. These trips are scheduled around work, usually over the weekend or during holidays.

Urban Transit

Urban-related trip demands fall into three broad categories that provide insights into origin-destination density patterns or **primary trip markets**. The first is the work or school trip. The need for this type of trip is the most consistent and repetitive because it has one origin and one destination. The work point is often a concentrated employment stop (office, factory, etc.). The second major trip needed in a household is the trip to shop for food and other necessities. This, too, can be repetitive in pattern. The third type of trip, miscellaneous, includes recreational and medical trips. Miscellaneous trips are the least repetitive and are not always conducive to transit service attraction.

The automobile has often been referred to as the "fifth freedom" held by Americans. It has pervaded life-styles to the extent that it is often used even in the face of alternative lower cost transportation options. The personal convenience and privacy of the auto has created, in many cases, an intolerance of the waiting, walking, and crowding often associated with public forms of transportation. The convenience and privacy factors, accompanied by the relatively inexpensive availability of gas and oil for several decades, created a dramatic diversion to the auto and away from public transport. This diversion was felt mostly in shopping and recreational intracity trips and to a lesser extent in commuting trips.

Urban sprawl has been accompanied by the growth of suburban shopping centers. This has caused retail stores, theaters, and restaurants to be concentrated in suburban locations, rather than downtown. Thus, shopping trips to downtown areas during the day or in the evening via public transit systems have tended to disappear.

The drop in the use of public transit systems for shopping and recreation has meant that these systems are not fully used during the day. Formerly, they were intensively used by commuters in the morning, shoppers during the day, commuters in the evening, and people attending theater, cultural events, and restaurants in the evening. Transit equipment was often used 12 to 15 hours per day, and employees operated public transit for full-shift periods.

When only commuting demand remains, a transit system experiences a travel demand similar to that shown in Figure 1.17. The peak situation calls for greater de-

FIGURE 1.17 Urban Travel Peaking Problem

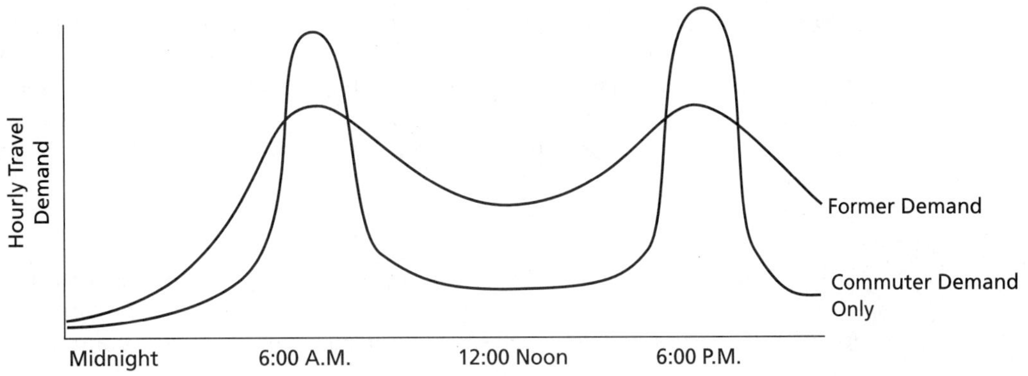

mand than before, but the demand is largely concentrated in two two-hour periods per day for only five days per week; roughly only six percent of the week is represented by full utilization. It is not uncommon for a city like Washington, D.C. to require 2,000 buses in service during rush hours, only to have half of them in service during the day, a quarter of them in the evening, and only five percent during the night and early morning. This **peak**/valley **demand** problem means that capital investments are largely underutilized and many operating employees who are paid full eight-hour shifts are only required to work runs that take half to three-quarters of that time. In many cities, some bus drivers and train crews are paid for a full day for one trip into the city in the morning and one trip at night.

Gradually over a two-decade period, the industry found it could not survive under private ownership. Whereas public urban transportation was viewed in the late 1960s and early 1970s as a *desirable* service for cities to retain, many public agencies began to subsidize urban transportation operations, to invest in them, or to purchase them outright for public agency operation. Since the beginning of the energy crunch in the 1970s, urban transportation services have been viewed as a necessary component to the viable function of cities and their environments.

Passenger Demand Characteristics

The demand characteristics of passenger transportation consist of many individual components. These range from very objective and tangible items to some that are very intangible.

Destination

The destination is where the traveler seeks to go. It can be important, such as a business destination (Chicago, Detroit, or Los Angeles) or it can have a vacation appeal (the Virgin Islands or Stowe, Vermont). Most locations represent a blend of these two destination segments, such as New York, which attracts many business as well as vacation travelers. In some situations, a destination is a means of getting to somewhere else. For example, Atlanta is an airline hub through which a person must transfer to get to his or her ultimate destination. In today's cruise travel, the destination is the origin and the important demand aspect of the cruise is the quality of the trip.

Schedules and speed

Many times a means of travel is selected because it is the only one with a convenient departure or arrival time. The consistency with which a carrier meets schedules is also an important factor, and many air travelers consult the U.S. DOT's on-time record of air carriers over a given origin-destination. Further, the speed of travel can be an advantage or disadvantage. The speed of the airplane allows travelers more productive time on the ground at the origin and destination. However, the arrival or destination time is of less importance and slow speed is an advantage when touring the Rocky Mountains via Amtrak.

Cost

Cost is one objective measure of the transportation product. It comprises the actual fare and several other costs. These other costs include access, parking, overnight lodging, food, and, in some cases, ability or opportunity to perform work or make sales calls.

Equipment

This factor can be part of the advertised appeal of travel. It was a key element in the airline industry when new jets were being built and many of the older and slower propeller airplanes were still in service. In other modes, equipment can make a difference if it represents cleanliness and the avoidance of maintenance delays. This was a travel problem with Amtrak when it first started and had to operate with equipment that was old and often broke down. In the cruise industry, the ship is the item that is advertised. It is a major component of the entire vacation.

Entertainment and Attention

These amenities are often important in vacation travel. This is the case with on-board entertainment, food, and available diversions on ships. Some airlines recognize the nature of business travel and promote their services as providing close in-flight attention only if the passenger wants it.

Terminals

These are the points from which persons board and depart the transportation vehicles. To be attractive to the traveling public, terminals must be accessible, clean, and safe. They should be designed to move baggage efficiently and to give easy access to other modes of transport.

Complaints and Experiences

Passenger travel is a highly visible service industry. Unlike industrial buying where many objective elements come into the buying decision, passenger travel can be subject to sudden shifts resulting from intangible perceptions.

Role of the Travel Agent

The travel agent is a valuable but often overlooked and misunderstood facilitator of passenger travel. Though not providing movement service themselves, travel agents provide a wide range of informational and arrangement services.

The travel agent is a link between the passenger, on the one hand, and carriers and hotels on the other. Their services include explaining the lowest cost and most direct transportation services as well as making reservations for and issuing tickets to the passenger. Agents also arrange for car rentals, hotels, and complete tour services. The cost of using a travel agent is minimal to the passenger. The cost of a ticket purchased directly from an airline, Amtrak, or steamship company, for example, is the same as that arranged and purchased through a travel agent. The travel agent is compensated through a commission paid by the carrier. The passenger has the advantage of learning and possibly using all the carrier's services through this one facilitator. The alternative would be to make arrangements and purchase tickets individually for each segment of a trip. The carriers would have to have offices in each town served, or passengers would have to make an additional trip to the terminal to make trip arrangements and purchase tickets. Travel agents, however, often have computer terminals with direct links to airline reservation systems that allow for fast travel arrangements.

Deregulation of the air industry has created the opportunity for firms to perform their own travel agency service, rather than use outside independent travel agents. Firms can now strike special fare arrangements with specific airlines and obtain the commission fee for writing the ticket. At the time of this writing, anyone with a home personal computer can link into TWA's reservation system, book flights, and obtain seat assignments. For business travel, this means diminished revenue for many travel agents in the country. This will probably cause a shakeout in this industry, and it will cause many to emphasize developing pure vacation market segments.

SUMMARY

- The decade of the 1990s brought many changes to the logistics and transportation activities through globalization, technology, deregulation, and restructuring.
- Transportation is an integral activity in a firm's implementation of the logistics and supply chain concepts.
- Total-cost analysis is an important part of the logistics system perspective because of the interactions of logistics decisions with the firm and other channel partners' decisions.
- A customer's perception of conformance to quality requirements results in the creation of value and satisfaction for that customer; over time this satisfaction can result in a positive attitude toward the service supplier.
- Transportation is a necessary activity for a modern society and it influences almost every aspect of our lives.
- Transportation helps to determine the value of goods by adding time and place utility to them.
- Transportation is an important part of the U.S. economy, contributing 16 percent to the Gross Domestic Product (GDP).
- Transportation has a significant impact on the environment because of its potential consequences to air and water quality, as well as its influence on noise levels.
- Freight demand is measured in ton-miles, a combination of weight and distance; the ton-mile is a heterogenous unit. The passenger-mile is a heterogenous unit of measure for passenger demand.
- The service components of freight demand include transit time, reliability, accessibility, capability, and security.

Key Terms

accessibility pg. 45
aggregate demand 40
bundle of services 20
business logistics 3
capability 45
cash flows 9
common carrier 34
comparative advantage 25
cost trade-offs 10
customer attitude 18
customer filters 14
customer perception 18
demand elasticity 40
deregulation 4
eminent domain 34
environmental concern 30
extent of the market 43
freight transportation 28
globalization 4
inbound 6
inelastic 41
information flows 9
integration 5
inventories 12
landed cost 43
landed cost advantage 43
Lardner's Law 23
logistics channel management 3
materials management 14
mobility 39
modal split 29
passenger service 46
passenger transportation 28
passenger-mile 40
peak demand 49
physical distribution 4
place utility 23
price inelastic 41
price-sensitive 48
primary trip markets 48
product flows 9
product demand 38
quality 12
quality gaps 15
reliability 45
security 45
service 12
service elastic 41
service provider perceptions 15
supply chain management 3
technology 5
time utility 24
ton-mile 40
total-cost analysis 10
transaction-specific 18
transit time 44
transportation 20
transportation interaction 36
utility creation 13
value added 3
value creation 18

Study Questions

1. The decade of the 1990s saw significant changes occurring in logistics and transportation. Discuss the factors that helped cause these changes.

2. Did the factors that caused changes in logistics during the 1990s also affect transportation? Discuss the impact and changes that occurred.

3. What is the nature of total-cost analysis? Why is it so important to the logistics systems approach?

4. Discuss the relationship between quality, value, satisfaction, and attitude.

5. What role did transportation play in the economic development of the United States? Is this role of transportation still important today?

6. How does transportation add value for manufacturing or distribution firms?

7. How does transportation contribute to geographic specialization and large-scale production? Is there a relationship between the two?

8. Describe the economic role of transportation in an economy and relate this role to the demand for transportation services. How has the movement toward a global economy impacted the demand for transportation?

9. The ton-mile is a heterogenous measure of transportation demand. Explain.

10. Distinguish between aggregate, modal, and specific demand.

11. Aggregate demand for freight is price and service inelastic, while modal and specific freight demand is price and service elastic. What is the rationale for this?

12. What is meant by *derived demand* and how does this demand characteristic impact freight demand?

NOTES

1. Council of Logistics Management, Oak Brook. IL.
2. For a more detailed discussion of logistics and supply chain management, see John J. Coyle, Edward J. Bardi, and C. John Langley, Jr., *The Management of Business Logistics,* 6th ed. (Minneapolis, MN: West Publishing Company, 1996), Ch. 1.
3. Donald J. Bowersox, Patricia J. Daugherty, Cornelia L. Droge, Dale S. Rogers, and Daniel L. Wardlow, *Leading Edge Logistics: Competitive Positioning for the 1990s, (Oakbrook, IL: CLM, 1989),* pp. 7–10.
4. Ibid.
5. Ibid., pp. 15–20.
6. Ibid., pp. 20–25.
7. Ibid.
8. John J. Coyle, Edward J. Bardi, and C. John Langley, *Management of Business Logistics,* 5th ed. (St. Paul, MN: West Publishing, 1992), p. 8.
9. Ibid., p. 9.
10. C.J. Smith, "Integrating Logistics in a Major Chemical Company," *Proceedings of Council of Logistics Management,* Vol. 2 (1990), pp. 173–176.
11. Ibid.
12. Ibid.
13. Coyle, et. al., *op. cit.,* pp. 23–26.
14. Allen W. Kiefer and Robert A. Novack, "An Empirical Assessment of Warehouse Performance Measurements in Supply Chain Management," submitted to the *Transportation Journal,* 1998.
15. See, for example, Robert A. Novack, C. John Langley, Jr., and Lloyd M. Rinehart, *Creating Logistics Value: Themes for the Future* (Oak Brook, IL: Council of Logistics Management, 1995), pp. 176–189.
16. The concept of quality gaps was introduced in Valeria A. Zeithaml, Leonard L. Berry, and A. Parasuraman, "Communication and Control Processes in the Delivery of Service Quality," *Journal of Marketing,* Vol. 52 (April 1998), pp. 35–48.
17. Robert A. Novack, Lloyd M. Rinehart, and C. John Langley, Jr., "An Internal Assessment of Logistics Value," *Journal of Business Logistics,* Vol. 15, No. 1 (Spring 1994), pp. 113–152.
18. Ibid.
19. U.S. Senate, Committee on Interstate and Foreign Commerce, *National Transportation Policy* (December 1960), p. 29.
20. Sang Youn Kim, "The Role of Transportation to African Famine Relief Operations," *Journal of Transportation Management,* Vol. 1, No. 1 (September 1988), pp. 369–377.
21. Donald Harper, *Transportation in America* (Englewood Cliffs, NJ: Prentice-Hall, 1978), p. 8.
22. See Robert B. Fetter and Winston C. Dalleck, *Decision Models for Inventory Management* (Homewood, IL: Richard D. Irwin, 1961), Udie Raumliche Ordnungder Wirtschaft (Jena: Gustav Fischerverlag, 1940).
23. John J. Coyle, Edward J. Bardi, and C. John Langley, Jr., *The Management of Business Logistics,* 6th ed. (St. Paul, MN: West Publishing, 1996), Ch. 10.

SUGGESTED READINGS

Abdelwahab, Walid, and Michael Sargious, "Modeling the Demand for Freight Transport," *Journal of Transport Economics and Policy,* Vol. 26, No. 1, January 1992, pp. 49–70.

Andel, Tom. "Parcel Shippers Are Put to the Test," *Transportation and Distribution,* Vol. 33, No. 4, April 1992, pp. 34–36.

Bloomberg, David J., and James W. Adams. "1991 Proceedings Issue," *Journal of Transportation Management,* 51st Annual International Education Conference, Snowmass Village, Colorado, October 9–12, 1991.

Burr, John T. "A New Name for a Not-So-New Concept," *Quality Progress,* March 1993, pp. 87–88.

Cooke, James Aaron. "Why It Pays to Be an 'Ideal Shipper,'" *Traffic Management,* Vol. 31, No. 2, February 1992, pp. 30–34.

Coyle, John J. "Future Manufacturing, Markets and Logistics Needs," *Proceedings of International Symposium on Motor Carrier Transportation,* Summer 1993, pp. 1–55.

Coyle, John J., Edward J. Bardi, and C. John Langley, Jr. *The Management of Business Logistics,* 6th ed. St. Paul, Minn: West Publishing, 1996.

Gattorna, John, and Abby Day. Strategic Issues in Logistics, Monograph Series. *International Journal of Physical Distribution & Materials Management,* Vol. 16, No. 2, 1986.

Gopalakrishnan, K. N., Barry E. McIntyre, and James C. Sprague. "Implementing Internal Quality Improvement With the House of Quality," *Quality Progress,* September 1992, pp. 57–60.

Helms, Marilyn M. "JIT Utilization: Shaping the Future of the Transportation Industry," *Journal of Trans-*

portation Management, Vol. 4, No. 1, Spring 1992, pp. 97–124.

Horsley, R. C. "The Value of an Integrated Transport System to the Logistician." *Focus on Logistics and Distribution Management,* Vol. 11, No. 8, October 1992, pp. 2–8.

Johnson, Richard S. "TQM: Leadership for the Quality Transformation," *Quality Progress,* January 1993, pp. 73–75.

Rakowski, James P., and David Bejou. "Structural Change and the Nature of Competition in the Deregulated U.S. Airline Industry," *Transportation Practitioners Journal,* Vol. 59, No. 3, Spring 1992, pp. 241–262.

Smith, R. I. "Transport to Match the Demands of the Market," *Management Accounting,* Vol. 70, No. 1, January 1992, pp. 32–36.

CASES

CASE 1.1
Soup to Nuts, Inc.

Soup to Nuts, Inc. (STN) was a wholesaler of various types of sundry items used to supply the electronics manufacturing industry. These items included everything from color monitors' control knobs to sophisticated computer chips. Chip N. Dale, STN's founder and president, felt that offering this broad product line to these manufacturers would give STN a market niche as a one-stop supplier. Coupled with its broad product line, STN prided itself on fast and accurate delivery to customers because of the critical nature of STN's products in the manufacture of electronic devices.

Through the efforts of STN's logistics manager, Jaba T. Hutt, STN had established a long and successful relationship with an overnight, small package delivery company called Century Express. STN was one of Century's largest customers with shipments originating at multiple origins to destinations all over the world. Century was not the lowest priced carrier in the market, but it was certainly one of the best on service. The relationship between the two companies was mutually beneficial.

Since STN placed a high priority on correct and prompt delivery to customers, it placed a great deal of emphasis on a carrier's ability to trace and expedite shipments. Historically, Century had used a manual phone system for tracing where the customer would call in to a local terminal with a bill of lading number or pro number. Century's tracing clerk would then begin the process to locate the shipment by using an internal computer system and, many times, through phone calls to other terminals. As far as STN was concerned, this process was acceptable for its service requirements.

Century decided to implement a fully computerized tracing system using bar codes and scanners, allowing the customer to perform the tracing function. This system could also be used to enter customer orders, generate bills of lading and freight bills, and transmit documents electronically. Each customer would have to learn Century's tracing system and would have to fill out a customer profile including such information as shipping locations, freight classifications, freight terms, and the like. With this information, Century felt it could speed up the tracing process.

The first shipment to be made under the new system by STN was an extremely time-sensitive part to a manufacturer who needed it to keep a production line running. With all of the appropriate documents generated and information input to the system, the shipment was picked up by Century with scheduled delivery the next morning to the customer. The following afternoon, Jaba T. Hutt received a call from his customer, who was not in a very good mood. "Jaba, I thought you said that part would be here this morning. I am really close to having to shut down my line. I am really in a difficult position with the plant manager. She wants that part now." Jaba replied, "Century was supposed to have delivered it this morning. I'm not sure what the problem is, but I plan to find out."

After he hung up the phone, Jaba attempted to get into Century's system to trace the shipment. After several attempts to log on to a system that was busy, he gave up and decided to try the old tracing method. He called his contact at the local Century terminal and explained his dilemma. His contact told him that tracing was no longer a local terminal activity but was centralized at Century's headquarters. Placing a call to Century's HQ got him in touch with the Customer Service department. He once again explained how important it was to find his customer's shipment immediately. The Customer Service rep reminded Jaba that he could trace his own shipments using the new system. Jaba informed the agent that the system had been busy when he tried to get into it. Reluctantly, the Customer Service rep took down the pertinent information concerning STN's shipment and informed Jaba that he would look into it and call Jaba back.

In the meantime, STN's customer had also called Chip N. Dale to complain about the non-delivery. Chip in turn called the regional manager for Century to voice his concerns. As in Jaba's case, Chip was reminded that he could use the new system to trace his own shipments.

About 12 hours after Jaba's initial call to Century, the Customer Service rep returned his call. He told Jaba that the shipment was not in the system at all, so he doubted that Century had even picked up the shipment. Jaba argued that this was impossible because he had a bill of lading number and a pro number. The rep responded by stating that it could be a number for another carrier. Because neither number showed up in the system, Century obviously never had the shipment. Jaba had other problems on his hands because his customer's line had to be shut down and he was threatening to cut off all business ties with STN.

Jaba and Chip N. Dale both had made numerous calls to Century executives demanding an explanation for the situation. Both also demanded full compensation for the shipment from Century and that Century make full restitution to STN's customer for the costs of shutting down its production line. Plus, STN wanted an apology from Century management for the embarrassment they suffered in the eyes of their customers. If they did not receive their requests, they were going to take their small package delivery business to a competitor.

Case Questions

1. If you were Century's management, what would you do?

2. Are some customers not worth keeping? In other words, are STN's requests too costly for Century?

3. How would you rate the effectiveness of the "new system?" Would you have instituted this new system in the same manner as Century?

CASE 1.2

Fly-By-Night Helicopter Service

In mid-July 1994, the Youngstown, Ohio community was shocked by an announcement from Crow Airline that it would discontinue flights to and from the Youngstown airport by the end of the year. Crow provides commuter airline service to major hub airports in Cleveland, Pittsburgh, and Chicago, as well as direct service to such cities as Buffalo, Rochester, Toledo, and Indianapolis. Although a number of very small air carriers provide service, Crow is the only major air carrier serving Youngstown.

The business community leaders became quite concerned with the possibility of two-hour drives to airports in Cleveland and Pittsburgh to catch flights. The Youngstown Port Authority met with the business leaders to ascertain suggestions to this blow to air travelers. A number of alternatives were suggested, including recruitment of a new commuter airline, establishment of an airport bus service, and formation of a joint-venture air commuter to connect Youngstown to Cleveland and Pittsburgh.

Following the announcement of the Port Authority's meeting in the local newspaper, Darrin Yugg, President of Fly-By-Night Helicopter Service (FBN), contacted the Port Authority executive director with the idea of providing helicopter service between Youngstown and the Cleveland and Pittsburgh airports. The initial discussion was positive and Mr. Yugg felt that enough interest existed to develop and present a formal proposal to the Port Authority.

Mr. Yugg was a seasoned helicopter pilot who had served with distinction in the Vietnam War. He had successfully built a helicopter service in the Youngstown area and currently had a fleet of 10 choppers. FBN's primary market was providing service to construction, agriculture, and pipeline companies. FBN would fly client personnel to construction job sites, spray farm fields, and provide surveillance of pipelines. FBN's service was highly regarded in the business community, and it enjoyed a reputation as a well-managed and financially strong company.

The shift from the FBN's current type of business into shuttling passengers between airports was a new business venture, one which Mr. Yugg did not know. He was somewhat concerned about the marketability of a helicopter shuttle service and, in particular, the acceptance of such a service by passengers not accustomed to flying in a helicopter. The helicopter flight would save passengers about 75 minutes on the commute to either Cleveland or Pittsburgh, but the cost of operating a helicopter would result in a round-trip charge approximately 2.5 times greater than a bus fare and 1.5 times greater than the current Crow fare.

Case Questions

1. What additional demand factors should Mr. Yugg consider as he develops his proposal?

2. As executive director of the Youngstown Port Authority, what areas would you want to see addressed in the proposal presented by FBN?

3. Given the information presented, would you recommend that FBN establish a helicopter shuttle service? Why or why not?

CHAPTER 2

TRANSPORTATION REGULATION AND PUBLIC POLICY

Resources in the United States are allocated through two main processes. The first is the political process wherein the public or its elected representatives vote with ballots. The second is the market process where the people vote with their dollars. In other words, people buy certain products or services and not others, and therefore commit resources or inputs to the products or services purchased in the marketplace.

The United States has traditionally relied on the market process to provide transportation. Since the early part of the century, however, Congress has created and funded a growing number of transportation programs. All three levels of government, however, have been reluctant to abandon the market process, particularly with respect to vehicle ownership and **operation**.

Overall, the current allocation of resources to transportation reflects both a market allocation process and a political allocation process. Ideally, the political process should recognize the potential inadequacies of an unrestrained market that provides for each individual's basic necessities and that acts to prevent or mitigate market imperfections. Furthermore, the market process should operate within such constraints to efficiently provide the transportation society wants and for which it is willing and able to pay. This blend of government and marketplace interaction in the transportation area is important to understand.

All facets of government's roles are important in this discussion. A convenient starting point for developing an understanding of this role is to discuss transportation regulation. Transportation regulation influences and constrains carrier operations and user services.

This chapter examines the basis of regulation along with the role of the regulatory commissions and the courts. Also presented in this chapter is a discussion of the development of transportation regulation from its inception in 1887 to its role today.

Regulation of Transportation

Nature of Regulation

In the United States, the government influences the activities of business in many different ways. The amount of influence in business activity varies from providing the legal foundation and framework in which business operates to governmental ownership and control. There has been a long history of governmental regulation and control, but even today there is still some opposition on the part of managers to the governmental activity that influences their operations.

The amount of governmental control and regulation has increased as the United States has grown and prospered. If one compared the controls exercised by the government 150 years ago with those in existence today, the former would probably seem insignificant. The expansion of governmental influence, however, has been necessitated to some extent by the increase in the scope of activity, complexity, and the size of individual firms.

In the United States, we tend to view our economic activity as one of private enterprise. Competition is a necessary requirement to a free-enterprise economy. The allocation of scarce resources can be decided in the competitive market. The case for free-market enterprise and competition has been developed by economists for more than 150 years.

The definitions of *pure competition* and *free market* involve a number of conditions that may not exist in reality. Products are justified only by people's willingness to buy them. A product should not be sold at a price below the marginal cost of the last unit. The theory also assumes that people are able to assess whether a given economic act will make them better off—either as producers or consumers—and that people will use personal resources to achieve a more positive life-style.

Our belief that competition is most conducive to the betterment of all is joined by a feeling that **monopoly** or monopolistic practices are undesirable. The problem would be simple if our market structures took the form of either perfect competition or monopoly. Most individuals would not quarrel with governmental regulation of monopoly and a valid case would be made for little or no governmental interference in an economy characterized by perfect competition. However, the prevailing situation is not this simple. The market structures usually take some form between the extremes of perfect competition and monopoly.

The imperfections in the marketplace in a free-enterprise economy provide the rationale for governmental control. The control exercised by the government can take one of several forms. One form is that of maintaining or enforcing competition—for example, the antitrust actions of the government. Second, the government can substitute regulation for competition as it did in transportation. Third, the government can assume ownership and direct control as it has done with the U.S. Post Office.

The basic problem of regulation in our society is that of establishing or maintaining the conditions necessary for the economical use of resources under a system of private enterprise. Regulation should seek to maintain a competitive framework and rely on the competitive forces whenever possible. The institutional framework for regulating transportation is provided by federal statute. A perspective on the overall legal basis for regulation is important to the student of transportation, and we will examine this topic in the next section.

Common Law

The legal system of the United States is based upon **common law** and civil or statutory law. The former is a system basic to most English-speaking countries since it was developed in England. Common law relies upon judicial precedent, or principles of law developed from former court decisions. Therefore, if one wants to find out what the law is on a particular topic, one must search out the court decisions to see what was originally decided about the topic. When a court decision establishes a rule for a situation, then that rule becomes part of the law of the land. As conditions change, the law sometimes needs further interpretation. Therefore, an important feature of the common law system is that it changes and evolves as society changes. We have many examples of such change in interpretation of the areas of federal and state control or responsibility for regulating transportation.[1] Common law involves a continuous process of court interpretation.

The common law approach fits well with a free-market enterprise system, since the individual is the focus of attention and can engage in any business that is not prohibited. Each individual is essentially regarded as possessing equal power and responsibility before the law.[2] The early regulation of transportation developed under the common law. The obvious connection is with the concept of common carriage.

Common law rules were developed for those common carriers, since they serve all shippers on a similar basis, at reasonable rates, and without discrimination.

Statutory law or civil law is based upon the Roman legal system and is characteristic of continental Europe and the parts of the world colonized by European countries. Statutory law is enacted by legislative bodies, but it is a specific enactment. It is in a sense a written law that is more apparent and easier to check. A large part of the laws pertaining to business control in general and to transportation in particular are based upon statutory law. However, two points are important to note in this regard. First, common law rules are still very important in the transportation area, since many statutes were in effect copied from common law principles. Second, statutes are usually general and need to be interpreted by the courts. Thus, in the United States, there is a very close relationship between common law and statutory law.

The regulation of transportation began at the state level under the common law system when a number of important rules for regulation were developed, as well as the basic issue of whether business could even be regulated at all. In the latter regard, a concept of "business affected with the public interest" was developed under the common law. **State regulation** also included use of charters for some of the early turnpike companies and canal operations. The development of the railroad necessitated a move to statutory regulation, which was in effect by 1870 with the passage of **granger laws** in various states. These granger laws were the product of the granger movement, which began about 1867 in states such as Illinois, Iowa, Minnesota, and Wisconsin. Granges were organizations formed by farmers in various states and functioned as political action groups where farmers could discuss problems. The granger movement was started by the farmers through their grange organizations because of their dissatisfaction with railroad rates and service. The development of state laws, and later federal laws, also gave rise to independent regulatory commissions, which are discussed next.

Role of the Independent Regulatory Commission

Our federal government is set up under a system of checks and balances in three separate branches—the executive, judicial, and legislative. The independent regulatory commission is an administrative body created by the legislative authority operating within the framework of the Constitution. The members of the commission are appointed by the president and approved by the Senate for a fixed term of office.

The Interstate Commerce Commission (ICC) was the first independent regulatory commission to be established in the United States at the federal level. It was set up under the Act to Regulate Commerce in 1887. Originally, the ICC had somewhat limited powers. However, over the years it evolved as the most comprehensive and powerful commission in the country. The independent regulatory commission is somewhat peculiar to the United States.

The ICC served as an expert body, providing a continuity to regulation that neither the courts nor the legislature could provide. The ICC exercised legislative, judicial, and executive powers. As a consequence, it was often labeled as a quasi-legislative, quasi-executive, and quasi-judicial body. Regulatory agencies can be regarded as a fourth branch of the government. When the ICC enforced statutes, it served in the executive capacity. When it ruled upon the reasonableness of a rate, it served in its judicial capacity. When it filled out legislation by promulgating rules or prescribing rules or prescribing rates, it exercised its legislative powers.

On December 31, 1995, the ICC was abolished. The ICC Termination Act of 1995 (ICCTA) ended the 108-year-old ICC and replaced it with the **Surface Transporta-**

tion Board (STB), which implements a greatly reduced body of economic regulation exercised over the modes of transportation. The STB is housed in the **U. S. Department of Transportation** (DOT), but it is constituted as an independent regulatory agency, immune from DOT direction and supervision. The three-member STB Board is appointed by the president with approval of the Senate.

The role of the STB in the economic operations of carriers has been greatly reduced from that of the ICC. Congress intended for the marketplace, not the STB, to be the primary control mechanism for rates and services. The STB exercises economic controls over railroads, motor carriers, motor carrier freight brokers, water carriers, freight forwarders, and pipelines. (See "Current Economic Regulations," later in this chapter, for more details on the ICCTA regulations.)

In addition to the ICC and STB, other independent regulatory commissions have been established for transportation. In 1938, the **Civil Aeronautics Board** (CAB) was established to administer the economic regulations imposed upon airlines. The CAB was abolished in 1985 under the provisions of the Airline Deregulation Act of 1978, and the remaining regulatory jurisdictions (safety issues) were transferred to the DOT.

The **Federal Maritime Commission** (FMC) was created in 1961 to administer the regulations imposed on international water carriers. The FMC exercises controls over the rates, practices, agreements, and services of common carrier water carriers operating in international trade and domestic trade to points beyond the continental United States. The laws under which the FMC operates have seen great change in 1998. This will be discussed in more detail in Chapter 9.

The **Federal Energy Regulatory Commission** (FERC) was created to administer the regulations governing rates and practices of oil and natural gas pipelines. However, the FERC is not an independent regulatory commission that reports to Congress, such as the ICC or FMC. Rather, it is a semi-independent regulatory commission that reports to the Department of Energy.

Our regulatory laws are often stated in vague terms such as reasonable rates, inherent advantages, and unjust discrimination. Therefore, in administering and interpreting the law, the regulatory commission exercises broad discretionary powers over the regulated transport firms. We must not, however, lose sight of the fact that the commission is still limited by the regulatory laws. It can only carry out the law to the best of its ability and is subject to the opinions of the courts.

Role of the Courts

Even though the independent commission plays a powerful role in regulating transportation, it is still subject to judicial review. The courts are the sole judges of the law, and only court decisions can serve as legal precedent under common law. The courts make the final ruling upon the constitutionality of regulatory statutes and the interpretation of the legislation. The review of the courts acts as a check upon arbitrary or capricious actions, actions that do not conform to statutory standards or authority, or actions that are not in accordance with fair procedure or substantial evidence. The parties involved in a commission decision have the right, therefore, to appeal the decision to the courts.

Over the years, the courts had come to recognize the ICC as an expert body on policy and the authority on matters of fact and, to some extent, the STB. Therefore, the courts limited their restrictions on ICC and STB authority. The courts would not substitute their judgment for that of the ICC and STB on such matters as what constitutes a reasonable rate or whether a discrimination is unjust, since such judgments would usurp the administrative function of the commission.

Safety Regulations

As will be noted in this chapter's appendix, which describes the DOT functions, various federal agencies administer transportation safety regulations. Some of these regulations are enacted into law by Congress, whereas others are promulgated by the respective agencies. A thorough discussion of the specific regulations pertaining to each type of transportation is beyond our scope, but a general description of safety regulations is presented below.

Safety regulations have been established to control the operations, personnel qualifications, vehicles, equipment, hours of service for vehicle operators, etc. The **Federal Aviation Administration** enforces and promulgates safety regulations governing the operation of air carriers and airports. The **Federal Highway Administration** administers motor carrier safety regulations, and the **National Highway Traffic Safety Administration** has jurisdiction over safety features and the performance of motor vehicles and motor vehicle equipment. The **Federal Railroad Administration** exercises railroad safety regulations, and the Coast Guard is responsible for marine safety standards for vessels and ports. The **Office of Hazardous Materials Transportation** develops hazardous materials transportation safety regulations for all modes. The **National Transportation Safety Board** is charged with investigating and reporting the causes, facts, and circumstances relating to transportation accidents.

In addition, the states, through the **police powers** contained in the Constitution, exercise various controls over the safe operation of vehicles. These safety regulations set standards for speed, vehicle size, operating practices, operator licensing, etc. The purpose of the state safety regulations is to protect the health and welfare of the citizens of that state.

Often, the federal and state safety regulations conflict. For example, the federal government restricted the automobile speed limit to 55 miles per hour during the energy crisis of the 1970s. Some states did not agree with the mandate, but followed the requirement to qualify for federal money to construct and maintain the highway system. In 1982, the Surface Transportation Act established federal standards for vehicle weight and length of trucks operating on the interstate highway system. The states complied with the standards for the interstate highways but not for the state highways.

State Regulations

The states establish various transportation safety regulations to protect the health and welfare of their citizens. In addition, the states exercise limited economic regulation over the transportation of commodities and passengers wholly within the state. The states' powers were greatly limited under various federal laws. States generally cannot impose stricter regulation than that imposed on that mode at the federal level. States can still regulate safety provided it does not impose an undue burden on interstate commerce. This type of transportation is known as **intrastate commerce,** and most states had a regulatory commission that was charged with enforcing these intrastate controls. The agencies may still exist to regulate utilities such as telephone or electric companies.

The intrastate economic regulations vary from state to state, but they are generally patterned after federal economic regulations.

In 1994, the federal government eliminated the intrastate economic regulation of motor carriers with the passage of the FAA Reauthorization Act of 1994. The law, which applies to all motor carriers of property except household good carriers, prohibits the states from requiring operating authority or regulating intrastate trucking rates, routes, and services. The states have the option to regulate the uniform business practices, cargo liability, and credit rules of intrastate motor carriers.

The determination as to what constitutes commerce subject to state economic regulations is generally based on whether the shipment crosses a state line. If the shipment has an origin in one state and a destination in another state, it is an interstate shipment and is subject to federal regulations, if any. However, for shipments that are moved into a distribution center from a point outside the state and then moved from the distribution center to a destination in the same state, the distinction is not that clear. The move within the state from the distribution center to the final destination can be considered interstate commerce and subject to federal regulations.

Development of Regulation

As has been seen in this chapter, transportation does not operate in a completely free-market environment. Government has controlled the economic operations of transportation since the 1860s. Regulatory constraints to entry, pricing, and customer relations have dictated the management practices of carriers and transportation users even after the deregulation laws of the late 1970s, 1980s, and 1990s. Transportation regulation has been a major force shaping the transportation industry.

Transportation has long been considered an industry that impacts public interest. In fact, transportation is so vital to the economic viability of the country that it has been argued that government should provide the service, rather than private enterprise. Without a sound transportation system, the level of economic activity, the exchange and movement of goods and services, would be greatly limited and the well-being of the citizens reduced. Thus, government involvement has been directed toward ensuring that the public has equal access to an economically viable transportation system.

Table 2.1 provides a a chronology of transportation regulation. The regulatory history is broken down into four areas. First, the initiation era from 1887 to 1920 saw the establishment of federal transportation regulation and the ICC. Second, the era of positive regulation from 1920 to 1935 was oriented toward promoting transportation. The third era, intermodal regulation from 1935 to 1960, witnessed the expansion of regulation to motor carriers, air carriers, water carriers, and freight forwarders. Finally, the deregulation era from 1976 to 1996 was the period of gradual lessening and elimination of economic regulation, culminating in the elimination of the ICC and most truck regulations in 1995.

In the next section, a summary of the current regulation applied to railroads and motor carriers is given.

Current Economic Regulations

As stated above, the air carrier industry is deregulated. Cargo and passenger rates are not controlled and domestic air carriers are permitted to serve any locale as long as the carrier meets safety regulations and landing slots are available.

The majority of the economic regulation over pipelines has been transferred to the Federal Energy Regulatory Commission. Since most water carrier operations are exempt from economic regulation, domestic water carrier economic regulation is a moot issue.

TABLE 2.1 Chronology of Major Transportation Regulation*

Date	Act	Nature of Regulation
Initiation Era		
1887	Act to Regulate Commerce	Regulated railroads and established ICC; rates must be reasonable; discrimination prohibited
1903	Elkins Act	Prohibited rebates and filed rate doctrine
1906	Hepburn Act	Established maximum and joint rate controls
1910	Mann-Elkins Act	Shipper given right to route shipment
1912	Panama Canal Act	Prohibited railroads from owning water carriers
Positive Era		
1920	Transportation Act of 1920	Established a rule of ratemaking; pooling and joint use of terminals permitted; began recapture clause
1933	Emergency Transportation Act	Financial assistance to railroads
Intermodal Era		
1935	Motor Carrier Act	Federal regulation of trucking, similar to rail
1938	Civil Aeronautics Act	Federal regulation of air carriers established Civil Aeronautics Board (CAB)
1940	Transportation Act	Provided for federal regulation of water carriers, declaration of national transportation policy
1942	Freight Forwarder Act	Federal regulation of surface freight forwarders
1948	Reed-Bulwinkle Act	Antitrust immunity for joint rate making
1958	Transportation Act	Eliminated umbrella (protective) ratemaking and provided financial aid to railroads
1966	Department of Transportation Act	Established the U.S. Department of Transportation
1970	Rail Passenger Service Act	Established Amtrak
1973	Regional Rail Reorganization Act	Established Consolidated Rail Corporation (Conrail)
Deregulation Era		
1976	Railroad Revitalization and Regulatory Reform Act	Rate freedom; ICC could exempt rail operations; abandonment and merger controls began
1977	Airline Deregulation Act	Deregulated air transportation, sunset CAB (1985)
1980	Motor Carrier Act	Eased entry restrictions and permitted rate negotiation
1980	Rail Staggers Act	Permitted railroads to negotiate contracts, allowed rate flexibility, and defined maximum rates
1993	Negotiated Rates Act	Provided for settlement options for motor carrier undercharges
1994	Trucking Industry Regulatory Reform Act	Eliminated motor carrier filing of individual tariffs; ICC given power to deregulate categories of traffic
1994	FAA Reauthorization Act	Prohibited states from regulating (economic) intrastate trucking
1995	ICC Termination Act	Abolished ICC, established STB, and eliminated most truck economic regulation

*For a detailed description of these acts, see John J. Coyle, Edward J. Bardi, and Robert A. Novack, *Transportation*, 4th ed., St. Paul, MN: West Publishing, 1994, pp. 58–83.

Effective January 1, 1996, the ICC Termination Act of 1995 abolished the Interstate Commerce Commission, further deregulated transportation, and transferred the remaining ICC functions to a three-person Surface Transportation Board located within the DOT. The STB now administers the remaining economic regulations exercised over railroads, motor carriers, freight forwarders, freight brokers, water carriers, and pipelines. The key provisions of the ICCTA are summarized below.

Railroad Regulations

- Rail economic regulation is basically unchanged by the ICCTA.
- The STB has jurisdiction over rates, classifications, rules, practices, routes, services, facilities, acquisitions, and abandonments.
- Railroads continue to be subject to the common carrier obligations (to serve, not discriminate, charge reasonable rates, and deliver).
- Rail tariff filling is eliminated; railroads must provide 20 days advance notice before changing a rate.
- Rail contract filing is eliminated except for agricultural contracts.

Motor Carriers

- All tariff filing and rate regulation is eliminated, except for household goods and noncontiguous trade (trade between the continental United States and Hawaii, for example).
- Motor carriers are required to provide tariffs to shippers upon request.
- Motor carriers are held liable for damage according to the conditions of the Carmack Act, i.e., the full value of the product at destination. However, motor carriers can use released value rates that set limits on liability.
- The Negotiated Rates Act undercharge resolution procedures are retained and the unreasonable practices defense is extended indefinitely for pending undercharge cases.
- Undercharge/overcharge claims must be filed within 180 days from receipt of the freight bill.
- The STB has broad powers to exempt operations from regulation with the existing exemptions remaining.
- Antitrust immunity for collective ratemaking (publishing the national motor freight classification, for example) is retained.
- The motor carrier is required to disclose to the person directly paying the freight bill whether and to whom discounts or allowances are given.
- The concept of common and contract carrier authority is eliminated; all regulated carriers can contract with shippers.
- The STB will develop a single registration system without the common or contract authority.
- Regulated carriers are to provide safe and adequate service, equipment, and facilities upon reasonable request; thus, the common carrier obligations are eliminated.

Freight Forwarders and Brokers

- Both are required to register with the STB.
- The freight forward is regulated as a carrier and is liable for freight damage.

- The broker is not a carrier and is not held liable for freight damage.
- The STB can impose insurance requirements for both.

In summary, the ICCTA has eliminated the ICC and substituted the STB as the administrator of remaining economic regulations. Railroads are no longer required to file tariffs and nonagricultural contracts. The historical railroad economic regulation remains in force including the common carrier obligations.

Motor carrier economic regulation has been drastically altered by the ICCTA. While the common carrier concept still exists, the requirements to file tariffs and the controls over rates has been removed, making this almost a moot point. Carriers are liable for the full value of damaged freight but are permitted to use release value rates that limit their liability value. Finally, any motor carriers can contract with shippers.

Antitrust Laws in Transportation

The deregulatory movement has exposed many practices to be in violation of antitrust laws. Antitrust regulations were first established in 1890 with passage of the **Sherman Antitrust Act**. The key points of this act are as follows:

> Trusts, etc., in restraint of trade illegal; penalty. Every contract, combination in the form of trust or otherwise, or conspiracy, in restraint of trade or commerce among the several States, or with foreign nations, is declared to be illegal. Every person who shall make any contract or engage in any combination or conspiracy declared by Sections 1 to 7 of this title to be illegal shall be deemed guilty of a felony, and, on conviction thereof, shall be punished by fine not exceeding one million dollars if a corporation, or if any other person, one hundred thousand dollars, or by imprisonment not exceeding three years, or both said punishments, in the discretion of the court.
>
> Monopolizing trade a felony; penalty. Every person who shall monopolize, or attempt to monopolize, or combine or conspire with any other person or persons, to monopolize any part of the trade or commerce among the several States, or with foreign nations, shall be deemed guilty of a felony. . . . [3]

The thrust of the Sherman Act was to outlaw price fixing among competing firms, eliminate business practices that tended toward monopolization, and prevent any firm or combination of firms from refusing to sell or deal with certain firms or avoiding geographic market allocations.

The law was strengthened in 1914 by the **Clayton Act**. This act specifically described some other practices that would be interpreted as attempts to monopolize or actual monopolization. These include exclusive dealing arrangements whereby a buyer and/or seller agree to deal only with the other party for a period of time. Another is a tying contract. This is where a seller agrees to sell goods only if the buyer also buys another product.

Also in 1914, legislation was passed that created the **Federal Trade Commission** (FTC). This agency was the primary overseer and enforcement agency in this business practice area.

Collective rate making by carriers was made exempt from antitrust laws by the **Reed-Bulwinkle Act of 1948,** which empowered the ICC to oversee carrier rate making. As such, it limited traditional jurisdiction by the FTC and Department of Justice in this area. A repeal of those parts of the Interstate Commerce Act that traditionally allowed collective rate making by carriers in rate bureaus caused this practice to become subject to the antitrust laws.

Collective rate making over single-line rates of rail, motor, air, and household goods carriers is not allowed by law as mandated by the regulatory changes. This means that any such practices would come under the jurisdiction and penalties of the Sherman Act and those that follow.

Another major law that might apply to the recent deregulation of transportation is the Robinson-Patman Act of 1936. This law prohibits sellers from practicing price discrimination among buyers unless the differences in price can be justified by true differences in manufacturing and marketing (distribution). Defenses against such a practice are: (1) differences in cost, (2) the need to meet competition, and (3) changing market conditions. Although this law was created for application to the buying and selling of goods, many observers of transportation state that it might be applied in carrier contracting (a service and not a physical good). Whether this law might be applied in carrier pricing will only be determined as deregulation evolves further and cases based on this theory are brought to the courts.

In the selling and purchase of transportation services, two types of antitrust violations can occur. The first is called a **per se violation.** This type of violation is illegal, regardless if any economic harm is done to competitors or other parties. Types of per se violations include price fixing, division of markets, boycotts, and tying agreements.

The second type of antitrust violation is called **rule of reason.** In this type of violation, economic harm must be shown to have been caused to competitors or other parties because these activities can be undertaken by firms with no antitrust implications. Rule of reason violations include exclusive deals, requirements contracts, joint bargaining, and joint action among affiliates.

Carriers, in the selling of transportation services, are normally thought to be the party to which antitrust regulations apply. However, in buying these services, shippers are also subject to these same laws and are at an equal risk of committing an antitrust violation. Because transportation has been subject to antitrust laws only since around 1980, these laws, as they relate to transportation, have not yet been fully tested in the courts.

Transportation Policy

The federal government has played an important role in molding the transportation system that exists in the United States today. The federal government's role has been defined through various laws, rules, and funding programs directed toward collecting and promoting the different modes of transportation. The federal government's policy toward transportation is a composite of these federal laws, rules, funding programs, and regulatory agencies; however, there is no unified federal transportation policy statement or goal that guides the federal government's actions.

In addition to the Congress and the president, more than 60 federal agencies and 30 congressional committees are involved in setting transportation policy. Two independent regulatory agencies interpret transport law, establish operating rules, and set policy. Lastly, the Justice Department interprets statutes involving transportation and reconciles differences between the carriers and the public. Each of these groups has made decisions that have affected the DOT.

The purpose of this chapter is to examine the national transportation policy, both explicit and implicit, that has molded the present U.S. transportation system. Although the national transportation policy is constantly evolving and changing, there are some major underpinnings upon which the basic policy is built. These basic

STOP OFF

Cutting Regulations

The DOT has increased its regulation of the Transportation industry despite President Clinton's efforts to reduce government regulation, according to the General Accounting Office (GAO).

In the 21 months since President Clinton pledged to cut the 140,000-page Code of Federal Regulations by 16,000 pages, DOT has increased its net regulations by 283 pages, the GAO reports. When President Clinton announced his regulatory reform program in June 1995, DOT's regulations comprised 10,663 pages. DOT promised to eliminate 1,221 pages. As of April 30, 1997, DOT had eliminated 1,282 pages and added 1,565 pages for a net increase of 283 pages.

DOT officials blamed statutory requirements imposed by Congress for the overall increase. The Federal Highway Administration and the National Highway Traffic Safety Administration were responsible for much of the increased regulations, GAO said. NHTSA added 68 pages of regulations in response to mandates imposed by the Intermodal Surface Transportation Efficiency Act and the American Automobile Labor Act. DOT's office of the secretary added 18 pages of rules describing procedures for statutorily mandated alcohol testing of safety-sensitive employees.

DOT said it did not eliminate some regulations at the request of regulated parties and added pages to clarify regulatory requirements, including adding charts and examples to clearly illustrate how to comply with the regulations. DOT said it also plans to use question-and-answer formats and checklists to assist regulated parties. The changes, while increasing the actual length of the rules, would decrease the burden imposed on the transportation industry, DOT said.

According to GAO, 38 percent of the 183 actions taken by DOT during the period studied substantially reduced regulatory burden, seven percent resulted in a minor reduction, 37 percent caused no change, while nine percent increased the burden. GAO was unable to determine what impact the remaining rules had.

Source: "GAO: DOT Not Cutting Regulations," *Traffic World*, December 8, 1997, p. 13. Reprinted with permission of *Traffic World*, the Logistics News Weekly.

policy issues will be examined as well as the declared statement of national transportation policy contained in the Transportation Act of 1940.

Why Do We Need a Transportation Policy?

A good starting point for examining the nature of our national transportation policy is the consideration of our need for such a policy. The answer to the question of need lies in the significance of transportation to the very life of the country. Transportation permeates every aspect of a community and touches the life of every member. The transportation system ties together the various communities of a country, making possible the movement of people, goods, and services. The physical connection that transportation gives to spatially separated communities permits a sense of unity to exist.

In addition, transportation is fundamental to the economic activity of a country. Transportation furthers economic activity—the exchange of goods that are mass-produced in one location to locations deficient in these goods. The carry-over benefits of economic activity—jobs, improved goods and services, and so on—would not be reaped by a country's citizens without a good transportation system.

An efficient transportation system is fundamental to national defense. In times of emergencies, people and materials must be deployed quickly to various trouble spots within the United States or throughout the world to protect American interests. Without an efficient transportation system, more resources would have to be dedicated to defense purposes in many more locations. Thus, an efficient transportation system reduces the amount of resources consumed for national defense.

Many of our transportation facilities could not be developed by private enterprise. For example, the capital required to build a transcontinental highway is very likely beyond the resources of the private sector. Efficient and economical rail and highway routes require governmental assistance in securing land from private owners; if the government did not assert its power of eminent domain, routes would be quite circuitous and inefficient. Furthermore, public ownership and the operation of certain transportation facilities, such as highways or waterways, is necessary to ensure access to all who desire to use the facilities.

The purpose of transportation policy is to provide direction for determining the amount of national resources that will be dedicated to transportation and for determining the quality of service that is essential for economic activity and national defense. National policy provides guidelines to the many agencies that exercise transportation decision-making powers and to Congress, the president, and the courts that make and interpret the laws affecting transportation. Thus, transportation policy provides the framework for the allocation of resources to the transportation modes.

The federal government has been a major factor in the development of transportation facilities—highways, waterways, ports, and airports. It also has assumed the responsibility to:

- Ensure the safety of travelers
- Protect the public from the abuse of monopoly power
- Promote fair competition
- Develop or continue vital transport services
- Balance environmental, energy, and social requirements in transportation
- Plan and make decisions[4]

This statement of the federal government's transportation responsibility indicates the diversity of public need that transportation policy must serve. The conflicts inherent in such a diverse set of responsibilities will be discussed in a later section.

Declaration of National Transportation Policy

The ICC Termination Act of 1995 included statements of national transportation policy. Congress made these statements to provide direction to the STB in administering transportation regulation over railroads, motor carriers, water carriers, and pipelines.

The declaration of national rail transportation policy is stated in Public Law 104-88:

> In regulating the railroad industry, it is the policy of the United States Government:
>
> (1) to allow, to the maximum extent possible, competition and the demand for services to establish reasonable rates for transportation by rail;
>
> (2) to minimize the need for Federal regulatory control over the rail transportation system and to require fair and expeditious regulatory decisions when regulation is required;
>
> (3) to promote a safe and efficient rail transportation system by allowing rail carriers to earn adequate revenues, as determined by the Board;
>
> (4) to ensure the development and continuation of a sound rail transportation system with effective competition among rail carriers and with other modes, to meet the needs of the public and the national defense;

(5) to foster sound economic conditions in transportation and to ensure effective competition and coordination between rail carriers and other modes;
(6) to maintain reasonable rates where there is an absence of effective competition and where rail rates provide revenues which exceed the amount necessary to maintain the rail system and to attract capital;
(7) to reduce regulatory barriers to entry into and exit from the industry;
(8) to operate transportation facilities and equipment without detriment to the public health and safety;
(9) to encourage honest and efficient management of railroads;
(10) to require rail carriers, to the maximum extent practicable, to rely on individual rate increases, and to limit the use of increases of general applicability;
(11) to encourage fair wages and safe and suitable working conditions in the railroad industry;
(12) to prohibit predatory pricing and practices, to avoid undue concentrations of market power, and to prohibit unlawful discrimination;
(13) to ensure the availability of accurate cost information in regulatory proceedings, while minimizing the burden on the rail carriers of developing and maintaining the capability of providing such information;
(14) to encourage and promote energy conservation; and
(15) to provide for the expeditious handling and resolution of all proceedings required or permitted to be brought this part.

The declaration of national transportation policy for motor carriers, water carriers, brokers, and freight forwarders is stated in the same document:

In General. To ensure the development, coordination, and preservation of a transportation system that meets the transportation needs of the United States Postal Service and national defense, it is the policy of the United States Government to oversee the modes of transportation and:
(1) in overseeing these modes:
(A) to recognize and preserve the inherent advantage of each mode of transportation
(B) to promote safe, adequate, economical, and efficient transportation;
(C) to encourage sound economic conditions in transportation, including sound economic conditions among carriers;
(D) to encourage the establishment and maintenance of reasonable rates of transportation, without unreasonable discrimination or unfair or destructive competitive practices;
(E) to cooperate with each State and the officials of each State on transportation matters; and
(F) to encourage fair wages and working conditions in the transportation industry;
(2) in overseeing transportation by motor carrier, to promote competitive and efficient transportation in order to:
(A) encourage fair competition, and reasonable rates for transportation by motor carriers of property;
(B) promote efficiency in the motor carrier transportation system and to require fair and expeditious decisions when required;
(C) meet the needs of shippers, receivers, passengers, and consumers;
(D) allow a variety of quality and price options to meet changing market demands and the diverse requirements of the shipping and traveling public;
(E) allow the most productive use of equipment and energy resources;
(F) enable efficient and well-managed carriers to earn adequate profits, attract capital and maintain fair wages and working conditions;
(G) provide and maintain service to small communities and small shippers and intrastate bus services;
(H) provide and maintain commuter bus operations;
(I) improve and maintain a sound, safe, and competitive privately owned motor carrier system;

(J) promote greater participation by minorities in the motor carrier system;
(K) promote intermodal transportation;
(3) in overseeing transportation by motor carriers of passengers:
(A) to cooperate with the States on transportation matters for the purpose of encouraging the States to exercise intrastate regulatory jurisdiction in accordance with the objectives of this part;
(B) to provide Federal procedures which ensure the intrastate regulation is exercised in accordance with this part; and
(C) to ensure that Federal reform initiatives enacted by section 31138 and the Bus Regulatory Reform Act of 1982 are not nullified by State regulatory actions; and
(4) in overseeing transportation by water carrier, to encourage and promote service and price competition in the noncontiguous domestic trade.

The declaration of pipeline national transportation policy is as follows:

In General. To ensure the development, coordination, and preservation of a transportation system that meets the transportation needs of the United States, including the national defense, it is the policy of the United States Government to oversee of the modes of transportation and in overseeing those modes:
(1) to recognize and preserve the inherent advantage of each mode of transportation;
(2) to promote safe, adequate, economical, and efficient transportation;
(3) to encourage sound economic conditions in transportation; including sound economic conditions among carriers;
(4) to encourage the establishment and maintenance of reasonable rates for transportation without unreasonable discrimination or unfair or destructive competitive practices;
(5) to cooperate with each State and the officials of each State on transportation matters; and
(6) to encourage fair wages and working conditions in the transportation industry.

Policy Interpretations

Although the declarations of national transportation policy are general and somewhat vague, the statements do provide a guide to the factors that should be considered in transportation decision making. However, the statements contain numerous conflicting provisions. This section analyzes the incompatibility of the various provisions.

Provisions

First, the declarations are statements of policy for those modes regulated by the STB. Therefore, only railroads, oil pipelines, motor carriers, and water carriers are considered. **Air carriers** are excluded from consideration.

The requirement of "fair and impartial regulation" also overlooks the **exempt carriers** in motor and water transportation. The exempt carriers are eliminated from the economic controls administered by the STB and therefore are not included in the stated policy provisions.

Congress requested the STB administer the transportation regulation in such a manner as to recognize and preserve the inherent advantage of each mode. An inherent advantage is the innate superiority one mode possesses in the form of cost or service characteristics. Such modal characteristics change over time as technology and infrastructure change.

It has been recognized that railroads have an inherent advantage of lower cost in transporting freight long distances and that motor carriers have the advantage for moving freight short distances, less than 300 miles. If the preservation of inherent advantage was the only concern, the STB would not permit trucks to haul freight long distances, more than 300 miles, nor railroads to haul freight short distances. However, the shippers demand long-distance moves from motor carriers and short-distance moves from railroads, and the STB permits these services to be provided.

Safe, adequate, economical, and efficient service is not totally attainable. An emphasis on safety may mean an uneconomical or inefficient service. Added safety features on equipment and added safety procedures for employees will increase total costs and cost per unit of output and may reduce the productivity of employees. However, when lives are involved, safety has taken precedence over economical and efficient service.

Providing adequate service has been construed to mean meeting normal demand. If carriers were forced to have capacity that is sufficient to meet peak demand, considerable excess capacity would exist, resulting in uneconomical and inefficient operations. Fostering sound economic conditions among the carriers does not mean ensuring an acceptable profit for all carriers. Nor does it imply that the STB should guarantee the survival of all carriers. The STB must consider the economic condition of carriers in rate rulings so as to foster stability of transportation supply.

The policy statement regarding reasonable charges, unjust discrimination, undue preference, and unfair competitive practices is merely a reiteration of the **common carrier** obligations. Congress made no attempt to define these concepts. The STB was given the task of interpreting them as it hears and decides individual cases.

Following the passage of the 1940 Transportation Act, a number of laws provided some degree of definition for these common carrier policy statements. For example, the Staggers Rail Act of 1980 defined a **reasonable** rail **rate** as one that is not more than 160 percent of variable costs. The Motor Carrier Act of 1980 defined a zone of rate freedom in which a rate change of ±10 percent in one year is presumed to be reasonable. Both acts defined the normal business entertainment of shippers as acceptable practice and not an instance of under preference.

The cooperative efforts between the federal and state governments have not always been smooth. The very foundation for federal regulation of transportation was the judicial decision that only the federal government could regulate interstate transportation. Through police powers, the states have the right to establish laws regarding transportation safety. Thus, for example, states have enacted laws governing the height, length, weight, and speed of motor carrier trucks. However, the federal government has standardized weight and speed laws on interstate highways. One approach the federal government has taken has been to threaten to withhold federal highway money from states that do not comply.

Finally, the STB was charged with the responsibility of encouraging fair wages and working conditions. No attempt was made to interpret the terms *fair wage* and *working conditions.* A wage that is deemed fair by an employee may be unfair to an employer. An air-conditioned cab may be equitable working conditions to a driver, but it is merely an added cost to the employer. In addition, both of the above examples may conflict with the policy statement regarding the promotion of economical and efficient service.

The stated goals of the national transportation policy are to provide a system of transportation that meets the needs of commerce, the U.S. Postal Service, *and* national defense. It is possible that a system that meets the needs of commerce may be insufficient to meet the needs of national defense during an emergency situation. In addition, a system that has the capacity to meet national defense needs will have excess capacity for commerce and postal service needs during peace times and will be inefficient and uneconomical.

For example, the United States maintains a merchant marine fleet that can be called into service to haul defense material during a national defense emergency. However, this fleet may be twice the size of that needed for commerce. Many government critics claim a fleet with such excess capacity is a waste of resources. Defense advocates argue that national defense needs dictate that such a fleet be operated to preclude dependency on a foreign country for water transportation during defense emergencies. As the arguments rage on, one can see the conflict that exists in the stated national policy goals.

The ICCTA provides specific direction regarding the railroads and motor carriers. For the railroads, the STB is directed to minimize the need for federal regulatory control, reduce regulatory barriers to entry and exit, prohibit predatory pricing, and promote energy conservation. For motor carriers, the STB is to allow pricing variety, serve small communities, promote greater participation by minorities, and promote transportation.

Who Establishes Policy?

National transportation policies are developed at various levels of government and by many different agencies. The specifics of a particular policy may reflect the persuasion of a group of individuals (for example, a consumer group) or of a single individual (for example, an elected official). The purpose of this section is to examine the basic institutional framework that aids in the development of national transportation policy.

Executive Branch[5]

Many departments within the executive branch of government influence (establish) transportation policy. At the top of the list is the office of the president. The president has authority over international air transportation and foreign air carriers operating into the United States. The president also appoints individuals to head the various agencies that influence transportation and to head the two regulatory agencies—the STB and Federal Maritime Commission (FMC).

The Department of State is directly involved in developing policy regarding international transportation by air and water. The policies and programs designed to encourage foreign visitors to the United States are implemented by the U.S. Travel Service. The Maritime Administration is involved with ocean (international) transportation policy. It determines ship requirements, service, and routes essential to foreign commerce. In addition, international transportation policies and programs are shaped by the Military Sealift Command, Military Airlift Command, and Military Traffic Management and Terminal Service—agencies responsible for the movement of military goods and personnel.

On the domestic level, the Department of Energy develops policies regarding energy availability and distribution (fuel and rationing). The U.S. Postal Service contracts for the transportation of the mail; such contracts have been used to promote air transportation as well as motor and rail transportation at other times. The Department of Housing and Urban Development (HUD) consults with the DOT regarding the compatibility of urban transportation systems within the HUD-administered housing and community development programs. The Army Corps of Engineers is responsible for constructing and maintaining rivers and harbors and for protecting the navigable waterways.

The DOT, however, is the most pervasive influence of policy at the domestic level. The secretary of transportation is responsible for assisting the president in all transportation matters, including public investment, safety, and research. (See Appendix 1 at the end of this chapter for a list of agencies within the DOT.)

Congressional Committees[6]

The laws that are formulated by Congress are the formal method by which Congress influences national transportation. The congressional committee structure is the forum in which Congress develops policy, programs, and funding for transportation.

Within the Senate, the two standing committees that influence transportation are the Commerce, Science, and Transportation Committee and the Environment and Public Works Committee. The Commerce, Science, and Transportation Committee is concerned with the regulations of the modes, the promotion of air transportation (subsidies and construction funding), and the promotion of water transportation (Maritime Administration programs). The Environment and Public Works Committee is concerned with internal waterway and harbor projects, highway construction and maintenance projects, and air and water pollution regulations.

The House of Representatives' standing committees relating to transportation include the Energy and Commerce Committee, Public Works and Transportation Committee, and Merchant Marine and Fisheries Committee. The Interstate and Foreign Commerce Committee has jurisdiction over railroads, the Railroad Labor Act, and air pollution. The Merchant Marine and Fisheries Committee is concerned with international water transportation and Maritime Administration programs. The Public Works and Transportation Committee is concerned with internal waterway and harbor projects, the regulation of all modes, and urban mass transportation.

In addition to the above standing committees, numerous other congressional committees have an impact on transportation. Federal funding can be decided in the Appropriations Committee, Senate Banking Committee, Housing and Urban Affairs Committee, House Ways and Means Committee, or Senate Finance Committee.

Regulatory Agencies

The STB and FMC are independent agencies charged with implementing the laws regulating transportation. The agencies have quasi-judicial and quasi-legislative powers, and when they decide on a case (for example, reasonableness of rates), the agencies are exercising quasi-judicial powers. The courts enforce agency decisions.

Judicial System

The courts have been called upon to interpret laws or reconcile conflicts. In doing so, the courts have an impact upon transportation policies. Carriers, shippers, and the general public may call upon the courts to change existing policy through interpretation of statutes. As the regulatory commissions exercise quasi-legislative and quasi-judicial powers, the affected parties seek recourse to the courts to determine the legality of the decisions. The role of the courts is basically to interpret the meaning of policy as stated in laws, regulations, and executive orders.

Industry Associations

One facet of national policy development that is often overlooked in the study of transportation is the role of industry associations in shaping national, state, and local promotion, regulation, and policy. These associations exist in most industries, and many of the transportation industry associations are based in Washington, DC.

Industry associations in transportation serve two basic purposes: establishment of industry standards, and policy formulation and influence. The organizations are nonprofit entities that derive their powers and resources from individual member firms. They act on the charges given them by their members. In transportation, the railroads in the Association of American Railroads (AAR) and the motor carriers in the American Trucking Associations (ATA) often meet to resolve matters of equipment conformity and loss and damage prevention. On the policy side, these associations develop legislative and administrative ruling concepts that favor the collective membership, or they serve as a united front against proposals that are perceived to be harmful to the group.

The major industry associations in the transportation field have evolved from specific modes. The AAR represents the larger railroads in the United States; it was instrumental in the passage of the Staggers Rail Act of 1980. The ATA is divided into subconferences including regular common carriers, household goods carriers, local and short-haul carriers, bulk tank firms, contract carriers, and automobile transporters. The Air Transport Association of America (ATAA) represents the airline industry in the United States. The American Waterways Operators (AWO) consists of barge operators on the inland waterway system. The Freight Forwarders' Institute (FFI) serves member carriers in that mode. The National Motor Bus Operators Organization (NAMBO) represents common and charter bus firms. The Committee of American Steamship Lines (CASL) represents the subsidized U.S. flag steamship firms.

Two major associations exist for the interests of large shippers. One is the National Industrial Traffic League (NITL), and the other is the National Small Shipment Transportation Conference (NASSTRAC). Both are active before congressional bodies, regulator agencies, and carrier groups.

The Transportation Association of America (TAA) (which ceased operation in 1982) had as its concern the health and vitality of the entire U.S. transportation system. It became involved in policy issues relating to two or more modes, or between modes and shippers as well as investors. The TAA was largely instrumental in the passage of the act that created the DOT, as well as the passage of the Uniform Time Standards Act, which caused all areas of the United States electing to recognize daylight savings time to do so at the same time in April. Previously, each state did so on different dates, which caused major confusion in railroad and airline scheduling systems and timetable publication. At one point, United Airlines had to publish 27 different timetables during the spring as various states recognized daylight savings time on different dates. Since it was enacted in 1967, the Uniform Time Standards Act has simplified these facets of transportation management.

Other groups and associations are involved in transportation policy, including nontransportation special interest groups such as the grange and labor unions. Various governmental agencies such as the Department of Agriculture and the Department of Defense influence existing and proposed transportation legislation, rules, and policies on their behalf, or on behalf of the groups within them.

One of the most important governmental policy issues has been the public promotion of transportation. All of the above groups and associations have been involved over the years in this important area. The topic is of such importance as a policy issue that it is considered in detail in the next section.

Public Promotion

This section presents an overview of the major transportation planning and promotion activities conducted in the United States public sector. Promotion connotes encouragement or provision of aid or assistance so transportation can grow or survive. *Planning* and *promotion* are general terms used to refer to programs, policies, and actual planning. Programs involve actual public cash investments into or funding for transportation activities both privately and publicly owned. Agencies make policies to encourage beneficial actions or impacts for transportation. Planning determines future transportation needs, and then establishes policies or programs to bring about certain goals through the public or private sector. All three activities promote transportation and cause it to grow or survive in instances in which pure market forces would not have done so.

Transportation Project Planning in the Public Sector

Transportation project planning is the process whereby federal, state, or local groups review the movement needs or demands of a region or population segment, develop transport alternatives, and usually propose or implement one of them. It enables the development of new movement functions or allows an existing one to continue in the face of adverse trends or change.

Transportation project planning is a public activity; purely financial returns and other concerns are not the overriding benefits sought. It is a major part of the public activity in the U.S. economy for several reasons. Public transportation processes can open trade or movement where private actions have not or would not have been enticed to do so for financial gain alone. Various cultural and political benefits often come from projects and programs provided publicly. Transportation planning also lowers the cost of living or reduces the social costs of delay or congestion. Finally, it provides services that are not remunerative but are deemed socially necessary or desirable.

Transportation planning has been and continues to be a critical factor in the last quarter of the twentieth century. There are many areas of transportation from which private firms have withdrawn. Many forms of carriage today are no longer economically profitable or compensatory. Urban bus systems, commuter railroads, rail and urban research and development, and many rail services are examples of transportation forms that would not now exist without public sector involvement.

Many forms of transportation require large capital investments that contain cost lumpiness that would normally discourage or basically prohibit private investment. Port dredging and development, as well as airport construction, are examples of capital items that are not affordable by the carriers using them. Instead, the ability of a public authority to attract capital enables the asset to be built; cost is recovered through user charges.

Public planning of transportation is generally found in situations where environmental or social needs override financial ones. A major argument used in modern subway construction is that, although the system might not recover its full costs from the fare box, the city as a whole will gain by increased access to already existing downtown facilities, including buildings, offices, stores, and water utility systems. Constructing other facilities in developing suburban areas will not be necessary. Also, commuters save money because the subway eliminates the need for a second family auto, long driving, excess fuel consumption, costly parking in downtown areas, and so on. It is apparent that public planning of transportation involves a different viewpoint and set of objectives than does capital investment analysis in private firms.

An Approach to Public Planning Project Analysis

Whereas the private firm is seeking a financial return to the firm itself, public planning agencies compare the initial costs of a project to the financial, environmental, and measurable social benefits to everyone affected by the project. Thus, it compares total societal cost to total societal benefits whether they be monetary or nonmonetary in nature.

The specific analytical tool typically used in public planning is the **benefit/cost ratio** (BCR). In essence, it is a measure of total measurable benefits to society divided by the initial capital cost. The formula for it in basic form is as follows:

$$BCR = \frac{\textit{Sum of yearly benefits to society}}{\textit{Sum of costs to agencies and those in society initially impacted}}$$

$$= \frac{\textit{Sum of benefits}}{\textit{Sum of initial costs}} = \frac{\textit{Year 1 benefit} + \textit{Year 2 benefit} + \ldots}{\textit{Sum of all initial costs}}$$

If the resulting answer is greater than one, the project is said to produce a "profit" for society. The figure one indicates the break-even point; less than one indicates that the agency will spend more on the project than society will ever reap in long-term benefits.

The major costs of a project include those expenses typically involved in private projects. Planning, engineering, constructing, and financing costs are critical. Other costs include delay or congestion measured in terms of dollars per hour and in terms of everyone in society who will be inconvenienced during the construction phase of a transportation project. This is certainly the case in new lock and dam construction with regard to barge operations. Project costs also can include a cost of lost sales to downtown businesses; for example, the stores are more difficult to access during several years of subway construction. The costs of bond financing incurred to construct the system are pertinent also. All costs are monetarily measured or translated into monetary measures and listed according to the year in which they will occur. Typically, the major expenses arise in the initial years of construction; financing is a major cost carried through the project's life.

The benefits of a project include any measurable benefit to the agency, other agencies, and the public at large. Benefits include increased employment, decreased prices for products, lowered costs of commuting or freight transfer, reduced maintenance, improved health due to lessened pollution, less travel time due to faster commuting or travel, increased travel, and often increased recreational benefits. Many benefit measures are easily quantified, though others pose analytical difficulties in the form of forecasting volumes and cost relationships in future periods.

Three analytical steps or checks must be undertaken to compute the actual benefit/cost ratio:

1. Both costs and benefits must be assessed in such a way that *all costs* and *benefits* to both agencies and the general public are included. It is wise to be analytically conservative about costs, assuming they will be incurred by everyone in society and assuming they may be higher than what current estimates show them to be. Similarly, benefits should only be limited to actual benefits that are sound and quantifiable in logical ways.

2. The individual costs and benefits should be summed for each year of occurrence and presented in the respective position of numerator or denominator as shown earlier.

3. A yearly discount rate should be used against each cost and benefit because most costs and benefits will not be incurred until the future.

The timing and **time value of funds** is an important part of any capital project analysis. Political controversy exists about the choice of the specific discount rate and its application. Several analytical points can be examined that will shed light on this task. One, the discount rate should reflect the interest cost and impact to the public agency that borrows the initial funds. Second, the rate should become higher in later years to reflect increasing risk, inflation, uncertainty, and forecasting difficulties. This is a conservative practice of private project financial managers, and the logic of it can be applied soundly in a public setting. Third, the counting of benefits should cease in some future period, even though the project might last longer. This is another practice that is an implicit way of conservatively considering only those benefits within the intermediate term, unless a logical case can be made for an extended period of time. These points are made so as to ensure that benefit overcounting is minimized, especially for those items such as recreation, which are generally not central to the main project need or justification. By including benefits for 25 years or more, it is easy to inflate the ratio or cause it to be above the breakeven point when it would not be otherwise. Conservative risk analysis states that costs should be analytically considered higher and benefits lower than what a first-glance measure indicates.

An example of a benefit/cost ratio application to a proposed subway line will show how public planning processes are employed. Costs include those of organization development, design, engineering, initial financing, land purchases, relocation, and disruption to the public. Costs projected into the future include operations, lost property taxes, interest costs, and any other costs directly tied to the project. Benefits to the agencies include lowered operational costs of city buses; alternative application of funds released from the bus operation (reduced street and highway requirements); decreased need to expand highways or downtown parking; increased property, sales, and wage taxes from higher economic activity downtown; avoidance of federal penalties for not reducing citywide auto emissions; and many others. Benefits to society include the income multiplier effect from the initial project investment in the form of employment, reduced unemployment, and general dollar spending and circulation from construction. The general public also gains from savings in direct commuting costs and greater area-wide mobility. The system will improve society in the form of time savings, less pollution, and reduced commuting stress. The subway will generally cause the downtown to become more fully utilized. Thus, industry and retail stores might not leave the downtown for the suburbs, and the overall region benefits from the reduced need to expand streets, fire protection, water, electricity, and so on. In this manner, the unit tax base of the city itself remains low.

As we have seen, public planning involves many of the basic concepts inherent in private project planning, but the application is different. The public agency is concerned about costs and benefits to all parties affected by the project. Thus, costs, benefits, and "profits" are measured for society as a whole in tangible and intangible ways. The following discussion presents those forms of modal promotion found in the United States.

Air

The domestic air system received the benefits of several government programs. Foremost is the Federal Aviation Administration's (FAA) **air traffic control system.** It is the right-of-way system for the airlines. The navigation and traffic flow control system is used by every aircraft in flight. It is a necessary standardized safety system, which is provided at little direct fee cost to the airlines. The FAA is part of the U.S. DOT.

Another direct air system benefit is the subsidy system. These subsidies generally apply to short and medium nonjet flights to cities that are unable to support high traffic volumes. The subsidy has been a significant support mechanism for regional airlines. In recent years, the growth of air commuter lines has enabled the regional airlines to discontinue service to small cities. The Air Deregulation Act of 1978 accelerated this trend, which results in a lessened need for regional airline subsidies. This act might also cause increased political pressure for subsidies for commuter lines serving very small cities.

The U.S. Postal Service also provides substantial support to airlines. In the airline industry's early years, its prime earnings came from this subsidy system. In recent years, mail income has not been as significant, but this subsidy still is a major revenue source for the industry.

State and local agencies help promote the airline industry through air terminal development and construction. Terminals represent substantial capital investments and would be difficult for the industry to finance and construct. State and local bodies are able to raise the necessary large construction funds at reasonable municipal bond interest rates, often backed by the taxing power of the community. The airlines then rent terminal and hangar facilities and pay landing fees for each flight. This system reduces the problem of capital investment cost for the airlines.

Many aircraft safety matters are handled by the federal government. The FAA provides aircraft construction and safety rules as well as pilot certification. This relieves the industry of many research, development, and information tasks related to safety of the system. In another capacity, the National Transportation Safety Board investigates accidents so that many can be avoided or reduced through aircraft specification or flight procedures.

Another indirect form of promotion to this industry comes from the military. Defense contracts for military airplane development often provide spillover benefits to commercial aviation in the form of mechanical or navigational aircraft improvements. Without military-related research and development activity, advancements in this area would no doubt occur at a slower pace.

A last form of airline promotion, which is not found in the United States system, is direct government ownership, operation, or subsidy of air service. This is common with foreign airlines that serve the United States and other routes. In these instances, African, Asian, many European, and the Latin American lines are subsidized so the countries can operate their airlines for purposes of national pride, have some degree of control over traffic to and from their nations, and gain balance of payment benefits and hard currencies through ticket sales and revenues.

A related form of such **home-flag airline** promotion exists here in the United States and in most foreign nations. In the United States, there is a requirement that only American flag carriers with domestically owned aircraft and domestic crews may originate and terminate domestic passengers and freight. Many foreign lines serve both New York and San Francisco, for example, with a flight originating abroad, but these flights are limited to international passengers. The only way in which a foreign line can originate and terminate a passenger in two U.S. cities is when that passenger is exercising stopover privileges as part of a tour or through movement. This home-flag requirement serves to protect the domestic lines.

Several forms of **user charges** are essentially designed, in whole or part, to have the modes pay for many of the public benefits they receive. As mentioned before, landing fees are charged to repay investments or incur revenue for specific airports. A major user charge is levied against passenger movements through ticket taxes. An international per head tax is also part of this user tax, as are some aircraft registration fees. Many of these funds go into the **Airport and Airway Trust Fund,** which is used for airport facility projects on a shared basis with local agencies.

Motor and Highway

With regard to public promotion, the highway system and motor carrier firms have a joint relationship. There is no direct promotion to motor carriers themselves, but indirect benefit comes to the industry through highway development since most highway projects are done with government funds.

The Federal Highway Administration branch of the DOT is responsible for federal highway construction and safety. A predecessor agency, the Bureau of Public Roads, carried out the mandate to build the Interstate Highway System, which was paid for on a 90 percent«minus»10 percent federal-state sharing basis. Today the agency is largely devoted to highway research, development, and safety. It also is charged with certain repair projects on critical parts of the Federal and Interstate Highway System. Motor carriers benefit from the increased access, speed, and safety of this system because without it they would have to travel more congested routes, presenting safety hazards.

The National Highway Traffic Safety Administration is responsible for highway and auto safety. It also conducts major research into vehicle safety, accidents, and highway design related to safety. This agency provides administrative regulations for certain minimum automobile safety features.

The Bureau of Motor Carrier Safety is a noneconomic regulatory body whose main purpose is truck safety. Though this agency imposes strict standards on truck safety, the long-term benefit is increased safety for everyone on the highways.

Highway development also comes from states and various regional planning commissions. One example is the Appalachian Development Commission, which is charged with improving the infrastructure and economy of that region. Many highway building and improvement projects are funded by this agency.

User charges are present in the highway systems in several forms. A major form is the gas and fuel tax. States look to this per-gallon tax as a major revenue source for highway construction and upkeep. The federal government fuel taxes go to the **Federal Highway Trust Fund,** which is the financing source of the Interstate Highway System. Some states are switching from a per-gallon to a percent-of-sales-price method of fuel-based taxation because in recent years the number of gallons of fuel sold has decreased, leaving state agencies with less revenue in times that demand greater highway maintenance. The percent-of-sales-price approach can avoid much of this decline. Another public revenue source is the federal excise tax on road tires. States also obtain revenues through vehicle registration fees. These mostly are assessed on a vehicle weight basis so as to recoup, somewhat, a proportionate share of construction costs related to heavier versus light vehicles. Further, some states assess a ton-mile tax. Finally, tolls are a form of user taxes on many turnpikes and bridges.

Two major controversies are currently taking place with regard to highway user charges. One concerns the Federal Highway Trust Fund. The tax money that goes into this fund is collected primarily for interstate highway construction. Approximately 96 percent of the interstate system has been built, but doubt exists over whether the remaining portions, mostly very costly urban sections, will ever be built. Meanwhile, the fuel tax continues to be collected and accumulated in the fund.

A second problem with user taxes is on the state level. Most states collecting vehicle fees and vehicle taxes only return a portion of them for highway purposes.

Some states have earmarked some of these funds for education and other uses. In addition, industry groups continue to seek a greater share of these funds for highway development and improvement.

Rail

The railroads currently can avail themselves of direct assistance from the Regional Railroad Reorganization Act of 1973, the Railroad Revitalization and Regulatory Reform Act of 1976, and the Staggers Rail Act of 1980. Most of the assistance is in the form of track repair and motive power acquisition financing. These provisions are attempts to overcome the problem of poor equipment and facilities, which lead to poorer service and blighted financial conditions, which usually perpetuate into a further downward spiral.

Another form of funding has been available as a subsidy to lines that are abandoned by railroads but that states and other groups continue to operate. This assistance was designed to make rail line abandonment easier by railroads while still allowing service to be continued.

The Consolidated Rail Corporation (Conrail) had been the subject of special federal funding and promotion. It has received special appropriations for operations and capital improvements, mainly through provisions of the Regional Railroad Reorganization Act of 1973. Recently, after a successful transformation, Conrail was purchased by the Norfolk Southern and CSX Railroads. Conrail's routes were integrated into those companies.

Research and development in this mode essentially disappeared in the late 1950s. Financial problems in most railroads caused cutbacks in the research and development area, thereby stagnating the technology. In response to this situation, the Federal Railroad Administration (FRA) was created as part of the DOT in 1966. The FRA has become a major source of gains in railroad technology as well as safety. A test facility at Pueblo, Colorado, originally owned by the FRA, is used to test improvements in existing power and rolling equipment and to develop advanced high-speed rail technologies for the future. This facility, now known as the Transportation Technology Center, has been privatized and is managed by the AAR.

Another form of help to the rail industry is **Amtrak.** In 1969, the industry's intercity passenger deficit reached more than $500 million. Because the ICC, DOT, and the public deemed many of these services essential to the public need, the railroads could only discontinue them slowly after major procedural steps were taken. Amtrak was created to relieve this burden from the railroads while at the same time providing some of the needed services to the public. Thus, much of the passenger train deficit was shifted from the railroads and their shippers and stockholders to the federal taxpayer.

Domestic Waterway Operations

The inland barge industry receives two major forms of federal promotion. The first is from the **Army Corps of Engineers,** which is responsible for river and port channel **dredging** and clearances, as well as lock and dam **construction**. Operation and maintenance of these facilities rest with corps as well. The second is provided by the **Coast Guard**, which is responsible for navigation aids and systems on the inland waterway system.

Historically, the barge industry paid no user charges except what could be interpreted as a very indirect form through general income taxes. A major controversy over a critical lock and dam on the upper Mississippi River at Alton, Illinois, brought the free-use issue to a head. The competing railroad industry lobbied to prevent this lock from being improved and enlarged. The resulting legislation and appropriation provided for improvement of that lock and initiated a fuel tax user charge for that industry.

International Water Carriage

The American flag overseas steamship industry receives major assistance from the federal government through the Maritime Administration (MARAD). The Merchant Marine Act of 1936 was designed to prevent economic decline of the U.S. steamship industry. One major facet of this act is construction differential subsidies (CDS). These are paid by the Maritime Administration to U.S. steamship yards that are constructing subsidized lines' ships. A ship that might only cost $20 to build in Asia might cost $30 million to build in a U.S. yard. Without CDS, U.S. lines would build their ships abroad and American ship-building capacity would cease to exist. Instead, the steamship line pays, say, $20 million and MARAD pays the other $10 million to construct the ship in the United States. The survival of the U.S. shipyard also is viewed as essential to U.S. military capability. The Merchant Marine Act of 1936 also provides for operating differential subsidies (ODS), which cover the higher-cost increment resulting from having higher-paid American crews on ships, rather than less costly foreign labor.

Several **indirect** forms of **promotion** exist in this industry as well. The U.S. cabotage laws state that freight or passengers originating and terminating in two U.S. points can only be transported in ships constructed in the United States and owned and manned by U.S. citizens. The United States also has a **cargo preference** law that assists the U.S. fleet. Enacted in 1954, it stipulates that at least 50 percent of the gross tonnage of certain U.S. government-owned and -sponsored cargoes must be carried by U.S. flagships. This law extends to Department of Defense military goods, foreign aid by the State Department, surplus food movements by the Department of Agriculture, and products whose financing is sponsored by the Export-Import Bank.

Several planning and facilitating promotional efforts also assist the American flag ocean fleet. MARAD continually studies and develops plans for port improvements and ways in which export–import movements can be made more efficient. The Department of Commerce has a subagency whose prime purpose is to stimulate export sales that also benefit the U.S. fleet.

Two points should be brought out here with regard to the major funding and support roles played by MARAD. One deals with the control MARAD has over the lines it subsidizes. The agency exercises decision powers over the design and construction of each ship. It also plays a major role in the routes taken by each one. In this manner, the agency makes certain decisions that are normally within the discretion of carrier managements. This form of control is unique to the transportation industry in the United States.

The other point relates to the rationale for such extensive assistance to this one industry. A strong home shipping fleet is a vital part of national defense sealift capacity in the event of war. Also, existence of the fleet tends to exert some influence on services and rates on various trade routes to the benefit of the United States and its interests. Further, export and import movements on U.S. flagships help retain U.S. dollars to accumulate certain other strong foreign currencies.

The **Shipping Act of 1984** is a further example of the U.S. policy toward supporting a strong U.S. ocean fleet. The act was designed to reduce the regulation on foreign ocean shipping with the following goals:

- Establishing a nondiscriminatory regulatory process for common ocean carriers with a minimum of government intervention and regulatory costs
- Providing an efficient and economic transportation system in the ocean commerce of the United States that is in harmony and responsive to international shipping practices
- Encouraging the development of an economically sound and efficient U.S. flag liner fleet capable of meeting national security needs

The St. Lawrence Seaway Development Corporation within the DOT functions as the U.S. financing and operating arm of the joint U.S./Canada venture to upgrade the Great Lakes waterway and lock system to accommodate oceangoing ships. This waterway opened a fourth seacoast for the United States, enabling oceangoing ships to call at Buffalo, Cleveland, Toledo, Detroit, Chicago, Duluth, and other inland ports.

A final, and major, positive role in the water carrier industry is played by various port authorities. These agencies provide financing, major construction, and leasing of facilities in much the same way that the airport authorities provide facilities to the air industry.

Pipeline

The pipeline industry receives no public financial support, but it has benefited in a legal sense from the right of eminent domain permitted to oil, gas, and petroleum product lines. Typically, a pipeline will negotiate for land acquisition or rental. If the landowner will not negotiate at all or in good faith, the law of eminent domain will uphold the use of the land for a pipeline right-of-way in a court of law.

Miscellaneous Forms of Promotion

Various other activities directly or indirectly benefit the transportation industry. The DOT conducts planning and research activities in several ways. The Office of Assistant Secretary for Policy Plans and International Affairs is involved with improving international goods flow and conducting studies about the transportation systems and data coordination. The assistant secretary for the Systems Development and Technology Department is responsible for research and development into improved transport vehicles and methods.

Other research and development studies of benefit to transportation are conducted by the Transportation Research Board and the National Science Foundation. A small but effective group within the Department of Agriculture is concerned with improving loading, unloading, packaging, and carriage methods of food products on all modes. Many of these efforts result in equipment design changes that make transportation equipment more efficient for food movements. The Department of Defense continually examines methods to improve shipping, and many improvements spill over into the commercial area.

Transportation Promotion in Perspective

Two major concepts override the entire topic of transportation promotion: user charges and nationalization. User charges often are created and assessed to pay for some or all of the services used by the carrier or mode. Nationalization represents an extreme form of public assistance or provision of transportation.

User Charges

These are assessments or fees charged by public bodies against carriers. They are created for a variety of reasons. One is to pay back the public for assistance during modal conception and encouragement. Some user charges are assessed to finance construction. The federal fuel tax on gasoline is an example, as is the barge fuel tax. Coverage of operating costs is often a reason for the origin of user charges. Examples here are airport landing fees, road tolls, and state fuel tax when it is applied to road maintenance. In addition, a user charge also can serve to equalize intermodal competitive conditions. The barge fuel tax, while paying for some lock construction, also makes barge operators bear some of the full cost of providing their service. This lessens, to a degree, some of the advantage that existed when right-of-way costs were borne by the public and not the barge firm.

Forms

User charges are present in three basic forms. The first is an **existence charge,** a charge related to existence. This is similar to driver's license and auto registration fees. A charge is made against the person or unit regardless of the extent of use made of the services.

A second user charge is a **unit charge.** This is a fee assessed for use of a facility or resource. This fee is variable according to use, but it does not distinguish between passengers or freight within each unit. Tolls and gas mileage taxes are examples. Thus, a bus with two passengers pays the same as does a bus with 40 passengers. An empty truck or one with scrap is charged the same as a truck carrying calculators and cameras. This form of fee assessment does not take into account the economic value of the service being performed.

A third user fee is based upon **relative use.** This form assesses fees according to the investment of cost incurred by the agency to provide the service. An increased truck registration fee for heavier vehicles is an example here. Deeper road bases are required for heavier trucks. Road and bridge wear and damage is believed to be experienced on the basis of vehicle weight. Another example of relative use charge is a commuter route bridge toll. In the San Francisco area, bridge tolls are assessed for each vehicle. However, cars and vans having four or more passengers can cross the bridge toll-free. In this instance, the user charge becomes a behavior inducement. A form of *nonuser fee* also has arisen in recent years. Atlanta and San Francisco and area counties are partially paying for their shares of rapid transit development through a one-cent additional sales tax on all retail transactions within those areas. Here, many persons do not, or might not, ever use the rapid transit system, but they do bear some of its costs. A major rationale behind this nonuser charge is that all persons in a community benefit at least indirectly from the improved infrastructure provided by the system.

Nationalization

Nationalization is an extreme form of public promotion. It basically consists of public ownership, financing, and operation of a business entity. No true forms of nationalization exist in the U.S. transportation system except the Alaska Railroad, which was owned by the DOT and is now owned by the state of Alaska. Nationalization is a method of providing transportation service where neither financing, ownership, nor operation is possible in a private manner. Railroads and airlines in foreign countries are examples of nationalization, but many countries, such as Mexico, New

Zealand, and Great Britain, are privatizing their railroads. Transportation service in many lands probably would not exist in a desirable form, or at all, without such government intervention. Advantages of nationalization that are often cited are that services can be provided that would not exist under private ownership, and capital can be attracted at favorable rates. But nationalized organizations have been criticized as being slow to innovate, unresponsive to the general public, subject to the same labor reduction as private enterprise, dependent on large management staffs, and subject to political influence.

Transportation Safety

As noted earlier, the federal government has assumed the responsibility of ensuring the safety of travelers. It has promulgated numerous safety regulations for all modes and has centralized safety enforcement in the DOT. Protection of the traveler and the general public is an increasing government concern in light of the reduced economic regulation of transportation and the resultant concerns that carriers will sacrifice safety matters for profitability or economic viability.

Since **economic deregulation,** greater attention has been given to the establishment and enforcement of safety regulations to ensure that the transportation providers do not defer required vehicle and operating safety requirements in the heat of competition. Critics of economic deregulation cite that the marketplace pressures carriers to increase productivity and improve efficiency at the expense of safety. The deregulation experience in the airline and motor-carrier industries has resulted in economic strains on the carriers and a deleterious effect on safety, whereas the opposite is true for the railroads, which have been able to increase profitability and safety.[7]

Federal safety regulations cover all aspects of transportation operations from labor qualifications and operating procedures to equipment specifications. The primary objective of the safety regulations is to establish a **minimum level of safety** for transportation providers to maintain. Many transportation companies establish higher safety levels than those required by law, and these companies have their own enforcement personnel to ensure compliance.

Labor safety regulations have established minimum qualifications for operating personnel, including such factors as age, health, training, licensing, and experience. Minimum age requirements were established for driving a tractor trailer in interstate commerce, and a nationwide commercial driver licensing program was initiated in 1988. Pilots are required to pass a physical examination, to have training and experience on specific types of aircraft, and to be certified for various types of flying conditions. Similar regulations govern rail engineers and ship captains.

The policy of safe transportation has been extended to the specification of standards for transportation vehicles. These standards range from design specifications for aircraft to required safety equipment for the automobile. The vehicle manufacturer is obligated to adhere to the safety specifications, and the vehicle operator is required to maintain the vehicle and equipment in good operating condition and to use the safety equipment. For example, the automobile manufacturer must equip the vehicle with seat belts, a minimum number of headlights and taillights, a horn, etc. The auto owner then is required by state law to use the seat belt and to ensure proper functioning of the lights, horn, etc.

Of all the commodities moved within the boundaries of the United States, **hazardous materials** pose the greatest threat to public safety. Consequently, the movement of hazardous materials and hazardous wastes has been subjected to considerable regulations. A hazardous material is a substance that poses more than a reasonable risk to the health and safety of individuals and includes products such as explosives, flammables, corrosives, oxidizers, and radioactive materials. The safety regulations govern the movement of hazardous wastes as well.

A plethora of hazardous material and hazardous waste safety regulations have been imposed upon the transportation of such commodities. The regulations govern loading and unloading practices, packaging, routing, commodity identification, and documentation. Transportation personnel must be trained to properly handle hazardous cargoes and to respond to emergencies.

These regulations overlap somewhat because of the overlapping jurisdiction of the regulatory agencies originating and enforcing the rules. For example, the DOT promulgates and enforces hazardous material regulations, while the Environmental Protection Agency regulates the movement of hazardous wastes. In addition, the various states and municipalities within the states establish various laws impacting the movement of hazardous commodities through their jurisdiction.

As indicated above, the states are involved in regulating the safe operation of transportation vehicles. The police powers of the Constitution grant the states the right to protect the health and welfare of their citizens. The states have used this power to establish safety regulations governing the safe operations of trains through a state, and to limit the maximum speed, height, length, and weight of trucks, etc. These regulations are not standard from state to state because of the differing political, economical, sociological, and geographical conditions. However, the common denominator in state safety regulations is that all states regulate transportation safety matters.

Transportation safety matters have been extended to include environmental safety. Auto emission standards are designed to protect air quality; flight take-off procedures and patterns are designed to reduce noise levels for the citizens living near airports; and tanker loading and unloading procedures for petroleum products are meant to protect the animals, sea life, and the landscape from the degradative effects of an oil spill.

One effect of these myriad safety regulations is an increase in the cost of transporting people and goods. The safety controls exercised by government usually add a direct cost to a transportation operation, making its service more costly to consumers. However, when the indirect social costs are considered, society feels that the benefits of safety regulations, including fewer deaths and injuries and a cleaner environment, more than offset the direct cost. In the future, the number and scope of safety regulations will increase as government expands its safety regulating authority into additional transportation areas.

SUMMARY

- Imperfections in the marketplace in a free-enterprise economy provide the rationale for government intervention in business operations.
- Potential monopolistic abuses in transportation motivated the federal government to create the Interstate Commerce Commission (ICC) to regulate the transportation industry. The Surface Transportation Board replaced the ICC.
- The U.S. court system, through decisions under a common law structure, also influences transportation regulation.

- All carriers are subject to safety regulations administered by both federal and state agencies.
- The Department of Transportation (DOT) is the federal organization responsible for developing and implementing the overall transportation policy for the United States.
- Transportation regulation has progressed through four phases: Era of Initiation, Era of Positive Regulation, Era of Intermodal Regulation, and the Era of Deregulation.
- In today's transportation environment, the federal government is a proponent of less regulation, preferring to allow market forces to regulate carrier prices and availability of supply.

Key Terms

air carriers pg. 71
air traffic control system 78
Airport and Airway Trust Fund 80
Amtrak 81
Army Corps of Engineers 81
benefit/cost ratio 77
cargo preference 82
Civil Aeronautics Board 61
Clayton Act 66
Coast Guard 81
common carrier 72
common law 59
Department of Transportation 61
dredging and construction aid 81
economic deregulation 85
exempt carriers 71
existence charge 84
federal-state conflict 62
Federal Aviation Administration 62
Federal Energy Regulatory Commission 61
Federal Highway Administration 62
Federal Highway Trust Fund 80
Federal Maritime Commission 61
Federal Railroad Administration 62
Federal Trade Commission 66
granger laws 60
hazardous material 85
highway construction and repair 80
home-flag airlines 79
indirect promotion 82
Interstate Commerce Commission 60
intrastate commerce 62
MARAD control 82
minimum safety level 85
monopoly 59
National Highway Traffic Safety Administration 62
National Transportation Safety Board 62
Office of Hazardous Materials Transportation 62
Nationalization 84
operation 58
per se violations 67
police powers 62
public investment 69
reasonable rate 72
Reed-Bulwinkle Act of 1948 66
relative use 84
resource allocation 58
rule of reason violations 67
Sherman Antitrust Act 66
Shipping Act of 1984 82
state regulation 60
statutory law 60
Surface Transporation Board 60
time value of funds 77
truck intrastate deregulation 62
unit charge 84
user charges 79
vehicle standards 85

Study Questions

1. Discuss the rationale for economic regulation of transportation.

2. How has common law provided a basis for the government's regulation of transportation in the United States?

3. Discuss the role of antitrust laws in transportation during the regulated era versus the deregulated era.

4. How do the police powers of the Constitution affect transportation?

5. Why does the United States need a national transportation policy? What purpose does it serve?

6. Analyze the major issues addressed by the ICC Termination Act national transportation policy statements.

7. Unlike many industrialized nations, the United States has fostered private ownership of transportation companies. What is the rationale for private ownership?

8. Which governmental entities develop transportation policy? What powers and limitations exist for these agencies?

9. Describe and contrast the types of public promotion that have been provided to the modes. What is the rationale for such public promotion?

10. What are transportation user charges? What is the purpose of such changes?

NOTES

1. Dudley F. Pegrum, *Public Regulation of business* (Homewood, IL: Richard D. Irwin, 1959), pp. 21–24.
2. Ibid.
3. Sherman Antitrust Act of 1890, Sections 1 and 2.
4. U.S. Department of Transportation, *A Statement of National Transportation Policy* (Washington, D.C.: 1975), p. 1.
5. The material in this section is adapted from: Transportation Policy Associates, *Transportation in America,* 4th ed. (Washington, D.C.: 1986), pp. 28–31.
6. Ibid., p. 31.
7. Paul Stephen Dempsey, "The Empirical Results of Deregulation: A Decade Later, and the Band Played On," *Transportation Law Journal,* Vol. 17 (1988), pp. 69–81.

SUGGESTED READINGS

Adrange, Bahram, Garland Chow, and Raffiee Kambiz. "Airline Deregulation, Safety, and Profitability in the U.S." *Transportation Journal,* Vol. 36, No. 4, Summer 1997, pp. 30–43.

Babcock, Michael W., M. Jarvin Emerson, and Marvin Pratter. "A Model-Procedure for Estimating Economic Impacts of Alternative Types of Highway Improvement," *Transportation Journal,* Vol. 36, No. 4, Summer 1997, pp. 17–29.

Brown, T. A., and J. Greenlee. "Private Trucking After Deregulation: Managers' Perceptions," *Transportation Journal,* Vol. 35, No. 1, Fall 1995, pp. 5–14.

Berskin, C. G. "Econometric Estimation of the Effects of Deregulation on Railway Productivity Growth," *Transportation Journal,* Vol. 35, No. 4, Summer 1996, pp. 34–43.

Charles, R. A., and H. K. Newman. "Public Policy and Technology Management: Changing the Role of Government in the Operations of Air Traffic Control," *Transportation Journal,* Vol. 35, No. 1, Fall 1995, pp. 39–48.

Hazard, John L. *Managing National Transportation Policy.* Wesport, CT: ENO Foundation for Transportation, Inc., 1988.

Pegrum, Dudley F. *Transportation Economics and Public Policy,* 3rd ed. Homewood, IL: Richard D. Irwin, 1973.

Proper, A. F. "In Defense of Antitrust Immunity for Collective Ratemaking: Life After the ICC Termination Act of 1995," *Transportation Journal,* Vol. 35, No. 4, Summer 1996, pp. 26–33.

Spychalski, John C. "From ICC to STB: Continuing Vestiges of U.S. Surface Transportation Regulation," *Journal of Transport Economics and Policy,* Vol. XXXI, No. 1, January 1997, pp. 131–136.

U.S. Department of Transportation, *National Transportation Strategic Planning Study.* Washington, D.C.: U.S. Government Printing Office, 1992.

CASES

CASE 2.1

Quart Trucking

The North American Free Trade Agreement (NAFTA), signed by the United States, Mexico, and Canada, is designed to reduce or eliminate duties, tariffs, and other trade barriers at the U.S., Canadian, and Mexican borders over the next 15 years. It will create the world's largest trading block. NAFTA took effect following governmental approval by all three countries.

Many manufacturers and transportation companies view NAFTA as a method of increasing business, while others see it as a means of utilizing cheaper labor in Mexico. Considerable interest has been expressed by U.S. and Canadian shippers as to the ability of Quart Trucking to handle shipments into and out of Mexico. Peter Quart, Vice President of Marketing, has been assigned to the project of establishing a Mexican operation to be fully operational in 2000.

Mr. Quart's first step in the project was to assess his shippers' anticipated Mexican transportation needs. In general, the shippers desired to have "seamless" transportation from Canada and the United States to Mexico; that is, the shippers want little, if any, delays at the Mexico-U.S. border. In addition, a number of the larger customers were contemplating the location of two or more plants in Mexico and therefore desired intra-plant transportation within Mexico.

Armed with this market research, Mr. Quart developed a plan to establish a Mexican division of Quart Trucking. He planned to establish a terminal in Laredo, Texas, to serve the Maquiladora operations, one in Monterey, and one in Mexico City. These locations coincided with the proposed Mexican plant locations of Quart Trucking customers.

As Mr. Quart prepared to present his plan to the Quart board, a marketing staff person gave him a copy of the trucking implications of NAFTA. According to the agreement, a 10-year-phase-in is proposed for international trucking companies in Mexico. Specifically the agreement states:

- After three years, up to 49 percent of the ownership of a Mexican trucking carrier providing international service can be controlled by U.S. investors. During the first three years, the trucks operating in Mexico must be owned by and driven by Mexican nations.
- After seven years, U.S. investors can own controlling interest (51 percent) of a Mexican fleet that handles international traffic.
- After ten years, U.S. investors can have 100 percent ownership of Mexican motor carriers involved in international transportation. Mexican investors would have the same rights in the United States.

After reading this NAFTA summary, Mr. Quart canceled his presentation to the board and began the development of a new strategy to serve Mexico.

Case Questions

1. What portions of Mr. Quart's original strategy to serve Mexico are viable?
2. Describe and analyze alternative strategies Mr. Quart could take with regard to serving Mexico as his customers desire.

CASE 2.2

The U.S. Ocean Carrier Industry's Financial Plight

The U.S. carriers did not have a banner year in 1998. All major carriers incurred operating losses for the year, and 1997 was no better. As each major passenger carrier reported first quarter 1999 financial results, the financial picture of the industry looked bleak. Many ocean carrier managers and public officials questioned how long the carriers could sustain such losses and continue to operate.

A citizens group calling itself SOS (Save Our Ships) was formed to lobby Congress to enact legislation to "bail out" the ocean carriers during this financial crisis and to ensure the survival of the remaining major carriers. SOS felt it was essential to the economy and national defense that the United States have a strong and viable ocean carrier industry. Its global business orientation, and the geographic vastness of the United States and national security demanded an ocean transportation industry that could transport people and freight great distances in relatively large quantities. Without a U.S. ocean carrier industry, the United States would be dependent on foreign carriers to move globally.

Living in a free-market economy, many U.S. citizens believe that government should not provide assistance to the ocean carrier industry. Private enterprise is the backbone of the transportation industry, and any assistance given to the ocean carriers will surely set a precedent for other modes to seek federal help. The end result: a nationalized transportation system.

Case Questions

1. What are the merits of the SOS arguments to have the federal government provide financial assistance to the U.S. ocean carrier industry?

2. Are there any other examples of the federal government providing assistance to financially ailing companies?

3. If federal assistance is granted, should the ocean carriers be expected to repay the government? If so, what method of repayment would you suggest? Why?

Appendix 2-A

Department of Transportation

The U.S. DOT was established in 1966 to coordinate the administration of government transportation programs and to establish overall transportation policy that enables the provision of fast, safe, efficient, and convenient transportation at the lowest cost. As indicated in Figure A.1, the DOT consists of nine different agencies with the secretary of transportation having the responsibility of coordinating the activities of these agencies as each administers the programs under its respective jurisdiction. The centralization of federal transportation activities under the auspices of one department in the executive branch focuses attention on the critical nature of transportation in the economy.

The operating programs of the individual agencies are basically organized by mode. The secretary and deputy secretary are responsible for overall planning, directing, and controlling the departmental activities but do not exercise direct operating control over the agencies. Rather, the secretary's office is concerned with policy development, resource allocation, program evaluation, agency coordination, and intermodal matters.

At times the secretary of transportation will issue a policy of ruling that impacts all agencies. For example, on November 14, 1988, then Secretary of Transportation Jim Burnley issued a ruling that required transportation workers to undergo

FIGURE A.1 Agencies of the U.S. Department of Transportation

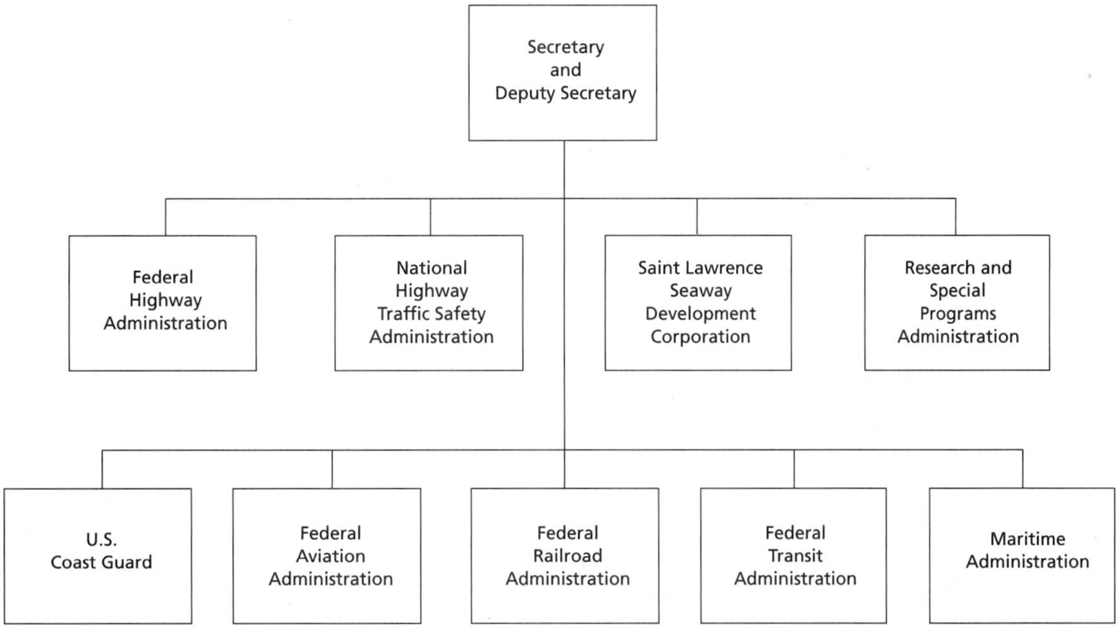

random drug testing beginning in 1989. The ruling would affect about four million workers: three million truck drivers, 538,000 airline employees, 195,000 transit personnel, 116,500 pipeline workers, and 90,000 railroad personnel. This controversial ruling was appealed to the courts, which issued an injunction blocking its implementation. Had this ruling not been blocked by the courts, the various modal agencies concerned with safety would have been charged with its implementation.

The secretary is the principal advisor to the president on matters relating to federal transportation. The responsibility for domestic and international transportation policy development and review is delegated to the assistant secretary for policy and international affairs. On the domestic level, this policy formulation is directed toward assessing the economic impact of government regulations and programs on the industry and the economy. Such policy issues as public trust funds, user charges, energy and environmental concerns, subsidy levels for subsidized carriers, international mail rates, aviation and maritime concerns in multilaterial and bilateral negotiations, and coordination of efforts to combat transportation-related terrorists acts and drug smuggling are representative of the wide range of policy responsibilities of the secretary of transportation.

Through its various agencies and departments, the DOT has responsibility and control over transportation safety, promotion, and research. The individual agency programs provide insight into the overall role of government in transportation matters other than economic regulation. A brief description of some of the activities included in the DOT can be found on the following pages.

United States Coast Guard

The U.S. Coast Guard is a branch of the armed forces at all times and is a service within the DOT, except when operating as part of the Navy in time of war. The Coast Guard is responsible for search and rescue efforts and maritime law enforcement, including the suppression of smuggling and illicit drug trafficking. It has the responsibility to enforce marine safety standards for commercial vessels and ports, protect marine environment, manage waterways, aid navigation, operate icebreaking vessels, and implement national boating safety programs for small craft. In addition, the Coast Guard is required to maintain a state of readiness to function as a specialized service in the navy in time of war, and it provides a group of trained individuals through the Coast Guard Reserve.

Federal Aviation Administration

The Federal Aviation Administration (FAA) is responsible for regulating air safety, promoting development of air commerce, and controlling navigable airspace in the interest of safety and efficiency. The FAA is most noted for its air safety regulations governing the manufacture, operation, and maintenance of aircraft, the certification of pilots and navigators, and the operation of air traffic control facilities. It conducts research and development of procedures, systems, and facilities to achieve safe and efficient air navigation and air traffic control. It also enforces the hazardous materials safety regulations.

The FAA administers a grant program for planning and developing public airports and provides technical guidance on airport planning, design, and safety operations. The agency maintains registration and records of aircraft, aircraft engines, propellers, and parts. It promotes international aviation safety by exchanging aeronautical information with foreign authorities, certifying foreign repair facilities and mechanics, and providing technical assistance in aviation safety training.

Federal Highway Administration

The Federal Highway Administration (FHWA) is concerned with the overall operation and environment of the highway systems, including the coordination of research and development activities aimed at improving the quality and durability of highways. In this capacity, the FHWA administers the federal-aid highway program, which provides financial assistance to the states for the construction and improvement of highways and traffic operations. For example, the interstate system is a 42,500-mile network financed on a 90 percent federal«minus»10 percent state basis. Improvements for other federal-aid highways are financed on a 75 percent federal −25 percent state basis. The monies are generated from special highway use taxes, which are deposited into the Highway Trust Fund. Congress authorizes disbursement of money from the trust fund for payment of the federal government's portion of the highway expenditures.

The second broad area of FHWA responsibility is motor carrier safety. It enforces the federal motor carrier safety regulations covering qualification of drivers, driver hours of service, equipment, employee safety and health, and hazardous materials. It oversees the national network for trucks, which provides minimum standards for size and weight limitations for trucks operating on the interstate system in the various states. Finally, the FHWA establishes the requirements for a single, national commercial vehicle driver's license that is issued by the states.

Federal Railroad Administration

The promulgation and enforcement of railroad safety regulations are major responsibilities of the Federal Railroad Administration (FRA). The safety regulations cover maintenance, inspection, and equipment standards and operating practices. It administers research and development of railroad safety improvements and operates the Transportation Test Center near Pueblo, Colorado, which tests advanced and conventional systems and techniques that improve ground transportation.

The FRA administers the federal assistance program for national, regional, and local rail services. The assistance is designed to support continuation of rail freight and passenger service and state rail planning. In addition, the FRA administers the programs designed to improve rail transportation in the northeast corridor of the United States.

National Highway Traffic Safety Administration

Motor vehicle safety performance is the major jurisdiction of the National Highway Traffic Safety Administration (NHTSA). In this capacity, the NHTSA issues prescribed safety features and safety-related performance standards for vehicles and motor vehicle equipment. The agency reports to Congress and to the public the damage susceptibility, crashworthiness, ease of repair, and theft prevention of motor vehicles. It is charged with the mandate of reducing the number of deaths, injuries, and economic losses resulting from traffic accidents. Finally, the NHTSA establishes fuel economy standards for automobiles and light trucks.

Federal Transit Administration

The Federal Transit Administration (FTA) is charged with improving mass transportation facilities, equipment, techniques, and methods; encouraging the planning and establishment of urban mass transportation systems; and providing financial assistance to state and local governments in operating mass transportation companies. Capital grants or loans of up to 75 percent of the project cost are made available to communities to purchase equipment and facilities. Formula grants are available in amounts of up to 80 percent of the project cost for capital and planning activities and 50 percent for operating subsidies. In addition, FTA makes funding available for research and training programs.

Maritime Administration

The Maritime Administration (MA) oversees programs designed to develop, promote, and operate the U.S. Merchant Marine and to organize and direct emergency merchant ship operations. The MA maintains a national defense reserve fleet of government-owned ships that are to be operated in time of national defense emergency. It also operates the U.S. Merchant Marine Academy, which operates training for future Merchant Marine officers.

The MA administers maritime subsidy programs through the Maritime Subsidy Board. The operating subsidy program provides U.S. flagships with an operating subsidy that represents the difference between the costs of operating a U.S. flagship and a foreign competitive flagship. A construction subsidy program provides funds for the difference between the costs of constructing ships in U.S. shipyards and in foreign shipyards. It also provides financing guarantees for construction of reconditioning of ships.

St. Lawrence Seaway Development Corporation

The St. Lawrence Seaway Development Corporation (SLSDC) is a government-owned operation that is responsible for the development, maintenance, and operation of the U.S. portion of the St. Lawrence Seaway; the SLSDC charges tolls to ship operators who use the seaway. These tolls are negotiated with the St. Lawrence Seaway Authority of Canada. The United States and Canadian seaway agencies coordinate activities involving seaway operations, traffic control, navigation aids, safety, and length of shipping season.

Research and Special Programs Administration

The Research and Special Programs Administration (RSPA) is responsible for a number of programs involving safety regulation, emergency preparedness, and research and development. The Office of Hazardous Materials Transportation develops and issues hazardous material transportation safety regulations for all modes. These regulations cover shipper and carrier operations, packaging specifications, and hazardous material definitions. The Office of Pipeline Safety establishes and enforces safety standards for the movement of gas and hazardous liquids by pipeline.

Through the auspices of the Transportation Systems Center in Cambridge, Massachusetts, numerous transportation research and development programs are conducted, including the development and maintenance of important national transportation statistics. The Office of Emergency Transportation administers the transportation civil emergency preparedness programs.

Summary

- The agencies that make up the DOT administer federal programs covering all transportation modes.
- DOT establishes national transportation policy, enforces safety regulations, provides funding for transportation programs, and coordinates transportation research efforts.
- The secretary of transportation is the principal advisor to the president on transportation matters.

PART 2

Overview of Carrier Operations

CHAPTER 3

Motor Carriers

Brief History

The trucking industry has played an important role in the development of the U. S. economy during the twentieth century. Its growth is noteworthy because the motor-carrier industry did not get started until about World War I when converted automobiles were utilized for pickup and delivery in local areas. The railroad industry, which traditionally had difficulty with small shipments that had to be moved short distances, encouraged the early trucking entrepreneurs. It was not until after World War II that the railroad industry began to seriously attempt to compete with the trucking industry, and by that time it was too late.

The United States has spent more than $120 billion to construct its **interstate highway system** and in the process has become increasingly dependent on this system for the movement of freight. The major portion of this network evolved as the result of a bill signed into law in 1954 by President Dwight D. Eisenhower to establish the National System of Interstate and Defense Highways, which was to be funded 90 percent by the federal government through fuel taxes.

As the interstate system of highways developed from the 1950s to 1980, trucks steadily replaced railroads as the mode of choice for transporting finished and unfinished manufactured products. In 1950, the railroad industry moved 1.4 billion tons of freight on an intercity basis, while motor carriers moved 800 million tons. In 1980, railroads moved 1.6 billion tons, compared to more than 200 billion tons by motor carriers. By 1997, motor carriers were handling 3.7 billion tons, compared with 1.97 billion tons by rail (see Figures 3.1 and 3.2). On a relative basis, however, the railroads did stabilize their market share.

FIGURE 3.1 Intercity Trucking Ton-miles

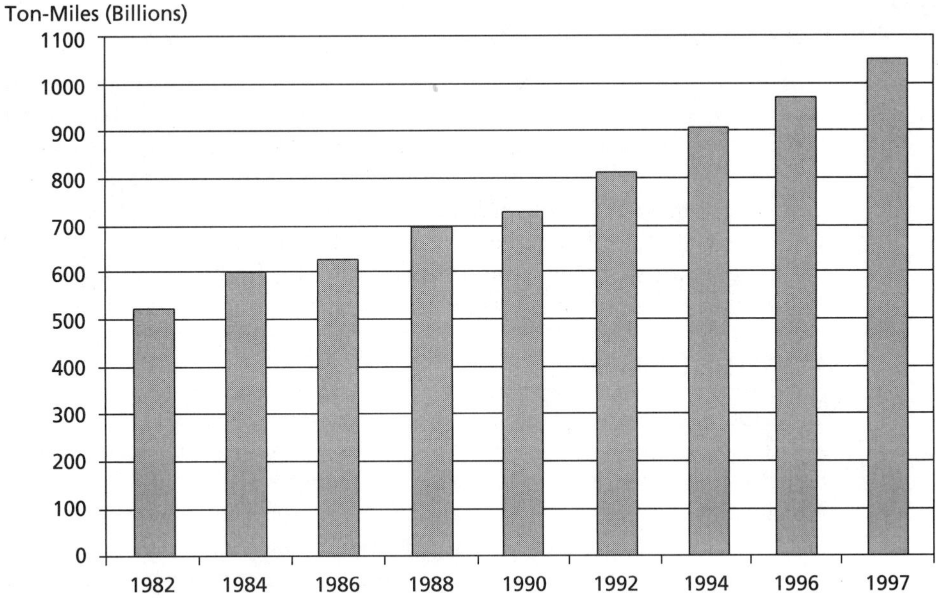

Source: Eno Transportation Foundation, *Transportation in America,* 16th ed., 1998.

FIGURE 3.2 Intercity Trucking Tons

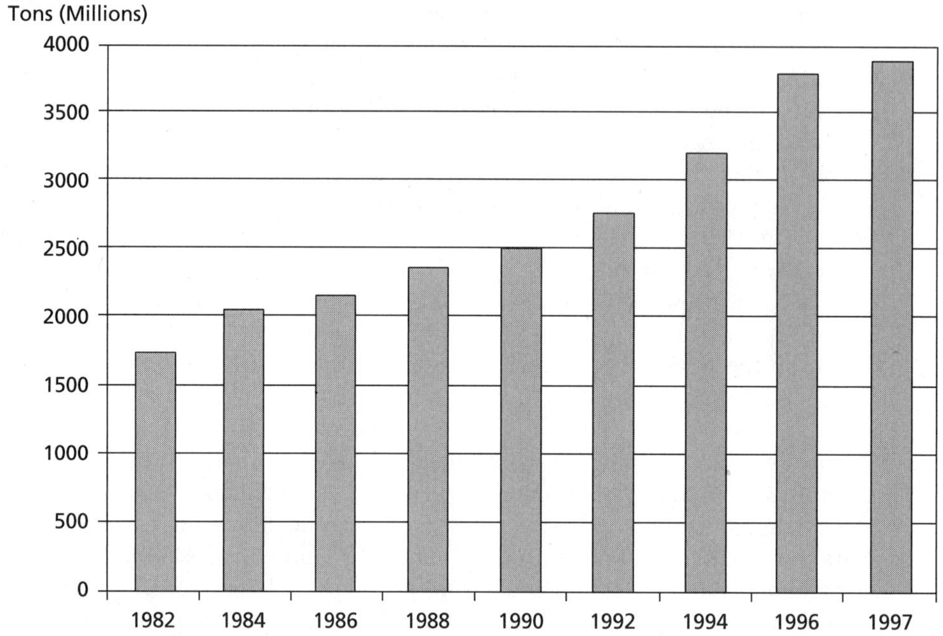

Source: Eno Transportation Foundation, *Transportation in America,* 16th ed., 1998.

Industry Overview

Significance

In 1998, the United States paid over $120 billion for highway transportation, approximately 86 percent of the total 1998 Nation's Freight Bill.[1] Trucks transported 10.51 billion revenue freight ton-miles in 1997, or 29.1 percent of the ton-miles transported by all modes.[2] During 1998, approximately 2.4 million people were employed in trucking with an average compensation of $37,036.[3] These figures clearly demonstrate the significant role that motor carriers play in our society and the dependence of U. S. companies on motor-carrier service. Finally, trucks logged 353 billion miles used for business purposes in 1994 (excluding government and farm).[4]

Types of Carriers

The first major division of motor carriers is between for-hire and private carriers. The **for-hire** carrier provides services to the public and charges a fee for the service. The private carrier provides a service to the industry or company that owns or leases the vehicles, and thus does not charge a fee, but obviously the service provider incurs cost. Private carriers may transport commodities for-hire, but when operating in such a capacity, the private carrier is really an exempt for-hire carrier.

For-hire carriers can be either local or intercity operators, or both. The local carriers pick up and deliver freight within the commercial zone of a city. The intercity carriers operate between specifically defined commercial zones to include the corporate limits of a municipality plus adjacent areas beyond the corporate limits determined by the municipal population. Local carriers frequently work in conjunction with intercity carriers to pick up or deliver freight in the commercial zone.

For-hire, **exempt carriers** are specifically exempt from economic regulation. The exempt carrier gains this status (free of economic regulatory control) by the type of commodity hauled (agricultural commodities, for example) or by the nature of its operation (incidental to air transportation). With the absence of economic regulation, the laws of the marketplace determine the rates charged, the services provided, and the number of vehicles supplied.

The for-hire carriers may be common and/or contract operators. The common carriers are required to serve the general public upon demand, at reasonable rates, and without discrimination. The contract carriers serve specific shippers with whom the carriers have a continuing contract; thus, the contract carrier is not available for general public use. Contract carriers also typically adapt their equipment and service to meet shipper needs.

Shippers must choose to use a commercial carrier or to operate their own private fleet. The decision is based on what is best for the business. Trade-offs exist for both, but it will ultimately be determined by the needs of the shippers. Table 3.1 compares the cost per mile of operating a private fleet versus using a for-hire carrier.

Another important distinction is the truckload (**TL**) and less-than-truckload (**LTL**) carriers. The truckload carriers provide service to shippers who tender sufficient volume to meet the minimum weights required for a truckload shipment and truckload rate or will pay the required amount. Less-than-truckload carriers provide service to shippers who tender shipments lower than the minimum truckload quantities, such as 50 to 10,000 pounds. Consequently, the LTL carrier must consolidate the numerous smaller shipments into truckload quantities for the linehaul (intercity) movement and disaggregate the full truckloads at the destination city for delivery in smaller quantities. In contrast, the truckload carrier picks up a truckload and delivers the same truckload at destination.

Finally, interstate common carriers may be classified by the type of commodity they are authorized to haul. Historically, motor carriers were required to have "operating authority" issued by either federal or state authorities. Since 1996, with the repeal

TABLE 3.1 Cost-per-mile Comparison

Private fleet versus For-hire			
1996 Estimates		**1995 Figures**	
For-hire truckload	$1.36 avg.	For-hire truckload	$1.33
Private fleet	$1.43 avg.	Private fleet	$1.42
For-hire van	$1.25	For-hire van	$1.23
Private-fleet van	$1.21	Private-fleet van	$1.20
For-hire refrigerated	$1.28	For-hire refrigerated	$1.23
Private-fleet refrigerated	$1.68	Private-fleet refrigerated	$1.75
For-hire tank	$1.72	For-hire tank	$1.74
Private-fleet tank	$1.76	Private-fleet Tank	$1.78
For-hire flatbed	$1.16	For-hire flatbed	$1.19
Private-fleet flatbed	$1.32	Private-fleet flatbed	$1.33

Source: International Fleet Management Consultants, Inc.
Source: Private Fleet Management Institute.

of the Interstate Commerce Act and the closing of the Interstate Commerce Commission, such authority is no longer required. The ICC Termination Act of 1995 removed virtually all motor-carrier regulation and preempted the states from exercising any economic control over the trucking industry. Carriers are now only required to register with the Federal Highway Administration and provide proof of insurance. They can then transport any commodity they wish, with only household goods and related items being subject to any economic oversight.

Number of Carriers

The motor-carrier industry consists of a large number of small carriers, particularly in the truckload segment of the industry. As illustrated in Figure 3.3, as of December 1998, 458,634 interstate motor carriers were on file with the Office of Motor Carriers (Figure 3.3 is based on older data but reflects approximated distributions). Of these carriers, 70 percent operate with six or fewer trucks.[5] This figure supports the for-hire carrier industry. Keep in mind that many businesses do use their own private fleet.

Since 1980, there has been a significant growth in the trucking industry but most of it has been in the carriers operating 30 or less trucks. There are currently nearly 459,000 firms registered with the U.S. Department of Transportation but only about

FIGURE 3.3 U.S. Distribution of Motor Carriers

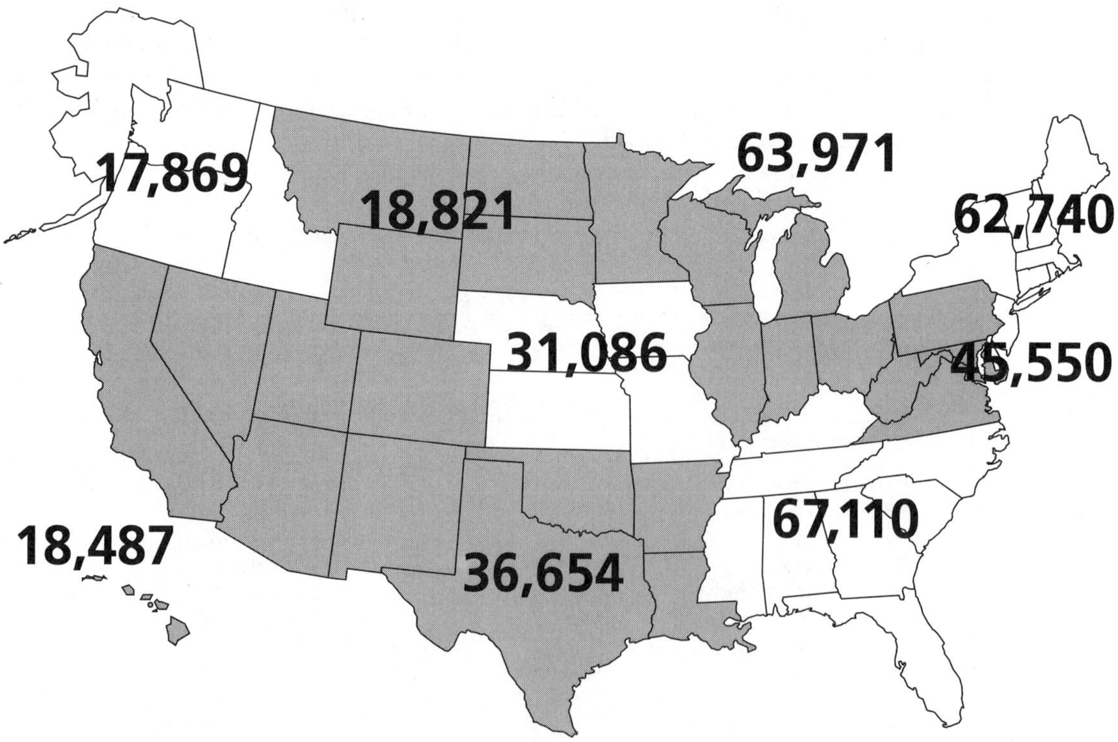

TABLE 3.2 Class Types of Motor Vehicles

(Classification by Revenue)	
Class	**Gross Revenue**
I	$10 million plus
II	$3-10 million
III	Less than $3 million

Source: Federal Highway Administration, Bureau of Statistics.

850 of these carriers have annual revenue of more than $20 million. There are just over 2,100 Class II carriers and approximately 9,500 Class III trucking firms. (See Table 3.2)

A further explanation of the large number of small carriers is the limited capital needed to enter the truckload industry. A trucking company can be formed with as little as $5,000 to $10,000 equity, and the balance can be financed with the vehicle serving as collateral for the loan. However, LTL carriers have terminals that increase the capital requirements and thus add a constraint to entry.

There is a significant difference between truckload (TL) and less-than-truckload (LTL) carriers, both in terms of number and start-up costs. The great growth that occurred in the 1980s, when regulated carriers more than doubled, happened primarily in small truckload carriers because of the low start-up costs indicated above.

The LTL segment of the motor-carrier industry requires a network of terminals to consolidate and distribute freight. The large LTL carriers moved to expand their geographic coverage after 1980, and many of them eliminated their truckload service. Since 1980, the pattern has developed in concentration of LTL traffic among the top 10 LTL carriers, and especially the top four companies. The concentration of traffic is such that the top 10 LTL carriers account for more than 60 percent of the intercity ton-miles carried by such carriers.

Perhaps a brief description of an LTL operation would be helpful here. Shippers that have shipping requirements that are small use LTL carriers (for example, the cubic capacity of a 53-foot trailer is not needed for the shipment). Also, the LTL shipper typically has shipments headed for more than one destination. The LTL carrier collects the shipments at the shipper's dock with a **pickup and delivery (PUD)** vehicle. This vehicle, as its name implies, does the collection and delivery of all shipments. After a PUD vehicle is finished collecting and delivering shipments, the PUD vehicle returns to a consolidation or break-bulk facility. Once at the consolidation facility, the packages collected are sorted with respect to their final destination. The next part of the trip is called the **line-haul** segment. For this portion of the trip, the shipments most often are loaded into 28-foot trailers. The trailers are hooked together in combinations of twos and threes, depending on the state's trailer configuration permitted over the route of travel. The 28-foot trailer is used in this situation because it is easier to unload two 28-foot trailers at separate bays than to unload one 48-foot trailer at one bay. Another reason for using the 28-foot trailer is better capacity utilization. LTL carriers find that it is easier to utilize the capacity of a 28-foot trailer. Following the line-haul portion of the trip, the trailers are unloaded at another break-bulk facility and are then sorted and reloaded into a PUD vehicle to be delivered to the receiver.

The TL segment of the industry has been experiencing some limited concentration. Carriers such as J. B. Hunt and Schneider National have become increasingly larger. The ability of the larger TL carriers to compete effectively with small TL companies with their value-added services may change the structure of the TL segment.

With the repeal of the Interstate Commerce Act, combined with changes in distribution patterns, a climate was created in which new truckload motor carriers could easily enter the business (see Figure 3.4). The "trucking recession" of 1994–1995, during which capacity greatly exceeded demand, removed many of the weaker firms either through bankruptcy or merger. However, low startup costs in this sector still enabled new entrants to attempt success in this area.

Market Structure

When discussing the motor-carrier industry, consideration must be given to the commodities hauled. Trucks, both for-hire and private, primarily transport manufactured, high-value products. Trucks carry more than 50 percent of the various manufactured

FIGURE 3.4 Overview of Interstate Motor Carrier Industry

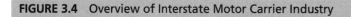

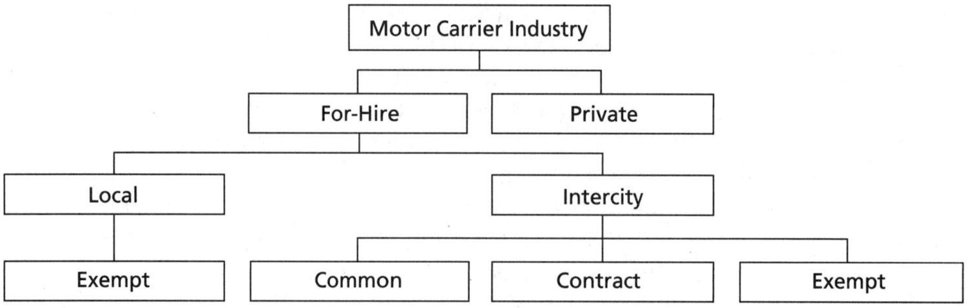

Types of Special Commodities
¥ Household goods
¥ Heavy machinery
¥ Petroleum products
¥ Refrigerated liquids
¥ Dump trucking
¥ Agricultural commodities
¥ Motor vehicles
¥ Armored truck service
¥ Building materials
¥ Films & associated commodities
¥ Forest products
¥ Mine ores excluding coal
¥ Retail store delivery
¥ Hazardous materials
¥ Other

commodity categories. The commodity list includes both food products and manufactured products, consumer goods, and industrial goods. In addition, trucks transport approximately 100 percent of the sheep, lambs, cattle, calves, and hogs moving to stockyards.[6]

Trucks transport less than 50 percent of commodities such as grain, primary nonferrous metal products, motor vehicles and equipment, and paper and allied products. Because such commodities generally must move long distances and in large volumes, shipping them by rail and water is usually less expensive.

Competition

Motor carriers compete vigorously with one another for freight. With almost 48,000 regulated trucking companies, rivalry between firms can be intense. In addition, regulated carriers compete to a limited extent with the approximately 40,000 exempt carriers. However, the most severe competition for for-hire carriers often comes from the private carrier.

As indicated earlier, the motor-carrier industry offers few capital constraints to entry. With a relatively small investment, an individual can start a trucking business and compete with an existing carrier. Thus, freedom on entry, discounting, and lack of regulatory constraints appear to dominate the industry and suggest that "competition" between trucking firms can control the industry. Such a conclusion has been the basis for greater reliance on the marketplace and less reliance on regulation. Even though the LTL segment is more concentrated, there is still intense competition between the top carriers. Other competitors also include United Parcel Service, FedEx, and recently Amtrak through its "express" operation.

Certain segments of trucking have higher capital requirements than others, as indicated, and therefore have some degree of capital constraint for entry. The major segment that has extensive capital requirements for entry is the LTL carrier. The LTL carrier must invest in terminals and freight-handling equipment that are simply not needed by the TL carrier. Special equipment carriers—carriers of liquefied gases or frozen products—usually have larger investments in equipment and terminals than those involved with general freight. The large TL carriers like J. B. Hunt and Schneider National also have significant capital investment.

On the whole, the motor-carrier industry, especially for contract carriers, has been market-oriented. Meeting customer requirements has been a common trait of motor carriers. The small size of the majority of for-hire carriers permits individualized attention to be given to customers. As carriers have grown in size, this close carrier-customer relationship has been strained. However, the responsiveness to customer demands for service still denominates all trucking organizations, and shippers expect carriers to respond to their needs.

Operating and Service Characteristics

General Service Characteristics

The growth and widespread use of motor-carrier transportation can be traced to the inherent service characteristics of this method. In particular, the motor carrier possesses a distinct advantage over other modes in the area of accessibility. The motor carrier can provide service to virtually any location, as operating authority of the regulated carrier no longer places restrictions on the areas served and commodities transported. Motor-carrier access is not constrained by waterways, rail tracks, or airport locations. The U.S. system of highways is so pervasive that virtually every shipping and receiving location is accessible via highways. Therefore, motor carriers have potential access to almost every origin and destination.

The accessibility advantage of motor carriers is evident in the pickup or delivery of freight in an urban area. It is very rare to find urban areas served by a pickup-delivery network or waterways (except possibly Venice, Italy), parkways (except possibly downtown Chicago), or runways (except possibly a town in Alaska). In fact, trucks provide the bridge between the pickup and delivery point and the facilities of other modes; that is, the motor carrier is referred to as the universal coordinator.

Another service advantage of the motor carrier is speed. For shipments going under 500 miles, the truck can usually deliver the goods in less time than other modes would take. Although the airplane travels at a higher speed, the problem of getting freight to and from the airport via truck adds to the air carrier's total transit time. In fact, the limited, fixed schedules of the air carriers may make trucks the faster method even for longer distances. For example, a delivery to a destination 600 miles away may take 12 hours by truck (600 miles at 50 mph). Although the flying time between airports is $1^1/_2$ hours, three hours may be needed for pickup and three hours for delivery, plus time for moving the freight from one vehicle to another. If the airline has scheduled only one flight per day, the shipment could wait up to 24 hours before being dispatched. The truck, however, proceeds directly from the shipper's door to the consignee's door.

When compared to the railcar and barge, the smaller cargo-**carrying capacity** of the truck enables the shipper to use the truckload (TL) rate, or volume discount, with a lower volume. Many TL minimum weights are established at 20,000–30,000 pounds. Rail carload minimum weights are often set at 40,000–60,000 pounds, and barge minimums are set in terms of hundreds of tons. The smaller shipping size of the motor carrier provides the buyer and seller with the benefits of lower inventory levels, lower inventory-carrying costs, and more frequent services.

Another positive service characteristic is the smoothness of transport. Given the suspension system and the pneumatic tires used on trucks, the motor-carrier ride is smoother than rail and water transport and less likely to result in damage to the cargo (although there can still be some cargo damage with truck transportation). This relatively damage-free service reduces the packaging requirements and thus packaging costs.

Lastly, the for-hire segment of the motor-carrier industry has been customer- or marketing-oriented. The small size of most carriers has enabled (forced) the carriers to respond to customer equipment and service needs.

In 1998, interstate truckload motor carriers had an average haul length of 289 miles.[7] This statistic, however, conceals the competitiveness of motor carriers for loads hauled 500 to 1,500 miles or more.[8] For 30,000- to 60,000-pound shipments, trucks dominate the market for hauls of 300 miles or less. On shipments of 90,000 pounds or more, moving more than 100 miles, railroads are the dominant mode. In between these ranges, both modes compete vigorously.

Equipment

Many of the motor-carrier service advantages emanate from the technical features of the truck. The high degree of flexibility, the relatively smooth ride, and the small carrying capacity of the truck are the unique characteristics that result in greater accessibility, capability, frequency of delivery and pickup, cargo safety, and lower transit time.

The truck can also be loaded quickly. A railroad operation needs to collect a number of freight cars to be pulled by the one power unit; the motor carrier has just one or two. The availability to operate one cargo unit separately eliminates the time needed to collect several cargo units.

The other dimension of motor-carrier equipment flexibility is the lack of highway constraint. Unlike the railroad and water carriers, the motor carrier is not constrained to providing service over a fixed railway or waterway. The truck can travel over the highway, and there is a road, paved or unpaved, servicing virtually every conceivable consignee in the United States.[9]

Types of Vehicles

Motor-carrier vehicles are either line-haul or city vehicles. Line-haul vehicles are used to haul freight long distances between cities. City trucks are used within a city to provide pickup and delivery service. On occasion, line-haul vehicles also will operate within a city, but the line-haul vehicle is normally not very efficient when operated this way.

Line-Haul Trucks

The line-haul vehicle is usually a tractor-trailer combination of three or more axles (see Figure 3.5). The cargo-carrying capacity of these vehicles depends on the size (length) and the state maximum weight limits. A tractor-trailer combination with five axles (tandem-axle tractor and trailer) is permitted in most states to haul a maximum of 80,000 pounds gross weight (110,000 pounds in Michigan). For a vehicle to run with more than five axles, a permit is required. If the empty vehicle weighs 30,000 pounds, the maximum net payload is 50,000 pounds or 25 tons.

The net carrying capacity of line-haul vehicles is also affected by the density of the freight. A 53' × 8' × 8' trailer has 3,392 cubic feet of space. If the commodity has a density of 10 pounds per cubic foot, then the maximum payload for the vehicle is 33,920 (3,392 $ft.^3 \times 10\ lb./ft.^3$). Shippers of low-density freight (below 16 $lbs./ft.^3$) advocate increased payload capacity of trucks.

City Trucks

City vehicles are normally smaller than line-haul vehicles and are single units (see Figure 3.5). The city truck has the cargo and power unit combined in one vehicle. The typical city truck is approximately 20 to 25 feet long with a cargo unit 15 to 20 feet long. However, there is growing use of small trailers (20 to 28 feet) to pick up and deliver freight in the city. These trailers can also be used for line-haul, which increases efficiency. Shipments can be "loaded to ride," meaning they will not require handling at the origin terminal.

Special Vehicles

In addition to the line-haul and city vehicle classifications, the following special vehicles are designed to meet special shipper needs:

- Dry van: Standard trailer or straight truck with all sides enclosed
- Open top: Trailer top is open to permit loading of odd-sized freight through the top
- Flatbed: Trailer has no top or sides; used extensively to haul steel
- Tank trailer: Used to haul liquids such as petroleum products
- Refrigerated vehicles: Cargo unit has controlled temperature

FIGURE 3.5 Equipment Types

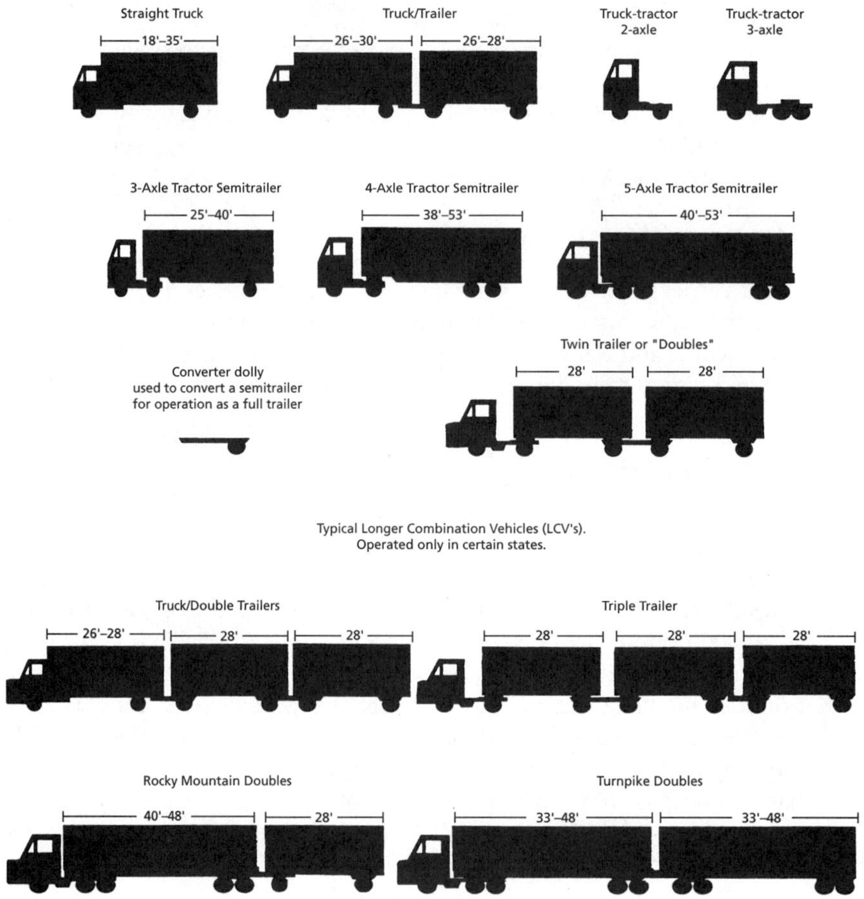

Source: American Trucking Associations

- High cube: Cargo unit has drop-frame design or is higher than normal to increase cubic capacity
- Special: Vehicle has a unique design to haul a special commodity, such as liquefied gas or automobiles

The Department of Transportation's Federal Highway Administration has established many rules and regulations governing the specifications of trucks. These regulations cover such areas as the number of lights on the vehicle, the type of brakes used, tire specifications, and other operating parts.[10] The overall allowable length and height of the vehicle are prescribed in the various states.[11]

Terminals

Some motor-carrier operations, namely TL operations, may not require terminals. The carrier uses the shipper's plant for loading and the consignee's plant for unloading. However, as indicated earlier, the LTL freight operations do require terminals. Some of the large LTL carriers, such as Yellow Freight or Roadway Express, have more than 400 terminals. A driver will leave a terminal to make deliveries throughout the country but will always return to its domicile. A driver's domicile is the terminal that the driver left originally. The terminals used by motor carriers can be classified as pickup or delivery, break-bulk, and relay. A discussion of functions performed at each type of terminal follows.

Pickup and Delivery Terminals

Freight is collected from shippers and brought to their terminals where it is consolidated with other loads going in the same direction or to the same destination. The consolidated shipments are loaded onto a line-haul vehicle for movement to the destination terminal. At the destination terminal, the line-haul vehicle is emptied, and the combined shipments are separated and reloaded onto city trucks. The city trucks complete the delivery to the ultimate consignee.

At the pickup and delivery (PUD) terminals, other carrier functions, such as sales, billing, and claim handling, are performed. Some limited vehicle maintenance can be performed at such terminals.

Carriers also will use the PUD terminal to change freight from one carrier to another. While a carrier may have operating authority to transport the shipment to the destination, it may choose to cooperate with one or more carriers to complete the movement. When the shipment reaches the end of one carrier's line, it is transferred, via the terminal, to another carrier. Usually the transfer entails the unloading of the shipment onto the terminal floor, then reloading it onto the subsequent carrier's vehicle.

The PUD terminal, also known as the *end-of-line terminal,* serves many purposes. The break-bulk and relay terminals serve a much more limited function.

Break-Bulk Terminals

The basic function performed at the break-bulk terminal is the separation of combined shipments. As shown in Figure 3.6, a consolidated shipment from PUD terminals travels the majority of the distance toward the respective shipment destinations. Such consolidated moves permit the carrier to realize economies of operation.

Consolidated truckloads arrive from many pickup terminals. Freight is unloaded, sorted by destination, and reloaded for dispatch to destination. For greater efficiency, break-bulk terminals usually are centrally located within the carrier's operating scope and at the juncture of major east-west and north-south highways. For example, a major carrier has a break-bulk terminal located at Toledo, Ohio, which is at the juncture of Interstate 80 (east-west) and Interstate 75 (north-south).

Relay Terminals

Relay terminals are different from the PUD and break-bulk terminals in that freight is never touched. The relay terminal is necessitated by the maximum hours-of-service regulation that is imposed on drivers. Under DOT enforcement, drivers are permitted to drive a maximum of 10 hours after eight consecutive hours off-duty. At the relay terminal, one driver substitutes for another who has accumulated the maximum hours of service. (The term **slip seat** also has been used to describe the relay terminal operation.)

As indicated in Figure 3.7, the location of the relay terminal is a maximum driving time of 10 hours from an origin. If the relay terminal is located five hours from an origin, the driver can drive to the relay terminal and return within the maximum 10 hours.

FIGURE 3.6 Break-Bulk Terminal

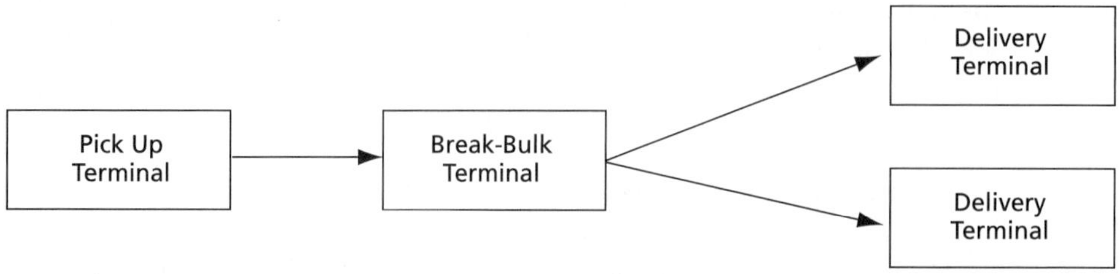

FIGURE 3.7 Relay Terminal

Using the example given in Figure 3.7, assume that the driving time is 15 hours between origin and destination. Without the relay terminal, the transit time is 23 hours. After 10 hours of driving, the driver goes off-duty for eight consecutive hours. Upon resuming duty, the driver drives five hours to the destination. The total elapsed time is 23 hours (10 + 8 + 5). The driver drives 10 hours to the relay terminal and another driver takes over and drives the vehicle to the destination. In this instance, the relay terminal reduces the transit time by eight hours, the mandated driver off-duty time.

An alternative to the relay terminal is the use of a sleeper team—two drivers. While one driver accumulates the off-duty time in the sleeper berth of the tractor, the other driver is driving. The sleeper team has been most successful for long trips with many destinations.

Cost Structure

Fixed Versus Variable Cost Components

The cost structure of the motor-carrier industry consists of high levels of variable costs and relatively low fixed costs. Approximately 70 to 90 percent of the cost is variable, and 10 to 30 percent is fixed. The public investment in the highway system is a major factor contributing to this low fixed-costs structure. In addition, the motor carrier is able to increase or decrease the number of vehicles used in short periods of time and in small increments of capacity. Lastly, the carriers as a group (with the exception of the LTL carrier) do not require expensive terminals. The small investment in terminals also contributes to low fixed costs. The bulk of the motor carrier's cost then is associated with daily operating costs of the carrier—the variable costs of fuel, wages, and maintenance.

The discussion of motor-carrier cost will begin with the vehicle operating costs of long-distance fleets transporting perishable agricultural products and refrigerated solid products in tractor-trailers. These data can be compared only to similar operations; that is, comparisons cannot be made to local trucking (pickup and delivery). Figure 3.8 indicates that in 1995 the total cost to operate a tractor-trailer was 130.2 cents per mile. As indicated, approximately 70 percent of the cost to operate an intercity tractor-trailer is the variable. The remaining 30 percent is associated with the fixed costs of vehicle interest; depreciation and interest on terminals, garages, and offices; management; and overhead (such as utilities). For carriers handling LTL freight, the fixed cost is higher. That is, additional terminals, management, and overhead expenses are required to handle small-sized shipments.

The two categories with the largest share of the variable costs are labor and fuel. A discussion of each of these two variable costs will follow.

Labor

The cost of drivers accounts for 29 percent of the total costs per vehicle mile, as shown in Figure 3.8. Labor costs (wages plus fringe benefits) usually absorb about 50 percent of a carrier's revenue dollar. That is, 50 cents out of every dollar in revenue goes to labor. The average annual wage in 1997 was $37,036[12]; and the average hourly compensation for trucking and warehousing was $12.83.[13]

The over-the-road (intercity) driver is typically paid on a mileage basis, such as 32.5 cents per mile; local drivers are paid by the hour. Over-the-road driver normally are paid an hourly rate for operating delays resulting from loading/unloading, accidents, weather, and the like.

The DOT enforces maximum hours of service regulation. As mentioned earlier, the DOT's **driving time regulations** permit drivers to drive a maximum of 10 hours after being off-duty for eight consecutive hours. A driver is permitted to be on-duty

FIGURE 3.8 Cost of Operating a Tractor Trailer, 1995

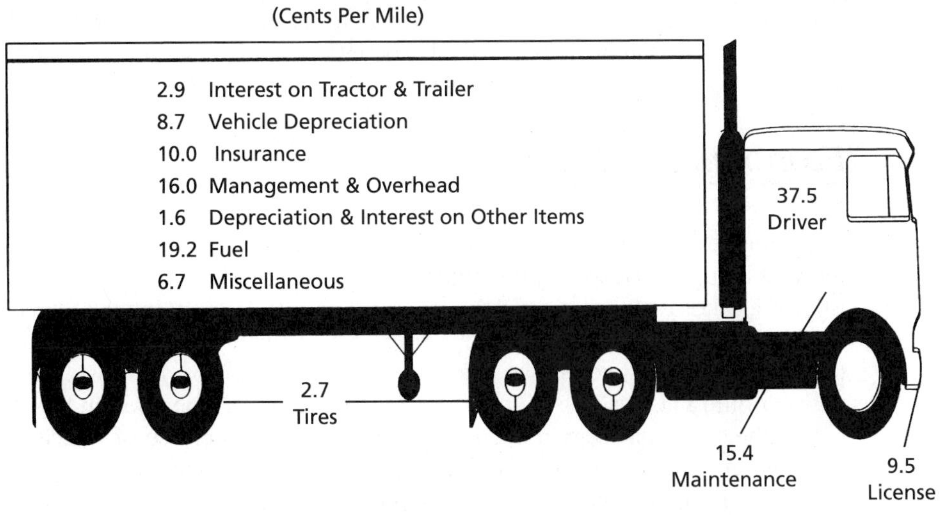

Source: USDA AMS Market News Service, Fruit and Vegetable Truck Rate Report.

a maximum of 15 hours after eight consecutive hours off-duty. In addition, no driver can drive after accumulating 60 hours on-duty in seven consecutive days, or 70 hours in eight consecutive days.

The most pressing labor issue facing trucking companies, particularly truckload carriers, is the shortage of drivers. Part of the problem is that the federal government, as part of an overall safety program, imposed stringent driver licensing requirements. Since April 1992, all operators of trucks over 26,000 pounds gross vehicle weight must hold a commerce driver's license (CDL). Although CDLs are issued by the driver's home state, the requirements are mandated by the federal DOT. Along with the new licensing requirements, the DOT also imposed stringent rules dealing with drug and alcohol abuse. Poor driving records and inability to pass the CDL test eliminated many marginal drivers.

The hardships imposed by the very nature of long-haul trucking have also impacted the availability of drivers. Drivers are frequently away from home for long periods and often have to assist with the loading and unloading of trailers. This lifestyle is not as attractive as other career choices, so the available pool from which drivers may be drawn has declined. The trucking industry has undertaken several initiatives to counteract the problem of driver retention and recruitment. They have raised the per-mile and per-hour pay rates, scheduled drivers more frequently, and worked with shippers and consignees to make freight more "driver-friendly."

Fuel

Since 1974 the higher price of fuel has resulted in a rise in the relative proportion of fuel cost to total cost. For example, in 1976, fuel cost was 11.6 cents per mile or 19.8 percent of the total cost per mile, but in 1985 fuel cost was 24.6 cents per mile or 21.1 percent of total cost. In 1995, fuel cost was lower at 19.2 cents per mile or 14.7 percent of total costs (see Figure 3.8). Carriers have experienced a 130 percent increase in diesel fuel prices from 1976 to 1985—approximately 53 cents per gallon in 1976, to about $1.14 per gallon in 1999.[14] Ever since 1974, fuel prices have changed more frequently over a larger range due to fluctuations in supply.

Included in the price of the diesel fuel is a highway user tax imposed by both the federal and state governments. The fuel tax plus other taxes for highway use are payments made by the carrier to the government for the construction, maintenance, and control of the highways. In 1995, the motor-carrier industry paid $23.8 billion in federal and state highway user taxes.[15] The federal fuel tax is $24.3 plus any amount added by states. The state amount varied from $.02 to $0.245.

Economies of Scale

There does not appear to be major economies for large-scale trucking operations. Economies of scale are realized through more extensive use of large-sized plants or indivisible inputs. However, the extensive use of indivisible inputs is not characteristic of all motor-carrier operations. In addition, the large number of small firms—about 95 percent of the regulated carriers have annual operating revenues of less than $1 million—suggests that small-sized operations are competitive. The concentration of the LTL business is indicative of economies of operation in this segment.

In the short run, certain economies exist in the greater use of indivisible inputs such as terminals, management specialists, and information systems. The average cost of such inputs will decrease as output (greater use) increases. Such economies of use justify the rather large-sized firms that operate transcontinentally, especially in the truckload segment. Carriers that operate over wide geographic areas require more terminals, elaborate information systems, and more management specialists than those carriers that operate over narrow geographic areas.

For truckload operations, very limited investment is required for terminals, but information systems are becoming increasingly important to efficient operations. Computers in tractors, direct satellite communication to drivers, and bar coding with optical scanners are a few examples of the sophisticated information systems and technology that now exist in the trucking industry. Many of the truckload carrier inputs (vehicle, labor, fuel) can be increased one truck at a time in response to the small increases in demand.

Operational cost trade-offs exist between large and small carriers. A large-scale operation affords savings in purchase economies of equipment and in such inputs as fuel, parts, and interest in loans. (The small carrier may enjoy some of these purchase economies from larger retailers of truck suppliers, such as truck stops.) On the other hand, large LTL trucking companies may be unionized and thus pay higher labor rates, but the trucking industry is less unionized today than it was in, say, 1980.

Overall, long-term economies of scale appear not to be significant in motor-carrier transportation. This lack of scale economies has implications for competition and the market's capability to control such competition.

Operation Ratio

A measure of operating efficiency used by motor carriers is the **operation ratio.** The operation ratio measures the portion of operating revenues that covers operating expenses.

$$\textit{Operation ratio} = \frac{\textit{Operating expenses}}{\textit{Operating revenue}} \times 100$$

Operating expenses are those expenses directly associated with the transportation of freight, excluding nontransportation expenses and interest costs. Operating revenues are the total operating revenues generated from freight transportation services; nontransportation services are excluded. Motor carriers use the operation ratio to support a rate increase request. The closer the operation ratio is to 100, the more indicative of the possible need to raise rates to increase total revenues.

An operation ratio of 94 indicates that 94 cents of every operating revenue dollar is consumed by operating expenses, leaving six cents of every operating dollar to cover interest costs and a return to the owners. Motor-carrier operation ratios usually range between 93 and 96. The operation ratio is also a benchmark or barometer of financial viability. Obviously, if the operation ratio is equal to or greater than 100, there is no revenue available to cover fixed or overhead costs or to return a profit to owners or stockholders. Increasing revenues and/or reducing costs are viable approaches to resolving the problem of a high operation ratio.

Since the founding of the United States, the federal government has felt that the government has the responsibility to provide highways to meet the national defense and commerce needs of the country. At first, the federal government was the sole financier of highways, but over the years, state and local governments have assumed a greater role. Today, the state and local governments assume the responsibility for maintaining the highways, while the federal governments provide up to 90 percent of the construction cost of new highways with the designated network. The Federal Highway Administration, part of the DOT, oversees the National Highway System (NHS). The NHS was defined in 1995 and consists of the 42,000 mile interstate highway system, 113,7000 miles of existing state and federal non-interstate highways and 3,000 additional miles devoted to specialized freight transportation needs. Although the NHS includes slightly over four percent of the total road mileage, this network sees the transportation of more than 75 percent of intercity freight traffic.

The Intermodal Surface Transportation Efficiency Act (ISTEA), has been replaced by the Transporation Equity Act for the Twenty-first Century (TEA21), which has continued the role of FHWA in this area. Additional funds were added under TEA21, which will remain in place until 2003. More than $73 billion is expected to be spent on roads and related projects during this period.

Funding

Highway users—truck and automobile operators—pay for the construction, maintenance, and policing of highways through highway user taxes. The total amount of taxes paid depends on the use of the highway. The motor carrier incurs a cost for the use of the highway that is related to its amount of use. This situation contributes to the high variable cost structure of the motor carrier.

Federal and state governments assess highway user taxes. The federal highway user taxes are paid into the Federal Highway Trust Fund. From the Federal Highway Trust Fund, the federal government pays 90 percent of the construction costs for the interstate system and 50 percent of the construction costs for all other federal-aid roads. Table 3.3 indicates items taxed and the rate assessed by the Federal Highway Trust Fund.

The state also assesses highway user taxes to defray the cost of construction, maintenance, and policing of highways. The state taxes include fuel tax, vehicle registration fees, ton-mile taxes, and special-use permits.

Implied in the highway user tax concept is the philosophy that the highway predominantly confers benefits on specific groups and individuals. Although the general public benefits from increased mobility and the availability of a wide variety of goods and services, the motor vehicle user is presumed to be the major benefactor and therefore is expected to pay a larger share of the costs. An analogy that illustrates this concept is the property owner who pays property taxes that include an assessment for streets (access to the property). Much debate exists as to whether trucks pay a fair share of the total cost of highways. In 1990, all motor vehicles paid $74.9 billion[17], of which trucks paid $19.36 billion, or 25.8 percent.[18] The central issue is whether trucks should pay for the added construction and maintenance costs caused by their heavier weight.

TABLE 3.3 Federal Highway Trust Fund Tax Rates

Commodity	Tax
Gasoline	18.3 cents/gallon
Diesel fuel	24.3 cents/gallon
Gasohol	12.3–15.2 cents/gallon
Tires	15 cents/lbs. for tires 40–70 lbs. $4.50 + 30 cents/lbs. for tires 70–90 lbs. $10.50 + 50 cents/lbs. for tires over 90 lbs.
New truck and trailer sales	12% of manufacturer's sales price on trucks weighing more than 33,000 lbs. and trailers exceeding 26,000 lbs.
Highway vehicle use tax	For trucks weighing 55,000 lbs. or more, $100 + $22 for each additional 1,000 lbs. up to a maximum of $550

Source: Federal Highway Administration, Highway Trust Fund Primer, Page 2.

Because each state must pay for the maintenance, policing, and construction of the highways within its boundaries, each state attempts to ensure receipt of taxes for using its highways. For a motor-carrier operation over many states, this means buying vehicle registrations in many states and maintaining records of miles driven in a particular state so that the state will receive a fuel tax or ton-mile tax. Such record keeping adds a cost to the carrier's operation.

Current Issues

Safety

Some members of the trucking industry have come to realize that improved safety can mean improved profitability. After the regulatory reform that took place in the early 1980s, motor carriers found themselves with more direct control of their economic and operating policies. Deficiencies in safety can translate into decreased profitability because of expensive claims for lost or damaged goods, increased insurance premiums, accidents, fines, and so on. These consequences are not unique to the trucking industry; in fact, they apply to the entire transportation industry.[19]

The Federal Highway Administration (FHWA) has developed rules under which its inspectors determine whether a carrier is fit from a safety rule compliance perspective. The system includes the three categories: Satisfactory, Conditional, and Unsatisfactory. The FHWA has the right to force a carrier to stop operating after a specific time period has passed if the carrier has received an Unsatisfactory rating and improvement is not made. The period varies depending on the type of traffic the carrier is transporting. If the carrier is hauling non-hazardous materials, they must cease operations 61 days after their safety rating is found to be Unsatisfactory. If the company hauls hazardous materials, the time period is reduced to 41 days. This only applies if the carrier does not correct the problems discovered in the FHWA safety audit. There is also an appeal process that allows the carrier to correct any concerns as may be necessary.

The carrier may be allowed to continue to operate if there is a "good faith" effort on its part to correct the defects. Government regulations require that the FHWA review a carrier who is found in violation within 45 days of that company's request. If the carrier transports hazardous materials, the time period for review upon request drops to 30 days.

Many shippers seek safety fitness information as part of their selection process, so there is considerable pressure on carriers to operate safely. Many transportation contracts contain clauses that permit the shipper to cancel the contract if the carrier's safety rating is Unsatisfactory.

A major related concern is that of alcohol and drug abuse. It has been estimated that American industry pays $50 to 100 billion for the effects and results of substance abuse in the workplace every year, either for the cost of accidents or losses in productivity. In response to this problem, the trucking industry has begun to move toward drug screening for its employees. Drug and alcohol testing are required in the following circumstances:

- As a requirement for employment
- As a part of a regular physical exam required of current employees
- For "cause," required after any accident
- On a random selection basis

Drug and alcohol rules require motor carriers to have an anti-drug program, as well as drug testing that includes random and post-accident testing. All fleets, regardless of size, are required to have a complete program, including random and post accident testing in place. These rules apply to the owner/operator as well. Many states have drug testing programs of their own as well, with which the carrier must comply.

Each carrier must test a specified number of drivers on an annual basis. FHWA will adjust this number based on test results. Although it started at 50 percent, now (1999) only five percent of the total driver pool is tested for alcohol and 25 percent for drugs. Both alcohol and drug use of motor-carrier employees has fallen to extremely low levels, indicating the programs put in place by the trucking industry has been beneficial.

When proper care is taken to implement a substance abuse program, most drivers support the program because it makes their job safer. Proper care in implementing a substance abuse program involves relating substance abuse to health and problems, while leaving moral judgments to the individual. Such care also includes setting consistent policies that are enforceable and apply to every employee, making policies for violations known, and providing counseling and rehabilitation services for those employees who have substance abuse problems.[20] Support of the employees with problems is critical for any substance abuse program to be successful.

Other actions that are being taken by the trucking industry to ensure safety are improving training programs that stress proper ways to drive and perform other job-related duties. This also includes giving positive reinforcement to employees who do follow safety rules and closely monitoring drivers to allow management to identify employees who violate safety rules.[21]

Other areas of safety concerns are drivers' hour of service and fatigue issues. The hours of service rules date from before World War II and do not reflect modern realities. Under a complex formula of allowed driving and required rest periods, a driver can be on duty for not more that 60 hours in seven days or 70 hours in eight days. Several recent studies point to the need to change these rules and it is likely that a significant rewriting will be done in an effort to improve highway safety.

Another safety issue receiving attention deals with truck size and weight. As shown earlier, there are a number of different sizes of vehicles and each has its own weight-carrying regulations. Recent studies have analyzed increasing total weight to 94,000 pounds with the addition of a third axle to the trailer. The studies have also addressed increased use of triples. All these issues include safety concerns and will require federal legislation before any changes can be made. In addition to safety, there are significant economic issues for the motor-carrier industry, as these larger trucks will improve productivity and lower cost.

Technology

The use of satellite technology has a major impact on the motor-carrier industry. Using global positioning technology (GPS), satellites are being used to track trucks throughout their movement from origin to destination. The use of satellites allows the carriers to pinpoint the location of the truck and relay this information to the customer. The interaction between the driver, using an on-board computer, and a home-base computer allows route or arrival adjustment for poor weather or road conditions, and these adjustments can be communicated to the customers.

One area where satellite communication has had a very positive effect is in the movement of hazardous materials. For example, phosphorous pentasulfide (P^2S^5), a very dangerous chemical if not handled properly, is shipped by Bee Line Trucking

STOP OFF

SCHNEIDER NATIONAL, INC.

"An information system masquerading as a trucking line." "The orange on-time machine." These phrases describe the motor carrier Schneider National, Inc. and its thousands of motor vehicles. Schneider owns 35,000 of the trademark orange semitrailers and 13,000 tractors. These vehicles are used to ship freight for two-thirds of the Fortune 500 companies.

Schneider is headquartered in Green Bay, Wisconsin. This site receives updated information on every one of its trucks every 18 minutes. This and many other capabilities are made possible by satellite technology. Each vehicle is equipped with a STAR Serv satellite communication receiver and a laptop for sending and receiving information.

This technology benefits both the customer and the driver. First, the customer receives unprecedented levels of service and on-time reliability. They are able to receive information about where their freight is and when they will receive it. On the other hand, the technology protects and saves time for the driver. For instance, Brian Betram, a driver for Schneider, was driving through Wisconsin one stormy night. He punched a key in his laptop and watched the following message appear: "ICY ROAD CONDITIONS EXIST IN MUCH OF WISCONSIN AND ILLINOIS." He was extremely grateful for that warning. As well as protecting the drivers, the technology also provides directions, monitors and transmits vehicle performance data, and pinpoints exact location to within 1,000 feet.

During a typical day before the technology was implemented, a driver would have to phone a dispatcher two to three times per day to check in, pick up lead assignments, and receive the latest pronouncements from the front office. The driver wasted time by parking the truck, searching for a pay phone, and being put on hold by the dispatcher. Today, the driver never has to leave his or her truck. The satellite communication device provides up-to-date information for the driver.

Overall, Schneider National, Inc., provides excellent customer service both internally and externally, that is, to its drivers and its customers. The satellite technology allows Schneider's operations to run efficiently and effectively, which is what customers are looking for today in a transportation provider.

Source: Lappin, Todd. "Truckin." *Wired.* January, 1995, and Schneider National, Inc. at www.schneider.com © Copyright 1997.

for the Monsanto Company, a corporation in the food, medicine, and health industries. The two companies have teamed up to provide safe transportation for this dangerous chemical. The satellites used in the transport allow communication between the driver and a terminal in San Diego, which forwards the information on location and status to both Bee Line and Monsanto. This tracking allows for quick reaction to any accidents or spills, and the computers can give the name of the authority in the area to call in case any emergency action needs to be taken. Satellite communication will continue to play a role in improved safety and customer service for motor carriers into the future.[22]

LTL Rates

Since the early 1980s, the LTL segment of the motor-carrier industry has used discounts from published tariffs as a means of pricing segments to attract traffic of large shippers.

The Interstate Commerce Commission (ICC) was eliminated under the ICC Termination Act of 1995 (ICCTA1995) and with it, most of the last vestiges of motor-carrier rate regulation. Although certain portions of rate oversight were transferred to the then newly created Surface Transportation Board, for all practical purposes

LTL rates are subject to the free market environment. In addition, the common carrier obligation to serve was preserved but absent an enforcement mechanism, which the market place will control as well. As it currently stands, the shipper has more choices for LTL today than existed during the height of regulation.

A limited amount of anti-trust immunity was also preserved but only for classifications, mileage guides rules, and general rate adjustments. Individual carrier rates are subject to anti-trust action but cannot be challenged that the rate is unreasonably high. This is a direct reversal of the situation that existed under the old ICC.

There is no longer any requirement to file tariffs, and contracts can be used instead. Although carriers are still required to maintain rates, rules, and classifications, they only need be furnished to the shipper upon request. In a departure from previous regulation, rates need not be in writing to be enforceable. Shippers, however, must exercise due caution since federal oversight and enforcement is greatly diminished.

This law also reduced the time period for recovery of disputed freight charges from three years to 18 months. If either the carrier or the shipper feels that the charges are incorrect, they must file suit in not more than 18 months from the date of the shipment. The lack of tariffs may make this more difficult unless the shippers have obtained the carrier's prices and rules in writing prior to tendering the shipment to the carrier.

Financial Stability

Another major concern in the motor-carrier industry is financial stability. The operating rates of many motor carriers have been in excess of 95 percent, and some companies have operating ratios of over 100. The high operating ratios are a clear indicator of the financial plight of many motor carriers and an indication of the low competitive rates.

Immediately after the initial lessening of economic regulation in 1980, a large number of motor carriers failed as the competitive environment became severe. Of the top 100 motor carriers in 1980, less than 10 were still in business in 1990. Only one new LTL was formed in this period which has survived to the 1990s. The failures after 1990 were fewer but usually involved larger firms that could not continue to compete. In some cases, the unionized carriers were victims of labor unrest or shipper concerns about stability. In other cases, mergers and buyout reduced the number of Class I carriers. Recent consolidations have also occurred in the truckload sector as the larger carriers have taken over smaller firms to achieve market share.

TABLE 3.4 Summary of Motor Carrier Industry Characteristics

• General Service Characteristics	• Low investments/equipment
• Investments/Capital Outlays	• 90% Variable Costs, 10% Fixed
• Cost Structure	• High
• Ease of Entry	• Pure competition
• Market Structure	• On Price
• How they Compete	• High-valued products
• Types of Commodities	• Large number of small carriers (with few exceptions)
• Number of Carriers	
• Markets in which they compete	• Long distance/metropolitan destinations
• Accessibility, speed, reliability, frequency, and lower loss and damage rates	

Overcapacity has periodically been a severe problem for the trucking industry, most recently during 1994–1995. Given that there is a finite amount of freight to be transported at any one time and there is little, if anything, that carriers can do to influence this, market share changes generally occur at the expense of one carrier over another. These periods of overcapacity also lead to severe pricing pressure which can cause weaker carriers to exit the market. Shippers often exploit these factors and the "spot" market can drive prices below costs as carriers seek to move empty equipment.

Shippers have become increasingly cognizant of the failure rate among motor carriers, and many have introduced a financial evaluation of carriers into their overall decision framework for selecting carriers. When a carrier goes out of business, the interruption of service could have serious consequences.

SUMMARY

- Motor carriers have developed rapidly during the twentieth century and now represent one of the most important modes of transportation for freight movement. U.S. business and most individuals depend in whole or in part upon motor carriers for the movement of goods.
- The public provision (federal, state, and local government units) of highways has played a major role in the development of the motor carrier because of the ubiquitous level of accessibility provided by the comprehensive U.S. highway system.
- The private carrier is a very important part of the motor-carrier industry and a viable option to large and small companies requiring special services, such as grocery or food deliveries. The need of the U.S. industry for dependable and controlled service has also contributed to the development.
- For-hire motor carriers can be classified in a number of useful ways including local versus intercity, common versus contract, regulated versus exempt, general versus specialized, and TL versus LTL.
- One of the manifestations of deregulation has been the tremendous growth in the truckload segment of the motor-carrier business, especially among the small truckload carriers, which has significantly escalated the degree of intramodal competition.
- The LTL segment of the motor-carrier industry has experienced increased concentration; that is, the larger carriers have generated a larger share of the total tonnage, as they have aggressively expanded and marketed their services.
- The motor-carrier industry plays a major role in the movement of manufactured and food products, that is, higher-valued, time-sensitive traffic, because of its generally higher quality of service compared to other modes of transportation.
- The general service characteristics of motor carriers, including accessibility, speed, reliability, frequency, and lower loss and damage rates, have given motor carriers an advantage over other modes.
- Motor carriers offer a variety of equipment for use by shippers that reflect the distance of service and customer requirements.
- The cost structure of motor carriers is dominated by variable costs largely due to the carriers' ability to utilize a publicly provided right-of-way (highways) where payment is based upon user charges such as fuel taxes and licenses.

- Labor costs are an important element of the motor-carrier industry, which tends to be much more labor-intensive than other modes. Increased equipment size and more non-union drivers have lessened the impact of wage costs during the 1980s.
- In contrast to railroads, motor carriers are regarded as having limited economies of scale; that is, small-scale operations are viable and competitive. The major exception would be the LTL carriers with their required investment in terminals. There is increasing evidence that there are some economies of scale among large TL carriers.
- Public funding of highways and the level of user charges paid by motor carriers continue to be arguable issues since it is frequently maintained that motor carriers do not pay their fair share.
- A number of current issues face motor carriers, including safety, substance abuse, technology, undercharge claims, and state regulation.

Key Terms

carrying capacity pg. 104
driving regulations 109
exempt carriers 99
for-hire 98
interstate highway system 97
line-haul 101
LTL (less than truckload) 99
operation ratio 111
pickup and delivery (PUD) 101
slip seat operation 107
TL (truckload) 99

Study Questions

1. The motor carrier is probably the most visible segment of the transportation system in the United States, but in many ways the motor carrier is also the most significant element of the freight transport industry. What factors account for the motor carrier's visibility and significance?

2. The railroad industry played a significant role in the development and growth of many cities and geographic regions during the nineteenth century. What role, if any, have motor carriers played during the twentieth century in terms of economic development?

3. Private carriage is more important in the motor-carrier segment of our transportation industry than any of the other four major modal segments. What factors have contributed to private carriage becoming so prevalent in the motor-carrier area?

4. The so-called local carrier is also almost unique to the motor-carrier industry. Why?

5. Compare and contrast the truckload segment of the motor-carrier industry with the LTL segment in terms of infrastructure, cost structure, market structure, and operation characteristics.

6. What is the nature of intramodal and intermodal competition in the motor-carrier industry? How have the motor carriers fared in terms of intermodal competition since 1980?

7. Describe the general service characteristics of motor carriers and explain how these service characteristics have contributed to the growth of the motor-carrier industry.

8. The cost structure of the motor-carrier industry is affected by its infrastructure (such as highways and terminals). Discuss the cost structure of motor carriers and how it is affected by the infrastructure. Should there be changes made in public policy with respect to the motor carriers' use of public highways?

9. Describe the nature of the operation ratio and its usefulness in analyzing a motor carrier's financial viability.

10. What are the major issues facing motor carriers as we approach the twenty-first century? How should these issues be addressed?

NOTES

1. *Transportation in America,* 16th ed. (Washington D.C.: Eno Transportation Foundation, 1998), p. 40.

2. Ibid., p. 44.

3. Ibid., p. 60.

4. American Trucking Associations, *American Trucking Trends* (Alexandra, VA: American Trucking Associations, Inc., 1996), p. 1.

5. Ibid., p. 2.

6. American Trucking Associations, *American Trucking Trends, 1977–1978.* (Washington, DC: American Trucking Associations, Inc.), p. 27.

7. *Transportation in America,* p. 71.

8. Roth, Ronald D., *An Approach to Measurement of Modal Advantage.* (Washington, DC: American Trucking Associations, Inc., 1977), p. 1–10.

9. There are no notable exceptions to this ability to serve. Shippers located on an island are served by water or air transportation. Other unique examples exist where the truck is physically unable to provide the transportation.

10. For a complete listing of federal equipment specifications, see the U.S. Department of Transportation, Federal Highway Administration, Bureau of Motor-carrier Safety, *Federal Motor Carrier Safety Regulations.* (Washington, DC: U.S. Government Printing Office, 1984), p. 2.

11. Through police powers contained in the U.S. Constitution, each state has the right to establish regulations to protect the health and welfare of its citizens. Vehicle length and height laws are within these police powers, as are vehicle speed and weight laws.

12. *Transportation in America,* p. 60.

13. American Trucking Associations, *American Trucking Trends, 1996.* (Alexandria, VA: American Trucking Association, Inc., 1996), p. 14.

14. Ibid., p. 29.

15. Ibid., pp. 19–20.

16. The Appalachian Highway System was designed to spur the depressed economy of that region.

17. American Trucking Associations, *Highway Statistics, 1990.* (Alexandria, VA: American Trucking Associations, 1990), p. 42.

18. American Trucking Associations, *American Trucking Trends, 1991–1992.* (Alexandria, VA: American Trucking Associations, 1992), p. 15.

19. October 1988, p. 45.

20. Kenneth B. Ackerman, "Is Substance Abuse Stealing Your Efficiency?", *Transportation & Distribution* (November 1988), p. 26.

21. Robert J. Baker, *Transportation & Distribution,* p. 46.

22. Daniel J. McConville, "Trucking the Hazmat Express," *Distribution,* June 1992, p. 51.

Cases

CASE 3.1

JEI Carrier Corporation

At its annual shareholders meeting, Jean Beierlein of JEI Carrier Corporation is braced for dissent from the JEI union employees. For some time, the company has attempted to negotiate for more flexibility in its operations with its union workers. Because of an agreement with the union, JEI has limits on when it can engage in intermodal operations. At present, intermodal transportation can only be used when there are no drivers available at the origin or at key relay points. The problem for the company is that the industry has become increasingly competitive since 1980 with the growth of other alternatives such as UPS and non-union carriers.

In many instances, nonunion carriers have taken away market shares that the JEI Carrier Corporation once held, because the nonunion companies are more flexible with respect to transporting goods. As a result, the nonunion carrier companies continue to grow and increase their share of the market.

The use of intermodal transportation gives carriers the opportunity to use a variety of modes of transportation when moving goods so they can better serve their customers. A frequent intermodal choice within the trucking industry is using rail. In addition, JEI wants to be able to use split shifts with its employees.

With the union not allowing the company to participate in intermodal operations for more than 28 percent of total line-haul, the company does not have much flexibility and is less competitive. The union does not want the company to participate in intermodal operations because it is afraid that some of its members will lose their jobs. Since deregulation, more than 400,000 union jobs have been lost within the trucking industry.

The company is in a bad position because it wants to be able to remain competitive. However, with the union restricting the use of intermodal operations, JEI's competitors may be in a good position to capture some of its customers. The trucking industry has become very competitive over the years, and a lot of companies are using intermodal operations as a competitive measure to attract and retain customers, as well as to lower cost.

Case Questions

1. What recommendations would you make to the company for increasing its flexibility while also providing job security for its union employees?

2. What strategies could JEI use to remain competitive if the union still restricts the use of intermodal operations?

3. Do you think that having union employees is an advantage or a disadvantage for JEI? Why or why not?

CASE 3.2
Retirement Funds

In the U.S. trucking industry there has been a coalition attempting to persuade Congress to place a limit on the amount of payouts of pension funds for workers in the industry. One important concern is that many of the pension funds are not fully funded, yet there continues to be an increase in the number of benefits being offered by these funds. Right now, in one union pension fund, an individual with 30 years of service who is 65 years of age will receive at least $2,500 a month.

Employers want to see an end to the trend of increasing benefits. The unfunded liabilities are growing year by year. In the trucking industry, in which many employees belong to a union, there has been a lot of conflict recently concerning this issue. The coalition feels that the only way to stop increasing benefits is to have Congress put a limit on the benefits of pension funds. However, there is union opposition to such a limit.

As a result of not having fully funded pension funds, if a company goes bankrupt and out of business, the government agency that oversees pension funds will be faced with a large number of claims for funds. The position of the union is that it wants to secure the maximum amount of benefits for its members. Employers are worried that by continuing to have increasing benefits, their respective companies will become more and more insolvent. Some employers may have to go out of business, depending on how insolvent they become. The result of going out of business means a loss of jobs and more unemployment. Congress has an important decision to make regarding whether or not to put a limit on the amount of benefits that pension funds will pay. The increasing liabilities of employers can affect the economy in a large way because many employers might pass on the increased liabilities to customers in the form of higher prices.

Case Questions

1. What decision should Congress make regarding the issue of putting a limit on the benefits of pension funds? Justify your answer.

2. Do you think that the unions are being too greedy by not wanting a limit put on the amount of benefits of pension funds? Why or why not?

3. What recommendations do you have for solving the pension fund issue between employers and unions?

CHAPTER 4

RAILROADS

Brief History

Throughout its history, the United States has viewed transportation as being vital to the well-being of commerce, and for well over a century railroads commanded a dominant position in the U.S. transport system. Rail transportation has played a significant role in the economic development of the nation from 1850 to 1950. The establishment of a transcontinental railway in 1869 contributed to the population migration to the land west of the Mississippi River because expansion was no longer dependent on U.S. inland waterways or slow travel by wagon over poor trails.

However, the railroad industry has declined in relative importance during the last half of the twentieth century. This decline has been well documented and can be attributed in part to the following events: the rise of alternate transport modes with superior services and/or cost characteristics, primarily motor carriers and pipelines; a resurgence in water transportation; and changing needs of the U.S. economy. In 1997, railroads transported only 39.2 percent of the total intercity ton-miles transported by all modes, which is approximately 39 percent less than 1929 on a relative basis.[1] It is important to note that, on an actual basis, rail ton-miles have continued to increase and railroads are still the largest carrier in terms of intercity ton-miles.

Starting in 1984, the railroad industry adopted a new depreciation accounting system, and **return on investment (ROI)** shot up to 5.7 percent. In 1987, ROI again showed a slight decrease to 5.6 percent and the railroad industry's ROI in 1996 reached 9.4 percent.[2]

The railroads are still vital to our transportation system and play an important role in our economy. For example, in 1997, rail revenues accounted for approximately one percent of the gross domestic product.[3] Railroads in 1998 employed almost 212,000 people or approximately .19 percent of the total civilian labor force.[4] Investment is another indication of importance. In recent years, rail investment in new plant and equipment has accounted for about 1.5 percent of total private investment. In 1989, for example, rail locomotive and freight car acquisition increased sharply over 1988 (i.e., an increase of more than 7,000 rail cars).[5] These indicators have been hailed as further evidence of the success of the Staggers Rail Act of 1980.

As mentioned earlier, in 1995, the railroads shipped about 40.6 percent of all ton-miles moved by all transport modes in the United States. This percentage of total ton-miles has been declining since its peak of 75 percent in 1929. However, actual ton-miles have, for the most part, been steadily increasing. In 1980, 932 billion ton-miles of domestic intercity freight was moved. The figure dropped to 810 billion ton-miles in 1982 due mostly to the recession of 1982–83. In 1997, the ton-miles moved were 1,375 billion, representing 40.6 percent of transportation's total 3,348 billion.[6]

These figures highlight the fact that, even though railroads continue to move record amounts of goods, they are capturing less of the total transportation market because other modes have been growing even faster. However, there are indications that railroads may experience a resurgence on a relative basis because of more aggressive marketing and growth in intermodal traffic.[7]

Industry Overview

Number of Carriers

Although there were 550 railroads listed in 1997, only nine were Class 1 companies (see Table 4.1). This meant that they did more than $256.4 million (1997) annually

TABLE 4.1 Number of Railroads

Line-Haul Railroads[a]				
Year	**Class I**	**Others**	**Switching and Terminal Companies**	**Total**
1920	186	686	245	1,117
1930	156	541	231	928
1940	131	397	208	736
1950	127	310	207	644
1960	106	304	197	607
1970	71	273	173	517
1980	39	288	153	480
1984	31	296	142	469
1987	18	481	—	499
1990	14	516	—	530
1996	10	543	—	553
1997	9	541	207	530

[a]A line-haul railroad conducts actual transportation service. A switching and terminal company performs switching services; furnishes terminal trackage, bridges, or other facilities such as union passenger or freight stations; operates ferries; or performs any one or a combination of these functions.

Source: Association of American Railroads, *Railroad Facts.* 1997, p. 9.

in revenue. The balance of the railroads is classified as "Regional," "Local," and "Switching" carriers.

Offsetting the decline in the number of Class 1 lines, significant growth occurred in short-line railroads known as Locals and larger lines known as Regionals. These new operators took over unwanted trackage of the Class 1 lines and sought to recover lost business. As of 1997, 34 regional railroads existed, of which the Wisconsin Central is the largest. There are also 507 Local lines, broken up by linehaul and switching. Some of the roads are as small as two or three miles but still contribute to the overall freight network.

In addition, a number of holding companies were formed to control a number of short lines scattered around the country. One of the largest is Railtex, which operates more than 20 separate railroads in the United States and Canada. The holding companies have economies of scale in purchasing and can share other corporate assets, which reduces the cost of operation.

Line mileage declined during the same 50-year period (see Table 4.2). Line mileage expanded rapidly during the initial construction period of 1830–1910 and reached a peak of 254,251 miles in 1916.[8] By 1929, line mileage was down to 249,433 and in 1997 it had been reduced to about 171,225 miles.[9] This reduction is traceable largely to the abandonment of duplicate trackage that was built during the "boom" periods of the industry's developmental years that was no longer needed because of technology, market shifts, and the rail merger movement.

Competition

The competitive position of the railroad industry has changed dramatically during the last 50 years. Railroads were the dominant mode of transportation prior to World War II; now the industry is faced with intense intermodal competition and selective intramodal competition. Consolidations within the industry have created a situation in which only nine Class I railroads handle 98 percent of the traffic. In addition, the

TABLE 4.2 U.S. Railroad Miles & Trackage (Class I)

Year	Miles of Line[a]	Miles of Track[b]
1939	220,915	364,174
1951	213,401	354,546
1955	211,459	350,217
1971	195,840	317,711
1975	191,520	310,941
1980	164,822	270,623
1982	159,123	263,330
1986	140,061	233,205
1988	127,555	213,669
1989	124,236	208,322
1990	119,758	200,074
1996	105,779	176,978
1997	103,290	171,285

[a]This represents the aggregate length of roadway of all line-haul railroads exclusive of yard tracks, sidings, and parallel lines.
[b]This includes the total miles of railroad track owned by U.S. railroads.

Source: Association of American Railroads, *Railroad Facts* (Washington, DC, 1998), p. 44.

railways must compete with the other modes of transportation that have either evolved or matured since the 1920s.

The industry's economic structure has developed into a fine example of differentiated oligopoly.

Intramodal

Today, only a few railroads serve a particular geographic region. This situation gives rise to an oligopolistic market structure because there are a small number of interdependent large sellers. Barriers to entry exist because of the large capital outlays and fixed costs required and, consequently, pricing can be controlled by the existing firms. For this reason, economic regulations implemented by the ICC prior to 1980 brought the geographic coverage and the ratemaking procedures of the railroads under federal scrutiny and control so that intramodal and intermodal competition might be promoted. Thus, because of the need to recover many of the high fixed costs while maintaining a market share, regulation influenced railroads to set prices in a competitive fashion.

With the merger trend discussed earlier, the intramodal competition has been further reduced. Many cities now have only one railroad serving them. Even major rail centers such as Chicago or Kansas City have seen the number of carriers serving those areas significantly reduced. Shippers are now concerned that there will be enough effective intramodal competition to preserve railroad-to-railroad competition.

Intermodal

As noted earlier, the relative market share of railroad intercity ton-miles has been steadily declining because of increased intermodal competition. Inroads into the lucrative commodity markets have been facilitated by governmental expenditures on infrastructure that have benefited competing modes. The government has provided an extensive local and national road system, including the interstate network, for motor-carrier use. When asking a railroad company president how his service compares to that offered by trucking firms, he responded:

> Our service is not as fast as truck, but we have discovered that customers will accept a slower transit time in exchange for a lower rate, as long as service is consistent and we can usually provide a lower freight rate because our costs are less than truck.[10]

Customers look for 100 percent on-time performance. Railroads must provide this service in order to stay competitive. Railroad companies cannot deliver freight early either because the customer then has to find a place to store it.

In addition, through improvements and maintenance of the inland waterway system by the U.S. Army Corps of Engineers, the government has also provided the right-of-way for water carriers. Because of the governmental programs and the response of the railroad industry to change, railways now account for only 27 percent of total tonnage and 37 percent of total ton-miles shipped, figures totaling one-half of the amounts from just 50 years ago.

Overall, the railroads have been rate-competitive. Government influence, either in the form of economic regulation or expenditure programs aimed at promoting other modes, together with intermodal competition, forced the railways into making a determined effort to forestall industry decline by becoming more competitive. The Staggars Rail Act, which removed significant economic regulation, has allowed railroads to be much more price-competitive through contract rates and a more tailored response to customers.

Mergers

Historically, many mergers have taken place in the railroad industry, and the size of the remaining carriers has correspondingly increased. Early rail mergers grew out of efforts to expand capacity in order to benefit from large-volume traffic efficiencies and economies. Later, **side-by-side** combinations were made to strengthen the financial positions of many of the railroads and eliminate duplication. More recently through, **end-to-end mergers** were created to provide more effective intermodal and intramodal competition.[11] Customer service and reliability can be improved by these mergers, since the many types of operating costs, such as car switching and clerical costs, such as record keeping, can be brought under control.

Previously we noted that the number of railroads (refer to Table 4.1) and the number of miles of track (refer to Table 4.2) have declined. One of the major reasons for this decline in both the number of companies and the miles of track has been the significant number of mergers or unifications that have occurred in the railroad industry during the past 30 years. Twenty-eight mergers have taken place during the last 30 years and 50 unifications overall. The latter included not only mergers but also consolidations and outright purchases for control. The decade of the 1970s was very active, but the tempo of the rail consolidations in the 1980s was hyperactive.

In 1920, there were 186 Class 1 railroads; by 1997, the number had declined to nine. One reason for this drop was the way in which railroads are classified by revenue, which, as it was adjusted for inflation, fewer roads qualified. The primary reason, however, was the acclerating trend of mergers. After the Staggers Act was passed in 1980, there was a significant increase in mergers and acquisitions so that, as of 1999, there are only four major rail lines, Norfolk Southern, CSX Transportation, Union Pacific, and the Burlington Northern Santa Fe.

Abandonments

Recall that in 1916, at its peak, the railroad industry owned 254,000 miles of track. Today, more than half of that is gone, enough to circle the Earth three times. The early overexpansion left extensive amounts of excess trackage in many areas, and the railroads had to abandon significant portions of rail trackage to remain competitive. Parallel and overlapping routes, therefore, have been eliminated wherever possible.

Many factors led to the abandonment of track around the country. In the late 1950s, the government opened the Interstate Highway System. This allowed trucking service to gain speed, which caused shippers to use motor carriers. To effectively compete with trucking companies for time-sensitive traffic, railroads had to focus on efficient routes. In the 1970s and 1980s, bankruptcies forced the shutdown of railroad systems such as Rock Island, Penn Central, and Milwaukee Road. Another critical issue that caused abandonment of railroad tracks occurred in 1980. Deregulation gave companies freedom to buy, sell, or abandon unprofitable track without federal interference. Cities such as Annapolis, Maryland, and Carson City, Nevada, lost all railroad service. Even famous tracks that carried the country's most famous passenger trains vanished. Once the railroad companies abandoned the tracks, they sold the rails and ties to scrap dealers. They received as much as $10,000 per mile.

The land used for rights-of-way could also be used unless the original deed required the return when the property was no longer being used for railroad purposes. In some cases, all or part of the right of way was turned into hiking trails with some bridges left in place. The 13-year-old program, "Rail to Trails Conservancy," has been highly successful in adding over 10,000 miles of trails to the country's recreational facilities. In other cases, the land and sometimes even the track was left in as part of a program known as "rail-banking." The theory behind this is should the line be needed in the future, it would be much easier to restore it. In one case, a major railroad company reopened a major line after it was closed for over 10 years.

Even though the railroad industry reduced its track mileage by more than half, the lines left still carried the majority of the freight. The abandonments were either rural branches or duplicate lines left over from mergers. The ICC, and later the STB, still regulate abandonments but changes in the law made it much easier for the railroad industry to close unprofitable lines. Not all the lines were scrapped, as discussed above, and regional and short line operators took over some of this property.

New developments, such as unit trains carrying one commodity like coal or grain from one shipper to one consignee, helped the railroads operate profitably. As more and more traffic was concentrated on fewer and fewer routes, overhead costs were spread over more businesses. Each time a railroad interchanges a car to another line, there was the chance for delay. As mergers reduced the number of railroads, fewer interchanges were needed. For example, until 1993, at least three railroads were needed to go from Chicago to San Francisco, but now one company owns all the track allowing more efficient service.

With less than half the amount of original track, railroads had to find a way to stay in business profitably. The best solution concentrated on improved service. For one, railroads developed special train units to carry the cargo of only one manufacturer at a time. This provided express service (no stop offs) for the shipper. Railroads also sold track to short lines that provided faster, customized service for smaller shippers who discontinued to use large shippers. Finally, railroads had to eliminate unnecessary delays in service by providing 24-hour service. They also used computer systems to track cargo.

Operating and Service Characteristics

General Service Characteristics

Commodities Hauled

In the nineteenth century, when the railroads were the primary source of transportation, they moved almost every available type of product or raw material. Today, the railroad system has evolved into a system that ships large quantities of heavyweight, low-value commodities (or bulk products).[12] Motor carriers concentrate on the handling of small-volume, high-value finished goods, whereas water and pipelines carry the larger volumes of the lowest value types of bulk commodities. The railroads therefore find themselves engaged in intense competition with these other modes for the opportunity to ship many product categories. Although railroads still handle a wide variety of commodities, more than 50 percent of total rail carloadings in 1996 involved the movement of bulk materials. Table 4.3 lists the products with more than 700,000 carloadings carried by the railroads. Of the six commodities shown in the table, only one, motor vehicles and equipment, is not a bulk commodity.

Coal

Railroads are the primary haulers of coal, accounting for 43.8 percent of the total tonnage transported in 1996.[13] In addition, coal constitutes almost one-third of the total tonnage handled by the railways. Its share of carloadings, which make up more than one out of every four rail freight cars loaded in 1996, represents a marked change in transport. Table 4.3 indicates that 6.7 million carloadings took place, up by more than one million from 1979 levels. Furthermore, rail coal traffic is concentrated among a few railroads, with four firms handling more than 60 percent of the railcar tonnage.[14] Coal is an alternative energy source that will probably continue to be an important commodity shipped by the railroads.

Farm Products

When considered together, farm products constitute the second largest commodity group hauled by railroads. Total movement by rail amounted to about 1.4 million tons in 1996.[15] The growth in domestic markets and the increase of exports to foreign customers have been steady for many years. For example, the exportation of

TABLE 4.3 Carloads Originated by Commodity

	Carloads (thousands)		Change	
Commodity Group	**1997**	**1996**	**Cars**	**Percent**
Coal	6,703	6,746	(43)	(0.6)
Chemicals and allied products	1,705	1,668	37	2.2
Farm products	1,408	1,530	(122)	(8.0)
Motor vehicles and equipment	1,380	1,341	39	2.9
Food and kindred products	1,295	1,302	(6)	(0.5)
Non-metallic minerals	1,160	1,176	(17)	(1.4)

Source: Association of American Railroads, (Washington, DC, 1998), P. 25.

grain and its related products accounted for more than 50 percent of the total grain market in 1989. Because of this growth, distribution patterns might change, but the transportation of farm products will continue to be an important rail commodity movement.

Chemicals

Chemicals and allied products, a great number of which are classified as "hazardous" by the U.S. Department of Transportation (DOT), are transported in specially designed tank cars. Most of this material is carried long distances (more than 500 miles) in 187,000 privately owned tank cars. One hundred and forty million tons of this highly rated traffic traveled by rail in 1996.[16] The railroads, in comparison with highway movements, safely transport chemicals, and this safety has been steadily increasing for years. This type of long-haul bulk material is ideally suited for rail movement.

Transportation Equipment

Transportation equipment carloadings, which are linked to the relative health of the domestic automobile industry, have increased to more than five percent of total carloadings, an increase of more than 40 percent since 1982.

Although the commodities shipped by the railroad industry have changed over the years, with the emphasis placed on the movement of low-value, high-volume bulk materials, the railroads are still an ideal mode of transport for many different types of goods, high-value merchandise and raw materials alike.

Constraints

Railroads are constrained by fixed rights-of-way and therefore provide differing degrees of service completeness. For example, if both the shipper and receiver possess rail sidings, then door-to-door service can be provided. However, if no sidings are available, the movement of goods must be completed by some other mode. If line-haul mileage continues to decline (as indicated by current industrial trends), the industry will become less service-complete and even more dependent on other modes of transportation for completion of many types of moves.

Unlike motor, air, or water transport, the railroad system provides a truly nationwide network of service. Each railroad serves a specific geographic region, and freight and equipment are exchanged at interchange points. For example, a shipment between Philadelphia, Pennsylvania, and Portland, Oregon, might be handled by two or three railroads, depending on the route chosen. The through service is unique, but multiple handlings can create rate-division problems and delays in delivery.

Although on-time delivery performance and the frequency of service had deteriorated in the past, improvements have been made in recent years. The current position of the industry has been restored to competitive levels and selected movements (particularly over long distances). Railroads dominate the market for hauling 30,000 pounds or more over distances exceeding 300 miles. The industry hopes to expand its service to certain short-haul markets and selected lanes for manufactured products.[17]

Strengths

A large carrying capacity enables the railroads to handle large-volume movements of low-value commodities over long distances. Motor carriers, on the other hand, are constrained by volume and weight to the smaller truckload (TL) and less-than-truckload

(LTL) markets. Furthermore, although pipelines compete directly with the railroads, they are restricted largely to the movements of liquid and gas (and then only in one direction).

This kind of carload capacity, along with a variety of car types, permits the railroads to handle almost any type of commodity. For the most part, the industry is not constrained to weight and volume restrictions, and customer service is available throughout the United States. In addition, railroads are able to use a variety of car types to provide a flexible service, since the rolling stock consists of boxcars, tankers, gondolas, hoppers, covered hoppers, flatcars, and other special types of cars.

Another important service is that the **liability** for loss and damage is usually assumed by the railroads. Railroads, however, have had a comparatively high percentage of goods damaged in transit (about three percent total tonnages shipped). In 1995, the total pay-out of freight claims for U.S. and Canadian railroads increased $11 million from $115.9 million in 1994.[18] Such damage occurs because rail freight often goes through a rough trip due to vibrations and shocks (steel wheel on steel rail). In addition, the incidence of loss is usually higher than on other modes because of the high degree of multiple handlings. Excessive loss and damage claims have tended to erode shipper confidence in the railroad's ability to provide adequate service.

In an attempt to regain traffic lost to other modes and gain new traffic share, the railroads have been placing an increasing amount of attention on equipment and technology. For one, to decrease damage statistics, railroads focus on new technologies. Multilevel suspension systems and end-of-car cushioning devices protect the goods in transit. Also, the Association of American Railroads has developed a quality certification program (M-1003) to ensure freight car quality and technical specifications. Finally, equipping cars with instrumentation packages to measure forces that might cause damage reduces the damage potential. One area that has received much attention has been the intermodal era, namely, trailer-on-flatcar (**TOFC**) and container-on-flatcar (**COFC**) service. The railroads realized the necessity of improving the TOFC and COFC service to compete effectively with motor carriers. The developments include terminal facilities for loading and unloading, as well as changes in the railcars and trailers and containers. However, the changes have not stopped here. The railroads have invested a significant amount of money recently in improving right-of-way and structures to help improve service by preventing delays.

Microprocessors have found their niche in the railroad industry, particularly in communications and signaling. The "chip" is also being used in vital circuits (safety-related). Fiber optics are used in this high-tech explosion to improve communications, which will in turn improve service and revenues. The railroad industry hopes that these service-related improvements will increase its traffic.

Equipment

The **carload** is the basic unit of measurement of freight handling by the railroads. A carload can vary in size and capacity depending on the type of car being used. Historically, the number of carloadings has declined since the turn of the century; there was a total of almost 53 million carloadings in 1929. In 1996, the total railroad carloadings equaled 24.2 million.[19] This decline has occurred primarily because of the introduction of larger cars and the increase in productivity per car type.

The increases in average carrying capacity of railroad freight cars over the past 50 years have been dramatic. In 1996, the average carrying capacity per car stood over at almost 91.9 tons, compared to 46.3 tons in 1929.[20] Most of today's new cars have more than twice the capacity of the typical boxcar used 50 years ago. However, the carrying capacity of a new or rebuilt car could easily exceed 100 tons, and the trend of increasing average capacity will continue in the near future. A car with a 100-ton capacity probably represents the most efficient size with the present support facilities.

The railroads own and maintain their own rolling stock. The characteristics of these cars have changed considerably to suit customer requirements; for example, the conventional boxcar has been deemphasized but has seen resurgence in the past few years. Today's car fleet is highly specialized and is designed to meet the needs of the individual shipper. Following is a list of eight generalized car types:

- Boxcar (plain): Standardized roofed freight car with sliding doors on the side used for general commodities
- Boxcar (equipped): Specially modified boxcar used for specialized merchandise, such as automobile parts
- Hopper car: A freight car with the floor sloping to one or more hinged doors used for discharging bulk materials
- Covered hopper: A hopper car with a roof designed to transport bulk commodities that need protection from the elements
- Flatcar: A freight car with no top or sides used primarily for TOFC service machinery and building materials

FIGURE 4.1 Types of Freight Equipment, 1997

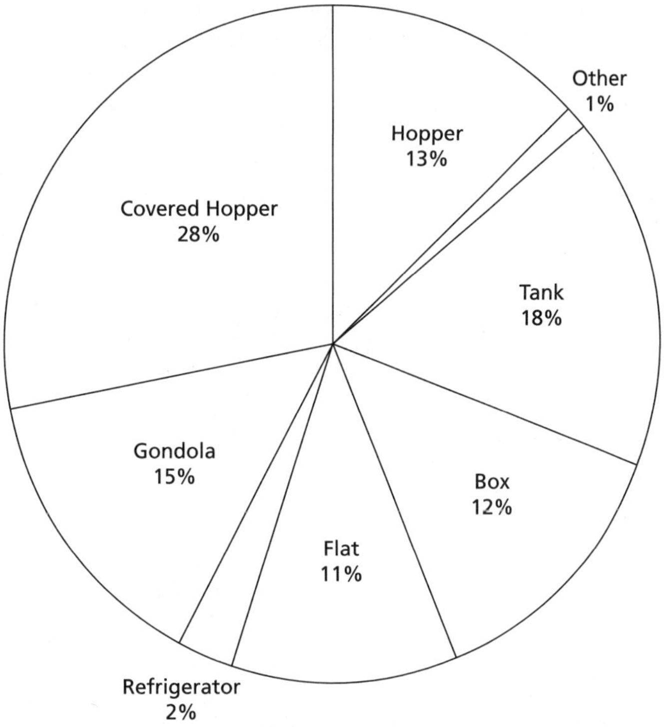

Source: Association of American Railroads, *Railroad Facts* (Washington, DC, 1998), p. 51.

- Refrigerator car: A freight car to which refrigeration equipment has been added for controlled temperature
- Gondola: A freight car with no top, a flat bottom, and fixed sides used primarily for hauling bulk commodities
- Tank car: Specialized car used for the transport of liquids and gases

The total number and percentage of freight cars in service in 1996 are shown in Table 4.4 and Figure 4.1. The boxcar has been surpassed by the covered hopper car, which is followed closely in number by the hopper car. In addition, the largest increase in total new cars was in covered hopper cars. The composition of the railroad fleet has shifted from the accommodation of manufactured commodities to the movement of bulk goods. In 1996, more than 65 percent of the total fleet was designed for the transport of bulk and raw materials.

Class I railroads own almost 46 percent of the rolling stock in use, private companies hold title to 37 percent, and other classes of railroads make up the remainder[21] (see Table 4.4). Car companies and shippers are becoming increasingly more important in the ownership of railroad cars. In 1991, they owned almost all of the specially designed tank cars in use, and in the last several years they have purchased a substantial number of covered hopper cars, more than 30,000.

To remain competitive with the other modes of transportation, the railroads have increased their capacity to about 134 million tons—an industry record. The average freight train load also has increased; in 1996, more than 2,912 tons per load were carried as compared to barely 800 tons per load in 1929.[22] This increase in capacity will be necessary if more bulk commodities are to be shipped longer distances in the future.

Service Innovations

The railroad cost structure makes it necessary to attract high and regular volumes of traffic to take advantage of scale economies and to operate efficiently. In recent years, rail management has developed or reemphasized a number of service innovations to increase traffic volume.

The concept of piggyback service was designed by railroad management to increase service levels to intermodal customers. Piggyback traffic, which includes both

TABLE 4.4 Types and Number of Freight Cars in Service in 1996

Type	Total	Class I Railroads	Other Railroads	Car Companies and Shippers
Box cars:	156,284	94,165	46,204	16,205
Plain box	31,681	5,017	12,889	13,775
Equipped box	124,893	89,148	33,315	2,430
Covered hoppers	365,196	150,121	20,255	194,820
Flat cars	134,233	83,745	10,893	39,595
Refrigerator cars	29,650	24,035	3,379	2,236
Gondolas	187,224	109,162	17,546	60,516
Hoppers	163,917	101,724	16,070	46,123
Tank cars	225,029	945	35	224,049
Others	8,596	4,596	1,726	2,274
Total	1,270,419	568,493	116,106	585,818

Source: Association of American Railroads, *Railroad Facts* (Washington, DC, 1998), p. 51.

TOFC and COFC services, accounted for 15.2 percent of total loadings in 1986, occupying a little less than three million cars and ranking second behind coal in total rail carloadings.[23] In 1997, more than 8.5 million trailers and containers were loaded. As can be seen in Table 4.5, intermodal carloadings have been growing at a rate of about 20 percent per year. When discussing piggyback service, consideration must be given to the individual concepts of TOFC and COFC movements.

TOFC service transports highway trailers on railroad flatcars. It combines the line-haul efficiencies of the railroads with the flexibility of local motor pickup and delivery service. On-time deliveries, regularly scheduled departures, and fuel efficiency are the major reasons for the present growth and future potential of TOFC service. For example, a 100-car train (which places two trailers on each flatcar) is more economical to run than 200 trucks over the road. Fuel is saved and railroad economies of scale are realized. Traffic congestion, road damage, and maintenance and repair costs are all reduced because of the reduction of number of trucks out on the highways.

Table 4.5 shows that the intermodal movement of trailers and containers grew rapidly during the 1980s. This growth was stimulated by the advent of double-stack containers used in international trade. Also, the railroads have placed new emphasis on their intermodal business after a number of years of doubting its profitability.

In recent years, the railroads have largely segregated their intermodal traffic from regular freight, with most of the intermodal trains operating on a priority schedule. One result of the new schedules has been more reliable service for shippers, which has led to increased growth in loadings. The railroads have also simplified their billing procedures and made their computers accessible to customers for service innovations.

The growing use of TOFC by motor-carrier companies has also contributed to the recent growth. United Parcel Service (UPS) has been a supporter of rail intermodal service for some time and is still their largest single customer. The LTL carriers began using intermodal service during the 1980s to handle their surges of traffic,

TABLE 4.5 Intermodal Carloadings

Year	Trailers and Containers
1965	1,664,929
1970	2,363,200
1975	2,238,117
1980	3,059,402
1981	3,150,522
1982	3,396,973
1983	4,090,078
1984	4,565,743
1985	4,590,952
1986	4,997,229
1987	5,503,819
1988	5,779,547
1989	5,987,355
1990	6,206,782
1996	8,143,258
1997	8,695,860

Source: Association of American Railroads, *Railroad Facts* (Washington, DC, 1998), p. 26.

FIGURE 4.2 Intermodal Traffic Flows

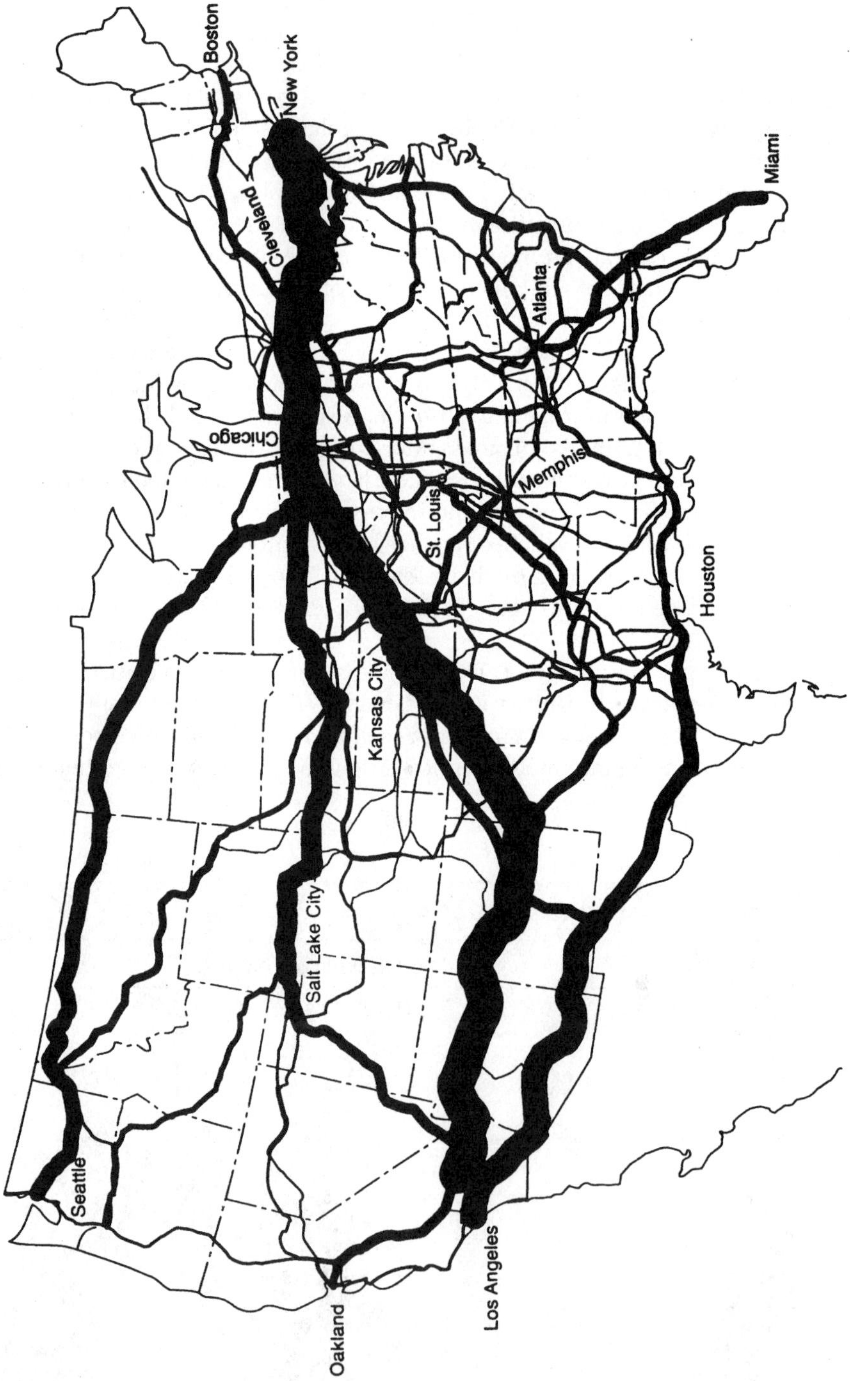

Note: Line thickness corresponds to intermodal volume.
Soruce: Double Stack Container Systems: Implications for U.S. Railroads and Ports (Washington: U.S. Dept. of Transportation, 1990).

and as rail service has become more reliable, they are using the rail service on a continuing basis. New union agreements allow truckers to substitute rail for over-the-road for up to 28 percent of the total traffic. The biggest change came recently when two of the largest truckload carriers, Schneider National and J. B. Hunt, purchased equipment to use rail intermodal service on an extensive basis. This commitment by these two large carriers has had a significant influence on the growth of rail intermodal service. Figure 4.2 shows the flows of traffic in the United States.

COFC is the international form of transportation for containers and is equivalent to domestic TOFC movements. A container does not have the wheels and must therefore be placed on a flatbed truck for ramp-to-door delivery. The amount of handling is reduced because the container can be loaded and sealed at the origin and shipped directly to the consignee. Economies are realized, because putting finished goods in containers means not only lower packaging and warehousing costs, but also faster transit times since time and effort are saved in the loading, unloading, and delivery of goods. In addition, the TOFC piggyback plans can apply to COFC shipments with the substitution of the container for the trailer in the movement. Furthermore, land-bridge traffic, which substitutes railroads for ocean vessels for part of the journey, has become more widely used in international commerce because it facilitates the handling of export-import commodities.[24] The double stacking of the containers on traffic to and from West Coast ports has improved the productivity of the rail COFC service dramatically.

The **unit train,** which evolved from the rent-a-train concept for the movement of goods, specializes in the transport of only one commodity, usually coal or grain, from origin to destination. Many times the shipper owns cars, and the train is, in effect, rented to the shipper for a particular period of time. For example, a typical utility coal unit train move would involve the transportation of 10,000 tons of coal in 100 hopper or gondola cars, each with a 100-ton capacity. The movement would be directly from the mine to an electric power-generating station with no stops in transit, and loading and unloading would be accomplished while the train was moving. Because of the single commodity nature of the concept and the need to maintain regularly scheduled movements, empty backhauls occur. However, this drawback is offset by the high revenue-producing capabilities of the unit train resulting from the improved overall car utilization.

The scale economies of the railroad industry have brought about the division and specialization of labor. Rail management has responded by increasing the use of computers and communications to help improve discipline and maintain control over rail operations. Elaborate information and communication systems have been developed so that a railroad's progress, status, and reliability can be monitored on an online basis. Car ordering and billing is simplified, while cars are traced and located, and orders are expedited at a faster rate. Computers are not a panacea, but they do help bring about increased efficiencies without any loss in service quality.

Cost Structure

Fixed Costs

The railroad industry's cost structure in the short run (a period when both plant and capacity remain constant) consists of a large proportion of indirect fixed costs, rather than variable costs.[25] This situation exists because the railroads, along with the pipelines, are the only modes that own and maintain their own network and terminals.

In addition, railroads, like other modes, operate their own rolling stocks. In the past, it has been estimated by some managers that up to two-thirds of the industry's cost did not vary with volume.[26] Today it is believed that this figure is closer to 30 percent. The investment in long-lived assets has had a major impact on the cost characteristics of the industry. Cost structures will be discussed in more detail in Chapter 11.

The major cost element borne by the railroad industry, and not found in the cost structure of other modes (excluding pipelines), is the operation, maintenance, and ownership of rights-of-way. **Rights-of-way** describe what a carrier's equipment uses to provide movement. For example, the railroads use track and ballast, while the motor carriers use highways. Initially, a large capital investment is required and annual maintenance costs become a substantial drain on earnings. Capital expenditures in 1996 alone amounted to $6.1 billion.[27]

Another major component of the railroad industry's high fixed costs is the extensive investment in private terminal facilities. These terminal facilities include freight yards, where trains are sorted and assembled, and terminal areas and sidings, where shippers and connecting railroads are serviced. Because of the large amount of fixed assets, the railroads as a group are not as responsive as other modes to the volume of traffic carried. Motor and water carriers, as well as the airline industry, are able to shift resources faster in response to changes in customer demand, because of their use of "free" rights-of-way. Motor carriers, for instance, pay for their costs through user charges, tolls, and various taxes (such as gasoline taxes). These charges are related and vary directly with the volume handled, thereby creating a variable rather than a fixed cost for the user. Circumstances place the railroads at a disadvantage.

The investment for equipment in rail transport, principally for locomotives and various types of rolling stock, has been enormous. In 1996, more than $6.9 billion was spent on plant and equipment.[28] The Class I railroads operated 19,269 locomotives and some 1,240,573 freight cars in 1996.[29] Other railroads, car companies, and shippers owned or leased about 500,000 cars. The costs associated with equipment are both fixed and variable depending on which costs are used and what time period is being considered.

It is apparent that the railroads have a high proportion of expenses that are fixed and constant in the short run. However, they also have costs that vary substantially with volume.

Semivariable Costs

Semivariable costs, which include maintenance of rights-of-way, structures, and equipment, have accounted for more than 40 percent of railroad outlays in recent years and have amounted to more than $10 billion per year. These figures, however, are deceptive because some railroads which were in poor financial health had allowed their physical plants and equipment to deteriorate at alarming rates. The Federal Railroad Administration estimated that the industry has deferred more than $4 billion in maintenance expenses in some years.[30] Railway management found it necessary to forego maintenance in order to pay other pressing expenses, such as increased fuel and labor. Recently, maintenance schedules have been implemented on a regular basis, so that service would not further deteriorate, and additional business would then be lost.

Variable Costs

Variable costs are one of the immediate concerns of railroad management, accounting for a large proportion of every revenue dollar spent by the railways. Labor cost is the largest single element of variable costs for railroads. Fuel and power costs are the next largest group of variable costs. Together these two categories account for a major portion of variable costs.

Labor

In 1996, the cost of labor was $10.9 billion for 33.2 cents of every revenue dollar.[31] The average hourly gross earning for all employees was $20.05 with an average annual earning of $50,611. Train and engine employees received an annual earning of $59,330, whereas maintenance workers received about $41,700. Together, these groups accounted for 76 percent of all the wages paid by the railroads.[32]

Railroad labor is represented by 14 different unions, as opposed to the trucking industry, the vast majority of whose unionized employees are members of one union, the Teamsters. There are three major classifications of labor unions: operating, non-operating craft, and non-operating industrial. Each represents a different category of employee. The large number of unions has created difficulties for railroad management because each union guards its rights. Recently, some unions have merged and have shown much more flexibility in allowing innovation.

Railroad management believes that several of the work rules for the operating unions are either out of date or inefficient. The railroad industry has been reducing the size of the standard train crew wherever possible. Many positions, such as that of fireman, a carryover from the steam engine era, are no longer needed. In addition, the dual basis for pay for a full day's work (either eight hours or 100 miles traveled) is inefficient in today's operating environment. Furthermore, "seniority districts," or the establishing of artificial boundaries beyond which an employee is not authorized to work, is another barrier to operating efficiency. Progress has been made with these issues, but they have not been completely resolved.

The railroad industry has been addressing the work rules and staffing requirements in a very aggressive manner in the past several years. Several railroads have negotiated new crew agreements that have reduced the number of personnel required for trains. Conrail started a program in 1981 to buy off unnecessary brakemen and firemen; this program eliminated more than 1,900 positions, yielding a savings of $85 million.[33]

Starting in 1982, rail management took steps to remove cabooses from railroad trains. It has been estimated that the elimination of cabooses had saved as much as $400 million per year. The rail brotherhood agreed that railroads could drop cabooses by local agreement, if possible, and by arbitration, if necessary.[34] Two-person crews are now the standard, with both riding on the locomotive.

Railroad managers feel that continuing changes in modifying or eliminating work rules for rail employees must be implemented in the near future if the industry is to survive in its present form. Mutual trust and cooperation should replace impediments between labor and management that restrict productivity gains, labor-savings methods, and technological advances. Progress in other industries has indicated the productivity gains that are possible.

Fuel

Fuel costs make up the second largest percentage of the revenue dollar. Fortunately, railroads have very efficient propulsion units, and productivity and fuel efficiency have increased dramatically since 1929. In the past 50 years, the railroads have more than doubled the revenue of ton-miles while reducing the locomotive units to less than one-half the 1929 level. Thus, the industry has been able to partially offset the increase in fuel costs by making locomotives more efficient. In 1996, only $2.4 billion was spent on fuel, showing a decrease of $0.7 billion from 1982's level of $3.1 billion. This is a result of using more fuel-efficient engines and other train devices, such as wind-resistance designs.[35] The railroad's efficiency in the use of fuel is an important factor making intermodal movements with the motor carrier more attractive.

Economies of Scale

As previously indicated, the railroads have a high level of fixed costs as contrasted with variable costs. Fixed costs, such as property taxes, are incurred regardless of traffic volume. Variable costs, on the other hand, vary or change with the volume of traffic moved; that is, they rise with increases and fall with decreases in traffic levels.

The development of any railroad requires a very large capital investment because of the cost incurred in buying land, laying tracks, building bridges, providing terminals, and providing right-of-way facilities. In addition, equipment investment is significant. Maintenance of right-of-way structures also results in fixed costs since it is usually the weather rather than use that necessitates such expenditures. The same is also true to some extent of equipment maintenance, since the equipment spends so much time in freight yards and on sidings.

All costs are generally regarded as being variable in the long run because, as traffic increases, capacity is reached and new investment is needed in plant and equipment. However, because railroads are so large and facilities are durable, the short run can be a long period of time.

Our focus here is primarily on the short run. Consequently, we should make special note of the impact of the high level of fixed costs in the railroad industry. When fixed costs are present, a business will operate under conditions of increasing returns until capacity is reached. In other words, an increase in output (traffic) will not be accompanied by a proportionate increase in total costs since only the variable costs will increase. This will mean a decline in the per-unit costs since the fixed costs will be spread out over an increased number of units with subsequent unit cost declines.

Let's consider several examples that illustrate the impact of fixed costs and economies of scale. Suppose that C. B. N. Railroad carries 200 million tons of freight at an average charge of $.035 per ton. It has fixed costs of $3.5 million and variable costs of $2.5 million:

Fixed costs	$3.5 million
Variable costs	+ $2.5 million
Total costs	*$6.0 million*
Revenue	$7.0 million
Profit	$1.0 million
Cost per ton	*$.03*

Let's assume a 20 percent increase in traffic at the same average charge of $.035 per ton and no need to increase plant size:

Fixed costs	$3.5 million
Variable costs	$3.0 million
Total costs	*$6.5 million*
Revenue	$8.4 million
Profit	$1.9 million
Cost per ton	*$.295*

It is obvious from the above example that, if average revenue stays the same, the economies of scale not only lower costs per unit but also increase profit.

Financial Plight

As was stated previously, the railroad industry once enjoyed a virtual monopoly on the efficient and dependable transportation of passengers and freight. Railroads played a very important role in achieving various national objectives during the nineteenth century. Because of this, the government promoted the growth of the industry until a distinct change in public attitudes toward railroads became apparent.

The establishment in 1887 of the ICC, which was created to regulate maximum rates and to prevent discrimination to protect the rail shipper, marked the beginning of this change. In later years, the ICC's objective was to promote competition between modes of transportation while ensuring the financial health of the regulated carriers. However, this objective was never completely accomplished.[36] Competition tended to be restrained under the regulatory environment prior to 1975.

Over the decades, competition from other modes of transportation increased dramatically. By the 1950s, more people selected buses and planes for transportation, rather than rail transportation. The rail industry's share of the intercity freight market also declined to less than 50 percent during this time period. Although competition from other modes became progressively more intense, the railroads were subject to strict regulations that frequently treated them as if they were still the dominant form of freight transportation.[37] Government funds were used to provide rail competitors with their rights-of-way without fully charging them the cost of constructing or maintaining them as with the rail industry. Between 1946 and 1975, the federal government spent more than $81 billion on highways, $24 billion on airports and supervision of airways, $10 billion on inland waterways, and only $1.3 billion on railroads.[38]

The financial position of the railroads grew increasingly worse after World War II. During the 1970s, the railroad industry's return on investment remained near two percent and never exceeded three percent. The railroads were plagued by decreasing market shares, poor future prospects, and high debt ratios. At least 20 percent of the industry was bankrupt by 1970. These poor conditions were evident in delayed or poor maintenance, increasing claims for damages, and accidents that cost the industry many of its much needed customers. The railroads' share of intercity freight revenues had fallen from 72 percent in 1929 to less than 18 percent in the mid-1970s.[39]

It became obvious that the railroad industry could not continue to survive under these conditions and that the main obstacle that needed to be cleared from the railroads' path to survival was probably excessive regulation that restricted their ability to compete. Poor earnings made it difficult for the railroads to earn or borrow sufficient funds to make improvements in track and rail facilities.[40]

Legislation Reform

The Rail Passenger Act of 1970 created the government-sponsored National Railroad Passenger Corporation (Amtrak), which relieved the railroads of their requirement to provide necessary passenger operations that were not profitable.[41] While only a few key "corridors" (the Northeast corridor, Boston, New York, and Washington, DC) were profitable enough to fully support regularly scheduled intercity passenger service, Congress still supports this service.

The **Regional Rail Reorganization Act of 1973 (3R Act)** attempted to maintain rail freight service in the Northeast by creating the Consolidated Rail Corporation (Conrail), which was formed from six bankrupt northeastern railroads. The act also created the United States Railroad Association (USRA) as the government agency responsible for planning and financing the restructuring. By 1980, the federal government had granted Conrail more than $3.3 billion in federal subsidies to cover its operating expenses.[42]

Conrail proved to be very successful and was "spun off" to the public with the sale of in 1992. Conrail's management was able to rationalize the excess track while preserving and improving service. After a failed attempt by CSX to takeover Conrail, CSX and the Norfolk Southern Railroad agreed to split Conrail between them and paid collectively over $10 billion for the property.

The **Railroad Revitalization and Regulatory Reform Act of 1976 (4R Act)** was the first attempt to deregulate the industry since the railroads had come under regulation in 1887. The goals of the 4R Act were to help the railroads obtain funds for capital investment and to allow the railroads more freedom concerning decisions on mergers, abandonments, and ratemaking.[43] Although the 4R Act was an attempt to deal with regulatory problems, the ICC's interpretation of the act negated much of its positive aspects and in some cases actually increased rail regulation.

The **Staggers Rail Act** did a great deal to enable the railroads to help themselves and avoid further deterioration of the industry, although they still face financial challenges because their return on equity is very low (about three percent) compared to many other industries. However, many railroad managers are optimistic that the industry will be able to keep its profitability and financial health if the Staggers Rail Act is not altered to introduce more regulatory control and is allowed to continue working.[44] Many railroads have continuously improved their financial situation during the 1980s.

The ICC Termination Act of 1995 eliminated the ICC and transferred economic rail regulation to the Surface Transportation Board (STB), which is part of the DOT. The STB has taken a relaxed posture on rail regulation, sometimes to the dismay of the shippers, so the railroads are now subject to market pressures more than economic regulations.

Improved Service to Customers

Since the Staggers Rail Act, the performance of the railroads has been improving in the eyes of some of its customers, and the railroads have shown a distinct increase in customer service levels. Rail freight declined by an inflation-adjusted 7.6 percent in the period 1981–1988. This decline in freight rates is evident in the two major areas of coal and grain rates. Coal rates dropped by 10 percent and grain rates dropped an inflation-adjusted 40.8 percent during this same period.

As shown in Table 4.8, **intermodal** traffic has expanded by 97 percent during the period 1981–1996, while productivity measures also have shown an increase.[45] An important indicator of improved performance is the railroads' continued good safety record. Train accidents declined by 52 percent from 1982 to 1986. Consequently, injuries and fatalities also have fallen.

A positive effect of the railroads' performance was shown in a survey of rail shippers. The survey showed that 86 percent of the shippers polled approved of government actions for allowing the railroads ratemaking freedom.[46] Many signs indicate that deregulation has brought improvement to the railroads (improved financial status) and to their customers. The industry has changed dramatically in many ways, including providing more tailored service and equipment and negotiating contract rates for volume movements. The railroads have worked hard at improving their operating performance times and reliability.

Current Issues

Alcohol and Drug Abuse

Alcohol and drug abuse has affected almost every workplace in the United States. Many industries, including the rail industry, are taking a close look at the problem and at possible methods of dealing with it.

The problem of substance abuse can be brought on by the very nature of the railroad work. Long hours, low supervision, and nights away from home can lead to loneliness and boredom, which can then lead to substance abuse. Because of this situation, the railroads have been dealing with the problem of substance abuse for a century. Rule G, which was established in 1897, prohibits the use of narcotics and alcohol on company property. Rail employees violating this rule could be subject to dismissal; however, the severity of this punishment led to the silence of many rail workers who did not want to jeopardize the jobs of their coworkers.

To deal with this problem, the railroad industry has attempted to identify and help employees with substance abuse problems. The industry has established employee assistance programs (EAPs) that enable these troubled employees to be rehabilitated.

Employees can voluntarily refer themselves to EAPs before a supervisor detects the problem and disciplinary actions become necessary. However, a Rule G violation —substance abuse while on the job—usually necessitates removal of the employee from the workplace to ensure his or her safety and the safety of coworkers. Employees who are removed can still use EAPs for rehabilitation and can apply for reinstatement after they have overcome their problem.

Railroad employee assistance programs have proven to be very effective. A recent Federal Railroad Administration report found that the rate of successful rehabilitation has risen by 70 percent. The success of these programs depends largely on support from rail workers as well as all levels of management.[47]

Energy

The energy shortages of the 1970s have made the United States increasingly more aware of the need to conserve natural resources. The U.S. government, for example, has decided to reduce the quantity of fuels and petroleum products that are imported into the country. Americans want to preserve and, wherever possible, clean up the environment. The railroads today are in a favorable position, especially when compared to motor carriers, because they are efficient energy consumers. For instance, a train locomotive uses less fuel than a tractor-trailer in pulling the same amount of weight. In fact, a study supported by the National Science Foundation indicates that railroads are more energy-efficient than any other freight mode except pipelines per ton-mile than most of the other modes, using only 670 BTUs per ton-mile (see Table 4.6).[48]

Another study by the U.S. DOT concluded that railroads are more energy-efficient than motor carriers, even when measured in terms of consumption per ton-mile.[49] In addition to being more energy-efficient, railroads cause less damage to the environment than do trucks. In 1980, railroad emissions (0.9 grams per net ton-mile)

TABLE 4.6 Relative Fuel Efficiency of Transportation Modes

Mode	Actual Btu[a] per Ton-Mile	Price (Cents per Ton-Mile)	Haul Length (Miles)	Speed (MPH)
Pipeline	490	0.27	300	5
Railroad	670	1.40	500	20
Waterway	680	0.30	1,000	—
Truck	2,800	7.50	300	40
Airplane	42,000	21.90	1,000	400

[a]Btu = British thermal units

Source: Association of American Railroads, *More Miles to the Gallon . . . The Railroads* (Washington, DC, 1974), p. 4.

TABLE 4.7 Summary: Railroad Industry Characteristics

• General service characteristics	• In competition with motor carriers; shippers of bulk products
• Investments/capital outlays	• High investments/equipment, track
• Cost structure	• High fixed costs, low variable costs
• Ease of entry	• Low
• Market structure	• Oligopoly/monopoly
• Ways in which they compete	• Price (intramodal) and service (intermodal)
• Types of commodities	• Low-value, high-volume bulk commodities
• Number of carriers	• Small number of large carriers
• Markets in which they compete	• High-value chemicals, long-haul but large commodities

were 75 percent less than truck emissions.[50] Railroads, therefore, in comparison to trucks—a major competitor—are able to move large amounts of freight with less energy and less harm to the environment.

The railroads economically shipped 5.5 million carloads of energy-yielding products in 1979; 94 percent of these loadings were coal movements. Because coal, which can be converted into electricity, is an abundant substitute for oil, electric utility companies can convert their present processes to coal whenever economically possible. Since the railroads already transport approximately three-quarters of all the coal moved, they would be able to increase service to the utilities and capture more of the market by using high-volume-unit coal trains. Hence, the railroads can be an important factor in the development of the nation's energy policy.

Technology

To become more efficient and consequently more competitive, the railroad industry is becoming a high-tech industry. Computers are playing a large role in every mode of transportation, and the railroads are no exception. A line of "smart" locomotives are being equipped with onboard computers that can identify mechanical problems, while the legendary "red caboose" was phased out by a small device weighing 30 pounds that attaches to the last car of the train. This electric device transmits important information to engineers and dispatchers alike, including information about the braking system. Other applications of computer technology are as follows:

- Advanced Train Control Systems (ATCS): A joint venture between the United States and Canada that will use computers to efficiently track the flow of trains through the entire rail system
- Railyard Control: Computer control of freight yards that is used to sort and classify as many as 2,500 railcars a day
- Communications and Signaling: Provides quick and efficient communications between dispatchers, yard workers, field workers, and train crews
- Customer Service: By calling a toll-free number, customers can receive information on the status of their shipments, correct billing errors, and plan new service schedules

The role of high technology and computers will continue to expand and increase the ability of the railroads to provide progressively higher levels of customer service.[51] Please refer to Chapter 13 "Information Management and Technology" for a further explanation of technology.

SUMMARY

- The railroads played a significant role in the economic and social development of the United States for about 100 years (1850–1950) and continue to be the leading mode of transportation in terms of intercity ton-miles, but they no longer dominate the economy.
- The railroad segment of the transportation industry is led by a decreasing number of large, Class I carriers, but the number of small (Class III) carriers has been increasing in number since the deregulation of railroads in 1980.
- Intermodal competition for railroads has increased dramatically since World War II, but the level of intramodal competition has decreased as the number of Class I railroads has decreased. The increased intermodal competition has led to more rate competition.
- Mergers have been occurring among railroads for many years, but the pace has accelerated during the last 30 years leading to rapid decrease in the number of Class I railroads.
- In recent years, the railroads have become more specialized in terms of the traffic they carry, with the emphasis being on low-value, high-density, bulk products, but there is some evidence of a resurgence of selected manufactured products such as transportation equipment.
- In recent years, railroads have been emphasizing new technologies and specialized equipment to improve their service performance and satisfy customers.
- Intermodal service (TOFC/COFC) has received renewed interest since 1980 and there has been a dramatic growth in the movement of such traffic by railroads. Long-distance truckload carriers and other motor-carrier companies such as UPS have also begun to use rail intermodal service.
- The railroads have a high level or proportion of fixed costs since they provide their own right-of-way and terminal facilities. Since the large railroads are multistate operators, the amount of fixed expenditures is significant.
- The cost of labor is the single most important component of variable costs for railroads, but the railroad industry has been striving to reduce labor costs on a relative basis by eliminating work rules that were a carryover from another era.

- The high level of fixed costs helps give rise to economies of scale in the railroad industry, which can have a dramatic impact upon profits when the volume of traffic increases.
- The financial plight of the railroads has improved since the deregulation in 1980 as railroads have been able to respond more quickly and aggressively to market pressures from other modes, particularly motor carriers.
- A number of important issues are facing railroads at present, including substance abuse, energy, and technology.

Key Terms

carloads pg. 130
Container-On-Flatcar (COFC) 130
end-to-end mergers 126
intermodal traffic 140
liability 130
Railroad Revitalization and Regulatory Reform Act of 1976 (4R Act) 140
Regional Rail Reorganization Act of 1973 (3R Act) 140
return on investment (ROI) 123
right-of-way 136
side-by-side mergers 126
Trainer-on-flatcar (TOFC) 130
types of mergers 126
unit train 135

Study Questions

1. After almost a century of dominating domestic transportation, what factors have led to the decline in the dominant position of the railroads? Are there any indicators of a resurgence of interest in railroads? Why?

2. The railroad industry has been referred to as an *oligopoly*. Has this situation changed since the Staggers Rail Act of 1980? Why or why not? What factors have led to the growth in the number of Class III railroads?

3. What is the nature of the competition faced by railroads on both an intramodal and intermodal basis?

4. What factors have contributed to the merger in the railroad industry? Is the merger movement over?

5. What is the nature of the traffic hauled by railroads? Has this changed over the years? Why?

6. If you were responsible for selling rail service to a prospective customer, what service characteristics would you emphasize?

7. What changes have occurred in railroad equipment in recent years?

8. What has been the impact of the Staggers Rail Act upon the railroads?

9. What is the nature of the railroad cost structure? Why is it so different from motor carriers?

10. What special challenges have railroads faced with labor? Has this situation been changing? How?

NOTES

1. *Transportation in America,* 16th ed. (Washington D.C.: Eno Transportation Foundation, 1998), p. 44.
2. Association of American Railroads, *Railroad Facts,* 1997, p. 5.
3. *Transportation in America,* p. 5.
4. Ibid., p. 61.
5. Ibid., pp. 8–9.
6. Ibid., p. 44.
7. Association of American Railroads, *Railroad Facts* (Washington, DC: Association of American Railroads, 1997), p. 3.
8. U.S. Department of Commerce, *Bureau of the Census, Historical Statistics of the United States: Colonial Times to 1975.* (Washington, DC: U.S. Government Printing Office, 1960), p. 429.
9. Association of American Railroads, *Railroad Facts* (1997), p. 44.
10. *Trains* (August 1996), p. 14.
11. The National Commission of Productivity, *Improving Railroad Productivity,* p. 161.
12. The commodity groups included here are metals and metal products; food and kindred products; stone, clay, and glass products; and grainmill products.
13. Association of American Railroads, *Railroad Facts* (1997), p. 5.
14. Reebie Associates, *The Railroad Situation: A Perspective on the Past, Present, and Future of the Railroad Industry* (Washington, DC: U.S. Department of Transportation, March 1979), p. 687.
15. Association of American Railroads, *Railroad Facts* (1997), p. 29.
16. Ibid., p. 29.
17. Roth, Donald D., *An Approach to Measurement of Modal Advantage* (Washington, DC: American Trucking Association, 1977), p. 11.
18. Judge, Tom, ed., "Shake, Rattle & Roll," *Progressive Railroading,* Vol. 39 (October 1996), pp. 30–32.
19. Association of American Railroads, *Railroad Facts* (1997), p. 24.
20. Ibid., p. 52.
21. Ibid., p. 51.
22. Ibid., p. 37.
23. Association of American Railroads, *Railroad Facts* (1991), p. 39.
24. Association of American Railroads, press release (Washington, DC: 1979), p. 342.
25. Fixed costs remain the same over a period of time or a range of output (such as labor costs). Semivariable costs contain some fixed variable elements (such as setup costs on a production line).
26. R. J. Sampson and M. I. Farris, *Domestic Transportation: Practice, Theory, and Policy,* 4th ed. (Boston: Houghton Mifflin, 1979), p. 59.
27. Association of American Railroads, *Railroad Facts* (1997), p. 9.
28. Ibid., p. 15.
29. Ibid., p. 48.
30. U.S. Department of Transportation, *A Prospectus for Change in the Freight Railroad Industry* (Washington, DC: U.S. Government Printing Office, 1978), p. 65.
31. Association of American Railroads, *Railroad Facts* (1997), p. 11.
32. Ibid., p. 56.
33. Frank Wilner, *Railroads and the Marketplace* (Washington, DC: Association of American Railroads, 1988), p. 7.
34. Ibid., p. 2.
35. Association of American Railroads, *Railroad Facts* (1997), p. 60.
36. Association of American Railroads, *Railroad Facts* (1988), p. 11.
37. Ibid., p. 9.
38. Frank Wilner, *Railroads and the Marketplace* (Washington, DC: Association of American Railroads, 1988), p. 7.
39. Ibid., p. 9.
40. Ibid., pp. 8–12.
41. Ibid., p. 2.
42. Consolidated Rail Corporation, *Summary of Business Plan* (Philadelphia: Consolidated Rail Corporation, 1979), p. 5.
43. Wilner, op cit., p. 15.
44. Ibid.
45. Association of American Railroads, *Railroad Facts* 1997), p. 26.
46. Association of American Railroads, *Railroad Facts* (1992), p. 3.
47. Association of American Railroads, *"What are the Railroads Doing About Drug Abuse?"* (Washington, DC: 1986), pp. 1–4.
48. Consolidated Rail Corporation, *Summary of Business Plan* (Philadelphia: Consolidated Rail Corporation, 1979), p. 5.
49. Wilner, op cit., p. 15.
50. Ibid.
51. American Association of Railroads, *High Technology Rides the Rails* (Washington, DC: American Association of Railroads, 1988), pp. 1–3.

Suggested Readings

"A Guide to Buying Rail Freight Services," *Traffic Management,* Vol. 31, No. 5, May 1992, pp. 49–52.

Armstrong, John H. "High Productivity Trains: How Integral? How Imminent?", *Railway Age,* Vol. 188, No. 9, September 1987, pp. 43–51.

Beier, Frederick J. "Cost of Locating On-Rail: Perceptions of Shippers and Practices of Carriers," *Transportation Journal,* Fall 1977, pp. 22–32.

Bierlein, Lawrence W. "Increasing Complexity in the Regulation of Hazardous Materials Transportation," *Transportation Practitioners Journal,* Vol. 54, No. 1, Fall 1986, pp. 68–77.

Bookbinder, James H., and Noreen A. Sereda. "A DRP-Approach to the Management of Rail Car Inventories," *The Logistics and Transportation Review,* August 1987, pp. 265–280.

Borts, George H. "Long-Term Rail Contracts—Handle with Care," *Transportation Journal,* Vol. 25., No. 3, Spring 1986, pp. 4–11.

Callari, James J. "Return of the RoadRailer," *Traffic Management,* Vol. 26, No. 9, September 1987, pp. 81–85.

Cross, James, and Frederick J. Beier. "Market Planning: Status and Need in Small and Medium Class I Motor Carriers," *Transportation Journal,* Vol. 25, No. 3, Spring 1986, pp. 12–19.

Crum, Michael R. "Public Interest Measures for Railroad Merger Evaluation," *Transportation Practitioners Journal,* Vol. 54, No. 1, Fall 1986, pp. 6–12.

Detmold, Peter J. "The Procurement of a More Efficient Railroad System," *Transportation Journal,* Winter 1986, pp. 4–11.

DeWitt, William J. "Railroads' Response to Marketing in a Deregulated Environment/Logistics: Transportation by Design." *Annual Conference Proceedings,* Vol. 11, September 27–30, 1987, Atlanta, GA (Oak Brook, IL: Council of Logistics Management), pp. 389–400.

Ditmeyer, Steven. "Deregulation and Technological Progress in Railroading: Some Reflections from the Perspective of a Particular Carrier," *Transportation Journal,* Vol. 27, No. 1, Fall 1987, pp. 5–9.

Feigenbaum, Armand F. "The Making of a World Class: Class I Railroad." *Railway Age,* Vol. 193, No. 2, February 1992, pp. 20–21, 86, 194.

Finerty, Peter J. "Current Maritime Issues: A Carrier's Viewpoint," *Annual Conference Proceedings,* Vol. I, September 27–30, 1987. Atlanta, GA (Oak Brook, IL: Council of Logistics Management), pp. 389–398.

Gellman, Aaron J. "Barriers to Innovation in the Railroad Industry," *Transportation Journal,* Vol. 25, No. 4, Summer 1986, pp. 4–11.

Gittings, Gary, and Evelyn Thomchick. "Some Logistics Implications of Rail Line Abandonment," *Transportation Journal,* Vol. 26, No. 4, Summer 1987, pp. 16–25.

Gordon, Jay. "Railroads Weather the Recession Well," *Distribution,* Vol. 91, No. 9, July 1992, pp. 40–43.

Holtman, William. "Staggers Act: History Pre-Post," *Annual Conference Proceedings,* Vol. II, September 27–30, 1987, Atlanta, GA (Oak Brook, IL: Council of Logistics Management).

Lemay, Stephen A. "Strategic Information Systems in LTL Carriers of General Commodities," *Transportation Journal,* Vol. 25, No. 3, September 1986, pp. 25–32.

"Managing for Profit: BN's Aim is 'Precision Execution'," *Railway Age,* Vol. 193, No. 7, July 1992, pp. 31–34.

Mentzer, Marc S. "Executive Career Paths in the Railroad Industry," *Transportation Journal,* Vol. 27, No. 2, Winter 1997, pp. 35–40.

Murphy, Paul R., and James M. Daly. "Customer Satisfaction in International Distribution: Do Water Ports Know What Shippers Really Want?", *Journal of Transportation Management,* Vol. 4, No. 1, Spring 1992, pp. 25–46.

Rockey, Crain F. "The Formation of Regional Railroads in the United States." *Transportation Journal,* Vol. 27, No. 2, Winter 1987, pp. 5–13.

Sipe, Samuel M., Jr. "Section 214 of the Staggers Act and the Preemption of State Regulation of Intrastate Rail Transportation." *Transportation Practitioners Journal,* Vol. 35, No. 3, Spring 1986, pp. 279–297.

Stasser, Sandra. "The Effect of Railroad Scheduling on Shipper Modal Selection: A Simulation." *Journal of Business Logistics,* Vol. 13, No. 2, 1992, pp. 175–198.

Tye, William B. "Preserving Postmerger Rail Competition via the Parity Principle," *Transportation Journal,* Winter 1986, pp. 39–54.

"Union Pacific: The Story Behind the Statistics," *Railway Age,* Vol. 193, No. 12, December 1992, pp. 19–23.

Weltey, Gus. "Rolling Stock for the 90s," *Railway Age,* Vol. 193, No. 9, September 1992, pp. 49–53.

Wilner, Frank N. "The Railway Labor Act: Why, What, and for How Much Longer—," *Transportation Practitioners Journal,* Vol. 55, No. 3, Spring 1988, pp. 242–287.

Wood, D. F., and J. C. Johnson. *Contemporary Transportation,* Tulsa, OK: Petroleum Publishing Company, 1980, Chapter 5.

Wyckoff, D. Daryl. *Railroad Management* (Boston, Lexington Books, 1976).

CASE

CASE 4.1
CBN Railway Company

CEO John Spychalski is concerned about a problem that has existed at CBN railroad for almost 20 years now. The continuous problem has been that the locomotives used by the company are not very reliable. Even with prior decisions to resolve the problem, there still has not been a change in the reliability of these locomotives. Between 1995 and 1997, 155 new locomotives were purchased and one of CBN's repair shops was renovated. The renovated shop has been very inefficient. Spychalski estimated that the shop would complete 300 overhauls on a yearly basis but instead it has only managed to complete an average of 160 overhauls per year.

The company has also been doing poorly servicing customers, i.e., providing equipment. CBN has averaged only 87 to 88 percent equipment availability compared to other railroads with availability figures greater than 90 percent. Increased business in the rail industry has been a reason for trying to reduce the time used for repairing the locomotives. CBN's mean time between failure rate is low, 45 days, compared to other railroads whose mean time between failure rates is higher than 75 days. This factor, Spychalski feels, has contributed to CBN's poor service record.

CBN is considering a new approach to the equipment problem: Spychalski is examining the possibility of leasing 135 locomotives from several sources. The leases would run between 90 days to five years. In addition, the equipment sources would maintain the repairs on 469 locomotives currently in CBN's fleet, but CBN's employees would do the actual labor on the locomotives. The lease arrangements, known as "power-by-the-mile" arrangements, call for the manufacturers doing the repair work to charge only for maintenance on the actual number of miles that a particular unit operates. The company expects the agreements to last an average of 15 years. John Thomchick, Executive Vice President, estimates that CBN would save about $5 million annually since the company will not have to pay for certain parts and materials. Problems with the locomotives exist throughout CBN's whole system, and delays to customers have been known to last up to five days. Spychalski and Thomchick feel that the leasing arrangement will solve CBN's problems.

Case Questions

1. What are potential advantages and disadvantages of entering into these "power-by-the-mile" arrangements?

2. What should be done if the problem with the locomotives continues even with the agreements?

3. Do you think that the decision to lease the locomotives was the best decision for CBN? Explain your answer.

CHAPTER 5

DOMESTIC WATER CARRIERS

Brief History

Ever since humankind discovered the buoyancy of water, the waterways have provided a vital transportation link for moving goods and people. Waterways are highways provided by nature; nature even provides the power currents to propel water vehicles. Although this **natural highway** and motive power have been improved upon by technological advancements in construction and engines, water transportation is still thought of by many individuals as a form of transportation provided by nature.

Water transportation played an **important role** in the development of the United States, providing the early settlers with a link to markets in England and Europe. In addition, many of our major cities developed around waterpower along the coasts. As the internal portions of the country developed, water transportation from the inland ports and the Great Lakes linked the settlements in the wilderness with the coastal cities. This natural highway, or waterway, was the only viable form of economical transportation available and was a prime determinant of population centers, as well as industrial and commercial concentration at port cities. Early private and public sector construction projects in transportation were the Erie, C&O and other canals to offer inexpensive water transportation.

This chapter focuses on the basic economic and operating characteristics of domestic water transportation. An overview of the industry is given first, followed by a consideration of types of carriers, market structure, operating and service characteristics, equipment cost structure, and current issues.

Industry Overview

This chapter focuses on domestic water transportation, which consists of all water movements where the origin and destination of the shipment is the United States. Shipments that have a foreign country as either the origin or destination are classified as international shipping and are not included in this discussion but will be covered in Chapter 10 "Private Transportation".

Significance of Water Transport

Today water transportation remains a viable mode of transportation for the movement of products and especially basic raw materials. Domestic water transportation competes vigorously with railroads for the movement of bulk **commodities** (such as grains, coal, ores, and chemicals) and with pipelines for the movement of bulk petroleum and petroleum products. In 1997, water carriers transported 508 billion ton-miles of intercity freight (using internal waterways and the Great Lakes), or 14 percent of the total national freight transported.[1]

There are more than 6,200 tugs and towboats with more than 31,000 barges which have a combined capacity of 89 million tons. The inland waterway system employs more than 30,000 persons and moves almost 800 million tons of freight annually.[2]

The addition of domestic deep-sea service to the above intercity freight tonnage shows that water carriers transported 26.5 percent of the total domestic ton-miles of freight in 1996 (948 billion out of a total 3,563 billion, including coastal traffic) at a cost of $7.7 billion to shippers.[3] To perform this level of service, water carrier owners **employed** 182,000 people at an average compensation, including fringes, of $44,605.[4] The next section will focus on the different types of carriers involved in domestic water transportation.

STOP OFF

Ocean Carriers Sail the Electronic Sea

The maritime industry has long been a user of electronic commerce. Information about a large number of the transactions in the U.S. maritime trades between shippers and carriers, as well as between ocean carriers and other modes of transport in intermodal transport movements, is communicated electronically. The data contained in bills of lading, dock receipts, certificates of insurance, and the carrier's manifest, as well as a host of other documents, are generated and transmitted electronically in an internationally agreed format.

International ocean liner carriers, both U.S. and foreign, as well as ocean freight rate conferences, are required to file their tariffs (rates charged their customers) with the Federal Maritime Commission, the agency of the U.S. government that regulates maritime transportation. The carriers and conferences also provide these rates to freight forwarders for their use in electronically booking cargo for their customers. The information System Agreement, a group of 11 shipping lines, recently put its members' shipping schedules on the World Wide Web (http://www.isaweb.com/isa).

Ocean carriers also file their manifests (a list of cargo on the vessel) with U.S. and other customs authorities electronically to expedite customs procedures at ports moving their cargo onward in a more efficient manner to its final destination. This is particularly important for intermodal movements and just-in-time deliveries.

Carriers track cargo through computer coding on containers. The customers with access to this system or the ocean carriers using it can inform shippers of the location of the cargo at any time and provide arrival times.

The next big step in the development of electronic commerce for the industry will be shipping contracts signed and transmitted electronically. Both shippers and carriers can incur substantial costs when the paper trail becomes congested. The use of electronic signatures for bills of lading and other documents can unclog the paper trail at every turn. Some carriers now have the electronic means to allow shippers to set up nonnegotiable bills of lading and charter party documents.

Electronic negotiable bills of lading, in addition to speeding the data movement process, could solve the problem of the ship arriving in port before the paperwork needed to release a cargo to the consignee. In the maritime industry, negotiable bills of lading provide evidence of ownership of the cargo. If the carrier turns the cargo over to someone without the original bill of lading, the carrier faces the risk of the actual holder appearing later to claim the cargo and liability for the loss of that cargo. A way is needed to verify that the electronic signature is valid.

The worldwide shipping community is working to achieve this objective. The European community, through a project known as Bolero, is seeking to establish a central clearinghouse where electronic trade documents, including negotiable bills of lading, would be registered and secured by digital signatures.

Source: Johnson, C. William. Maritime transportation: Ocean carriers sail the electronic sea. *Business America*. Vol. 119n1. Jan. 1998, p.37.

Types of Carriers

An overview of the domestic water carrier industry is given in Figure 5.1. Like motor carriers, the first major classification of the domestic water carrier industry is between for-hire and private carriers. A **private carrier** cannot be hired and only transports freight for the company that owns or leases the vessel. Private water carriers are permitted to transport, for a fee, exempt commodities; when they are hauling such exempt goods, they are technically exempt for-hire carriers. Bona fide private water carriers (transporting company-owned freight and exempt commodities) are excluded from federal economic regulation as are water shipments of three or less commodities within the same barge unit.

The **for-hire** water **carriers** consist of regulated and exempt carriers that charge a fee for their services. Exempt carriers are excluded from the federal economic reg-

FIGURE 5.1 Overview of Domestic Water Carrier Industry

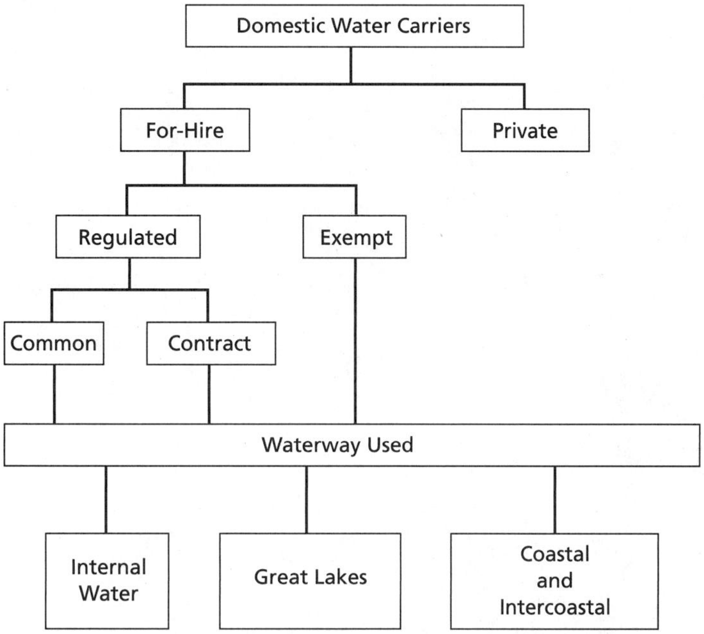

ulations administered by the Surface Transportation Board (STB). When authority was transferred to the STB under the ICC Termination Act of 1995, the STB's authority was expanded over domestic water traffic. In addition to inland river traffic, the STB has jurisdiction over port-to-port traffic when both ports are in the United States as well as transportation between the U.S. and its territories. Water carriers are exempt from economic regulation when transporting bulk commodities, both dry and liquid. Because the majority of freight transported by domestic water carriers consists of bulk commodities, exempt carriers dominate the for-hire segment of the industry.

Regulated water **carriers** are classified as either common or contract carriers. Economic regulation, similar to that controlling motor carriers (operating certificates, rates, etc.), is administered by the STB. (The Federal Maritime Commission administers federal economic controls over international water carriers.) Although the majority of water traffic is exempt from regulation, a small number of regulated common and contract carriers do exist. In 1993, fewer than 300 water carriers were regulated.

The domestic water carrier industry is most commonly classified by waterway used. Carriers that operate over the internal navigable waterways are classified as **internal** water **carriers**. Internal water carriers use barges and towboats and operate over the principal U.S. rivers—Mississippi, Ohio, Tennessee, Columbia, and Hudson—plus smaller arteries (see Figure 5.2). Internal water carriers dominate the north-south traffic through the central portion of the United States via the Mississippi, Missouri, and Ohio rivers.

The Great Lakes carriers operate along the northeastern portion of the United States and provide service between ports on the five Great Lakes (see Figure 5.3)

FIGURE 5.2 Waterways of the United States

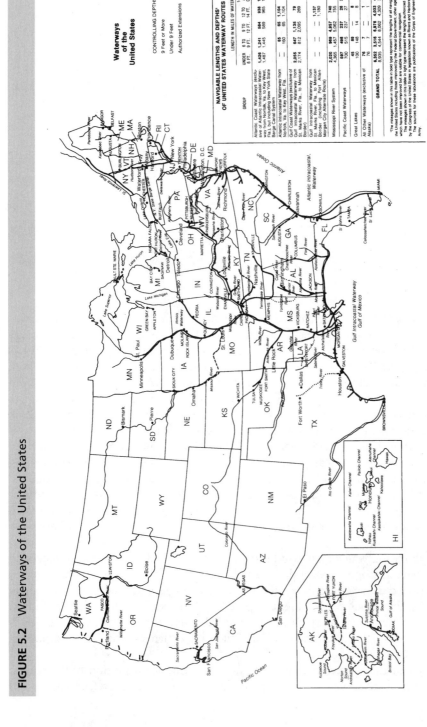

NAVIGABLE LENGTHS AND DEPTHS[1] OF UNITED STATES WATERWAY ROUTES

GROUP	LENGTH IN MILES OF WATERWAYS: UNDER 6 FT.	6 TO 9 FT.	9 TO 12 FT.	12 TO 14 FT.	14 FT. AND OVER	TOTAL
Atlantic Coast Waterways (exclusive of Atlantic Intracoastal Waterway from Norfolk, Va. to Key West, Fla.), but including New York State Barge Canal System	**1,426** 1,487	**1,241** 1,445	**584** 589	**938** 965	**1,581** 1,544	**5,768** 6,030
Atlantic Intracoastal Waterway from Norfolk, Va. to Key West, Fla.	— —	**65** 160	**65** 65	**1,104** 1,104	— —	**1,234** 1,329
Gulf Coast Waterways (exclusive of Gulf Intracoastal Waterway from St. Marks River, Fla., to Mexican Border)	**2,055** 2,174	**647** 812	**1,135** 2,095	**79** 269	**378** 388	**4,292** 5,738
Gulf Intracoastal Waterway from St. Marks River, Fla., to Mexican Border (including Port Allen-Morgan City Alternate Route)	— —	— —	— —	**1,137** 1,180	— —	**1,137** 1,180
Mississippi River System	**2,020** 4,365	**969** 1,457	**4,957** 5,062	**740** 755	**268** 268	**8,954** 11,907
Pacific Coast Waterways	**597** 700	**498** 515	**237** 237	**26** 27	**2,387** 825	**3,825** 2,554
Great Lakes	**45** 100	**89** 148	— 14	**8** 8	**348** 369	**490** 639
All Other Waterways (exclusive of Alaska)	**76** 76	**7** 7	— —	**1** 1	**7** 7	**91** 91
GRAND TOTAL	**6,352** 8,935	**3,516** 4,544	**6,976** 8,062	**4,033** 4,309	**4,666** 3,368	**25,543** 29,218

[1]The mileages shown in this table in bold type represent the lengths of all navigable channels of the United States including those improved by the Federal Government, other agencies, and those which have not been improved but are usable for commercial navigation.

The mileages shown in this table in light type represent the lengths authorized for improvement by the Congress of the United States in legislation known as Rivers and Harbors Acts.

The sources for these tabulations are publications of the Corps of Engineers, United States Army.

Source: The American Waterways Operators, Inc.

FIGURE 5.3 St. Lawrence–Great Lakes Waterway

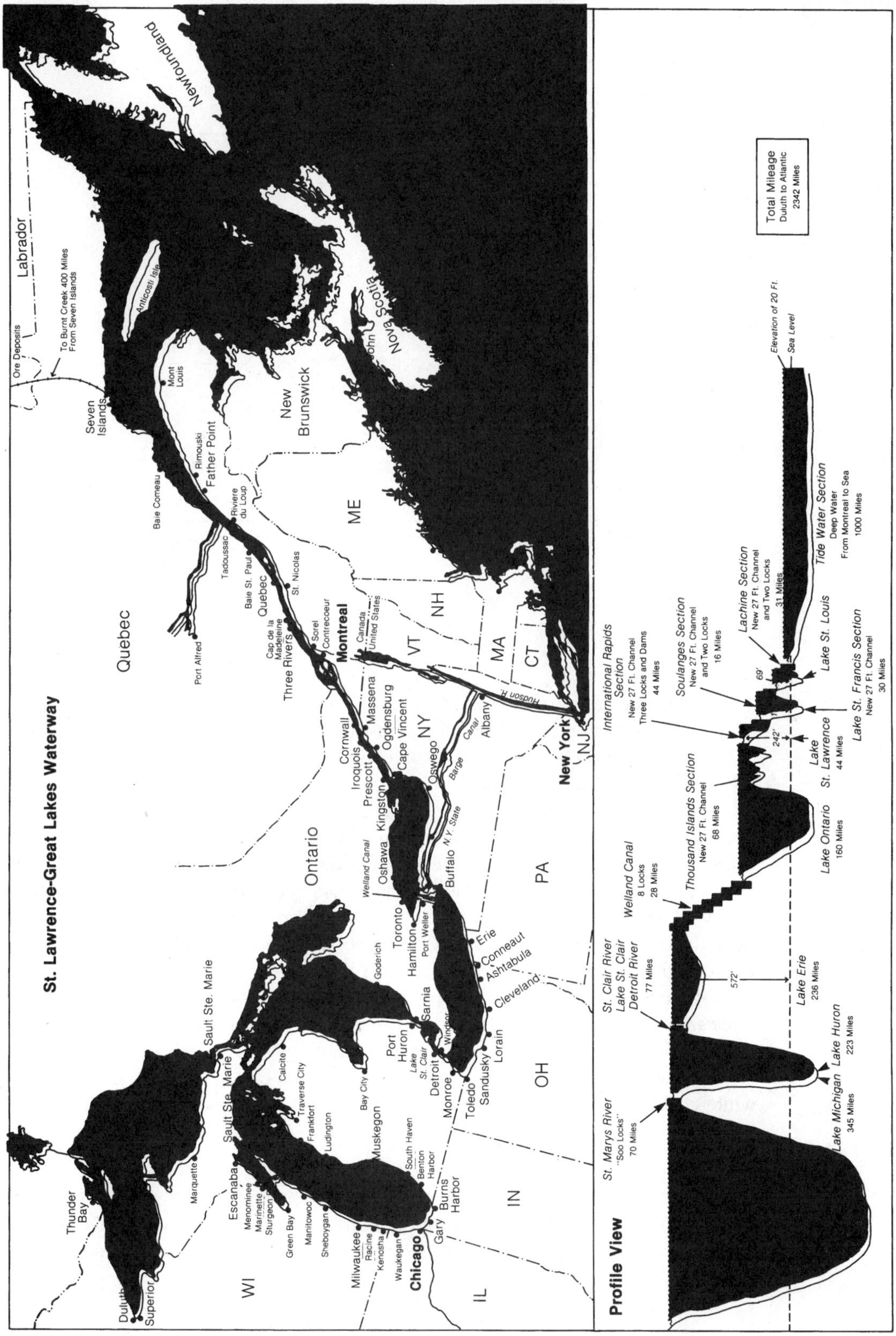

Source: The American Waterways Operators, Inc.

FIGURE 5.4 Distribution of Ton-Miles by Type of Waterway Used

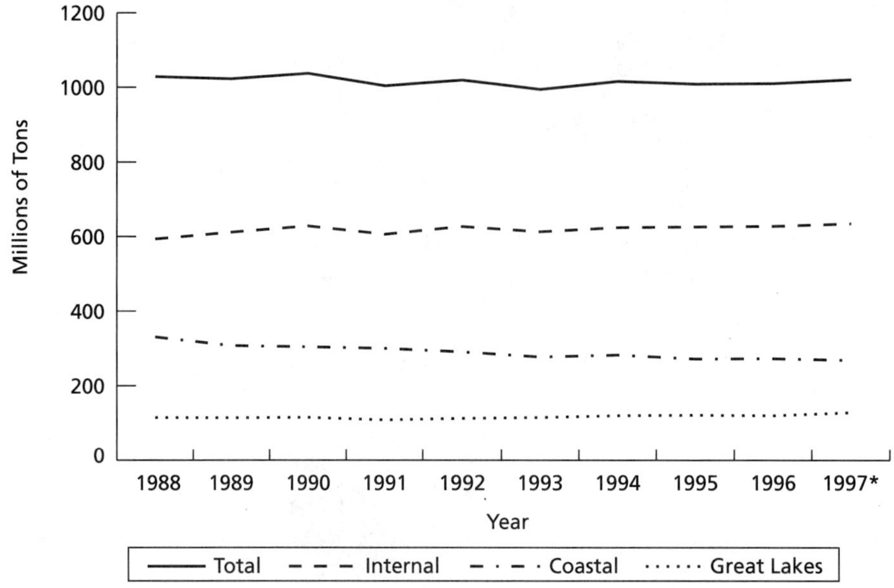

*Preliminary June 19, 1998

that border the states of New York, Pennsylvania, Ohio, Michigan, Indiana, Illinois, Wisconsin, and Minnesota. The lake ships normally remain on the lakes, but access to the Atlantic and Gulf ports is possible via the Saint Lawrence Seaway. This Great Lakes-to-Atlantic traffic is classified as a coastal operation.

Coastal carriers operate along the coasts serving ports on the Atlantic or Pacific oceans or the Gulf of Mexico. Intercoastal carriers transport freight between East Coast and West Coast ports via the Panama Canal. Coastal and intercoastal carriers use oceangoing vessels, but some operators use ocean-going barges (18,000-ton capacity). Currently, large quantities of petroleum, crude and refined, are moved between points on the Atlantic and Gulf of Mexico. Likewise, oil from Alaska moves via coastal carriers to refineries along the Pacific coast.

Figure 5.4 shows the relative distribution of the ton-miles hauled for each of the three major types of waterways used. Figure 5.5 shows a distribution of the domestic ton-miles by type of service and type of traffic.

Petroleum and related products account for about 32 percent of water traffic while coal is second in volume with 26 percent of water borne commerce.[5]

Market Structure

This section presents a discussion of the number and type of categories of domestic water carriers and an overview of the competitive marketplace for domestic water carriers.

FIGURE 5.5 Distribution of Domestic Ton-Miles by Type of Service and Types of Traffic Exempt, For-Hire

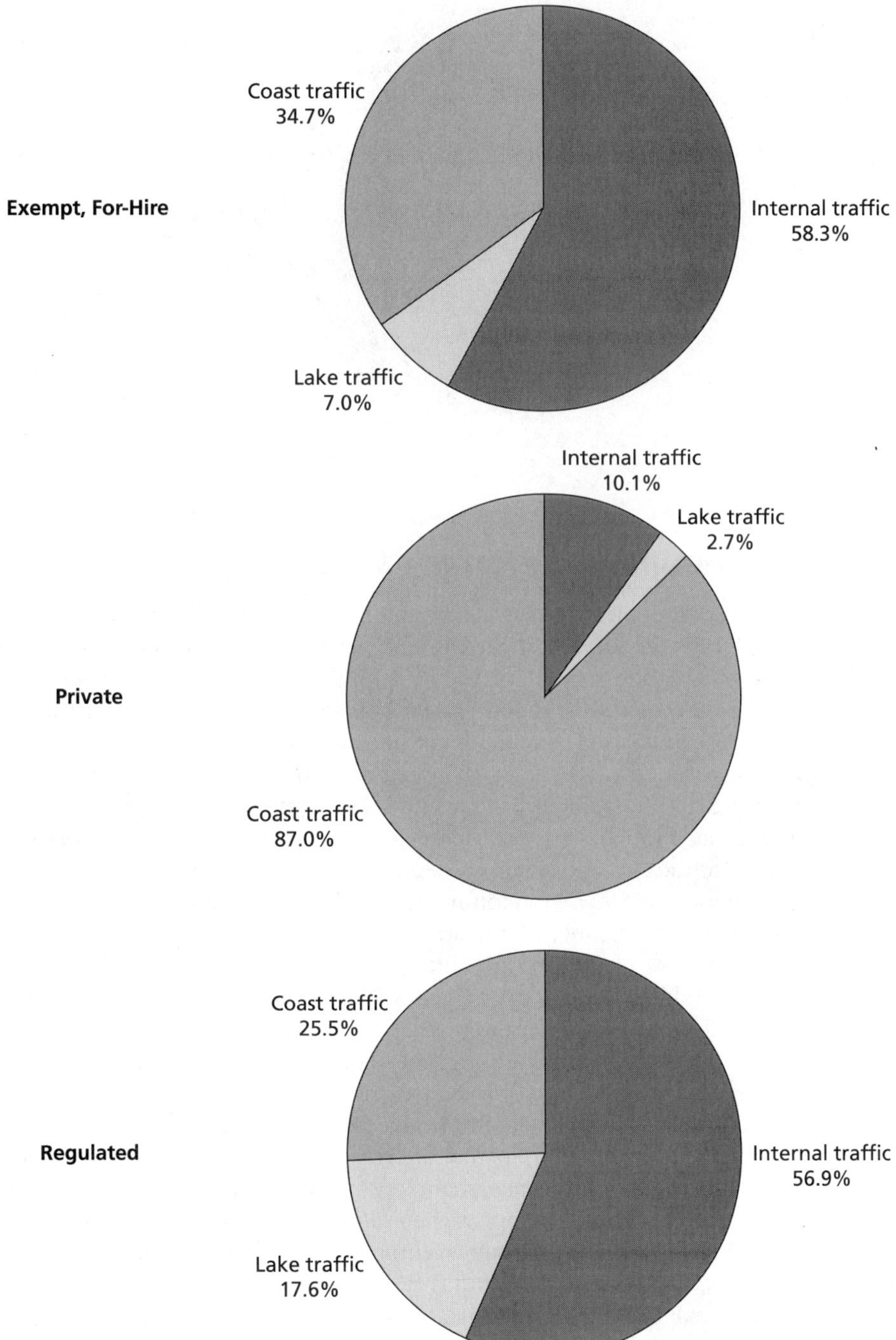

FIGURE 5.6 Domestic Ton-Miles by Type of Service

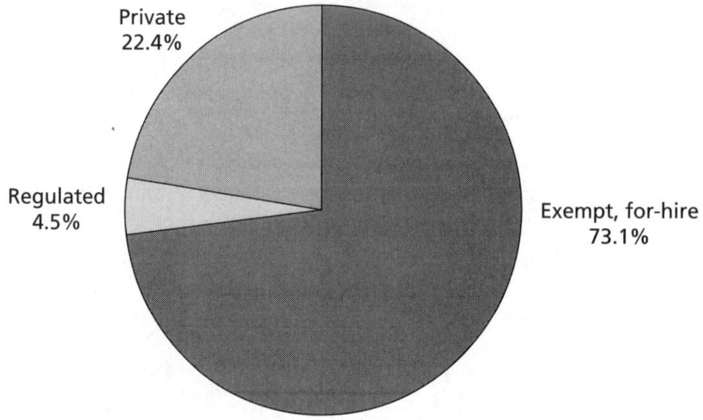

Number and Categories of Carriers

The regulated domestic water carrier industry consists of a limited number of small firms. In 1990, about 180 water carriers were subject to STB regulation. Out of this total, 100 earned less than $100,000 in annual gross operating revenues.

According to an ICC report on the operation of 135 inland (internal) and coastal carriers, 67 carriers earned more than $100,000 per year and had an average 1978 gross operating revenue of $8,110,000 from regulated freight.[6] For the 68 carriers that earned less than $100,000 per year, the average 1978 gross operating revenue was $78,700 from regulated freight. The conclusion to be drawn is that the regulated water carriers reporting to the ICC are small businesses. In 1988, regulated carriers transported only 4.5 percent of the 890 billion ton-miles of waterborne traffic, whereas exempt carriers transported 73.1 percent and private carriers handled 22.4 percent (see Figure 5.6).[7]

The number of carriers operating on the Great Lakes and the Mississippi River is given in Table 5.1. Only 5.8 percent of the Great Lakes carriers and 3.5 percent of the Mississippi River carriers are regulated (common or contract carriers) by the ICC. The majority of the carriers are exempt—66.7 percent of the Great Lakes carriers and 70.7 percent of the Mississippi River carriers. Private water carriers account for approximately one-fourth of the total carriers.

The percentage of carriers that are regulated, exempt, and private closely parallels the percentage of ton-miles handled by each type of carrier as indicated above (see Figure 5.4). Thus, exempt carriers dominate the domestic inland water carrier industry. The dominance of the exempt water carriers has been a tradition in this segment of the transportation industry because of the importance of large shippers who can qualify for exempt status.

Competition

Water carriers vigorously compete for traffic with other **modes** and, to a limited degree, with other water carriers. The rather small number of water carriers (see Table 5.1) elicits a limited degree of competition among water carriers. Because the num-

TABLE 5.1 Number of Water Carriers Operating on the Great Lakes and the Mississippi River

Carriers	Number	Percent
Great Lakes		
Regulated	7	5.8
Exempt	80	66.7
Private	33	27.5
Total	120	100.0
Mississippi River and Gulf Intracoastal (1975)		
Regulated	33	3.5
Exempt	662	70.7
Private	241	25.8
Total	936	100.0

Source: U.S. Army Corps of Engineers, *Transportation Lines on the Great Lakes Systems,* 1980 and *Transportation Lines on the Mississippi River System and Gulf Intercoastal Waterway,* 1975 (Washington, D.C.: U.S. Government Printing Office, 1978).

ber of carriers on a given waterway is limited, there is little incentive for the water carriers to compete with one another as long as local traffic volume is sufficient for all who are capable of transporting a particular cargo.

The major water carrier competition is with two other modes, those being **rail** and **pipelines.** Water carriers compete with railroads for the movement of dry bulk commodities such as grain, coal, and ores. The movement of grains from the Midwest to New Orleans (export traffic) is possible by rail as well as by water carrier. The water carriers can use the Mississippi and Missouri river systems to connect the plain states with New Orleans. Both modes move sizable amounts of grain along this traffic corridor.

Rail and water carriers compete heavily to move coal out of the coal-producing states of Pennsylvania, West Virginia, and Kentucky. The water carriers are capable of transporting coal via the Ohio and Mississippi rivers to southern domestic consuming points (utilities) as well as to export markets.

On the **Great Lakes,** water carriers compete with railroads for the movement of coal, ores, and grain. Iron ore and grain originating in Minnesota, Michigan, and Wisconsin are moved across the Great Lakes to other Great Lakes ports, or out of the Great Lakes region via the Saint Lawrence Seaway to Atlantic and Gulf ports or to export markets.

The Port of **Toledo** has become an interchange point between rail and water carriers for the transport of coal. Railroads haul coal out of the coal-producing states to Toledo, where the coal is loaded onto laker ships for movement to northern Great Lakes ports. In essence, the railroads have overcome the water carrier accessibility problem by moving coal from the mines to Toledo, which suggests that the modes are partners rather than competitors. Because the cost of the water-rail combination is lower than the all-rail route, shippers continue to request the combined water-rail service.

Water carriers and pipelines are vigorous competitors for the movement of bulk liquids (petroleum and petroleum products). As indicated in Figure 5.7, bulk liquids (petroleum, petroleum products, and chemicals) account for about 32.8 percent of the total tonnage transported by domestic water carriers. Bulk liquids are important commodities to both modes, and rigorous competition exists for moving bulk liquids along the Gulf, Atlantic, and Pacific coasts, as well as the Mississippi River system.

To a very limited degree, water carriers compete with trucks. In most cases, trucks are used to overcome the accessibility constraints of water carriers because trucks tie inland areas to the waterways for pickup and/or delivery. Shipment quantities argue against motor carriers since one barge can transport the equivalent of 58 tractor trailers.

Operating and Service Characteristics

Commodities Hauled

As indicated in Figure 5.7, petroleum and petroleum products accounted for 24.4 percent (151.8 million tons) of the total tonnage of domestic water commerce in 1996. Chemicals accounted for 8.4 percent of the total tonnage and, when combined with petroleum and petroleum products, represent the largest type (liquid) of traffic.

The **dry bulk** commodities transported by water carriers are basic raw materials, such as coal and coke (176.3 million tons). Bulk, basic raw materials account for 28.3 percent of the total tonnage transported by water carriers.[8] The "other" commodities transported, 123.4 million tons, include such items as waste and scrap, water, pulp and paper products, and motor vehicles, as well as non-metallic products and lumber. Figure 5.7 shows the relative distribution of the commodities hauled. Dry bulk products provide a wider variety of traffic for water carriers than **liquid products**.

High-value manufactured **products,** such as electrical equipment and photographic instruments, account for a small portion of the total tonnage transported by

FIGURE 5.7 Distribution of Commodities Hauled by Domestic Water Carriers

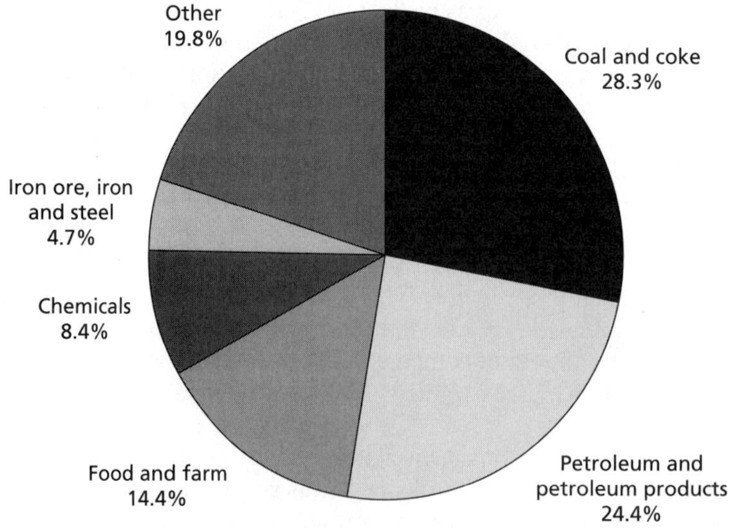

Source: Waterborne Commerce in the U.S., 1988.

domestic water carriers. The conclusion that can be drawn from Figure 5.7 is that domestic water carriers transport primarily basic raw materials in bulk form (liquid and dry). International carriers have a greater opportunity to compete for high-value, manufactured products because the alternative modes of transportation are much more limited.

Length of Haul

The average length of **haul** via water carriage varies by type of carrier. In 1994, the average length of haul was 482 miles for internal carriers, 508 miles for Great Lakes carriers and 1,652 miles for coastal and intercoastal carriers.[9] The railroad average length of haul is greater than that of internal and Great Lakes water carriers, but the water carrier shipping distance is greater than pipeline and motor carriers.

As noted in Table 5.2, shipping distances are quite long over internal waterway routes, 1,400–2,200 miles long. For example, a shipment of grain from Kansas City or Minneapolis can be transported to New Orleans, a major exporting port of grain. The mileage to New Orleans from Kansas City is 1,434 miles, from Minneapolis, 1,731 miles. Petroleum and petroleum products are the majority of products that move from New Orleans to northern cities.

Load Size

The cargo-carrying **capacity** of water carrier vehicles is large. Barges are capable of handling 3,000 tons, with normal carrying capacities of 1,000 to 1,500 tons. Great Lakes carriers average approximately 20,000 tons of carrying capacity, with one ship, the *Columbia Star*, which has a capacity of 61,000 tons. The carrying capacity of a 1,500-ton barge is equivalent to about 15 railcars and 60 trucks. This high-volume capability contributes to the water carriers' ability to offer such low-cost service (see Figure 5.8).

Low-Cost Service

The major advantage of water transportation is low-cost service. Water transportation is generally the lowest transportation cost mode for the shipment of non-liquid products. For liquid petroleum products, the pipeline is usually the lowest transportation cost mode. In 1997, barge revenues per ton-mile were $0.73, compared to $2.40 for rail, $26.12 for truck, $56.25 for air, and $1.37 for oil pipelines.[10] The volume loads and low operating costs make the cost per ton-mile by water carrier extremely low.

TABLE 5.2 Typical Transit Times and Distances via Barge

Route	Miles	Upstream Transit Time (Hours)	Downstream Transit Time (Hours)
Pittsburgh–New Orleans	1,852	338	210
St. Louis–New Orleans	1,053	211	105
Pittsburgh–Houston	2,257	405	260
Kansas City–New Orleans	1,434	324	190
Minneapolis–New Orleans	1,731	272	152

Source: The American Waterways Operators, Inc., *The Big Load Afloat* (Washington, D.C., 1955), p. 15.

FIGURE 5.8 Comparison of Cargo-Carrying Capacity

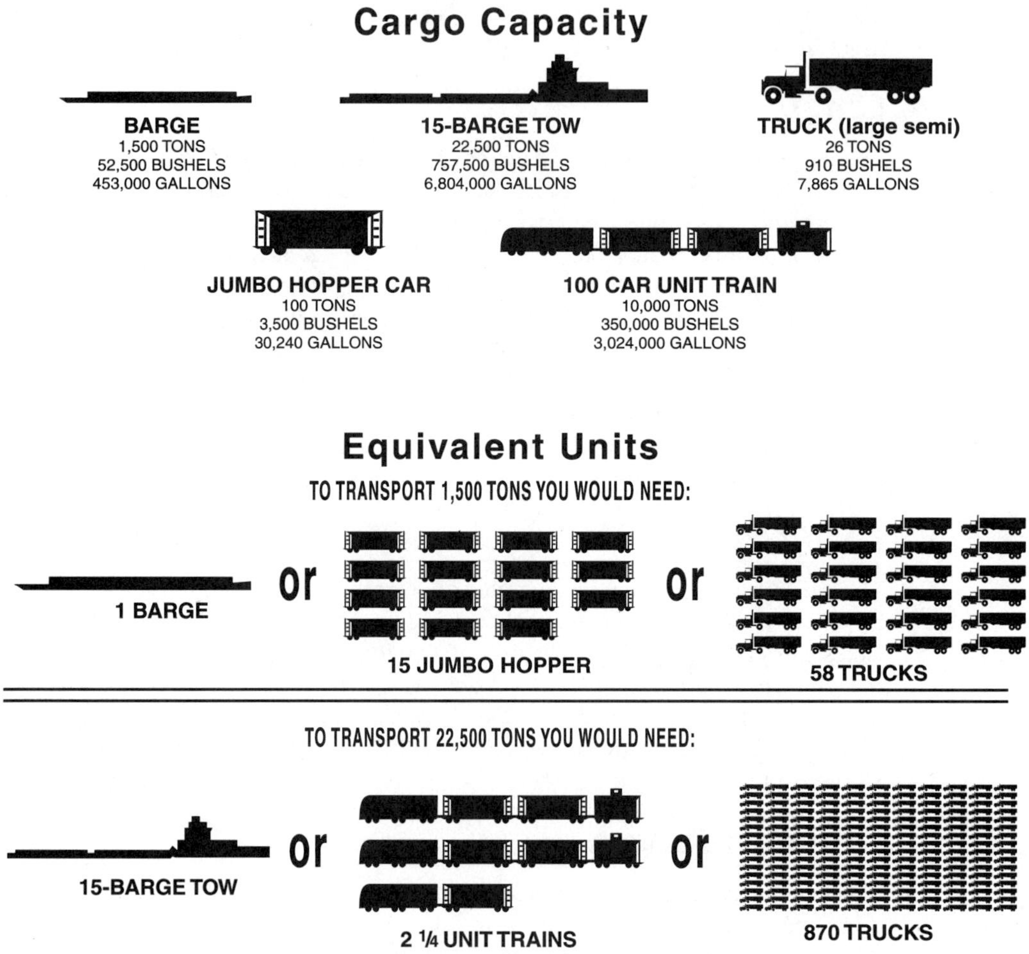

Source: The American Waterways Operators, Inc., *The Industry Today.*

Speed of Service

The low transportation cost advantage for nonliquid products is associated with slow speeds. **Transit time** via water transportation is the longest (or slowest speed) of the four modes that move nonliquids. The typical transit time under ideal conditions by barge is given in Table 5.2. For example, the transit time upstream from New Orleans to Pittsburgh is 338 hours, or 14 days and two hours. The average speed over this route is 5.5 miles per hour (1,852 miles/338 hours). The downstream time for the Pittsburgh-New Orleans route is 210 hours, or eight days and 18 hours. The average speed on this downstream route is 8.8 miles per hour (1,852 miles/210 hours). Obviously, slow speed is a disadvantage for water carriers and must be traded off against the low cost. The trade-off analysis usually makes water carriers more attractive for low-value products. Some firms use water carriers as "in transit" warehouses. This is common with commodities such as anti-freeze and other seasonal goods.

Service Disruption

In addition to long transit times, water carrier transportation is subject to disruption during **winter** months. Ice conditions from late December to early March preclude water transportation on the upper Mississippi and the Great Lakes. Lowered water levels resulting from droughts also have curtailed normal operations on segments on the lower Mississippi River system, at times reducing the movement by 30–35 percent of normal flow patterns.

Such disruption in service for two or three months during the winter increases the inventory costs of water transportation users. Users will increase inventories before the winter months to ensure adequate supplies for operation during the water transportation stoppage. This added inventory cost is the reason that primarily low-value commodities are transported by water because the relative cost of carrying inventory for such products as iron or coal is low.

Other Characteristics

Poor **accessibility** is another characteristic of water transportation. To use water carriers, the shipper and receiver must have access to the waterway. Most volume users of water transportation have facilities located adjacent to a waterway. If the shipper or receiver is not located on the waterway, truck or rail transportation is required to bridge the accessibility gap.

Finally, the ride and freight-handling characteristics of water transportation are more demanding than those of other modes. The freight is subject to inclement weather, rough waters, and numerous handlings that necessitate stringent, high-cost **packaging** for protection. For example, a wooden crate is used to ship electronic equipment by water transportation, whereas a plastic covering has sufficed for air transportation. However, given that the majority of commodities transported by water are bulk commodities that require little, if any, packaging, the packaging factor is not a serious concern to most water shippers.

When compared to other modes of transportation, water carriers have many disadvantages, but their best advantage (low cost) can offset the service disadvantages for certain products.

Equipment

Types of Vehicles

Because most domestic water carriers transport bulk materials, they use ships with very large **hold** openings to facilitate easy loading and unloading. Watertight walls dividing the holds allow a ship to carry more than one commodity at a time.[11] However, most carriers will carry a limited variety of products at one time.

The largest ship in the domestic water carriage industry is the tanker. A **tanker** can carry anywhere from 18,000 tons to 500,000 tons of liquid, generally petroleum or petroleum products. Due to oil spill problems, the use of double-hulled tankers has become preferable to the use of the more conventional single-hulled tankers.[12] However, the building of these ships has diminished greatly since 1991 with only three merchant vessels built in the last six years.[13]

Another type of vessel is the **barge,** a powerless vessel towed by a tugboat. Barges (Figure 5.9) are most commonly used by internal waterway carriers. Additional barges can be added to a tow at very little additional cost. Oceangoing barges

FIGURE 5.9 Types of Barges Used

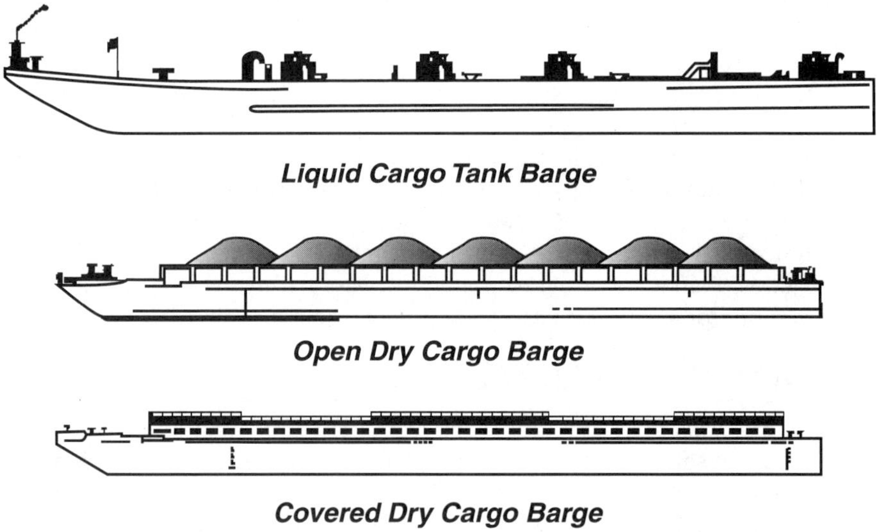

Source: The American Waterways Operators, Inc., *The Industry Today.*

FIGURE 5.10 Coastal Ocean Going Barge

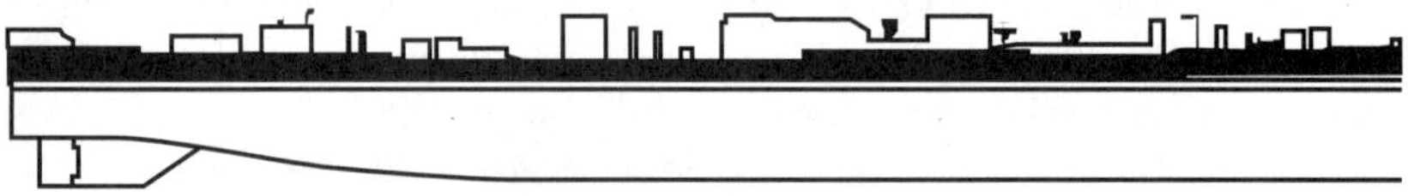

Source: The American Waterways Operators, Inc., *The Industry Today.*

(Figure 5.10) also exist as an option for inexpensive transport in the coastal traffic lanes. Thus, barge transportation is a very efficient form of transportation.

Terminals

Water carrier terminals are often provided by the **public.** Most ports are operated by local government agencies, and many ports have publicly operated storage facilities. It has been recognized for a long time that water transportation is a catalyst to economic activity in the community, and it is this belief that has spurred public investment in the operation of ports.

Many volume users of transportation invest in and operate port facilities or shipper run **terminals**. Individual firms that handle such commodities as grain, coal, and oil commonly build docks, terminals, and commodity-handling facilities to meet their unique needs. The water carriers have the opportunity to use these private facilities owned by shippers.

Over the past few decades, major port improvements have centered on the mechanization of materials-handling systems, especially for internal waterway ports.

Efficient handling of large volumes of bulk commodities has been a prerequisite for ports that desire to remain economically competitive with other ports along the waterway, and for water carriers that seek to be competitive with other modes.

The port facilitates ship loading and unloading, which means that the port must be equipped with cranes, forklifts, etc. Certain commodities like oil, grain, and coal require more technically advanced loading equipment, such as pneumatic loaders and railcar dumping equipment. Such materials-handling equipment reduces unproductive port delays and enables water carriers and ports to remain economically viable.

The port also facilitates the **transfer** of freight from one mode to another. The port is usually served by railroads and motor carriers. Terminals at the port will have railroad sidings to handle inbound and outbound rail freight as well as parking lots for motor carrier equipment. Ports play a key role in promoting the efficiency of intermodal transportation.

Because barges and ships carry larger loads than rail or motor-carrier vehicles, **storage** facilities are necessary at the port. The storage areas receive cargo from many trucks and railcars. This freight is held until sufficient volume is obtained to be handled effectively by barge or ship. Conversely, when a loaded vessel arrives at port, the freight is unloaded, stored, and then dispatched in hundreds of railcars or trucks at some later date.

Cost Structure

Fixed Versus Variable Cost Components

The basic cost structure of water carriers consists of high variable costs and low fixed costs. Like the motor carriers and air carriers, water carriers do not provide their own highways (rights-of-way). The waterways are provided by nature (except canals) but are maintained, improved, and controlled by the government. The carriers pay **user charges**—lock fees, dock fees, fuel taxes—for the use of the government-provided facilities. These user charges are directly related to the volume of business and therefore add to the variable costs.

The **operating costs** for water carriers reported to the ICC are given in Table 5.3. The data indicate that 13.48 percent of the total costs is fixed and 86.52 percent is variable. Fixed costs include depreciation and amortization and general expenses. General expenses exceed depreciation and amortization by almost two to one.

The major variable expenses listed in Table 5.3 are line-operating costs, operating rents, and maintenance. Line-operating costs, 50.89 percent of the total costs, include labor, fuel, user charges, and other direct operating costs. Operating rents, 13.05 percent of total costs, are those expenses associated with renting operating equipment and facilities. Maintenance expenses amount to 9.04 percent of total costs.

Water carrier owners purchase insurance to hedge against the risk of loss and damage resulting from the forces of nature. The carriers take out insurance to subrogate losses, or they directly incur the cost of accidents as self-insurers. The type of commodities moved by many domestic water carriers (such as basic raw materials) reduces their liability risk for damage.

Infrastructure

As indicated earlier, the domestic water carrier's low fixed costs can be attributed to **public aids** in the area of infrastructure. For water carriers, the major public aid is

TABLE 5.3 Domestic Water Carrier[a] 1978 Operating Costs

Functional Expense	Amount (In Millions of Dollars)	Percent of Total Cost
Fixed		
Depreciation × amortization	32.76	4.66
General expenses	61.98	8.82
Total fixed	94.74	13.48
Variable		
Line perating	357.82	50.89
Terminal	32.44	4.61
Traffic	10.63	1.52
Casualties and insurance	38.16	5.43
Operating rents	91.77	13.05
Maintenance	63.59	9.04
Taxes	13.95	1.98
Total variable	608.36	86.52
Total cost	703.10	100.00

[a]Great Lakes and internal carriers with revenues of $500,000 or more.

Source: Interstate Commerce Commission, *Transport Statistics in the United States, 1978: Part 5, Carriers by Water* (Washington, D.C.: U.S. Government Printing Office), pp. 8–9.

in the construction and maintenance of waterways. The construction of canals with public funds opens new markets and sources of revenue for water carriers. The construction of locks and dams on rivers makes the waterways navigable for domestic water carriers. The dredging of the Mississippi River, for example, is performed by the Army Corps of Engineers to maintain channel depth and width. Port facilities are maintained by federal and local monies.

An example of a major public aid for domestic water carriers is the Tennessee Tombigbee (Tenn-Tom) project. Opened in 1985, the project connects the Tennessee River and the Warrior River via the Tombigbee River. This new water route provides access to the mid-portion of the United States via the port of Mobile, Alabama, and offers an additional north-south route, in lieu of the Mississippi River, for such commodities as Kentucky coal exiting the United States and for upstream traffic entering the states of Alabama, Kentucky, and Tennessee. Another example of public aid was when, in 1986, the federal government built two 1,200-foot locks and a new dam at Lock and Dam Number 26 on the Mississippi River systems.

Critics of waterway projects like Tenn-Tom often refer to them as "pork barrel projects," suggesting that they are funded by government funds for the benefit of only a small number of the legislator's constituents. Critics question their value to society and maintain that these projects probably would not have been constructed if the actual users or local taxpayers had to assume the full burden of the costs. The U.S. Army Corps of Engineers has been responsible for conducting benefit/cost analysis to determine if such projects deserve to be funded by federal dollars, but critics question whether the Corps' analysis are realistic and whether the projects' expected benefits will ever be realized.

Another public aid that domestic water carriers receive from the federal government is in the form of U.S. cabotage laws. The cabotage laws require that coastal and intercoastal traffic be conducted in ships built and registered in the United States. The **cabotage laws** do not provide a direct subsidy to domestic water carries, but they do provide a monopoly for U.S. coastal and intercoastal carriers. This monopoly results from a complete prohibition against foreign-registered or foreign-built ships hauling domestic coastal and intercoastal traffic.

To a limited extent, the water carriers repay the government agencies for the various aids received. Lock fees on the Saint Lawrence Seaway (but not on the inland waterways) are paid to traverse locks, and port fees are paid to use the port facilities. Barge carriers are assessed a fuel tax of $.10 per gallon, comparable to the motor-carrier fuel tax per gallon.

Labor

Water transportation is not labor-intensive. In 1997, 2.72 million ton-miles of freight were transported for each water carrier employee. This compares to 4.74 million ton-miles for each rail employee, 0.4 million ton-miles for each motor carrier employee, and 39.3 million ton-miles for each pipeline employee.[14]

The 1978 ICC Statistical Report for Water Carriers[15] indicated that labor compensation paid by one intercoastal carrier amounted to 173.5 million dollars, or 19.6 percent of the total operating costs. In 1997, the annual compensation paid to water carrier employees, including fringes, was $46,672.[16]

Labor is required at the terminal to load and unload general commodities. The freight is moved from the dock onto the ship and into the appropriate hold for the voyage (and vice versa for unloading). In addition, the labor is required to handle the loading of freight from connecting modes, such as truck and rail, and to store the freight waiting to be loaded onto the ship or connection carriers.

Domestic water carriers, however, do not require much labor at the terminal, because the carriers primarily transport bulk commodities that can be loaded mechanically. Great Lakes carrier companies have developed ships that are equipped with automatic unloading devices that reduce the amount of labor required to unload the ships.

Fuel

Compared to the other modes, ships often consume more fuel per mile. According to an ICC study, intercoastal carriers consumed 15.2 million barrels of fuel, or 638.4 million gallons, and operated 8.16 million miles. The mileage rate was .0128 miles per gallon, which means that ships consumed 78.2 gallons of fuel per mile.[17] In 1998, water carriers, international and domestic, consumed 223.89 million barrels of fuel, or 5.4 percent of the fuel consumed by all modes.[18]

The total fuel consumption was less than that used by trucks, rail, an air, although the water carriers transported more ton-miles of freight than some other modes. Thus, it might be fair to conclude that water transportation is a more fuel-efficient mode in terms of fuel consumed per ton-mile.

Economies of Scale

Like the motor carrier, the water carrier does not have significant economies of scale. The large portion of variable costs (approximately 90 percent), the small size of the carriers in the industry, and the ability to add small increments of capacity (one barge, for example) suggest that the economies of large-scale operations are not great.

In the **short run,** however, the water carrier is capable of achieving economies of operation (productivity). A good example is the movement of 25–40 barges in one tow with one towboat. On the lower portion of the Mississippi, a 40-barge tow, hauling 40,000–60,000 tons, is quite common. As the tow moves upstream, the channel width narrows, requiring that the tow be reduced to 5–20 barges hauling 5,000–20,000 tons. The incremental cost of additional fuel, labor, and maintenance to push a 40-barge tow is relatively small compared to a five-barge tow. But the improvements in the economies of operation cause an increase from 5,000–20,000 tons hauled to 40,000–60,000 tons, or an increase in output of 200–1,200 percent.

Current Issues

Drug and Alcohol Abuse

The grounding of the Exxon tanker ***Valdez*** off the shores of Alaska in March 1989 exemplifies the need for strong measure against drug and alcohol abuse in the water transportation industry. The captain of the *Valdez* was found to be intoxicated at the time the ship ran aground and spilled 10 million gallons of oil off Alaska's shores. The full impact of this disaster will not be known for many years to come; however, it is known that the environmental damage resulted in the deaths of hundreds of animals, including some endangered species, and the loss of income and jobs for many of Alaska's citizens (such as fishermen, for example).

In recognition of the problem of substance abuse, the U.S. Coast Guard now tests American seamen for **drug abuse** before they are issued a seamen's license and before they can be employed. Seamen are also tested randomly during their employment.

Port Development

Because of today's environmental concerns, ports are having trouble keeping pace with the accelerated developments in global trade. Ports are now having to balance competitive economic concerns with the concerns of the public, which, rightly or wrongly, often view ports as a main source of air, water, and noise pollution.

An example of the struggle would be the problems the port of Oakland, California, faced in trying to get permission to dredge its harbors to a lower depth in order to berth new, larger vessels. Without the dredging, Oakland's competitiveness would sink. But proposals for dumping the spoil from the dredging were shot down at every turn. Soon another problem came up. The city's mayor decided to siphon port revenues into the city's coffers to alleviate budget problems. After local and international business people united in support of the port's autonomy, the mayor backed down. Months later, thanks to the concerted efforts of two U.S. representatives and California's governor, the port got the O.K. to dredge and dump the spoil in a cost-effective spot in the bay. Although that issue was resolved, now California is considering a bill that would allow the state to take revenue from the ports to replenish the state's depleted treasury.

These problems are not exclusive to the port of Oakland; they exist all around the country. Some people believe that federal government attention is needed to alleviate port problems. Competitiveness between the ports seems to preclude a joint lobbying effort for White House action on a new subsidy reform policy.[19]

Also, a current issue facing North American ports is the growth of multicarrier alliances leading to the expansion of the already gargantuan ships. An increase from

TABLE 5.4 Current U.S. Port Depths From Coast to Coast

Port	Depth (in Ft.)
New York/New Jersey Kill van Kull (deepening to 45)	35
Philadelphia	40
Savannah	38
Miami	38
New Orleans	45
Houston (deepening to 45)	40
Los Angeles	45
Oakland (deepening to 42)	35
Seattle	40–60

Source: AAPA

6,000 20-foot equivalent units (TEU) to 8,000 TEUs has many ports worried for the future. The larger the ships are, the deeper they go, meaning that many of the smaller ports will need to begin the dredging process as soon as possible to be able to compete in the future. Table 5.4[20] shows examples of current U.S. port depths from coast to coast and their plans to expand in the future. The dredging process will allow ports to make their waterways deeper and wider in order to accommodate these new, larger ships and allow them to stay competitive.

SUMMARY

- Water carriers are the oldest economic mode of transportation and have played a key role in the development of many early U.S. cities and regions.
- The water carrier system is still a viable part of the total transportation system and competes with the railroad system for the movement of many bulk, low-value commodities.
- The water carrier system includes all four legal forms of transportation (common, contract, exempt, and private), but the majority of the water carrier traffic is exempt from economic regulation.
- The domestic water carrier system can also be classified in terms of inland carriers (rivers, canals, and Great Lakes) and coastal/intercoastal carriers, all three of which are vital to water transportation.
- Intramodal competition among water carriers is not nearly as important as intermodal competition with other types of carriers, especially railroads and pipelines.
- Water carriers compete actively for the movement of bulk liquid and dry/low-value, high-density items, especially on the inland water system. Coastal and intercoastal carriers, and especially international water carriers, compete for higher valued products that move via containers.
- Water carriers offer very low-cost services, but their transit time is slow and can be interrupted by weather conditions. Accessibility and potential product damage are also service disadvantages.
- Water carriers use a limited variety of types of equipment and typically use public- or shipper-provided terminals.

- Water carriers have relatively low fixed costs because they use a right-of-way provided by the government for which they pay user charges like motor carriers and airlines.
- Water carriers are not highly labor-intensive in terms of their movement operations but may require more labor in terminal areas for certain types of freight.
- Water carriers do not have significant economies of scale but can achieve economies of operating in the short run.
- Substance abuse and port development are two major issues facing the water-carrier industry.

Key Terms

accessibility pg. 161
average haul 159
barge 161
cabotage laws 165
capacity 159
coastal carriers 154
commodities 149
criticism of projects 164
drug abuse 166
dry-bulk products 158
early importance 149
efficient materials handling 162
employment 149
equipment improvement 162
fixed costs 163
for-hire carriers 150
Great Lakes 157
high-value products 158
holds 161
intermodal competition 156
intermodal transfer 163
internal carriers 151
intramodal competition 156
liquid products 158
natural highway 149
operating costs 163
packaging 161
pipeline competition 157
port storage 163
private carriers 150
public aid 163
public terminals 162
rail competition 157
regulated carriers 151
shipper terminals 62
short run 166
tanker 161
terminal labor 165
Toledo 157
transit time 160
user charges 163
Valdez incident 166
winter conditions 161

Study Questions

1. What are the primary commodities carried by domestic water carriers? What other carrier or carriers would be competitors of the inland water carriers?

2. How would water carriers work with other modes to provide a complete service?

3. Describe the various classifications used in connection with water carriers. How do the participants in this group differ?

4. Discuss the speed of service for inland waterways carriers and how this could impact inventory requirements of users of the commodities carried.

5. Discuss the components of the cost structure of water carriers. How are carrier costs impacted by governmental actions?

6. Is water transportation labor intensive? Discuss and support your answer with examples.

7. Do the water carriers have economies of scale at any level? Discuss and support your answer with examples.

8. What are some of the current challenges and opportunities facing the domestic water carriers in this time?

NOTES

1. *Transportation in America,* 16th ed. (Washington, D.C.: Eno Transportation Foundation, 1998), p. 44.
2. American Waterways Association.
3. Ibid.
4. Ibid.
5. American Waterways Association.
6. ICC, *Transport Statistics in the United* States: *Carriers by Water* (Washington, D.C.: U.S. Government Printing office, 1978).
7. Department of Army Corps of Engineers, *Waterborne Commerce of the United States* (Washington, D.C.: U.S. Government Printing office, 1997).
8. Ibid., p. 4
9. *National Transportation Statistics, 1997* (United States Department of Transportation, Bureau of Transportation Statistics, 1997).
10. *Transportation in America, p. 49.*
11. John J. Coyle, Edward J. Bardi, C. John Langley, *The Management of Business Logistics* (St. Paul, Minnesota: West Publishing Company, 1992), p. 282.
12. Ibid., p. 282.
13. *Transportation in America,* p. 30.
14. Ibid., p. 61.
15. Interstate Commerce Commission, *Statistical Report for Water Carriers* (Washington, D.C.: U.S. Government Printing Office, 1978).
16. *Transportation in America,* p.60.
17. *Statistical Report for Water Carriers.*
18. *Transportation in America,* p. 56.
19. E. J. Muller, "Development Is Stuck in the Mud," *Chilton's Distribution* (July 1992), pp. 48–49.
20. Colleen Gourley, "From Sea to Shining Sea," *Distribution* (February 1997), pp. 48–49.

SUGGESTED READINGS

Bowman, Robert J., "Ocean shippers call the shots," *Distribution,* July 1997, pp. 70–71

Bradley, Peter. "The Giants of Information", *Logistics,* September 1998, pp. 55–64.

Gillis, Chris, and Mottley, Robert. "Ports face 6,000-TEU question", *American Shipper,* July 1998, pp. 73–75.

Gooley, Toby B. "Ocean Shipping: Feeling the pinch," *Logistics,* July 1998, pp.48–51. Harrington, Lisa, and Knee, Richard. "The Maritime Industry is Changing with the Times," *Transportation & Distribution,* October 1998, pp. 97–109.

"Ocean Reform bill passes Senate," *Logistics,* May 1998, p. 22.

"Politics beach ocean reform," *Logistics,* April 1998, p. 24.

"Supreme Court strikes down harbor tax," *Logistics,* May 1998, pp. 19–20. "The Big Yawn", *Distribution,* September 1997, pp. 48–49.

CHAPTER 6

Air Carriers

Brief History

From the first flight that lasted less than one minute to space shuttles orbiting the earth, air transportation has come a long way in a short period of time. Wilbur and Orville Wright made their first flight in 1903 at Kitty Hawk and sold their invention to the federal government. In 1908, the development of air transportation began with the **U.S. Post Office** examining the feasibility of providing air mail service. Although airplanes were used in World War I, the use of airplanes for mail transport can be considered the beginning of the modern airline industry. Passenger transportation services developed as a by-product of the mail business and began to flourish in selected markets. Since that time, airplanes have become faster, bigger, and relatively more fuel-efficient. Although the level and degree of technological improvement have slowed in the airline industry, there is still opportunity for further innovation.

Airline travel is a common form of transportation for long-distance passenger travel and the only reasonable alternative when **time** is of the essence. The tremendous speed of the airplane coupled with more competitive pricing have led to the growth of air transportation, particularly in the movement of passengers.

Industry Overview and Significance

In 1997, for-hire air carriers had total operating revenues of $109.54 billion, of which $79.47 billion (72.6 percent) came from passenger service.[1] In 1997, air carriers transported 20.51 billion revenue ton-miles, or .4 percent of total intercity ton-miles.[2] **Employment** in the air carrier industry totaled 586,509 people in 1997, with an average annual compensation of over $65,000 for persons employed by scheduled carriers.[3]

The airline industry is very dependent on **passenger** revenues to maintain its financial viability. However, to characterize airlines simply as movers of people presents too simplistic a view of their role in our transportation system. The airlines are a unique and important group of carriers that meet some particular needs in our society. Although their share of the freight movement on a ton-mile basis is small, the type of traffic that they carry (high-value, perishable, or emergency) makes them an important part of our total transportation system. Emphasis upon total logistics cost in a quick-response lead time environment will continue to contribute to their growth in freight movements.

Types of Carriers

Private Carriers

Air carriers can be segmented into for-hire carriers and private carriers. A private air carrier is a firm that transports **company personnel** or freight in planes that it owns or leases. The preponderance of private air transportation is used to transport company personnel, although emergency freight is sometimes carried on private airplanes as well. Rarely, however, is a private air carrier established to routinely carry freight. The private air carrier is subject to the federal safety regulations administered by the Federal Aviation Administration (FAA) of the U.S. Department of Transportation. This category also includes firms such as U.P.S. and FedEx which operate large fleets of aircraft to provide transporation in connection with service offered by these firms.

For-Hire Carriers

The for-hire carriers are no longer regulated on an economic basis by the federal government and cannot be easily categorized into specific types because carriers provide many **types** of services. For our purposes, the for-hire carriers will be discussed according to type of service offered (all-cargo, air taxi, commuter, charter, and international) and annual revenue (majors, nationals, and regionals).

A classification frequently used by U.S. air carriers is one based on annual operating **revenues.** The categories used to classify air carriers in terms of revenue are as follows:

Majors — annual revenues of more than $1 billion

Nationals — annual revenues of $75 million to $1 billion

Regionals — annual revenues of less than $75 million

U.S. major carriers have $1 billion or more in annual revenues and provide service between major population areas within the United States such as New York, Chicago, and Los Angeles. The routes served by these carriers are usually high-density corridors, and the carriers use high-capacity planes. The U.S. **majors** also serve medium-sized population centers such as Toledo, Ohio. Examples of major U.S. carriers are United, Delta, U.S. Airways, and American.

U.S. **national** carriers have revenues of $75 million to $1 billion and operate between less populated areas and major population centers. These carriers operate scheduled service over relatively short routes with smaller planes. They "feed" passengers from outlying areas into airports served by the U.S. majors. Today, many of the U.S. national carriers operate over relatively large, regional areas and are stiff competition for the U.S. majors on many routes. Examples of U.S. nationals include Southwest Airlines and America West.

Regional carriers have annual revenues of less than $75 million and have operations similar to the nationals. The carriers operate within a particular region of the country, such as New England or the Midwest, and connect lesser populated areas with larger population centers. Included in the regional category are the following: Mesa, Air Wisconsin, and Alaska. The regional carriers are grouped into two categories: large ($10–75 million) and medium (less than $10 million).

The **all-cargo carrier,** as the name implies, transports cargo primarily. The transportation of air cargo was deregulated in 1977, permitting the all-cargo carriers to set rates, serve routes, and use any size plane dictated by the market. Examples of all-cargo carriers include Federal Express and Air Borne Express.

The **commuter** air carrier is technically a regional carrier. The commuter publishes timetables on specific routes that connect lesser populated routes with major cities. As certified carriers abandon routes, usually low-density ones, the commuter enters into a working relationship with the certified carrier to continue service to the community. The commuter then connects small communities that have reduced or no air service with larger communities that have better scheduled service. The commuter's schedule is closely aligned with connecting flight schedules at a larger airport. In 1985, 133 commuter airline firms were in operation, down from 148 firms in 1978. During the period 1978–1985, 257 firms entered the commuter airline business, while 271 went out of business. This was largely due to airline deregulation.[4] Many commuter operators are franchised by the majors, such as U.S. Air Express.

The **charter** carriers use large planes to transport people or freight. The supplemental carrier has no time schedule or designated route. The carrier charters the entire plane to transport a group of people or cargo between specified origins and destinations. Many travel tour groups use charter carriers. However, a big customer for charters is the Department of Defense; it uses charter carriers to transport personnel and supplies. For example, the Vietnam conflict relied upon charters. The rates charged and schedules followed are negotiated in the contract. As a result of increased fare competition and the end of the United States' involvement in the Vietnam War, the number of charter airlines decreased. However, many of the majors have separated charter operations to more fully utilize equipment.

Many U.S. carriers are also international carriers and operate between the continental United States and foreign countries, and between the United States and its territories (such as Puerto Rico). Because service to other countries has an effect on U.S. international trade and relations, the president of the United States is involved in awarding the international routes. Examples of international carriers include United and American. Many foreign carriers provide services between the U.S. and their country, such as British Air and Air France.

Market Structure

Number of Carriers

In comparison to the motor carrier industry, which has more than 69,000 for-hire **carriers** (regulated and exempt), the air carrier industry is made up of under 5,000 for-hire carriers. Of these carriers, very few have a major market impact. A look at

TABLE 6.1 Number of Carriers

Carriers	1982	1984	1987	1994	1996
Majors	12	11	14	11	11
Nationals	17	19	20	24	26
Large Regionals	18	37	32	20	24
Medium Regionals	51	28	27	20	28
Total	98	95	93	85	89

Source: Air Transport Association, "Air Carrier Traffic Statistics," Washington, DC, 1998.

STOP OFF

THE WORLD IS GETTING SMALLER

In 1800, it took a traveler about 12 days to travel by pack horse from Philadelphia to Pittsburgh. This was an average speed of three miles per hour, but the trip was only possible during daylight hours. The traveler had to carry his own food and bedding and make sure the horse had something to eat along the way. The trip was also dangerous.

By 1840, a canal and railroad system linked Philadelphia and Pittsburgh. The trip was reduced to seven days, and it required stopping each night in inns along the way. Charles Dickens described his accommodations on this trip as dirty and cramped with often questionable food.

In the 1850s, a direct all-rail line opened that cut the trip to two days. An overnight stay was often required in either Harrisburg or Altoona. Improvements in the rail lines and equipment speeded the trip to one day by the early 1870s. And, by 1910, a fast train made the trip in just over eight hours. Thus, in one century the travel time had been cut from twelve days to one-third of one day — nearly a 97 percent reduction in time!

The twin-engine passenger plane called the DC–3 was introduced during the middle 1930s. With the capability to travel 180 miles per hour, this plane cut the trip to just under two hours. In the late 1940s, the 300-mph Constellation reduced the trip further to one hour and 15 minutes (including take-off and landing time). Allegheny Airlines introduced jets on the route in the 1960s that cut the trip to 50 minutes. Since 1900, the trip was cut again by 90 percent!

In the 1930s, an automobile trip took about two and a half days. The opening of the Pennsylvania Turnpike in 1939 cut this trip to six hours. Advances in the highway and automobiles cut the trip to about five hours by the 1950s. The speed limit reduction to 55 mph in 1974 lengthened the trip to 6 hours again.

The supersonic Concorde can travel 1,400 mph today. This plane can cover 300 miles (the distance from Philadelphia to Pittsburgh) in just 13 minutes! The U.S. government and two aerospace firms predict that hypersonic planes of the late 1990s will travel at 3,500 mph (300 miles in just five minutes). Such a plane will travel in "near-space" at an altitude of about 90,000 feet. Still another proposed plane is projected to be similar to the current space shuttle. It will supposedly take off and land at conventional airports and use rocket engines once it attains low orbit in space. This 17,000-mph plane will travel between any two airports in the world in no more than two hours, traversing a distance of 300 miles in just one minute!

carrier revenues shows a concentration of earnings by the small group of majors, nationals, and regionals (Table 6.1 provides numbers for these three categories). These carriers, which represent less than three percent of the total number of carriers in the industry, receive more than 90 percent of the total air revenue.[5] The remaining industry revenue is distributed among the 4,000 (approximate) air taxi, commuter, and cargo carriers.

Private air transportation has been estimated to include approximately 60,000 company-owned planes, with over 500 U.S. corporations operating a private air fleet.[6] In addition, thousands of planes are used for personal, recreational, and instructional purposes.

Deregulation was expected to result in a larger number of airlines competing for passengers and freight traffic. The number of airlines did increase initially, but as Table 6.1 indicates, the number of airlines had decreased by 1984. Table 6.2 provides a clearer picture of entry and exit into and out of the airline industry in the period following the initiation of deregulation. As indicated, 205 carriers entered the market, and 132 carriers existed in this period.

Another aspect of the deregulation is that in 1978 there were 43 national and regional carriers operating. Twenty-eight have exited the market—13 because of merg-

TABLE 6.2 Market Entry and Exit Since 1978. National and Regional Air Carriers*

			Reasons for Exit		
Entered Market	**Exited Market**	**Still Operating**	**Merger**	**Waivers**	**Financial**
205	132	73	23	22	87

*43 carriers operating in 1978 and 28 of them have exited.

Source: Air Transport Association: Washington, DC, 1997.

ers, 14 for financial reasons, and one for a status waiver. Overall, the market has been turbulent with deregulation.

Competition

Intermodal

Due to their unique service, air carriers face **limited** competition from other modes for either passengers or freight. Air carriers have an advantage in providing time-sensitive, long-distance movement of people or freight. Airlines compete to some extent with trucking for the movement of higher-valued manufactured goods; they face competition from automobiles for the movement of passengers and, to a limited extent, from trains and buses. For short distances (under 300 miles), the access time and terminal time offsets the speed of the airline for the line-haul.

Intramodal

Competition in rates and service among the air carriers is very **intense,** even though the number of carriers is small. As noted, air carrier regulation was significantly reduced in 1978, and new carriers entered selected routes (markets), thereby increasing the amount of competition. Also, existing carriers expanded their market coverage, which significantly increased intramodal competition in certain markets. Table 6.3 indicates that the top 10 air carriers accounted for about 95 percent of the passenger revenues, freight revenue, and total operating revenue when competition has increased and fare wars have developed on high-density routes, even though operating costs may have increased. Carriers may also have **excess capacity** (too many flights and seat miles on a route) and attempt to attract passengers by selectively lowering fares to fill the empty seats. As evidence of this price competition, in 1991, 95 percent of the U.S. majors' domestic revenue passenger miles was sold at a discount rate, with the average being 66 percent off full fare.[7] Recent years have been more stable, but competition exists between certain pairs, particularly when carriers such as Southern Airlines provide service.

As new carriers start to serve a route, fares are lowered, as are profits for many carriers. The end result has been a reduction in the number of carriers and flights on many routes, in particular, low-traffic routes. After the passage of the Airline Deregulation Act in 1978, many communities experienced an influx of new carriers, many of whom exited within 12–18 months. Now these same communities (lesser populated areas) have fewer flights than before the deregulation act took effect. Table 6.2

TABLE 6.3 Top 25 Airlines by Various Rankings—1996

	Passengers (000)			Revenue Passenger Miles (000)	
1	Delta	97,201	1	United	116,554,641
2	United	81,863	2	American	104,521,123
3	American	79,324	3	Delta	93,876,999
4	US Airways	56,639	4	Northwest	68,626,530
5	Southwest	55,372	5	US Airways	38,942,794
6	Northwest	52,682	6	Continental	37,344,225
7	Continental	35,743	7	Trans World	27,110,708
8	Trans World	23,281	8	Southwest	27,085,489
9	America West	18,130	9	America West	15,275,989
10	Alaska	11,758	10	Alaska	9,793,978
11	Simmons	6,010	11	American Trans Air	4,914,897
12	Hawaiian	5,338	12	Continental Micronesia	4,569,143
13	Aloha	5,059	13	Tower	3,327,961
14	Reno	4,930	14	Hawaiian	3,297,979
15	Mesa	4,307	15	Reno	2,765,805
16	Continental Express	4,100	16	Carnival	2,121,312
17	Horizon Air	3,753	17	Western Pacific	1,519,889
18	Atlantic Southeast	3,632	18	Value Jet	1,467,959
19	American Trans Air	3,431	19	Simmons	1,316,845
20	Value Jet	3,003	20	Midwest Express	1,239,147
21	Continental Micronesia	2,601	21	Mesa	998,608
22	Trans States	2,121	22	Midway	988,433
23	Carnival	1,770	23	Airtran	929,699
24	Air Wisconsin	1,757	24	Continental Express	903,757
25	Western Pacific	1,754	25	Kiwi	900,064
	Freight Ton Miles (000)			**Total Operating Revenues ($000)**	
1	Federal Express	5,353,490	1	United	16,316,749
2	United Parcel Service*	3,351,121	2	American	15,136,003
3	Northwest	1,910,689	3	Delta	13,317,693
4	United	1,785,759	4	Federal Express	10,950,187
5	American	1,641,172	5	Northwest	9,751,383
6	Delta	1,000,133	6	US Airways	7,704,057
7	Emery*	965,205	7	Continental	5,487,150
8	Polar Air	769,342	8	Trans World	3,554,407
9	Continental	359,142	9	Southwest	3,407,361
10	DHL Airways	358,215	10	United Parcel Service	1,792,199
11	Evergreen*	451,248	11	America West	1,751,813
12	Trans World	268,840	12	Alaska	1,306,621
13	Challenge Air Cargo	181,360	13	DHL Airways	1,085,360
14	US Airways	151,905	14	Continental Micronesia	777,246
15	Continental Micronesia	79,057	15	American Trans Air	716,123
16	Arrow	79,037	16	Simmons	465,401
17	American Int'l	63,639	17	American Int'l	448,763
18	Alaska	63,639	18	Tower	417,819
19	Amerijet	62,522	19	Mesa	394,938
20	Hawaiian	50,815	20	Continental Express	386,762
21	America West	47,279	21	Hawaiian	384,473
22	Southwest	36,714	22	Atlantic Southeast	375,300
23	Tower	26,656	23	World	356,409
24	Carnival	22,080	24	Reno	351,188
25	Fine Airlines	17,409	25	Atlas	315,659

*Includes non-scheduled service.

Source: Air Transport Association: Washington, DC, 1998.

clearly indicates this competitive turbulence with new entrants into the air market, but it also shows the many who have exited the business for various reasons.

Service Competition

Competition in airline service takes many forms, but the primary service competition is the **frequency and timing** of flights on a route. Carriers attempt to provide flights at the time of day when passengers want to fly. Flight departures are most frequent in the early morning (7:00 A.M. to 10:00 P.M.) and late afternoon (4:00 P.M. to 6:00 P.M.).

In addition to the frequency and timing of flights, air carriers attempt to differentiate their service through the **advertising** of passenger amenities. Carriers promote such things as on-time arrival and friendly employees to convince travelers that it has the desired quality of service. Gourmet meals and on-board movies are some of the amenities that a carrier uses to entice passengers to use and reuse its service. Frequent flyer programs and special services for high-mileage customers are popular examples of other services to attract loyal customers.

A post-deregulation development in service competition was **no-frills service.** The no-frills air carriers (for example, Southwest Airlines and American Trans Air) charge a fare that is lower than that of a full-service air carrier. However, passengers receive limited snacks and drinks (coffee, tea, or soft drinks). Another hallmark of such carriers is that they only provide one class of service. Also, the passengers provide their own magazines or other reading materials. Overall, there are fewer airline employees involved in no-frills services operations, which contribute to lower costs. The "no-frills" carriers have had a significant impact upon fares where their service is available.

Cargo Competition

For cargo service, competition has become intense. As a result of the complete deregulation of air cargo, air carriers have published competitive **rates,** but these rates are still higher than those available via surface carriers. Freight schedules have been published that emphasize low transit times between given points. To overcome accessibility problems, some carriers provide door-to-door service through contacts with trucking companies.

Although the number of major and national carriers is small (approximately 20), the competition among carriers is great. An interesting development has been the number of surface carriers that have added air cargo service, such as United Parcel Service. Competition for non-passenger business will become even greater as more carriers attempt to eliminate excess capacity resulting from currently reduced passenger travel patterns. Another interesting dimension has been the growth in volume of express carrier traffic, which is an important reason for the attraction of surface carriers into this segment of the business.

Operating and Service Characteristics

General

As indicated above, the major revenue source for air carriers is passenger transportation. In 1997, approximately 73 percent of total operating revenues was derived from passenger transport. This **revenue** was generated from about 600 million passenger enplanements in 1997.[8] Air transportation dominates the for-hire, long-distance passenger transportation market.

In 1997, approximately 10.0 percent of the total operating revenues was generated from **freight** transportation.[9] The majority of freight using air service is high-value and/or emergency shipments. The high cost of air transportation is usually prohibitive for shipping low-value routine commodities unless there is an emergency.

For **emergency shipments,** the cost of air transportation is often inconsequential compared to the cost of delaying the goods. For example, an urgently needed part of an assembly line may have a $20 value, but if the air-freighted part arrives on time to prevent the assembly line from stopping, the "opportunity" value of the part may become worth hundreds of thousands of dollars. Thus, the $20 part may have an emergency value of $200,000, and the air freight cost is a small portion of this emergency value.

Examples of **commodities** that move via air carriers include mail, clothing, communication products and parts, photography equipment, mushrooms, fresh flowers, industrial machines, high-priced livestock, race horses, expensive automobiles, and jewelry. Normally basic raw materials such as coal, lumber, iron ore, or steel are not moved by air carriage. The high value of these products provides a cost savings trade-off, usually but not always from inventory, that offsets the higher cost of air service. The old adage, time is money, is quite appropriate here.

Speed of Service

Undoubtedly, the **major** service **advantage** of air transportation is speed. The terminal-to-terminal time for a given trip is lower via air transportation than via any of the other modes. Commercial jets are capable of routinely flying at speeds of 500 to 600 miles per hour, thus making a New York to California trip, approximately 3,000 miles, a mere six-hour journey.

This advantage of high terminal-to-terminal **speed** has been dampened somewhat by reduced frequency of flights and congestion at airports. As a result of deregulation, the air traffic controllers strike of 1981, and lower carrier demand, the number of flights offered to and from low-density communities has been reduced to increase the utilization of a given plane. As previously noted, commuter airlines have been substituted on some routes where major and national lines find the traffic volume to be too low to justify using large planes. The use of commuters requires transfer and rehandling of freight because the commuter service does not cover long distances.

Air carriers have been concentrating their service on the **high-density** routes like New York to Chicago, for example. In addition, most carriers have adopted the hub terminal approach in which most flights go through a hub terminal; Atlanta and Chicago are examples. These two factors have aggravated the air traffic congestion and ground congestion at major airports and increased the overall transit time. Also, some carriers have been unable to expand because of limited "slots" at major airports.

The shippers who use air carriers to transport freight are primarily interested in the speed of the service and the resultant benefits, such as reduced inventory levels and inventory carrying costs. Acceptable or improved service levels can be achieved by using air carriers to deliver orders in short time periods. Stockouts can be controlled, reduced, or eliminated by responding to shortages via air carriers.

Length of Haul and Capacity

Air carriers transport freight long distances. In 1997, the average length of domestic haul was over 1,400 miles, compared with an average of about 600 miles for rail and 400 miles for truck.[10] The high speed of the airplane makes a 1,000-mile trip a matter of hours versus days for other modes.

For passenger travel, air carriers dominate the long-distance moves. In 1997, the average length of haul for passenger travel was about 1,000 miles for air carriers.[11] This distance was approximately six times greater than for intercity bus and 20 times that of rail. The capacity of airplanes is dependent on its type. A wide-body, four-engine jet has a seating **capacity** of about 375 people and an all-cargo carrying capacity of 90–100 tons, whereas a regular-body, four-engine has an all-cargo carrying capacity of 35–40 tons. However, the same planes used for both passenger and cargo have carrying capacities of about 50 and 20 tons, respectively. Many medium-size planes are in use today with a seating capacity of 100–150 people and an all-cargo capacity of 90–100 tons. A 10- to 40-passenger capacity is common for the commuter plane (see Table 6.4).

Normally, **small shipments,** less than 500 pounds, are moved by air carriers. Rates have been established for weights as low as 10 pounds, and rate discounts are available for shipments weighing a few hundred pounds. Adding freight to the baggage compartment on passenger flights necessitates rather small-size shipments and thus supports rate-making practices for these shipments.

In addition to small shipment sizes, the *packaging* required for freight shipped by air transportation is usually less than other modes. It is not uncommon in air transportation to find a palletized shipment that is shrink wrapped instead of

TABLE 6.4 Aircraft Operating Characteristics—1996

Model	Number of Seats	Average Cargo Payload (Tons)	Speed Airborne	Flight Length	Fuel (Gallons Per Hour)	Aircraft Operating Cost Per Hour
B747–400	400	8.49	539	5,063	3,445	$7,075
L-1011–100/200	305	4.50	498	1,363	2,399	5,081
B777	291	9.70	513	2,451	2,037	4,194
DC-10–10	286	8.54	498	1,493	2,233	5,092
A300–600	266	11.63	467	1,126	1,671	5,123
MD–11	260	10.24*	524	3,253	2,400	6,335
L-1011–500	222	5.06	523	2,995	2,454	4,764
B767–300ER	216	7.32	495	2,331	1,590	3,616
B757–200	187	2.39	464	1,167	1,048	2,637
MD–90	154	0.43	441	782	817	1,711
B727–200	148	0.63	440	742	1,288	2,396
A320–100/200	148	0.75	458	1,101	816	2,126
B737–400	144	0.49	414	702	792	2,106
MD–80	141	0.48	432	798	924	2,033
DC-9–50	121	0.47	374	345	898	1,925
DC-9–40	109	0.41	387	487	837	1,789
F-100	97	0.17	384	500	705	1,858

*Cargo Carriers have been excluded.

Source: Air Transport Association: Washington, DC, 1998.

banded. The relatively smooth ride through the air and the automated ground handling systems contribute to lower damage and thus reduce packaging needs.

Accessibility and Dependability

Except in adverse conditions such as fog or snow, air carriers are capable of providing **reliable** service. The carriers may not always be on time to the exact minute, but the variations in transit time are small. Sophisticated navigational instrumentation permits operation during most weather conditions.

Poor **accessibility** is one disadvantage of air carriers. Passengers and freight must be transported to an airport for air service to be rendered. This accessibility problem is reduced when smaller planes and helicopters are used to transport freight to and from airports, and most passengers use automobiles. Limited accessibility adds time and cost to the air service provided.

Even with the accessibility problem, air transportation remains a fast method of movement and the only logical mode when distance is great and time is restricted. The cost of this fast freight service is high, about three times greater than truck and 10 times greater than rail. Nevertheless, the high speed and cost make air carriage a premium mode of transportation.

Equipment

Types of Vehicles

As previously mentioned, there are several different **sizes** of airplanes in use, from small commuter planes to huge wide-body, four-engine planes used by the nationals. These various sized planes all have differing costs associated with using them; these costs will be addressed later in the section titled "Cost Structure." Generally speaking, airlines have limited flexibility in designing equipment to meet the special needs of shippers. Table 6.4 compares some of the major aircraft types in terms of seats, cargo payload, speed, fuel consumption, and operating cost per hour. Airlines have many options to select from when purchasing equipment.

Terminals

The air carriers' **terminals** (airports) are financed by the government. The carriers pay for the use of the airport through landing fees, rent and lease payments for space, taxes on fuel, and aircraft registration taxes. In addition, users pay a tax on airline tickets and air freight charges. Terminal charges are becoming increasingly more commonplace for passenger traffic.

The growth and development of air transportation is dependent upon adequate airport facilities. Therefore, to ensure the viability of air transportation, the federal **government** has the responsibility of financially assisting the states in the construction of airport facilities. The various state and local governments assume the responsibility for operating and maintaining the airports.

At the airport, the carriers perform passenger, cargo, and aircraft servicing. Passengers are ticketed, loaded, and unloaded, and their luggage is collected and dispersed. Cargo is routed to specific planes for shipment to the destination airport or to delivery trucks. Aircraft servicing includes refueling; loading of passengers, cargo, luggage, and supplies (food); and maintenance. Major aircraft maintenance is done at specific airports.

As carrier operations become more complex, certain airports in the carriers' scope of operation become hubs. Flights from outlying, lesser populated areas are fed into the hub airport, where connecting flights are available to other areas of the region or country.

For example, Chicago and Denver are major **hub** airports for United Airlines. Flights from cities such as Toledo and Kansas City go to Chicago, where connecting flights are available to New York, Los Angeles, and Dallas. Delta Airlines uses the Atlanta airport in the same way. By using the hub airport approach, the carriers are able to assign aircraft to feed passengers into the hub over low-density routes and to assign larger planes to the higher-density routes between the hub and an airport serving a major metropolitan area. In essence, the hub airport is similar to the motor carrier's break-bulk terminal.

Airport terminals also provide services to passengers, such as restaurants, banking centers, souvenir and gift shops, and snack bars. The new Denver airport also includes some major general purpose attractions similar to a shopping mall. The success of the Pittsburgh airport has resulted in other airports expanding restaurants to include many popular chains (McDonald's, TGI Friday's, Pizza Hut, etc.) and popular shops for clothing, accessories, books, and other items.

Cost Structure

Fixed Versus Variable Cost Components

Like the motor carriers, the air carriers' cost structure consists of **high variable** and low fixed costs. Approximately 80 percent of total operating costs is variable and 20 percent is fixed. The relatively low fixed cost structure is attributable to government (state and local) investment and operations of airports and airways. The carriers pay for the use of these facilities through landing fees, which are variable in nature.

As indicated in Table 6.5, 29.3 percent of airline operating costs in 1997 was incurred for flying operations and amounted to $29.6 billion; maintenance costs equaled 12.3 percent of total operating costs. Both of these expenses are variable costs. The next major category of expense is general services and administrative costs, which totaled $43.9 billion in 1997 and about 43 percent of total operating costs. In 1997, depreciation accounted for about 5.2 percent of total operating expenses.

Table 6.5 provides a comparison of operating costs for 1982, 1988, 1991, and 1997. The cost of flying operations increased from 1982 to 1991, but total costs decreased in 1991 compared to 1988. The decrease in total costs was caused by the decrease in maintenance costs, general services and administrative expenses, and depreciation. However, overall costs increased again in 1997 because of the growth in passenger and freight demand, which increased the number of scheduled trips. The increased price competition in the airline industry has caused airlines to try to operate more efficiently by cutting costs where possible. There has been much effort put forth to decrease labor costs since the airline industry tends to be labor-intensive compared to other modes such as railroads and pipelines.

Fuel

Escalating **fuel costs** have caused problems in the past for the airlines. The average price per gallon of fuel for domestic operations was about 89 cents in 1983

TABLE 6.5 U.S. Scheduled Airlines Operating Costs

	($ Billions)			
Expense	**1982**	**1988**	**1991**	**1997**
Flying operations	14.7	16.7	16.8	29.6
Maintenance	3.4	7.2	6.7	12.3
General services and administration				
Passenger services	3.3	5.7	5.1	8.58
Aircraft and traffic servicing	5.6	11.8	9.1	15.85
Promotion and sales	5.2	11.0	8.8	14.23
Administrative	2.6	3.6	2.9	5.25
Depreciation	2.3	3.7	3.2	5.25
Total costs	37.1	59.7	56.7	88.96

Source: Air Transport Association of America, *Air Transport 1998* (Washington, DC, 1998).

compared to 57 cents in 1979 and 30 cents in 1978. It dropped to under 60 cents in 1986 but rose again in 1990 to above the 1983 level. They decreased again by 1998 to about 55 cents per gallon.

The impact that such fuel increases have had can be shown by analyzing fuel consumption for certain aircraft that are commonly used today. The Air Transportation Association's annual report shows that the number of gallons of fuel consumed per hour for the following planes is as follows.[12]

400-seat 747	3,445 gallons/hour
286-seat DC-10	2,233 gallons/hour
148-seat 727	1,288 gallons/hour
109-seat DC-9	837 gallons/hour

Using a cost of $1.00 per gallon, the fuel cost per hour is $3,268 for a 747, $2,133 for a DC-10, $1,260 for a 727, and $801 for DC-9. Consequently, the lower fuel costs in recent years has helped airlines to improve their financial performance and increase their stock prices.

When fuel costs have risen, carriers have scrutinized planes in the fleet as well as routes served. More **fuel-efficient** planes have been developed and added to carrier fleets. In the short run, carriers are substituting smaller planes on low-density (low demand) routes and eliminating service completely on other routes. Commuter lines have provided substitute service on the routes abandoned by major and national carriers. Fuel costs were as high as 30 percent of operating expenses in 1981 but are now about 10 percent.

Labor

Labor costs represent over one-third of total operating expenses in the airline industry. In 1997, carriers employed about 586,000 people at an average annual compensation of $65,000.[13] Average compensation includes wages and fringe benefits.

Airlines employ people with a variety of different **skills.** To operate the planes, the carrier must employ pilots, copilots, and flight engineers. The plane crew also includes the flight attendants, who serve the passengers. Communications personnel are required to tie together the different geographic locations. Mechanics and ground crews for aircraft and traffic service provide the necessary maintenance and servicing of the planes. The final component of airline employment consists of the office personnel and management. Overall employment has decreased as airlines have moved aggressively to reduce costs to improve their competitiveness and lower prices in selected markets.

Strict **safety** regulations are administered by the FAA. Acceptable flight operations, as well as hours of service, are specified for pilots. Both mechanics and pilots are subject to examinations on safety regulations and prescribed operations. FAA regulations also dictate appropriate procedures for flight attendants to follow during take-off and landing.

The **wages** paid to a pilot usually vary according to the pilot's equipment rating. A pilot who is technically capable (has passed a flight examination for a given type of aircraft) of flying a jumbo jet will receive a higher compensation than one who flies a single-engine, six-passenger plane.

Wages can also vary according to whether a person works for a **union** airline or not. In 1996, the average salary for a captain with 10 years of experience who belonged to a union was well over $100,000, whereas an employee with the same credentials and a position at a nonunion airline, received about $52,000.

Equipment

As mentioned earlier, the cost of operating airplanes varies. Larger planes are more costly to operate per hour than smaller planes, but the cost per seat mile is lower for larger planes. That is, the larger plane has the capability to carry more passengers; thus, the higher cost is spread out over a large number of output units.

Table 6.4 shows the hourly operating costs for four aircraft used by major carriers in 1996. The cost per *block hour* was $7,075 for the 400-seat 747 and $1,925 for the 121-seat DC-9. However, the cost per seat mile was $0.003 for the 747 and $0.050 for the DC-9. This reduced operating cost per seat mile for the larger planes indicates that economies of scale exist in air equipment.

Economies of Scale

Large-scale air carrier operations do have some economies of scale, which result from more extensive use of large-size planes or indivisible units. The small number of major and national carriers, approximately 30, that transport 90 percent of the passengers indicates that large-scale operations exist.

The information contained in Table 6.4 suggests the existence of economies of scale with large-size planes. Market conditions (sufficient demand) must exist to permit the efficient utilization of larger planes; i.e., if the planes are flown near capacity, the seat mile costs will obviously decrease.

Another factor indicating large-scale operations for air carriers is the integrated **communication** network required for factors such as operating controls and passenger reservations. Small local or regional carriers find the investment required for such a communication system rather staggering, but without the communication system, the emerging carrier cannot effectively operate (provide connecting service with other carriers and through ticketing to passengers). Such carriers have purchased passenger reservation systems from large carriers in order to be competitive.

The air carrier industry overall has a cost structure that closely resembles that of motor carriers. Long-run economies of scale, as compared to short-run economies of plane size and utilization, are not significant in the air carrier industry.

Over the years the federal government has provided direct operating **subsidies,** that is, public service revenues, to air carriers. The subsidies have been provided to ensure air carrier service over particular routes where operating expenses exceed operating incomes. The subsidies enable regional carriers to provide service to lesser populated areas that otherwise would probably not have air service.

In the fiscal year 1983, for example, the federal government paid $54.6 million in subsidies to 43 regional carriers. This compares to $79.8 million paid in fiscal year 1982. Such subsidies were administered by the Civil Aeronautics Board (CAB), which reviewed the operating efficiency of the carrier as well as the public interest. Since 1968, the subsidies have totaled less than $100 million per year.

Rates

Pricing

Airline pricing for passenger service is characterized by the **discounts** from full fare. Seats on the same plane can have substantially different prices, depending on restrictions attached to the purchase, such as having to stay over a weekend or having to purchase the ticket in advance. Business people generally pay more for their airline travel due to the more rigid schedules they are on and the fact that they usually depart and return during the high-demand times. In 1991, 95 percent of the U.S. majors' domestic revenue passenger miles sold at a discount rate, with the average being 66 percent of full fare.[14] The price of seats on different flights and the price of the same seat on a particular flight can vary due to competition with other airlines, the time and day of departure and return, the level of service (first class versus coach or no-frills service), and advance ticket purchase. Discount pricing has continued throughout the 1990s as airlines have attempted to increase their "payload." Some sales on flights are tracked closely for pricing purposes.

Cargo pricing is dependent mainly on **weight** and/or cubic dimensions. Some shipments that have a very low density can be assessed an overdimensional charge, usually based on 8 pounds per cubic foot. This overdimensional charge is used to gain a more appropriate revenue from shipments that take up a lot of space but do not weigh much. An exaggerated example of a shipment to which this rule would apply is a shipment of inflated beach balls. Other factors affecting the price paid to ship freight via air transportation include completeness of service and special services, such as providing armed guards.

Operating Efficiency

An important measure of operating efficiency used by air carriers is the **operating ratio.** The operating ratio measures the portion of operating income that goes to operating expenses:

$$\text{Operating Ratio} = \frac{\text{Operating Expense}}{\text{Operating Income}} \times 100$$

Only income and expenses generated from passenger and freight transportation are considered.

Like the motor carrier industry, the air carrier industry's operating ratio was in the high 90s. Between 1978 and 1991, the air carrier industry had an operating ratio ranging from 94 to 103. In 1997, the airline operating ratio was 92, due to improved

STOP OFF

MERGER REPORT: U.S. AIRLINES AND RAILROADS REAP BENEFITS OF THE CONTINUED DECLINE IN THE PRICE OF OIL

Anyone who drives a car knows falling oil prices eventually show up at the gasoline pump. But declining crude prices also are felt at factories, power plants, and airports, creating far more winners than losers for the United State's business sector.

Oil prices fell again Tuesday, with the January crude contract slipping nine cents to settle at $11.13 a barrel. In early New York Mercantile Exchange trading Wednesday, the January contract was off one cent at $11.12 a barrel. Once factoring in inflation, oil prices are at lows not seen since 1972, according to Merrill Lynch & Co.'s Michael Rothman. Meanwhile, the U.S. Department of Energy said the average price for regular unleaded gasoline fell this week to 97.4 cents a gallon, down from $1.15 a gallon a year ago.

The biggest beneficiaries, of course, are everyday consumers who buy more refined oil products than does any single U.S. industry. But beyond them, the companies and industries that buy oil and natural gas in great quantities—for vehicles with big fuel tanks, like airplanes and trains—are enjoying a nice boost.

Indeed, low oil prices are helping many companies remain competitive in an increasingly cutthroat global business environment by allowing them to reduce costs and maintain profits—all while keeping consumer prices in check.

Some benefits of lower oil prices are indirect, said Frantz Price, Senior Vice President at WEFA Inc., an economic consulting firm in Eddystone, Pennsylvania. Consider what tends to happen to the price of other energy sources, such as natural gas, when oil prices go down: They go down, too. So even a company that uses very little oil in its own processes stands to benefit.

So who wins? Airlines, for one. For airlines, fuel is the second-biggest expense behind labor—and any change in fuel prices drops swiftly to the bottom line. A one-cent shift in the price of jet fuel translates into $180 million annually for the U.S. airline industry, said David Swierenga, chief economist for the Air Transport Association (ATA).

The ATA estimates airlines will end the year having paid an average of 51 cents a gallon for jet fuel. Current spot prices are now near 40 cents a gallon, but many airlines won't see as big an immediate savings because they are locked into hedging contracts, where they agreed to pay a certain price for fuel. Last year, U.S. airlines paid an average 63.2 cents a gallon, according to the ATA. Next year, ATA estimates fuel will average 49 cents a gallon for the major carriers.

Source: *Wall Street Journal:* Brussels, Dec. 3, 1998.

operating efficiencies.[15] The overall profit margin is small, and a loss is incurred when the operating ratio exceeds 100. Another widely used measure of operating efficiency is the load factor. The load factor measures the percentage of a plane's capacity that is utilized.

$$\text{Load Factor} = \frac{\text{Number of Passengers}}{\text{Total Number of Seats}} \times 100$$

Airlines have raised plane load factors to the 65–70 percent range. The particular route and type of plane (capacity) directly affect the load factor as does price, service level, and competition.

Again, referring to Table 6.4, the **relationship** among load factor, cost, plane size, and profitability can be seen. Assume that a route requires one hour to traverse and has a load factor of 65 percent; the average operating cost per passenger for a 747 is $22.76 ($5,946 per hour/(402 [capacity] × .65 [load factor]). If the demand drops to 80 passengers on the route, the load factor for the 747 would be 19.9 percent (80/402), and the hourly operating cost per passenger would be $74.32 ($5, 946/80). At this level of demand, the carrier would substitute a smaller capacity plane, a 727 or DC-9. With 80 passengers, the load factor for the DC-9 would be 78 percent (80/103) and the average operating cost would be $20.47 ($1,638/80). The small aircraft would be more economical to operate over this lower-density (demand) route, and the carrier would substitute this more efficient plane (DC-9) on this hypothetical route.

Equipment substitution, however, may not be possible, and substitution may result in excess capacity. The jumbo planes have large carrying capacities that may not be utilized in low-demand routes. Thus, large-capacity planes are used on high-demand routes such as New York–Chicago and New York–Los Angeles, and smaller capacity planes are used on low-demand routes such as Toledo–Chicago and Pittsburgh–Memphis.

Current Issues

Safety

The issue of airline safety is of great importance to the airline industry. Any incident involving airplanes receives a great deal of publicity from the media because of the large number of people affected at one time. (Accidents involving motor vehicles affect only a few people in each incident but affect a greater number of people than do airline accidents in the long run.)

Several factors affect airline safety. First, airport security has come under close scrutiny over the past several years. In 1988, a bomb exploded on Pan Am flight 203, and the plane crashed into the town of Lockerbie, Scotland, killing all passengers on board and several people on the ground. In 1987, a former airline employee shot his supervisor on a flight to Los Angeles and then caused the plane to crash. Such tragedies have spurred many people to take a closer look at airline security. International terrorism has also heightened concern about airport security.

Air travel is more popular than ever, as indicated previously, but there is still great concern about safety. The 1990s had some major air disasters among major carriers, such as TWA, American, U.S. Airways, SwissAir, and the ValuJet crash in the Florida Everglades. In addition, the frequent reportings of near collisions, minor accidents, and airplane recalls have heightened public awareness of the air safety problem. The aging air fleet and the number of flights will almost certainly result in more safety concerns. Finally, as with other transportation modes, the issue of substance abuse concerning pilots and ground crews has become important.

In spite of these concerns, airline travel is still a very safe form of transportation; however, these issues are currently being addressed by the airlines to ensure that airline transportation remains safe.

Technology

Because the airline industry must offer quick and efficient service to attract business, it constantly needs more sophisticated equipment. With other modes such as railroads and water carriers, travel times are measured in days; however, air carriers measure travel time in hours.

For this reason, the airline industry has developed automated information processing programs like the Air Cargo Fast Flow Program, which was designed by the Port Authority of New York/New Jersey. The Fast Flow Program is a paperless system that speeds the processing of air freight cargo through customs processing, which was found to take 106 out of 126 hours of processing time for international shipments. The system allows the air freight community to tie into customs-clearing systems and thus reduce paperwork and time requirements dramatically. The system also will provide better tracking of shipments and better communication between connecting carriers. These improvements will allow customers to receive their inbound shipments faster than ever before.[16]

SUMMARY

- The airline industry began its development in the early part of the twentieth century, and its growth was influenced to a great extent initially by government interest and policy.
- The airline industry is dominated by revenue from passenger service, but air freight revenue is growing in importance.
- Both private and for-hire carriers operate as part of the airline industry, but private carrier service is predominantly passenger movement.
- For-hire carriers can be classified based on service offered (all cargo, air taxi, charter, etc.) or annual operating revenue (majors, nationals, or regionals).
- All cargo carriers and commuter operators have grown in importance in recent years and play a more important role in the total airline industry.
- A relatively large number of airline companies exist, but a small number (less than three percent) account for more than 90 percent of the total earnings.
- Deregulation of airlines was rationalized to some extent with the argument that an increase in the number of carriers would increase competition. Initially, there was an increase, but subsequently the number has declined.
- Airlines are unique in that they face limited intermodal competition, but intramodal competition is very keen in terms of pricing and service and has been exacerbated by unused capacity.
- Airline service competition is usually in terms of frequency and timing of flights, but special passenger services and programs are important.
- The express portion of air freight has grown dramatically. A growing number of commodities use air freight service, and increased growth is expected.
- Speed is the major advantage of airlines for both passengers and freight, but the airlines' speed of service has been offset recently by congestion and fewer flights.
- The higher cost of airline service can be a trade-off against lower inventory and warehousing costs, as well as other logistics-related savings.
- Airline carriers are essentially long-haul service providers for passengers and freight since the cost of take-offs and landings makes short hauls relatively uneconomical.
- Airlines usually provide service for small shipments where value is high and/or the product may be perishable.
- Airlines offer a generally reliable/consistent service, but their accessibility is limited.
- Airlines use different types of equipment that limits their carrying capacity, but their overall equipment variety is also limited.
- Airlines use publicly provided airways and terminals, but pay user charges on both, which helps make their cost structure highly variable.

- Major and national airlines use a hub approach to their service, which contributes to operating efficiency, but often adds travel time.
- Fuel and labor costs are important expense categories for airlines and have received much managerial attention. The low fuel cost of the late 1990s has helped the airlines improve their profitability.
- Economies of scale affect the airline industry, making larger-scale carriers usually more efficient, based on equipment and communications.
- In the era of deregulation, discount pricing has become very popular, and it has made the rate schedules of airlines for passenger services complex.
- Airline safety is a very important issue, but overall airlines have a very good record.
- Traditionally, airlines have capitalized on new equipment technology to improve their operating efficiency and to expand capacity. In recent years, technology improvements have come in a variety of other areas.

Key Terms

advertising pg. 177
all-cargo carriers 172
capacity 179
changing fuel costs 181
charters 173
commodity examples 178
communication 183
commuters 173
company personnel 172
different types 172
discount pricing 184
emergency shipments 178
employee skill variety 182
employment 171
equipment size 180
equipment substitution 186
excess capacity 175
explanation of costs 181
freight revenue 178
frequency and timing 177
fuel efficiency 182
government role 180
high operating ratios 184
high variable cost 181
high-density corridors 178
hub systems 181
importance of passengers 171
intense intramodal competition 175
limited accessibility 180
limited intermodal competition 175
major advantage 178
majors 172
many carriers 173
nationals 172
no-frills service 177
passenger revenue 178
pilot wages 183
private carriers 174
public terminals 180
rates and service 177
regionals 172
relationships 185
reliability 180
revenue classes 172
safety 183
small shipments 179
speed 178
speed offsets 178
subsidies 184
time factor 171
U.S. Post Office 171
union wages 183
weight based 184

Study Questions

1. What are the types of carriers as defined by revenue class? Who are some of the members of each class? Do you think the members of each class would compete against or work together with members of the other classes? What about members of their own class? Use examples obtained from advertising or Websites.

2. Discuss the ways in which air carriers compete with each other. How have regulatory changes affected this competition?

3. What is the major advantage of air carriers? How does this advantage impact the inventory levels of those firms using air transportation? Explain how this advantage relates to the choice of modes when choosing between air carriage and other modes of freight and passengers.

4. Discuss the length of haul and carrying capacity of the air carriers. Explain how this both favors and hinders air carriers from a competitive standpoint.

5. What is the role of government in air transportation? Include both economic and safety regulations in your answer.

6. How does fuel cost and efficiency affect both air carrier costs and pricing?

7. What is the current situation of labor within the air industry? Are unions a major factor? How does skill level cary within the industry? Do you think this situation is similar to other modes? If so, which one(s) and explain why.

8. Do air carriers have economies of scale at any level? Discuss and support your answer with examples.

9. How do air carriers price their services? Is the weight or density of the shipment a factor? Explain this factor as part of your answer. How does air carrier pricing relate to the value of the goods being transported?

10. What are the current issues facing the air industry? Discuss how each impacts the industry, its customers and employees?

11. What is the cost structure of the air industry? How does it compare with other modes? How does this affect pricing, particularly passengers? Be sure your answer includes examples from either advertising or the Internet.

Notes

1. Air Transportation Association Annual Reports.
2. Ibid.
3. Ibid.
4. Ibid.
5. Ibid.
6. Ibid.
7. Ibid.
8. Ibid.
9. Ibid.
10. Ibid.
11. Ibid.
12. Ibid.
13. Ibid.
14. Ibid.
15. Ibid.
16. Ibid.

Suggested Readings

Cotrill, Ken, "Air Express Carriers Stress Time-Definite Services in U.S.–Europe Trade," *Global Sites and Logistics,* October 1998, pp. 28–35.

Gooley, T. B., "Air Freight Gears Up for the 21st Century," *Logistics Management and Distribution Report,* March 1998, pp. 87–90.

Herbert, Lisa, "Information Must Fly With Air Cargo," *Transportation and Distribution,* April 1998, pp. 115–118.

Krause, Kristin S., "Goodbye Southern Air," *Traffic World,* October 5, 1998, pp. 34–35.

James, B., "Turbulent Times for Asia's Air Carriers," *Global Sites and Logistics,* February 1998, pp. 46–52.

Nall, S., "Air Cargo Alliances Take Tentative First Steps into Cargo Arena," *Global Sites and Logistics,* June 1998, pp. 54–63.

Oster, Jr., C.V., Rubin, B.M., and Strong, J. S., "Economic Impacts of Transportation Investments: the Case of Federal Express," *Transportation Journal,* Winter 1997, pp. 34–44.

Reyes, Brian, "Belly Carriers Hungry for Air Cargo," *American Shipper,* April 1998, pp. 48–51.

Reyes, Brian, and Gillis, C., "Bumpy Flight Toward Open Skies," *American Shipper,* May 1998, pp. 93–95.

Schwartz, B. M., "Soaring to Meet Rising Expectations," *Transportation and Distribution,* May 1998, pp. 70–74.

Windle, R. J. and Dresner, "The Short and Long Run Effects of Entry on U.S. Domestic Air Routes," *Transportation Journal,* Winter 1995, pp. 14–25.

Cases

Case 6.1

CBN Airways

Pete Swan, CEO of CBN Airways, was having a bad day. Several weeks ago, Scott Keller, Executive Vice President of Arkansas Wiener Corporation, had promised Pete that they were going to start air freighting the deliveries of their new line of "prime cut wieners" to the Northeast market area. Pete had really been excited at that point because CBN was a relatively new company that was struggling to break even, and he was worried about meeting the growing financial obligations of the company. Now it seemed that Mr. Keller was having second thoughts and had been solicited by one of the large Arkansas-based motor carriers, I. M. Hurting.

Background

CBN Airways was the product of many years of planning by Pete Swan while he worked for U.S. Airways in Pittsburgh. Pete was Director of Freight Transportation with U.S. Airways, but was dissatisfied with the focus and emphasis that they placed upon freight movements. Pete felt that freight movements were an afterthought after passengers. In other words, the basic network and services were designed and focused upon efficient passenger movements.

It was Pete's opinion that U.S. Airways should set up a separate subsidiary for air freight and aggressively market freight movements of high-value, perishable products. However, he was not able to persuade them that his vision would be a profitable venture.

In 1995, Pete met with Gordon Mulkey, a venture capital manager with a large Midwestern company. In a casual conversation he mentioned his dream and struck a responsive chord. Gordon asked Pete to draft a strategic plan with his goals and objectives. Pete Swan's focus in his strategic demand emphasized the need for high quality, guaranteed service of medium to high-value products and perishable products. He emphasized the Northeastern area of the United States because of its large population base and income level.

Pete also pointed out in his strategic plan that food products were usually moved by motor carriers. He believed, however, that there was a potential market niche for air freight movement of high-quality, packaged meat that could be shipped fresh instead of frozen. Pete had identified a select number of states that dominated the meat production including Arkansas and Iowa. He also felt that fresh fish was another potential niche.

Gordon Mulkey was impressed when he read Pete's strategic plan for CBN Airways. He approached the board of his venture capital company, Far Out Investments, and the board approved an initial capital outlay of $25 million for the start of CBN Airways.

Arkansas Wieners

Pete Swan met Scott Keller at a Young President's Club meeting in Chicago during the first year of CBN's operations. Pete hoped to identify some potential customers at the meetings because CBN had only been marginally successful during the first nine months. Pete was hoping that some of the young presidents would be sympathetic to his plight and be willing to try his service.

Scott Keller responded almost immediately when Pete Swan talked to him at the cocktail reception to kick off the Y.P.C. meetings. Scott was explaining his plan to introduce a high-quality wiener made with steak to appeal to the younger professionals who were always pressed for time. Scott wanted to ship the wieners to select outlets in the Northwest. He asked Pete what he thought about the plan and Pete was enthusiastic. Peter quickly suggested a relationship with CBN Airways as the prime transporter of the prime-cut wieners. Scott liked the idea and asked for a proposal including rates.

Current Picture

Pete Swan finished his proposal for Scott Keller in about five days after returning from a visit to Scott's offices in Pickle Gap, Arkansas, and followed up with a telephone call. Scott informed Pete at that point that the Vice President of Sales of the I. M. Hurting Truckline was coming to his office that day with a proposal for expedited, express truck service. It was now two weeks later and Pete had not heard anything from Scott Keller. Pete was worried. CBN had finished its first year of operations and the revenue deficit was larger than expected. Gordon Mulkey had called to express concern on behalf of Far Out Investments.

Case Questions

1. What is your evaluation of Pete Swan's strategic vision for CBN Airways?

2. Help Pete Swan by writing a one- to two-page memo to him suggesting how he can persuade Scott Keller to buy CBN's services. (Hint: What are the trade-offs for air service?)

3. Recommend with appropriate rationale, some other products for CBN to focus upon to enhance their revenues.

CASE 6.2

Southwest Airlines

Southwest Airlines started its passenger service as an intrastate carrier in Texas. Initially, they offered service between Dallas, Houston, and San Antonio. The original founders of Southwest were probably considered eccentric or even crazy during the early years of the company's development. After all, their strategies were contrary to the conventional wisdom of the 1970s and 1980s.

Most airline executives felt that interstate service offered the most potential for profit and that an important ingredient of efficiency was to use the hub concept for service. These same executives also felt that in-flight service of beverages, snacks, and/or food should be included in the fare and that guaranteed seating and baggage checking were necessary ingredients also for success. Perhaps even more important was their vision that air service was a premium transportation alternative and should be priced accordingly.

The Southwest Approach

Dissatisfied with the then-current airline service, the founders of Southwest Airlines felt that there was a great opportunity for an intrastate carrier to serve the growing metropolitan areas of Dallas, Houston, and San Antonio. Southwest also, after a while, switched its service to the old airports in Dallas and Houston that had been almost abandoned by the larger carriers.

Southwest used a no-frills, low-price service approach in their marketing strategy. After deregulation of the airline industry in 1978, there was greater opportunity to offer "rock bottom" fares, point-to-point, in selected market areas.

Another important ingredient of the Southwest strategy was their approach with their employees. Southwest is run like a democracy, with all of its employees given the opportunity to participate in running the company and having an ownership stake through stock investment. Employees are viewed as the most important asset of the company and the number one priority. Underlying this philosophy is the action that happy employees will help make the company efficient and will provide better overall customer service. This approach has worked for Southwest—their profitability, customer service, and employee morale are the stuff that legends are made of.

The key points of their continuing success have been:

- Dominance of the short-haul, high-density markets using secondary airports
- Rock bottom fares
- Aggressive advertising
- High level of service
- Employees' attitude and buy-in
- Fiscally sound and conservative

Future Opportunity

Southwest has ventured away from its Southwestern U.S. market focus and into other cities throughout the country while still maintaining its culture. Now the company needs to reexamine its strategies for the twenty-first century.

Case Questions

1. What is your evaluation of Southwest Airlines?
2. What changes, if any, would you recommend?
3. What difficulties would a new entrant to this low-cost market likely face?

CHAPTER 7

PIPELINES

Brief History

Pipelines have played an important role in the transportation industry in the post-World War II era. Originally, pipelines were used to feed other modes of transportation, such as railroads or water carriers. The Pennsylvania Railroad initiated the development of pipelines in the oil fields of Pennsylvania in the nineteenth century and then sold out to the Standard Oil Company, establishing the precedent of pipelines being owned by the oil companies. Early in the twentieth century, the oil companies operated the pipelines as integrated subsidiaries and often used them to control the oil industry by not providing needed transportation service to new producers. Consequently, after World War II, in a decision rendered by the U.S. Supreme Court known as the Champlin Oil Case, pipelines would operate as common carriers if there were a demand by shippers of oil for their services.

Industry Overview

The pipeline industry is unique in a number of important aspects, including the type of commodity hauled, ownership, and visibility. The industry is relatively unknown to the general public, which has little appreciation of the role and importance of pipelines. Pipelines are limited in the markets they serve and very limited in the commodities they can haul. Furthermore, pipelines are the only mode with no **backhaul,**; i.e., they are unidirectional with products that only move in one direction through the line.

Significance of Pipelines

As seen in Table 7.1, pipelines accounted for more than 57.5 percent of the total intercity ton-miles shipped in the United States in 1995. This figure is comparable to motor carriers, while pipelines' relative position on a strict tonnage basis is comparable to that of the railroads. Few people in the United States would guess that pipelines compare to motor carriers and rail companies in terms of traffic relevance. They are virtually unknown to the general public but represent a key component in our transportation system.

TABLE 7.1 Pipeline Share of Intercity Traffic

Year	Ton-miles Shipped (Billions)	Total Transportation Intercity Ton-miles (%)
1945	129	12.4
1950	129	12.1
1955	203	15.9
1960	229	17.4
1965	306	18.7
1970	431	22.3
1975	507	59.9
1980	588	47.2
1985	564	47.2
1990	584	54.2
1995	601	57.5
1997	628	64.4

Source: *Transportation in America,* 16th ed., (Washington D.C.: Eno Transportation Foundation, 1998).

TABLE 7.2 Pipeline Network

Oil (000)		Gas (000)	
Year	**Miles**	**Year**	**Miles**
1960	191	1960	631
1970	219	1970	913
1980	218	1980	1,052
1985	214	1985	1,119
1990	209	1990	1,207
1995	201	1995	1,262

Source: *Transportation in America,* 16th ed., (Washington D.C.: Eno Transportation Foundation, 1998).

TABLE 7.3 Revenue Position of Pipelines

Oil (Millions)		Gas (Millions)	
Year	**Revenue**	**Year**	**Revenue**
1960	900	1960	8,700
1970	1,400	1970	16,400
1980	7,500	1980	85,900
1985	8,900	1985	103,900
1990	8,500	1990	66,000
1995	9,100	1995	58,400

Source: *Transportation in America,* 16th ed., (Washington D.C.: Eno Transportation Foundation, 1998).

As shown in Table 7.2, the pipeline network grew steadily until the early 1980s, allowing pipelines to move an increased amount of tonnage. However, Table 7.2 does not adequately reflect the increase in total capacity because it does not show the diameter of pipelines. As we will discuss later, pipeline diameters have increased in recent years, and the larger diameters have increased capacity significantly because of the increased volume that can move through the pipeline. The larger diameter has also allowed the total network shown in Table 7.2 to decrease since the early 1980s.

The tonnage comparison shown in Table 7.1 is a sharp contrast to the revenue picture indicated in Table 7.3. Here the low rates of the pipeline, which are discussed later in this chapter, are reflected in the very low percentage of the total intercity revenue paid to all pipeline carriers. The pipelines account for approximately four percent of total transportation revenues, compared to the motor carriers, which account for more than 75 percent of the total revenue for almost the same share of intercity ton-miles.

Types of Carriers

As noted earlier, due to the decision rendered by the U.S. Supreme Court in the Champlin Oil Case, pipelines operate as **common carriers.** Hence, although some private carriers exist today, the for-hire carriers dominate the industry. Common carriers account for approximately 92 percent of all pipeline carriers.

Ownership

With some minor exceptions, oil companies have been the owners of the oil pipelines. Beginning with Standard Oil Company buying out the Pennsylvania Railroad and developing pipelines more extensively in order to control the industry and enhance its market dominance, oil companies have been the principal owners of pipelines. The federal government entered the pipeline business briefly during World War II when it developed two pipelines to bring crude oil and oil products from the oil fields of the Southwest to the Northeast in order to ensure an uninterrupted flow of oil. These two pipelines, known as the Big Inch and the Little Inch, were sold to private companies after the war.

As discussed previously, most of the pipelines are operated as common carriers on a for-hire basis, even though most oil pipelines are owned by the oil industry. Some pipelines are joint ventures because of the capital investment unnecessary for large-diameter pipelines. Individual, vertically integrated oil companies control about 46 percent of the pipeline revenues with an additional 27 percent controlled by jointly owned pipeline companies. Railroads, independent oil companies, and other industrial companies control the remaining percentage.[1]

Number of Carriers

Like the railroad industry, the pipeline has a small number of very large carriers that dominate the industry. In 1992, approximately 145 carriers of oil and oil products offerred for-hire service, accounting for approximately 85 percent of the ton-miles carried. The remaining 15 percent were carried by approximately 12 private carrier operations. The oligopolistic nature of the industry is demonstrated by the fact that 20 major integrated oil companies control about two-thirds of the crude oil pipeline mileage.[2]

There are a number of reasons for the limited number of pipeline companies. First, start-up costs (capital costs) are high. Second, like railroads and public utilities, the economies of scale are such that duplication or parallel competing lines would be uneconomic. Large-size operations are most economical because capacity rises more than proportionately with increases in the diameter of the pipeline and investment-per-mile decreases, as do operating costs per barrel.[3] For example, a 12-inch pipeline operating at capacity can transport three times as much oil as an eight-inch pipeline.

The procedural requirements for entry and the associated legal costs also contribute to the limited number of companies. An additional factor is the industry itself, which has been dominated by the large oil companies that joined together in the post-World War II era to develop from major fields and entry ports.

Oil Carriers

The pipeline industry experienced rapid growth after World War II, but the rate of growth has since decreased dramatically, as indicated in Table 7.4. Intercity ton-miles increased to 628 billion in 1997. The reported operating revenue decreased from 1985 to 1992 by almost 4 percent. There were corresponding changes in other data, including the number of employees, which also decreased (by five percent).[4] Overall, however, oil pipelines play a major role in our transportation network, because, as previously mentioned, they transport more than 20 percent of the total intercity ton-miles.

TABLE 7.4 Oil Pipeline Performance Data

	1975	1985	1995	1997
Intercity Ton-Miles (Millions)	507,000	564,000	601,400	628,400
Tons Transported (Millions)	879	1,019	1,121	1,142
Average Length of Haul (Crude)	633	777	752	—
Transportation Mileage (Crude)	145,679	117,812	114,000	—
Number of Employees	17,000	19,000	16,000	16,000
Operating Revenue ($ Millions)	2,220	8,910	9,061	8,735

Source: *Transportation in America,* 16th ed., (Washington D.C.: Eno Transportation Foundation, 1998).

TABLE 7.5 Gas Pipeline Profile

	1975	1984	1985	1992
Total Production[a]	20,108,661	18,229,638	17,197,999	18,711,808
Total Delivered[a]	17,558,353	16,344,893	15,811,130	17,785,833
Number of Companies	122	137	139	126
Number of Employees	88,500	93,400	108,100	130,100
Operating Revenue[b]	17,836	70,685	67,248	66,289
Operating Expenses[b]	13,148	61,432	57,965	59,936

[a]Million Cubic ft.

[b]Transmission and Distribution Companies ($ Millions)

Source: U.S. Department of Transportation, *National Transportation Statistics* (Washington, D.C.: 1992), pp. 47–48.

Natural Gas Carriers

Another part of the industry is involved with the transportation of natural gas, which, like oil, is an important source of energy. Table 7.5 presents a profile of the gas pipeline industry. The movement data for natural gas are presented in cubic feet, rather than ton-miles. The industry is comparable in size to the oil pipeline industry in terms of the number of companies and, as in the oil pipeline industry, there has been a growth in the number of companies since 1975 (in spite of a decrease in the volume moved). It should be noted that there has been a reclassification of some companies since 1975, so the growth numbers are not exactly comparable. Finally, this profile shows that operating revenues also decreased in 1985 with the decline of the volume moved.

Operating and Service Characteristics

Commodities Hauled

Pipelines are a very specialized carrier in that they transport a very limited variety of products. The four main commodities hauled by pipeline are oil and oil products, natural gas, coal, and chemicals.

TABLE 7.6 Crude Oil and Oil Products Movement Modal Share by Percentage

	Pipelines (%)	Water (%)	Truck (%)	Rail (%)
1980	47.24	49.61	2.15	1.00
1983	45.45	51.53	2.05	0.97
1986	48.65	47.83	2.50	1.02
1989	53.39	42.61	2.78	1.22
1991	53.27	42.81	2.65	1.27
1994	56.50	39.31	2.68	1.51
1997	64.45	30.90	2.90	1.75

Source: *Transportation in America,* 16th ed., (Washington D.C.: Eno Transportation Foundation, 1998).

Oil and Oil Products

The bulk of pipeline movements are crude oil and oil products. In 1994, crude oil and oil products accounted for approximately 57 percent of total pipeline use. Table 7.6 shows the relationships of crude oil and oil product movements by the major modes of the transportation industry with pipelines moving the largest individual share.

The total volume of petroleum transported domestically in the United States has remained relatively stable during the 1980s. However, the split by modes between pipeline and water carrier has changed for several reasons. A pipeline was built across Panama during the 1800s, virtually eliminating long movements of Alaskan crude oil tankers around South America. The Alaskan crude is now transshipped via the pipeline to Atlanta tankers for Gulf and Atlantic Coast deliveries to refineries. Also, another large crude oil pipeline has been built, providing service from the West Coast to Midwest refineries and reducing the need for tanker movements even further.

The length of haul in the oil pipeline industry is medium in length compared to other modes. Crude oil movements average about 800 miles per shipment, and product lines average about 400 miles per movement. The average shipment size for these movements is very large (this will be discussed later in the section titled "Equipment").

Natural Gas

Natural gas pipelines are an important part of our total pipeline network. They account for the second largest number of miles of intercity pipelines—266,900 miles (Table 7.7). The natural gas companies produce about 10 percent of the gas they transport. Independent companies produce the remaining 90 percent.[5]

Coal

Coal pipelines are frequently called **slurry lines** because the coal is moved in a pulverized form in water (one-to-one ratio by weight). Once the coal has reached its destination, the water is removed and the coal is ready for use. Coal pipelines are primarily used for transporting coal to utility companies for generating electricity.[6] The large slurry pipeline that operates between Arizona and Nevada covers 273 miles and moves 4.8 million tons of coal per year. Coal pipelines use enormous quantities of water, which causes concern in the several western states where their installation has been proposed because there is a scarcity of water and the water is not reusable (no backhaul).

TABLE 7.7 Type of Intercity Pipeline and Mileage

Type of Pipeline	Miles of Pipeline
Natural Gas	266,900
Crude Oil	145,770
Petroleum Products	81,296
Coal Slurry	273
Chemicals	4,050

Source: U.S. Department of Transportation, National Transportation Trends and Choices (Washington, D.C.: 1977), and *Association of Oil Pipelines, Oil Pipelines of the U.S. Progress and Outlook* (Washington, D.C.: 1985).

Chemicals

Chemical lines are another type of product line, although only a limited number of different types of chemicals are carried by pipelines. The three major chemicals are anhydrous ammonia, which is used in fertilizer; proplyene, which is used for manufacturing detergents; and ethylene, which is used for making antifreeze.

Relative Advantages

A major advantage offered by the pipeline industry is low rates. Pipeline transportation can be extremely efficient, with large-diameter pipelines operating near capacity. Average revenues for pipeline companies are below one-half of a cent per ton-mile, which is indicative of their low-cost service.

Two additional user cost advantages complement the low rates. First, pipelines have a very good **loss and damage record** (L and D). This record is attributed in part to the types of products transported, but it is also related to the nature of the pipeline service, which provides underground and completely encased movement.

The second important cost advantage is that pipelines can provide a warehousing function because their service is slow. In other words, if the product is not needed immediately, the slow pipeline service can be regarded as a form of free warehousing storage. (Products move through pipelines at an average of three to five miles per hour.)

Another positive service advantage of pipelines is their dependability. They are virtually unaffected by weather conditions, and they very rarely have mechanical failures. Although the service time is slow, scheduled deliveries can be forecasted very accurately, diminishing the need for safety stock. In addition, carriers assume full liability for loss with no extra charges.

Relative Disadvantages

Although the pipeline's slow speed can be considered an advantage due to its use as a free form of warehousing, in some instances the pipeline's slow speed can be considered a disadvantage. For example, if a company's demand is uncertain or erratic, it will have to hold higher levels of inventory to compensate for possible shortages because the pipeline will not be able to deliver an extra amount of the product in a short period of time.

Pipelines are also at a disadvantage when it comes to completeness of service, because they offer a relatively fixed route of service that cannot be easily extended to complete door-to-door service. That is, they have limited geographic flexibility or accessibility. However, because the source of the pipelines and the location of the refineries are known and are fixed for a long period of time, the fixed route service factor may not be a critical problem. Frequently, pipelines depend on railroads and motor carriers to complete delivery, which adds to user costs.

The use of pipelines is limited to a rather select number of products: crude oil, oil products, natural gas, coal, and a limited number of chemicals. There is interest in using pipelines for other products because of their cost advantage, but the technology for such use has not yet been fully developed. Capsule and pneumatic pipelines can carry and extend the low-cost, high-volume, reliable service to other bulk products. Frequency of service, the number of times a mode can pick up and deliver during a particular period, is a characteristic of interest to some users. On one hand, the large tenders (shipment size requirements) and slow speed of pipelines reduces the frequency. On the other hand, service is offered 24 hours a day, seven days a week.

Pipelines are generally regarded as somewhat inflexible because they serve limited geographic areas and limited points within that area. Also, they carry limited types of commodities and only offer one-way service. Finally, the operations technology precludes small shipment sizes.

In summary, pipelines offer a good set of services for particular types of products, but they have some serious limitations for many other products.

Competition

Intramodal

Intramodal competition in the pipeline industry is limited by a number of factors. First, there are a small number of companies—slightly more than 100. The industry, as noted previously, is oligopolistic in market structure, which generally leads to limited price competition. Second, the economies of scale and high fixed costs have led to joint ownership of large-diameter pipelines because the construction of smaller parallel lines is not very efficient. Finally, the high capital costs preclude duplication of facilities to a large extent.

Intermodal

The serious threats to the pipeline industry, in terms of traffic diversion, are other modes of transportation. Technically, pipelines compete with railroads, water carriers, and motor carriers for traffic. However, even with these forms of transportation, the level of competition is limited. The most serious competition is water, or tanker, operations. The only mode that comes close to pipeline costs and rates for transportation is water carriers. However, the limited coverage of water carrier service limits its effective competition also. Trucks have increased the number of products they carry that can also be carried by pipelines. However, truck service complements rather than competes with the pipeline, because trucks perform a distribution function for pipelines (i.e., delivery).

Once a pipeline has been constructed between two points, it is difficult for other modes to compete. Pipeline costs are extremely low, dependability is quite high, and there is limited risk of damage to the product being transported. The major exception is probably coal slurry pipelines because of the need to move the pulverized coal in water can make the costs comparable to rail movements. Water carriers come closest to matching pipeline costs and rates as indicated.

Equipment

The U.S. Department of Transportation estimates that the total pipeline investment is in excess of $21 billion, based on historical costs. Also, the department estimates it would cost about $70 billion to replace the system at today's costs. This great investment in the equipment is necessary to finance the complex operation of getting oil from the well to the market.

Pipelines can be grouped into other categories in addition to for-hire versus private carriers. For instance, they are frequently classified as gathering lines or trunk lines, particularly in reference to the movement of oil. The trunk lines are further classified or subdivided into two types: crude and product lines. The gathering lines are used to bring the oil from the fields to storage areas before the oil is processed into refined products or transmitted as crude oil over the trunk lines to distant refineries (see Figures 7.1 and 7.2). Trunk lines are used for long-distance movement of crude oil or other products, such as jet fuel, kerosene, chemicals, or coal.

Early in the history of the oil industry, the refineries were located primarily in the eastern part of the United States, and thus the long-distance movement of oil was basically the movement of crude oil. The state of technology in the industry also made it much easier to control leakage with crude oil than with refined oil products such as gasoline for kerosene. After World War II, however, refineries were developed at other locations, especially in the Southwest, when better technology (limited seams and welding techniques) made the long-distance movement of oil products easy to accomplish.

When comparing **gathering lines** and trunk lines, there are several important differences to note. First, gathering lines are smaller in diameter, usually not exceeding eight inches, whereas trunk lines are usually 30–50 inches in diameter. Gathering lines are frequently laid on the surface of the ground to ensure ease of relocation when a well or field runs dry. Trunk lines, on the other hand, are usually seen as permanent and are laid underground.

The term **trunk line** is often used on conjunction with oil movements and can refer to crude oil trunk lines or oil product lines. Oil trunk lines move oil to tank farms or refineries in distant locations while oil product lines move the gasoline, jet fuel, and home heating oil from refineries to market areas. Technically, however, any long-distance movement via a large-diameter, permanent pipeline implies a trunk-line movement. Therefore, when coal, natural gas, or chemicals move via pipelines, such movement is usually classified as trunk-line movement.

Commodity Movement

Gathering lines bring oil from the fields to a gathering station, where the oil is stored in sufficient quantity to ship by trunk line to a refinery. After the oil is refined, the various products are stored at a **tank farm** before they are shipped via product line to another tank farm with a market-oriented location. A motor carrier most frequently makes the last segment of the trip, from the market-oriented tank farm to the distributor or ultimate customer.

Trunk lines, as indicated previously, are usually more than 30 inches in diameter and are the major component of the pipeline system. Stations that provide the power to push the commodities through the pipeline are interspersed along the trunk line. For oil movements, pumps are located at the stations, which vary in distance from 20 to 100 miles, depending on the viscosity of the oil and the terrain.

FIGURE 7.1 Major Interstate and Intrastate Crude Oil Pipelines

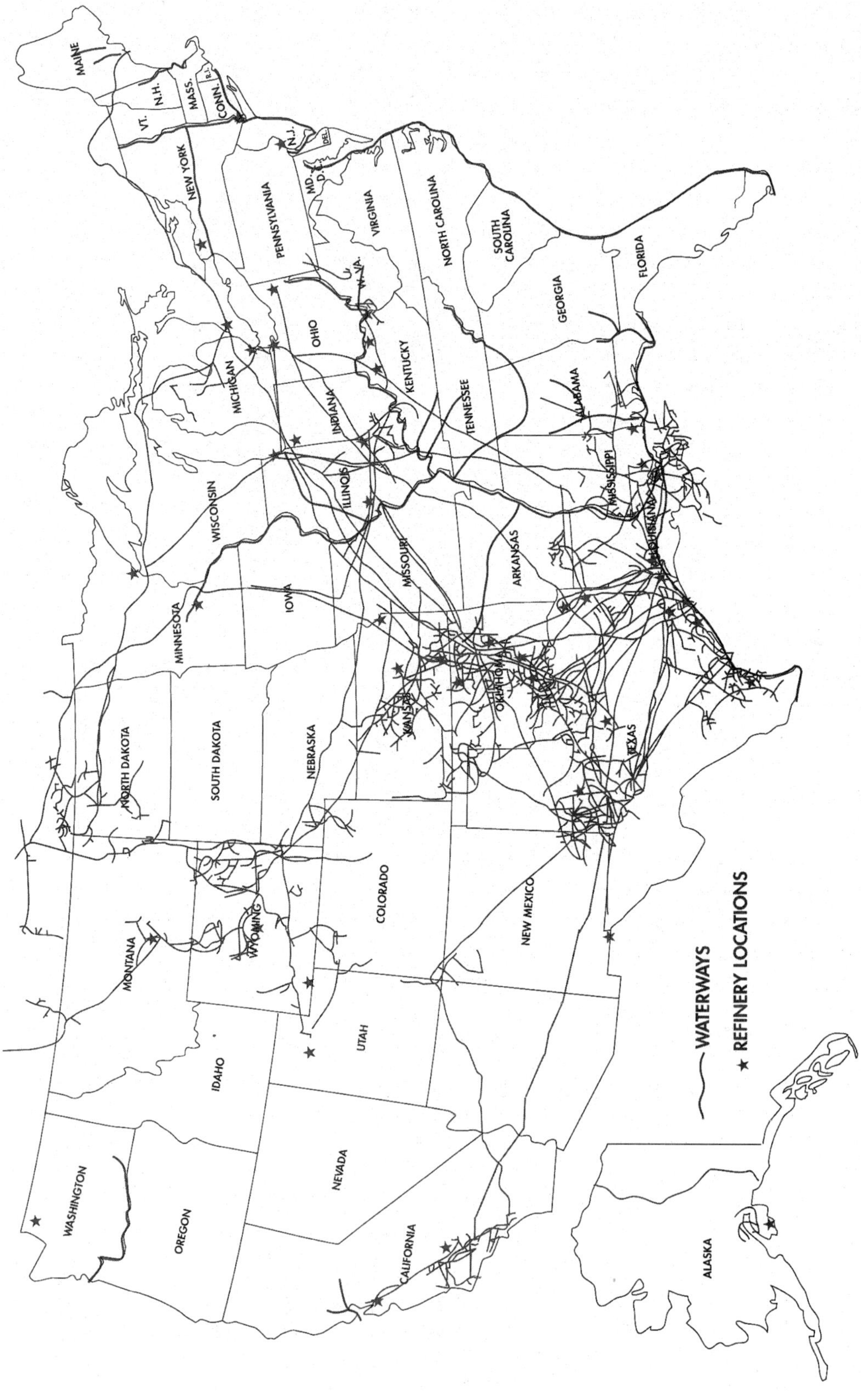

Source: Association of Oil Pipelines, 1997.

FIGURE 7.2 Major Interstate and Intrastate Products Pipelines

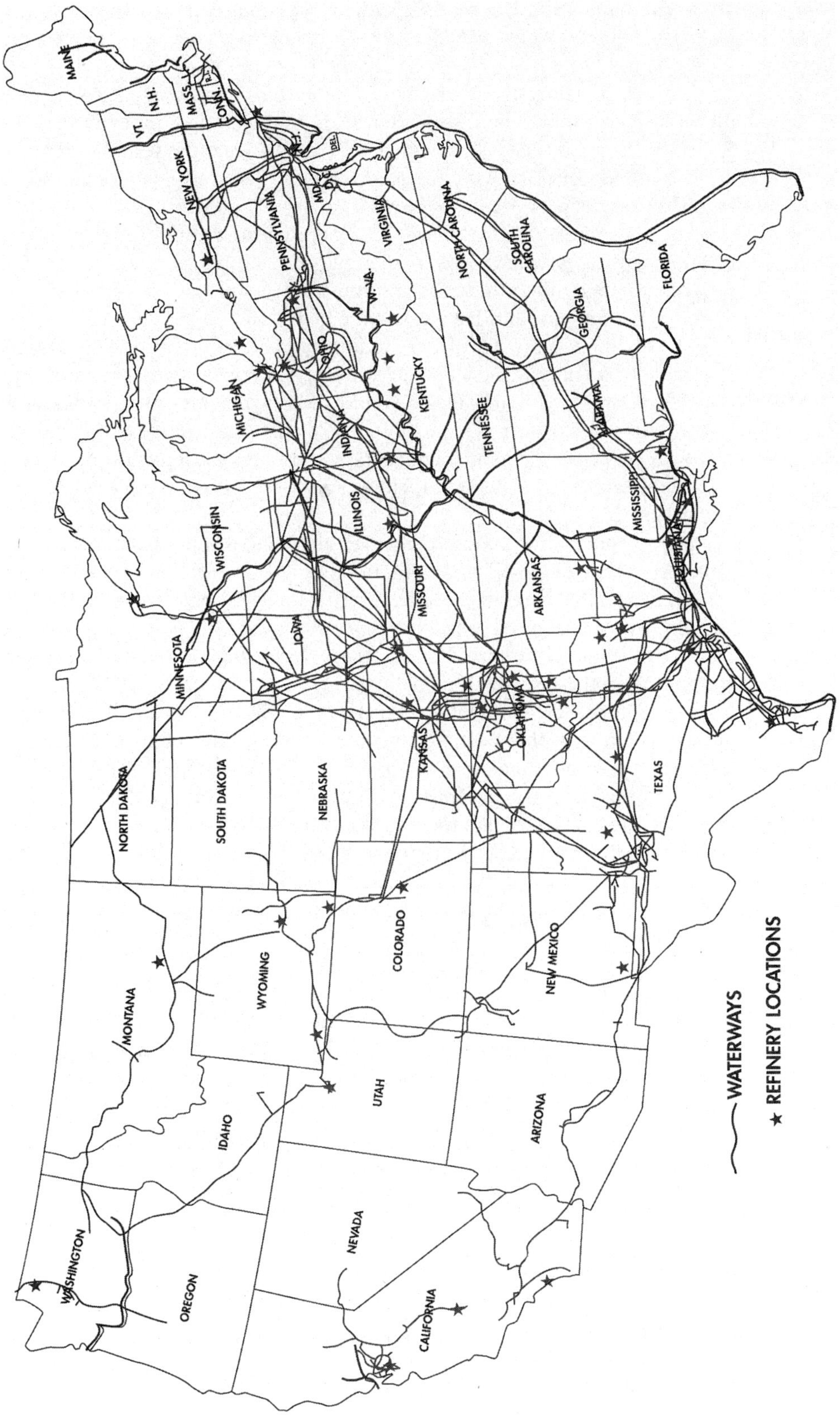

Source: Association of Oil Pipelines, 1997.

These pumping stations for large-diameter pipelines can provide 3,000–6,000 horsepower.[7] Compressors are used for the movement of natural gas, and pumps are used for the liquid items that move through the pipelines.

Today's pipelines have a record of limited loss and damage, which stems from the industry's sophisticated approach to operations. The pipes are constructed of special high-quality alloy steel with a life expectancy of 50 years or more. The pipes are laid in long sections with a limited number of seams. High-quality electric welding of the seams prevents leakage.

The U.S. Department of Transportation, Research and Special Programs Administration (RSPA), Office of Pipeline Safety (OPS) administers the national regulatory program to assure the safe and environmentally sound transportation of natural gas, liquefied natural gas, and hazardous liquids by pipeline.

The Pipeline Safety Act of 1992 requires that RSPA adopt rules requiring pipeline operators to identify facilities located in unusually sensitive areas and high density population areas, to maintain maps and records detailing that information, and to provide those maps to federal and state officials upon request. OPS currently does not have access to a reasonably accurate and national depiction of natural gas and hazardous liquid transmission pipelines and liquefied natural gas facilities operating in the United States.

A preventative approach to maintenance and sophisticated monitoring of the pipeline system are also key factors in limiting loss and damage and protecting the environment. The pipeline is coated with protective paints and resins, and special techniques are used to control corrosion after the pipeline is in the ground. Electric current is used to neutralize the corroding electrical forces that come naturally from the ground to the pipeline.[8]

Computers at the pumping stations continually monitor the flow and pressure of the oil system. Any change indicating a leak is easily detected. Routine visual checks and searches by airplane are sometimes used to locate leaks. Great care is rendered, not only because of the potential losses, but also because of the lawsuits that could ensue as a result of damage to property and the environment.

In the oil segment of the pipeline industry, sophisticated operating and monitoring techniques are used because of the different petroleum products moving through the product lines and the different grades of crude moving through the crude oil lines. There are 15 grades of crude oil and a range of products including jet fuel, kerosene, and aviation fuel. When two or more grades of crude oil or two or more products move through a system at one time, the "batches" may need to be separated by a rubber ball called a **batching** pig. However, this is not always necessary because the different specific grades of the products help to keep them separated.[9] Any mixing (shop) that does occur is only of minor lower-grade items with which they are mixed. Usually, products are scheduled one month in advance with kerosene moving first, then high-grade gasoline, then medium-grade gasoline, then various other products, with home heating oil last. Before the cycle starts again, the pipeline is usually scoured to prevent mixing problems.[10]

Cost Structure

Fixed Versus Variable Cost Components

Like the railroad industry, the pipeline industry has a high proportion of fixed costs with low capital turnover. The pipeline owners have to provide their own right-of-way by purchasing or leasing land and constructing the pipeline and pumping stations along the right-of-way. The property taxes, amortization of depreciation, the return to investors, and preventative maintenance all contribute to the high ratio of fixed to variable expenses.

In addition to the right-of-way coats, the terminal facilities of pipelines contribute to the high level of fixed costs. The same types of expenses associated with the right-of-way, such as depreciation and property taxes, are incurred by the pipeline terminals.

As stated previously, the pipeline industry has significant economies of scale. The high fixed costs and the economies of scale help to explain the common pattern of joint ownership and investment in large-diameter pipelines. Pipelines do not operate vehicles like other modes of transportation because the carrying capacity is the pipe itself, which is best regarded as part of the right-of-way. This unique element of the pipeline operation helps to explain the low variable costs, because vehicles are frequently a major source of variable expense.

Labor costs are very low in the pipeline industry because of the high level of automation. One example is the Trans-Alaska Pipeline System, built at a cost of $9.2 billion, operated by 450 employees.[11] Another variable cost is the cost of fuel for the power system. The pipelines employ about 8,000 people compared to about 10 million in the motor carrier industry for comparable ton-miles on an intercity basis.

Overall, many experts estimate that carrier costs are only 30–40 percent of total costs in the pipeline industry and may be as low as 25 percent in some pipeline systems.

Rates

Pricing in the pipeline industry is unique compared to its major modal competitors. First of all, pipelines do not use the freight classification system that underlies the class rates of railroads and motor carriers. The limited number and specialization of commodities make such a practice unnecessary. A crude oil pipeline or natural gas pipeline has little need for an elaborate classification system.

Even though pipelines have high fixed costs, the differential pricing practices so common in the railroad industry are virtually nonexistent among pipelines. The nature of operation (one-way movement, limited geographic coverage of points, limited products, etc.) provides little opportunity to provide differential pricing practices. Pipelines quote rates on a per-barrel basis (one barrel equals 42 gallons). Quotes for rates are typically point-to-point or zone-to-zone. Also, minimum shipment sizes, usually called **tenders,** are required; these range from 500 barrels to 10,000 barrels.

Pipeline rates are very low, which is reflected in the fact that they carry more than 20 percent of the total intercity ton-miles and receive only about two percent of the total revenues. One gallon of crude oil can be sent from Texas to New York for only 1.8 cents.[12]

Water carrier costs come closest to pipeline costs, and, in fact, international supertankers have lower costs than most pipelines. However, these supertankers do not really compete with domestic pipelines. When considering pipelines with diameters of 30 inches or more, even ocean carriers have difficulty matching pipeline costs.

Current Issues

The pipeline industry can have a powerful impact on the environment and the people who live in it. Because pipelines carry oil products and chemicals, a leak could have disastrous effects. Pipelines generally are built in rural areas, but increases in housing needs could create a situation in which people would live close to the pipelines and be exposed to the effects of a potentially harmful product leak (such as oil or gasoline). Even when people would not be directly affected by a leak, a leak could have a serious impact on wildlife living around the pipeline. Although the U.S. DOT inspects pipelines for safety, it only manages to inspect a small percentage each year; this means the pipeline industry is basically responsible for its own safety level. With the decreasing amount of wildlife areas (such as the reserve in Alaska) and the increased number of people who reside or work near pipelines, the concern for pipeline safety will continue to grow and be an important concern for the industry. However, the overall record of the industry in this area is outstanding. There is a much higher risk of product leakage/damage with oil tankers as evidenced by the number of spills in recent years.

SUMMARY

- The development of pipelines began in the nineteenth century in Pennsylvania by the Pennsylvania Railroad, but subsequently the ownership and development was taken on by the oil companies, who operated them as integrated subsidiaries.
- Ownership by oil companies has continued to the present, but some oil pipelines are owned by non-oil companies. Also, joint ownership by several companies has become common because of the large investment of capital necessary.
- The pipeline industry is a large component of our transportation industry (more than 20 percent of intercity ton-miles), but it is largely invisible to many people.
- Because of market control tactics used by some oil companies, an important U.S. Supreme Court ruling after World War II required pipelines to operate as common carriers, even if owned by an oil company.
- Pipelines are very specialized in terms of the commodities that they carry. Most of the traffic is oil and oil products, but they also carry natural gas, chemicals, and coal.
- Only a small number of pipeline companies exist (about 100), and they only have limited intermodal competition.
- Pipelines are low-cost carriers when operated at capacity, but they have high levels of fixed cost because of the heavy investment necessary in infrastructure.
- Pipeline service is slow and has limited accessibility but is also very reliable with little or no loss and damage.
- Intercity pipeline service is provided by large-diameter (30–50 inches) pipelines called **trunk lines.** Small-diameter pipelines, called **gathering lines,** are used to bring the oil from the producing area to the terminals for storage before processing and/or transporting.
- Pipelines are a highly automated, efficient form of transportation. Oil moves in one direction in large volumes at a steady, slow speed.
- Although there is always some concern about safety and the environment, pipelines have been a relatively safe mode of transportation.

KEY TERMS

backhaul pg. 194
batching 204
classification 195
common carriers 195
gathering lines 201
loss and damage record (L and D) 199
slurry lines 198
tank farms 201
tenders 205
trunk lines 201

STUDY QUESTIONS

1. The integrated ownership of pipelines was used initially by some oil companies to gain control of oil-producing areas. What other reasons can be offered for integrated ownership? Are these reasons valid in today's business environment?

2. The pipeline industry has approximately 100 companies, as constrated to the motor-carrier industry with more than 50,000. How do you account for this difference, given the fact that they both carry approximately the same volume of intercity ton-miles?

3. The typical pipeline company has high fixed costs. What economic factors account for this situation? What special problems does this present?

4. Pipelines account for more than 20 percent of the intercity ton-miles but less than five percent of the revenue paid by shippers to transportation companies. What factors account for this contrast? Is this situation likely to change? Why or why not?

5. Three major modes of transportation—airlines, railroads, and motor carriers—have been deregulated, but no federal legislation has been developed to deregulate the pipeline industry. Why? Is this situation likely to change in the future? Why or why not?

6. The economic and market position of the pipelines has been described as mature and stable with little likelihood of significant growth in the near future. Do you agree? Why or why not?

7. Pipelines are very specialized in terms of the type of products that they transport. What products do they carry? Why are they so specialized? What technological changes would be necessary to expand the variety of products carried by pipeline?

8. Given the present concern about environmental pollution, what are the major environmental concerns related to the pipelines? How do pipelines compare to other modes in terms of safety?

9. "Pipeline companies face limited competition." Do you agree with this statement? Why or why not? What market competition do pipelines actually face?

10. Why are pipelines unknown to many individuals? Do you think the pipelines should advertise to change this?

NOTES

1. U.S. Department of Transportation. *National Transportation Report* (Washington, D.C.: U.S. Government Printing Office, July 1975), p. 40.

2. Association of American Railroads, *Railroad Facts* (Washington, D.C.: Association of American Railroads, 1990), p. 34.

3. Arthur M. Johnson, *The Development of American Petroleum Products* (Ithaca, NY: Cornell University Press, 1956), p. 3.
4. *Transportation in America,* 16th ed. (Washington, D.C.: Eno Transportation Foundation, 1998).
5. Donald Wood and James Johnson. *Contemporary Transportation* (New York: Macmillan, 1989), p. 164.
6. Ibid., p. 164.
7. Ibid., p. 156.
8. Ibid., p. 156.
9. Ibid., p. 157.
10. Ibid., p. 158.
11. Ibid., p. 169.
12. Amoco Educational Services, *Oil on the Move* (Chicago, IL: Amoco Educational Services, 1983).

Suggested Readings

Alberstadt, Milton L. "Ten Years of TAPS," *The Lamp,* Fall 1987, pp. 14–17.

Barfield, R.S. "Trans-Panama Pipeline System Links Alaska Oil to Eastern U.S.," *Pipeline Gas Journal,* June 1983, p. 28.

Bright, Donald B. "Sohio Crude Oil Pipeline: A Case History of Conflict," *Transportation Law Journal,* Vol. 2, No. 2, 1980, pp. 243–289.

Campbell, Thomas C. "Eminent Domain: Its Origin, Meaning, and Relevance to Coal Slurry Pipelines," *Transportation Journal,* Vol. 17, No. 1, Fall 1977, pp. 5–21.

Chancellor, Andrea. "Will Coal Slurry Pipelines Survive?", *Modern Railroads,* August 1988, pp. 37–40.

Coburn, Leonard L. "Petroleum Pipeline Deregulation: A Critical Analysis of the Primary Analytical Justification of Deregulation," *Journal of the Transportation Research Forum,* 1978, pp. 346–352.

Courtney, J. L. "Arctic Natural Gas Transport Systems," *Annual Proceedings of the Transportation Research Forum,* 1978, pp. 68–72.

Energy Journal, Vol. 3, No. 4, October 1981. A special issue on natural gas deregulation.

Farris, Martin T., and David L. Schrock. "The Economics of Coal Slurry Pipelining: Transportation and Nontransportation Factors," *Transportation Journal,* Vol. 18, No. 1, Fall 1978, pp. 45–57.

Hale, Dean, and Jim Watts. "Pipeline Construction Forecast: Modest Construction Year Seen for U.S., Canada Pipelines," *Pipeline & Gas Journal,* January 1984, pp. 28–30.

Hyman, Eric L. "For Want of Water: Rail Versus Slurry Pipeline Transport of Coal in the Northern Great Plains," *Annual Proceedings of the Transportation Research Forum,* 1978, pp. 533–542.

Johnson, James C., and Kenneth C. Schneider. "Coal Slurry Pipelines: An Economic and Political Dilemma," *ICC Practitioners Journal,* Vol. 48, No. 1, 1980, pp. 24–37.

Rohleder, Gilbert V. "Pipelines—The Challenge of Regulation in a Free Economy," *Annual Proceedings of the American Society of Traffic and Transportation,* 1978, pp. 111–115.

Rose, Warren. "Facilitating U.S. Oil Imports: Deepwater Ports in the Gulf of Mexico," *Transportation Journal,* Vol. 20, No. 2, Winter 1980, pp. 41–49.

"Ships May Tap Giant Arctic Wells," *Resource Development,* Fall 1981, pp. 43–45.

Sims, Lee S., and Neal A. Irwin. "Transportation of LNG from the Arctic to Eastern Canada," *Annual Proceedings of the Transportation Research Forum,* 1981, pp. 578–586.

U.S. Congress House Committee on Energy and Commerce. *Coal Slurry Pipeline Issues. Hearing Before the Subcommittee on Commerce, Transportation, and Tourism,* 98th Cong., 1st Sess., July 14, 1983, Serial 98–3.

______*Coal Slurry Pipelines. Hearing Before the Subcommittee on Commerce, Transportation and Tourism,* 97th Cong., 2nd sess., August 6, 1982, Serial 97–1.

______*Natural Gas Contract Renegotiations and FERC Authorities. Hearings Before the Subcommittee on Fossil and Synthetic Fuels,* 98th Cong., 1st sess., February 10 and 22, 1983, Serial 98–??.

______*Oil Pipeline Deregulation. Hearings Before the Subcommittee on Fossil and Synthetic Fuels on H.R. 4488 and H.R. 6815,* 97th Cong., 2nd sess., May 10 and 23, September 23, 1982, Serial 97–1.

______*U.S. Energy Outlook: A Demand Perspective for the Eighties,* 9th Cong., 1st sess., July 1981, Committee Print 97–Q.

U.S. Congress House Committee on Public Works and Transportation. *The Coal Pipeline Act of 1983. Hearings Before the Subcommittee on Surface Transportation on H.R. 1010,* 98th Cong., 1st sess., April 13 and 19, 1983.

U.S. Congress Senate Committee on Energy and Natural Resources. *Petroleum Pipeline Regulatory Reform Bill.* Hearing before the Subcommittee on Energy Regulation on S. 1626. 97th Cong., 2nd sess., May 21, 1982, Publication 97–95.

U.S. Department of Energy, Federal Energy Regulatory Committee. *Proceedings of the Informal Public Conference on the Availability and Pricing of Natural Gas and Alternative Fuels,* Vol. 2, April 1980.

Wald, Haskell P. "Rate Report for Electric Utilities and Gas Pipeline Companies," *Transportation Journal,* Spring 1975, pp. 30–41.

Weissbrod, Richard, and Stephen Veseris. "Regulation of the Coal Slurry Industry," *Annual Proceedings of the Transportation Research Forum,* 1978, pp. 83–92.

"West Coast Crude Oil Pipeline System," *Annual Proceedings of the American Society of Traffic and Transportation,* 1978, pp. 210–228.

Wildenradt, Wayne C. "Changing Economic Factors Affect Pipeline Design Variables," *Pipeline & Gas Journal,* July 1983, p. 20.

Wood, Donald F., and James C. Johnson. *Contemporary Transportation,* 4th ed. (New York: Macmillan, 1993), Chapter 7.

Cases

Case 7.1

Bestway Pipeline

The Bestway Pipeline Expansion Project has come under investigation by federal authorities since the project was completed with limited compliance with environmental regulations. The pipeline stretches for 370 miles from the United States to Canada. John Bagby, CEO of Bestway, does not understand why the investigation is underway and contends that it is the result of opposition of the expansion project.

Currently, the pipeline is in operation even though numerous lawsuits have been filed against the 12 U.S. companies involved in the Bestway project. In one phase of construction, workers were arrested because they were supposedly using the wrong method to construct part of the pipeline. But Bagby claims that using the suggested method would have resulted in a violation.

Numerous stop-work orders have been issued since construction began on the project. According to Bagby, Bestway has received conflicting advice from the various regulatory agencies involved. The Bestway Pipeline Expansion Project has been the center of much controversy, and officials seem to be in trouble no matter what they do. At the moment, the officials could be in serious trouble depending on whether or not they are found guilty of violating environmental regulations. Bagby claims that the various agencies that have opposed the project have not been reasonable with them, and the companies involved with the pipeline claim that the environmental precautions taken in the construction of this project have been more than for any other pipeline project in history.

Case Questions

1. What are some ways, if any, that the officials of this pipeline project could have avoided the investigation?

2. With environmental issues becoming increasingly important, do you think that pipeline projects are going to be stymied?

Case 7.2

BJS Pipeline Case

For the BJS Pipeline Corporation, the thought of constructing a pipeline in the western part of the country seemed like a good idea. Economically, the project would create many jobs, provide millions of dollars in tax revenues, and pump millions of dollars into the economy. What officials of the project did not expect was the opposition that would develop.

BJS proposed building an underground pipeline that would eliminate the need for 300 crude tankers on an annual basis and run 155 miles to supply oil to four refineries. In the process, the risk of an oil spill would be significantly decreased. However, once word of the proposed project was publicized, there was a groundswell of opposition to it. BJS Pipeline Corporation needed to persuade the public that the pipeline project was worthwhile and would benefit the community.

Prior to the announcement of the proposed pipeline, there had been a major oil spill that caused a lot of damage to the environment. Surveys had been sent out to many registered voters in the area asking for their opinions on the proposed pipeline. One concern expressed by many citizens was the fear of an oil spill. The task for the company was to gain support from enough constituents so that it could find the political support that it needed. However, after gaining the support it needed for building a pipeline, BJS then decided to postpone the project. Reasons given for the postponement were increasing concerns about operating and construction costs.

Case Questions

1. Do you think that BJS wasted its time in gathering support for its proposal since the project was postponed?

2. With the increased awareness of environmental concerns, do you think that BJS Pipeline Corporation's proposal was not given a fair chance initially? Why or why not?

3. What effects, if any, will stricter environmental laws and increased awareness of the environment have on the pipeline industry?

CHAPTER 8

INTERMODAL AND SPECIAL CARRIERS

Historically, transportation service was purchased directly from providers such as railroads, motor carriers, or air lines. Shippers dealt directly with the carrier and, to the extent possible under the old regulatory scheme, negotiated rates and service requirements. Freight forwarders existed since just after World War I as the railroads found they could not profitably handle Less Than Carload (LCL) traffic. These firms collected small shipments, loaded them into boxcars, sending these consignments to the destination city where the process is reversed. Shipper cooperatives began in the 1930s to provide this type of service to their members on a not-for-profit basis. Prior to 1980, most brokers were confined to the produce business acting as the go-between for truckers and growers. When piggyback service started growing during the 1950s, railroads were concerned that shippers would move freight from boxcars to trailers, so they created a number of rules designed to prevent this from happening. In so doing, they created yet another agency, the consolidator. These firms grew to the point where they became the major intermodal customers of the railroads. This trend was also helped by the railroad industry's decision to become wholesalers.

With the removal of economic regulation starting in 1980, these various agencies grew and prospered. With the easing of entry for brokers, the number of these firms grew to more than 6,000 by mid-decade. Freight forwarders were treated similarly in 1982 and the growth was equally explosive.

During this period, a new entity came on the scene, that being third-party providers. These firms were either linked to motor carriers or were started specially to manage the transportation sector of a shipper's business. These firms have since expanded into supplying related services such as warehousing and inventory control.

Intermodal Transportation

Intermodal transportation involves the use of **two or more modes** of transportation in moving a shipment from origin to destination, primarily through the use of the "container." The development of the container allowed the growth of intermodealism to be possible. In the mid«minus»1950s, Malcolm McLean, a successful truck line owner, developed the concept of using a trailer to move freight by both highway and water. McLean's operation grew into sea-land services, one of the largest water carriers. Although this was a logical outgrowth of the use of the highway trailers for railroad piggyback service, the development of a standard container that could be interchanged among all modes made modern intermodalism possible. Standarization of dimensions, hold down devices, and related items allowed the service providers to design ships, railcars, and highway chassis knowing the container or "box" would fit.

The intermodal service combines the advantages (and disadvantages) of each mode used. For example, air-truck intermodal transportation combines the advantages of the motor carrier's accessibility and lower cost with the speed of the air carrier. At the same time, the combined service includes the air carrier's high cost and the motor carrier's slow speed. Air-truck intermodal rates are lower than all-air rates, but higher than all-truck rates, and the transit times are shorter than by all-truck but longer than by all-air.

The **growth** of intermodal transportation has been aided by the deregulation of U.S. transportation, the growth in global business, and the changes in the business environment. The economic deregulation of rail piggyback transportation and air cargo reduced the regulatory barriers to modes working together to provide through service. Substantial growth in global business, particularly in the off-shore sourcing of goods in the Pacific Rim countries by the U. S., led to the increased use of water-rail-truck intermodal service. Lastly, the economic reality of higher operating costs and driver shortages caused numerous motor carriers to divert long-haul traffic from all truck to piggyback in order to save costs and remain competitive.

The motor carrier industry experienced a severe driver shortage staring in 1986 with the commencement of stringent licensing of truck drivers. This, combined with the promise of lower costs, induced the motor carriers to make greater efforts to utilize piggyback. Recent teamster union agreements also permitted the diversion of up to 28 percent of linehaul LTL movement to intermodal, which made this sector one of the railroad industries largest customers.

A mode common to most forms of intermodal transportation is the motor carrier. The motor carrier's high degree of **accessibility** enables it to serve points that other modes are physically incapable of serving. Trucks can go to the shipper's door, pick up the freight, deliver it to the airport, and at the destination airport deliver the freight from the airport to the consignee. The air carrier is incapable of providing service to points beyond the airport. Similar conditions exist for rail, water, and pipeline transportation.

Piggyback

Piggyback transportation includes the movement of motor-carrier trailers on flatcars **(TOFC)** plus containers in flatcars **(COFC).** In 1992, railroads moved approximately 6.7 million containers and trailers, a record of successive annual volume increases since 1980. This continued growth is due in part due to economic deregulation of piggyback and technological advancements such as the double-stack train. With a double-stack train, two containers are loaded onto one flatcar, increasing the operating efficiency of the railroad and lowering the cost per container, thereby making possible a lower rate per container (see Figure 8.1).

Piggyback also permitted the railroads to follow their industrial customers to the suburbs. As manufacturers moved from the cities to build new and more efficient plants, many of these new sites did not have rail carload access. Without the ability to provide intermodal, the railroads would have lost this business to truck. Their success is illustrated by the fact that 8.7 million trailers and containers were transported during 1997.

In principal rail corridors such as Los Angeles or Chicago, transit time is motor carrier-competitive as well as cost-effective. In recent years, the rail industry has concentrated on major point pair lanes, focusing resources on providing truck-competitive offerings. Many small, older ramps were closed with service either being withdrawn or truck-substituted service being provided. By doing this, the railroad industry has acknowledged that motor carriers are their primary competitors. Recent railroad mergers have created new options for intermodal service. The acquisition of Conrail by CSX and Norfolk Southern created several new corridors for intermodal. The longer hauls within the merged railroads mean fewer interchanges. This has speeded intermodal service while reducing the number of times the trailer must be handled between origin and destination.

A new innovation is the RoadRailer®, which provides a railroad with the ability to haul trailers on special wheel sets and avoid the use of flatcars. (See Figure 8.2) RoadRailers® do not require special mechanical equipment for loading or unloading as the train can be made up on a paved area with a spur track. The cost structure of RoadRailer® operation is such that railroads are now competitive within a 500–800 mile range. Historically, intermodal shipments had to travel more than 1,000 miles

FIGURE 8.1 Examples of a Piggyback and Double-Stack Train Car

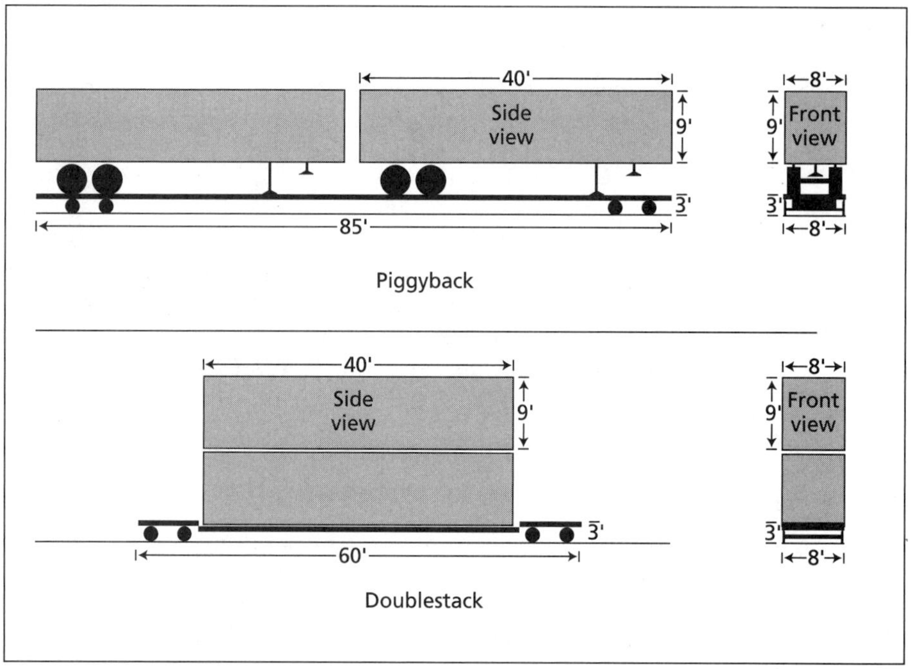

FIGURE 8.2 RoadRailer®

Source: Photo courtesy Wabash National.

before the railroad could complete effectively. RoadRailers® are available in 48' and 53' lengths, and refrigeration units have been introduced. Amtrak has added RoadRailers® to their fleet, allowing them to compete for truckload shipments. Amtrak also uses RoadRailers® to transport mail as the postal sorting facilities, similar to their industrial counterparts, have also moved to the suburbs. Swift Transportation, a major motor carrier, has contracted with The Union Pacific to operate two dedicated RoadRailer® trains between Los Angeles and Seattle.

Increased use is being made of piggyback (COFC) for the domestic portion of product movements between the U.S. and foreign countries. In such moves, the container is commonly used because of its easy transferability from one mode to another and minimal additions to handling costs and total transit times. For example, Japanese automobile plants located in the U.S. are supplied with some parts produced in Japan. These parts are loaded into containers at the Japan supply sources, moved by ship to the West Coast (Long Beach or Seattle) and hauled into the Midwest plant locations via double-stack railroad service. If the rail terminus is not within the plant, a motor carrier is used to deliver the containers from the rail siding. The items in the container are handled only two times: once at loading in Japan and once at unloading in the Midwest.

Recently, major long haul motor carriers such as J.B. Hunt have made significant investments in containers designed for movement by rail or highway. Other truckers such as Schneider National and KLLM have modified conventional trailers for use in intermodal service. Swift Transportation purchased a fleet of RoadRailers® for use along the West Coast in what is called the I–5 corridor between Los Angeles and Seattle. In recent years, motor carriers have experienced problems with an adequate supply of drivers. In addition to assisting with this problem, carriers can address an imbalance of loaded and empty trailers as well. These carriers can also offer their customers alternative service and pricing problems that provide a greater range of options.

Under the old regulations of the Interstate Commerce Commission, a number of "plans" prescribed the type of intermodal service that could be offered. For example, Plan I, for trucking companies, required that the trucker supply their trailer. Under Plan II, their railroad supplied the trailer, flat car, and all related services. Each plan was detailed, and this limited customer choice.

With the end of most economic regulation in 1996, these plans were scrapped and the free market took over. Service providers, whether they are motor carriers, intermodal service companies, or railroads, can offer any type of service combination that the customer desires. Current offerings range from intermodal service offered through motor carriers to transporting shipper-owned trailers with the customer providing the highway portion of the service.

Containerization

As noted above, the container, which is nothing more than a big box into which the freight is loaded, improves the efficiency of interchange among modes. The container also reduces the potential for damage and theft because the actual freight is not rehandled after it is loaded at the shipper's facility. Cargo interchange efficiency increases with the container, and both overall transit time and the transit time consistency of containerized intermodal shipments improve.

The motor carrier trailer is essentially a container on wheels. The trailer comes in various sizes, ranging in length from 28 to 53 feet. The railroad flatcar is capable of handling various sizes of trailers, but longer trailers preclude loading two trailers on one flatcar, thereby increasing the cost per freight unit hauled. The trailer is loaded onto the flatcar by a variety of methods including driving, hoisting with a crane, or lifting by means of a forklift-type device.

The use of trailers as containers for movement by ship presents technical problems. Therefore, the containers used for water transportation are boxes without wheels or a chassis. The water container comes in two standard lengths: 20 feet (TEU or 20 feet equivalent unit) or 40 feet (FEU or 40 feet equivalent unit). Container rates are quoted by water carriers on a TEU or FEU basis.

In an effort to address the varying sizes of containers, both marine and highway, the railroads developed a method whereby containers can be "double stacked" on specially designed rail cars. These cars can accommodate a wide variety of sizes and placing the smaller containers in the "well" of the cars, larger containers can be stacked on top. This has also increased the efficiency of the railroads. Under the old method of placing two trailers on a flat car, as many as three or four containers can be shipped on a double-stack car. The elimination of chassis from the rail portion of the move has also reduced the gross weight, allowing more units to hauled by the same number of engines.

Containers are unloaded from the ship by crane and are transferred to either railroad or motor carriers. As noted above, containers can be placed two high on double-stack cars or one high on regular flatcars. For movement by motor carriers, the containers are either placed on a flatbed trailer or on a chassis (frame with wheels). The transfer of the container from water to either railroad or truck takes less than one day and usually is accomplished in a matter of hours.

The most recent trend in rail-ocean transfer has been to load or unload the containers from the rail cars directly at shipside. The "on-dock" transfer saves both time and money by eliminating the drayage between the pier and the rail yard.

The container used in intermodal air shipments is not the standard rectangular, 40-foot-long shape. Rather, the air container is smaller (usually under 20 feet), narrower than the standard eight-foot ocean container, and typically rounded at the top to fit the contours of the aircraft. Many air carriers utilize hydraulic handling equipment to quickly and easily move the container into and out of the aircraft.

Third-Party Transportation

This trend towards the use of outside firms to provide logistics support grew out of many companies' desire to concentrate their resources on what they do and leave other, non-income producing tasks to these specialists. The trend towards focusing on "core competencies" has also benefited from management's desire to streamline operations and move such non-productive facilities as warehouses off the firm's balance sheet by transferring that activity to a third party. Many of these third-party firms enjoy economies of scale that allow them to provide a manufacturer with logistics services for fewer costs than the firm could do themselves.

Table 8.1 shows the different **types** of third-party transportation providers in operation today. These include either management of information-based providers or asset and operation-based providers. The management-based firms tend to be either shipper or consultant spin offs, while the asset firms are outgrowths of either carriers or leasing firms. Each has its own unique benefits and must be considered in light of the tasks to be performed for the customer. The information-based third-party providers generally, but not exclusively, provide freight bill payment, auditing, reporting, and consulting services.

TABLE 8.1 Types of Third-Party Transportation Providers

Company	Source Entity
Information-Based	
Numerax	Subsidiary of Trategic Technologies, Inc.
Cass Logistics	Cass Commercial Corporation (financial institution)
Bank of Boston	Bank of Boston
Shipper-Based	
USCO Distribution Services	Spun off from Uniroyal
Caterpillar Logistics Services	Subsidiary of Caterpillar, Inc.
Tower Group International	Subsidiary of McGraw-Hill, Inc.
Carrier-Based	
CTI, Inc.	Subsidiary of Baronial Transportation Corp.
Yellow Logistics Services	Subsidiary of Yellow Freight System, Inc.

Source: E.J. Muller, "Third Party Catches On," *Distribution* (July 1992), pp. 60–67.

In all of these third-party arrangements, information **links** exist between the shipper and/or receiver, and the third-party "carrier" is part of an integral link. Many of them have over-the-road trucking equipment with computer-transponder links to satellites that can give the exact location of the truck at all times and information regarding specific package pickups and deliveries to company headquarters at the exact moment the transfers are taking place.

The people typically initiating these new forms of **services** have been innovative and entrepreneurial transportation experts who see valuable opportunities in the efficient linking of shippers and receivers. The benefits to shippers and receivers are more efficient processes, lower labor rates, and/or improved services.

Another recent development has been for third-party firms to place their own personnel at the manufacturer's plant or the consignee's warehouse to handle the details of outsourced services. This frees the client's staff to devote their attention to those areas which are beyond the day to day details.

Use of third party firms allows McDonald's Corporation, the fast food chain, to have less than 50 employees oversee food shipments to more than 33,000 stores.

Schneider Logistics of Green Bay, Wisconsin, and Ryder Integrated Logistics of Miami, Florida, provide two excellent examples of the new third-party providers. Schneider, an outgrowth of a truckload motor carrier, provides logistics support to a major farm equipment manufacturer for both raw materials and finished goods as well as parts and international shipments. They coordinate not only shipments moving on their trucks, they also manage services provided by other firms. Ryder, a division of what started as truck leasing firm, provides a major retailer with onsite management atone of its distribution centers as well handling all store deliveries from that facility.

This trend is expected to accelerate and one study[1] predicted that growth in this sector will be about 19 percent annually through 2000. The same study suggests that this sector will produce revenue of $50 billion annually by 2000.

Customized Transportation Inc. (CTI) of Jacksonville Florida provides a service to an auto manufacturer that starts when the final assembly plant communicates a specific automobile production schedule to both the strut plant and to CTI. CTI picks up the struts and moves them to the former warehouse that is now leased by CTI. CTI's lower-cost labor inspects the struts in a quality-control process and arranges them in boxes for the specific automobile production sequence. CTI then delivers the struts by way of forklift to the production line within two hours of final automobile production. This system requires less costly labor. Quality and sequence errors have been greatly reduced in the system, and the automobile manufacturer has the added benefit of less total inventory in its entire materials management system. Although CTS is performing transportation as its primary services, its total service provides several other benefits to the auto firm.

Single Sourcing LTL

Caliber Logistics, a unit of FDX Global Logistics, based in Hudon, Ohio, and Libby-Owen-Ford (LOF), a Toldeo-based glassmaker, entered into a third-party arrangement whereby Caliber makes the carrier selection and routing decisions for 80,000 LTL (less than 10,000 pounds) inbound and outbound shipments. Prior to utilizing Caliber, LOF used more than 500 different carriers to move products from 12,000 suppliers to 105 shipping and receiving locations.

Through the use of a computer software system Caliber exercises centralized control over LTL shipment routings. Vendors and LOF shipping personnel are required to call the Caliber routing toll-free number to obtain routing instructions for an LTL shipment. Caliber has contracts with 21 carriers; approximately half of the carriers are Caliber Logicistics carriers. Time-sensitive shipments verified by LOF personnel are moved by surface or air express carriers. By concentrating the 80,000 LTL shipments in 21 carriers, lower rates and improved srvices are obtained. The system is completely paperless, which has reduced the "backroom" paper handling cost associated with freight bill payment and auditing.

Special Carrier Forms

Several special types of carrier services represent a significant segment of the transportation services purchased by shippers. These forms of transportation often use the long-haul services of the five basic transportation modes.

Surface Forwarders

Surface freight forwarders hold a unique place among carriers. A forwarder is both a carrier and shipper in as much as they are recognized as a "carrier" by their customer, while being treated a "shipper" by the company who actually provides the transportation service. Once regulated as another form of common carriage, forwarders are now exempt from economic over sight. Forwarders must still register with the Department of Transportation and maintain cargo insurance in the amount prescribed.

A forwarder's role is still defined under current regulations as found at 49 United States Code, Section 13102, Part 8. A forwarder is a "person" that offers itself to the general public (other than a railroad, motor, or water carrier) to provide transportation or property for compensation in the ordinary course of its business. The definition goes on to state that the forwarder assumes responsibility for the transportation from the place of receipt to the place of destination and uses the services of another mode, such as a motor or rail carrier. Air freight forwarders are specifically exempted from this definition.

Operations

Historically, forwarders consolidated small shipments into truckloads or carloads. (See figure 8.3) In most cases, the forwarder provided local pickup and delivery but

FIGURE 8.3 Surface Forwarder Operation

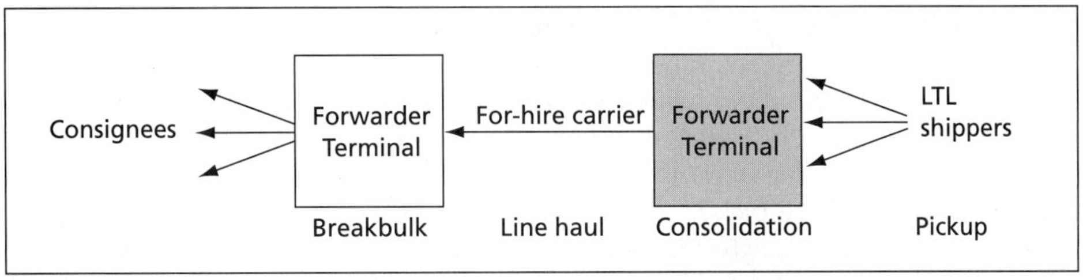

historically used boxcars to provide linehaul service. Since the 1960s motor carriers, and to some extent intermodal, have become the primary means of transport used by the forwarder.

The forwarding industry nearly died out by the mid-1980s because of severe competition from LTL motor carriers. The LTL carriers were able to provide better service and, in many cases, lower prices including generous discounts from their base rates. Passage of the Freight Forwarder Act of 1986 removed nearly all regulatory oversight from this industry. The industry rebounded quickly and has become a significant factor as a transportation service provider. It is estimated that several thousand surface freight forwarding companies are in business today.

With the elimination of economic regulation, forwarders have evolved into a role similar to truckers. They have moved away from the traditional LTL market and have concentrated on volume shipments. Some forwarders still provide the classic consolidation or small shipment service, but most have expanded into the intermodal and truckload areas.

A forwarder must "issue" a bill of lading to the shipper, the same as a railroad or motor carrier. In so doing, the forwarder accepts responsibility for the shipment. Because of this, a forwarder must maintain cargo insurance and accept liability for loss and/or damage to a shipment that it accepts. A copy of the insurance policy must be filled with the Surface Transportation Board for the protection of the forwarder's customers.

As with other carriers, for the most part, forwarders are no longer required to file their prices with the federal government. The exception relates to those forwarders who handle household goods. This allows forwarders the freedom to negotiate prices on a shipment-by-shipment basis with their customers, giving them the same flexibility as motor or oil carriers. Since they are required to "issue" bills of lading, they are subject to the same terms and conditions as other carriers.

Air Freight Forwarders

These firms act in much the same way as surface forwarders by consolidating small shipments for long-haul and eventual distribution. They primarily use the services of major passenger and freight airlines for long-haul service. The air freight forwarder serves the shipping public with similar pickup, a single bill of lading and freight bill, one-firm tracing, and delivery service, as does the surface forwarder. The air freight forwarder, though, is generally used by shippers of goods having high-product-dollar value or time-sensitivity value, or both.

Characteristics

Use of air freight **forwarders** has grown over the past two decades. As the air industry grew, so did acceptance of this generally high-cost form of transportation for emergency and high-time-value moves. A reason often also stated for air forwarder growth has been that these firms have concentrated upon offering door-to-door service from shipper to consignee. This service relieves a significant traffic arrangement burden from shippers and consignees. It also fills a void because airlines tend to emphasize terminal-to-terminal services and have been involved only to a limited degree in surface pickup and delivery services.

Many air freight forwarders have expanded into aircraft operations as the airline industry consolidated because of mergers and bankruptcies. Emery and Airborne are examples of two such firms that started as pure forwarders but now operate a large fleet of aircraft. This trend was accelerated by increased passenger loads brought about by deregulation of air fares. As the passenger aircraft became more crowded, there was little room for freight after the baggage and mail was loaded. Changes in passenger schedules eliminated many flights that forwarders relied on for overnight service. This, along with basic changes in air service patterns as the airlines moved towards "hub and spoke" operations, forced many forwarders to acquire their own freight airplanes.

Service Benefits

The air freight forwarder industry presents some major transportation service benefits to the shipping community. For one, speed of service is vital for many movements such as spare parts, emergency replenishment goods, medical components, and business documents. Further, this industry represents a single-carrier, full door-to-door service. Its main disadvantage lies in its high rates, but these are usually considered by shippers in light of the service benefit received relative to the product's value and time-sensitivity. New "deferred" rate plans provide for second or third day shipment at significant savings. In some areas, these new plans are truck competitive.

Air Forwarder Future

The future of air freight forwarding is mixed. On the positive side, the pickup and delivery movements of air freight are unrestricted. Air freight movements became unregulated in 1977, and the pickup and delivery portions of the moves were unregulated in 1980. Thus new origin and destination points far from terminal cities presented expanded opportunities for these firms. However, deregulation of air freight has brought about price and service competition and innovation. Mergers and acquisitions have strengthened the industry so that most firms are well positioned for the new century.

In the international arena, air freight forwarders provide the shipping public with transportation movement and the handling and processing of many international documents. Thus, in this sector, the air forwarders provide a value-added service in addition to simple movement.

Freight Brokers

Brokers function as "middlemen" between the shipper and the carrier much the same as a real estate broker does in the sale of property. The definition of a broker is still found in the United States Code under Title 49, section 13102, subpart (2). This regulation defines as broker as a "person" other than a motor carrier, an agent, or an employee that, as a principal or agent, sells, offers for sale, negotiates for, or holds itself out by solicitation, advertisement, or otherwise selling, providing, or arranging for transportation by motor carrier.[2]

Most truckload motor carriers cannot afford to maintain a nationwide sales force, but their trucks operate throughout the U.S. The broker normally represents the carrier and seeks freight on their behalf to avoid moving empty equipment. They may also represent the shipper and will provide trucks for loading. Brokers can provide intermodal services as well as other logistics offerings, such as warehousing and cross docking.

Historically, brokers were confined to the agricultural area, but after the partial repeal of economic regulation in 1980, combined with the elimination of the Interstate Commerce Act in 1996, the brokerage industry saw explosive growth. The restrictions to entry into the brokerage business were removed with the only requirement being retained was that broker post a $10,000 surety bond. This bond is for the protection of the carrier since many brokers bill the shipper and pay the trucker. In the event the broker fails to do so, the bond would be available to make good on the lost revenue.

Brokers do not have to file any price schedules with the federal government. A broker does not issue a bill of lading and they are not required to maintain cargo liability insurance since they are not considered to be a carrier. These two factors are the primary difference between a broker and a freight forwarder. Many brokers provide cargo insurance at their expense for the protection of their customers so as relieve the shipper of that concern.

Brokers and surface freight forwarders are represented by a trade association, Transportation Intermediaries Association (TIA) located in Alexandria, Virginia. TIA conducts educational programs and holds annual meetings while representing these carriers before Congress and federal agencies.

Roles

Brokers assume some of the functions of shippers and truckers. They also relieve shippers of a major traffic function burden. Client truckers use brokers to relieve them of a major fixed cost burden and communicating expense. These are both traffic management and carrier sales and pricing roles.

Surveys indicate that individual brokers service anywhere from a few to several thousand shippers. Basic shipper services include the arrangement of service, the verification of the trucker's insurance and safety rating, verification of equipment condition, and the negotiation of a freight transportation price. Brokers also are involved in LTL and warehouse consolidation for shippers, as well as insurance acquisition for truckers. Although brokers traditionally dealt with owner-operators, today they also deal with regular for-hire carriers, acting in a sales role for these firms. The broker typically charges the shipper for the freight movement, deducts a brokerage fee between eight and 10 percent, and then remits the net amount to the trucker.

Deregulation increased the number and roles of brokers. In the past, it was a relatively small, locally based industry in the agricultural commodity area. Between 1980 and 1988, the ICC issued 6,000 licenses to new brokers. Today many are quite large and represent major sources of revenues for motor carriers and piggyback operations.[3]

The future is quite bright for brokers, and one of the largest transportation firms, C.H. Robinson, does more than $1 billion in revenue, much of it from brokerage.

The computer and communications networks available today provide access to information about current and upcoming shipments and the availability of equipment. The broker industry will no doubt grow as it seeks ways to expand solicitation, movement availability, and third-party service opportunities.

Shippers' Associations

These transportation entities are **nonprofit** cooperative consolidators or distributors of shipments owned or shipped by member firms. Their prime purpose is to group together members' shipments for line haul in much the same way as for-hire, for-profit freight forwarders. In the past, these organizations consolidated many local shippers' small shipments into line-haul piggyback shipments. In this role, they were a form of nonprofit surface freight forwarder.

Services

Shippers' associations benefit members through better service and lower total transportation costs. Washington Oregon Shippers Cooperative Association (WOSCA) is an example of today's shipper association. The Seattle-based organization, founded in 1953, generated $61 million in revenue in 1998 and performs a range of services for its member firms. These include broker-like services for line-haul truckload movements, piggyback consolidations services for smaller shipments, the arrangement of over-the-road truckload services, and tailored third-party services for special transportation needs. The breadth of services and buying power enables the shippers' association to provide traffic management services to small and medium shippers.

The **future** for shippers' associations is bright. In an unregulated environment with changing transportation supply and price settings, the shippers' association provides shippers with a high level of expertise and buying power.

Shippers' Agents and Consolidators

Shippers' agents are also referred to as **intermodal marketing companies** (IMC), as well as consolidators or agents. They are facilitators or arrangers of transportation only. They assume little or no legal liability; the legal shipping arrangement is between the shipper and long-haul carrier and not with the agent. Freight charge payment usually is made to the agent who, in turn, pays the long-haul carrier.

Piggyback shipments were exempted from regulation by the ICC in 1981. This expanded the market opportunities available to shippers' agents and consolidators. The deregulation meant that specific service features and rates could be established through negotiation and contracting.

Characteristics

Shippers' agents maintain simple management structures. They are either locally or nationally based and rely upon personal solicitation and advertising.

The trend of this shipping sector is generally positive. Agents play a cost-savings role for both the shipper and the railroad. Little specific industry-wide knowledge exists as to the number, size, and particular services they perform since they are not subject to regulation. Most IMCs have volume, wholesale contracts with the railroads. They can offer lower prices than most shippers could obtain on their own.

Rail equipment use is enhanced as trailers are matched and shipped by the IMC. Many IMCs actively assist in managing rail equipment for better turnaround. These agents solicit freight for the carriers, sparing the railroad this expense.

A disadvantage associated with agents is in the area of liability. The shipper usually pays the freight agent who, in turn, pays the rail carrier. Ultimate freight payment liability, however, still rests with the shipper. There is the possibility, and it has occurred occasionally, that the agent will retain the freight charges and cease operations, leaving the shippers with, in effect, a second freight bill. Therefore, before hiring any agent, the shipper should investigate the agent's reputation and stature.

Shippers often find that these firms can save transportation costs for them even after their fee is paid. The segment of the industry is represented by the Intermodal Association of North America, based in Greenbelt, Maryland. IANA, who has 630 members and does gather some data, holds annual meetings and provides information on participants in this area of transportation.

The future is also relatively bright for shippers' agents, especially in light of the increased use of intermodal transportation by long-haul motor carriers and international container shippers. Agents represent the pooled buying power of shippers. Opportunities exist for these firms to negotiate low rail contract rates and better service.

Owner-Operators

The term *owner-operator* was traditionally applied to a person who owned or leased a truck and often a trailer and made his or her equipment and driving service available to for-hire carriers. Owner-operators were confined to serving regular for-hire carrier firms that needed the service on an overflow basis when carrier equipment and labor were not available. They also commonly worked for special-commodity carriers that did not have the equipment but booked freight and used owner-operators to carry it from origin to destination. The owner-operator rented his or her services and equipment to the carrier that possessed the operating rights to move the goods. Owner-operators are often paid a percentage of the amount received in exchange for the carrier's retention of the operating rights.

Regulatory changes now allow private carriers to single-source owner-operator's equipment and driving services.

Owner-operators are playing a key role for some newly evolving for-hire carriers. Some new carriers do not have employee drivers or company-owned equipment. That is, long-haul movement as well as regular pickup and delivery operations are often performed under an arrangement between the carrier and the terminals and owner-operators. These relationships are often contractual, but they give the carrier flexibility in operations and reduced financial risk. Many of these carriers offer incentive plans and pay scales that allow them to be very competitive against the unionized, traditional for-hire carriers.

The owner-operator does not seem to be involved in some of the new advanced truckload firms, such as J. B. Hunt and Builders' Transport. These firms find that using their own nonunion drivers and vehicles provides greater economies and flexibilities of movement.[4]

Express Services and Courier Services

This carrier group started by offering fast service, usually door-to-door, for small, high-value goods and documents. Recent changes in the regulation and the market have reshaped this section significantly.

Although these carriers were limited as to the size of the shipments that they would handle, firms such as United Parcel Service (UPS), RPS, and Federal Express (FedEx) have moved aggressively into the LTL market. These firms are now competing directly against companies such as Consolidated Freightways and Roadway Express. These package and express carriers provide both air and surface transportation and offer a variety of pricing and service plans designed to offer the customer a range of options. Although they started as package carriers, most firms in this category offer a full range of services; the distinction between a package and express carrier and a LTL company is becoming much less clear. Many of these companies have expanded into the international market as well.

Express firms operate with large networks of terminals, pickup and delivery vehicles, and line-haul service. UPS is most notable in this regard.

It began as a retail store delivery system and has since grown to a worldwide firm with 1998 revenues of $20.65 billion domestically while billing another $2.3 billion in Europe. UPS has operations in over 200 countries and territories worldwide. UPS transported 3.14 billion packages in 1998, making it by far the largest firm in this category.

RPS, the major competitor of UPS, started in 1985, grew quickly and reported revenue of $1.7 billion in 1998, and handled an average day volume of 1.4 million packages. RPS has been very innovative, being the first carrier of its type to use bar code scanning for tracing. RPS also uses "owner-operators" for both long haul and local delivery versus UPS, which uses company employees. RPS was recently acquired by FedEx and will be integrated into its system.

The United States Postal Service (USPS) provides package service and in 1998 handled 971 million packages generating revenues of $1,626 billion. Other package and express services include those provided by national and local bus companies such as Greyhound and the recently expand offerings of Amtrak, the national railroad passenger service provider.

The trend for these services has been positive. Deregulation of the air freight and trucking industries in 1977 and 1980 cleared the way for more operational efficiency by reducing many of the former restrictive routings, limited certificates, and hindrances to intermodal operations. The shipper experiences fast service when using these firms, but it is at a high-rate cost.

The future is good for this sector because expansion and service innovations can take place without the impediment of the high legal costs incurred when confronting regulatory bodies.

Household Goods Industry

This industry sector consists of a group of motor carriers that are specifically organized to move the household goods of people and businesses. These firms, often called van lines, are geared to serve the market with specialized vehicles, local agencies with warehouses for storage, and pickup and delivery equipment, as well as central dispatching operations. In all areas, however, the overall corporate name, or franchise, will appear on vehicles, local agencies, and in national advertising.

The top 10 household goods carriers generated 1997 revenues of $3.018 billion, an increase of six percent over 1996. This compares with $8.619 billion of the top 10 truckload carriers for the same period.

The specific segments of this industry fall into four groups. The first is the **central franchise firms** whose corporate name and operating certificate are used by the agencies and over-the-road vehicles. The franchise firms also provide a central dispatch to coordinate the most efficient possible flow of vehicles between all points.

The second group is the **local agencies,** each of which consists of a terminal and storage warehouse. The terminal is the local contact point for customer contact and shipment initiation. It generally supplies the packing and the pickup vehicle loading labor, as well as delivery and unpacking manpower. In the event the household goods owners wish to move goods when vehicles are not available, or they wish to store goods temporarily, local agencies provide storage facilities.

STOP OFF

QUIET REVOLUTION IN THE MAKING

The J.B. Hunt Co., one of the largest truckload carriers, teamed up with the Sante Fe Railway several years ago for the long-haul movement of its trailers and has since expanded its intermodal partnerships with other railroads. Then the press announced J.B. Hunt has ordered 10,000 containers and 13,500 chassis. The company also plans to phase out most, if not all, of its 12,000 trailers. If so, its fleet in the near future will comprise containers and accompanying chassis.

Many truck drivers are so upset at J.B. Hunt they can hardly talk about it. Why? If tens of thousands of trailers are moved via rail instead of highway, there go thousands of drivers' jobs.

Another item of interest is C.H. Robinson Co.'s proposal to create a national shippers association of large over-the-road carriers. C.H. Robinson would manage the business by tendering large volumes of truck trailers and containers to the railroads for intermodal movement.

Then there are personal difficulties and ongoing experiences in obtaining service and rail carload rates. That and the current railroad industry reduction in personnel all indicate railroads' approach to carload business.

The last item of interest is an advertisement by one of the seven largest railroads that offered to fully refund your transportation charges if you are not satisfied with the service on one of its inaugural intermodal trains. The only conditions are that you must ship within the first 30 days and mail the written complaint on company letterhead. What is so remarkable about this offer? The statement is almost totally unheard of in the railroad industry.

These four pieces of information indicate the following:

- Railroads see the U.S. carload pie as relatively fixed and that minor market share shifts between railroads are basically the only variables in this pie.
- Most large rail carriers are aggressively pursuing the growing intermodal market. They have the capacity, profit incentive, and historical motivation to recapture motor carrier traffic.
- If J.B. Hunt continues to have economic success with its rail venture, it will have a definite market advantage—cost. If the company begins to reduce its rates, other large truckload carriers will have to reduce their rates, become partners with the railroads, join the C.H. Robinson family, become a regional carrier, or go out of business.
- No one is sure at this stage if any of these scenarios will come to pass. There are real and perceived problems and challenges. The success factor is a 70-plus rating because of economics, bottom-line accounting, world competition, environmental concerns, and our mostly free-market driven economy.
- If successful, tens of thousands of additional trailers will be taken off the highways. The implications are enormous: highway damage will decrease, as will taxes paid to the highway trust fund. Railroad employment will increase, but truck driver employment will decrease.

And as a colleague recently noted, those "truck" companies, such as J.B. Hunt, with large fleets of containers, will be in a prime position to market internationally. This major shift in transportation is overdue and on its way. It can be thwarted by protectionism legislation, such as "job security" for truck drivers or tax breaks for long-haul truck companies. I am in favor of allowing the market to work. Yes, it creates bumps. But in the long run, it benefits us all with lower costs, less air pollution, and better allocation of scarce resources such as fuel and labor.

Adapted from Douglas Cheaney, "Quiet Revolution in the Making," *Inbound Logistics* (February 1993), p. 24. Reprinted with permission.

The third segment of this industry is the **over-the-road vehicle** owned by the local agency. Many local agents own their own tractor and trailer and hire employees who will perform outbound and inbound moves dispatched by the central firm.

A fourth entity in this industry is the **owner-operator** who displays the corporate identity on the vehicle and loads, hauls, and unloads shipments that are dispatched by the central franchise firm and are coordinated by local agents.

This four-party system is not apparent to individual shippers who typically think that they are dealing with one corporate entity that has direct supervisory control over drivers and vehicles as well as all agencies. Instead, the household goods industry is a loose alliance of entities that share a single franchised **identity** and a communication system.

Shipment Process

The household goods shipment process reveals the makeup of the functional relationships in this transport sector. Initially, the individual agent joins the franchise by paying an entry fee and adhering to certain centrally established standards. An individual owner-operator who generally performs long-haul services acquires a vehicle and moving firm identity in much the same way.

The actual shipment process is as follows. First, a home or apartment dweller contacts the local agent, who generally visits the pickup point, estimates the shipment weight, and evaluates the need for any special move tasks. The agent, in turn, estimates a total move cost for the shipper. The shipper-carrier relationship is initiated when the shipper signs an **"order for service"** document that is transmitted to the central firm dispatch office for over-the-road vehicle assignment and scheduling. Generally, if an individual shipment is 7,500 pounds or more, a new run will be created based on that shipment. Smaller shipments are tacked onto existing runs and the home owner is then informed of the estimated arrival date. If packing is to be part of the hired service, local agency personnel perform this task a few days prior to pickup.

The over-the-road vehicle then arrives, after the driver has determined the total vehicle weight prior to loading. The driver will inspect the possessions, label them, and log them onto an inventory tally sheet along with notations about the condition of each item. The goods are then loaded, and the shipper is given a receipt (bill of lading). The pickup goods are usually loaded into a vehicle with other shipments that are often dropped off to other homes along the route (and where others might be picked up) prior to the specific shipment delivery. The vehicle is then reweighed to determine the total shipment weight.

The actual **charges** are based on that weight as well as special charges that might be added for such things as weekend work; movement of large, heavy, special, or fragile items; or the need to climb stairs or use an elevator. Agency packing, too, is included in these charges, all of which can boost the total shipment cost by 30 to 50 percent.

The shipment then moves to the delivery point. The driver can, and usually does, demand payment of freight charges in cash or by certified check unless certain credit arrangements are made in advance. Then the shipment is unloaded. The new local agency then unpacks the boxes, if packing and unpacking are part of the hired service. Any loss and damage claims are then filed through the new local agency.

Revenue distribution is usually made on the following basis: 10 percent to the corporate franchise, 50 percent to the vehicle owner (agency or owner-operator), 25 percent to the pickup agency, and 15 percent to the destination agency. Packing service charges are distributed in various ways between the two local agencies.

Problems

Many problems exist in this industry. First, people's possessions are being handled and moved—a major event for the shipper and family. Second, moving causes the shipper and his or her family a significant degree of stress, and problems in the actual move may aggravate the entire process. Third, the industry is made up of three or four separate parties (franchise, pickup, vehicle, and destination agencies). Fourth, unless the shipper is being transferred by the military or a major national firm, the individual has little influence over the movers. Traditionally, none of these agencies has had any direct control over the others. The Household Goods Transportation Act of 1980 now binds actions by any agent or vehicle to the parent franchise holder.[5] Further, long-distance communications are necessary between all of them.

Trends in this industry are mixed. The market basically consists of about 17 percent military moves; the remainder is divided equally between individual shipper moves and moves booked under supervision of employers. It is a very seasonal business. Typically 70 percent of all moves take place in the five-month period between May to September (representing only 42 percent of the year). This peak situation creates a great demand during a short period, and manpower and equipment use is low for the remaining part of the year.

Some household goods moving firms have withdrawn completely from the field, while a few have discontinued shipping household goods in favor of moving fragile electronic items, such as computers and copying equipment. This traffic requires the special equipment and handling expertise of the moving firms, but it is less seasonal in nature. Other firms divested from the household goods operations altogether in the 1970s when the military and corporations began what appears to be a long-term trend toward reducing the number of employee transfers.

Legislation

The Household Goods Transportation Act of 1980 has brought some forms of deregulation and reregulation to this sector of the industry as well.[6] This legislation allows carriers some flexibility in the pricing and services they offer the shipping public, and it provides for greater STB jurisdiction over the agents in addition to the parent corporation.

Some of the innovations now allowed, and in fact encouraged, by the new law are:

- discounts for senior citizens
- promotions allowing reduced or free transportation
- charges by cube rather than weight
- space reservations
- choice of levels of service
- binding estimates
- guaranteed delivery dates
- full-value insurance in place of the traditional released value rates
- volume discounts on line-haul rates
- volume discounts on accessorial services[7]

The act also extends Surface Transportation Board jurisdiction over negative actions of individual agents in the industry. Many observers think that the act does not fully correct the inherent relational and organizational weaknesses of this industry.

As with the other modes, the future will tell what shakeout or innovative actions will take place in this part of the industry.

SUMMARY

The transportation user is not confined to firms and services of the basic modes. Carriers that appear as hybrids of these modes, as well as special forms within each, are also available forms of transportation service.

- Regulatory changes governing air, motor, rail, and household goods transportation aided the development of the special carriers.
- Intermodal transportation involves the joint efforts of two or more modes to complete the through movement. The most common forms of intermodal include piggyback (rail-truck), water-rail (container on flatcar), and truck-air. The container improves the freight interchange efficiency between the modes and enhances the value of intermodal service.
- Third-party transportation providers offer a total package of logistics services in which transportation is one component. Third-party transportation involves outsourcing transportation services ranging from simple freight bill payment to carrier selection and routing of shipments to storage, partial assembly of parts, and transportation.
- Today's transportation system is supported by a number of intermediaries who provide shipment consolidation, marketing, information, and premium services to both carriers and shippers. Forwarders, shippers' associations, brokers, shippers' agents, owner-operators, and express and courier companies are the primary providers of these intermediary services.
- The household goods moving industry consists of specialized motor carriers who move the household goods of people and businesses. The industry faces peak demand during the summer months and utilizes a system of local agents and owner-operators to provide service.

KEY TERMS

air forwarder trends pg. 220
central franchise firm 224
charges 226
COFC 213
common identity 226
future 222
growth 212
intermodal marketing companies 222
key links 217
local agency 224
nonprofit forwarders 222
ordering service 226
over-the-road vehicle 225
owner-operator 226
prime example 217
revenue distribution 226
services 217
TOFC 213
truck accessibility 213
two or more modes 212
types 216
user benefits 222

STUDY QUESTIONS

1. The use of TOFC and COFC has been steadily rising since 1980. What factors have contributed to its growth in intermodal transportation?

2. How has freight forwarding changed in the past 15 years? Compare the historical role of forwarders with their current place among carriers.

3. The broker industry has become a major factor in the "Special Carrier" sector. Discuss their role as it relates to both shippers and motor carriers.

4. Intermodal Marketing Companies and similar organizations control about 75 percent of all intermodal rail traffic. Explain why this is true and its implications for the railroad industry.

5. What new roles do shippers' associations play in today's transportation market?

6. Explain the difference between an Intermodal Marketing Company (IMC) or shipper's agent and a freight forwarder. What do you think the role IMCs will have in the future?

7. What are the primary components of the household goods movement industry?

8. Why have there been problems with service reliability in the household goods industry?

9. Discuss the current state of economic regulations of the household goods industry. Do you feel that such regulation will continue? Why?

10. What is an owner-operator? What is their role in motor carrier transportation?

Notes

1. Gregory E. Burns; Gerard, Klauer & Mattison, Co. Inc. "Freight Forwarding/Logistics, Toward a New Era in Transportation," June 1997.
2. Michael R. Crum, "The Expanded Role of Motor Freight Brokers in the Wake of Regulatory Reform," *Transportation Journal,* Vol. 24, No. 4 (Summer 1985), pp. 5–15.
3. Terrence A. Brown, "Freight Brokers and General Commodity Trucking," *Transportation Journal,* Vol. 24, No. 2 (Winter 1984), pp. 4–14.
4. Thomas M. Corsi and Curtis M. Grimm, "Changes in Owner-Operator Use, 1977–1985: Implications for Management Strategy," *Transportation Journal,* Vol. 26, No. 3 (Spring 1987), pp. 4–16.
5. *Household Goods Transportation Act of 1980,* L. 196–454.
6. Ibid.
7. Edward Morash, "A Critique of the Household Goods Transportation Act of 1980: Impact and Limitations," *Transportation Journal,* Vol. 21, No. 2 (Winter 1981), pp. 16–27.

Suggested Readings

Allen, Benjamin, and Roy Voorhees. "Constraints to Rail-Barge Movements: An Identification and Assessment," *Transportation Journal,* Vol. 26, No. 2, Winter 1986.

Bardi, Edward J., and Michael Tracey. "Transportation Outsourcing: A Survey of U.S. Practices," *International Journal of Physical Distribution and Logistics Management,* Vol. 21, No. 3, 1991, pp. 15–21.

Bradley, Peter. "Intermodal Puts the Parts Together," *Purchasing,* Vol. 108, No. 5, March 22, 1990, pp. 104–109.

____"Railroads, The Big Get Bigger," *Logistics Management,* July 1998.

Brown, Terrence A. "Producer Owned Truck Brokerage," *Journal of Transportation Management,* Vol. 111, No. 1, Spring 1991, pp. 13–29.

______*The Role of Intermediaries in Unregulated Markets: Transportation Brokers.* Washington, D.C.: U.S. Small Business Administration, 1989.

Burns, Gregory. "Freight Forwarding/Logistics," Gerard, Klauer Mattison & Co., New York, NY 10017, June 1997.

Cohan, Paul. "Truck, Rail Cooperation Boosts Intermodal," *Container News,* Vol. 26, No. 4, April 1991, pp. 12–14.

Crum, Michael R. "The Expanded Role of Motor Freight Brokers in the Wake of Regulatory Reform," *Transportation Journal,* Vol. 24, No. 4, Summer 1985.

Dillon, Thomas F. "Containerization: An Idea That Made Sense," *Inbound Logistics,* Vol. 11, No. 4, April 1991, pp. 25–28.

Gillis, Chris. "Third Party Managers," American Shipper, April 1996.

Gooley, Toby B. "Express: The Competition Heats Up," Logistics Management, July 1998.

Jedd, Marcia. "Big Battle for Small Packages," Logistics Management, February 1999.

Krause, Kristin S. "Taking off the Gloves — FedEx expands freight business," Traffic World, March 1, 1999.

Mele, Jim. "Living with the Driver Shortage," Fleet Owner. April 1995.

Mueller, E. J. "Avoiding the Traps of Consolidation," *Distribution,* Vol. 90, No. 11, October 1991, pp. 42–48.

Pope, David J., and Evelyn A. Thomchick, "U.S. Foreign Freight Forwarders and NVOCCs," *Transportation Journal,* Vol. 24, No. 3, Spring 1985.

Saccomano, Ann. "Third-Party Logistics: The Heat Is On," Traffic World, February 8, 1999

Sheffi, Yosef. "Third Party Logistics: Present and Future Prospects," *Journal of Business Logistics,* Vol. 11, No. 2, 1990, pp. 27–40.

Thomas, Jim. "Transportation Intermediaries — How David Lives with Goliath," *Logistics Management,* December 1998.

Thomas, J. M. "Quality Competition and Regulatory Reform: New Evidence of the Impact of the Household Goods Transportation Act of 1980," *Transportation Journal,* Vol. 29, No. 4, Summer 1990, pp. 42–51.

Various, "Third-Party Logistics, From Contract to Contract," *Inbound Logistics,* July 1997.

Vellenga, David G., Jake Semizn, and Daniel R. Vellenga, "One-Stop Shipping for Logistics Services: A Review of the Evidence and Implications for Multi-Modal Companies," *Journal of Transportation Management,* Vol. 111, No. 1, Spring 1991, pp. 31–58.

Unknown, "Rebound, Intermodal Markets," Logistics Management, March 1997.

Cases

Case 8.1
Fast Forward Air Freight

Mr. John Klinker, president of Fast Forward Air Freight, has just hung up the phone after a two-hour conversation with Carol Burdinski, vice president of Cargo Marketing for Fly Right Air Lines. Burdinski informed Fast Forward that, effective at the end of the current contract, Fly Right would not extend the current guaranteed space and rate agreement. In other words, after the contract expires, Fast Forward will have to pay the tariff rate in effect for the commodity, shipment size, and destination at the time of the shipment and will be subject to space availability. This is bad news, because for the past 10 years, Fast Forward has been able to contract with Fly Right for a guaranteed amount of space on particular flights with appropriate volume rate discounts.

Fast Forward is an air freight forwarder formed by John Klinker in 1978, following deregulation of the airline industry. Klinker was a cargo marketing manager for Fly Right prior to 1978 and saw the opportunity presented by deregulation to provide a value-added service to air cargo shippers. From its inception, Fast Forward provided guaranteed pickup and delivery service to the shippers and, by contracting for space on flights, guaranteed overall transit times.

The Fast Forward-Fly Right alliance prospered. Fast Forward concentrated on the marketing of air cargo service and developed a strong reputation among shippers for being able to deliver the service promised. In addition, Fast Forward developed state-of-the-art material-handling systems and vehicle-routing techniques, which enhanced the level of service provided. The Fast Forward cargo enabled Fly Right to reduce empty capacity and generate additional revenue without the marketing, freight handling, and pickup and delivery expense.

However, during the past two years, Fly Right has been experiencing a sizable growth in air cargo. A number of large consumer products shippers increased the freight volume tendered to Fly Right, as did Fast Forward. During the past six months, this increased demand resulted in 20 percent of the flights leaving the airport with cargo sitting on the tarmac waiting for available space on another flight. The waiting time exceeded three days on more than 50 percent of the delayed shipments. Given the contract Fly Right had with Fast Forward, the Fast Forward cargo had to be shipped on the first flight, causing the shipment delays to fall exclusively on the Fly Right's direct customers. The large consumer-products-shippers were threatening to pull all of their business from Fly Right if service delays continued.

The Fly Right board of directors denied a request by management to purchase additional aircraft specifically to haul cargo, reminding management that Fly Right is a passenger airline first and foremost, and an air cargo line last.

Given the constraints on cargo capacity and the increased demand, Burdinski concluded that the only prudent strategy to follow was to allocate the cargo capacity on the basis of price. It made no economic sense to haul Fast Forward cargo at rates below those charged with large consumer products shippers. Because Fast Forward did not pass on the discounted rate to its shippers, Fly Right felt it could bypass Freight Forward and service those shippers directly, thereby increasing revenues and profits.

Case Questions

1. Discuss the advantages and disadvantages of the current Fast Forward-Fly Right alliance. Who has benefited the most? The least?

2. Analyze the strategy developed by Fly Right to allocate available space. What are the short-run and long-run results of the strategy to eliminate the Fast Forward space contract?

3. What actions would you recommend for John Klinker?

Case 8.2

Fragle Van Lines

Fragle Van Lines is a household goods motor carrier operating primarily in the southeast United States and maintains agency relationship with American Van Lines. American is a 48-state operator and uses companies like Fragle to offer complete service both locally and nationally. Fragle has help operating authority for the past 20 years and, even though entry and expansion are unregulated, until now Fragle has never sought to expand its operation. Within in its region, Fragle uses their own equipment, but when the destination is beyond this area, Fragle relies on American to provide line-haul and destination services. Fragle also supplies destination services for American and its other agents when they have shipments destined to Fragle's region.

As part of its arrangement with American, Fragle supplies an agreed number of tractor trailers for use by American. American is responsible for repairs and maintenance of these units while they are under American's control.

Revenue is shared with American unless Fragle provides all services at pick up, delivery, and line haul. Fragle then pays an "advertising fee" to American to support its sales and marketing program. If the move originates or terminates outside of Fragle's territory, Fragle receives a share of the revenue dependent on the services it provides.

Since the early 1980s, Fragle's region has experienced significant industrial growth. Not only have new firms, both domestic and foreign, located in the Southeast, other companies have located their corporate headquarters in this area. Fragle has aggressively pursued these firms and built up a large national account base. Many of these firms move employees both nationwide and internationally. When the shipments originate or terminate outside of Fragle's region, American collects a minimum of 25 percent of the total revenue as its share for its "services." If the shipment is international, American collects a minimum of 35 percent.

Strong competition for these national accounts has placed great pressure on rates and Fragle finds its margins slim. When forced to share its income on these percentage levels outlined above, Fragle's business is at the near break-even level.

Fragle's management plans to expand its operation and rely less on American for support. Since deregulation, expansion from a regulatory standpoint is simple. However, many other factors to consider must be considered. Fragle has asked you to assist them in forming a plan to manage this expansion.

Case Questions

1. Discuss the resources, non-carrier alliances, information systems needed, and management requirements for not only a 48-states operation, but international as well.

2. Develop a high-level plan for Fragle's top management to implement this expanded operation. Include your plan for sales and marketing.

3. Should you consider intermodal? What about ocean shipping? What will be required to insure that motor vehicles operated by Fragle are maintained, repaired, and fueled?

4. What will American do? What steps can you take to meet this concern?

CHAPTER 9

INTERNATIONAL TRANSPORTATION

International transportation is an integral part of the study of transportation. Foreign trade is growing in tonnage and value for the United States and for most other nations of the world. Further, it is a purchase or sales activity engaged in by more and more firms, even medium and small firms and carriers. Although the primary economics and techniques of carrier management efficiencies are similar in an international setting to those in domestic settings, the processes, the supply of transportation, and the public policy require separate treatment.

This chapter examines foreign trade and the international transportation process and presents the basic forms of transportation found in this realm. Rate-making systems are examined for both air and ocean trades. Several major areas of policy concern are covered that bear on the carriers, the United States, and relations with foreign nations. Finally, often overlooked in many texts, but a crucial part of international transportation, is the role of port planning.

Extent and Magnitude of Trade

The United States is a large trading partner in the world. Although foreign trade is not as significant to the United States as it is to the gross national product of some other nations, the magnitude and value of U.S. tonnage imported and exported makes U.S. global trade an important area of study. The United States trades with nearly all nations of the world, with the exception of a few nations that are excluded due to political reasons.

The U.S. trading partners are indicated in Table 9.1. The largest U.S. trading partner is Canada, with a first quarter 1997 trade value of $77.97 billion. Japan is the second largest, with an annual trade value of $46.40 billion. Mexico, the United Kingdom, and Germany are the next largest trading partners, with annual trade values of $35.35 billion, $17.20 billion, and $16.22 billion, respectively. These 10 countries account for 70 percent of U.S. imports and 64 percent of U.S. exports of goods.

Trading with Canada and Mexico is a relatively simple procedure because truck and rail transportation can be used in a manner similar to that used for domestic moves. Documentation and custom processes still exist, but this form of international transportation does not require differentiation from that of domestic U.S. transporta-

TABLE 9.1 U.S. Trading Partners

Country	Trade Value (1 Q 1997)[a] ($ in Billions)
Canada	77.97
Japan	46.40
Mexico	35.35
United Kingdom	17.20
Germany	16.22
China	15.31
South Korea	11.52
Taiwan	11.82
Singapore	8.92
France	8.43

[a]In 1997 U.S. dollars.

Source: U.S. Census Bureau, as reported in *Distribution,* July 1997, p. 88.

tion. Both countries are adjacent to the United States, and both serve as markets for U.S. goods as well as sources of raw materials and production and assembly operations. The United States, Mexico, and Canada have signed the **North American Free Trade Agreement (NAFTA),** easing import duties and encouraging trade among the three countries.

Overview of the North American Free Trade Agreement

The North American Free Trade Agreement (NAFTA) was signed by leaders of Canada, the United States and Mexico in 1993 and was ratified by Congress in early 1994. NAFTA establishes free-trade between these three countries and provides the way the Agreement is to be interpreted. The Treaty states the objectives of the three countries is based on the principles of an unimpeded flow of goods, most-favored-nation (MFN) status, and a commitment to enhance the cross-border movement of goods and services. MFN status provides the lowest duties or customs fees, if any and simplifies the paperwork required to move goods between the partner countries.

Canada and the U.S. have agreed to suspend the operation of the Canada–U.S. Free Trade Agreement (FTA) in order to allow NAFTA to prevail. Any sections of the FTA which are not covered by NAFTA remain in place.

From a transportation standpoint, by 2000, motor carriers of each country were to have been able to operate freely in all three countries. There have been meetings between trucking executives and government officials the U.S., Canada and Mexico but no overall agreement has been put in place. While cross border operations between the U.S. and Mexico were to have started in 1995, a number of problems remain to be resolved and such operations are still prohibited. The original agreement allowed U.S. or Mexican carriers to pick up or deliver but not both, in each country's border states with their own equipment and employees. A number of concerns including safety issues remain to be addressed.

A problem has been the allowable trailers which could operate into Mexico. While American carriers have standardized on the 53' van, many Mexican carriers do not operate this type of trailer. The Mexican government announced new size regulations in early 1997 which would seem to permit 53' trailers in Mexico. These regulations limit overall combination tractor and trailer length to just over 68 feet. This requires an extremely short wheel base tractor which very few Mexican or American carriers operate. This issue is the subject of an ongoing negotiations between the U.S. and Mexico.

Since June 1996, Mexican regulations will not allow American owned trailers to operate more than 12.5 miles from the border without obtaining a permit from the Mexican government for each vehicle. The Department of Commerce and Industrial Development issues the permit and the U.S. trucking company is required to post a bond. The permit is good for 30 days and will allow only one entrance and one exit for that trailer during the life of the permit. The other alternative is to transfer the freight to a trailer owned and operated by a Mexican based trucking company. A bond is required for each separate trailer and the bond fee is not refundable.

Much work has still to be done in connection with NAFTA implementation as it relates to the U.S. and Mexico. However, there has been significant change related to Canadian motor carriers operation in the U.S.

Canadian motor carriers now have the same rights in the U.S. as American truckers have in Canada. Historically a "foreign" carrier was not allowed to pick up and deliver shipments within the U.S. Recent changes in regulations have been changed so that Canadian and U.S. carriers enjoy the same privileges while operating in the other's country.

Canadian carriers are now allowed to transport domestic U.S. traffic when such transportation is incidental to a return trip to Canada. For example, a Canadian trucker could deliver a load in Chicago, pick up a shipment for Detroit and upon arrival in Detroit, pick up a shipment destined to Canada. However, the truck must be driven by a citizen of the country in which the truck is operated.

An example of the trading arrangement between the United States and Mexico is a unique international operation known as a **Maquiladora.** A Maquiladora is a U.S. manufacturing or assembly operation located along the U.S.–Mexico border or other locations specified by the Mexican government. U.S. raw materials and component parts are sent to the Maquiladora, where the semi-finished or finished product is manufactured or assembled. All or part of the Maquiladora output is subsequently returned to the United States without any Mexican import duties being paid. The U.S. companies with Maquiladora operations are taking advantage of the lower labor rates in Mexico.

International Transportation Process

From the shipper's perspective, the management of international transportation involves the planning, implementation, and control of the procurement and use of freight transportation and related service providers to achieve company objectives. Managing the international transportation process is more complex than that of domestic transportation because of the many differences between the trading nations' transportation and customs regulations, infrastructure, exchange rates, culture, and language.

Figure 9.1 depicts the international transportation process. It begins with the buyer-seller agreement and the management areas of order preparation, transportation, and documentation. Each of these process elements is discussed below.

Buyer–Seller Agreement

The agreement between the buyer and seller determines the specific transportation criteria the seller must meet. These criteria include the product to be shipped, financial terms, delivery requirements (date and location), packing, the transportation method(s) to be used, and cargo insurance. In addition, the INCOTERMS agreed to delineate the transportation responsibility between the buyer and seller.

*INCOTERMS**

The international terms of sale are known as **INCOTERMS.** Unlike domestic terms of sale, in which the buyers and sellers primarily use Free On Board (FOB), origin and FOB, and destination terms, there are 13 different INCOTERMS. Developed by the International Chamber of Commerce, these INCOTERMS are internationally accepted rules defining trade terms.

The INCOTERMS define responsibilities of both the buyer and seller in any international contract of sale. For exporting, the terms delineate buyer or seller responsibility for the following:

*This section is based on the material found in John J. Coyle, Edward J. Bardi, and C. John Langley, *The Management of Business Logistics,* 6th ed. (St. Paul, MN: West Publishing Co., 1996), pp. 367–369.

FIGURE 9.1 International Transportation Process

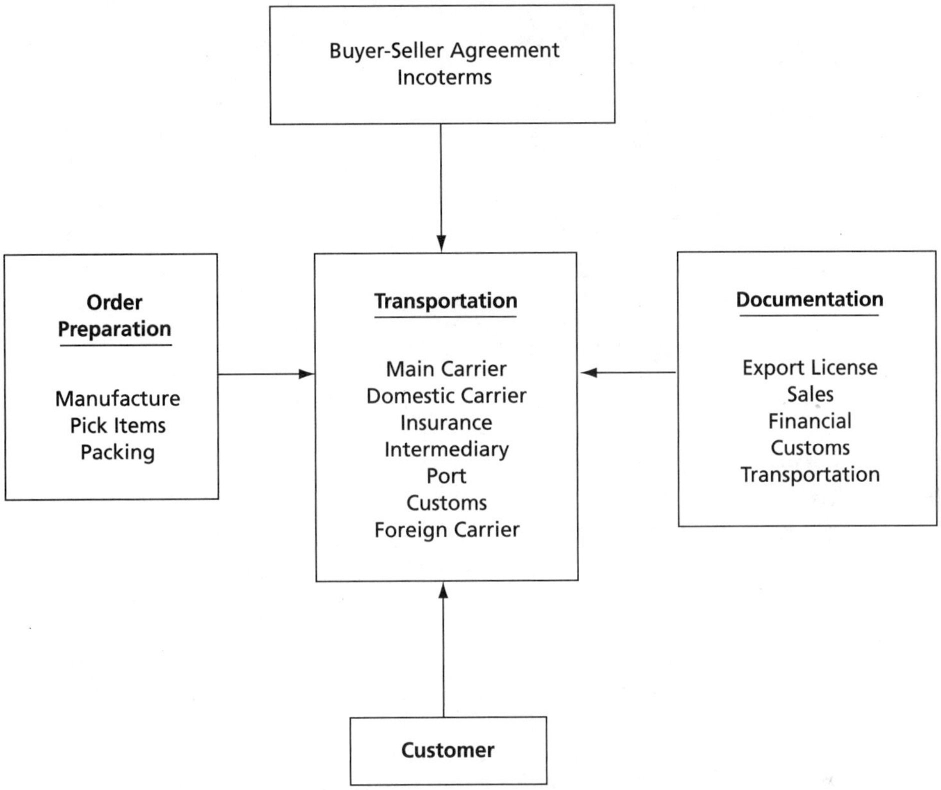

- Export packing cost
- Inland transportation (to the port of export)
- Export clearance
- Vessel or plane loading
- Main transportation cost
- Cargo insurance
- Customs duties
- Risk of loss or damage in transit

E Terms

The E terms consist of one INCOTERM, **Ex Works.** This is a departure contract that gives the buyer total responsibility for the shipment. The seller's responsibility is to make the shipment available at its facility. The buyer agrees to take possession of the shipment at the point of origin and to bear all of the cost and risk of transporting the goods to the destination (see Figure 9.2 for additional responsibilities of the E Terms).

FIGURE 9.2 Summary of INCOTERMS Cost Obligations

Cost or Activity	EXW	FCA	FAS	FOB	CFR	CIF	CPT	CIP	DAF	DES	DEQ	DDU	DDP
Export packing	B	S	S	S	S	S	S	S	S	S	S	S	S
Export clearance	B	S	B	S	S	S	S	S	S	S	S	S	S
Inland transport (Dom.)	B	S	S	S	S	S	S	S	S	S	S	S	S
Vessel/plane loading	B	B	B	S	S	S	S	S	S	S	S	S	S
Main transport	B	B	B	B	S	S	S	S	S	S	S	S	S
Cargo insurance	B	B	B	B	B	S	B	S	S	S	S	S	S
Customs duties	B	B	B	B	B	B	B	B	B	B	S	B	S
Inland transport (For.)	B	B	B	B	B	B	B	B	B	B	B	B	S
Mode applicability	X	X	W	W	W	W	X	X	X	W	W	X	X

B = Buyer; S = Seller; W = Water Carrier; X = Air, Motor, Rail, Intermodal.

F Terms

The three F terms obligate the seller to incur the cost of delivering the shipment cleared for export to the carrier designated by the buyer. The buyer selects and incurs the cost of main transportation, insurance, and customs clearance. **Free Carrier (FCA)** can be used with any mode of transportation. Risk of damage is transferred to the buyer when the seller delivers the goods to the carrier named by the buyer. **Free Alongside Ship (FAS)** is used for water transportation shipments only. The risk of damage is transferred to the buyer when the goods are delivered alongside the ship. The buyer must pay the cost of "lifting" the cargo or container on board the vessel. **Free On Board (FOB)** is used for only water transportation shipments. The risk of damage is transferred to the buyer when the shipment crosses the ship's rail (when the goods are actually loaded on the vessel). The seller pays the lifting charge (see Figure 9.2 for additional responsibilities on the F Terms).

C Terms

The four C terms are shipment contracts that obligate the seller to obtain and pay for the main carriage and/or cargo insurance. **Cost and Freight (CFR)** and **Carriage Paid To (CPT)** are similar in that both obligate the seller to select and pay for the main carriage (ocean or air to the foreign country). CFR is only used for shipments by water transportation, while CPT is used for any mode. In both terms, the seller incurs all costs to the port of destination. Risk of damage passes to the buyer when the goods pass the ship's rail, CFR, or when delivered to the main carrier, CPT.

Cost, Insurance, Freight (CIF) and **Carriage and Insurance Paid To (CIP)** require the seller to pay for both main carriage and cargo insurance. The risk of damage is the same as that for CFR and CPT (see Figure 9.2 for additional responsibilities of the C Terms).

D Terms

The D terms obligate the seller to incur all costs related to delivery of the shipment to the foreign destination. There are five D terms; two apply to water transportation only and three to any mode used. All five D terms require the seller to incur all costs and the risk of damage up to the destination port.

Delivered At Frontier (DAF) means the seller is responsible for transportation and incurs the risk of damage to the named point at the place of delivery at the frontier of the destination country. For example, DAF, Laredo, Texas, indicates the seller is responsible for making the goods available at Laredo, Texas. The buyer is responsible for customs duties and clearance into Mexico. DAF can be used with all modes.

Delivered Ex Ship (DES) and **Delivered Ex Quay (or wharf) (DEQ)** are used with shipments by water transportation. Both terms require the seller to pay for the main carriage. Under DES, risk of damage is transferred when the goods are made available to the buyer on board the ship uncleared for import at the port of destination. The buyer is responsible for customs clearance. With DEQ, risk of damage is transferred to the buyer when the goods cleared for import are unloaded onto the quay (wharf) at the named port of destination.

Delivered Duty Unpaid (DDU) and **Delivered Duty Paid (DDP)** are available for all modes. DDU requires the seller to incur all cost, except import duties, to the named place in the country of importation. Risk of damage passes to the buyer when the goods are made available, duties unpaid, at the named place. (DDU is similar to DES.) DDP imposes the same obligations on the seller as DDU, plus the additional responsibility of clearing the goods for import and paying the customs duties (DDP is similar to DEQ). See Figure 9.2 for additional responsibilities of the D Terms.

Order Preparation

Order preparation involves either picking items ordered from inventory or manufacturing them. In either case, the seller must make sure the item prepared for shipping matches exactly what is ordered. Failure to comply with the product specifications contained in the buyer's purchase order indicates the buyer's refusal to accept the shipment or to pay the invoice.

Packing for international water shipments is usually more stringent than for domestic shipments because of the increased potential for damage. Shippers typically use an export packing company to pack the shipment for the rigors of frequent handling, lifting, and storage, as well as the rough ride of international water carriage. For international air shipments, the domestic packing is usually sufficient.

Documentation

International shipments movement is controlled by paper; without proper documentation the shipment does not move. A missing or incorrect document can delay a shipment and/or prevent the shipment from entering a country. These documents are governed by the customs regulations of the shipping and receiving nations.

Substantial improvements have been made to computerize the documentation process, but these automation improvements have not been made in all countries. In the United States, the Customs Service has developed the Automated Brokers Interface System and the Automated Export System. Canada has a computerized system called the Pre-Arrival Review Process for Canadian imports.

Export License

No special authorization is needed to export, but the president of the United States is authorized to control exports for national security, foreign policy, and items in short supply. In addition, licensing by a federal agency having jurisdiction over a commodity can exercise licensing requirements for a given product, such as the Department of Agriculture having jurisdiction over grain.

The Department of Commerce issues two types of licenses: validated and general. The validated export license is required for commodities and destinations deemed important to national security, foreign policy, and items in short supply. A formal application for a license is required; after the authorized shipments are made, the license is returned to the Bureau of Export Administration.

If the commodities being exported do not require a validated license, the general license is needed. However, no actual general license is issued since U.S. law contains a blanket authorization for commodities and destinations not requiring a validated export license.

Sales Documents

Three sales documents are generally used in international trade: a pro-forma invoice, a commercial invoice, and a consular invoice. All three contain essentially the same information: buyer, seller, product descriptions, payment terms, selling price, and other information requested by the buyer, bank, or importing country.

The **pro-forma invoice** is issued by the seller to acquaint the importer and import government authorities with details of the shipment. It may be required to obtain necessary foreign exchange information and/or an import license or permit. The **commercial invoice,** issued by the seller, is a bill of sale for the goods sold to the buyer, a basis for determining shipment value and importing duty assessment, and a requirement for clearing goods through customs. The **consular invoice** is the same as the commercial invoice except it is a special form prescribed by the importing country and it must be completed in the language of the importing country.

Financial Documents

In the buyer-seller agreement, the credit extended by the seller to the buyer is delineated and takes the form of either a letter of credit or draft. The **letter of credit**, issued by the buyer's bank, is a guarantee by the buyer's bank to the seller that payment will be made if certain terms and conditions are met. These conditions include, for example, documentation, shipping date, time limits, and so on. If these conditions are not met, payment will be withheld.

The **draft** is credit extended by the seller directly to the buyer. It is a written order for a sum of money to be paid by the buyer on a certain date. Upon presentation of the draft to the buyer's bank, the buyer's bank collects the money from the buyer, releases the shipment documentation to permit the buyer to receive the shipment, and remits the money to the seller.

Customs Documents

As noted earlier, each nation has a unique set of customs regulations governing the international trade. In the United States, two common customs documents are the shipper's export declaration and the certificate of origin. To assist in identifying commodities throughout the world, an international commodity classification system, the Harmonized System, is used.

The **shipper's export declaration** is issued by the seller and acts to control the export of restricted goods (implements of war, high-level technology, etc.) and to provide statistics regarding exporting activity. The **certificate of origin** is used to certify the country of origin of the commodities and is particularly important for trade between countries that have special import duty treaties. For example, NAFTA provides lower import duties for commodities originating in the United States, Canada, or Mexico and destined for one of the respective countries.

Transportation Documents

As with domestic shipments, international shipments require a bill of lading. The **bill of lading** acts as a contract of carriage, a receipt for the goods, and provides carrier delivery instructions. For water shipments, an ocean bill of lading is used; an airway bill is used for air carrier shipments.

In addition to the bill of lading, most international shipments require a packing list that provides detailed information of the package contents, dimension, and weight. A dock receipt is issued by a water carrier when the goods arrive at the dock, but are not loaded onto the ship immediately; this transfers accountability, or liability, from the domestic carrier to the international carrier.

Transportation

The transportation elements include the selection of carriers, ports/gateways, intermediaries, and the acquisition of insurance. At least three carriers are involved in an international shipment: a domestic, an international, and an international carrier. The international transportation manager must select a domestic carrier to move the goods from the seller's door to the port or gateway, an international carrier to move it between countries, and a foreign carrier to move it to its final destination in the importing country. The responsibility for carrier selection is delineated by the INCOTERMS.

Selection of the port or gateway involves consideration of handling, carrier availability, handling equipment availability, convenience, frequency of damage, and freight rates. Cargo insurance is usually purchased for international shipments because of the complexity of international claim settlement associated with multinational laws. The buyer–seller agreement defines whether the buyer or seller is responsible for securing cargo liability insurance.

International Transportation Providers

International transportation is provided by all modes of transportation, including pipelines in North America. However, the majority of non-North American shipments are made via air and water transportation. Because the shipments from and to Canada and Mexico are quite similar to the domestic moves, this section will emphasize ocean and air transportation. In addition, attention is given to the transportation intermediaries who are critical components in most international shipments.

Ocean Transportation

The specific types of carriers that transport U.S. ocean-borne trade are liners, tramps, and private vessels. Each type provides specific service features to the international transportation user as discussed below.

Liners

Liners are ships that ply fixed routes on published schedules. They typically charge according to published tariffs that are either unique to the ship line or are made by several lines in a particular trade route. Liner services are either container or break-bulk types.

Freight must be moved to the liner company's terminal at the port after the shipper has arranged for the freight booking or reservation. This freight is loaded by machine if bulk or crane if containerized and stowed in accordance with ship weight and balance requirements. The frequency of various liner departures from New York and Oakland has caused these ports to be highly preferred by many shippers.

Container movement is gaining over the traditional **break-bulk** method of ocean carriage. When goods have to be heavily crated and packaged for break-bulk movement, a container often provides much of that needed protection. Further, whereas a break-bulk ship might require many days to unload and load its cargo by small crane and manpower, an entire container ship can enter, unload, load, and clear a port in less than 12 hours. Such speed has brought about labor savings to both the shipper and the liner company, as well as increased ship (and capital) utilization. Because a ship is only earning revenue at sea, it is easy to see why containers have become a dominant form of packaged goods shipping.

Container service, while saving port and ship time, has brought about different operating and management concerns for the ship company. For one, this service requires a large investment in containers because, while some are at sea, many others are being delivered inland or are being loaded there for movement to port. Although a ship might carry 1,000 containers, an investment of 1,500 to 2,500 containers is necessary to support that ship. Another concern is control over the containers. Previous shipping line managements were port-to-port-oriented. With inland movement of containers, control over this land movement becomes a necessity. The container itself is a large investment and is attractive to thieves in areas of warehouse or housing shortages.

The **lighter-aboard ship (LASH)** is a liner that carries barges that were loaded at an inland river point and moved to the ocean port via water tow. A specially designed ocean ship carries the payload and barge intact to a foreign port to be dropped off in the harbor. This system avoids port handling and enables fast ship turnaround and high utilization.

The economics of the LASH ship are similar to that of the container ship in that the ocean ship is high in capital cost, and the presence of barges or containers decreases high stowage density. These two factors are generally traded off against the fast port turnaround provided by these systems.

Another type of ship found in liner services is a **roll-on/roll-off ship,** often referred to as a **RORO** ship. These ships carry trucks, trailers, and construction equipment much like a multilevel ferryboat. When in service with trailers, a RORO ship is like a container ship except that it has the wheel chassis attached to the trailer body en route. RORO ships are especially useful in carrying heavy construction equipment because they are unable to maintain an even keel while the equipment is being loaded and unloaded. This stability allows loading and unloading without the use of dockside cranes that may not even be available.

Tramps

The **tramp ship** is one that is hired like a taxi or leased auto. That is, it is a bulk or tank ship that is hired on a voyage or time basis. On a voyage basis, a U.S. exporter of grain will seek a tramp ship that will become empty at a desired U.S. port. It will then be hired for one-way movement to a foreign port. Port fees, a daily operating rate and demurrage, will be part of the charter contract. Time charters are usually longer-term charters in which the shipper will make or arrange for more than a one-way move. Such charters are made with or without crews being provided by the ship owner.

Private Vessels

Private ships are ships that are owned or leased on a long-term basis by the firm moving the goods. Many oil ships fit this category as do automotive and lumber vessels. The economics of this form of ship movement are similar to those of private motor trucks.

Another element of interest in international shipping is that of ship registry. Although a ship might be owned by an American and ply a route between the United

States and the Persian Gulf, it might be registered in and fly the flag of Liberia or Panama. These nations represent what are called **flags of convenience.** That is, the owners derive certain benefits of taxes, manning, and some relaxed safety requirements by being registered in those countries, rather than in the United States, Canada, or wherever. However, some activity has taken place recently with regard to labor rules in these countries that might diminish the advantage of registering there.

Air Carriers

Just as with domestic moves, air transportation offers the international transportation user speed. The fastest method of movement for the non-North American international shipment is air carriage. Four types of air carriers are available for international shippers: air parcel post, express or courier, passenger, and cargo.

Air Parcel Post

Air parcel post service is provided by the postal service of a country and is designed to handle small packages. The postal service contracts with an air carrier to pick up and deliver the item from one country to another. There are restrictions as to the size and weight of the shipment handled by air parcel post, and these restrictions vary by country. In the United States, the maximum size permitted is 108 inches of length and girth and no more than 70 pounds of weight.

Express or Courier Service

Express or courier service is provided by air carriers and is generally restricted to small shipments weighing less than 70 pounds. Speed is the essential characteristic of this service, with next-day or second-day delivery a standard service level. Examples of major carriers providing this service include Federal Express, United Parcel Service (UPS), DHL, and Emery.

Passenger Carriers

Regularly scheduled international passenger flights haul freight in the "belly" of the plane. These carriers focus on the movement of passengers, but the excess capacity in the nonpassenger compartment permits the transporting of cargo along with passengers. Cargo capacity and cargo size are limited by the size of each plane, but the regular schedules afford the use of numerous flights between origin and destination. Examples of U.S. international passenger carriers that transport cargo are American, Delta, Northwest, and United.

All-Cargo Carriers

All-cargo carriers specialize in the movement of freight, not passengers. The airplanes are outfitted with larger hatch openings, cargo compartments, and floor-bearing ratings. Many air cargo planes have mechanized materials-handling devices on board to permit the movement of heavier cargo inside the plane. Some of the larger planes are capable of transporting a 40-foot container, trucks, and other motor vehicles. Generally, these carriers haul heavier shipments weighing more than 70 pounds. BAX Global, Federal Express, and UPS Air are examples of U.S. all-cargo carriers.

Ancillary Services

Other service firms exist in addition to the basic modes that are available to the international transportation user. These ancillary service companies provide a variety of functions that offer the user lower costs, improved service, and/or technical expertise.

Air Freight Forwarders

International air freight forwarding firms operate in a manner similar to domestic air freight forwarders. The air freight forwarder books space on an air carrier's plane and solicits freight from numerous shippers to fill the booked space. The air freight forwarder offers the shipper of small shipments a rate savings resulting from the advanced purchase of space. In addition, the air freight forwarder offers convenience to the shipper, especially when more than one airline must be used in an interline setting, or when ground transportation is necessary at one or both ends of the air move.

International Freight Forwarders

These firms arrange movement for the shipper. They do not necessarily act as consolidators or earn their revenues in that manner like domestic forwarders. International freight forwarders act as agents for shippers by applying familiarity and expertise with ocean shipping to facilitate through movement. They represent the shipper in arranging such activities as inland transportation, packaging, documentation, booking, and legal fees. They charge a percent of the costs incurred for arranging these services. They play an invaluable role for shippers who are not familiar with the intricacies of shipping or those who do not have the scale or volume to warrant having in-house expertise in this area.

Nonvessel Operating Common Carriers (NVOCC)

Nonvessel operating carriers assemble and disperse less-than-container shipments and move them as full-container shipments. They serve much the same role as the domestic freight forwarders. A shipper moving a small item would otherwise have to move it via break-bulk ocean carrier or air freight. The NVOCC consolidates this shipment with many others and gains the economies of container movement. Some NVOCCs operate from inland cities, where they unload inbound containers and distribute the goods to consignees. They in turn solicit outbound freight, **consolidate** shipments into the containers, and move them back to a seaport for outbound movement. The steamship line gains opportunities from broadened territorial traffic, and it gains services and control over containers from the NVOCC solicitations. Shippers and receivers gain from the shipping expertise and processes of the NVOCC, as well as from expanded and simplified import and export opportunities.

Ship Brokers

These firms act as middlemen between the tramp ship owner and a chartering shipper or receiver. The brokers' extensive exposure, contacts, and knowledge of the overall ship market make them valuable parties in these arrangements. They are compensated on the basis of a percentage of the chartering fees.

Ship Agents

Ship agents act on behalf of a liner company or tramp ship operator (either owner or charter company) to represent their interests in facilitating ship arrival, clearance, loading, unloading, and fee payment while at a specific port. Liner firms will use agents when the frequency of sailings are so sparse that it is not economical for them to invest in their own terminals or to have management personnel on-site.

Land, Mini-, and Micro-bridges

These three services have become significant parts of international shipping over the past decade. Their development is largely due to the carrier efficiencies they provide that also benefit the shippers.

The **land bridge** system consists of containers moving between Japan and Europe by rail and ship. That is, originally, containers were moved entirely by ship between Asia and Europe across the Pacific and Atlantic Oceans and through the Panama Canal. Ship fuel and capital costs as well as trouble in Panama created economies in moving the containers by water to a U.S. Pacific Coast port, then by entire trainload across the United States to another ship for transatlantic crossing to Europe. This system reduces transit time and liner company ship investment.

A **mini-bridge** is a similar system that is used for movements between, say, Japan and New York, Philadelphia, Baltimore, Charleston, New Orleans, or Houston. Rather than move all-water routes from Asia to these cities through the Panama Canal, a mini-bridge consists of transpacific water movement to Seattle, Oakland, or Long Beach, California, then by rail to the destination East Coast or Gulf Coast city. Mini-bridge services likewise operate from Europe to West Coast cities and New Orleans and Houston, with water–rail transfer taking place at New York or Charleston.

Examples of two mini-bridges are shown in Figure 9.3. The all-water route from Japan to New York requires about 21 to 24 days. This route is 9,700 miles and it involves transit through the Panama Canal, which requires a toll. The alternative is to unload the freight in Seattle and use rail to move it across the country. This route is only 7,400 miles long and takes about 16 days. The savings to the shipper is in the transit time. The second route is Europe to Houston. The all-water route is 4,600 miles, whereas unloading at Charleston and using rail to Houston is 4,500 miles. The mileage is not significant, but the savings here is in faster transit time. The steamship company can turn the ship around and return it to Europe faster than before. In fact, this option enables the steamship company to offer weekly service between Europe and Houston using one less ship than is used in the all-water route. That ship can be redeployed onto another route altogether. The mini-bridge gives the steamship company effective freight-hauling capacity while saving the investment in one ship.

A mini-bridge saves transit time and ship line separating costs and investment, but previously another benefit accrued to the shipper/receiver in loading and unloading cost savings was avoiding what was called a "50-mile rule." When containers replaced break-bulk shipping, many stevedores lost work and income. As part of a labor settlement, it was arranged that any consolidated container had to be loaded or unloaded by stevedores if it was stuffed or unstuffed within 50 miles of the container point of embarkation or debarkation. This system often required handling at times that were inconvenient for the shipper/receiver or were at a cost much higher than what would be incurred by the shipper's own labor. An all-water movement from a San Jose, California shipper to a consignee in Europe through ship loading at Oakland, California required such stevedore container packing. However, in a mini-bridge move by container train from California for containership movement from New York to Europe, San Jose was beyond the 50-mile radius of the New York containership loading point. Thus, the San Jose shipper avoided stevedore loading and enjoyed faster transit time to Europe.

In early 1989, the 50-mile rule was struck down in a court decision. This did not have a major impact upon traffic patterns. Mini-bridges are firmly entrenched because it provides faster transit time and avoids Panama Canal tolls and congestion.

Micro-bridge is an adaptation of mini-bridge, only it applies to interior nonport cities such as St. Louis. The origin or destination of the shipment is a U.S. interior, nonport city. Micro-bridges operate similarly to the NVOCC system. Here, too, a container is loaded at the interior point for transference to the ship at the port. This avoids truck movement to the port for actual loading of the container at the port terminal.

FIGURE 9.3 Mini-Bridge System

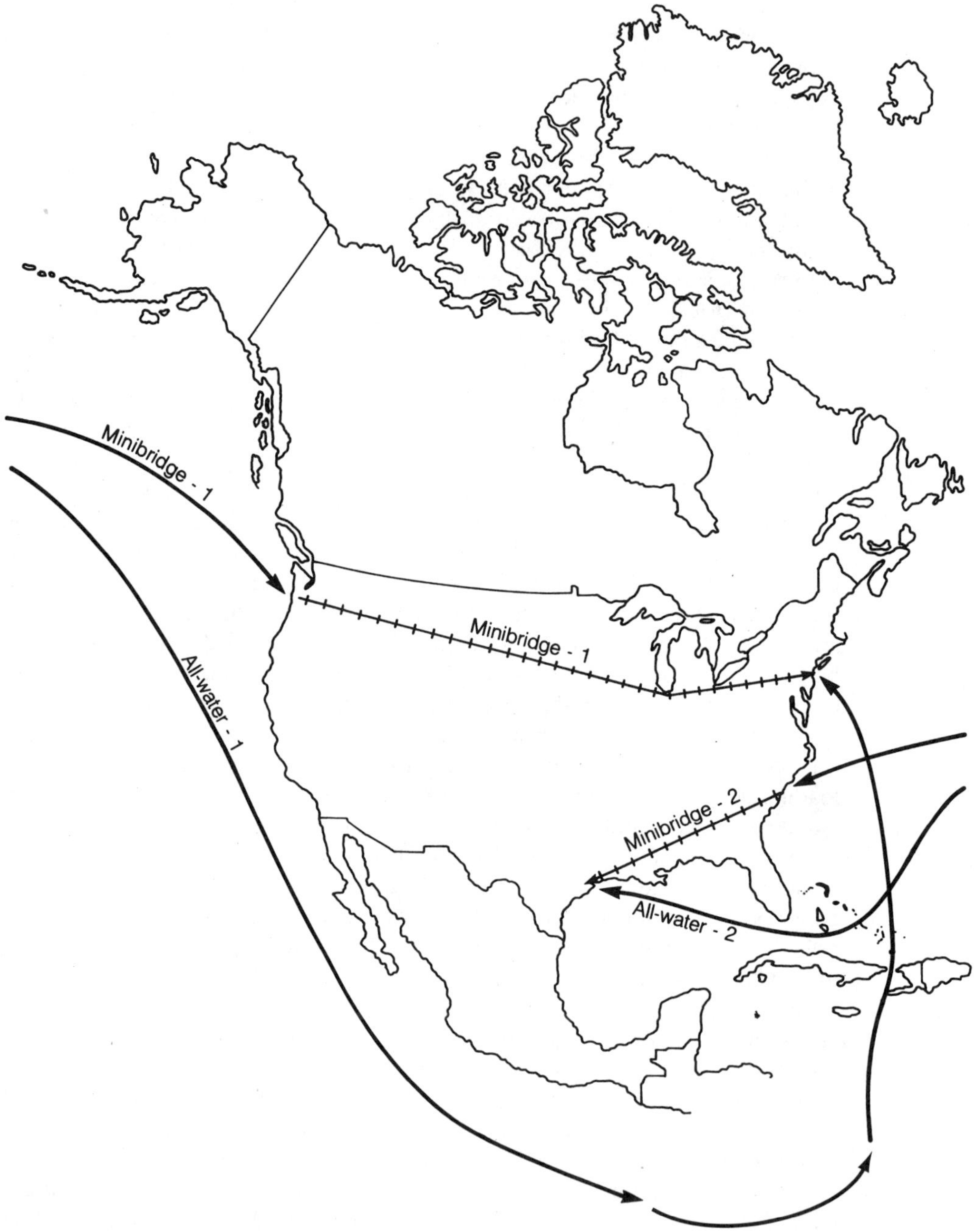

Rate Making in Foreign Transportation

Rate making is presented from the standpoint of three major transportation supply sources available to shippers: air, liners, and chartered tramp ships.

STOP OFF

Port of Hong Kong Challenged by Transition to China

Tiny as it may be, Hong Kong prides itself on objects that are the world's richest, biggest, bulkiest, most modern, and efficient. The port is trying to maintain that image with the help of the Hong Kong International Distribution Center (HIDC), billed as the world's largest warehouse at 40.4 square miles.

When Hong Kong was "ceded" by China to Great Britain after the 1841 Opium War, the island was ridiculed as a barren and remote territory. But soon the deep water port was prized as the only one in southern China.

Last year, Hong Kong evolved into the world's leading container port, carrying an estimated 11 million TEUs (20-foot equivalent units, or 20-foot containers) through the port annually.

Though the port serves Hong Kong and its five million people, its primary function as a transshipment port to and from the billion-plus residents of China serves Hong Kong's re-export market where the former colony derives its largest source of income. So the port has become the key access point to China's burgeoning economy.

The main port area is Kwai Chung, where the container terminals handled 4.71 million TEUs in the first eight months of 1994. Although the oldest terminal, Modern Terminals, handled 1.99 million TEUs, it was Hutchinson Whampoa Ltd.'s Hong Kong International Terminal (HIT) that handled about 60 percent of the break-bulk cargo. It was with this business in mind that Li Ka-Shing, Chairman of Hutchinson, erected the HIDC.

HIT started operations 20 years ago and today serves more than 30 shipping lines. Its computer system is rated among the most advanced in the world, controlling yard operations, ship planning, reporting, and communication systems. It was voted the region's best container terminal operator in 1991 and 1993, winning the Asian Freight Industry Award both years.

Equally important, HIT and Hutchinson Whampoa Group have invested heavily in Chinese southern ports, which serve to link, not compete with, Kwai Chung. This is one of the ironies of Hong Kong business.

A decade ago, Hong Kong was absolutely essential to doing business in China. Today, however, Shanghai is vying to reclaim its former glory as the gateway to China, while other ports throughout the booming southern region of China are opening each month. In nearly every case, the new ports are run by the same Hong Kong businessmen, many natives of the mainland, who helped make Hong Kong what it is today. Some observers feel these businessmen's efforts may undermine Hong Kong's future, but others seem less concerned. They contend that China's ports will not be able to catch Hong Kong for decades.

No matter how efficiently the terminal and adjacent warehouses are run, Hong Kong is facing a major problem. The port is overcrowded and needs a ninth container terminal, but China so far has blocked construction.

Where Hong Kong had previously eschewed politics for the business of business, becoming the darling of libertarian economist Milton Friedman, China does business with political brute force. When Chinese officials expressed their disapproval of one of the contractors scheduled to build the proposed terminal, planning stopped. As a result, the port is becoming overcrowded and inefficient.

But due to the strong ties between Hong Kong businessmen and their Chinese counterparts, new port facilities will be built north of what used to be Hong Kong's border with China. New container terminal or not, Li and Hutchison Whampoa will be able to direct container traffic wherever it needs to go from the "world's largest warehouse."

HIDC's uniqueness — with its miles of roads, total climatic control, minimal paperwork, and location at the port — means it will continue to prosper. If nothing else, its expertise may serve as an example for China's "baby terminals" in the future.

Source: Gordon Feller, *Distribution*, October 1997, p.16. Reprint with permission granted by *Logistics* (formerly *Distribution)* Magazine.

Shipping Conferences

A steamship conference is a voluntary organization of vessel-operating carriers whose main function is to set acceptable rates for steamships and shippers. The goal of the conference is to maintain a stable market and fair competition among carriers. Another important element of the steamship conference is to administer operating rules that guarantee the shipper a consistent level of service from participating lines.

For many years it was believed that the members of steamship conferences were "the cream of the crop"—providing the best service coupled with the highest cost. On the other hand, a shipper could get a cheaper price than what was offered by choosing a non-conference carrier but at the cost of a lower service level. Several factors have begun to erase this line between conference and nonconference carriers. First, the demand for highly sophisticated services has forced all carriers, conference and nonconference alike, to upgrade their service level to remain in business. Second, the development of containerization has enabled even the smallest carrier to compete in the door-to-door markets. Third, the Shipping Act of 1984 granted service and ratemaking freedoms to conference carriers that were available only to nonconference carriers before the act.[1] This has changed even more under the Ocean Shipping Reform Act of 1998.

International Air

The economies of international air freight carriage are largely similar to those of domestic movement. The differences lie primarily in institutional factors relating to national agreements and the International Air Transport Association (IATA). This is an international air carrier rate bureau for both passenger and freight movement. IATA has long served as a collective rate-making body composed of the U.S. overseas airlines in various trade routes. Prices for both passenger and freight traditionally tend to be set at sufficient levels so as to cover most costs of the higher-cost or lower-load factor carriers. This system enhances a supply of service and brings a stability to the rate structure. U.S. government policy shifts in the late 1970s tended to encourage rate flexibility and greater route expansion; these factors were initially seen as decreasing the effectiveness of IATA-made prices. This situation is discussed further in this chapter along with other policies.

Air Cargo Rate

Air cargo rates are based on the value of service or the cost of service. **The value of service,** as discussed in Chapter 2, "Transportation Regulation and Public Policy," is demand-based and considers the sensitivity of the cargo being shipped to freight rates. The less sensitive cargo is to rates, the higher the rate will be. On traffic lanes where demand is strong and plane capacity is limited, the air rates will be high, and vice versa for traffic lanes where supply exceeds demand. Also, products with high prices or emergency conditions surrounding the move will be charged high rates because the freight rate is a small portion (less than one percent) of the landed selling price.

Cost factors enter into air carrier pricing of cargo. Given the limited cargo-carrying capacity of a plane, space is a premium. The utilization of this space is related to the **density** of the cargo, with low-density cargo requiring more space per weight unit than high-density cargo. Rates are based on a product density of 10.4 pounds per cubic foot. For shipments with lower densities, the air carrier calculates the weight based on the shipment's number of cubic feet times the standard density of 10.4 pounds per cubic foot. For shipments with densities greater then 10.4 pounds per cubic foot, the actual weight is used.

For example, an international shipment weighing 480 pounds and measuring 6 feet × 3 feet × 5 feet, or 90 cubic feet, has a density of 5.33 pounds per cubic foot (480 pounds/90 cubic feet). The international air carrier will charge the shipper a calculated weight of 936 pounds (90 cubic feet × 10.4 pounds per cubic foot) for moving the shipment.

Three types of international air carrier rates are based on the commodity shipped: general cargo, class, and specific commodity rates. The **general cargo rate** is a standard rate that applies to commodities for which there is no other applicable rate (class or specific). The general cargo rate is available for any commodity, can vary with distance and direction, and/or is applicable between specific origin-destination pairs. Discounts are available for larger shipment sizes and may or may not include ground transportation to and from the airport

The **class rate** is applicable to cargo grouped into classes. There is no classification system in international air transportation as is found in domestic surface transportation. The rate for a particular class expressed as a percentage of the general cargo rate, is usually lower than the general cargo rate and can be door-to-door or airport-to-airport.

The specific **commodity rate** is applicable to a specific commodity between a specific origin-destination pair. The specific commodity rate is generally lower than the general cargo rate. A high minimum weight is usually required for each shipment. Because the air carrier utilizes the specific commodity rate to attract freight and to enable shippers to penetrate certain market areas, it may have a time limit. As with the other commodity-based rates, the specific commodity rate can be either door-to-door or airport-to-airport.

Container rates are also available for cargo shipped in a container. The rate is cost-based, rather than value of service- or commodity-based. The rate applies to a minimum weight in the container. Some carriers offer a container rate discount per container shipped over any route of the individual carrier. The discount is deducted from the tariff rate applicable to the commodity being moved in noncontainerized form and a charge is assessed for returning the empty container.

Liner Rate Making

Costs

Liner operation, as with most ship operation, is largely fixed and common in nature. It has been estimated that roughly 10 to 20 percent of the total costs of ship operation is variable and is in fuel, loading, and unloading costs.[2] Liner companies tend to have large overhead costs in the form of managements that are necessary for solicitation purposes.

The liner ship is often specifically constructed for a particular trade route. That is, such things as ship size and type, dimension, hatches, cargo space configuration, and engine type are designed around the ports to be visited, cargoes to be moved, and even the wave patterns experienced in a particular trade. These factors cause a ship that is designed for, say, Asian traffic to be less economical for United States-to-European trades.

A majority of the total costs of operating a ship are fixed. Because cargo loading, unloading, and fuel are the only primary variable costs, the ship's operation cost is roughly the same regardless of the commodity hauled. The problem of determining a cost per pound entails a difficult fixed cost allocation process, which can be arbitrary at best. Ship operators will often determine unit costs in terms of cost per cubic foot of ship space so as to better evaluate and price for the range of commodities handled.

Because the cost of owning and operating the ship manifests itself as a relatively fixed cost per day regardless of the commodity hauled, ship operators attempt to solicit and charge rates that will maximize the total revenue of the entire ship. This condition brings about the tendency to price according to the principles of value of service. That is, a floor of variable costs must be covered as a minimum; then the blend of high- and low-value-per-pound commodities, as well as the host of traffic elasticities, leads to pricing according to what the traffic will bear to maximize revenue.

The Conference of Rate Making

Liner firms have long banded together into collective rate-making bodies called **steamship conferences**. These serve a similar purpose as those provided by domestic rail and motor rate bureaus. Conferences date back to the last century, when several liner firms banded together in the United Kingdom to calculate Calcutta trade. Since then they have developed into their current state in which several characteristics can be noted.

Conferences comprise member liner firms only. The organization is international in scope since liner firms of many nations will belong to one. They are also territorial in scope. For example, the Pacific Westbound Conference includes the United States and foreign carriers originating freight at Pacific Coast ports between California, Alaska, and Canada for destinations in Japan, Korea, Taiwan, and Hong Kong. Another conference made up of some of the same countries as well as others will cover eastbound traffic between the same points. A range of firms belongs to conferences. Some operate on sparse schedules, whereas others might offer weekly service. American carriers with new ships costing up to $15,000 per day to operate will be in the trade, along with foreign carriers, some of whose ships might cost only $6,000 to $7,000 per day to operate.

The actual rate system in conferences reflects the ship and liner firm economics previously discussed. Because ship operators experience a relatively fixed cost per day, and weight is not necessarily a variable cost expense, rates are constructed to also accommodate the density of freight. Many rates are assessed on a weight basis, either on a 2,000-pound short ton or a 2,240-pound long ton. Products that might occupy more of a proportionate share of space relative to their weight are often charged on a "weight or measure" (W/M) basis. That is, the carrier would charge a dollar rate per ton based upon shipment weight or "cubic tons," which are computed at every 40 cubic feet. A shipment assessed at $60 W/M that weighs five weight tons but occupies 280 cubic feet would be charged $420 (seven cubic tons at $60). This system somewhat enables the carrier to recoup a minimum cost per cubic foot of space of ship capacity.

Another feature of conference rate making deals with contract rates and noncontract rates. Noncontract rates are the base rates, while contract rates are charged to shippers who have signed "exclusive patronage agreements" with the conference. This means that the shipper is charged rates approximately 10 to 15 percent lower than noncontract rates in exchange for using only member liner firms of the conference. The exclusive patronage agreement evolved from a deferred rebate system, but that was replaced by the agreement in U.S. trade as a result of American regulatory policy. The two rates are the reason this system is referred to as a dual-rate system. A shipper not having signed an agreement must pay the noncontract rate. Contract shippers unable to book space on a conference ship can use a nonconference liner without jeopardizing the discount. Further, a contract shipper can use tramp ships for bulk cargoes without conflicting with the agreement. Competitive pressures in the late 1970s caused a few steamship lines to eliminate the contract/noncontract system and replace it with a single-rate system.

Time/volume rates are a rate feature new to ocean shipping to and from the United States. These rates are much like the service contracts found in motor carriage transport. They often provide for a rate reduction in exchange for a guaranteed amount of tonnage or containers over a certain time period. The carrier or conference receives the benefit of a larger or guaranteed amount of tonnage.

One problem facing conferences and shippers in recent times is fluctuating international currency levels. That is, a Japanese steamship firm receiving revenues in dollars might find that rate and revenue to be unprofitable due to an upward relationship of the yen against the dollar. This does not necessarily harm the American flag carrier that pays the ship mortgage and wages in dollars, but the Japanese ship is hurt because its obligations must be paid in yen. The conferences consequently developed a currency adjustment factor (CAF), which is a surcharge on the rates used to recover any such related losses. These surcharges also fluctuate with currency relationship shifts. Problems have occurred with different conferences charging different CAFs, as well as land portions of mini-bridges also being subject to the charge. In essence, the CAFs tend to harm U.S. exports. Carriers charge extra fees for moving U.S. exports; thus, a low dollar that makes exports cheaper to foreigners is actually charged at a proportionally higher rate. This is a continuing subject of debate and policy consideration by the Federal Maritime Commission.

Another problem relating to ocean export and import movements is the competitiveness, location, and rail network relationship of various U.S. ports. Some ports are in direct lines between producing and consuming areas of the nation and major ocean routes, but others require longer land moves or experience less frequent ship sailings. As a result, railroads traditionally serving the less-competitive ports often charge a rate for inland moves on export and import shipments that cause a through-move to be the same rate as that over a direct port route. This traditionally was encouraged by the Interstate Commerce Commission (ICC) in an effort to equalize port relationships. Since the ICC has been eliminated, the STB is not following the same course of action.

The conference system has withstood a great amount of pressure and criticism over the years. The criticism has focused mainly on two situations. One is over tonnage of shipping capacity. That is, the amount of ship-carrying space plying the oceans is greater than the freight being moved. This situation leads to price cutting in any cartel-like relationship, and in the late 1970s ship conferences experienced the pressure when some line firms withdrew from the conference.

Another problem area has been with price cuttings by ship firms owned and operated by the Soviet Union in United States-to-Japan and United States-to-European markets. The Atlantic and Pacific Ocean arms of the Russian steamship organizations entered into these markets in the 1970s with significant rate cutting that severely affected the traditional firms. In many instances, this practice was seen by many as unfair, because the Russian firms appeared to be operating at below variable cost. However, labor and capital costs of these ships were paid in Russian currency, and profit was not necessarily the motive. Market entry and obtaining hard Western currencies was no doubt the objective; that is, the motive for operating was different than the other liners' long-run profit objective. The situation came to a head in 1980 when U.S. stevedores refused to service these ships as a result of the Russian invasion of Afghanistan.

The conference system has often been criticized from several vantage points. These criticisms are similar to those against domestic rate bureaus because rates are higher than they would be under free-market competition. Inefficient liner firms are protected, and rate innovations are not encouraged. Further, the practice of restricted conference membership by liner firms might leave poor-quality service to some areas.

For example, in the 1980s, 10 conferences existed between Western Europe and the East Coast of the United States. One superconference, Trans-Atlantic Conference Agreement (TACA), was available to shippers on this trade route. In 1992, TACA, then the Trans-Atlantic Agreement (TAA), reduced the available supply of ship space, increased rates by approximately 20 percent, and eliminated the door-to-door rate. That is, the shippers faced an ocean rate 20 percent greater than the previous door-to-door rate, plus they had to incur additional inland transportation charges. Also, certain ports, such as Philadelphia, were eliminated from the regular TAA schedule, thereby reducing the shippers' flexibility and negotiating abilities for inland transportation. This trend toward superconferences was evident on other major trade routes such as U.S.–Asia (Transpacific Westbound Rate Agreement).

Rate conferences do provide some benefits that contribute to their long-term existence. They provide a somewhat stable rate structure that fosters uniformity of rates and procedures. Further, individual shipper discrimination is reduced because any economic discrimination that is taking place is done uniformly.

The changes made by the Ocean Shipping Reform Act of 1998 may spell the end of the conference system. The new flexibility granted ship lines and their customers may see much ratemaking activity done outside the conference environment. The new freedom to enter into contracts will also impact the conferences.

Tramp Ship Cost Rate Factors

Costs

Tramp ships are generally not controlled by a specific route with a single commodity. Large oil tankers that are built for time charters for specific origin–destination markets are the exception. The basic tramp vessel might haul coal, grain, fertilizers, and lumber in the same year. Adaptability is necessary to minimize lost revenue possibilities that will arise. These vessels might not always be of low-cost, optimal design for any of the movements, but that is a basic trade-off to being flexible. This general construction means general internal features and hatches as well as the capability to enter into most ports of the world.[3]

The economies of ship construction are critical to the tramp vessel, especially the tanker. The nontanker vessel is generally built to hold between 5,000 and 8,000 tons of cargo. This is a good range for a majority of cargo lot sizes shipped by firms. The tanker, on the other hand, is usually designed for crude oil movements, and here the large tankers can competitively move oil at costs much lower than small vessels. This is due to economies of scale in both construction and operation. In fact, many 200,000 deadweight ton (DWT) tankers have the same number of crew members as those carrying only 40,000 DWT. Labor economies exist on new ships through the technological advances in navigation and operating systems. Whereas boiler rooms previously required a large number of personnel, many now function through computerized and automated control direct from the bridge. Navigational safety and optimum route planning are even enhanced with direct satellite links that can pinpoint ships' locations within a few hundred yards.

A major consideration of tramp owners is the nation in which the ship is registered. The nation of registry requires the shipowner to comply with specific manning, safety, and tax provisions. Liberia, Greece, and Panama are nations imposing relatively loose requirements in such areas. For this reason, many of the world ships are registered in these countries.

Tramp Ship Rate Making

A tramp ship owner experiences costs, like those of the liner, that are largely fixed in nature. Ownership costs present themselves in depreciation and interest costs. Fuel is not as greatly variable with the commodity weight load, as is ship speed or at-sea versus port time. The key is that the shipowner minimizes empty nonrevenue miles and days.

Three primary forms of ship rental or chartering systems are in use. These are the voyage, time, and bareboat or demise charter. Each one is distinct. The **voyage charter** is one in which the shipowner mans, operates, and charters the vessel, similar to a taxicab. Shippers seek voyage charters for primarily one-way and sometimes two-way trips. The owner is constantly seeking charters subsequent to present charters to minimize empty moves to the next charter.

The **time charter** is one in which the shipowner rents the vessel and crew to a shipper for use over a period of time that often includes use for several shipments. The owner has his or her ship productively tied up for a longer period of time than in the voyage charter and the shipper might judiciously arrange the moves, making the time charter more economical than several voyage charters.

The **bareboat** or demise **charter** is one in which the owner usually rents the vessel for a long period of time while the chartering party supplies the crew and performs the physical operation of the vessel. In this setting, the owner is seeking to recoup capital and interest costs and to be assured that the ship will be safely operated. Ship brokers in New York and London handle most ship chartering in this area.

The market for ship chartering is a fluid supply-and-demand situation. At any one time, the charter rate situation can be one of feast or famine for shipowners. This market can fluctuate over both the short and long term. In the short run, the demand for a ship and charter rates at a single port area will depend on shipper movement needs and available ship supply within a time span as short as a month. In another way, the market can be considered glutted or tight, depending on the number of ships or types of ships that are available in the world during a span of a year.

Long-run conditions have affected the work charter market in several ways. In one context, the growth in world oil consumption dropped after the 1973 energy crisis. Much ship tonnage was still being constructed at the time that was expected to be profitably used throughout the 1970s. So the growth rate of new ship capacity coming online continued to exceed the growth rate of oil demand. Another market-depressing factor was the reopening of the Suez Canal in the mid-1970s. For several years, ships carrying oil from the Persian Gulf to Europe and North America had to travel around Africa. Once the Suez Canal reopened, a medium-sized ship could make a round trip in much less time. With the same number of ships in the market suddenly capable of making more trips per year, the world capacity of ship carriage effectively increased, which caused supply to exceed demand. A major U.S. grain sale to Russian or China had the effect of boosting charter markets in both existing grain-carrying ships and tankers that can be converted for such cargoes. This market was not very continuous during the 1970s and, in fact, the 1980 U.S. grain embargo to Russia harmed this market until other nation sales took up some of the supply. All of these factors point to the high capital commitment and risk situation in this area of shipowners.

International Transportation Problems, Issues, and Policies

Two major policy areas are of concern in international transportation. One relates to the Federal Maritime Commission (FMC) and to foreign policy in regulation of international waterborne rates and practices to and from the United States. The other revolves around international air transportation.

Federal Maritime Commission Regulation of U.S. Ocean Rates

Ocean Shipping Reform Act

President Clinton signed the Ocean Shipping Reform Act into law October 14, 1998. This new law made significant changes in the Shipping Act of 1984. The Act requires the FMC to develop regulations to implement the legislation on or before March 1, 1999 and the Act itself will become effective on May 1, 1999. There are a number of significant provisions of the Ocean Shipping Reform Act. Some of them are listed below.

As with the domestic, surface carriers the new law eliminated the requirement that ocean carriers file rates and tariffs with the Federal Maritime Commission. Carriers are now required to maintain and post pricing information on the Internet or other such methods.

Ocean carriers now have the authority to enter confidential contracts with shippers. This also parallels the deregulation of domestic carriers. Only certain details must be released to the public.

Antitrust immunity for ocean carriers is continued but some new restrictions have been added. A primary one is the degree to which such agreements can restrict independent rate actions by individual ocean carriers.

Freight forwarders and Non Vessel Operating Common Carriers (NVOCC) will now be referred to as "ocean transportation intermediaries." They will be licensed and bonded and it will remain unlawful for carriers to provide service to a NVOCC which is not in compliance with the FMC's regulation.

The new Act will quickly change the traditional common carrier, tariff-based pricing to contracts as has occurred with domestic surface carriers. Now that carriers or groups of carriers can legally enter into confidential contracts with shippers or groups of shippers, it is expected that this will replace the old tariff based system.

Freight forwarders and NVOCCs are becoming more significant in international distribution. The companies are moving into the role of "retailers" of ocean freight similarly to domestic intermodal service providers. However, they can be both an asset and a competitor with ocean carriers. This new law increases regulatory control over these firms more than it does over companies who actually operate ships. Under the Act, an NVOCC shipping 10,000 TEUs (20 Foot Equivalent) per year must be bonded and licensed. A major exclusion deals with an "ocean carrier" which does not own or operate ships but charters space aboard another company's ships, does not have to comply with the bonding and licensing requirements, can offer confidential contracts, and has immunities from the antitrust laws.

United Nations Conference on Trade and Development (UNCTAD) and Foreign Trade Allocations

The United Nations (UN) has long been concerned with problems of ocean shipping industry development in third-world nations. This concern relates to the inability of many nations to develop home flag shipping industries, because of the presence of flag of convenience shipping lines and their low costs of operation. A proposal has been developed that would impose a worldwide requirement that trade by ship between nations be allocated according to a percentage formula. This formula, called the **40-40-20 division**, would permit a nation to use its own flagship in trade with a second nation-for up to 40 percent of the volume shipped. The second trading nation partner can use its flag ships for up to 40 percent of the bilateral trade also. Ships of third-world nations can handle only up to 20 percent of the remaining trade between the two nations.

Though this system would no doubt tend to develop shipping industries in nations that do not currently have such industries, or have only weak ones, it is being resisted by the United States and many other nations because it would create inefficiencies. World trade routes would tend toward hub and spoke patterns for each nation, and little cross trading would exist. When traffic imbalances take place between two nations, much empty hauling would exist. In all, it would represent an artificial restraint of trade in the form of transportation.[4]

International Air Regulation

Matters of concern in international air carriage relate to air safety and economic regulation. No single international regulatory body covers rate and route matters in the international air area. Instead, the pattern of route and rate establishment has evolved from national policy, use of the bilateral system of operating rights as negotiated after World War II by many nations of the world, the new U.S. policy of open competition, and policies of the **International Air Transport Association (IATA)**, a long-standing international rate bureau.

Safety

International air safety issues are addressed by the International Civil Aviation Organization (ICAO), which is part of the United Nations. ICAO, headquartered in Montreal, is concerned with the technical and safety issues of aircraft operation. The organization has developed operating standards such as navigating practices, rules of the air, navigation charts, and communications. In addition, it is concerned with maintenance personnel and practices, meteorology, search and rescue, air accident investigation, and air traffic control. The focus of ICAO is international flying safety and is similar to the U.S. Federal Aviation Administration.

U.S. Open Policy

The deregulatory shift in the U.S. rail and motor modes has spilled over into a more liberal U.S. international air policy. Many U.S. cities, other than New York, Miami, Los Angeles, and San Francisco, are originating or developing sufficient traffic volumes to warrant direct overseas air service. The Civil Aeronautics Board (CAB), and White House policy during the late 1970s and early 1980s encouraged the opening up of more U.S. cities to direct service. This coincides with a shifted national policy of seeking more competition between the airlines. As a result, the United States has awarded international routes to both U.S. and foreign carriers at cities such as Atlanta, Boston, Dallas, Denver, Minneapolis, and St. Louis. The open policy has brought direct service, which is a convenience over having to change airlines at gateway cities such as New York. Whether true price reductions come about will remain to be seen as carriers experience post-introduction route traffic patterns. Many foreign nations are slow to accept the new open policy because the policy is expected

STOP OFF

Ocean Shipping Reform Act of 1998

This overview is intended to answer some basic questions about the Ocean Shipping Reform Act. It is reproduced with the permission of the American Association of Port Authorities (AAPA) which was founded in 1912 and today represents more than 150 public port authorities in the United States, Canada, Latin America and the Caribbean. The Association promotes the common interests of the port community and provides leadership on trade, transportation, environmental and other issues related to port development and operations.

Status of the Federal Maritime Commission

Under the law, the Federal Maritime Commission (FMC) will remain a separate, independent agency. (In earlier versions of the bill, the FMC would have been combined with the Surface Transportation Board.)

Port Antitrust Immunity

The new law retains antitrust immunity for carriers and ports. As under the 1984 Act, antitrust immunity applied to activity pursuant to an agreement filed with the FMC. Filing requirements for such agreements remain largely unchanged.

The new law expands the scope of antitrust immunity for ports to include jointly set rates or conditions of service offered to carriers in domestic as well as foreign commerce. The change was designed to address the "mixed use" terminal problem where a port might charge wharfage or dockage rates set by a terminal conference at a facility used by both foreign and domestic carriers—under the 1984 act, the port was not protected by antitrust immunity as to the domestic carrier. Even under the new law, port antitrust immunity for engaging in exclusive, preferential or cooperative working arrangements is limited to the extent that such agreements involve ocean transportation in the foreign commerce of the U.S.

Service Contracts

All service contracts between carriers and shippers will be filed with the agency (as under current law) and the following essential terms will be made available for all contracts: the origin and destination port ranges, the commodity or commodities involved, the minimum volume or portion and the duration of the contract. Such information as rates, the origin and destination geographic areas and in the case of through intermodal movements, service commitments and liquidated damages for nonperformance would no longer be public. Ports that may have used this information for internal marketing purposes will not have access to it through the FMC, but may through other sources such as PIERS.

Labor unions have the ability to request more information regarding specific dock or port areas cargo movements governed by a collective bargaining agreement.

Shippers may enter into service contracts individually and as a shippers association (as under current law) and now also as a group subject to antitrust laws.

As under the 1984 Act, non-vessel-operating common carriers may not enter into service contracts as carriers.

While under the 1984 Act, conferences could prohibit their members from entering into service contracts, under the 1998 Act, conferences may not (1) prohibit or restrict a member or members from engaging in negotiations for service contracts, (2) require a member or members to disclose a negotiation or the terms and conditions of a contract, or (3) adopt mandatory rules affecting the right of a member or members to negotiate or enter into service contracts. However, a conference may adopt voluntary guidelines relating to the terms and conditions of service contracts.

Tariff Filing

Neither carriers nor ports will be required to file tariffs with the FMC under the new law. However, common carriers must make tariffs open to public inspection in an automated tariff format.

Port tariffs, while not filed with the agency, would be enforceable as implied contracts, providing relief from years of court precedent that prevented terminal operators from enforcing liability provisions. The new law includes a provision requested by AAPA and the National Association of Waterfront Employers (NAWE) that marine terminal operators may make available to the public a schedule of rates, regulations, and practices, including limitations of liability for cargo loss or damage. If such a schedule is made available to the public, it is enforceable as an implied contract without proof of actual knowledge of its provisions. The FMC is authorized to prescribe the form and manner in which marine terminal operator schedules are published.

The new law reduces the notice requirement for independent actions from 10 business days to 5 calendar days. (This allows rates to become effective on shorter notice.)

Continued

STOP OFF

Ocean Shipping Reform Act of 1998

Continued

Port Leases and Other Agreements

The new law makes no changes with regard to the filing of terminal leases or port agreements with carriers.

Under current FMC regulations, agreements between marine terminal operators and carriers for marine terminal services (and terminal facilities furnished in connection with such services) are exempt from filing (Docket 91–20). However, a port would not have antitrust immunity unless the agreement is filed voluntarily with the FMC.

Marine terminal facilities programs (i.e. terminal leases) are also exempt from filing (Docket 92–33). Copies must be made available upon request for a reasonable copying and mailing fee. Even though exempt from filing, under the terms of the exemption, the agreements are still exempt from antitrust laws.

Any agreement filed voluntarily or filed before the exemptions were established must be updated—the FMC would like to receive supplements and/or notification if an agreement is canceled.

Exempt Commodities

The list of exempt commodities, for which service contracts do not have to be filed nor tariffs published, is expanded to include new assembled motor vehicles. Commodities continuing to be exempt are bulk cargo, forest products, recycled metal scrap, waste paper and paper waste.

In addition, the bill eases the standard for the Commision to grant other general exemptions.

Prohibited Acts

The ability of ports to challenge unfair or discriminatory behavior is unchanged by the law. At the same time, the ability of shippers, private terminal operators or others to challenge port behavior as unfair or discriminatory is also unchanged.

By contrast, the ability of shippers to challenge unfair and discriminatory behavior by carriers is limited under the new law in many cases to service pursuant to a tariff (but not pursuant to a service contract).

Common Carrier Obligation/Undercharges

The new law significantly erodes the common carrier obligation. Carriers will no longer be required to match service contract terms for "similarly situated shippers"; however, tariff rates must be applied without discrimination or rebates.

Shippers would not have to pay agreed-upon undercharges, but shippers and carriers remain subject to FMC undercharge penalties.

Joint Carrier Inland Transportation

The new law allows groups of ocean carriers to negotiate with non-ocean carriers for rates and service for inland transportation, subject to antitrust laws.

to open up other major foreign cities in exchange for gaining access to other U.S. cities. Again, the price benefit to the traveler is as yet unknown; the future role of the IATA is a major factor in this area.

IATA

The IATA is a collective rate-making body of international air carriers that is based in Montreal and has traditionally functioned in ways similar to a domestic rate bureau.

Collective fare and rate making in international air carriage under the IATA has fostered a relatively stable pricing system over the past few decades. New York to London fares have usually been the same regardless of the carrier. "Competition" under this type of system is generally limited to schedule positionings and in-flight amenities. This system also protects the higher-cost carrier while providing possibly higher than normal economic profits to the low-cost carrier.

The IATA has been the subject of official government criticism under the recent deregulatory thrusts in the United States. The more liberal route award actions by the CAB in the late 1970s and early 1980s along with the White House administration tended to weaken the strength of the IATA, since these awards are often predicted upon the applicant airliners' promotional fare plans.

The future picture of international air policy is unlcear. On one hand, nearly every nation of the world has a home airline operating on routes emanating from it as well as leading to prime third-flag routes. The opportunity for monopoly profits and strong one-nation influence upon a route (something more common in the past) is perhaps a diminishing phenomenon. The influence of the United States and major Western European nations in international air markets is not as great as it once was because modern equipment can be acquired by almost any airline in the world. Finally, many major nation governments are reluctant to subsidize the home nation airline deficits. These lines will then be seeking strategies for profit or positive cash flow opportunities in ways heretofore not used in their management approaches. This trend might cause the foreign governments to protect the home carrier, thereby enabling it to earn a profit. Such moves might include, but are not limited to, a strengthening of an IATA-like fare setting, and schedule and flight limitations by competing flag carriers.

Port and airport development represents large capital outlays and planning activities that are often beyond the normal capabilities of individual carriers. For these reasons, nations, states, and cities throughout the world are deeply involved in port and airport development. The vitality of a region's economic activity is closely linked with that of the capacity and efficiency of the airports and ports it uses to interface with other regions and nations.

Role of Port Authorities in International Transportation

The term **port authority** applies to a state or local government that owns, operates, or otherwise provides wharf, dock, and other terminal investments at ports. In many instances, these include the major city airport as well. The primary reasons for the existence of these organizations are to allow for comprehensive planning, to provide the large physical investment base, and to provide for certain political needs within the area.

Port authorities are organized along various lines. One is local to the port or terminal. This body seeks to maximize benefits to one particular port site. An example is Oakland, California, which actively competes against and, in fact, has diverted significant amounts of traffic away from the Port of San Francisco, which is in the same bay area. Another authority organization is statewide. Maryland, Virginia, Georgia, and Louisiana are examples. Here, one agency oversees all the ports within the state. The general taxing authority of the state backs up the financing efforts of these bodies. The third major authority organizational structure is concerned with a port area across state lines. The Port of New York and New Jersey covers the water area and airports in New York City, and the Delaware River Ports Authority spans Philadelphia and Camden, New Jersey.

Port authorities serve various roles. Some own all waterfront rights and rent waterside access rights to shipping companies and terminal firms. This is the case under Louisiana law, which evolved from French legal precedent in which the state controls access to the water. Some others actually develop waterways and pier terminal facilities and rent them to users (on short- and long-term bases) who do not have the scale of operations to support or perhaps do not wish to actually own such assets. This capital financing role is perhaps the major benefit provided by these port authorities. In the container boom of the 1960s and 1970s, ports acquired container-loading facilities to develop such traffic through them. These assets, in many cases, would not exist, nor would the traffic be found there today were it not for these public investments. Port authorities also promote overall trade through their port areas. This includes industrial development efforts, the offering of favorable financing, representation before regulatory bodies, and the encouragement of adequate transportation facilities on land.

Future of International Transportation

International transportation will grow in importance as more manufacturing and merchandising firms become involved in overseas sourcing and marketing. Long-standing domestic firms in many industries face competition against foreign-based manufacturers that can produce and load goods at customer docks as cheaply as the goods can be produced locally. This phenomenon is fostered by reduced trade barriers, relative currency fluctuations, and the competitiveness of ocean carriers. This exporting and importing used to be confined to the large firm; it is now a basic activity in many medium and small U.S. firms.

The cloud on the international trade horizon is nationalism. This ranges from tariff protection to political constraints and home flag carrier protection. Such nationalism tends to appear whenever a home industry is threatened by foreign competition or forces. The Jones Act in the United States, which requires domestic movements only by U.S. flag ships and domestic airlines, is one such example, though not a significant one on the world scene.[5] Be that as it may, pressures in supply-short or economically sluggish nations can tend to cause constraints that hinder international trade and transportation.

A final point on this topic relates to individual traffic and distribution managers. Most firms are becoming involved in international purchasing and marketing. The process requires different procedures than those for domestic trade. It is a discipline that is different in many ways from related domestic activities. The supply of transportation, rate making, and public policy concerns are somewhat different than counterpart domestic areas.

SUMMARY

International transportation is governed by the same set of underlying economic principles as domestic forms of carriage, but its ownership patterns, processes, procedures, and government policies are different. Today companies view markets as global, rather than domestic, and the international transportation system is being called upon to move ever-increasing quantities of goods between the countries of the world.

- The U.S. trades with nearly all countries of the world; Canada, Japan, Mexico, the United Kingdom, and Germany are the largest U.S. trading partners.
- The international transportation process begins with the buyer–seller agreement, including the INCOTERMS, and incorporates order preparation, transportation, and documentation.
- All modes of transportation are available for shipments from the United States to Mexico and Canada, but air and water are the dominant forms of shipments to other countries.
- Ocean carriers consist of liners, tramps, and private carriers. Liner or conference carriers offer scheduled services over fixed routes at a published rate. Tramp carriers follow the trade with no fixed schedules or rates. Private carriers are ships operated by the firm moving the goods, which are usually basic raw materials moving in large quantities.
- Air carriers offer low transit times and high rates. Four types of air carriers exist: air parcel post, express or courier service, passenger, and all cargo.
- Ancillary service companies provide numerous functions to assist the international shipper. These companies provide technical expertise, freight consolidation,

vehicle booking, and other services that offer users lower cost and improved service.

- International carrier rates are established on the basis of cost and service. Air carrier rates tend to be value of service-based, while ocean rates are cost-based. Line carriers publish rates via conferences; the international Air Transport Association acts as a domestic rate bureau. Both published and contract rates are available from both modes, and ship/plane chartering is available.
- The Federal Maritime Commission regulates ocean carrier rates. No federal agency regulates international air rates. Major changes in regulation have taken place under the Ocean Shipping Reform Act of 1998.
- Port authorities are state or local government agencies that own, operate, finance, or provide services at local ports and/or airports.

Key Terms

40-40-20 proposal pg. 255
all-cargo carriers 243
bareboat charter 253
bill of lading 240
break-bulk 241
Carriage and Insurance Paid To (CIP) 238
Carriage Paid to (CPT) 238
certificate of origin 240
class rate 249
commercial invoice 240
consolidate 244
consular invoice 240
container rate 249
containers 242
Cost and Freight (CFR) 238
Cost, Insurance, Freight (CIF) 238
Delivered at Frontier (DAF) 238
Delivered Ex Quay (DEQ) 238
Delivered Ex Ship (DES) 238
Delivered Duty Paid (DDP) 238
Delivered Duty Unpaid (DDU) 238
density 248
draft 240
Ex Works 237
flags of convenience 243
Free Alongside Ship (FAS) 238
Free Carrier (FCA) 238
Free On Board (FOB) 238
general cargo rate 249
INCOTERMS 236
International Air Transport Association (IATA) 255
land bridge 245
letter of credit 240
lighter-aboard ship (LASH) 242
liners 241
Maquiladora 236
micro-bridge 247
mini-bridge 246
North American Free Trade Agreement (NAFTA) 235
nonvessel owning carriers 244
port authority 256
private ships 242
pro-forma invoice 240
RORO ship 242
shippers' export declaration 240
steamship conferences 250
time charter 253
tramp ships 242
value of service 248
voyage charter 253

Study Questions

1. Describe the economic factors that indicate international transportation will become increasingly important in the future.

2. Why would a shipper select a liner ocean carrier? What are the disadvantages of using a liner carrier?

3. Describe the international transportation process a shipper uses and discuss the decisions required of each process element.

4. Discuss the business conditions necessary for air transportation to be an economical international carrier choice. Compare this to domestic air modal choice.

5. Discuss the advantages and disadvantages of using an international freight forwarder.

6. The use of the land, mini-, and micro-bridges has improved international water transportation. Describe these "bridges" and discuss their economic advantage.

7. Discuss the advantages and disadvantages of conference rate making.

8. Both air and water carriers establish container rates. What are the similarities and differences between air and water container rates?

9. What forms of economic regulation are imposed upon international air and water carriers by the United States?

10. Describe the role of port authorities in international transportation.

Notes

1. Toby B. Estes, "Are Steamship Conferences Obsolete," *Traffic Management* (October 1988), p. 91.
2. Roy Nersesian, *Ships and Shipping* (Tulsa: Penn Well Publishing, 1981), Ch. 9.
3. U.S. Maritime Administration, *Relative Costs of Shipbuilding* (Washington, D.C.: U.S. Government Printing Office, 1979), Ch. 2.
4. U.S. Maritime Administration, *The Impact of Bilateral Shipping Agreements in the U.S. Liner Trades* (Washington, D.C.: U.S. Government Printing Office, May 1979) Ch. 5.
5. The Jones Act, 46 U.S.C.A.

Suggested Readings

Bowman, Robert J. "The Two Faces of Vessel-Sharing," *Distribution*, Vol. 95, No. 3, March 1996. pp. 40–42.

Brooks, M. R. and J. J. Button, "The Determinants of Shipping Rates: A North Atlantic Case Study," *Transport Logistics*, Vol. 2, No. 1, 1996, pp. 21–30.

Clarke, Richard L. "An Analysis of the International Ocean Conference System," *Transportation Journal*, Vol. 36, No. 4, Summer 1997, pp. 17–29.

Foster, Thomas A. "Volvo: It's Swedish for Logistics," Distribution, Vol. 94, No. 5, May 1995, pp. 38–44.

Harley, Stephen. "Transportation: The Cornerstone of Global Supply Chain Management," *Council of Logistics Management Annual Conference Proceedings*, 1996, pp. 635–641.

Hayuth, Y. "The Overweight Container Problem and International and Intermodal Transportation," Vol. 34, No. 2, Spring 1995, pp. 18–28.

Maltz, Arnold B., James R. Giermanski, and David Molina. "The U.S.-Mexico Cross-border Freight Market: Prospects for Mexican Truckers," *Transportation Journal*, Vol. 36, No. 1, Fall 1996, pp. 5–19.

Morash, Edward A. and Steven R. Clinton, "The Role of Transportation Capabilities in International Supply Chain Management," *Transportation Journal*, Vol. 36, No. 3, Spring 1997, pp. 5–17.

Wood, Donald F., Anthony Barone, Paul Murphy, and Daniel L. Wardlow. *International Logistics* (New York: Chapman & Hall, 1995).

Cases

Case 9.1
Natural Footwear Company

Natural Footwear Company, located in Detroit, Michigan, is a manufacturer of specialty shoes. The company was started in 1990 by Mary Crawled, who is an avid mountain climber and hiker. In early 1985, following a fruitless search for a comfortable pair of hiking boots, Crawled designed and produced a model hiking boot that was comfortable and durable. The design was patented, and she began limited production and marketing of the Natural Hiker in 1987.

In 1995, Crawled attended an international footwear trade show in Paris. She received many positive inquiries from shoe distributors throughout Europe, and in July of 1995, she selected Barrett Brothers of Liverpool, England, to be the exclusive distributor of the Natural Hiker and other Natural Footwear products. The demand for the Natural Hiker in Europe exceeded Crawled's wildest expectations. As of January 1997, Crawled committed to producing and shipping 100 40-foot containers (FEU) per year to Barrett Brothers. The delivery requirement specified the receipt of one container on Monday and Thursday of each week, except the first two weeks of July.

John Vangen, traffic manager for Natural Footwear, was not experienced in international shipping. During the initial start-up period with Barrett Brothers, Vangen merely called the local international freight forwarder, described the shipment specifics, and let the freight forwarder make all the arrangements. Vangen felt that he had learned a considerable amount from the freight forwarder and decided to manage the international shipping for the new Barrett Brothers contract for 100 FEUs.

After contacting a number of liner and nonliner ocean carriers, Vangen discovered the FEU rate from Baltimore to Liverpool was $2,850 by the liner carriers and $2,668 by the nonliner carriers. The liner carriers published a biweekly departure schedule from Baltimore and a five-day sailing schedule to Liverpool. The nonline carriers promised a biweekly departure schedule but would not give Vangen a commitment as to this sailing schedule or the sailing time. The cost to transport a container to Baltimore by truck is $590 and requires one day.

A sales representative from Canadian Maritime learned of Vangen's shipping needs and presented a proposal to move containers from Detroit via railroad to Montreal and from Montreal to Liverpool via ship. The Canadian Maritime quoted Vangen a total cost from Detroit to Liverpool of $3,300 per container. The total transit time, including the rail move from Detroit to Montreal, is six days and the published departure schedule is four sailings per week.

Case Questions

1. What additional information would you require before making a decision?
2. What ocean route would you recommend John Vangen use?

CASE 9.2

Medical Supply Company

Carol Parsons, vice president of International Logistics for Medical Supply Company (MSC), recently returned from a series of negotiating sessions with the Trans-Atlantic Conference Agreement (TACA) conference carriers. The negotiations resulted in Parson signing a service contract with the TAA for a 20 percent increase in ocean rates for MSC shipments to the EU from the United States. In addition, the ocean rates do not include the ground transportation costs to and from the ports. This rate increase will place a great strain on MSC's ability to compete effectively in the EU market with European manufacturers of medical supplies and equipment.

MSC, which is located in Allentown, Pennsylvania, ships approximately 2,500 FEU containers per year from the East Coast ports of Philadelphia and Baltimore, with the majority moving through Philadelphia. The 1996 service agreement Parson negotiated with the TACA established a through rate from Allentown through the two ports to final inland destinations in Europe; the rate included ground transportation costs. Now, not only is the TACA charging MSC a 20 percent higher rate and excluding ground transportation, it is also excluding Philadelphia as a port of call, which means MSC containers will now move through either Baltimore or New York. This will increase the ground transportation costs from what they would have been via Philadelphia.

During the negotiations, Parsons emphasized the large block of business MSC shipped with TACA in 1996, but the TACA did not retreat from its position of increasing the rate and excluding the ground transportation portion. To fortify its position, the TACA members agreed to reduce ship capacity by approximately 20 percent over eight years and establish stiff penalties for TACA members who independently offer capacity above the agreed-upon levels.

Before signing the 1998 TACA agreement, Parsons contacted the non-TACA carriers to establish a rate agreement for the 2,500 FEU containers. But the TACA capacity reduction strategy caused most large and medium-sized shippers to seek space on these four carriers, thereby increasing the pressure on rates. The demand for space on the non-TACA carriers was so great that Parsons could not secure guaranteed space for the first three months of 1998, which excluded this as a viable option.

Parson also explored the possibility of shipping to Europe via Canada. The containers would move by rail to Montreal, and then be transloaded to a Canadian vessel for the ocean voyage to Europe. However, seeing the increased demand for space and the higher rates charged by the TACA carriers serving the United States, the Canadian carriers adjusted their rates to conform to those charged by TACA.

Faced with these cost increases in 1998, Parsons is attempting to develop a strategy to deal with the TACA in 1999, in part because she believes similar actions will be taken by the U.S.–Asia conferences in 1999 and that the TACA superconference strategy signals a trend for all major trade routes.

Case Questions

1. What is the economic rationale for the TACA actions and the short- and long-run implications of them?

2. Discuss the legality of the TACA actions.

3. What possible course of action would you recommend for Carol Parsons for 1999? For the next eight years?

4. In light of the changes brought about by the Ocean Shipping Reform Act of 1998, what would you recommend.

CHAPTER 10

Private Transportation

Private transportation may be construed as "do-it-yourself" rather than "buy it" transportation services. The firm engaged in private transportation is vertically integrated to perform the services provided by for-hire carriers. The private transportation decision is a classic "make" versus "buy" decision in which a company must determine if it is cheaper to make (engage in private transportation) or buy transportation (use a for-hire carrier).

In this chapter, the private transportation issue is examined for all modes, but emphasis is given to private trucking, the most pervasive form of private transportation. Attention will be directed on the decision to enter into private trucking and the operation of a private truck fleet.

What Is Private Transportation?

Private transportation is *not* the opposite of public (government) transportation. Private transportation is defined as not-for-hire transportation of goods owned by the firm that also owns (leases) and operates the transportation equipment for the furtherance of its primary business.

A **private carrier,** or **not-for-hire** carrier, does not service the general public. Rather, the private carrier serves itself by hauling its own raw materials and finished products. The private carrier is technically permitted to haul goods for others (the public), and under current regulation, may charge for this service.

Historically, the federal government had strictly enforced the prohibition of private carriers hauling public goods for a fee. This enforcement was an extension of the control over entry for regulated carriers. However, the ICC Termination Act of 1995 greatly reduced controls over entry into regulated trucking, and grants of authority are very easy to obtain for an existing private motor carrier.

Although private trucking is the most prevalent, private transportation is found in other modes as well. Following is a brief analysis of private transportation in rail, air, and water.

Private Rail Transportation

Private transportation in the railroad industry takes the form of privately owned railcars moved by a common carrier railroad. Private rail transportation does not exist in the form of a business operating a railroad to transport its goods between cities, yet some private railroads exist to transport products in large industrial complexes or in logging operations.

Many businesses purchase or lease specialized rail equipment, such as hopper, temperature-controlled, and tank cars, to ensure an adequate supply of vehicles. It is common for agribusiness firms to own (or lease) a supply of hopper cars to haul grain from the farms to the grain elevators to end users during the harvest season. Railroads normally do not have a sufficient supply of hopper cars to meet the peak demands during the harvest season. Thus, many agribusiness firms have acquired a private fleet of rail equipment to ensure an adequate supply of railcars and the continued operation of the company.

As stated above, no business owns a private railroad to transport its freight intercity. The private railcars are moved intercity by a for-hire railroad. The railroad grants the shipper permission to have the private car moved over its lines and the railroad provides an allowance to the shipper for use of the private railcar. This car allowance takes the form of either a **mileage allowance** or a reduction from the published rate for the specific commodity movement. The car allowance recognizes that the user is incurring a portion of the transportation expense (the capital cost of the vehicle) that is normally incurred by the railroad.

Private rail transportation includes the cost of a private siding or spur track that connects the railroad's track with the user's plant or warehouse. The rail transportation user desiring service to its door must provide and maintain the rail track on its property. In the absence of a private siding or spur track, the shipper must use a public side track and incur an additional transportation (accessibility) cost to move the freight between the public siding and the user's facility.

Some large manufacturing firms have built small railroads within the confines of their plants to shuttle railcars from building to building. Such private railroads may be construed as materials handling systems that move railcars loaded with goods such as raw materials. The switch engine performs the same function as the forklift; that is, the switch engine places the railcars in the proper location to permit loading and unloading. The switch engine of such private railroads does not operate outside the plant limits.

A number of large firms own for-hire railroads that primarily connect the owner's facilities with other for-hire railroads. These railroads are legally classified as for-hire common carriers, not private rail carriers. As an example, consider a large forest products company that owns and operates a short-line railroad in a rural community. The railroad is classified as a common carrier but provides service primarily to the area's major rail shipper, the forest products company. Some mining, logging, and paper-making firms operate extensive rail lines to serve their needs. In a few cases they also serve other firms, but this is very limited.

Private rail transportation is not a common form of private carriage. Private rail transportation basically means that the user buys or leases railcars, provides rail tracks on its property, and, in some limited cases, provides switching within the plant.

Private Air Transportation

Private air transportation, unlike the other model forms of private carriage, is used extensively, if not exclusively, to transport people. The private airplane fleets are purchased and operated to serve the travel needs of executives. The company plane is normally used by top management, with lower-level managers using commercial flights.

The private airplane fleet is also used to transport freight in certain emergency situations. Documents that are needed to consummate an important sale or repair parts that will prevent an assembly line from closing are typical examples of emergency situations in which the corporate jet is called to freight duty. The objective of the fleet is to serve the travel needs of management, not to make routine deliveries of freight.

The corporate jet has become somewhat of a status symbol. The private airplane projects an image of success—success both for the company and its managers. Within the organization, the manager who has access to the company plane is viewed by contemporaries as "having made it."

The cost of flying via a company plane is rather expensive—possibly three, four, or more times greater than commercial flights. Thus, the importance attached to managers using the private plane must be high enough to offset and justify the higher cost. At other times, access to certain communities is rather difficult. This is especially true for smaller communities that have lost many commercial flights as a result of air carrier deregulation. The cost of the manager's time while waiting for commercial flights often can and does justify the expense of a private plane.

Private Water Transportation

The use of company-owned or -leased ships and barges is quite common in the transportation of bulk, large-volume products. The private water carrier transportation of coal, ore, and oil is widely practiced.

Most private domestic water transportation takes the form of barge operations. Firms lease or buy barges and towboats to push barges carrying their own bulk product over the internal waterways of the United States. Some firms operate ships that carry ore and coal over the Great Lakes and along the Atlantic, Gulf of Mexico, and Pacific Coasts.

Private water transportation is most advantageous for the movement of bulk, low-value products that move in large volume between limited origins and destinations. As indicated above, coal, ores, and petroleum products are typical commodities moved by private water carrier fleets. These products are moved regularly and in large volumes from places such as mines and ports of entry to steel mills, electrical generating plants, refineries, and the like.

Considerable investment (capital) is required to begin private water carrier operation. This investment includes the capital required for the vehicles (barges, towboats, ships) and for the dock facilities. It should be noted that the dock facility expenses would be incurred if either private *or* for-hire water transportation was used. The shipper (receiver) is responsible for providing docking facilities to load and unload cargo at the shipper's plant just as the side track is used for rail operations to a shipper's plant. Public ports are available, but the private water carrier would be required to use some form of land transportation (truck or rail) to move the cargo between the public port and the shipper's plant.

The relatively large investment required supports the need for larger, large-volume shipments. Also, firms that operate private water fleets tend to have plants adjacent to waterways. The mining, steel, petroleum, and agriculture industries are significant users of private water transportation.

Private Oil Pipeline Transportation

Private oil pipeline transportation exists in a modified form, similar to that found with railroads. Although the vast majority of the oil pipelines are regulated, for-hire transportation companies, it is common for the major shippers to own the for-hire oil pipelines. Essentially, the owners of the oil pipeline have invested in a transportation company that provides service to them as well as to other shippers of petroleum products. The regulation of oil-company-owned oil pipelines is meant to ensure the independent, non-owner oil companies access to the pipeline transportation at reasonable rates.

The reason for the shipper-owned oil pipelines is basically economic. A huge investment is required to start a pipeline. The high fixed costs necessitate high traffic volume for the service to be economical. Like the railroads, duplicate or parallel oil pipelines create excess capacity and economic waste. Thus, shipper ownership, especially multiple shipper ownership, minimizes the high start-up cost barrier to entry and provides a guaranteed minimum amount of shipper–owner traffic to be moved through the oil pipeline.

Private Trucking

Private trucking is the most frequently used and most pervasive form of transportation in the United States. One estimate suggests private trucking accounted for 52 percent of the 1996 intercity truck expenditures of $230 billion.[1]

The exact number of private fleets in operation is very difficult to determine because firms are not required to report private trucking operations to the Surface Transportation Boad (STB). However, a Department of Transportation (DOT) requirement that private trucking firms register with the DOT should provide more accurate data in the future.

Whatever the number of private fleets, private trucking is an integral segment of the transportation system employed by the shipping public. At one time or another, almost every company will study or actually operate a private truck fleet, even if the fleet consists of only one truck. For this reason, an in-depth analysis of private trucking—from the reasons for private trucking to the operation of a fleet—is provided below.

Why Private Trucking?

The primary reasons for a firm having a private truck fleet are improved service and lower costs. In either case, the private fleet operator is attempting to improve the marketability and profitability of its products. Through improved levels of service, the firm attempts to differentiate its product (lower transit time) and increase its sales and profits. Reduced costs permit the company to keep prices constant (a price reduction during inflationary times), to lower prices, or to increase profits directly. These private trucking advantages are summarized in Table 10.1.

Improved Service

The private truck fleet permits the firm to have greater control and flexibility in its transportation system so it can respond to customer needs, both external (for

TABLE 10.1 Advantages and Disadvantages of Private Trucking

Advantages	Disadvantages
Improved Service	Higher Cost
Convenience	Transportation cost higher than for-hire
Flexible operation	Empty backhaul
Greater control	Lack of managerial talent
Lower transit times	Added overhead and managerial burden
Lower inventory levels	Capital requirements
Reduced damage	Cargo damage and theft responsibility
Driver/salesperson	Liability for accidents
Last resort (special needs)	Increased paperwork
Lower Cost	Breakdown on the roads
Reduced transportation costs	Labor union
(Eliminates carrier profit)	
Reduced inventory levels	
Advertising	
Bargaining power with for-hire carriers	

finished goods) and internal (for raw materials). This increased responsiveness is derived from the direct control that the private carrier has over the dispatching, routing, and delivery schedules of the fleet. Such control means the private carrier can lower transit times to the customer, lower inventory levels, and possibly lower stockouts.

Because the driver is really an employee of the seller, improved customer relations can result from private trucking. The driver now has a vested interest in satisfying customer need and in being courteous. In addition, the private carrier driver would probably exercise greater care in handling freight, and this would reduce the frequency of freight damage.

Some firms use the private truck as a moving store, calling on many customers along a route to take orders and to deliver merchandise. The route sales trucks used by some consumer goods firms to handle soft drinks, snack items, and bakery goods are current examples. For such merchandising operations, the for-hire carrier does not permit the firm to exercise the necessary control and direction, and private trucking is the only viable alternative.

The last-resort advantage of private trucking emanates from a lack of acceptable for-hire carrier service. Firms that ship products requiring special equipment have difficulty finding for-hire carriers with such special equipment and are virtually forced into private trucking to remain in business (for example, cryogenics, or liquid gas, require a pressurized tank trailer). In addition, firms that ship easily damaged products sometimes find it difficult to get for-hire carriers willing to provide service within a reasonable time frame or at a reasonable rate. This last-resort turn to private trucking comes from utter frustration with the service levels and the cost of for-hire carriage.

Lower Cost

For firms that ship high-valued and, consequently, high-rated traffic, private carriage affords the opportunity of moving goods at a lower cost than for-hire carriers. Private trucking can produce savings in transportation costs because it eliminates the for-hire carrier's profit. This advantage is especially true for private carrier operations that have vehicles loaded in both directions with high-value products.

Greater control and flexibility over transportation and the resultant lower lead time enable the private carrier to reduce the inventory levels of the firm and its customers. The possible cost savings depend on the total value of the inventory. For example, if a firm using a private fleet can reduce its inventory level by one day with each day of inventory valued at $1 million, a $1-million savings in inventory level is translated into a cost savings of $200,000 or more a year.[2]

A by-product of private trucking is free advertising space. A company trailer is a 45-by-eight-foot-high moving billboard. The company's name, products, and other information can be exposed to literally millions of potential customers. Such advertising benefits are more significant for consumer products than for industrial products. The advertisement has a disadvantage also: It informs thieves of the truck's contents.

Finally, private trucking can be a negotiating tool for seeking lower rates from for-hire carriers. The freight that moves via the private fleet is lost revenue to the for-hire carrier. Firms with a private fleet can threaten to divert traffic to the private fleet if the for-hire carrier does not provide a lower rate. Many companies have used this negotiating strategy very effectively to secure favorable for-hire rates.[3]

Disadvantages

Private trucking does have disadvantages. As indicated in Table 10.1, the disadvantages of private trucking all result in higher costs of transportation. Probably the most significant cause of higher cost is the **empty backhaul**. The cost of returning empty must be included in the outbound (inbound) loaded movement. Therefore, the cost of moving freight is really double the cost of the one-way move. For example, if the cost of operating a tractor-trailer is $1 per mile, the cost to move a shipment 1,000 miles and return empty is $2,000 ($1,000 loaded and $1,000 empty), or $2 per loaded mile. (The empty backhaul can be offset by engaging in for-hire transportation.) These concepts are discussed later in this chapter in the section titled "Fleet Operation and Control."

Newly formed private carriers may be hampered by a lack of trucking management expertise. The private fleet is really a trucking business that has some unique managerial requirements. Management time of transportation/traffic managers is diverted to private fleet operation. In many cases, the existing management does not have the trucking background to effectively operate the fleet. As a result of a lack of in-house talent, the firm must hire outside managers for the specific purpose of managing the fleet. This increases management costs.

Capital availability has been a problem for some firms. The money tied up in trucks, trailers, and maintenance facilities is money that is not available for use in the company's primary business. This capital problem can be eliminated by leasing the equipment. Even drivers can be leased, avoiding possible union problems.

As a private carrier, the firm bears the risk of loss and damage to its freight. To hedge against possible loss, the private carrier can buy cargo insurance or act as a self-insured carrier (merely absorb all losses). Customers receiving damaged goods will contact the seller (private carrier) for reimbursement, and failure (or delay) to pay is a direct indictment against the seller. When a for-hire carrier is used, the seller may be able to "wash its hands" of the claim because the dispute is between the buyer and the carrier, assuming FOB origin terms of sale.

The risk of public liability resulting from a vehicle accident is incurred by the private fleet. This risk can be mitigated by insurance, but the possibility of excessive court judgments is present.

The cost of paperwork and maintenance for long-distance, multistate operations is greater than for short-distance or local operations. The clerical costs associated with accounting for mileage driven in various states, gallons of fuel purchased in different states, and vehicle licenses or permits required by different states escalate as the scope of the private carriage operation becomes multistate.

Breakdowns away from the home terminal or garage requiring emergency road service are more expensive than normal maintenance service. The possibility of such emergency service increases as the operating scope increases. Breakdowns also reduce the service levels and have an impact on customer service and eventually sales and profits. Leasing equipment from national firms can minimize this concern.

The final disadvantage of private trucking is the possible addition of another union, the Teamsters, into the company. It is quite common for private fleet drivers to be unionized by the Teamsters, and then the Teamsters attempt to represent the other employees who are not drivers. In some companies, the private fleet drivers are members of the union representing the non-driver employees. Obtaining drivers from leasing firms may greatly reduce this problem.

Although there are such disadvantages to private trucking, the fact that so many private truck fleets exist suggests that the advantages outweigh the disadvantages for many firms. The firm's analysis of costs and benefits of private trucking is very critical at the evaluation stage as well as throughout the operation of the fleet.

Private Trucking Cost Analysis

Efficient and economical private truck operation requires a working knowledge of the actual cost of operating the fleet. The manager must know the facts affecting the individual cost elements of private trucking to make effective decisions that lower costs and improve service. The costs are categorized into fixed and operating (variable) costs and are presented in Table 10.2.

Fixed Costs

Fixed costs are those that do not vary in the short run. For private trucking, fixed costs can be grouped into four areas: depreciation (lease payments), interest on investment, management, and office and garage. As indicated in Table 10.3, fixed costs are approximately 29.9 cents per mile (22.1 percent of total cost) for fleets of long-distance haulers of refrigerated products.

The fixed cost per mile varies inversely with the number of miles operated per year. The greater the number of miles driven, the lower the fixed cost per mile; that is, the total fixed cost is spread over a larger number of miles. Therefore, most private truck fleet managers who refer to the economies associated with increased vehicle utilization are concerned with spreading fixed costs over a larger number of miles.

TABLE 10.2 Private Truck Costs

Fixed Costs	Operating Costs
Depreciation (lease)	Labor (drivers)
Trucks	Wages
Trailers	Fringe benefits
Garage	FICA, Worker's compensation
Office	Layover allowances
Interest on investment	Vehicle operating costs
Vehicles	Fuel
Garage	Oil, grease, filters
Office	Maintenance (Labor + parts)
Management costs	Road service
Salaries	Tolls
Fringe benefits	Insurance
Travel and entertainment	Liability
FICA, Worker's compensation	Collision and comprehensive
Office and garage costs	Cargo
Salaries	License and registration fees
Utilities	Highway user taxes
Rent or property cost	Fuel
Supplies	Ton-mile
Communication	Federal use tax

TABLE 10.3 Cost of Operating a Tractor-Trailer[a]

Cost Items	Cents/Mile
Fixed Costs	
Depreciation on vehicle	8.7
Interest on vehicle	2.9
Depreciation and interest on other items	1.6
Management and overhead	16.7
Total fixed	29.9
Operating Costs	
Fuel	21.0
Drivers	38.6
Maintenance	15.7
Insurance	10.7
License	9.9
Tires	2.6
Miscellaneous	6.8
Total Operating	105.3
Total Cost	135.2

[a]Based on long-distance haulers of refrigerated products.

Source: U.S. Department of Agriculture, *Fruit and Vegetable Truck Cost Report,* Vol. 18, No. 4 (April 1997).

For example, if annual use equals 140,000 miles, total fixed cost for the operation described in Table 10.3 is $41,860 (140,000 miles × $0.299). If the vehicle is operated 200,000 miles, approximately 43 percent greater utilization than the 140,000 miles per year, the fixed cost per mile would decrease to 20.9 cents per mile ($41,860 ÷ 200,000).

Interest

Interest on vehicles (investment) accounts for 2.9 cents per mile, or approximately 10 percent of the total fixed cost per mile in Table 10.3. Because of the relatively low cost of borrowing money, vehicle interest cost has dropped from 25 percent in 1989 to 10 percent of total fixed costs in 1997.

Management and Overhead

In 1997, management and overhead (office and garage) costs were 16.7 cents per mile or about 56 percent of total fixed costs. It is quite common to find management costs being understated in a private trucking operation. Management time, and therefore costs, is siphoned from the primary business of the firm to assist in managing the fleet. Rarely is this "free" management talent accounted for in the private fleet cost analysis.

Depreciation

Vehicle depreciation represented 29.1 percent of total fixed costs or 8.7 cents per mile. Vehicle costs have decreased in recent years but, in all likelihood, will rise in the future. The actual cost of a truck depends on the size, carrying capacity, engine, and market conditions.

Operating Costs

Operating costs are those costs that vary in the short run. Private trucking operating costs consist of fuel, drivers, maintenance, insurance, license, tires, and user taxes.

STOP OFF

WHY PPG INDUSTRIES OUTSOURCED ITS FLEET

PPG Industries, Inc., of Pittsburgh is one of many companies that converted its private fleet (200 tractors, 430 trailers, and five maintenance shops) to dedicated contract carriage. The conversion, in place now for about two years, saves the company $500,000 a year. The dedicated fleet, managed by Schneider National of Green Bay, Wisconsin, handles about 30 percent of PPG's truckload business.

At a recent Council of Logistics Management meeting, James Carr, manager of PPG's Transportation Center, itemized the reasons that PPG opted to outsource:

- Decreasing common carriage rates. "After deregulation, lane rates had fallen tremendously," noted Carr. "We benchmarked against these rates and found our private fleet costs weren't competitive."
- Competition for funds. Capital constraints meant money for the fleet was scarce or nonexistent.
- Inflexible work rules. A unionized driver corps and restrictive work rules had a negative effect on fleet productivity and flexibility.
- Liability exposure. PPG's fleet carried large quantities of hazardous materials, thereby exposing the corporation to considerable liability.
- Administrative headaches. Lastly, owning a large private fleet was an administrative burden. "Our small staff had trouble keeping up with all the work," Carr reported.

Source: *Distribution*, April 1996, p. 29. Reprint permission granted by *Logistics* (formerly *Distribution*) Magazine.

As indicated in Table 10.3, operating cost in 1997 was 105.3 cents per mile (77.9 percent of total).

The total operating cost varies directly with the number of miles operated per year. The greater the number of miles operated, the greater the total operating costs. The operating cost per mile will remain approximately the same.

For example, the total operating cost for 140,000 miles per year is $147,420 (140,000 miles × 1.053). If the mileage per year is increased to 200,000 miles, the total operating cost will increase to about $210,600, with the operating cost per mile at about 105.3 cents. In reality, license, insurance, and certain miscellaneous costs will remain constant per year and then decrease per mile. Maintenance costs, however, will increase.

Fuel

Fuel cost represents 19.9 percent (21.0 cents per mile) of the total operating cost. A diesel tractor averages about 5.0 to 6.5 miles per gallon, and a gasoline tractor averages a little less.

Fleet operators try hard to improve fuel mileage because the savings potential is great. For example, assume the fleet depicted in Table 10.3 was able to increase vehicle mileage per gallon by 10 percent, from five miles per gallon to 5.5 miles per gallon. The total fuel cost savings for 140,000 miles per year would amount to $2,800 per truck, or 9.1 percent.[4] Such a potential savings is justification for a $200 to $400 expenditure for an air deflector or for radial tires.

Labor

Driver cost (non-union) was 38.6 cents per mile or 36.6 percent of the total operating cost as given in Table 10.3. Over-the-road drivers are paid on the basis of the miles driven. City drivers are paid on an hourly basis.

Maintenance

From Table 10.3 we see that maintenance cost (including tire cost) was 18.3 cents per mile or 17.4 percent of total operating cost. Maintenance cost includes the cost of normal prevantative maintenance such as oil lubrication and new tires, as well as major and minor repairs. The cost of tires, parts, and labor is included in the 18.3 cents-per-mile cost, with tire cost representing one-sixth of the maintenance cost.

Other Operating Costs

The remaining operating costs—insurance, license, and miscellaneous—account for 27.4 cents per mile, or 26.0 percent of the total operating cost. Insurance cost includes the cost of vehicle collision and comprehensive protection, public and personal liability, and cargo insurance. The company's rate of accidents determines the insurance premium assessed.

The cost of licensing and registering the vehicle is determined by the size of the vehicle and by the individual state and the number of other states in which the vehicle operates. The license fee for a given truck is not uniform among the states. Most states require a registration fee to use state highways. Thus, the greater the geographic scope of the private truck operation, the greater the license and registration cost.

Miscellaneous costs include such operating items as tolls, overload fines, and driver road expenses (such as lodging and meals). A private truck fleet manager must watch miscellaneous operating costs closely because those costs can "hide" inefficient and uneconomical operations.

A fundamental requirement for an economical private truck fleet is knowing the costs. Once the costs are known and analyzed, effective decisions can be made.[5] In the next section, our attention is directed to the major operating decisions in private trucking.

Equipment

The private trucking manager is concerned with two basic equipment questions: What type of equipment should be selected? and Should this equipment be purchased or leased? Each of these questions is discussed below.

Selection

Choosing such things as the type, size, make, model, and type of engine of the vehicle used in private trucking seems to be an overwhelming challenge. However, the equipment used is determined by the firm's transportation requirements. The size of the shipment, product density, length of haul, terrain, city versus intercity operation, and special equipment needs are the equipment determinants to be examined. Table 10.4 provides a summary of the equipment selection factors and implications.

Shipment Size and Density

The size of the shipment and product density determine the carrying capacity desired in the vehicle. Shipments averaging 45,000 pounds will require five-axle, tractor-trailer combinations. However, a low-density commodity such as fiberglass insulation requires a large carrying capacity, even though the weight of the shipment is low (10,000 pounds of fiberglass insulation can be carried in a trailer 48 feet long).

TABLE 10.4 Equipment Selection Factors and Implications

Selection Factor/Characteristics	Equipment Implication
Shipment size	
Large-sized shipment (>35,000 lbs.)	Vehicles that can haul 80,000 lbs.
Small-sized shipments (<10,000 lbs.)	Vehicles that can haul 30,000 lbs.
Product density	
Low density (<15 lbs./ft^3)	High-cube-capacity vehicles (Trailers that are 110-inches-high, 102-inches-wide, 57-feet-long)
High density (>15 lbs./ft^3)	Normal cube capacity
Length of haul	
<75,000 miles annually	Gasoline-powered
>75,000 miles annually	Diesel-powered
Trips >1,000 one-way miles	Diesel-powered with sleeper cabs
City operations	Gasoline-powered
Intercity operations	Diesel-powered
Terrain	
Mountainous	Higher-powered engines
Level	Lower-powered engines
Special needs	
Controlled temperature	Refrigerated trailers
Customer required unloading	Power tailgate

Length of Haul

Long-distance operations, 300 miles or more one way and 75,000 or more miles per year, usually indicate the use of diesel-powered equipment. Diesel engines have a longer life and get better mileage than gasoline engines, but diesel engines have a higher initial cost. Some recent developments in diesel engine design have produced an economical, short-range, city diesel engine.

City Versus Intercity

For intercity operations, the tractor-trailer combination is commonly used along with a diesel engine if the distance justifies it. City operations use straight trucks that are gasoline-powered. However, some city operations, such as furniture delivery, use small, single-axle trailers with gasoline-powered tractors. The reason for using trailers is to permit loading of one trailer, while deliveries are being made with another; service to the customer is improved, and the firm reduces congestion and improves efficiency at the warehouse.

Terrain

The terrain over which the vehicle travels affects the selection of certain equipment component parts—the engine and drive train. For mountainous operations, the truck will require a high-powered engine and a low-geared drive train. For level, interstate highway operations, a lower-powered engine with a high-geared drive train is in order. Vehicles designed for mountainous operations usually are restricted to the mountainous regions because it makes sense to use different powered units in different regions.

Special Needs

Another transportation factor to be considered is the need for special equipment—refrigeration, power tailgates, high cube capacity, and so on. The nature of the product and customer requirements will dictate the type of special equipment to be considered.

A final consideration is the use of sleeper cabs for tractors. The sleeper cab adds a few thousand dollars ($2,000–$4,000) to the initial price of the vehicle and is usually only considered when the trips are more than 1,000 miles one way. The sleeper permits the use of two drivers: One can accumulate the required off-duty time in the sleeper berth while the other driver continues to drive. The two-driver team produces lower transit time and better service. However, lower transit time can also be accomplished by substituting drivers every 10 hours.

The sleeper cab can also eliminate the cost of loading for a one-driver operation. Instead of paying for a room, the driver accumulates the required eight hours off-duty in the sleeping berth. However, there is a fuel cost to run the engine to produce heat or cooling for the driver in the sleeper. This fuel cost for a large diesel engine is two to four gallons of fuel per hour, or $2.20 to $4.40 per hour (at $1.10 per gallon). The sleeper cost per eight-hour rest could be $17.60 to $35.20.

Leasing

One of the disadvantages of private trucking, identified in Table 10.1, is the capital requirement for the equipment. Leasing the equipment for a private truck operation reduces demands on company funds and enables existing capital to be used in the primary business of the company.

Two basic types of lease arrangements are available: the full-service lease and the **finance lease**. Both types are available with a lease-buy option that gives the lessee the option to buy the equipment, at book value, at the end of the lease.

Full Service

The **full-service lease** includes the leased vehicle plus a variety of operating support services. The full service may require the lessor to provide fuel, license, registration, payment of highway user taxes, insurance, towing, road service, tire repair, washing, substitute vehicles for out-of-service equipment, and normal preventative maintenance. The more services requested by the lessee, the greater the lease fee. The full-service leasing fee consists of a weekly or monthly fixed fee per vehicle, plus a mileage fee. In addition, the cost of fuel purchased from the lessor will be charged to the lessee. The full-service lease is a popular method of leasing trucks and tractors that require maintenance and other services.

Finance

The finance lease is only a means of financing equipment. Under the finance lease, the lessee pays a monthly fee that covers the purchase cost of the equipment and the lessor's finance charge. No services are provided by the lessor; all maintenance is the responsibility of the lessee. The finance lease is a common method of leasing trailers that require little maintenance.

Advantages

As noted earlier, leasing increases working capital. Existing funds are not drained off into trucking equipment but remain available for use in the primary business. In addition, leasing sometimes does not have an impact on the borrowing limits negotiated with lending institutions.

Leasing permits a company to reduce or eliminate much of the risk associated with private trucking. A company can use full-service leasing to conduct a trial private trucking operation. The monthly fixed operating costs will be known throughout the lease period; this gives a great deal of certainty to the trial operation. If the trial private trucking is too expensive, the firm can quit operating at the end of the lease or even during the lease term if there is a cancellation clause. (However, there may be a cancellation penalty.) Most companies just starting a private trucking operation would be well advised to use full-service leasing.

Other advantages of leasing include purchase discounts for equipment, fuel, and parts that the lessee is able to realize through large-volume purchases. During the fuel shortages or price instability, major full-service leasing companies offered a source of fuel that kept many lessees' private fleets operating. The wide geographic scope of operating major leasing companies offers full maintenance service throughout the country, which is especially important to private fleets that operate nationwide.

Disadvantages

Leasing does have its disadvantages. First, leasing may cost more than owning. Further, for large fleets (30 or more vehicles), the private fleet operator already has a volume purchase advantage and maintenance expertise. Finally, some companies may have excess funds to employ, and a truck fleet may offer an acceptable return on investment.

The economic test of buying versus leasing is a comparison of the net present cost of buying versus leasing. The net present cost is a discounted cash flow approach that considers the cost and savings of both buying and leasing, as well as the tax adjustments.

Fleet Operation and Control

The daily operation of a private fleet is a complex undertaking, and the discussion of daily operations is beyond the scope of this text. However, attention is given to the operational areas of organization, regulation, driver utilization, the empty backhaul, and control mechanisms.

Organizing the Private Fleet

Once the fleet is in operation, many intraorganizational conflicts will arise. These conflicts center on the incompatibility of departmental (user) demands and the private fleet goals.

Cost Center

The private fleet operating goals usually provide good service or lower transportation costs. These goals together pose problems for the private fleet manager and open the door for intra-organizational conflict. For example, a division may request the fleet manager to provide fifth-day delivery to Houston from New York. To do so would increase transportation costs beyond what was incurred previously by private or for-hire trucks. Although the service is desirable to the customer, it is not cost-efficient. The manager is unable to meet both goals.

To combat this conflict, the goal of the fleet is normally a cost-constrained service goal. That is, the goal is to provide good service at a given level of cost. Now the fleet manager can provide the best service that a given level of cost will permit.

Another organizational problem is the user's concept that private trucking is free transportation. Many shipments become emergencies that must be made, regardless of the cost, or a customer will be lost. A department may have the idea that the private fleet is already purchased (leased), so it should be used rather than sit idle. As pointed out earlier, operating cost is approximately 78 percent of the total cost, or 105.3 cents per mile; therefore, the truck is not free.

Profit Center

One organizational approach to eliminate the idea of free transportation is to establish the private fleet as a **profit center**. The income generated by the fleet is a paper or internal budget fee assessed to the active departments. The real costs are subtracted from the paper income to generate a paper profit, on which the manager's performance is evaluated. To guard against the idea that the private fleet must make a profit at any cost to the user, the departments must be given the option of using the private fleet or for-hire carriers (competition).

The profit center organizational structure was encouraged by deregulation provisions. Basically, the provisions permitted private trucking to be operated as a for-hire carrier through intercorporate hauling and eased constraints to securing operating authority.

The use of a profit center concept is ideally suited for a fleet operation that is designed to operate as a for-hire carrier. By establishing the fleet as a profit center, the fleet is operated as a separate business entity with management responsible for profitability and asset utilization. The establishment of a separate corporate entity for the fleet that has secured operating authority permits the fleet to solicit business from other shippers, thereby increasing the fleet utilization, eliminating the empty backhaul, and possibly generating a profit for the parent firm.

Organizational Positioning

The question of where to position the fleet in the organization (in which department) is another perplexing question. Usually a profit-center fleet is set up as a separate department reporting to the chief executive officer of the parent company. Placing the cost-center fleet under the control of the marketing, finance, production, or traffic departments tends to give the fleet the bias of the controlling department. For example, marketing tends to provide service at any cost, whereas traffic tends to minimize costs at the expense of service.

The solution reached by a multifaceted manufacturing/retailing company was to place the private fleet under the control of the division that made the greatest use of the fleet. This division was charged with the cost of operating the fleet and was given credit (paper income via budget transfers) for service provided to other divisions.

Many private fleets are centralized. Centralized organization permits the fleet manager to provide service to many different departments and divisions, thus increasing the fleet utilization. A decentralized operation usually is found where separate divisions have different operating and vehicle requirements, which eliminates the possibility of joint divisional utilization of equipment and operating economies possible through centralized control.

Controlling the Private Fleet

A key element to an effective and efficient private truck fleet is control over cost and performances. Table 10.5 is a list of cost and performance criteria for effective private truck fleet control.

Functional Costs

Costs by function must be collected at the source. Fuel costs (and gallons) should be noted for each vehicle. This notation of functional costs at the cost source permits analysis of individual cost centers for the actual costs incurred. It is very difficult to analyze the fuel efficiency of individual vehicles in a fleet when fuel costs are aggregated for the entire fleet.

Further, the collection of functional costs by driver, vehicle, plant, and so on will permit analysis of problem areas within the fleet. The use of fleet averages only may conceal inefficient operations at particular markets or plants. However, functional costs by vehicle, plant, and driver can be compared to fleetwide averages, and a management-by-exception approach can be practiced. That is, if the specific costs (fuel cost/given driver) are within acceptable limits, nothing is done. Management action is taken when the specific costs are out of line with the desired level.

Performance Criteria

The performance criteria to be considered are miles operated (loaded and empty), human resource hours expanded, vehicle operating hours, number of trips made, tonnage hauled, and the number of stops made. By collecting the above performance data, the fleet manager is able to measure the fleet's utilization and the drivers' productivity. Control measures such as overall cost per mile, per hour, and per trip can be computed and used in determining unacceptable performance areas in the fleet. Such information is also valuable to marketing and purchasing departments that determine the landed cost of goods sold or purchased.

TABLE 10.5 Private Cost and Performance Control Criteria

Cost	Performance
By function	Miles operated
Fuel (and gallons)	By vehicle
Driver	By driver
Maintenance	Empty miles
Interest	Total
Depreciation	By location
Tires	Human resource hours
Parts	Total
Management	Driving
Overhead	Loading and unloading
License and registration	Breakdown
Functional cost by	Vehicle operating hours
Vehicle	By vehicle
Driver	Number of trips
Plant	By vehicle/time period
Market	Tonnage
Warehouse	By vehicle
Customer	Number of stops (Deliveries)
	By driver

Likewise, performance measures must be collected and identified at the source. Total fleet mileage and total fleet fuel (gallons) consumption will permit determination of overall fleet fuel efficiency. However, collection of fuel consumption and mileage per individual vehicle will provide the information necessary for purchasing fuel-efficient vehicles as replacements or additions to the fleet.

The performance criteria enable the fleet manager to analyze the productivity of drivers. The number of miles driven per day, the number of stops (deliveries) made per day, or the number of hours per run or trip are driver productivity measures that can be collected for each driver. From this productivity data, individual drivers who drive fewer miles per day, make fewer stops per day, or take a longer time to make a run than the standards (fleet average, for example) are singled out for further investigation and corrective action.

Regulations

As stated earlier, bona fide private trucking is exempt from federal economic regulations. The private carrier need not secure authorization from the STB to transport the firm's products. Because private coverage is not for-hire service, no tariffs are published.

Economic

To be excluded from these economic regulations, the trucking operations must be truly private carriage. The trucking service must be incidental to and in the furtherance of the primary business of the firm—the **Primary Business Test.** Thus, the transportation of the firm's raw materials and finished goods in private trucks is bona fide private trucking if the firm takes the normal business risks associated with such products. Normal business risk would include the existence of production facilities, sales outlets, product inventories, and a sales force for the products being transported.

Historically, private carriers were restricted as to the activities in which they could engage, yet recent changes in regulatory law have placed these carriers on the same footing as any other motor carrier. Originally, privately owned trucks could only transport products that were owned by the firm that also owned the vehicle. Culminating with the passage of the ICC Termination Act of 1995, such prohibitions were removed. Upon registration with the Federal Highway Administration of the DOT, private fleets can now transport shipments for any firm. The private carrier must file proof of insurance, but, just as hire carriers, their rates are not filed with the STB.

A common problem many private fleets face is how to eliminate the empty backhaul and still operate legally. One solution is the transportation of **exempt commodities.** Exempt commodities can be hauled without STB authority and other economic regulations. Some examples of exempt commodities are ordinary livestock, agricultural products (grain, fruits, vegetables), horticultural goods (Christmas trees), newspapers, freight incidental-to-air transportation (to and from airports), used shipping containers, and fish.

In addition to hauling exempt and for-hire shipments, the National Private Truck Council (NPTC) has joined with the Transportation Intermediaries Association (TIA) to provide backhaul shipments to private fleet operators. TIA's members are comprised of third-party service providers including both brokers and freight forwarders. These firms represent shippers and have significant volumes of freight available. An NPTC member who has an empty truck in a particular city can contact a TIA member and determine if they have any shipments destined to the city to which the private truck wishes to go. With the freedom under the current regulatory system, the carrier and the TIA member can negotiate a price and service terms "on the spot."

Many shippers find that the use of private fleets in this situation is advantageous. Private fleets tend to be well maintained and operated. The fleet manager is interested in getting their truck back quickly, so service levels tend to be high. A drawback is that private fleets lack the ability to provide support services so any unusual situations with loading or unloading can create serious problems.

As noted above, a number of private fleets have been turned into for-hire operations by establishing the fleet as a separate trucking subsidiary and securing authority from the STB. As a common carrier, the fleet provides service to the parent firm and solicits business from other shippers. The additional freight business is selected to complement the service provided to the parent company, that is, to offset the empty backhaul. The carrier is not obligated to serve the general public and thereby is permitted to be selective in the shippers that it serves under contract.

In addition to the above for-hire operations, the private motor carrier may **trip lease** its equipment to a regulated motor carrier to eliminate an empty backhaul. With the trip lease, the private carrier hauls the freight solicited by the for-hire common carrier, realizing a portion of the freight revenue generated by the common carrier and thus offsetting the otherwise empty backhaul. The private carrier may trip-lease to another private carrier and charge a fee for the service provided.

Safety

Private trucking is subjected to all federal safety requirements in the following areas:

- Driver qualifications
- Driving practices
- Vehicle parts and accessories
- Accident reporting
- Driver hours of service
- Vehicle inspection and maintenance
- Hazardous materials transportation

These safety regulations are enforced by the DOT Federal Highway Administration (FHWA) and its Office of Motor Carriers, and the private carrier must register with the FHWA.

In addition, the private fleet must comply with the state safety regulations governing speed, weight, and vehicle length, height, and width. Such state regulations fall within the preview of the constitutionally granted police powers that permit states to enact laws to protect the health and welfare of their citizens. Because the safety regulations are not uniform among the states, the fleet management must be aware of specific regulations in each of the states in which the fleet operates.

Driving time regulations establish the maximum number of hours (minimum safety level) a driver may operate a vehicle in interstate commerce, and consequently they affect the utilization of drivers. Basically, a driver operating in interstate transportation is permitted to drive a maximum of 10 hours following eight consecutive hours off duty. A driver is prohibited from driving after having been on duty 15 hours following eight consecutive hours off duty. Further, on a weekly basis, no driver can be on duty more than 60 hours in seven consecutive days, or 70 hours in eight consecutive days. Entries of driving activities are recorded on a driver's daily log, as shown in Figure 10.1.

FIGURE 10.1 Driver's Daily Log

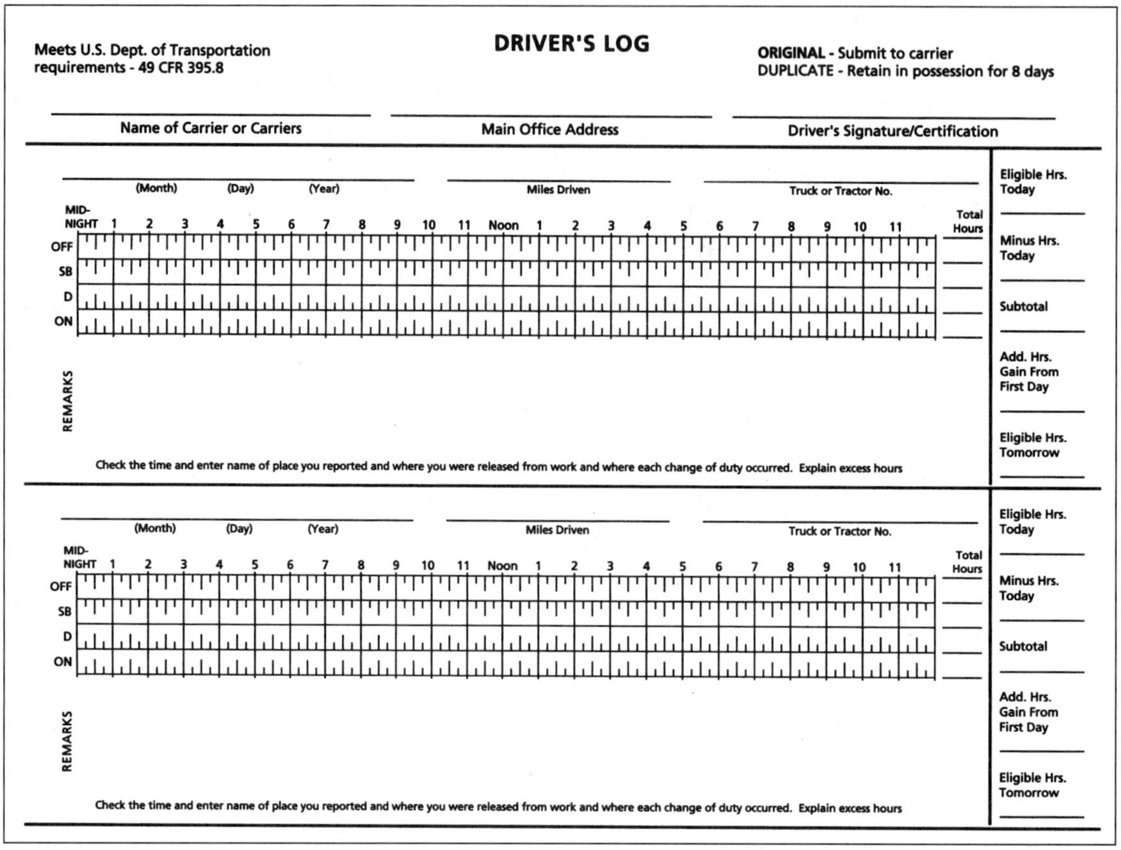

The driver's daily log entries must be kept current to the time of the last change of duty, and the driver and carrier (private) can be held liable to legal prosecution for failure to maintain logs.

The logbook is also an excellent source of performance data if the entries are accurate. The driver, vehicle, hours operated, miles driven, trip origin, and destination are found in the log entries. As the fleet management reviews the log to ensure driver availability, performance data can be compiled for each driver and vehicle.

SUMMARY

Private transportation is found in various forms in all modes of transportation. In air, water, and truck transportation, a firm owns or leases and operates the equipment. For rail, a firm owns or leases the equipment (cars and trucks), but the common carrier railroad actually operates the vehicles. Shipper-owned oil pipelines are common, but the oil pipelines are regulated as for-hire transportation companies. Private trucking is the most pervasive form of private transportation with thousands of companies operating truck fleets.

KEY TERMS

cost center pg. 277
driving time regulations 281
empty backhaul 270
exempt commodities 280
finance lease 276
full service lease 276
mileage allowance 265
not-for-hire 265
primary business test 280
private carrier 265
profit center 278
trip lease 281

STUDY QUESTIONS

1. What is private transportation?

2. The nature of private carriage varies among the modes. Describe the private differences among the modes.

3. Private trucking is the most pervasive form of private carriage. Comment on the reason why private trucking is so widely used in the United States.

4. Service and cost are the two areas most often cited as reasons for establishing a private trucking operation. Discuss the service and cost advantages afforded by private trucking.

5. What are the disadvantages of private trucking?

6. Using the data in Table 10.3, determine the managerial impact of (1) an increase in the annual miles operated per tractor/trailer from 100,000 to 125,000, (b) a decrease in the average load per trip from 40,000 pounds to 34,000 pounds, and (c) a 20 percent increase in the price of fuel from $1.10 to $1.32 per gallon.

7. If you were going to select trucks to operate over-the-road from Denver to Los Angeles, what type of equipment would you specify? Why? Would you specify the same type of equipment for a delivery operation within the county of Los Angeles? Why?

8. Why would a private fleet be organized on the basis of a cost center? A profit center?

9. Describe the methods available to a private carrier to operate as a for-hire carrier.

10. Discuss the economic and safety regulations imposed on private trucking by the federal government.

NOTES

1. Robert Delaney, "Eighth Annual State of Logistics Report," *Cass/Prologis,* June 2, 1997, Figure 19.

2. This is based on an inventory carrying cost of 20 percent per dollar inventory per year. For a further discussion of inventory costs, see John J. Coyle, Edward J. Bardi, and C. John Langley, Jr., *The Management of Business Logistics,* 5th ed. (St. Paul, MN: West Publishing, 1992), Chs. 5 and 6.

3. Some companies have been too successful in negotiating lower rates. The lower for-hire rates have made the long-haul intercity private fleet uneconomical.

4. Assuming fuel costs are $1.10/gallon and each vehicle is operated 140,000 miles per year, fuel cost per truck is $30,800 at five mpg ($1.10/gal. × 140,000 mi./5 mpg) and $28,000 at 5.5 mpg ($1.10/gal. × 140,000 mi./5.5 mpg). The 10 percent increase in mpg saved $2,800 per truck, or 9.1 percent.

5. For additional costing information, see Herman Granberry, "A Private Carrier Costing Guide," *The Private Carrier* (October, 1988), pp. 7–13.

SUGGESTED READINGS

Andel, Tom. "Load Plans Make Room for Profit," *Transportation & Distribution,* Vol. 37, No. 3, March 1996, pp. 58–62.

Bradley, Peter. "Fleets Change With the Times," *Logistics Management,* Vol. 35, No. 5, May 1996, pp. 35–43.

Brown, Terrence A., and Janet Greenlee, "Private Trucking After Deregulation: Managers' Perceptions," *Transportation Journal,* Vol. 35, No. 1, Fall 1995, pp. 5–13.

Cooke, James Aaron. "Dedicated to Savings," *Logistics Management,* Vol. 35, No. 10, October 1996, pp. 67–68.

Cooke, James Aaron. "High-Tech Gear Lets Private Fleets Work Smarter," *Traffic Management,* Vol. 34, No. 5, May 1995, pp. 51–55.

Granberry, Herman. "A Private Carrier Costing Guide," *The Private Carrier,* October 1988, pp. 7–13.

Harrington, Lisa. "Fleets Catch up With Technology," *Transportation & Distribution,* Vol. 36, No. 4, April 1995, pp. 30–36.

Harrington, Lisa. "New Dimensions in Truck Leasing," *Transportation & Distribution,* Vol. 36, No. 2, pp. 30–32.

Hoffman, Kurt. "A Piece of the Private Fleet Pie," *Distribution,* Vol. 94, No. 13, December 1995, pp. 32–35.

Truth, L. J., and S. E. Tarry. "The Rise and Fall of General Aviation: Product Liability, Market Structure, and Technological Innovation" *Transportation Journal,* Vol. 34, No. 4, Summer 1995, pp. 52–70.

CASES

CASE 10.1
Apex Soap Products

Apex Soap Products (ASP) started business in 1987 following the development of a biodegradable, environmentally safe laundry detergent by ASP's founder John Apex. Apex is a chemist and inventor, the day-to-day operations of ASP are managed by Allen Flash. During the early 1990s, Flash concentrated his attention on market development of ASP's laundry soap, and by 1997 ASP had gained a sizable share of the laundry detergent market. Recently, however, more and more of Flash's time has been directed toward ASP operations.

As Flash reviewed the 1997 operating results, he was concerned about the negative profit margin trend. Sales volume increased 10 percent from 1996, but profits decreased five percent. Part of this profit squeeze is attributable to the price decreases ASP granted its larger customers in response to the price war that developed in this very competitive market for biodegradable laundry detergent. Of greater concern, though, was the 17 percent increase in distribution costs and, in particular, the cost of transportation.

Recently, Flash read an article reporting on a 1997 private fleet benchmark study conducted by a private trucking organization. This article interested Flash because ASP operates a large private fleet consisting of 50 tractors, 180 trailers, and 80 drivers. The fleet delivers 80 percent of ASP's soap.

For 1996, the private fleet benchmark study reported the cost to operate a dry van tractor trailer fleet was $1.30 per mile. Flash calculated ASP's fleet cost per mile to be $1.65, or 27 percent more than the benchmark average. The study indicated the average miles per tractor was 100,000 miles, the miles per driver equaled 87,000 miles, and the trailer/tractor ratio to be 2.5/1. ASP's comparable statistics were 85,000 miles per tractor, 62,500 miles per driver, and a 3.5/1 trailer/tractor ratio. Also, the study indicated the cost of for-hire truckload carriers was $1.10 per mile.

Upon returning to the office, Flash asked Erica Gratchet, manager of the private fleet, to prepare a report on the feasibility of eliminating the fleet. The request to analyze the elimination of the private fleet caught Gratchet completely off-guard. The fleet has been an integral part of ASP from the founding of the company. In 1987, ASP purchased a truck to deliver the initial soap order to its first and currently largest customer. The fleet has since been a symbol of ASP's environmental orientation with the equipment maintained in top condition and always clean. The trailers are used as 48-foot moving billboards and have won national awards from the private trucking organization for their design, color, and advertising customer delivery problems. Gratchet could not understand why Flash would even consider eliminating the fleet.

The feasibility study is due in two months and Gratchet is concerned with the data requirements and areas she should address in the study. Of particular concern is the methodology she should use to justify the fleet on the basis of service.

Case Questions

1. What areas should Gratchet examine to explain the higher per mile cost of ASP's fleet?

2. What factors should Gratchet examine to analyze the efficiency of the private fleet?

3. What would you recommend as a method to quantify the value of the service provided by the fleet?

4. How would you develop the cost of outside transportation to compare against the private fleet cost?

5. Should the fleet be "outsourced"? Why or why not?

CASE 10.2

Coastal Chemical Company

Linda Thorton is vice-president of traffic and distribution for Coastal Chemical Company (CCC). CCC is a multinational basic and specialty chemical company based in the Midwest.

The company operates a fleet of about 50 tank and van truck-trailer combinations from nine of its 14 plants. The fleet is dedicated to the nine plants, that is, the fleet serves only the nine plants and not the other five. To date, the fleet operations have been limited, picking up inbound raw materials from suppliers and moving semiprocessed chemicals between plants.

With the passage of the ICC Termination Act of 1995 and the virtual deregulation of trucking, Linda sees new opportunities for the private trucking operations at the nine plants. She and her staff visualize opportunities for reducing the cost of freight outbound to customers and making inbound moves for the other plants that are along the return routes. The new law allows the firm to register as a regulated carrier with the STB to move freight or other firms when these moves are part of a private backhaul run. Further, there is also the option to set up a completely new trucking corporation and handle freight for any firm. This last situation would be managed like a trucking firm in that it would solicit freight from CCC and any other shipper firm. It would be operated as a separate profit center subsidiary.

Case Questions

1. What are the strategic issues raised with this proposal?
2. How would you organize the proposed fleet operations?
3. How would you structure the relationship between CCC and the new trucking operation?

PART 3

Carrier Management

CHAPTER

11

Costing and Pricing in Transportation

The regulation of business on a comprehensive basis by federal statute was initiated in the United States in 1887 when Congress passed the original Act to Regulate Commerce. This legislation established a framework of control over interstate rail transportation. The federal government continued intensive regulation of the modes until 1978 when air carriers were deregulated. This was followed by significant changes in motor carriers (the Motor Carrier Act of 1980) and railroads (the Staggers Act of 1980). In the 1980s, further regulatory reduction efforts continued with buses being deregulated in 1982 and surface, domestic freight forwarders being given similar treatment in 1986. The deregulation efforts that have swept through various segments of the transportation industry in recent years have focused on issues associated with rate control.

Problems created by the partial deregulation under the preceding laws created the need for more attention from Congress. The ICC Termination Act took effect in 1996. This legislation removed virtually all motor carrier economic regulation and significantly reduced the remaining oversight of the railroad industry. The ICC was terminated, and some of its functions were referred to the newly created Surface Transportation Board, part of the Department of Transportation (DOT).

With the removal of economic regulation, the marketplace prevails as to pricing. Due the monopolistic nature of the railroad industry, some rate regulation has been retained.

The motor-carrier industry is totally free to operate wherever and charge any rates. Certain functions within the LTL sector remain, including the classification that assigns products to a "category" based on transportation characteristics and the use of rate bureaus that publish "class rates." However, all aspects of the transportation cycle are negotiable.

The use of contracts has ensured that both the carrier and the shipper have a clear understanding of each other's requirements. The material discussed in this chapter is no less relevant than in the past. If anything, it is even more important, as no federal agency is available to assist should a shipper fail to negotiate wisely.

Individuals studying transportation should understand the theoretical underpinnings of the rates and prices of transportation agencies. A key point to master at the outset is the idea that a difference exists between the terms *rate* and *price.*

In the recent past when transport regulation was at its peak, it was more appropriate to use the term *rate* than *price.* A rate is an amount that can be found in a rate tariff book, as payment to a carrier for performing a given transport service. This rate is the *lawful* charge that a carrier can impose on a given commodity movement; therefore, a rate has the full force of the law behind it for its timely payment. A rate is determined primarily by considering a carrier's costs only and not by assessing the overall market situation at that moment in time and how these market forces influence supply and demand. A discussion of cost concepts can be found in this chapter's Appendix 11-A.

A price, however, is a much clearer notion of how post-deregulation transportation firms determine and impose charges for their services. A price implies a value or level that is determined based on prevailing market forces. Clearly, the notion of price implies a dynamic economic environment, one that is receptive to changes in customer supply and demand.

Although the transportation industry is not completely unique compared to other industries, there are enough differences to justify a thorough discussion of transportation pricing. The first part of this chapter on transport prices will explore the market structure of the transportation industry. The section on market structure will be followed by an analysis of cost-of-service pricing. This analysis will provide the basis for a discussion on value-of-service pricing. The final part of the chapter will address rate systems and pricing in transportation.

Market Considerations

Before discussing the characteristics of the transportation market, a brief review of basic market structure models is appropriate. Such a discussion will provide some insights into the unique nature of the transportation market situations.

Market Structure Models

The necessary conditions for **pure competition** are generally stated as follows: There are a large number of sellers, all sellers and buyers are of such a small size that no one can influence prices or supply, there is a homogeneous product or service, and there is unrestricted entry. The demand curve facing the individual firm is one of perfect elasticity, which means the producer can sell all output at the one market price, but none above that price. Although pure competition is not a predominant market structure, it is frequently used as a standard to judge optimal allocation of resources.

If pure competition is one type of market structure, the other extreme is a perfectly monopolistic market with only one seller of a product or service for which there is no close competitor or substitute. In such a situation, the single seller is able to set the price for the service offered and should adjust the price to its advantage, given the demand curve. To remain in this situation, the single seller must be able to restrict entry. The single seller maximizes profits by equating marginal cost and marginal revenue and may make excess profit.

A third type of market structure is **oligopoly.** Oligopoly can be defined as competition between a "few" large sellers of a relatively homogeneous product that has enough cross-elasticity of demand (substitutability) so that each seller must, in pricing decisions, take into account competitors' reactions. In other words, it is characterized by mutual interdependence among the various sellers. The individual seller is aware that in changing price, output, sales promotion activities, or the quality of the product the reactions of competitors must be taken into account. All modes encounter some form of oligopolistic competition.

The fourth type of market structure is **monopolistic competition.** In this type of market structure, there are many small sellers, but there is some differentiation of products. The number of sellers is great enough and the largest seller small enough that no one controls a significant portion of the market. No recognized interdependence of the related sellers' prices or price policies is usually present. Therefore, any seller can lower price to increase sales volume without necessarily eliciting a retaliatory reaction from competitors.

This brief description of the four basic market models is by no means complete. The interested student can obtain additional perspectives from any standard microeconomics text. For our purposes, the above discussion provides enough background to focus more closely on transportation markets.

Theory of Contestable Markets[1]

The relevant market structure faced by each mode of transportation provided the basis for arguments made by proponents of deregulation. This was especially the case with airline deregulation. For deregulation to work for a mode, its market structure must closely resemble pure competition. On the surface, it appeared that the passenger airline industry was oligopolistic and therefore would prevent the free entry of competitors. However, there was some consensus that the airline industry could perform in a competitive manner. This rationale resulted in what can be called *the theory of contestable markets,* which substitutes potential competition for the active participation of many sellers.[2]

For this theory to work, several conditions had to be met. First, barriers to entry could not exist. Such barriers could include physical barriers, informational barriers, and capital barriers.[3] Second, economies of scale could not be present. In the airline industry, this meant that operating many aircraft could not have a cost advantage over operating a single aircraft. Third, consumers had to be willing and able to switch quickly among carriers.[4] Finally, existing carriers had to be prevented from responding to new entrants' lower prices, assuming that the entrant possessed a lower cost structure than the incumbent.[5]

Although the theory of contestable markets proved to be correct in the early days of deregulation, incumbent airlines have been able to remove the potential threat of new entrants in today's operating environment, thus weakening the theory's application.[6] This conclusion points to the importance of understanding the market structures of the modes and how they will behave in a deregulated environment. It also leads to the conclusion that the passenger airline industry is indeed an oligopoly, and thus is subject to the potential abuses of this type of market.

Relevant Market Areas

A general statement classifying the market structure of the entire transportation industry cannot be made because it is necessary to view structures in particular market areas. In the railroad industry, for example, there exists a variety of different services, involving the transportation of thousands of different commodities between tens of thousands of different stations or geographic points, via a multiplicity of different routes, and under various conditions of carriage.[7] The market structure in transportation must describe the situation at any one point, and even then the situation will differ between commodities. Therefore, to determine pricing in transportation, we must describe the situation between two points for one commodity in one shipment size.[8]

For example, a particular railroad that provides service between Pittsburgh and Cincinnati may find that the movement of ordinary steel approximates what we have described as monopolistic competition. There is likely to be a large number of other carriers, especially common and contract motor carriers, that provide essentially the same service.

However, for the movement of a very large, sophisticated generator, the railroad may face an oligopolistic market on the move between Pittsburgh and Cincinnati because none of the motor carriers might be able to haul such a large piece of equipment, and the railroad might be competing with only a few water carriers. It is possible that we could find some commodity where the railroad would be operating in a monopolistic position because of restrictions on operating authorities. Finally, there might even be a product for which the situation approaches pure competition. In fact, this may be true for certain steel products, given the availability or rail, motor, water, and private carrier. In summary, the relevant market situation for transportation consists of one commodity moving between two points in one shipment size.

We could describe, of course, the market structure for a particular mode of transportation in one market in more detail. This is especially true with respect to the railroad industry, the water carrier industry, and the pipeline industry. We could describe a typical situation in *each* of these industries and make it fit one of the economic models described. For example, we could say that between two particular cities the water carriers are faced with oligopolistic conditions. From this, we could discuss the general pricing behavior of the industry.[9] However, there is intermodal competition present in transportation, and it is necessary to take this fact into consideration to adequately describe the market situations. Also, as we have stated, the situation varies by commodity.

The complexity of the situation does not eliminate the validity of the economic models described above. It only means that in order to make use of these models we must have knowledge of the situation that exists in the particular market. Although this may seem to be too much to expect at first, it can be accomplished. The elaborate classification system for rates (discussed in Appendix 11-B) distorts the situation somewhat, but in our economy commodity rates are the most important in terms of total intercity ton-miles. Commodity rates are competitive on commodities between specific points. In setting prices, a carrier must have knowledge of the relevant market area. With this knowledge, it is possible to use one of the economic models described. Although there will be instances when carriers may find it expedient to generalize in adjusting prices, a much narrower focus is customary in the day-to-day negotiation and analysis of these prices.

The deregulation that has occurred in transportation in the last 18 years has made these conclusions even more appropriate. Although it is true that there has been a general increase in competition, the competition has been uneven among market areas, commodities, and shipment sizes. The new competitive environment has made carriers and shippers more sensitive to the importance of the relevant market area concept. More prices are being negotiated by shippers and carriers and are taking into account the particular demand and supply situations for the movements affected.

The important point about our analysis is that, although transportation competition has indeed become more intense in the last three or four decades, the intensity is uneven. Therefore, all four types of markets can be found in transportation markets. This makes pricing very challenging. In addition, the derived nature of transportation demand further complicates the pricing situation.

Cost-of-Service Pricing[10]

There are two separate concepts in **cost-of-service pricing:** basing prices upon average cost or basing prices upon marginal cost. To give adequate treatment to both sides, let us make some simplifying assumptions and make use of diagrams. The assumptions are that the product or service is homogeneous, only one group of customers is involved, and this group of customers is responsible for all costs.

If the firm desires to maximize its profits (see Figure 11.1), it will produce quantity Q_m and charge price P_m. The firm would be making excess profits in the economic sense because the price is above average cost and the firm is not producing at a point for optimal allocation of resources.

Based on what may appear to be undesirable features, we might decide to impose regulation upon this firm. Now, if the "regulators" want to set a single price that would cover the firm's cost of production and at the same time sell all the output, then the price should be P_r and the output Q_r. In this instance, we would be basing the price on **average cost.** There would not be any excess profit in the economic sense, and consumers would be receiving more output at a lower price.

FIGURE 11.1 Cost-of-Service Pricing

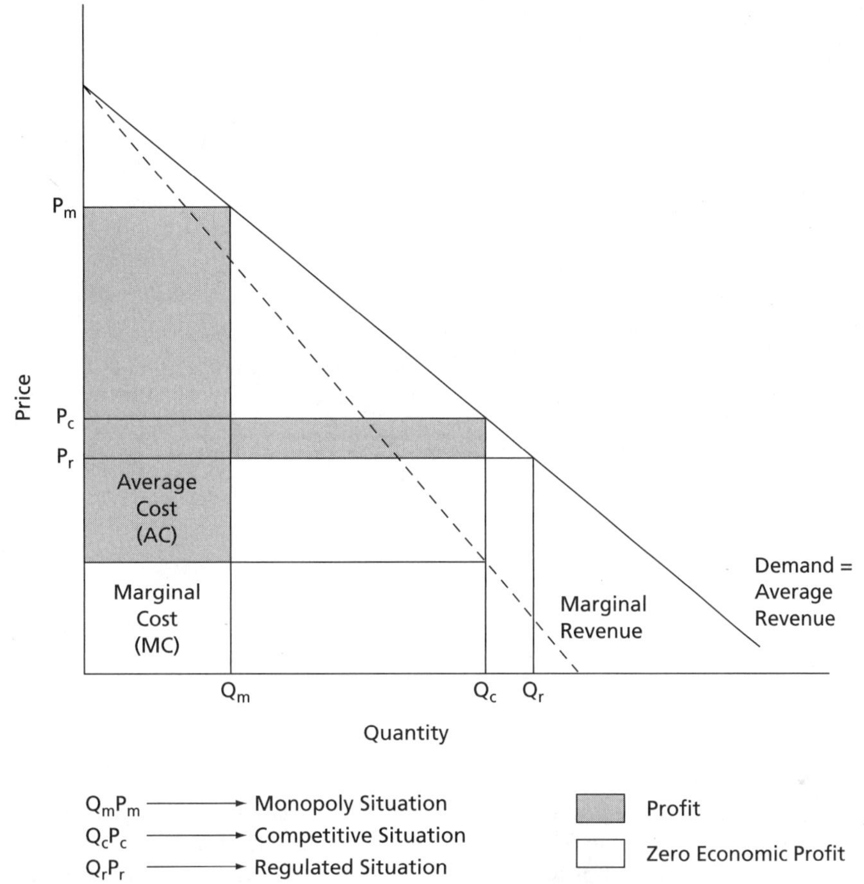

P = Profit, Q = Quantity, Q_mP_m Monopoly situation, Q_cP_c Competitive situation, Q_rP_r Regulatory situation

It appears that the average-cost approach is more socially desirable than the unregulated, profit-maximizing approach. What are the attributes of the marginal-cost approach? If price is set at **marginal cost** equal to marginal revenue, we have a higher price (P_c) and less output (Q_c) than the average-cost approach yields. The advocates of an absolute marginal-cost approach argue that the output between Q_c and Q_r is such that the marginal cost of producing these additional units of output is greater than what buyers are willing to pay for the extra units supplied, because the marginal-cost curve is above the demand curve over this range of output.[11]

In Adam Smith's terminology, we are saying that the value in use is not as great as the cost of producing the additional output. Therefore, there are alternate uses in which the resources used to produce this additional output are valued more highly by consumers. When stated in this manner, the argument is based upon logic usually advanced under a label of "welfare economics."[12] Under the marginal-cost solution presented in Figure 11.1, there would be excess profits because price is above

FIGURE 11.2 Decreasing Cost Situation

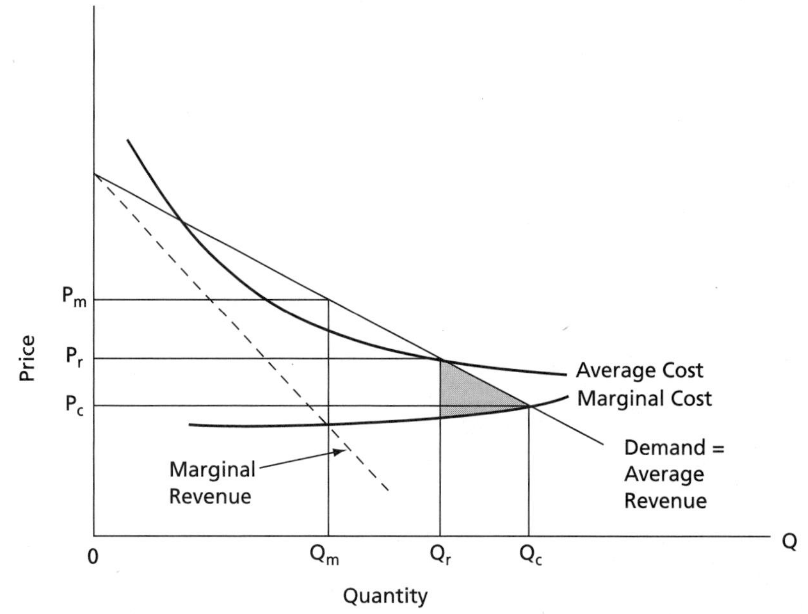

the average cost. However, this need not be a problem because the excess profits can be used to pay taxes.

One of the arguments frequently raised against a strict marginal-cost approach to pricing is that, under decreasing cost conditions, if the firm equates marginal cost with demand, then it will necessitate the firm's operating at a loss (see Figure 11.2). However, the advocates of a strict marginal-cost approach would still present the argument that individuals are willing to pay the marginal cost of the additional output between Q_m and Q_r and therefore it should be produced. There is one obvious solution, and that is to allow the government to make up the deficit through a subsidy.[13] These subsidies could be offset by the taxes collected in the previous example. These are also additional ways to offset governmental subsidies.

Thus far in our discussion, no attempt has been made to substantiate one approach or the other. We have merely presented the arguments advanced by advocates of each approach. Before any critique can be presented of these alternate approaches, we should examine the assumptions that were made at the outset.

In regard to the assumption that only one group of customers is served, this is not the typical situation, except in very special cases among transportation companies. Likewise, costs are not usually separable according to the classes of customers, but rather, common costs are quite typical, particularly with respect to railroads. We have already mentioned that output is not homogeneous in many instances; rather, what we have are heterogeneous or multiple services. Transportation firms are not peculiar in this respect because so many firms have common costs.

The presence of **common costs** raises some problems for cost-of-service pricing, particularly the average-cost approach. If we are to base rates upon average or fully allocated costs, it becomes necessary to apportion these costs by some arbitrary means. Average cost pricing with fixed or common costs, or both, makes these costs price-determining when they should be price-determined. In other words, fixed costs per unit depend on the volume of traffic, and the volume of traffic depends on the rate charged. To some extent then, cost is a function of the prices, not the prices a function of the cost.[14] In fact, it could be argued that not only do costs determine prices, but that prices determine cost; in other words, the situation is analogous to the chicken and egg argument.

The presence of common costs does not raise the same theoretical problem for marginal-cost pricing because no arbitrary allocation of these costs is technically necessary. However, we may encounter problems because marginal cost can only be determinable with large blocks of output as a trainload or even a truckload. The output unit we want to price can be smaller with less-than-truckload (LTL) shipments. There are some additional problems of a more practical nature, however, with respect to strict marginal-cost pricing. For example, in transportation, marginal costs could fluctuate widely, depending on the volume of traffic offered. The requirement of published rates would necessitate the averaging of these marginal costs to stabilize them, which would make them unequal with theoretical marginal costs.

We have raised some theoretical and practical problems with cost-of-service pricing. An obvious question is whether cost-of-service pricing has any relevance for establishing prices.

Prices charged by transportation companies are actually one of the criteria that guide intelligent shippers in selecting the mode of transportation or carrier that is most appropriate for their shipment. When the modal choice or carrier decision is made properly, the shipper will balance the carrier's price against the carrier's service characteristics such as transit time, reliability, and loss and damage record.

For the transportation decision to be properly made, the price charged should reflect the cost of providing the service to ensure carrier and economic system efficiency. The price(s) of carriers should be related to cost, but not to some arbitrary allocation of cost.

Railroads and pipelines require large, indivisible capital inputs because of their rights-of-way, terminals, and so on. The associated high fixed costs that are common costs to most of the traffic, if averaged over the units of traffic, will have to be allocated on an arbitrary basis, which will in turn lead to unwise and uneconomical pricing decisions. Adherence to an average cost or fully allocated cost approach does not make any sense in such situations.

Cost-oriented prices should be related to what we have defined as marginal cost or variable cost. Such costs, measuring as precisely as possible, should serve as the conceptual floor for individual prices. Some traffic will move if prices are above marginal or variable cost, whereas other traffic will move at prices close to marginal cost, particularly under competitive circumstances. In other words, differential pricing seems to make sense in most instances, but our rationale needs further explanation.

In the presentation of cost-of-service pricing, mention was made of **decreasing cost industries**. Some transportation firms fall into this category. If prices are based on strict marginal cost, the firm experiences a loss. A subsidy could be paid, but this is not likely to be done. Therefore, the firm has to recover its fixed costs. To accomplish this on the basis of an average-cost approach is not acceptable. However, it can be accomplished by using marginal cost as a floor for prices and using the value of service, or demand, to establish how far above this minimum the rate or price should be set.

Value-of-service pricing is sometimes defined as **charging what the traffic will bear**. In actuality, this phrase can assume two meanings. First, it can be used to mean that prices are set so that on each unit the maximum revenue is obtained regardless of the particular costs involved. That is, no service should be charged a lower price when it could bear a higher price. The second meaning, which can be more conveniently expressed in a negative form and which is germane to our discussion, is that no service should be charged a price that it will not bear when, at a lower price, the service could be purchased. This lower price will always cover the marginal cost incurred by the company in providing the service.

The differences in the elasticities of demand for the different services will determine the actual level of the prices. The presence of indivisibilities in the cost structure necessitates the dissimilar pricing. Therefore, the greater the amount of the indivisibilities in the cost structure, the greater the need for dissimilar pricing and its consequent practice of segregating services according to demand elasticity.

One final point should be treated, and that is the desirability of dissimilar pricing. Dissimilar pricing allows common and fixed costs to be spread out over large volumes of traffic. In other words, dissimilar pricing may render economical benefits because prices may be lower than they otherwise would be. It is not unusual to hear statements in the railroad industry that the prices on captive traffic subsidize competitive traffic; coal, for example, will not move unless the rates are relatively low. It could be argued that, as long as the coal rates cover more than the marginal cost of the movement, they allow the railroad to charge lower rates on other traffic.

As previously mentioned, the variable, or marginal, cost of providing the service should serve as the floor for carriers when setting prices. This is going to rely entirely on how marginal, or variable, cost is defined, as we will see in this discussion. With this mentality, a carrier will be able to recover at least the short-run related costs of providing a service. This relationship can be seen in Figure 11.3. In this example, a carrier's variable cost for a particular move is $90, its average cost (also called *fully allocated cost*) is $100, and its potential price is $110 (which could result in a $10 profit). This example assumes that (1) the carrier knows its costs and (2) it is able to charge a price that will result in a profit. This second assumption can be called *value-of-service pricing,* which will be discussed in the next section.

We can say that dissimilar pricing is the logical approach for pricing in regulated industries. Cost indivisibilities necessitate the practice of discriminatory pricing, but

FIGURE 11.3 Cost of Service as Price Floor—Generic Example

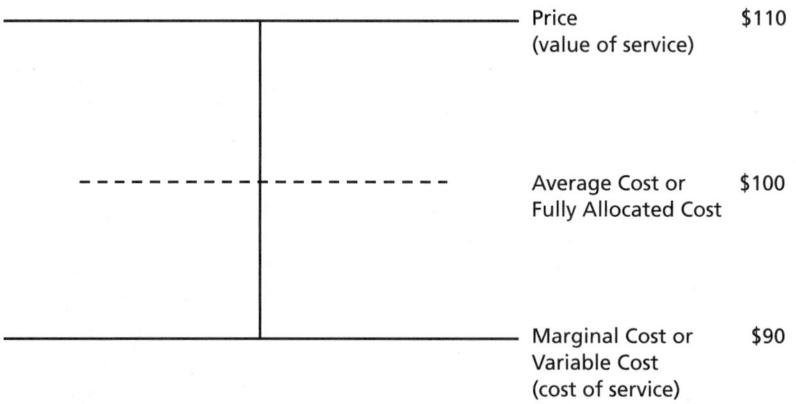

STOP OFF

DISCOUNT TARIFFS

Carriers' discount tariffs may be confusing, but they can result in considerable savings for your company if used correctly. Below are some ways to take maximum advantage of the various options available to you:

- **Measure net cost:** Carriers often have their own regional and national rate bases, from which they calculate discounts. In some cases, multiple rate bases apply to a customer or location. National rate bases can vary as much as 10 percent from one carrier to another, and regional rate bases can vary even more. Compute the actual net cost after applying the discount to the base for each alternative, rather than just compare discount percentages.
- **Negotiate a floor limit:** A floor limit is the minimum charge for a shipment, regardless of the size of the discount. This is of particular concern to the direct marketing industry, in which shipments often fall under 300 lbs. For example, take a tariff with a $55 floor limit. If the gross charge for the shipment is $80 and the carrier offers a 50 percent discount, the discounted rate would be $40. But the floor limit puts the charge at $55, making the discount only about 31 percent.
- **Review extra charges:** The two most common extra charges are the single shipment charge and the notification charge, which can range from $14 to $20. These are not appropriate for inbound situations and should not be included in the carrier's tariff.
- **Reduce COD fees:** Carriers' charges for COD service are high because they are usually based on a percentage of the shipment. (For instance, a rate of 3.5 percent of a $100,000 shipment results in a $3,500 charge). If you need COD service, negotiate a flat fee.
- **Arrange special non-direct service rates:** Most tariffs allow discounts only on direct point-to-point shipments. But your vendor, for instance, may call your carrier for pickup outside its service area. If this happens frequently, negotiate special discounted rates for non-direct service.
- **Consider FAK rates:** Freight-all-kinds (FAK) tariffs cover a whole range of products with one rate classification. For example, if your products range from books, class 70, to comforters, class 150, your weighted average class may be 100. Where you have limited control over the accuracy of the vendor's classification, these rates may be advantageous. Carefully evaluate the difference between using an average classification (FAK) and classifying products separately. FAK rates may offer some cost and control advantages. Companies such as Superior Products and Potpourri Collections, offering a broad range of products, have reduced their expense and improved control with FAK rates.

Source: Bill Wilson, *Operations & Fulfillment,* November/December 1997, p. 38. Copyright *Operations & Fullment* Magazine, 1997.

we have approached this within what we might call a cost framework. Marginal cost sets the minimum basis for prices, whereas fixed or common costs are, in effect, allocated on the basis of demand elasticity.

Value-of-Service Pricing

Value-of-service pricing is a frequently mentioned and often criticized approach to pricing that has generally been associated with the railroad industry. Part of the problem associated with value-of-service pricing is that a number of different definitions of it are offered by various sources. Therefore, we will first develop a workable definition of the term.

One rather common definition of value-of-service pricing in transportation is pricing according to the value of the product; for example, high-valued products are accorded high prices for their movement, and low-valued commodities are accorded

FIGURE 11.4 Influence of Value and Demand Elasticity on Price

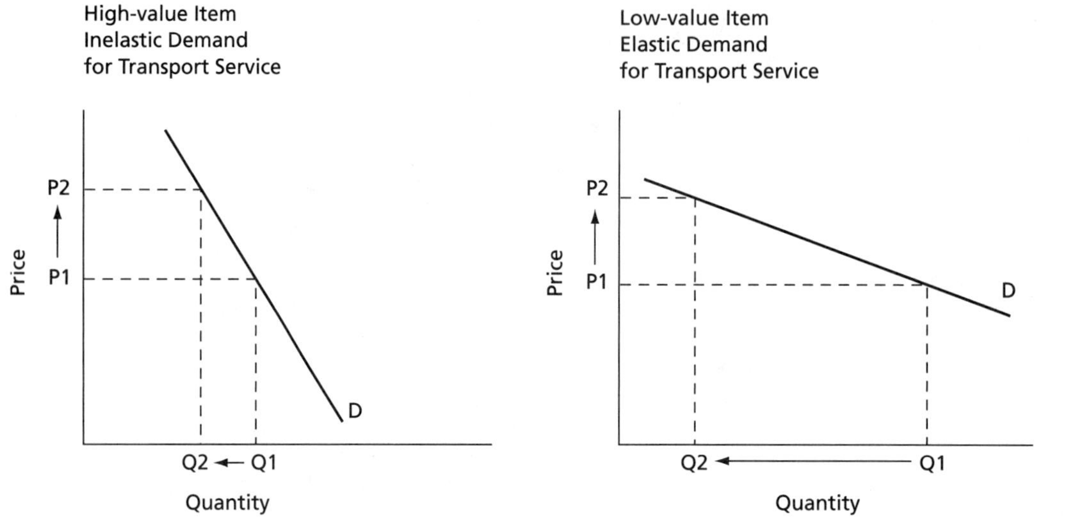

low prices. Evidence can be found to substantiate this definition by examining the class-rate structure of railroads.

Several points are in order here. First, even if we took a cost-based approach to setting prices, high-valued commodities would usually be charged higher prices because they are typically more expensive to transport. There is generally more risk involved in moving high-valued commodities, and more expensive equipment is necessary. Second, the value of the commodity is a legitimate indicator of elasticity of demand; for example, high-valued commodities can usually bear higher prices because transportation cost is such a small percentage of the final selling price.

This concept can be seen in Figure 11.4. The demand curves of two different types of commodities for transportation services are shown. The high-value item has a steeply sloping demand curve implying price inelasticity. On the other hand, the low-value item has a gradual slope, implying price elasticity. To see how these elasticities relate to how a transportation firm can set prices based on product value, consider a price increase from price P1 to price P2. When the price of the transport service increases for the high-value product, a small quantity-demanded decrease is observed from quantity Q1 to quantity Q2. For the same price increase, the low-value product cannot absorb the increased price. This inability to support the added price of the service is seen as a drop in the quantity demanded from Q1 to Q2. Clearly the decrease in quantity demanded for the low-value product is of a larger magnitude than the decrease for the higher-value product for the same price increase.

In a situation where a carrier has a complete monopoly, to consider value-of-service pricing only in terms of the commodity's value would not lead to serious traffic losses. It would be analogous to the idea behind progressive income taxes, that is, setting prices upon the ability or willingness to pay.[15] But where alternatives are present at a lower price, shippers are not willing to pay higher prices based upon the value of the product alone. This is one of the reasons why the motor carriers were able to make serious inroads in rail traffic during their early development. They undercut the prices on high-valued commodities when the railroads were the most susceptible to competition. In essence, we are saying that the value of the commodity gives some indication of demand or the ability to bear a charge, but competition also will affect the demand for the service, that is, the height and slope of the demand curve.

Value-of-service pricing also has been defined as **third-degree price discrimination** or a situation in which a seller sets two or more different market prices for two or more separate groups of buyers of essentially the same commodity or service.[16] Three necessary conditions must exist before a seller can practice third-degree price discrimination. First, the seller must be able to separate buyers into groups or submarkets according to their different elasticities of demand; this separation enables the seller to charge different prices in the various markets. The second condition is that the seller must be able to prevent the transfer of sales between the submarkets. That is, the buyer must not buy in the lower-priced market and sell in the higher-priced markets. Third, the seller must possess some degree of monopoly power.

Another name given to value-of-service pricing is **differential** pricing. Differential pricing can be done based on several methods of segregating the buyers into distinct groups. It can be done by commodity (such as coal versus computers), by time (seasonal discounts/premium rates), by place, as Figure 11.5 demonstrates, or by individual person. It should be noted, however, that discrimination based on an individual person is illegal per se on traffic that remains economically regulated by the STB.[17]

These conditions for third-degree price discrimination can be fulfilled in the transportation industry as well as in other regulated industries such as the telephone industry. For example, in transportation, shippers are separated according to commodities transported and between points of movement. Our previous discussion of the relevant market area in transportation implied that there were different or separable customer-related markets—for example, one commodity between each pair of shipping points, each with a separate elasticity.

FIGURE 11.5 Differential Pricing Based on Place Route

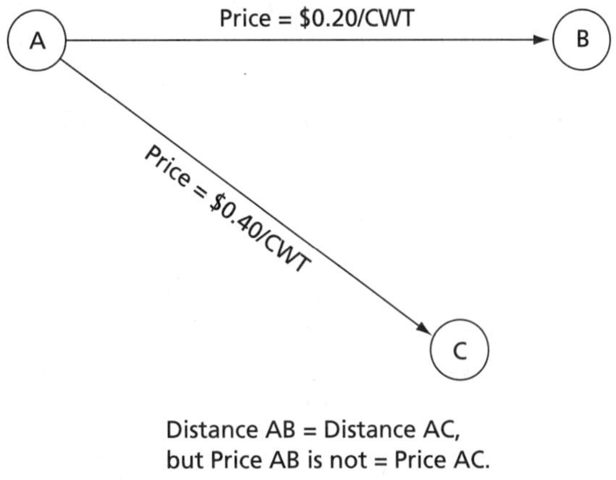

Another point that is relevant to our discussion is the nature of "essentially the same commodity or service."[18] Actually, we need only recognize that many transportation companies sell multiple or heterogeneous services that are technically similar. For example, rail movements of television sets or glassware are very different in terms of time, equipment, terminal facilities, and so on.

If we think back to a point that was made earlier about railroad costs, that is, the high level of fixed costs and the need to attract traffic, value-of-service or differential pricing makes sense from the perspective of the railroad. Remember that railroads will experience declining average costs with increases in volume. If shipments are priced properly, this could mean increased revenues from higher volumes with more profit.

The key to success lies in being able to determine the appropriate costs and to estimate demand elasticity in the various markets. This essentially means determining what the shipper is willing to pay for the service, given the competition in the market from other carriers, the demand for the product itself, and any other factors affecting demand.

Let us assume that a particular railroad is establishing prices on three different commodities.[19] One of the commodities is large computer systems, which have a very high value and for which there is limited substitutability. The second commodity is color television sets, which are of medium value and have some substitutes. The third commodity is coal, which is low in value and has substitutes.

Let us assume further that the value of a particular computer system is $200,000 and that it weighs one ton. If the rate charged for movement was $1,000 per ton, it would still only be one-half percent (.005) of the value of the product. The color television may have a value of $10,000 per ton. Therefore, a rate of $1,000 between the same points would represent 10 percent of the value. Finally, the coal may be worth $50 a ton. A rate of $1,000 would represent 2,000 percent of its value. Therefore, charging a common price would discourage some shippers, particularly of low-value products.

Our example is obviously simplified. However, it does point out some of the underlying logic behind value-of-service or differential pricing. In all three instances, each particular commodity is paying more than its variable cost and making a contribution to what we have labeled average cost, which also might be a concept of fully allocated cost.

Someone might argue that the coal shippers are not paying their full share and the computer shippers are paying too much. However, another argument that is frequently advanced in such instances is that, if the coal did not move (remember it is paying more than the associated variable cost), then the other traffic (computers and televisions) would have to pay an even higher price to help cover the costs of running the railroad. The same analogy applies to the supersaver fares charged by the airlines. Full-fare passengers complain sometimes that they are subsidizing discount-fare passengers. Actually, full fares might be higher if the special fares were not offered.

The essential ingredient in the value-of-service analysis is the notion that each commodity movement has its own unique demand characteristics. If the railroad placed the same price on all commodities shipped, it would discourage some shippers from moving their goods at that price. Consider what would happen if the meat counter at the local supermarket priced all the various cuts and types of meats at the same level. Obviously, it would sell the T-bone steaks quickly and have only chopped steak left.

Several points about our example need to be emphasized. First, the example is simplified. The determination of cost is a difficult task. Second, most railroads and many other carriers would be considering more than three commodities between two points. Third, the example applies to the railroad because it is more attractive in situations with high fixed costs, yet other carriers, even motor carriers, may find differential pricing attractive. Fourth, some difference would exist in rates among commodities because of cost differences; for instance, televisions cost more to handle than coal. Finally, the elasticity of demand for a particular commodity may change with competition, or because of some other factors. Therefore, high rates on higher-valued commodities have to be continually evaluated.

The three commodity examples presented here are extensions of the example presented for cost-of-service pricing, as shown in Figure 11.3. Conceptually, if cost-of-service pricing serves as the floor for carrier pricing, then value-of-service pricing can serve as the ceiling. This can be especially seen in the color television and computer examples. However, if we accept the notion that value-of-service pricing is pricing based on "what the traffic will bear," then an argument can be made that value-of-service pricing is also the floor for carrier prices, rather than the marginal cost of providing the service. This will depend on how marginal cost is defined in the context of the move.

An example might best represent this hypothesis. Assume that a truckload carrier moves a shipment from point A to point B with a variable cost of $90, an average cost of $100, and a price of $110. This relationship can be seen in Figure 11.6. This is called the carrier's **headhaul** because it is this move that initiated the original movement of the carrier's equipment and the shipper's goods. As such, the carrier might be able to use value-of-service pricing, charging $110 (profit maximization), because of commodity and competitive circumstances. With the carrier's equipment at point B, it is necessary to bring the equipment and driver back to point A. This is called a *backhaul* because it is the result of the original move (headhaul). The carrier now faces a totally different market in this backhaul lane. Assume that marginal

FIGURE 11.6 Value of Service as Price Floor and Price Ceiling

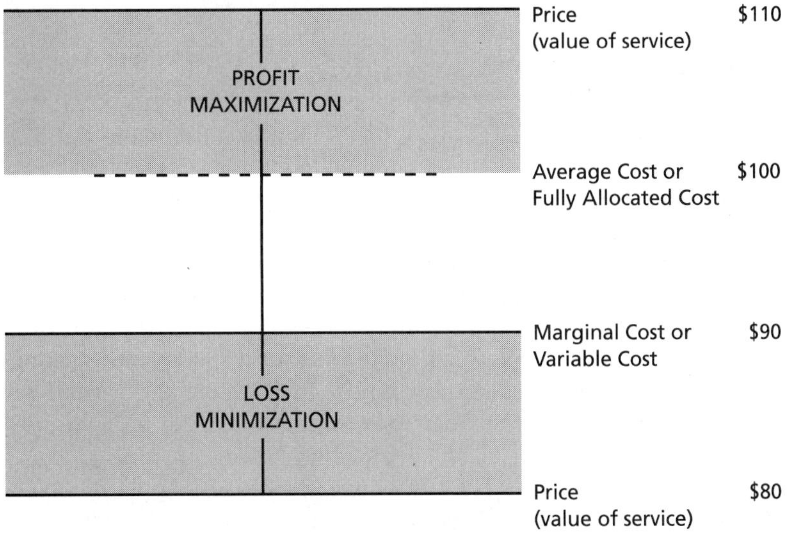

cost in this backhaul lane is defined as the variable cost of fuel and driver wages, or $90. If the carrier decides to price based on its marginal cost of $90 (cost-of-service pricing), it is very possible that the market from point B to point A will not "bear" this price and the carrier will be forced to return empty. This will result in a loss to the carrier of $90. Now suppose that the carrier prices this backhaul in accordance with market demands at a level of $80. Although this results in a price below marginal cost, the carrier has minimized its losses by losing only $10 on the move instead of $90. Pricing in this manner can be called *loss minimization*. So it can be argued that value-of-service pricing can be used as the price ceiling (profit maximization) and as the price floor (loss minimization). Both situations can be seen in Figure 11.6 and both assume that the carrier knows its costs and the market environment.

Now assume that the marginal cost in this backhaul lane is defined as those costs that would be avoided if the carrier, in fact, returned empty; that is, because the vehicle and driver are going to return anyway, the $90 for fuel and wages now becomes the fixed cost, which will now be included in the average cost figure. Marginal cost now becomes the added cost of loading the shipment and the reduced fuel efficiency, which will be assumed to be $20. Figure 11.7 shows these relationships. On the headhaul, the price of $110 covers both the average cost of $100 and the marginal cost of $90. On the backhaul, the $90 is allocated as a fixed cost over the units of output to result in an average cost of $50. Now the $80 price charged covers both the average cost and marginal cost and results in a profit, just as the price produced a profit in the headhaul example. In this example, value of service provided the price ceiling and cost of service provided the price floor, as shown in Figure 11.3. The point of showing how different price floors can be justified is that prices will be set depending on how costs are defined. In Figure 11.6, backhaul variable costs were defined from an accounting perspective, that is, those costs directly related to the return move. In Figure 11.7, backhaul variable costs were defined from an economic perspective, that is, those costs that would be avoided if the carrier, in fact, returned empty. These two definitions result in two distinctly different perspectives on the profitability of the move for the carrier and would probably affect pricing and operations decisions of the carrier. Thus, when using costs as a base for price, care must be taken to identify the proper role and definition of those costs in the pricing decision.

Rate Systems Under Deregulation

General rate structures (discussed in Appendix 11-B) were the basis of tariffs published by rate bureaus. These rate-making bodies consisted of carriers that collectively met, established rates, published them in tariff form, and sold them on a subscription basis. Deregulation changes in both rail and motor modes have prohibited rate bureaus from discussing or voting on rates that involve only a single carrier. Similarly, joint rate making is limited to only those carriers involved in a movement and not all carriers in the bureau.

The diminished role of the rate bureau in carrier rate making has resulted in a plethora of individual carrier tariffs. In addition, the greater reliance upon the marketplace to control carrier rates has enabled the shippers to greatly increase *negotiations,* resulting in rate reductions, discounts, and contract rates. Although deregulation has somewhat diminished the use and application of the class, exception, and commodity tariff systems, various features of these tariff systems are widely used today for the pricing of small LTL freight.

FIGURE 11.7 Cost of Service as Price, Floor, and Value of Service as Price Ceiling—Headhaul/Backhaul Example

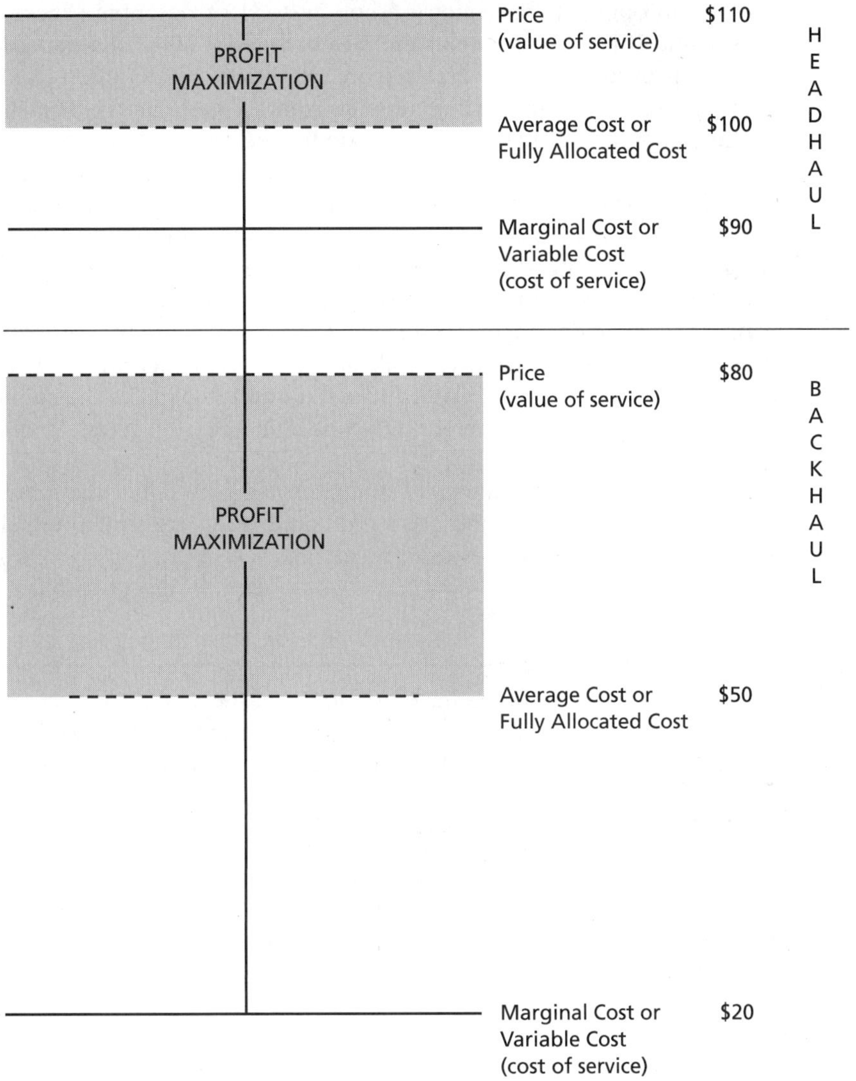

The product classification feature of the former class rate system will no doubt survive for some time to come. This system of describing and classifying products simplifies the entire product description processes for all carriers. Carriers that are not even a part of the classification process often refer to these groupings to simplify their rate-making processes.

The class rate system also serves as a benchmark against which specific carrier rates and contract rates are created. Discount plans for specific shippers often are published as a percentage from the published class or exceptions-based rate.

Commodity rates published by individual carriers are similar in form to those published by the former rate bureaus. Most individual carriers publish commodity rates in a form similar to the one shown in Table B.5, Appendix 11-B.

Many innovative carriers have simplified their own class and commodity rate structure further. One way of accomplishing this is by providing shippers with small tariffs for moves from one or a few shipper points to any points within three-digit zip codes throughout the country. Thus, instead of describing more than 30,000 points in the United States, as in the rate base-point system, a maximum of 1,000 groupings is used. For a five-state region, one carrier has 85 three-digit groupings.

Many large truck lines have computerized zip code tariffs. The shipper enters into the computer the three-digit zip code for the origin, destination, and class rating of the commodity being shipped. The computer program searches for the appropriate rate and determines the freight charges with any applicable discounts. These computerized zip code tariffs are simply a variation of the class rate structure, relying on the classification rating and zip codes to delineate the product being shipped and the origin and destination (rate basis points) of the shipment.

Another variation on the commodity tariff system is the **mileage rate.** The mileage rate is quoted in cents per mile and not in cents per hundredweight. For example, the shipper pays $1.25/mile times the number of miles the shipment moves, regardless of the shipment weight, which is limited by the physical or legal operating constraints.

In summary, the innovative rate structures being used in today's deregulated environment are variations of the class and commodity rate structures. The next section discusses the special rates used by carriers.

Special Rates

A myriad of special rate forms have evolved over the years either as a result of special cost factors or in order to induce certain shipment patterns. In their basic form, these special rates appear as either class, exception, or commodity rates.

Character-of-Shipment Rates

One set of special rates relates to the size or character of the shipment. Carriers generally have certain fixed costs for each shipment. Many rate forms have been developed that take advantage of the fact that additional units or weight in each shipment do not incur additional amounts of these fixed costs.

LTL/TL Rates

Less-than-truckload (LTL) shipments require several handlings. Each one of these handlings requires dock personnel, materials-handling equipment, terminal investment, and additional communications and tracking effort. A truckload (TL) shipment, on the other hand, is generally loaded by the shipper and moved intact to the destination, where the consignee unloads it. No intermediate handlings are required, nor does it have to be loaded or unloaded by carrier personnel. The direct movement also avoids intermediate terminals. As a result of these factors, larger TL shipments have lower rates than LTL shipments. As a result of carrier practices, the LTL/TL destinations were replaced by multiple weight groups.

Multiple-car Rates

Railroads offer volume discounts for moves of more than one carload that are shipped as a single string of cars from one point to another. The cost of moving several cars in a single shipment is proportionally less than the cost of each car moved singly. The multiple-car movement of, say, 10 cars can be handled by the same effort (empty car drop-off, pickup, intermediate and delivery efforts, and documentation) as a single-car shipment. The only basic difference is the additional weight moved in the larger string of cars. Because of this economy of movement, railroads offer such rates in coal, grain, fertilizer, chemical, and many other basic commodity moves.

Incentive Rates

The term **incentive rates** generally applies to a rate designed to induce the shipper to load existing movements and equipment more fully. These special rates usually apply only to weight or units loaded over and above the normally shipped quantities. For example, suppose an appliance manufacturer typically ships in carload quantities that only fill a car to 80 percent of its actual capacity. That is, the carload rate minimum is, say, 40,000 pounds and the car is typically loaded to 48,000 pounds, but 60,000 pounds of appliances can physically be loaded into it. The carrier would prefer to have this car more fully loaded. In an incentive rate situation, the carrier would offer a rate lower than the carload rate that would only apply to the weight above the 48,000-pound norm in this example. It is more economical for the carrier to move more weight in existing moves, than to move additional moves. By inducing the shipper to load each car more fully, fewer cars and moves would be required over the course of a year, and the same actual volume would be shipped.

Unit-train Rates

Unit trains are integrated movements between an origin and destination. These trains usually avoid terminals and so do not require intermediate switching or handling of individual cars. In many situations, the shipper or consignee provides the car investment. The railroad experiences economies through high car utilization and reduced costs of movement, because the rates are low in comparison to individual moves. Again, it is more economical to handle larger single movements than many individual moves. Rail carriers many times use this type of rate for TOFC or COFC movements.

Per-car and Per-truckload Rates

Per-car or per-truckload rates are single-charge rates for specific origin-destination moves regardless of shipment commodity or weight. These rates also apply to container movements where the carriers' costs of movement are dominated by moving the equipment and not specifically by the weight of the shipment.

Any-quantity Rates

Any-quantity (AQ) rates provide no discount or rate break for larger movements. That is, there exists an LTL rate but no TL rate for large shipments. The AQ rates apply to any weight in a shipment. They are usually found with large, bulky commodities such as boats, suitcases, and cages where no economies are realized by the carrier for larger shipments.

Density Rates

Some rates are published according to density and shipment weight, rather than by commodity or weight alone. These rates are common in air container shipments. Here a rate is published as, say, $10 per hundredweight for shipments up to 10 ponds per cubic foot, $9 per hundredweight for 11 to 20 pounds per cubic foot, and $8 per hundredweight for 21 pounds per cubic foot and up. These are applied when the carrier assesses rates on the basis of weight but does not experience fewer costs for lighter-weight containers. Here, in fact, the carrier would experience a loss of revenue (due to a low weight) when moving a given amount of cubic footage.

A recent motor-carrier variation on the density rate is the linear foot rule. The generalized linear foot rule applies on shipments that weigh more than 2,000 pounds and occupy more than one linear foot of space for every 350 pounds. If the shipment meets these criteria, the carrier reconstructs the weight of the shipment based on 350 pounds times the number of linear feet of space occupied and eliminates any discounts the shipper has negotiated. Air carriers use a similar approach to handling low-density articles. All rates except household goods (HHG) are exempt.

Area, Location, or Route Rates

A number of rates relate to area, location, or route. These special rates deserve consideration and discussion.

Local Rates

Local rates apply to any rate between two points served by the same carrier. These rates include full-cost factors for pickup, documentation, rating, billing, and delivery.

Joint Rates

Joint rates are single rates published from a point on one carrier's route to another carrier's destination. They are usually lower in total charges than the combination of the local rates because of through movement economy.

Proportional Rates

Many carriers experience a competitive disadvantage when their line is part of a through line that competes with another, more direct line. If a combination of local rates were charged, the through movement cost might still be higher than the charges over the direct route. In this situation, the carrier might publish a proportional rate (lower than the regular local rate) that applies only to through moves to certain destination points beyond its line.

Differential Rates

The term *differential rates* generally applies to a rate published by a carrier that faces a service time disadvantage compared to a faster carrier or mode. For example, water carriers often publish differential rates that are below those of railroads. In this way, the lower rate somewhat overcomes the longer transit time disadvantage inherent to the water carriers. The term *differential* is also found in situations where an extra charge is assessed for high-cost services such as branch lines. With all the recent mergers, this type of rate making has fallen from widespread use.

Per-mile Rates

Some rail, motor, and air carriers provide rates that are based purely upon the mileage involved. This is a common practice in bulk chemical truck moves and air charter movements. Railroads also use these rates in special train movements (high, wide, and heavy). Similarly, special moves, such as the movement of circus trains and some postal moves, are based on these rates.

Terminal-to-Terminal Rates

Terminal-to-terminal rates, often referred to as *ramp-to-ramp rates,* apply between terminal points on the carrier's lines. These rates require the shipper and consignee to perform the traditional pickup and delivery functions. Many air freight rates and some piggyback rates are found in this form.

Blanket or Group Rates

These rates apply to or from whole regions, rather than points. For example, all shippers of lumber from an area in Oregon and Washington are generally treated as having the same origin. Destinations eastward are grouped into zones in which all receivers in an entire state pay the same rates regardless of the special origin point in the Pacific Northwest. Blanket systems are found in food shipments from California and Florida. These rates equalize shippers and consignees because plant location is not a factor in determining the rate charged.

Time/Service Rate Structures

The Staggers Rail Act of 1980 specifically sanctioned rail contract rates, many of which can be classified as time/service rate structures. These rates are generally dependent on the transit time performance of the railroad in a particular service. One such contract provides for a standard rate for a transit time service norm. The shipper pays a higher rate for faster service and a lower rate for longer service. Another contract calls for additional shipper payments to the carrier for the fast return of empty backhaul shipper-leased cars. These rate forms either place incentives and penalties in areas where they tend to create desired results, or they reduce undesirable performance.

Contract Rates

Contract services are commonplace in motor carriage and rail moves, as well as in water and some air moves. These services are governed by contracts negotiated between the shipper and carrier, not by generally published tariffs. Some specific contract service features that are typically found are described here.

One basic contract calls for a reduced rate in exchange for a guarantee of a certain minimum tonnage to be shipped over a specified period. Another contract calls for a reduced rate in exchange for the shipper tendering a certain percentage of all tonnage over to the contracting carrier. In both these instances, a penalty clause requires the shipper to pay up to the regular rate if the minimum tonnage is not shipped.

Another type of rail contract calls for the rate to be higher or lower depending on the specific type of car supplied for loading and shipment, called a **car-supply charge.** The higher rates apply on cars whose contents have not been braced or blocked by the shipper; the higher charge is used to compensate the carrier for a potentially higher level of damage to the contents and ultimately to the higher liability level of the carrier. These are also the same cars that represent higher capital investment or daily per diem expense for the railroads.

A few contracts require the shipper to pay a monthly charge to the railroad that supplies certain special equipment for the shipper's exclusive use. This charge tends to increase the shipper's use of the cars; the shipper no longer views them as free capital goods that can be used for temporary storage or loosely routed and controlled. Here the shipper firm has the incentive to use these cars in a way that benefits the firm and the carrier.

Many different rate and service configurations are found in motor carriage. These contract rates call for such services as scheduled service, special equipment movements, storage service in addition to movement, services beyond the vehicle (such as retail store shelf stocking by the driver), small package pickup and movement, bulk commodity movement, or hauling a shipper-owned trailer.

A great degree of flexibility surrounds the contracts of both rail and motor carriage. Carriers and shippers are relatively free to specifically tailor contract services to particular movements, equipment, and time-related services. The key in any contract service is to identify the service and cost factors important to each party and to construct inducements and penalties for each.

Deferred Delivery

The deferred delivery rate is common in air transportation. In general, the carrier charges a lower rate in return for the privilege of deferring the arrival time of the shipment. For example, air express companies offer a discount of 25 percent or more for second- or third-day delivery, as opposed to the standard next-day delivery. The deferred delivery rate gives the carrier operating flexibility to achieve greater vehicle utilization and lower costs.

Other Rate Structures

Several other rate forms serve particular cost or service purposes.

Corporate Volume Rates

A new rate form called the corporate volume rate came into existence in 1981. It is a discounted rate for each LTL shipment that is related to the total volume of LTL shipments that a firm ships via a specific carrier from all shipping points. Generally, the more volume a shipper tenders to a particular carrier, the greater the discount.

The corporate volume rate is not widely used today, but the principle of gaining lower rates for shipping larger volumes via a carrier is the basis of many negotiated rates. The corporate volume concept brings the full market power of the shipper (total dollars spent on moving all inbound and outbound company freight) to bear on negotiations. Also, the practice of placing blocks of freight up for bid, such as all the freight moving into and out of the southeastern United States, uses the corporate volume approach to gain special rates from the accepted bidder.

Discounts

In the trucking industry, a discount is a common pricing practice for LTL shipments moving under class rates. The typical discount ranges from 25 to 50 percent, with some discounts as high as 60 to 65 percent, off the published class rate. The discounts may apply to specific classes of LTL traffic moving between given origins and destinations, or all LTL commodities moving between any origin and destination. For the smaller shipper that does not have the corporate volume to effectively negotiate lower rates, the discount is a viable alternative to achieving reduced rates.

Loading Allowances

A loading (unloading) allowance is a reduced rate or discount granted to the shipper that loads LTL shipments into the carrier's vehicle. Motor carriers are required to load and unload LTL shipments and their LTL rate structures include this loading and unloading cost. The shipper/receiver that performs this function is incurring a cost that would have been incurred by the carrier. Thus, the carrier agrees to reimburse the shipper for this expense in the form of a lower rate.

Aggregate Tender Rates

A reduced rate or discount is given to the shipper that tenders two or more class-rated shipments to the carrier at one time. Usually, the aggregate shipment weight must equal 5,000 pounds or some other minimum established by the carrier. By tendering two or more shipments to the carrier at one time, the shipper reduces the carrier's pickup costs by reducing the number of times the carrier goes to the shipper's facility to pick up freight. With the aggregate tender rate, the shipper reaps part of the cost reduction benefit that the carrier realizes from the multiple shipment pickup.

FAK Rates

FAK rates, also known as *all-commodity rates,* are rates expressed in cents per hundredweight or total cost per shipment. The specific commodity being shipped is not important, which means the carrier is basing the rate on the cost of service, not the value of service. The FAK rate is most valuable to shippers that ship mixed commodity shipments to a single destination, such as a grocery distributor shipping a wide variety of canned goods, paper products, and so on, to a local warehouse.

Released Rates

Released rates are lower than the regular full-value rates that provide for up to total value carrier compensation in the event of loss or damage. Instead, released rates only provide for carrier obligation up to certain limited dollar amounts per pound shipped. They traditionally are found in air freight, household goods, and a small number of motor- and rail-hauled commodities. The 1980 regulatory changes allowed flexible use of this rate form in most types of service and commodities.

Empty-haul Rates

An empty-haul rate is a charge for moving empty rail or motor equipment that is owned or leased by or assigned to a particular shipper. The existence of this type of rate tends to induce the shipper to fully load all miles of the equipment movements.

Two-way or Three-way Rates

The terms *two-way rates* and *three-way rates* apply to rates that are constructed and charged when backhaul or triangular moves can be made. The intent here is to tie a fronthaul move with what would have been another firm's backhaul move. In this way, neither firm incurs the penalty for empty backhauls. Some bulk chemical motor carriers offer these rates. They reduce total transportation charges for the shippers, and the carrier's equipment is more fully utilized than it would be otherwise.

Spot-Market Rates

"Spot-market" rates can be used to facilitate the movement of the equipment or product. For example, if an excess supply of empty trailers begins to accumulate in a geographic region, spot-market rates can be quoted to allow the trailers to begin moving full back to their origin. These are similar to those types of prices used in the buying and selling of commodities on the "spot market." This is also common in air freight.

Menu Pricing

Carriers are beginning to provide more and more value-added services for shippers, such as loading/unloading, packaging, and sorting, along with traditional transportation services. "Menu" pricing allows the shipper to pick and choose those services the carrier should perform, and the shipper is charged accordingly. This concept is the same used in "a la carte" menus in restaurants. This type of pricing also requires the carrier to understand and know its costs of providing these services.

The regulatory standards legislated in 1980 and 1995, as well as altered administrative STB policies, have created a realm of flexibility and creativity in rate forms. Carriers are relatively free to develop rate systems to benefit them and shippers in ways that were neither common in the past, nor even existent. Any pricing system, however, should induce the buyer to buy in ways beneficial to the seller, be simple to understand and apply, and maximize the financial resources of the seller.

Many carriers have published their rate forms and structure in computerized form. These are then made available to shippers and receivers via phone links or disks that are mailed to them. Computerization of the former rate structures in the 1960s and 1970s was frustrated by the multitude of product classifications, locations, and footnote items that applied to specific movements. Tariffs of today are often greatly simplified, and computers are capable of greater memories and computational processes.

Pricing in Transportation Management

For many years, carriers relied on tariffs as their "price" lists for their services. Under traditional economic regulation, little incentive was present for carriers to differentiate themselves through either service enhancements or pricing strategies. Today, however, both of these differentiating tactics are critical to carriers in all modes, regardless of market structure. Unfortunately, however, many carriers still rely on the "tariff" mentality when setting prices as a competitive weapon. This way of thinking normally uses cost as a base and pays little or no attention to price as a part of the marketing mix. Many carriers will admit that they know their costs but do not know how to price.

This section will present a basic discussion on pricing for transportation management. Its intent is to introduce some common pricing strategies and techniques that are commonly used in such industries as retailing. Further in-depth discussions on these topics can be found in any basic marketing textbook.[20]

Factors Affecting Pricing Decisions

Many carrier pricing decisions are based on some reaction to a stimulus from the business environment. In transportation, the environment comprises many constituencies, four of which include customers (market), government, other channel members, and competition.

The discussion presented on value-of-service pricing in this chapter focused on the role of the market to determine prices. Obviously, a profit maximizing-oriented carrier will not set a price in the long run that prohibits the movement of freight or passengers. The carrier's price will be set at that level, which maximizes its return. This, however, is dependent on what the market perceives to be a reasonable price and/or what the market is forced to pay (in monopolistic situations). The concept of price elasticity also plays an important role in the market's impact on carrier prices. For example, business travelers might be willing to absorb increases in air fares in exchange for the convenience of short-notice reservations while leisure travelers might not. Customers then have a formidable impact on carrier prices.

Transportation had been economically regulated by the federal government for well over 100 years because of potentially monopolistic abuses. Part of this regulation dealt with carrier prices in the forms of how they are constructed and how they are quoted. Most of the economic transportation regulation falls under the responsibility of the STB. After the deregulatory efforts of the late 1970s, the 1980s, and the

1990s, however, the Justice Department also entered the carrier pricing arena to monitor for antitrust violations. In some respects, these government agencies help mitigate the imperfections in the marketplace to control carrier pricing. As such, governmental controls affect how carriers price their services. (Government impact on carrier pricing is discussed at length in Chapter 2, "Transportation Regulation and Public Policy.")

In the case of carriers, other **channel members** can include other carriers in the same mode and in different modes. For example, interline movements between different carriers that involve revenue splits will certainly impact how each carrier prices its services. If one carrier decides to raise its price, the other carrier either has to reduce its price or risk losing business, given that the market has a high price elasticity. This can be especially true in airline movements using two different trunkline carriers or using trunkline/commuter combinations. Another case involves interline agreements between railroads for track usage. Because there is no single transcontinental railroad, it is quite likely that a shipment will have to use the tracks of more than one railroad. If costs increase, rail carriers might have to either increase their prices to customers, reduce their operating margins, or risk losing tonnage on that move.

Finally, competitors will impact carrier-pricing strategies. History has shown that even in transportation oligopolies (such as airlines and LTL trucking firms), price leaders that offer discounts to customers will find that competitors will match those discounts, even at the risk of reducing industry profits. This could be a symptom of the continual pressure on carrier customers to reduce transportation costs in their firms. Across-the-board price increases are also usually matched by all the major competitors in a particular mode. However, occasions do occur when competitors do not follow price leader actions. An attempt by one airline to simplify its pricing structure by reducing the number of special fares was not matched by its competitors. Because of this, that airline was forced to abandon its original simplification strategy and return to normal airline pricing tactics.

Carriers then must respond to changes and directions from their operating environment. Sometimes these changes might not favor the carriers, such as when government regulations force carriers to make a change that reduces efficiency. However, these environmental forces do exert pressure on carrier-pricing strategies and price levels.

Major Pricing Decisions

Every firm involved in delivering either a product or service faces major pricing decisions. These decisions can range from the very simple to the extremely complex. However, pricing decisions can be grouped into three categories. First, a carrier faces a decision when setting prices on a new service. For example, Federal Express had no precedent when setting prices on its first overnight delivery service. Such a decision could be difficult because it is based on little knowledge concerning the elasticity of the market to prices and the actual cost of providing the service. Also, if the price is set high enough to generate substantial profits, competitors will be enticed to enter the market at perhaps a lower price. On the other hand, if the price is set too low, although significant traffic might be generated, the carrier will not be maximizing its profits.

Second, a carrier must make decisions to modify prices over time. Market changes, operating changes, and service changes will require prices to be changed. An important aspect of this decision is how and when to announce the changes to the market. For example, a major price increase by a carrier after announcing record company profits might get negative reactions in the market. In a manufacturing or retailing environment, price increases are sometimes announced in advance so customers can increase purchases to help offset the higher price. However, in transportation, services cannot be inventoried, so prior notification of a price increase does not accomplish the same objective, yet prior notification does allow for customers to seek alternative sources of supply.

Finally, carriers will make decisions initiating and responding to price changes. The concept of a "price leader" within an industry is not new. If you are the price leader, then you initiate the change; if not, then you respond to the change. In transportation, where many of the markets are oligopolistic, price changes downward can be dangerous because of their potential to decrease industry revenues. Upward price changes can make a carrier the sole high-price service provider if competition does not follow the change, so how this decision is made can have a substantial impact on market share and profits.

Although there might be other types of price decisions, these represent the major ones that carriers will make. These can be considered strategic decisions because of the importance they have on carrier market position within the industry. For example, People's Express once offered a low-price, no-frills airline service and did not expect other carriers to match the low fares. However, some of the major trunk lines actually offered fares below People's, even though it meant a loss. With a high debt and stiff competition, People's eventually went out of business. Pricing then is a major marketing decision for every carrier.

STOP OFF

Bohman on Pricing
A Closer Look at the January 1, 1997 Rate Increases

In line with recent practice, most LTL motor carriers implemented general rate increases (GRIs) on January 1. Three major carriers—Viking Freight, Pitt-Ohio Express, and Preston Trucking—jumped the gun and came in with GRIs several weeks earlier.

For many carriers, this year's magic percentage figure was 5.9, but variations abounded. Here are the percentage increases taken by some of the larger carriers:

Yellow Freight System	5.2% on average
Consolidated Freightways	Approximately 5.65%
Roadway Express	Approximately 5.7%
ABF Freight System	About 5.5% overall
Overnite Transportation	Approximately 5.9%
American Freightways	5.9%

In press releases announcing their increases, most carriers were careful to note that these were not across-the-board increases. Instead, they prefaced their percentage figures with words such as "averaging," "approximately," and "about." Others elaborated even further by stating that "additional adjustments will be made in certain longer-haul and over-balanced lanes." And some said they would "adjust rates for specific lanes and certain connecting-line routes."

Although there was speculation last fall that carriers might roll in their fuel surcharges as part of their first-of-the-year general rate increases, practically all elected to retain separate surcharges, many of which now are on a sliding scale, adjusted weekly.

A number of carriers weren't reluctant to raise their minimum charge floors, with some, such as ABF Freight System, raising its for the first time in five years. Most are raising those floors by about $2 per shipment.

Some carriers also took the opportunity to tack on additional charges for certain special services they provide. Yellow, for example, added a $10 "transaction charge" to adjust freight to proper weight and classification where the shipper's error boosts freight charges by $20 or more, and Consolidated Freightways announced a new $6 per-shipment fee for handling hazardous materials.

Source: Ray Bohman, *Logistics Management,* January 1997, p. 31.

Establishing the Pricing Objective

Pricing objectives for a carrier should reflect overall company objectives and reflect, in many ways, how the carrier will compete in its markets. Pricing objectives might also change for a particular service offering as it progresses through its product life cycle. Carriers with multiple markets might also establish various pricing objectives for these markets. For example, passenger airlines have separate pricing objectives for first-class and coach markets as well as for business and leisure travelers. This section will present several different pricing objectives that can be utilized in the transportation industry.

Especially in the case of ailing passenger airlines, survival-based pricing is aimed at increasing cash flow through the use of low prices. With this price level, the carrier attempts to increase volume and also encourage the higher utilization of equipment. Because an empty airline seat cannot be inventoried and is lost at take-off, the marginal cost of filling that seat is small. Survival pricing then tries to take advantage of the marginal cost concept. Closely related is a **unit volume pricing** objective. This attempts to utilize a carrier's existing capacity to the fullest, so the price is set to encourage the market to fill that capacity. Multiple pickup allowances in the LTL industry, space-available prices in the freight airline industry, and multiple-car prices in the railroad industry are examples of this type of pricing objective.

Another price objective is called *profit maximization,* which can occur in the short run or in the long run. Carriers using this type of pricing usually are concerned with measures such as return on investment. This type of objective also can utilize what is called a **skimming price.** A skimming price is a high price intended to attract a market that is more concerned with quality, uniqueness, or status and is insensitive to price.[21] For example, although a high-cost move, pricing for the maiden flight of the Concorde was certainly aimed at those who would be willing to pay a high price because of the limited amount of seats. This strategy works if competition can be kept out of a market through high investment costs or firm loyalty.

Many times a skimming price strategy is followed by a **penetration price** strategy. This can lead to a sales-based pricing objective, which can be an effective strategy because (1) a high price can be charged until competition starts to enter; (2) a higher price can help offset initial outlays for advertising and development; (3) a high price portrays a high-quality service; (4) if price changes need to be made, it is more favorable to reduce a price than to raise it; and (5) after market saturation is achieved, a lower price can appeal to a mass market with the objective of increasing sales.[22] A sales-based pricing objective also follows the life cycle approach of using skimming during the introduction and growth stages and penetration during the maturation stage. The recent reintroduction of luxury passenger railroad service might be a good example of this type of strategy. In transportation, this strategy would more likely be successful with passenger movements because of the reliance it places on the price-value relationship.

A market share pricing objective can be used in an industry whose revenues are stagnant or declining. This objective tries to take market share from competitors through the use of lower prices. This strategy is used frequently in passenger airlines and the LTL trucking industries. In some cases, this strategy assumes that competitors' offerings are substitutes and that competitors are not in a position to match the lower prices; if the services were not substitutes, a lower price would not provide a competitive advantage. For example, an airline that lowers its fares for business travelers to gain more of this market but does not offer the same number of departures and arrivals as a competitor might not succeed at gaining any market share.

Finally, a social responsibility pricing objective forgoes sales and profits and puts the welfare of society and customers first.[23] For example, after Hurricane Andrew hit the state of Florida in 1992, many carriers offered to carry such items as food, clothing, and building supplies into the storm-devastated area at greatly reduced prices or for free.

Because carriers in the various transportation industries service multiple markets, it is quite possible for them to employ several pricing objectives at one time. A carrier must be careful when setting an overall company pricing strategy that these multiple pricing objectives are complementary, not conflicting.

Estimating Demand

Probably one of the most difficult tasks associated with pricing is estimating demand. In a perfectly competitive market, unit demand will decrease as price increases. This is reflected in the traditional demand-and-supply curve offered in basic economic theory. However, transportation carriers do not function in perfectly competitive markets. Demand estimation can become very tedious and difficult. However, certain concepts and procedures can be used in this process. One of these is the concept of price elasticity. Price elasticity refers to the change in demand because of a change in price. In an established market for a carrier, this relationship should be well developed to the point where demand implications from a price change should be easy to estimate. We can again use the example of business versus leisure travelers in the airline industry. Business travelers are relatively price inelastic because demand for business travel by air does not fluctuate widely with increases in price. However, leisure travelers are very price elastic and might tend to delay travel or seek travel by an alternative mode if there is an increase in air fares. In a new market, estimations of price elasticity can be made by comparing the new market with a similar existing market.

A direct attitude survey might also be used in determining demand under a new pricing structure. For example, asking customers and/or potential customers how much business they would provide at certain price levels might produce some feel of how sensitive demand is to price. Caution has to be used in this method in how this question is asked because customers will usually tend to favor the lowest price.

Finally, a market test is a possible way to determine potential demand when market testing is feasible. This might involve a carrier introducing a new service at a high price in one area and at a higher price in another area to see how sensitive demand is to price. Important in this method is choosing test market areas that resemble the entire market for which the service is applicable.

Although not a science, demand estimation is a critical part of pricing strategy. Demand estimation results in potential revenue estimation. (Some of the theory behind demand estimation was presented earlier in this chapter under the topic, "Value-of-Service Pricing.") With revenue estimated, costs should next be established.

Estimating Costs

A significant portion of this chapter is devoted to the concepts of costs and cost-of-service pricing, so a detailed explanation of either is not necessary here. However, a decision must be made as to which costs should be included in the total cost analysis. In the example given under value-of-service pricing, the fuel expense and driver wages generated on a backhaul can be considered a fixed cost and, as such, need not be included in the backhaul pricing decision.

Another cost relationship that must be examined is how costs behave at different levels of output or capacity. The existence or nonexistence of scale economies in transportation, for example, will affect how costs behave at different capacity levels. This information can be used to determine such concepts as break-even points. Regardless of the methods used, the cost of providing a service must be calculated to determine the attractiveness of a market for a carrier.

Price Levels and Price Adjustments

With demand and cost estimates generated, it is possible to set the actual price. Many methods for doing this exist, including demand-based methods, cost-based methods, profit-based methods, and competition-based methods. Lengthy discussions of these can be found in any basic marketing-text chapter on pricing.[24] However, a discussion of price adjustments might be warranted because of the federal government regulations over such concepts as rebates.

Discounts are a reduction from a published price that rewards a buyer for doing something that is beneficial for the supplier.[25] In transportation, LTL versus TL prices reflect carrier savings from larger shipments, a portion of which is passed on to the customer in the form of a lower price. This could be called a quantity discount. Airlines use a form of seasonal discounts to encourage vacation passengers to travel during carrier off-peak periods. Cash discounts, relatively new to the transportation industry, reward customers who pay their bills within a stated period of time. A common form of a cash discount is "2/10, net 30," which means that the customer can take a two percent discount if the bill is paid within 10 days, or pay the full amount within 30 days. This helps speed the cash flow for carriers, which is important for their financial stability.

Geographical adjustments are common in the transportation industry. Although not directly used by carriers, geographical adjustments are used by shippers and receivers to compensate for transportation costs in the final price to the customer. One common type of geographical price is FOB origin or FOB destination pricing. In FOB origin pricing, the buyer is responsible for transportation costs; in destination pricing, the shipper is responsible (see Table 11.1).

Uniform-delivered pricing, a form of FOB destination pricing, offers a final price to customers for a product that includes all transportation costs. Related to this is **zone pricing,** in which every customer within a certain zone pays exactly the same price for a product based on average transportation costs within the zone.

When using discounts and allowances in the transportation industry, an important rule to remember is that a discount or allowance passed on to a customer must be the result of a reduction in carrier costs because of an action by the customer. Also, the discount or allowance given to the customer may not exceed the cost savings to the carrier. Violating either of these rules of thumb exposes the carrier to the jurisdiction of the STB (rebates) and the Justice Department (antitrust and rebates).

Most Common Mistakes in Pricing

As previously mentioned, carriers have not had many years of experience in setting and managing prices on a strategic level. However, just like firms in any other industry, they are prone to certain mistakes. The first common mistake is to make pricing too reliant on costs. Although it is important to know the costs of providing a service, many other factors play a role in setting the appropriate price for a market. Competitive factors, customer preferences and values, and government regulations will affect the level at which the price will be most beneficial to the carrier.

TABLE 11.1 The Variety of F.O.B. Pricing Arrangements

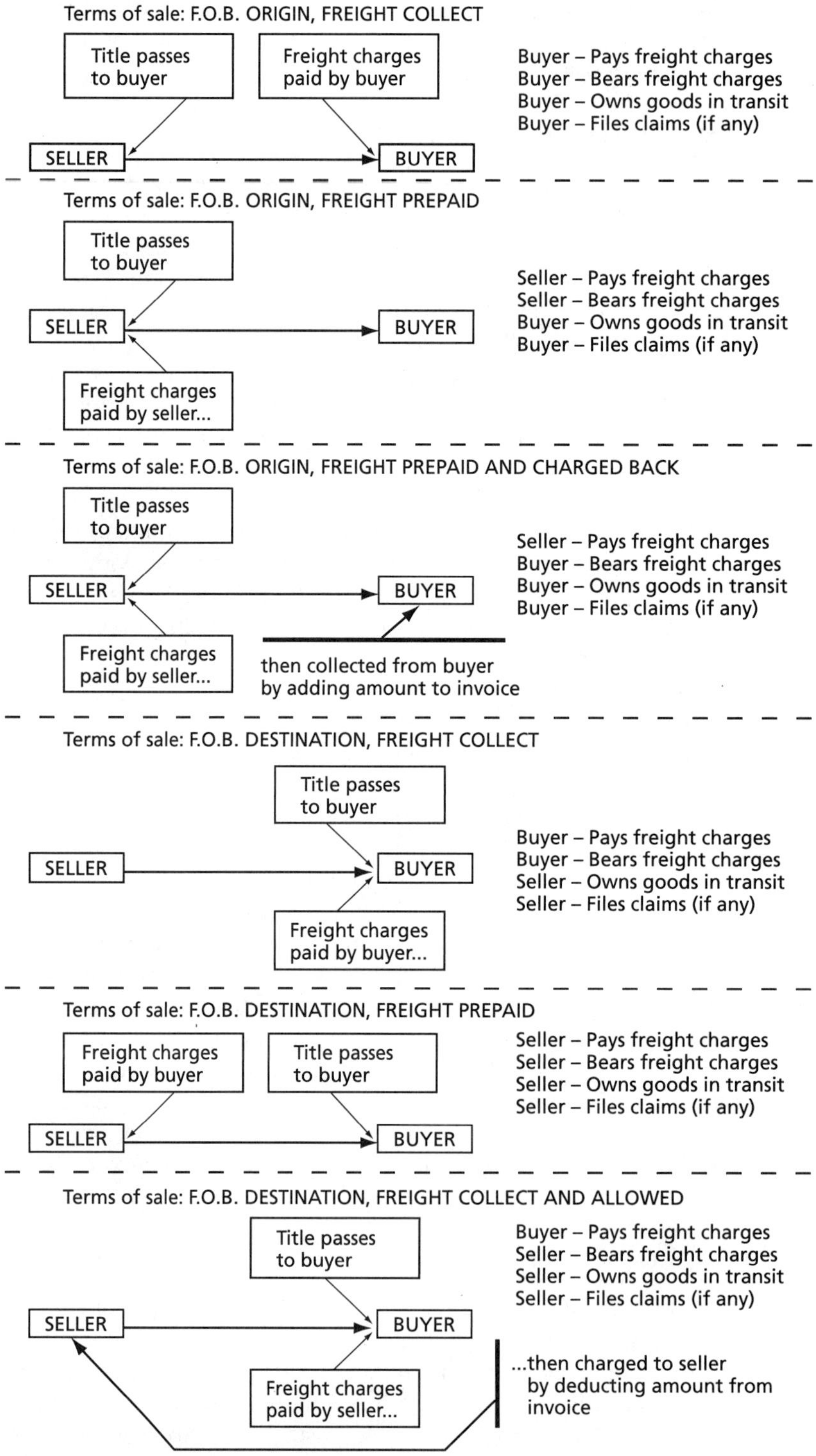

Source: Bruce J. Riggs, "The Traffic Manager in Physical Distribution Management," *Transportation & Distribution Management* (June, 1968), p. 45.

The second common mistake is that prices are not revised frequently enough to capitalize on market changes. Under the previous regulatory environment, it was difficult for carriers to change prices because of the requirement of public notice and the burden of proof on the carrier. However, today's environment has allowed tremendous freedom and the flexibility for carriers to change prices. Unfortunately, for some carriers, the traditional mentality remains and can prevent a carrier from entering a market or, in some cases, creating a new market.

Setting the price independently of the marketing mix is a third common mistake. The **marketing mix,** also known as the "4Ps," consists of product, price, promotion, and place. A carrier's product or output is transportation; its promotion is how it creates demand or advertises itself to customers; price is what it charges for its product or output; place is how it delivers its service to customers. All of these interact within a carrier's organization to provide access to and, it is hoped, success in current and potential markets. Managing one of these areas independently of the others will result in a suboptimization of the carrier's resources and its profits.

Finally, price is sometimes not varied enough for different service offerings and market segments. A "one price for all" mentality does not work in the transportation industry. As previously stated, carriers service multiple markets with differing service/price requirements. Airlines use a concept called "yield management" pricing, a form of value-of-service pricing, which relates price to the availability of capacity and the willingness of passengers to pay, or to address this situation.[26] Charging one price for all services is not going to maximize the profits for the carrier.

Pricing is a complex and challenging process that applies to all business entities. Pricing is also critical to a business's competitive advantage, position within its markets, and overall profitability. It must, however, be managed within the context of the carrier's overall strategic plan, not independently of it.

Summary

- The market structure for a carrier will be related to its cost structure; having a knowledge of this cost structure is necessary for the development of carrier prices.
- Cost-of-service pricing relies on the marginal cost of providing a service.
- Value-of-service pricing relies on the average cost of providing the service or on "what the market will bear."
- Various types of special rates exist that allow carriers and shippers the flexibility to tailor rate structures to meet market needs.
- Pricing in transportation can be a strategic advantage if managed within the context of corporate strategy.
- Setting and managing prices in transportation are affected by actions of government, customers, competition, and other channel members.

Key Terms

average cost pg. 292
car-supply charge 307
channel members 311
charging what the traffic will bear 295
common costs 294
cost-of-service pricing 292
decreasing cost industries 295
differential 299

freight-all-kinds (FAK) rates 309
headhaul 301
heavier loading 305
incentive rates 305
marginal cost 293
marketing mix 317
mileage rate 304
monopolistic competition 290
oligopoly 290
penetration price 313
pure competition 290
skimming price 313
third-degree price discrimination 299
unit-volume pricing 313
value-of-service pricing 295
zone pricing 315

Study Questions

1. Compare and contrast pure competition with monopoly from a pricing perspective. If you were a shipper, which would you prefer? Which would a carrier prefer?

2. Describe an oligopolistic market structure. What alternatives to price competition exist in such markets? Why would these alternatives be important to shippers?

3. What is value-of-service pricing? Is this approach to pricing valid today?

4. What is cost-of-service pricing? What is the relationship between value-of-service pricing and cost-of-service pricing?

5. What is a released value rate and how does its use affect a shipper's transportation costs?

6. What are the major forces that affect carrier pricing strategies?

7. How might pricing strategies differ among carriers in competitive markets, oligopolistic markets, and monopolistic markets?

Notes

1. For a more thorough discussion of contestable market theory, see W. J. Baumol, J. C. Panzar, and R. D. Willig, *Contestable Markets and the Theory of Industry Structure* (New York: Harcourt, Brace, Jovanovich, 1982).

2. Stanley E. Fawcett and Martin T. Farris, "Contestable Markets and Airline Adaptability Under Deregulation," *Transportation Journal,* Vol. 29, No. 1 (Fall 1989), pp. 12–24.

3. Ibid., p. 17.

4. Ibid., p. 14.

5. Ibid.

6. For a more detailed discussion of this conclusion, see Fawcett and Farris, op. cit.

7. Winthrop M. Daniels, *The Price of Transportation Service* (New York: Harper and Brothers, 1942), p. 1.

8. John R. Meyer, et al., *The Economics of Competition in the Transportation Industries* (Cambridge, MA: Harvard University Press, 1959), p. 205.

9. For an excellent analysis of industry pricing behavior, see Meyer, *The Economics of Competition,* pp. 203–211.

10. This section is based on the discussion in J. J. Coyle, "Cost-of-Service Pricing in Transportation," *Quarterly Review of Economics and Business,* Vol. 57 (1964), pp. 69–74.

11. Ibid., p. 27.

12. Harold Hotelling, "The General Welfare in Relation to Problems of Taxation and of Railway and Utility Rates," *Econometrics,* Vol. 6, No. 3 (July 1938), p. 242.

13. R. W. Harbeson, "The Cost Concept and Economic Control," *Harvard Business Review,* Vol. 17 (1939), pp. 257–263.

14. Ibid.

15. George W. Wilson, "Freight Rates and Transportation Costs," *The Business Quarterly* (Summer 1960), pp. 161–162.

16. John J. Coyle, "A Reconsideration of Value of Service Pricing," *Land Economics* (Winter 1964), pp. 193–199.

17. George W. Wilson, *Theory of Transportation Pricing* (Bloomington, IN: Indiana University, 1985), p. 160.

18. For an extended discussion, see Coyle, "A Reconsideration of Value of Service Pricing," pp. 195–198.

19. This example is adapted from Wilson and Smerk, "Rate Theory," pp. 7–10.

20. See, for example, Eric N. Berkowitz, Roger A. Kerin, Steven W. Hartley, and William Rudelius, *Marketing,* 3rd ed. (Homewood, IL: Richard D. Irwin, 1992).

21. Joel R. Evans and Barry Berman, *Marketing* (New York: Macmillan, 1982), p. 532.

22. Ibid.

23. Berkowitz, et. al., op. cit., p. 321.

24. Berkowitz, et. al., op. cit., pp. 339–352.

25. Ibid., p. 354.

26. For a discussion of yield management pricing, see Sheryl Kimes, "The Basics of Yield Management," *The Cornell H.R.A. Quarterly* (November 1989), pp. 14–19; Walter J. Relihan III, "The Yield Management Approach to Hotel Room Pricing," *The Cornell H.R.A. Quarterly* (May 1989), pp. 40–45; Peter P. Belobaba, "Application of a Probabilistic Decision Model to Airline Seat Inventory Control," *Operations Research,* Vol. 37, No. 2 (March–April 1989).

Suggested Readings

Baker, Jace A. "Emergent Pricing Structures in LTL Transportation," *Journal of Business Logistics,* Vol. 12, No. 1, 1991, pp. 169–190.

Barrett, Colin. "Wiz Your Way Through Freight Rates," *Distribution,* January 1991, pp. 71–73.

Benson, Gregory E. "Principled Negotiation: A Four-Step Process," *NAPM Insights,* September 1992, pp. 6–7.

Bohman, Ray, "What You Need to Know About LTL Rates," *Traffic Management* (May 1992), pp. 37–41.

Borts, George H. "Long-Term Rail Contracts—Handle with Care," *Transportation Journal,* Vol. 25, No. 3, Spring 1986, pp. 4–11.

Calderwood, James A. "Collective Ratemaking," *Transportation and Distribution* (July 1991), p. 36.

Cavinato, Joseph L. "Tips for Negotiating Rates," *Distribution,* February 1991, pp. 66–68.

Cooper, Robin, and Robert S. Kaplan. "Profit Priorities from Activity-Based Costing," *Harvard Business Review,* May–June 1992, pp. 130–135.

Coyle, John J., Edward J. Bardi, and C. John Langley. *The Management of Business Logistics,* 4th ed. St. Paul, MN: West Publishing Company, 1988.

Cunningham, William, and Grant Davis, "Collective Ratemaking in Trucking: An Interminable Issue?" *Transportation Practitioners Journal,* Vol. 54, No. 4, Summer 1987, pp. 361–377.

Curley, Jim. "How to Use Air Without Going Broke: The Deferred Air Option," *Inbound Logistics,* January 1987, pp. 22–28.

Harmatuck, Donald J. "Motor Cost Function Comparisons," *Transportation Journal,* Vol. 31, No. 4, Summer 1992, pp. 31–46.

Harper, Donald V. *Transportation in America: Users, Carriers, Government.* (Englewood Cliffs, NJ: Prentice-Hall, 1978), Chs. 7 and 8.

Hoover, Jr., H. "Pricing Behavior of Deregulated Motor Carriers," *Transportation Journal,* Vol. 25, Fall 1985, pp. 55–62.

Kahn, Alfred E. *The Economics of Regulation: Principles and Institutions,* Vol. 1 (New York: John Wiley and Sons, 1970), Part 3.

Keller, Robert E. "Preparing for Negotiations: The Sales Side," *NAPM Insights,* September 1992, pp. 16–17.

Kortge, G. Dean, and Okonkwo, Patrick A. "Perceived Value Approach to Pricing," *Industrial Marketing Management,* Vol. 22, 1993, pp. 133–140.

Krick, Pat. "BN's New Move-Specific Price Measurement System Offers More Reliable Data," *Modern Railroads* (September 1988), p. 10.

Locklin, D. Philip. *Economics of Transportation,* 7th ed. Homewood, IL: Richard D. Irwin, 1972, Ch. 7.

Locklin, D. Philip. *Economics of Transportation,* 7th ed. (Homewood, IL Richard D. Irwin, 1972), Chs. 3 and 8.

Long, Brain. "Training Your Negotiating Team for Success," *NAPM Insights,* September 1992, pp.14–15.

Nelson, James R. ed. *Criteria for Transport Pricing.* Cambridge, MD: Cornell Maritime Press, 1973.

Pegrum, Dudley F. *Transportation: Economics and Public Policy* (Homewood, IL: Richard D. Irwin, 1973), Chs. 7 and 8.

Pegrum, Dudley F. *Transportation: Economics and Public Policy* (Homewood, IL: Richard D. Irwin, 1973), Chs. 9 and 10.

Rakowski, James P., R. Neil Southern, and Judith L. Jarrell. "The Changing Nature of the U.S. Trucking Industry: Implications for Logistics Managers," *Journal of Business Logistics,* Vol. 14, No. 1, 1993, pp. 111–130.

Schultz, John D. "Yield Management Rate Strategies May Boost Truckers' Ailing Fortunes," *Traffic World,* October 7, 1991, pp. 33–34.

Simon, Hermann. "Pricing Opportunities—and How to Exploit Them," *Sloan Management Review,* Winter 1992, pp. 55–65.

CASE

CASE 11.1

Startruck, Inc.

Startruck, Inc., is a small parcel trucking firm specializing in overnight deliveries of small parcels and documents. The introduction of facsimile (fax) machine technology has significantly impacted the volume of overnight document business that Startruck handles. Because of this shrinking market, Startruck decided to focus its efforts on building its small parcel business. However, Startruck's president, John T. Work, knew that to leapfrog the competition in the industry would require a significant technological breakthrough. His chief scientist, Mr. Shock, was able to provide that breakthrough in the form of a transporter device that could instantly transport freight and small parcels by disassembling their molecules, transporting them through space, and reassembling them at destination. This technology would eliminate the need for transportation vehicles and could provide immediate transportation for freight and small parcels. It was, in effect, a fax-type technology for packages. In fact, shippers and receivers would only require an investment in what could be called a "transporter bay" to use this technology.

The key to this technology was imbedded in a special computer chip that was invented by Mr. Shock. Both he and Mr. Work realized that it would not be long before competitors were able to copy this chip and expand on it. In fact, a major competitor, Hang-On Shipping, was working on technology that could also transport people through space. Work and Shock realized that they too would soon have that technology but felt it important to quickly boost market share in small packages before getting into a new line of business.

Scotty, Startruck's Chief of Marketing, was asked by Mr. Work to devise a marketing plan to introduce this new service and technology. Because of the reduced investment in transportation equipment needed by Startruck and the significant improvement in speed of transportation, Scotty felt that the pricing strategy used by Startruck for this new service would be critical to its success in the marketplace.

Case Questions

1. What should Startruck's pricing objective be for this new service?

2. How will Startruck estimate demand for this service? Where will the market(s) be?

3. Which costs will be incurred by Startruck in offering this service?

4. Should any type of price adjustments be included in Startruck's pricing strategy for this service?

Appendix 11-A

Cost Concepts

Accounting Cost

The simplest concept or measure of cost is what has sometimes been labeled accounting cost, or even more simply as money cost. These are the so-called bookkeeping costs of a company and include all cash outlays of the firm. This particular concept of cost is not difficult to grasp. The most difficult problem with accounting costs is their allocation among the various products or services of a company.

If the owner of a trucking company, for example, were interested in determining the cost associated with moving a particular truckload of traffic, we could quickly arrive at all the cost of fuel, oil, and the driver's wages associated with the movement. It might also be possible to determine how much wear and tear would occur on the vehicle during the trip. However, we must also consider how much of the president's salary, the terminal expenses, and the advertising expense should be included in the price. These costs should be included in part, but how much should be included is frequently a perplexing question. Our computation becomes even more complex when a small shipment is combined with other small shipments in one truckload. Some allocation would then be necessary for the fuel expense and the driver's wages.

Economic Cost

A second concept of cost is economic cost, which is different from accounting cost. The economic definition of cost is associated with the alternative cost doctrine or the opportunity cost doctrine. Costs of production, as defined by economists, are futuristic and are the values of the alternative products that could have been produced with the resources used in production. Therefore, the costs of resources are their values in their best alternative uses. To secure the service or use of resources, such as labor or capital, a company must pay an amount at least equal to what the resource could obtain in its best alternative use. Implicit in this definition of cost is the principle that if a resource has no alternative use, then its cost in economic terms is zero.

The futuristic aspect of economic costs has special relevance in transportation because, once investment has been made, one should not be concerned with recovering what is sometimes referred to as **sunk costs.**[1] Resources in some industries are so durable that they can be regarded as virtually everlasting. Therefore, if no replacement is anticipated, and there is no alternative use, then the use of the resource is costless in an economic sense. This is of special importance in the railroad industry.

Railroads have long been regarded as having durable and therefore costless resources. That is, some of the resources of railroads, such as concrete ties, some signaling equipment, and even some rolling stock, are so durable and so highly specialized that they have no alternative production or use potential. So the use of such resources, apart from maintenance, is costless in an economic sense. Consequently, in a competitive pricing situation, such resources could be excluded from the calculation of fixed costs. Also, such specialized resources can be eliminated in comparing cost structures.[2]

Although the economic logic of the above argument on the use of durable, specialized resources is impeccable, it is frequently disregarded by pricing analysts and regulators. In a sense, the elimination of such costs from pricing calculations defies common sense. From the money or accounting cost perspective, these costs usually should be included.

The conclusion that must be drawn is that economic costs differ from money or accounting costs. Money costs are by their very nature a measure of past costs. This does not mean that money costs do not have any relevance in the economic sense. Past costs do perform a very important function because they provide a guide to future cost estimates. However, complete reliance should not be put upon historical costs for pricing in the transportation industry.

Social Cost

A third category of costs—social cost—might also be considered. Some businesses might not concern themselves with social costs unless required to do so by law. These costs take into consideration the cost to society of some particular operation and, in fact, might outweigh money cost. For example, what is the cost to society when a company releases its waste materials into a stream? Today many regulations and controls are administered by various regulatory agencies to protect society from such costs. These agencies make the business organizations responsible for social costs. (For example, strip-mining operators are customarily required to backfill and plant.) In spite of such controls, however, there are still instances when chemicals or other hazardous materials are discharged or leak out and society has to bear the cost of the cleanup operations as well as the health hazards.

We are not trying to castigate business organizations or suggest that all investment decisions result in negative social costs because, in fact, there can be social benefits from business investments. However, to ensure that our discussion is complete, social costs must be considered.

Analysis of Cost Structures

There are two general approaches to an analysis of a particular cost structure. Under one approach, costs can be classified as those that are directly assignable to particular segments of the business (such as products or services) and those that are incurred for the business as a whole. These two types of cost are generally designated as separable and common costs, respectively. Usually, common costs are further classified as joint common costs or nonjoint common costs. **Separable costs** refer to a situation in which products are necessarily produced in fixed proportions. The classic example is that of hides and beef. Stated simply, the production or generation of one product or service necessarily entails the production or generation of another product. In terms of transportation, joint costs occur when two or more services are *necessarily* produced together in fixed proportions. One of these services is said to be a by-product of the other. The most obvious illustration is that of the backhaul situation; the return capacity is the by-product of the loaded trip to the destination.[3]

It is a generally accepted fact that large transportation companies, especially railroads, have a significant element of common costs because they have roadbed, terminals, freight yards, and so on, the cost of which is common to all traffic. However, the only evidence of true jointness appears to be the backhaul.[4] Nonjoint common costs are those that do not require the production of fixed proportions of products or services. Nonjoint common costs are more customary in transportation. For example, on a typical train journey on which hundreds of items are carried, the expenses of the crew and fuel are common costs incurred for all the items hauled (see Figure A.1).

Recently, a new technique for allocating costs directly to activity centers has been implemented in both the carrier and shipper communities. **Activity-Based Costing (ABC)** identifies costs specifically generated by performing a service or producing a product. ABC does not allocate direct and indirect costs based on volume alone; it determines which activities are responsible for these costs and burdens these activities with their respective portion of overhead costs. One application for ABC today by both carriers and shippers is the calculation of customer profitability.[5]

Under the other basic approach to analyzing a particular cost structure, costs are divided into those that do not fluctuate with the volume of business in the short term and those that do. The time period here is assumed to be that in which the plant or physical capacity of the business remains unchanged, or the "short run." The two types of costs described are usually referred to as fixed and variable costs, respectively.

In the first approach, the distinction between common and separable costs is made with the idea that costs can be traced to specific accounts or products of the business. In the second approach, the distinction between fixed and variable is made to study variations in business as a whole over a period of time and the effect of

FIGURE A.1 Directly Assignable Cost Approach

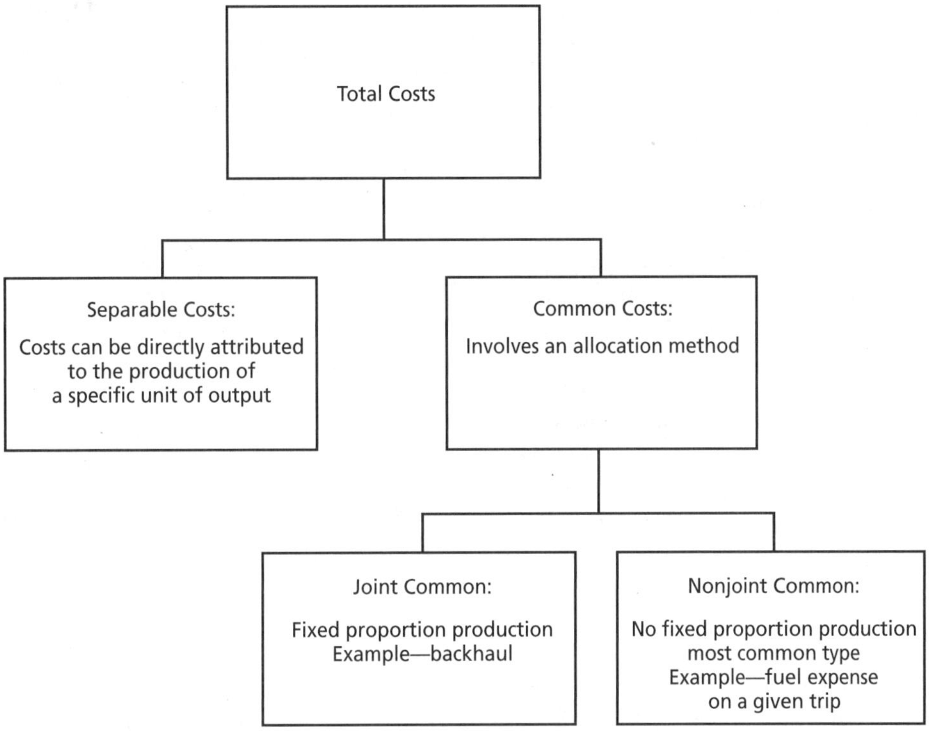

these variations upon expenses. In other words, with fixed and variable costs we are interested in the fact that some costs increase and decrease with expansion and contraction of business volume, whereas other costs do not vary as business levels change.

Because of the two different approaches to studying costs, it is possible that a certain cost might be classified as common on one hand and variable on the other, or common under one approach and fixed under the other, and so on for all the possible combinations. Therefore, the only costs directly traceable or separable are the variable costs, which are also separable. For example, fuel expense is generally regarded as a variable cost, but it would be a common cost with a vehicle loaded with less-than-truckload (LTL) traffic.

The second approach of cost analysis—namely, fixed and variable costs—is important and should be discussed further. As indicated previously, **fixed costs** are constant regardless of the enterprise's volume of business. These fixed costs can include maintenance expenses on equipment or right-of-way (track) caused by time and weather (not use), property taxes, certain management salaries, interest on bonds, and payments on long-term leases.

A business has a commitment to its fixed costs even with a zero level of output. Fixed costs might, in certain instances, be delayed, or to use the more common term, deferred. The railroads frequently delay or defer costs. For example, maintenance of railroad right-of-way should probably be done each spring or summer, particularly in the northern states. Freezing and thawing, along with spring rains, wash away gravel and stone (ballast) and may do other damage. Although this maintenance can be postponed, just as, for example, house painting might be postponed for a year or two, sooner or later it has to be done if the business wants to continue to operate. There is a fixed commitment or necessity that requires the corrective action and associated expense.[6] The important point is that the fixed expenses occur independently of the volume of business experienced by the organization.

Variable costs, on the other hand, are closely related to the volume of business. In other words, firms do not experience any variable costs unless they are operating. The fuel expense for trains or tractor-trailers is an excellent example of a variable cost. If a locomotive or vehicle does not make a run or trip, there is no fuel cost. Additional examples of variable costs include the wear and tear on tractor-trailers and the cost for tires and engine parts.

Another related point is that railroads and pipelines, like many public utility companies, are frequently labeled as decreasing cost industries. The relevance of this phenomenon to pricing was discussed earlier in this chapter, but it also deserves some additional explanation now. (Economies of scale was discussed in Chapter 3, "Motor Carriers.")

Railroads and pipelines have a high proportion of fixed costs in their cost structures. There is some debate about the percentage, but the estimates range from 20 to 50 percent. Contrast this with motor carriers whose average is 10 percent. As railroads produce more units, the proportion of fixed costs on each item will be lower. More importantly, this decline will occur over a long range of output because of the large-scale capacity of most railroads.

An example of the above situation is useful here. Let us assume that a particular railroad incurs $5 million of fixed costs on an annual basis. In addition, let us assume that the railroad is analyzing costs for pricing purposes between Bellefonte, Pennsylvania, and Chicago. In its examination of cost, the railroad determines that the variable cost on a carload is $250 between Bellefonte and Chicago.

Although it may be unrealistic, let us assume that the railroad only moves 10 cars per year. The cost would be as follows:

Fixed cost	$5,000,000	
Variable cost	2,500	(10 cars × $250)
Total cost	$5,002,500	
Average cost per car	500,250	

If it moves 1,000 cars, the cost would be

Fixed cost	$5,000,000	
Variable cost	250,000	(1,000 cars × $250)
Total cost	$5,250,000	
Average cost per car	5,250	

If it moves 100,000 cars, the cost would be

Fixed cost	$5,000,000	
Variable cost	25,000,000	(100,000 × $250)
Total cost	$30,000,000	
Average cost per car	300	

The relationship is easy to see. If we continued adding cars to our example, the average cost would continue to decline. Theoretically, average

FIGURE A.2 Average Cost and Output

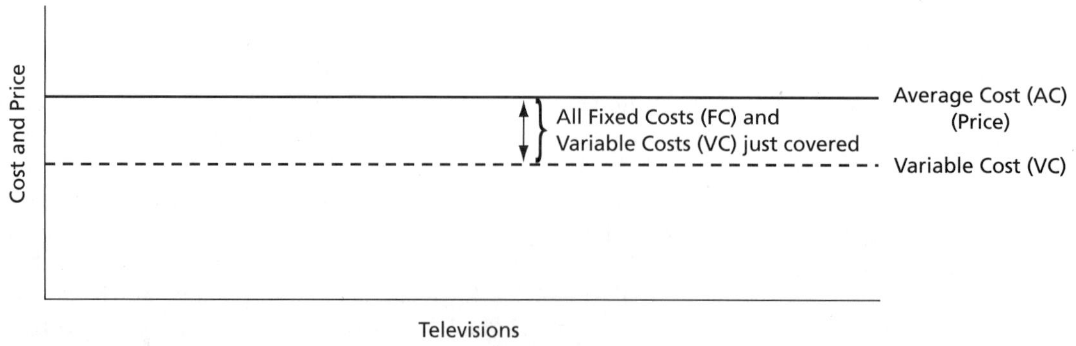

cost would have to level out and eventually increase due to decreasing returns, but the important point is that the high proportion of fixed costs and the large capacity cause the average cost to decline over a great range of output (see Figure A.2). There would be a point, however, at which additional cars would require another investment in fixed cost, thus shifting the average cost curve.

The significance of the declining cost phenomenon to a railroad is that volume is a very important determinant of cost and efficiency. Furthermore, pricing the service to attract traffic is a critical factor in determining profitability, particularly where there is competition from alternate modes of transportation.

Another cost concept that is of major importance in our analysis is marginal cost because of its key role in understanding pricing decisions. Marginal cost can be defined as the change in total cost resulting from a one-unit change in output, or as additions to aggregate cost for given additions to output. This latter definition probably makes more sense in transportation because of the difficulties of defining the output unit. Marginal cost also can be defined as the change in total variable cost resulting from a one-unit change in output, because a change in output changes total variable cost and total cost by exactly the same amounts. Marginal cost is sometimes referred to as *incremental cost,* especially in the transportation industry.

There is one other type of cost that should be mentioned because of its importance in price decision—**out-of-pocket costs.** Out-of-pocket costs are usually defined as those costs that are directly assignable to a particular unit of traffic and that would not have been incurred if the service or movement had not been performed. Within the framework of this definition, out-of-pocket costs could also be either separable costs or variable costs. Although the above definition states that out-of-pocket costs are specifically assignable to a certain movement, which implies separable costs, they can definitely be considered as variable costs because they would not have occurred if a particular shipment had not been moved. The definition also encompasses marginal cost because marginal cost can be associated with a unit increase in cost.

The vagueness of the out-of-pocket costs definition has left the door open to the types of cost included as a part of their calculation. The difficulty lies in the fact that from a narrow viewpoint, out-of-pocket costs could be classified as only those expenses incurred because a particular unit was moved. For example, the loading and unloading expense attributable to moving a particular shipment, plus the extra fuel and wear and tear on equipment (relatively low for railroads) could be classified as out-of-pocket costs. On the other hand, a broad approach might be used in defining out-of-pocket costs in regard to a particular shipment, thereby including a share of all of the common variable expenses attributable to a particular movement between two points.

The confusion surrounding the concept of out-of-pocket costs would seem to justify elimination of its use. However, the continued use of the term would be acceptable if its definition was made synonymous with the definition of one of the particular economic costs that its definition implies—marginal costs—because this term is important in price and output decisions and evaluations of pricing economics. Typically, out-of-pocket costs are most important to the firm's accounting system because they are payments that must be made almost immediately as an operating expense. The out-of-pocket cost concept is useful in that it is used as a way to estimate the amount of liquid funds that a transportation firm must keep on hand for daily operations.[7]

Figure A.3 gives a good breakdown of the methods of cost analysis. It illustrates the close relationship between the three cost concepts of variable, marginal, and out-of-pocket costs.

Although attention is devoted to cost structure in the separate chapters dealing with each of the modes of transportation, some consideration will be given in this section to an analysis of modal cost structures. Such discussion is useful and necessary background to the analysis of the approaches to pricing.

Rail Cost Structure

One of the characteristics of railroads, as previously noted, is the level of fixed costs present in their cost structures. It is a commonly accepted fact that a relatively large proportion of railway costs are fixed in the short run. At one time it was believed that more than half of rail costs were

FIGURE A.3 Short-Run Cost/Volume Output Approach

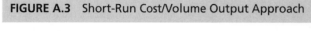

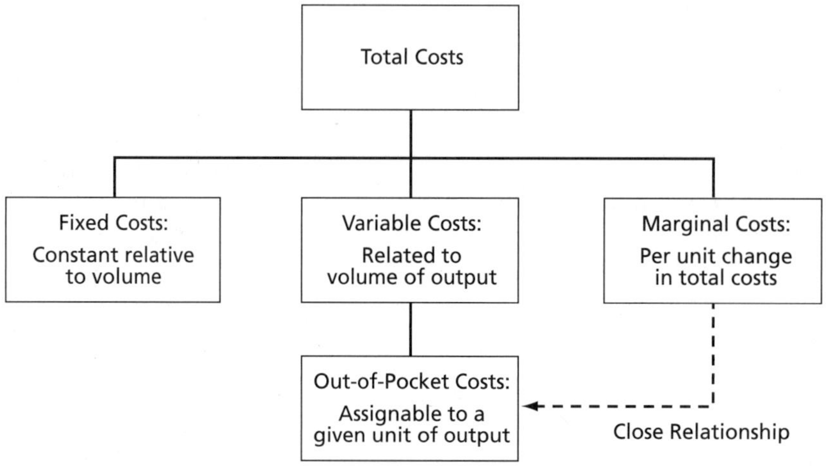

fixed, and some individuals estimated that these costs ran as high as 70 percent of total cost. The exact proportion of fixed expenses is subject to some debate; however, it is generally accepted that fixed expenses constitute a significant portion of railroad total costs, ranging from 20 to 50 percent. The high proportion of fixed costs can be explained by railroad investment (in such things as track, terminals, and freight yards), which is much larger than the investment of motor carriers, for example. For this reason, railroads are generally regarded as having increasing returns, or decreasing costs per unit of output.[8]

As has been indicated, a significant amount of railroad costs also include common expenses because replacement costs of a stretch of track are shared by all traffic moving over it. This is also true with respect to other items of cost, including officers' salaries. Some of these common costs are also fixed costs, while others are variable costs (refer to Chapter 4, "Railroads").

Motor-Carrier Cost Structure

The motor-carrier industry is exemplified by a high proportion of variable costs. It has been estimated that variable costs in the motor-carrier industry are 90 percent or more of total costs.[9] This high degree of variability is explained to a large extent by the fact that motor carriers do not have to provide their own right-of-way because roads are publicly provided. It is true that motor carriers do pay fuel taxes and other taxes to defray the cost of providing the highways, but these expenses are variable because they depend on the use made of the highway.

The economic concept of the "long run" is a shorter period in the motor-carrier industry than in the railroad industry. The operating unit, the truck, has a shorter life span than the rail operating unit. It is smaller and therefore more adaptable to fluctuating business conditions. The capital investment required is smaller too and fleets can be expanded and contracted easier.

The motor-carrier situation varies greatly with respect to common costs. Companies that specialize in LTL traffic will have a significant proportion of common cost, whereas contract carriers with only two or three customers who move only truckload (TL) traffic will have a high proportion of separable costs. Other companies that carry a mixture of TL and LTL traffic will be in the middle of the two extremes (refer to Chapter 3).

Other Carriers' Cost Structures

Information on water carrier cost structure is less prevalent because many companies are privately owned or exempt from economic regulation. The cost structure is probably very similar to that of motor carriers because their right-of-way is also publicly provided. There are some differences, however, because the investment per unit of output is greater, and a large volume of traffic is necessary to realize mass movement potentialities.[10] (See Chapter 5, "Domestic Water Carriers.")

The pipeline companies have a cost structure similar to that of railroads. The fact that they have to provide their own right-of-way and the fact that their terminal facilities are very specialized mean that they have a large element of fixed and usually sunk costs. They also usually have significant common costs because they move a variety of oil products through the pipeline (see Chapter 7, "Pipelines").

The airline companies have a cost structure similar to that of water carriers and motor carriers because of the public provision of their right-of-way. Also, terminal facilities are publicly provided to a large extent, and the airlines pay landing fees based upon use. Airlines tend to have a significant element of common cost because of small freight shipments and the individual nature of passenger movements; for example, airlines very seldom sell a planeload to one customer (see Chapter 6, "Air Carriers").

The differences in the cost structures of the modes of transportation and their differing service characteristics make pricing of their services very important. If motor-carrier service is better than rail service, motor-carrier prices can exceed rail prices. The cost structure of the motor carrier may dictate that their prices can exceed rail prices. The cost structure of the motor carrier may dictate that their prices have to be higher than the rail prices. The critical question is what is the relationship between demand and cost (supply) in such cases.

Appendix 11-A Terms

activity-based costing (ABC) pg. 322
fixed costs 323
future costs 321
out-of-pocket costs 325
separable costs 322
sunk costs 321
variable cost 324

Notes

1. William J. Baumol, et al., "The Role of Cost in the Minimum Pricing of Railroad Services," *Journal of Business,* Vol. 35 (October 1962), pp. 5–6. This article succinctly presents the essence of sunk versus prospective costs.
2. A. M. Milne, *The Economics of Inland Transport* (London: Pitman and Sons, 1955), p. 146.
3. Robert C. Lieb, *Transportation, the Domestic System,* 2nd ed. (Reston, VA: Reston Publishing), p. 138.
4. This problem was argued in the economic journals at an early date by two notable economists. See F. W. Taussig, "Railway Rates and Joint Cost Once More," *Quarterly Journal of Economics,* Vol. 27 (May 1913), p. 378; F. W. Taussig and A. C. Pigou, "Railway Rates and Joint Costs," *Quarterly Journal of Economics,* Vol. 27 (August 1913), pp. 535 and 687; A. C. Pigou, *The Economics of Welfare,* 4th ed. (London: Macmillan, 1950), Chs. 17 and 18. An excellent discussion of this debate is contained in D. P. Locklin, "A Review of the Literature on Railway Rate Theory," *Quarterly Journal of Economics,* Vol. 47 (1933), p. 174.
5. For a more thorough discussion of this topic, see Terrance L. Pohlen and Bernard J. LaLonde, "Implementing Activity-Based Costing (ABC) in Logistics," *Journal of Business Logistics,* Vol. 15, No. 2 (1994), pp. 1–23.
6. For an excellent discussion, see George W. Wilson and George W. Smerk, "Rate theory" in *Physical Distribution Management* (Bloomington, IN: Indiana University, 1963), pp. 2–4.
7. Wayne K. Talley, *Introduction to Transportation,* 1st ed. (Cincinnati, OH: Southwestern, 1983), p. 27.
8. George W. Wilson, *Essays on Some Unsettled Questions in the Economics of Transportation* (Bloomington, IN: Foundation for Economic and Business Studies, 1962), pp. 32–33.
9. Interstate Commerce Commission, Bureau of Accounts and Cost Finding, *Explanation of Rail Cost Finding Principles and Procedures* (Washington, D.C.: Government Printing Office, 1948), p. 88.
10. Meyer, et al., *The Economics of Competition in the Transportation Industries,* pp. 112–113.

Appendix 11-B

RATEMAKING IN PRACTICE

A complete understanding of carrier cost economics and behavior is a necessary prerequisite to effective management of carrier pricing. This appendix presents an overview of the general forms of pricing that are employed by carriers of all types. The form of each rate is discussed and analyzed along with the primary inducements for the carrier and its users.

The overall carrier pricing function revolves around costing, rates, and tariffs. Carriers employ costing personnel who are responsible for determining the overall cost and productivity of the carrier operations as well as the specific routes, customer services, or equipment needs. The work of cost analysts should serve as a pricing input to rate personnel who are responsible for establishing specific rates and general rate levels for the carrier. Tariffs are the actual publications in which most rates are printed. Some firms print their own tariffs, which are often referred to as *individual tariffs,* or they use a rate bureau that is common to many carriers to establish and publish rates. These tariffs are referred to as *bureau tariffs.*

General Rates

These are the class, exception, and commodity rate structures in the United States. The **class rate** system provides a rate for any commodity between any two points. It is constructed from uniform distance and product systems. **Exception rates** are designed so that carriers in particular regions can depart from the product scale system for any one of many possible reasons, which will be discussed later. **Commodity rates,** on the other hand, are employed for specific origin-destination shipping patterns of specific commodities. Each one of these three systems has a particular purpose.

It would be simple if all transportation services were sold on the basis of ton-miles; that is, we would have to pay X dollars to move one ton, one mile. But, in fact, transportation services are not sold in ton-miles; they are sold for moving a specific commodity between two specific points —for example, moving glass from Toledo to New York City. This fact gives some insight into the enormous magnitude of the transportation pricing problem. There are more than 33,000 important shipping and receiving points in the United States. Theoretically, the number of different possible routes would be all the permutations of the 33,000 points. The result is in the trillions of trillions. In addition, it is necessary to consider the thousands and thousands of different commodities and products that might be shipped over any of these routes. There are also the different modes to consider and different companies within each mode. It also may be necessary to consider the specific supply-demand situation for each commodity over each route.

Class Rates

Because it is obviously impossible to quote trillions and trillions of rates, the transportation industry has taken three major steps toward simplification. Figure B.1 summarizes this class rate simplification.

The first step consolidated the 33,000 shipping points into groups by dividing the nation into geographic squares. The most important shipping point for all other shipping points (based on tonnage) in each square serves as the **rate base point** for all other shipping points in the square. These grouped points are found in a groupings tariff. This reduces the potential number of distance variations for rate-making purposes. The distance from each base point to each other base point was determined by the railroads and placed on file with the Interstate Commerce Commission (ICC, now the STB) and published in the National Rate Basis Tariff. The distance between any two

FIGURE B.1 Class Rate Simplification

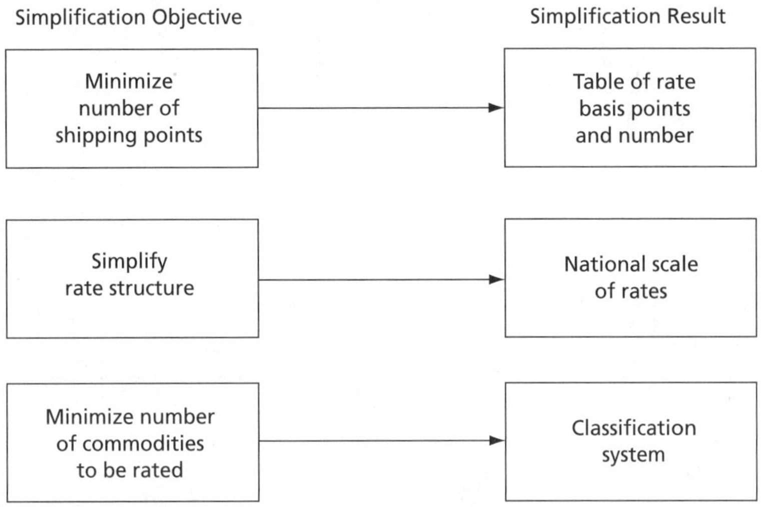

TABLE B.1 Groupings Tariff Example[a]

State	Point	Apply Rates From or To
Michigan	Climax	Battle Creek
	Coleman	Clare
	Comstock	Kalamazoo
	Columbiaville	Flint
	Crossvillage	Cheyboygan
Ohio	Clay Center	Toledo
	Clifford	Chillicothe
	Clement	Dayton
	Cleves	Cincinnati
	Climax	Marion

[a]Alphabetical listing of points by states from and to which rates apply.
Source: Tariff ICC CMB 575-C.

base points is referred to as the **rate basis number.** The first simplifying step reduced the number of possible origins and destinations for pricing purposes. (See Tables B.1 and B.2 for examples of grouping and rate basis number tariffs.)

The second step deals with the thousands and thousands of different items that might be shipped between any two base points. The railroads have established a national scale of rates that has been placed on file with the ICC (now the STB) and gives a rate in dollars per hundredweight (cwt), which is dollars per cwt for each rate basis number. (The motor carriers established a similar rate structure.) The actual rate to move a commodity considered the commodity's transportation characteristic by means of the classification, the third simplification step.

The third step simply groups together products with similar transportation characteristics so that one rating can be applied to the whole

TABLE B.2 Rate Basis Numbers Tariff Example

And Points Taking the Following Basing Points	Between Points Taking the Following Basing Points			
	Chilicothe OH	Cincinnati OH	Columbus OH	Dayton OH
	Rate Basis Numbers			
Cheboygan, MI	550	570	490	510
Clare, MI	400	420	360	380
Flint, MI	275	300	227	214

Source: Tariff ICC CMB 575-C.

group. Now one rate is quoted for the group into which a number of different commodities has been placed, thereby reducing the number of rates quoted by the carriers. Items that are placed into class 125 will be charged 125 percent of the first-class rate found in the uniform scales of rates. This percentage number is called a *class rating,* and it is the group into which the commodity is placed for rate-making purposes. Table B.3 is a classification example from the National Motor Freight Classification.

Classification Factors

The factors that are used to determine the rating of a specific commodity are the product characteristics that impact the carrier's costs. In particular, the ICC has ruled and the STB has maintained that four factors are to be considered: product density, stowability, handling, and liability. Although no specific formulas are used to assign a commodity to a particular class, the four factors are considered in conjunction by a carrier classification committee. An individual carrier can establish a commodity classification that differs from the national classification; this individual carrier classification is termed an exception and takes precedence over the national classification.

Product density directly impacts the use of the carrier's vehicle and the cost per hundredweight. The higher the product density, the greater the amount of weight that can be hauled and the lower the cost per hundredweight. Conversely, the lower the product density, the lower the amount of weight that can be hauled and the higher the cost per hundredweight hauled.

As shown in Table B.4, only 6,000 lbs. of a product that has a density of two lbs./ft^3 can be loaded into the trailer, which means the cost per hundredweight shipped is $6.67. However, 48,000 lbs. of a product with a density of 16 lbs./ft^3 can be hauled at a cost of $0.83/cwt. Therefore, the higher the product density, the lower the carrier's cost per weight unit and the lower the classification rating assigned to the product.

Stowability and handling reflect the cost the carrier will incur in securing and handling the product in the vehicle. Such product characteristics as excessive weight, length, and height result in higher stowage costs for the carrier and a corresponding higher classification rating. Likewise, products that require manual handling or special handling equipment increase the carrier's costs and are given a higher rating.

The final classification factor, **liability,** considers the value of the product. When a product is damaged in transit, the common carrier is liable for the value of the product. Because higher valued products pose a greater liability risk (potential cost), higher valued products are classified higher than lower valued products. In addition, products that are more susceptible to damage or are likely to damage other freight increase the potential liability cost and are placed into a higher classification rating.

TABLE B.3 National Motor Freight Classification

Item	Articles	Classes LTL	TL	MW
	PLASTIC MATERIALS, OTHER THAN EXPANDED, GROUP: subject to item 156100			
156300	Sheet or Plate, NOI. Self-supporting (rigid), see Note, item 156302, other than in rolls or coils, in boxes, crates or Packages 248, 384, 930, 1029, 2187, 2207 or 2310			
Sub 1	Exceeding 9 feet, 6 inches in two dimensions or 20 feet in one dimension	85	45	30
Sub 2	Not exceeding 9 feet, 6 inches in more than one dimension nor 20 feet in one dimension	60	35	30
156500	PLASTIC OR RUBBER ARTICLES, OTHER THAN EXPANDED, GROUP: Articles consist of Plastic or Rubber Articles, other than foam, cellular, expanded or sponge articles, see Item 110, Sec. 15 and Note, item 156502, as described in items subject to this grouping.			
156600	Articles, NOI, in barrels, boxes or crates, see Note, item 156602, also in Packages 870, 1078, 1170, 1241, 1273, 1409, 1456, 2195, 2212, 2213 or 2230:			
Sub 1	LTL, having a density of, subject to Item 170:			
Sub 2	Less than one pound per cubic foot, see Note, item 156608	400		
Sub 3	One pound per cubic foot, but less than two pounds, see Note, item 156608	300		
Sub 4	Two pounds per cubic foot, but less than four pounds, see Note, item 156608	250		
Sub 5	Four pounds per cubic foot, but less than five pounds, see Note, item 156608	150		
Sub 6	Six pounds per cubic foot, but less than 12 pounds, see Note, item 156608	100		
Sub 7	12 pounds per cubic foot, but less than 15 pounds, see Note, item 156608	85		
Sub 8	15 pounds or greater per cubic foot	70		
Sub 9	TL		100	10
			70	16
			60	21
			45	30
155000	Personal effects, other than household effects or furnishings, of commissioned or enlisted personnel of the U.S. Army, Air Force, Navy, or Marine Corps, or deceased veterans, moving on government bills of lading, see Note, item 155024, in bags, traveling bags, boxes, or in army trunk lockers or navy cruise boxes or foot lockers securely locked or sealed:			
Sub 1	Each article in value in accordance with the following, see Note, item 155022:			
Sub 2	Released value not exceeding 10 cents per pounds	100	70	16
Sub 3	Released to value exceeding 10 cents per pounds, but not exceeding 20 cents per pounds	125	77½	16
Sub 4	Released to value exceeding 20 cents per pounds, but not exceeding 50 cents per pound	150	85	16
Sub 5	Released to value exceeding 50 cents per pounds, but not exceeding $2.00 per pound	200	110	16
Sub 6	Released to value exceeding $2.00 per pound, but not exceeding $5.00 per pound	300	150	16

Source: National Motor Freight Classification 100-H.

In Table B.3, the stowability and handling factors are evidenced in the classification of item 156300. Plastic sheets or plates that exceed nine feet, six inches (Sub 1) have a higher rating than the same product that does not exceed nine feet, six inches (Sub 2). The density factor is embodied in the classification item 156600, subs. 1–8; the higher the density, the lower the rating. Finally, product liability is a primary factor in the classification of item 155000, personal effects of military personnel; the higher the declared value of the shipment, the higher the rating.

Determining a Class Rate

The procedure for determining a class rate for moving a specific commodity between two points is outlined in Figure B.2. The first step is to determine the rate base points for the specific

TABLE B.4 Product Density and Carrier Cost Per Hundredweight (cwt) Hauled

	Product Density		
	16 lbs./ft³	10 lbs./ft³	2 lbs./ft³
Shipment weight (lbs.)[1]	48,000	30,000	6,000
Carrier cost[2]	$400.00	$400.00	$400.00
Cost/cwt[3]	$0.83	$1.33	$6.67

[1]Shipment weight = product density × 3,000 ft³ assumed capacity of 48-ft. trailer

[2]Carrier cost assumed for a given distance to be the same for each shipment weight

[3]Carrier cost/shipment weight/100

FIGURE B.2 Procedure for Determining a Class Rate

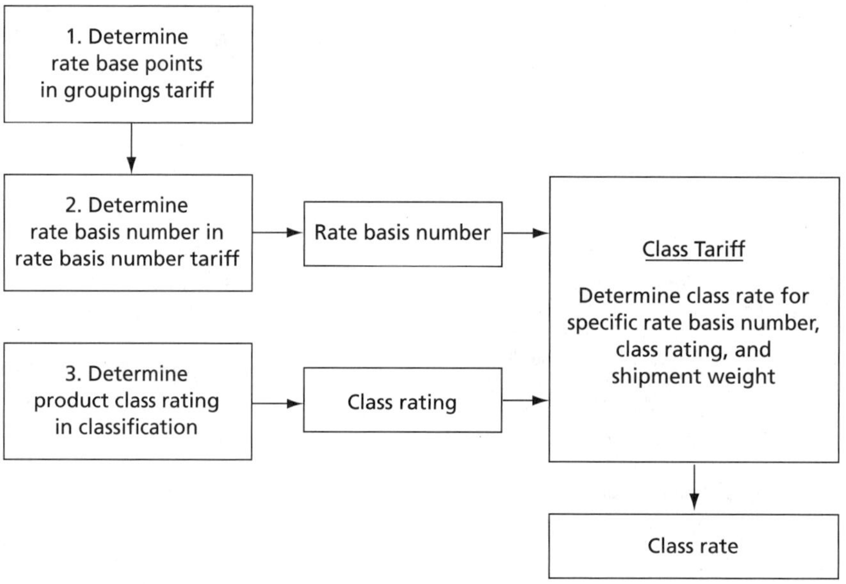

origin and destination from the groupings tariff. Next, from the rate basis number tariff, determine the rate basis number for the relevant rate basis points. The class rating for the particular commodity being shipped is found in the classification. Finally, the rate is found in the class rate tariff for the appropriate rate basis number and class rating. The shipping charge for moving a product between a specific origin and desintation is determined by multiplying the class rate, which is in cents per hundredweight, by the total shipment weight in hundredweight.

As an example, we will determine the total shipping charges for moving 11,000 lb. of plastic sheets, exceeding 9 ft. 6 in., from Crossvillage, Michigan, to Clifford, Ohio. From the groupings tariff (Table B.1), we find that the rate basis point for Crossvillage, Michigan, is Cheboygan, Michigan, and that for Clifford, Ohio, it is Chillicothe, Ohio. Next, the rate basis numbers tariff (Table B.2) indicates that the rate basis number for rate basis points Cheboygan, Michigan, and Chillicothe, Ohio, is 550. From the classification (Table B.3), we find the class rating for plastic sheets

Table B.5 Example of Commodity Rate

Item	Commodity	From	To	Rate	Minimum Weight (Lbs.)
2315	Rubber (reclaimed, dispersed, liquid, or paste)	Akron, OH Barberton, OH Ravenna, OH Cleveland, OH[1]	Warren, MI	726 518 496	2,000 5,000 10,000

(item 156300, sub 1) is 85. Consulting the class tariff (Table B.5) for a rate basis number of 550 and a class rating of 85, we find the class rate is 846 cents/cwt for the weight group M10M (minimum of 10,000 lb.)

The computation of total shipping charges is as follows:

$$\text{Shipment weight in cwt} = 11{,}000/100 \text{ cwt}$$
$$\text{Shipping charges at class rate} = \$8.46/\text{cwt} \times 110 \text{ cwt} = \$9.30$$

The term *tariff* is commonly used to mean almost any publication put out by a carrier or publishing agency that concerns itself with the pricing of services performed by the carrier. All the information needed to determine the cost of a move is in one or more tariffs.

Exception Rates

An exception rate is a modification (change in rating, minimum weight, density groups, etc.) to the national classification instituted by an individual carrier. Exception ratings are published when the transportation characteristics of an item in a particular area differ from those of the same article in other areas. For example, large-volume movements or intensive competition in one area may require the publication of a lower exception rating; in this case, the exception rating applies, rather than the classification rating. The same procedures described above apply to determining the exception rate, except now the exception rating (class) is used instead of the classification rating. There does not have to be an exception rate for every class rate.

Commodity Rates

A commodity rate can be constructed on a variety of bases, but the most common is a specific rate published on a specific commodity or group of related commodities between specific points and generally via specific routes in specific directions. Commodity rates are complete in themselves and are not part of the classification system. If the commodity being shipped is not specifically stated, or if the origin-destination is not specifically spelled out in the commodity rate, then the commodity rate for the particular movement is not applicable. When the commodity rate is published, it takes precedence over the class rate or exception rate on the same article between the specific points. A sample is shown in Table B.5. The commodity rate in the table applies only to reclaimed, dispersed, liquid, or paste rubber. In addition, the commodity is directional-specific and applies from Akron, Barberton, Ravenna, and Cleveland, Ohio, to Warren, Michigan. This commodity rate is not applicable from Warren to Akron, for example.

This type of rate is offered for those commodities that are moved regularly in large quantities. Such a pricing system, however, completely undermines the attempts to simplify transportation pricing through the class-rate structure. It has caused transportation pricing to revert to the publication of a multiplicity of rates and adds to the complexity of the pricing system.

Appendix 11-B Terms

class rate pg. 328
commodity rate 328
exception rate 328
liability 330
rate base point 328
rate basis number 329
stowability and handling 330

Appendix 11-C

LTL and TL Costing Models

Introduction

As mentioned in this chapter, understanding costs for costing purposes is critical to a carrier's ability to price in order to maximize profits. Costing and pricing can be extremely complex exercises, depending on the amount and complexity of inputs. However, if we look at LTL and TL operations, we might find that defining their activities for costing purposes can be relatively simple. The purpose of this appendix is to offer basic and simplistic costing models for LTL and TL that can be used to get a feel for the costs associated with a particular move. Obviously, these are not complex models and would need to be adjusted for actual costing purposes. The authors would like to give special thanks to the late Dr. Pete Patton, Professor of Transportation and Logistics at the University of Tennessee, for his pioneering efforts on these costing models.

Operational Activities

If we look at LTL and TL operations, we might think that they are significantly different in how they operate. Actually, they are very similar. The major difference between the two is in the dock rehandling that is associated with the LTL operations, not the TL. However, to move a shipment, both operations provide a pickup service, a line-haul service, and a delivery service. We can use these three activities, along with dock rehandling for LTL, to begin to break out the appropriate costs associated with a move.

Cost/Service Elements

Within each operational activity, we need to identify those cost/service elements that will actually be responsible for shipment costs. These cost/service elements can be defined as time, distance, and support. The time it takes a carrier to pick up, cross-dock, line-haul, and deliver a shipment will impact its fixed costs, such as depreciation and interest, because these costs are allocated and determined by units of time. The distance a carrier has to move a shipment during these operational activities will affect its variable costs, such as fuel and wages. Support costs, such as equipment insurance and maintenance, are considered semifixed and semivariable because they will exist if no activity takes place but will increase as activity increases. Finally, shipment billing can be considered a fixed cost because normally the cost to generate a freight bill is not related to shipment size or distance.

Having identified four operational activities (pickup, cross-dock, line-haul, and delivery) and three cost/service elements (time, distance, and support), it is possible to develop a costing methodology that will allow us to approximate the costs a carrier could incur for moving a shipment.

TL Costing

This section will present a simplified TL costing model that can be used to approximate the costs of moving a shipment between two points. This model can be used for calculating headhaul costs but does not include an adjustment for a possible empty return trip. However, as will be seen, headhaul costs could be adjusted to compensate for variable costs of an empty backhaul. The following scenario is used.

Shipment and Equipment Characteristics

The shipment consists of 400 cartons at 90 pounds each with each carton measuring three cubic feet. Carriers' trailers have a weight capacity of 40,000 pounds and 2,880 cubic feet. The shipment weighs 36,000 pounds (90 percent of weight capacity) and occupies 1,200 cubic feet (almost 50 percent of trailer cubic capacity).

Equipment Cost Data

Equipment Purchase Price

1. Line-haul tractors = $32,000

2. Trailers = $413,000

Depreciation

1. Tractors = five-year straight line

2. Trailers = eight-year straight line

Interest

1. Tractors = 10 percent APR for five years

2. Trailers = 10 percent APR for eight years

Fuel

1. $1.00 per gallon for diesel

2. Line-haul tractors = 4.5 miles per gallon

Labor Cost

1. Line-haul drivers = $.30 per mile

2. PUD operation drivers = $22 per hour

Miscellaneous

1. Insurance cost = $.03 per mile

2. Maintenance cost = $.15 per mile

3. Billing cost = $1.95 per freight bill

4. Tractors and trailers are available for use 365 days, 24 hours per day

5. Administrative/overhead cost = 10 percent of total cost of move

Route and Time of Move

The shipment originates on June 1, 1993, from Pennsylvania State University (located 35 miles from the carrier's dispatch/maintenance facility). A line-haul tractor and trailer are dispatched from the terminal at 0730 EST and arrive at the shipper's dock at 0830 EST. The shipment is loaded from 0830 EST to 1200 EST. Driver and tractor remain at Penn State during loading to visit the famous Nittany Lion statue. Driver and vehicle return to the carrier's terminal at 1300 EST to pick up paperwork.

Total time for pickup = 5.5 hours
Total distance for pickup = 70 miles

The vehicle and the driver depart from the terminal at 1300 EST on the same day for Dallas, Texas. The driver operates from 1300 EST to 2300 EST and travels 450 miles. The driver rests from 3200 EST to 0700 EST (on June 2) in Knoxville, Tennessee, and then operates another eight hours (0700 EST to 1500 EST) and 375 miles. The driver rests again from 1500 EST to 2300 EST in Memphis, Tennessee. The driver concludes the trip by traveling 450 miles from 2300 EST to 0900 EST (June 3) to the consignee in Dallas, George Bush's new home.

Total time for line-haul = 44 hours or 1.83 days
Total distance for line-haul = 1,275 miles

The trailer is unloaded from 0900 EST to 1200 EST with the driver and tractor remaining at the home to tour the museum dedicated to George Bush's college baseball days. The driver and vehicle then go to the carrier's Dallas terminal, located 45 miles from Bush's home, arriving at 1300 EST to wait for further dispatch instructions.

Total time for delivery = four hours
Total distance for delivery = 45 miles

Cost Analysis

Using the equipment cost data and the distance traveled and time elapsed for the shipment, we can calculate an approximate cost for this move. This analysis can be seen in Table C.1. In a real costing situation, certain changes might need to be made to the cost data included in this example. Tractor fuel economy, for example, might need to be increased or maintenance cost per mile might need to be decreased. The cost analyst would need to determine the appropriate levels for each cost element, depending on the type of equipment and nature of the move.

Pickup

As can be seen in Table C.1, the pickup operation generated seven types of costs. *Depreciation expense* per hour is calculated by *equipment cost/years depreciation/365/24.* This formula gives the hourly cost for depreciation for both the tractor and the trailer. *Interest expense* per hour can be calculated using the appropriate annuity compound factor (ACF) for each piece of equipment. The ACF can be found in tables in any introductory finance text. This formula is *annual interest = amount borrowed/ACF for the length of the loan, annual percentage rate;*

TABLE C.1 TL Costing Example

I.	**Pickup**				
	1. Depreciation:	tractor	5.5 hrs. @ $.73/hr. =	$4.02	
		trailer	5.5 hrs. @ $.186/hr. =	$1.02	
	2. Interest:	tractor	5.5 hrs. @ $.60/hr. =	$3.30	
		trailer	5.5 hrs. @ $.13/hr. =	$0.72	
	3. Fuel		70 mi. @ $.22/mi. =	$15.40	
	4. Labor		5.5 hrs. @ $22/hr. =	$121.00	
	5. Maintenance		70 mi. @ $.15/mi. =	$10.50	
	6. Insurance		70 mi. @ $.03/mi. =	$2.10	
	7. Billing			$1.95	
			TOTAL PICKUP COST		**$160.01**
II.	**Line-haul**				
	1. Depreciation:	tractor	44 hrs. @ $.73/hr. =	$32.12	
		trailer	44 hrs. @ $.186/hr. =	$8.18	
	2. Interest:	tractor	44 hrs. @ $.60/hr. =	$26.40	
		trailer	44 hrs. @ $.13 hr. =	$5.72	
	3. Fuel		1,275 mi. @ $.22/mi. =	$280.50	
	4. Labor		1,275 mi. @ $.30/mi. =	$382.50	
	5. Maintenance		1,275 mi. @ $.15/mi. =	$191.25	
	6. Insurance		1,275 mi. @ $.03/mi. =	$38.25	
			TOTAL LINE-HAUL COST		**$964.92**
III.	**Delivery**				
	1. Depreciation:	tractor	four hrs. @ $.73/hr. =	$2.92	
		trailer	four hrs. @ $.186/hr. =	$0.74	
	2. Interest:	tractor	four hrs. @ $.60/hr. =	$2.40	
		trailer	four hrs. @ $.13/hr. =	$0.52	
	3. Fuel		45 mi. @ $.22/mi. =	$9.90	
	4. Labor		four hrs. @ $22/hr. =	$88.00	
	5. Maintenance		45 mi. @ $.15/mi. =	$6.75	
	6. Insurance	45 mi. @ $.03/mi. =		$1.35	
			TOTAL DELIVERY COST		**$112.58**
IV.	**Total Cost**				
	1. Pickup, line-haul, delivery			$1237.51	
	2. Administrative/overhead (10%)			$123.75	
			TOTAL TL COST		**$1361.26**
V.	**Revenue Needs**				
	1. Per cwt ($1361.26/360) = **$3.78**				
	2. Per revenue mile ($1361.26/1310 miles) = **$1.04**				

interest per hour = annual interest/365/24. In this example, the ACF for five years at 10 percent APR is 6.105 and for eight years at 10 percent APR it is 11.436. Fuel cost per gallon and tractor fuel economy determine *fuel cost per mile.* This formula is *fuel cost per gallon/miles per gallon.* Labor, maintenance, insurance, and billing costs are given and are relatively easy to calculate. *Total pickup costs for this move are $160.01.*

Line-haul

Notice that the line-haul costs categories for this move are the same as for the pickup operation, except for the billing expense. This is simply because only one freight bill needs to be generated for this move. This will also be seen by the absence of a billing cost in the delivery section. Also, during the pickup operation, the driver was paid by the hour because waiting time was involved. In the line-haul section, the driver was paid by the mile. Obviously, pay scales for drivers will be determined by company or union policies. *Costs in the line-haul section are calculated in the same manner as they were in the pickup section.* Obviously, however, the time and distance generated by the line-haul activity are used. *Total line-haul costs for this move are $964.92.*

Delivery

The delivery activity generates the same type of costs as did the pickup activity, except for billing. Again, the time and distance associated with delivery need to be used in calculating costs. *Costs for delivery are calculated in the same manner as they were in the pickup section. Total costs for delivery for this move are $112.58.*

Total Cost

Adding the costs associated with pickup, line-haul, and delivery generates the total cost for this move of $1,237.51. Remember, however, that a 10 percent additional cost is added to make a contribution to the carrier's administration and overhead, so the *total cost for this move is $1,361.26.*

Revenue Needs

Carriers quote prices in many forms. Two of the more common methods are price per hundredweight (cwt) and price per revenue, or loaded, mile. In this example, although profit has not yet been added, to recover the fully allocated or average cost for this move, the carrier would quote a *price per cwt of $3.78 ($1,361.26/360.00 cwt)* or a *price per revenue mile of $1.04 ($1,361.26/1310 miles).*

Once again, this model is a simplified version of the types used by carriers. Certain adjustments and additions would need to be made to this model to make it more reflective of an actual move. However, it does give the analyst some idea of the approximate costs associated with a shipment.

LTL Costing

This section will present a simplified version of an LTL costing model. LTL costing is more difficult than TL costing because it requires arbitrary allocations of common and fixed costs to individual shipments. Although this does not make costing an LTL shipment impossible, it does require that the individual using the costs understand that averages and allocations were used. Thus, the resulting costs might not be as accurate as would be desired. However, this model will produce "ballpark" estimates for the cost of moving an individual shipment. *All* of the formulas for calculating depreciation costs, interest costs, and fuel costs are the same as those used in the TL costing example.

Shipment and Equipment Characteristics

The shipment to be costed consists of 15 cartons, each weighing 40 pounds and measuring 16 cubic feet. The carrier's trailers have a weight capacity of 40,000 pounds and 2,880 cubic feet. This shipment then occupies 1.5 percent of the trailer's weight capacity and 8.3 percent of its cubic capacity. Because the cubic feet requirement is greater, it will be used to allocate costs in the line-haul move.

Equipment Cost Data

Equipment Purchase Price

1. PUD tractor = $23,600

2. PH tractor = $32,000

3. PUD trailer = $10,000

4. LH trailer = $13,000

Depreciation

1. Tractors = five-year straight line

2. Trailers = eight-year straight line

Interest

1. Tractors = 10 percent APR for five years

2. Trailers = 10 percent APR for eight years

Fuel

1. $1.00 per gallon for diesel

2. PUD tractors = five miles per gallon

3. LH tractors = 4.5 miles per gallon

Labor Cost

1. PUD drivers = $22 per hour

2. Dock handlers = $20 per hour

3. LH drivers = $22 per hour

Miscellaneous

1. Terminal variable cost per shipment at both origin and destination = $1.00
2. Terminal fixed cost per shipment at both origin and destination = $1.50
3. PUD equipment maintenance cost = $.15 per mile
4. LH equipment maintenance cost = $.15 per mile
5. PUD equipment insurance cost = $.03 per mile
6. LH equipment insurance cost = $.03 per mile
7. Billing cost = $1.95 per bill
8. Equipment is available 365 days, 24 hours per day
9. Administrative/overhead cost = 10 percent of total cost of move

Route and Time of Movement

The shipment is picked up by the carrier's driver in a pickup and delivery (PUD) city tractor/trailer unit on June 1, 1993, as one of 23 stops made by the driver that day from 0730 EST to 1830 EST. The stops covered a total of 60 miles within the Altoona, Pennsylvania satellite terminal service area. The shipment was one of four handled by the carrier at this particular shipper's location. Once the pickup vehicle returns to the Altoona terminal, it takes 15 minutes to move the shipment from the city unit across the dock to the line-haul trailer.

Total time for pickup = 11 hours
Total distance for pickup = 60 miles
Total dock time = 15 minutes

The line-haul tractor/trailer departs from the Altoona terminal at 2300 EST on June 1 and arrives at the Cleveland breakbulk terminal, which is approximately 200 miles from the Altoona satellite, at 0400 EST on June 2. The shipment moves from the line-haul trailer across the dock to a PUD city tractor/trailer unit in 15 minutes.

Total time of line-haul = five hours
Total distance for line-haul = 200 miles
Total dock time = 15 minutes

The shipment is delivered to the Cleveland consignee by the PUD driver in a PUD city tractor/trailer unit on June 2 as one of 16 stops made by the driver over the period 0730 EST to 1800 EST. The stops covered a total of 45 miles in the Cleveland area. This shipment is one of three delivered to this particular consignee by the driver.

Total time for delivery = 10.5 hours
Total distance for delivery = 45 miles

Cost Analysis

With the equipment cost data and route and time of movement, an individual LTL shipment can be costed. This analysis can be seen in Table C.2. Once again, *the calculations for depreciation, interest, and fuel costs are the same as they were in the TL example.*

Pickup

In this example, a PUD tractor and trailer were used in the pickup operation. This is specialized equipment that really has no alternative uses in the line-haul operation. As such, when this equipment is done with the PUD operation during the day, it will normally sit idle at the satellite terminal. This explains why a full day's depreciation and interest are charged to both the PUD tractor and PUD trailer, even though they were only utilized for 11 hours during this particular day. Some arguments might exist that this places an excessive cost burden on these shipments through fixed cost allocation. This might be true. However, the cost analyst must make the decision as to where fixed costs will be recovered. If not through this allocation, then fixed costs must be covered by some other method so debt can be serviced and plans for equipment replacement can be implemented.

The fuel, labor, maintenance, and insurance cost calculations are relatively straightforward. *Total route costs for this move are $294.14.* Remember, however, that this cost is for all shipments picked up and delivered by the driver during the day. We want to calculate the cost of only one shipment. To do this, we must first divide the total route cost by the number of stops made by the driver. *This results in a route cost per stop of $12.79.* Second, we must divide the per stop cost by the number of shipments at the shipper's location that had our individual shipment. *This results in a route cost per shipment of $3.20.* Both the stop cost and the shipment cost

TABLE C.2 LTL Costing Example

I. Pickup					
A. Route Costs					
	1. Depreciation	PUD tractor	one day @ $12.93/day =	$12.93	
		PUD trailer	one day @ $3.42/day =	$3.42	
	2. Interest	tractor	one day @ $10.59/day =	$10.59	
		trailer	one day @ $2.40/mi. =	$2.40	
	3. Fuel		60 mi. @ $.20/mi. =	$12.00	
	4. Labor		11 hrs. @ $22/hr. =	$242.00	
	5. Maintenance		60 mi. @ $.15/mi. =	$9.00	
	6. Insurance		60 mi. @ $.03/mi. =	$1.80	
		SUBTOTAL		**$294.14**	
		# Stops		23	
		COST PER STOP		**$12.79**	
		# Shipments at stop		4	
		ROUTE COST PER SHIPMENT		**$3.20**	
B. Shipment Costs					
	1. Billing			$1.95	
	2. Terminal variable cost			$1.00	
	3. Terminal fixed cost			$1.50	
	4. Dock		.25 hr @ $20/hr. =	$5.00	
		INDIVIDUAL SHIPMENT COST		**$9.45**	
C. Total Pickup Cost Per Shipment					**$12.65**
II. Line-haul					
	1. Depreciation	PUD tractor	five hrs. @ $.73/hr. =	$3.65	
		PUD trailer	five hrs. @ $.186/hr. =	$0.93	
	2. Interest	PUD tractor	five hrs. @ $.60/hr. =	$3.00	
		PUD trailer	five hrs. @ $.13/hr. =	$0.65	
	3. Fuel		200 mi. @ $.22/mi. =	$44.00	
	4. Labor		five hrs. @ $22/hr. =	$110.00	
	5. Maintenance		200 mi. @ $.15/mi. =	$30.00	
	6. Insurance		200 mi. @ $.03/mi. =	$6.00	
		TOTAL LINE-HAUL FULL TRAILER		**$198.23**	
		% capacity occupied by shipment		8.3%	
		SHIPMENT LINE-HAUL COST			**$16.45**
III. Delivery					
A. Route Costs					
	1. Depreciation	PUD tractor	one day @ $12.93/day =	$12.93	
		PUD trailer	one day @ $3.42/day =	$3.42	
	2. Interest	PUD tractor	one day @ $10.59/day =	$10.59	
		PUD trailer	one day @ $2.40/mi. =	$2.40	
	3. Fuel		45 mi. @ $.20/mi. =	$9.00	
	4. Labor		10.5 hrs. @ $22/hr. =	$231.00	
	5. Maintenance		45 mi. @ $.15/mi. =	$6.75	
	6. Insurance		45 mi. @ $.03/mi. =	$1.35	
		SUBTOTAL		**$277.44**	
		# Stops		16	
		COST PER STOP		**$17.34**	
		# Shipments at stop		3	
		ROUTE COST PER SHIPMENT		**$5.78**	
B. Shipment Costs					
	1. Terminal variable cost			$1.00	
	2. Terminal fixed cost			$1.50	
	3. Dock		.25 hrs. @ $20/hr. =	$5.00	
		INDIVIDUAL SHIPMENT COST		**$7.50**	
C. Total Delivery Cost Per Shipment					**$13.28**

Continued

TABLE C.2 LTL Costing Example (Cont.)

IV. Total Cost Per Shipment			
	1. Pickup, dock, line-haul, delivery	$42.38	
	2. Administrative/overhead (10 percent)	$4.24	
	TOTAL COST PER SHIPMENT		**$46.62**
V. Revenue Needs			
	1. Per cwt ($46.62/6)	**$7.77**	

are averages that assume that each stop is basically the same and each shipment is the same. Adjustments could be made to these figures to more accurately reflect the time and distance actually used for our individual shipment. Remember, however, the per shipment route costs used in this example are averages.

Shipment costs are those assigned to each individual shipment that are not generated by the PUD operation. Billing, terminal variable cost, and terminal fixed cost are not dependent on shipment size but are allocated to each shipment. Our shipment took 15 minutes for its cross-dock operation resulting in the dock charge of $5.00. *Total shipment cost for this move is $9.45. Combining the route cost per shipment and the shipment cost results in a total pickup cost per shipment of $12.65.*

Line-haul

Depreciation and interest for the line-haul equipment is charged only for the actual time our shipment is on this equipment. This is the same as in the TL example. Unlike the PUD equipment, this assumes that the line-haul equipment has alternative uses and is 100 percent utilized. Again, actual utilization rates can be used to adjust the allocation of depreciation and interest charges.

As previously mentioned, our shipment occupied 8.3 percent of the cubic capacity of the line-haul trailer. This is the basis used for allocating line-haul costs in a *line-haul cost per shipment of $16.45.* This allocation method assumes that all shipments in the line-haul trailer have approximately the same pounds per cubic foot requirement and that the trailer would probably be cubed out. The analyst might want to make adjustments for this based on the known average weight and cube per shipment in the carrier's system.

Delivery

The calculations for delivery cost are the same as those used for pickup costs. For route shipment cost, 16 stops and three stops per shipment are used to determine the *average route cost per shipment of $5.78.* Shipment costs are also the same, except that billing cost is not included, resulting in a *shipment cost of $7.50 and a total delivery cost per shipment of $13.28.*

Total Shipment Cost

Combining the pickup cost of $12.65, the line-haul cost of $16.45, and the delivery cost of $13.28 results in total cost per shipment of $42.38. Remember, like the TL example, a 10 percent cost is added to cover administrative and other overhead expenses, resulting in a *total cost for our shipment of $46.62.*

Revenue Needs

Although prices are quoted in many different forms in the LTL industry, one popular form is in price per cwt. Taking our total shipment charge of $46.62 and dividing it by six cwt results in a *price per cwt of $7.77.* Remember this price does not yet include an allowance for profit for the carrier.

Conclusion

Determining the cost for a particular shipment can be a very complex and time-consuming task. Detailed data requirements and knowledge of a carrier's operations are necessary inputs to developing accurate costs. However, a simplified approach can be taken to shipment costing that does not need these complex requirements and results in approximate shipment costs. Thus, the advantage of these costing models is their simplicity and ease of calculation. Their disadvantage is that they use general data, allocations, and averages to determine shipment costs. The analyst must trade off these characteristics to determine the level of complexity needed for costing and whether these models will provide a sufficient level of cost detail.

CHAPTER 12

Relationship Management

By its very nature, logistics is a boundary-spanning discipline, i.e., it relies on establishing relationships with organizations outside its own in order to meet its service and cost goals. This is especially true because logistics encompasses many activities, and an organization must decide which it will provide itself and which it will buy from the market. Once an organization decides to approach the market for a particular service, it must develop the proper relationship with the selected supplier(s) to assure quality and continuity of service at the lowest total cost to the buying organization. This is especially true with the transportation requirements of an organization.

Buyers and sellers of transportation services realize the importance of this activity to a tangible product. In many organizations, transportation is the single largest logistics cost expenditure. In some industries, transportation speed and reliability provide a significant competitive advantage. In most firms, transportation is the last link between a shipper and its customers. It has the opportunity to create positive or negative customer perceptions based on how well the delivery process is performed. Taking these facts into consideration, it is easy to see that managing relationships between buyers and sellers of transportation services is a process that is critical to successfully meeting the transportation requirements of an organization. This chapter will discuss the different types of relationships that firms can be involved in, with special attention given to contracts and partnerships. Also discussed will be the concepts of outsourcing and third parties.

Types of Buyer/Seller Relationships

Buyers and sellers in a market achieve their mutual goals by establishing and managing a relationship between their respective organizations. The type of relationship that is necessary in each situation is determined by many factors. In general, however, three types of relationships exist: arm's length, contract, and partnership. These three are not as distinct as they might seem. Some research has proposed that relationship styles are positioned on a continuum, with one end anchored by arm's length relationships and the other end anchored by a true partnership.[1] This makes sense because an arm's length relationship between a carrier and a shipper can be implemented with a contract (such as a trip lease) or without one (such as common carriage, although this relationship is managed by the bill of lading contract rules), whereas a partnership can have a formalized document managing that relationship or can be consummated by a "handshake." Even though it might be difficult to determine a distinct difference among relationship types, specific types of relationships are better in some situations than they are in others.

Other efforts have been made to offer some insights to specific types of relationships and which ones are appropriate in different situations.[2] Six specific types of relationships have been identified: arm's length, Type I partnership, Type II partnership, Type III partnership, joint ventures, and vertical integration. Recognizing these different types is also important in determining the method used to establish relationships. The role these different types of relationships play in establishing relationships can be seen in Figure 12.1, which will be discussed later in this chapter.

Arm's Length Relationships

These types of relationships last for a single transaction between two parties and no commitments are made for future transactions. Normally, the single deciding factor in these relationships is price. For example, a shipper who has a low value commodity that is not time-sensitive might decide to offer that load to a broker (defined in Chapter 9, "International Transportation"). The **standard service** required is the movement of one shipment between two points, a service any carrier should be able to provide. If the shipment is time-sensitive, a different type of relationship between the shipper and the carrier might be necessary.

Another example would be a shipper who has daily small packages to ship over a wide geographic area. Some days the shipments are tendered to UPS, some days to RPS, and some days to the United States Postal Service. Over the course of the year, each carrier receives multiple shipments. However, there is no commitment on the part of the shipper to guarantee volume to any one carrier on any given day. As such, each shipment is transactual. In both examples here, no commitment exists on the part of either the shipper or carrier to continue to do business together. Both examples also show relationships that are very short term in nature, i.e., each shipment represents the length of the relationship. This type of relationship can minimize the risk to both the carrier and the shipper because neither has to commit volume or capacity to the relationship. However, the transaction might not result in the lowest price to the shipper because the carrier would not have had an opportunity to reduce its operating costs. Thus, arm's length relationships are appropriate in certain situations. Carriers and shippers must assess the risks and rewards associated with these types of transactions. Many organizations consider an arm's length, or transactual, relationship to be inefficient. This feeling is based on the notion that the carrier and shipper have little opportunity to interact, to get to know one another, to leverage volume, and to decrease transaction costs. However, these notions are more indicative of a contractual or partnership relationship than they are of an arm's length relationship. An arm's length relationship is appropriate when a carrier's service offerings are considered a commodity or are standard.[3,4]

Type I Partnerships[5]

Many definitions have been offered for the concept of a partnership. Some authors have even made the analogy between a partnership and a marriage.[6] The definition used here will be that offered by Ellram and Hendrick: a partnership is an ongoing relationship between two firms that involves a commitment over an extended time period and a mutual sharing of information and the risks and rewards of the relationship.[7] A Type I partnership can be described as a **short-term** contractual relationship that requires little investment on the part of either party and which has a limited scope of activities.

For example, a one-year contract for truckload transportation service between Chicago and Dallas would be a Type I partnership. The service offered is not much different than what would be offered to the market in general. The only difference might be guaranteed delivery times and a minimum dedicated fleet on the part of the carrier and a guaranteed minimum volume on the part of the shipper. More than likely, the price for this service will be based primarily on volume. This type of relationship is very common in the transportation industry.

Type II Partnerships

These relationships can also be described as contractual in nature. However, these contracts are longer term in nature, might require investment from either party, and have a larger scope of activities. A good example of this type of relationship can be found in many carrier certification programs and core carrier programs. Those carriers that have gained the status of "core carrier" enjoy a more integrated relationship with the shipper than other carriers. These carriers usually participate in guaranteed annual volume or dedicated freight lanes, are given incentives for cost-reduction efforts, perform more than basic transportation service, and are involved in a longer term relationship with the shipper. This type of partnership takes longer to develop simply because of the trust and commitment that are necessary for this relationship to work. For some shippers, carrier certification can be a three- to five-year process. Although this type of time frame can **increase** the **risk** because of the potential loss of investment by either the carrier or shipper, the rewards of success can be substantial.

STOP-OFF:

Schneider Logistics Targets World Markets

Schneider Logistics is going global.

The Green Bay, Wisconsin-based third-party logistics provider owned by Schneider National Inc. plans to expand its non-asset-based services first to Europe and then move into Latin America and Asia.

The expansion was revealed by Schneider National President Donald J. Schneider Jan. 15 during his keynote address to the Transportation Research Board annual meeting in Washington, D.C.

"North American customers are very desirous of having logistics expertise transferred to a lot of locations throughout the world," he said. "We are transforming many of the systems and modeling techniques we have to a European operation.

"We won't have any equipment over there, but we will be managing other carriers much as our logistics business does in North America. The same thing is going to be true in South America and in Australia and in the Far East."

The impetus for entering Europe grew out of the company's participation in a strategic logistics alliance with GATX Corp. and Fritz Cos. to serve Case Corp., the Racine, Wisconsin-based manufacturer of heavy equipment (TT, 10–21–96, p. 18).

Under the terms of the original five-year agreement with Case, Schneider Logistics supplies all of the company's transportation needs in North America. Alliance partner GATX handles warehousing and Fritz manages all international shipments.

"Basically they said to us last year, 'Can you follow us around the globe and would you be interested in doing Europe?'" Schneider Logistics President Larry Sur said in a telephone interview. "We looked at that and decided we would like to do Europe."

Schneider Logistics responded by sending four managers to Europe during the fourth quarter of 1996 to prepare a proposal. Implementation began Jan. 1.

"We are doing the transportation management function, aimed at trying to reduce the cost of their transportation, improving their service and reducing their inventory levels," Mr. Sur said.

"We take the same kind of approach there that we do in North America. We start by looking at where the opportunities are. The first part of it that we're taking on is the inbound transportation from suppliers to Case's assembly plants."

After that the company plans to analyze Case's outbound transportation needs and then will look at anything that moves between plants, followed by addressing the needs of its service parts operation. Schneider Logistics will work only within the scope of Case's European operations. Fritz will continue to handle import and export shipments.

"We use computer systems and engineering people to look at how we can re-engineer their network," Mr. Sur observed. "We also have people who manage the transactions and work with the carriers."

Case will pay Schneider Logistics for the work it performs in Europe on a fee plus gain-sharing basis, he said.

Mr. Sur expects that the initial steps taken by his company on Case's behalf will serve to support Schneider Logistics' growth in the European market and beyond.

"We're really excited about it; it's nice to be asked to go some place by a customer. We are interested in expanding in Europe and Case wants us to expand. They don't want us to be our only customer because there's more leverage when you have more customers and it spreads out systems development costs."

Schneider Logistics is starting out by working with Case's farm tractor and construction equipment manufacturing plants in France, Germany and England. The company also operates a primary parts distribution center in France.

Schneider Logistics also is looking at moving into other parts of the world right now, according to Mr. Sur. "We would like to expand by following our customers' lead. We've been getting a lot of interest in our moving into South America, but we haven't made any decision yet."

The company's top priority is ensuring the Case European initiative is a solid success before moving on to other customers or parts of the world, he emphasized.

"The first thing we want to do is make the Case implementation very successful, and then use that as our trophy account. We've already talked to other potential customers in Europe, but we want to do this one really well and expand from there."

Source: Sparkman, David L. *Transport Topics.* January 20, 1997, Pg. 3

Type III Partnerships

A Type III partnership is not governed by a typical contract mechanism. Although a document might exist between the two parties, its purpose is to outline general operations and management philosophy. The relationship has **no formal endpoint**. Assets in the relationship can be jointly owned and the scope of activities that is shared is substantial. Type III partnerships can be seen, in some instances, between carriers and firms in the automobile industry. In fact, these carriers are often referred to as "third parties" because of the scope of their responsibilities for the shipper (third parties will be discussed later in this chapter). These carriers perform pickup at supplier locations for assembly line delivery, provide break-bulk and consolidation, provide light manufacturing and assembly, handle returns of materials and storage media to suppliers, and, in some cases, provide inventory management for the automobile manufacturer. Planning and control of this relationship is done at a high executive level because of the significant economic impact that the success or failure of this relationship would have. Obviously, this type of relationship has a high risk and high investment on the part of both parties. This is why very few true Type III partnerships exist in the transportation industry. However, the success of this type of relationship can create a significant competitive advantage for both firms, the type of competitive advantage that neither firm could generate on its own.

Joint Ventures

Joint ventures represent a different type of relationship between two firms because the result of the relationship is usually the creation of another firm. This relationship obviously requires investments from both parties. The focus of a joint venture is for each party to benefit from the other party's expertise. For example, Encompass was the result of a joint venture between AMR (American Airlines) and CSX Railroad. Encompass was created to develop a global booking and tracking information system for freight movements. CSX brought its multimodal expertise to the joint venture because of its operation of a railroad, SeaLand Container Lines, and a motor-carrier concern. AMR brought its system design expertise to the firm because of its experience with the development of SABRE, the booking system used by all the major airlines. These types of relationships, by definition, are long term in nature because of the need to generate a return on initial and continuing investments made by each firm.

Vertical Integration

Every firm requires some type of transportation support. To fill this need, a decision is made to either provide the transportation internally (make) or acquire it from the market (buy). If the decision is made to provide it internally, then the firm is vertically integrating transportation. The most common usage of vertical integration in transportation is the use of **private fleets,** which is discussed further in Chapter 9, "Private Transportation." Many cost and service reasons are used to justify the investment in vertical integration. For example, Harley-Davidson Motorcycles uses a private fleet to transport motorcycles to dealers and pick up parts and raw materials on the backhaul to be used in the manufacturing process. Their decision to utilize a fleet for a major portion of their transportation needs is based on both cost and service criteria.

Conclusion

Every type of business relationship has its appropriate business application. Relationships fail because the parties attempt to implement the wrong type of relationship to fit the situation or one party exercises their dominance in a detrimental manner over the other party. The first step, then, to a successful relationship might be to determine what type of relationship is appropriate based on what each party brings to and wants from that relationship.[8] Fitting the right relationship model to the situation can result in a successful endeavor.

Why Enter Relationships?

As previously mentioned, logistics and transportation are conducive to establishing relationships with external organizations because of their boundary-spanning responsibilities. The nature of the relationship will depend on what each party needs from the exchange, what each party offers, and how each treats the other. However, several general reasons can be offered as to why an organization would enter into a relationship with another organization. These relationships are many times called "third-party" relationships. Before beginning the discussion concerning why to enter a relationship with a third party, a short discussion on third parties is necessary.

The concept of third parties in logistics has existed for many years. When farmers moved their grain on rail cars they were utilizing third parties. The first time the owner of goods put them in a public or contract warehouse, a third party was used. The term "third party" today has developed many definitions and is many times misused. Although this term can be used to represent a relationship between a carrier and a shipper, it is more appropriately used to represent a relationship between a shipper and a firm where more than a single function (such as transportation) is performed. This discussion will adopt the following definition of a third party: "A third-party logistics provider is a company that supplies/coordinates logistics functions across multiple links in the logistics supply chain. The company thus acts as a third party facilitator between seller/manufacturer (the first party) and the buyer/user (the second party).[9] Many third-party relationships begin with carriers assuming responsibility for a firm's private fleet operations. This relationship could grow with the carrier assuming coordination for all freight activities and possibly freight payment and claims. Because of this close relationship between asset-based carriers and third parties, the term third party will be used for the remainder of the chapter to represent any type of firm that has a relationship with a shipper. This will include asset-based carriers as well as non-asset-based firms that provide both transportation and logistics services.

The **third-party** industry has enjoyed a tremendous **growth** over the last several years. One source estimates that its size in 1996 was $25 billion.[10] This same source predicts the market to grow to $60 billion by the year 2000. Regardless of the actual size of the market, one statement is true: third-party use by shippers is growing.

As previously mentioned, transportation is the most commonly outsourced activity to third parties. Research has identified various services provided by third parties and their current and future use by shippers. Table 12.1 shows the results of this research.[11] As this table shows, transportation is the most common logistics activity given to third parties to manage. Other activities include warehousing, information systems, inventory management, and light manufacturing.

Many third-party firms have also begun to offer consulting services for shippers because of the expertise third parties have developed in these various areas.

TABLE 12.1 Outsourcing of Logistics Services

Logistics Services	Current	Future	Not Applicable
Outbound Transportation	77.1%	20.8%	2.1%
Inbound Transportation	63.6	29.5	6.8
Freight Bill Auditing/Payment	79.3	17.2	3.4
Information Systems	33.3	40.0	26.7
Freight Consolidation/Distribution	58.8	33.3	7.8
Cross-Docking	33.3	40.5	26.2
Product Assembly/Installation	31.0	24.1	44.8
Warehousing	74.6	22.0	3.4
Selected Manufacturing Activities	45.9	18.9	35.1
Product Marking, Labeling, Packaging	52.9	23.5	23.5
Traffic Management/Fleet Operating	39.4	45.5	15.2
Product Returns and Repair	36.8	36.8	26.3
Inventory Management	28.0	40.0	32.0
Order Entry/Order Processing	38.5	11.5	50.0
Network Design/Consulting	24.0	40.0	36.0
Other	6.7	2.7	90.6

Note: Data reported from survey of 75 industry executives who indicated their firm used third-party logistics services.

Source: Harry L. Sink and C. John Langley, "A Managerial Framework for the Acquisition of Third-Party Logistics Services," *Journal of Business Logistics,* Vol. 18, No. 2 (1997), p. 171. Permission to reprint this information was granted by the Council of Logistics Management.

Having defined a third party and identified the nature of their markets, the remaining discussion will focus on the reasons shippers enter into relationships with third parties.

Availability of External Suppliers

An obvious reason for shippers to enter into a relationship with a third party is simply because of the large number of third parties that already exist. In many instances, no reason exists for a shipper to operate its own fleet of transportation vehicles (refer to Chapter 9 for more information on private transportation). As such, relationships with third parties currently in the market are sufficient to meet a shipper's needs. This is especially true since many of the activities transferred to a third party involve assets and a given level of expertise in their management. Little incentive exists for a shipper to duplicate assets or expertise when they exist in the marketplace.

Cost Efficiencies

Many third-party providers are asset-based organizations; in other words, they own vehicles, warehouses, or both. With the ownership of these assets comes some **economies of scale** and **economies of scope.** The fixed costs associated with these assets can be allocated across various shippers, thus reducing fully allocated costs per unit. Shippers who own assets (vehicles or warehouses) to provide logistics service cannot generate similar economies. Many organizations have shed private fleets in exchange for a dedicated fleet operation run by a third party. For example, PPG Automotive Products Division as well as Kimberly-Clark Corporation have given the operation of their private fleets over to Schneider Logistics. Because Schneider is an asset-based third party, it is able to operate these fleets at a very competitive cost.

In fact, the results of a study published by the University of Tennessee showed that approximately 58 percent of the third-party users surveyed reported that operating costs of the activities transferred to third parties were reduced.[12] Many times the costs that are reduced are operating costs (like fuel and wages) and overhead costs (salaries and administration).

In some instances, corporate profitability issues force an organization to shed assets to **improve financial performance.** Private fleets and warehouses are prime targets for this asset reduction. However, since there is a high availability of third-party suppliers in these markets, the final impact on the firm from a service and cost perspective can be minimized.

The financial impact of using a third party to shed assets needs to be given adequate attention by the shipper organization. Assets, like fleets or warehouses, impact assets and liabilities on a shipper's balance sheet. The shipper gets the advantage of the asset as collateral for future market funding as well as the use of depreciation to reduce taxes. Along with advantages comes the liability associated with the asset. This would involve the fact that the shipper has an obligation to repay the debt associated with the asset as well as the fact that as assets increase, without a resulting increase in profits, return on investment will decrease.

Eliminating the asset from the balance sheet should have an immediate impact on the shipper's balance sheet. However, the operating expenses of providing transportation will still be present and will impact the expense portion of the income statement. Along with this expense comes the management fee charged by the third party. This will also be a variable expense captured by the income statement. This increase in variable expenses might very well decrease short-term profitability. The use of a third party by a shipper to reduce assets is a trade-off between balance sheet impacts (and ROI) and income statement impacts (and profitability). Asset reduction might not be in the best interest of the shipper from a financial perspective. This aspect of the third-party relationship must be analyzed carefully.[13]

Third Party Expertise

Many organizations believe that some of their activities are better performed by outside providers. The rationale for this decision is based on the principle of **core competency,** i.e., do what you do best and let someone else do the rest. Although it sounds simple, it is obviously not. Very few arguments would be made by any organization that transportation is not important to their success. However, for many firms (like manufacturers) transportation is not an area of expertise. Some firms decide to develop the expertise by owning their own fleet. Other firms decide to let the experts provide the transportation: third-party providers. These firms are in the business of providing transportation; it is their core competency. Also, these firms bring a tremendous amount of expertise to a shipper from having done business with other shippers in similar industries. This expertise in transportation also allows these third parties to better manage the costs of transportation by utilizing their equipment and personnel in a more efficient manner.

Customer Service

Some research has identified service as being a problem when using third parties.[14] Other research has shown that relationships with third parties can actually improve service.[15] What makes the difference between whether service improves or not when using a third party is how the shipper and third party develop and manage the relationship. Many times the cause of service reductions when using a third party has been attributed to a loss of control over that service by the shipper. Control is lost only if the shipper allows it to be lost. A carefully managed and phased-in relationship between the third party and the shipper can actually improve service. L.L. Bean is in a very close relationship with Federal Express for the delivery of its merchandise. FedEx employees work in the L.L. Bean warehouse to facilitate the processing of shipments. This relationship is a strategic decision on the part of L.L. Bean to improve the speed and reliability of its delivery service.[16] The service experienced by PPG and Kimberly-Clark has been very acceptable since Schneider Logistics has taken over their fleets. In all of these operations, care was taken to build customer service into the relationship and to make it a critical element in the performance evaluation of the third party.

Over time, customers develop expectations for logistics service from a supplier. Changing the provider of this service can have a negative impact on the relationships a supplier has with its customers. Care must be taken to maintain and/or strengthen customer relationships when transferring transportation or logistics service to a third party.

Conclusion

The reasons used for entering third-party relationships also end up providing the largest benefits. One of the most significant benefits of using third-party relationships is lower cost.[17] The other most frequently cited benefits of third-party relationships can be seen in Table 12.2.

Lower-cost and improved operational efficiency can be classified as cost/productivity benefits, improved expertise and the ability to focus on core business can be classified as third-party expertise benefits, and improved customer service and greater flexibility can be classified as customer service benefits.

The use of third-party organizations is a viable way for a shipping firm to supplement or provide its logistics services. When these operations are transferred to a third party, the management of the relationship between the shipper and the third-party provider magnifies in importance. This is why relationship management has become so important for logistics managers today.

The word "logistics" as it is used for the balance of this chapter is meant to include transportation within its meaning. Logistics is so closely linked to transportation

TABLE 12.2 The Most Frequently Cited Benefits Related to Use of Third-Party Logistics Services, 1995

Benefits	Percent of Respondents Indicating That Benefit
Lower Cost	38%
Improved Expertise/Market Knowledge and Access to Data	24%
Improved Operational Efficiency	11%
Improved Customer Service	9%
Ability to Focus on Core Business	7%
Greater Flexibility	5%

Source: Robert C. Lieb and Hugh L. Randall, "A Comparison of the Use of Third-party Logistics Services by Large American Manufacturers, 1991, 1994, and 1995," *Journal of Business Logistics,* Vol. 17, No. 1 (1996), p.314. Permission to reprint this information was granted by the Council of Logistics Management.

that one management area cannot be considered without the other. Most logistics strategies rely on transportation for the execution of the plan and transportation is generally the largest single component of logistics. Traffic and transportation managers must "think outside the transportation box" if they are to be fully successful in a logistics environment.

Third-Party Relationship Characteristics

The relationship between a third party and a shipper is usually different than traditional relationships. These relationships are often called partnerships, although many times they are not the same as they were defined earlier in this discussion. Regardless of what they are called, these relationships have certain characteristics that differentiate them from others. Previous research endeavors have found many common characteristics of third-party relationships.[18] In some instances, these characteristics have even been found to be instrumental to the success of the relationship, i.e., for a relationship to be successful it must include these characteristics.

Planning

Planning can be done at multiple levels within both organizations, from the operational to the strategic. In a third-party relationship, joint planning becomes effective at all levels. **Joint planning** requires input from both parties as well as "buy-in" from them. Once this occurs, both parties are in agreement on how the relationship is to be managed and how it is to grow. Penske Logistics and Lucent Technologies share in the planning process as it relates to volumes, product mix, and supplier selection. Allowing a third party into this type of process allows Lucent to treat Penske Logistics as more of a partner in their business, rather than just a supplier to their business.

Communications

Probably one of the most important aspects of a successful relationship, communications is also one of the most difficult to design and implement. However, successful communications between the appropriate individuals in a relationship are critical to making it work. As with planning, these communications take place at all levels within both organizations. Daily orders, weekly staffing requirements, monthly forecasts, and yearly long range plans are all examples of communications. Also critical, however, is identifying who has the information and who needs it so the communication process can take place. For example, Schneider National can determine if a trailer is going to be late for a delivery by using data from its Qualcomm satellite system (this will be discussed further in Chapter 13, "Information Management and Technology"). This information is communicated to the fleet manager, who is responsible for notifying the consignee of the potential delivery delay. This allows the receiving location to take measures to minimize the resulting problems from the late shipment. The two critical questions in these relationships are *what* information? and for *whom?* These need to be identified in the planning stages of the relationship, rather than developed on an ad hoc basis.

Risk/Reward Sharing

A characteristic of a successful relationship is a true sharing of benefits and burdens. This can be very difficult because each organization in this relationship has its own financial goals to achieve. Sharing successes and losses can prevent one or both firms from achieving these goals. Another difficult decision is how much to share. Should the third party bear a majority of the burden and a minority of the success? This type of decision needs to be clarified very early in the negotiating stages of the relationship. Many agreements between third parties and shippers include sliding goal and management fee structures. For example, a service level of 98 percent provided by the third party will net the third party a management fee of $1 million, while a 96 percent level will net $750,000 and a 99 percent level a $1,250,000 fee. An increasing service level will benefit the shipper and the resulting fee increase will benefit the third party. This type of sharing also allows both organizations to meet their financial goals without penalizing either party unfairly.

Trust and Commitment

In many relationships, third parties are placing their employees onsite at their customer's location to manage some transportation or logistics activity. However, third-party relationships can often be distant relationships; in other words, the third party is managing a part of the shipper's business without having the shipper physically present. A certain level of trust needs to be in place for this situation to work. The shipper must have trust that the third party will act in the best interest of the shipper, whether it involves contact with a customer or a major cost reduction initiative. The third party must have trust that the shipper will act in the best interest of the third party, i.e., treat the relationship with integrity and a long-term focus. Trust needs to be one of the critical factors assessed at the beginning of the relationship. However, trust really develops over the life of the relationship. Commitment and trust are not mutually exclusive. The commitment of both parties to the success of the relationship is necessary. Commitment to the relationship means a long-term focus, a willingness to tolerate failures, an encouragement for innovation and growth, and a respect for each firm's expertise and contribution to the relationship.

Scope of the Relationship

As previously mentioned, today's third-party relationships are characterized by the performance of more than just a basic logistics service. The larger the scope of activities performed by the third party, the stronger the relationship. For example, Penske Logistics manages the inbound logistics process for a General Motors plant. This involves inbound consolidation of parts and sub-assemblies, staging for production delivery, cart return, quality control, and even some light manufacturing. As the scope of activities increases, the ability to determine where one firm begins and the other one ends decreases.

Figure 12.1 shows the relationship between the nature of a third party's product offering, or the scope of activity with a shipper, and the type of relationship that will probably exist.[19,20] This discussion will provide some general guidelines that exist in shipper/third-party arrangements. It must be remembered that exceptions to these guidelines will exist. Joint ventures and vertical integration are not included because they do not involve a traditional shipper/third-party service provider type of relationship. At the bottom of the triangle is what can be called "reliability" services. Third parties that interact with shippers at this level compete by offering such services as on-time delivery, zero damage, and accurate invoicing. These are called reliability services because the only measure of success is 100 percent accurate performance. This focus on 100 percent performance by a shipper indicates that these services are evaluated based on quality (for example, did the third party perform as

FIGURE 12.1 Third Party Product Offerings and Relationship Type

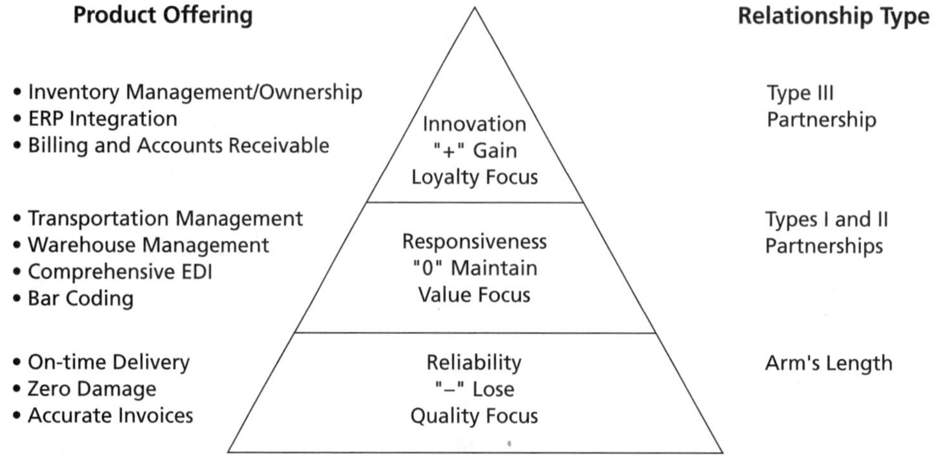

promised?). A third party cannot gain market share by performing these services well, but can lose market share by doing them poorly. In the logistics arena, these services are commodities and the relationship a shipper will have with a third party providing only these services will probably be arm's length. If a third party cannot provide basic on-time delivery on a consistent basis, another third party will. Consistently meeting shipper expectations for these services, however, will allow the third party an opportunity to elevate to the next level with the shipper.

"Responsiveness" services are evaluated by shippers as value adding. A value-adding service can increase market share if done well and lose market share if done poorly. Examples of value-adding services would be transportation management, custom-tailored delivery systems, bar coding, electronic data exchange (EDI), warehouse management, and so on. They all build on basic transportation service but provide more value to the shipper because they integrate more logistics activities. Type I or Type II partnerships would probably be used here because of the longer term nature of the relationship and the existence of a contract. Performing these services well over time can allow the third party the opportunity to advance to the next level in the triangle with a shipper.

Finally, the top-level product offering/relationship combination can be called "innovation." These services are meant to fully integrate a shipper's product, cash, and information flows. Third parties that reach this level with a shipper can gain significant market share by performing these services well but would probably not lose market share by not offering these service or doing them poorly. Service at this level might include inventory management/ownership, information system integration through an ERP system, billing and collections, and so on. These services build on those offered in the second level and are a result of and a cause of loyalty between the shipper and third party. This loyalty is developed between the shipper and third party by consistent performance by the third party at the reliability and responsiveness levels. A Type III partnership would more than likely exist at this level. An example of this relationship in the automotive industry is called the Lead Logistics Provider, or LLP. An LLP is a third party that is responsible for contracting all logistics services from other third parties on behalf of the automobile manufacturer. This LLP manages the logistics process for the manufacturer.

Third parties must be able to identify and market their product offerings so the scope of the relationship can be defined at the very beginning of the relationship. Many relationships begin between shippers and third parties at the very bottom of the triangle and develop over time to move into each succeeding level. Trying to enter a new relationship at the responsiveness or innovation levels can be difficult, but it can be done.

Financial Investment

Firms that share investments in assets, people, or information systems tend to have a stronger commitment to the success of the relationship. Obviously, financial rewards are a result of this success. However, trust in the relationship is a requirement for this type of financial investment. Profitable firms invest in relationships that will further their profitability. This involves a certain trust in the other firm that it will make the right decisions concerning this investment so both parties can benefit. Many third-party relationships will jointly develop information systems to manage logistics activities. With many manufacturers implementing enterprise resource planning systems, like SAP, third-party firms are developing and implementing compatible logistics information systems. Although a significant investment, these information systems provide a high level of synergy for the third-party firm across logistics activities within a single firm and across many firms (this will be discussed further in Chapter 13).

Future Orientation

This characteristic is related to trust and commitment. A future orientation in a relationship focuses on what can be, not on what is or was. This is also related to planning. As previously stated, many third-party relationships start out simple in order to allow them to develop and mature. For example, a third party might enter into a relationship with a shipper to manage its private fleet, rather than undertake all of the shipper's transportation needs, thus beginning with reliability services. This allows the third party to focus its attention on one aspect of the logistics of the shipper. Once it masters the fleet management aspect, the third party can begin to grow into other areas within transportation. This is where the future orientation enters. Both parties agree that the long-term goal is to have the third party take on not only all transportation activities but also all warehousing activities, evolving into responsiveness services. However, the relationship starts with a single activity. This gives both parties agreement on what the future will look like and how the relationship will possibly develop into an innovative type of relationship.

Organization/Culture Change

For many firms, third-party management of logistics represents an organizational culture shock. This occurs because of the fear of losing control over logistics cost and service and the fear of losing jobs. Also, the mentality of "we can do it better" is difficult to shed. Managing relationships can be more difficult than managing operations. For some shipper logistics managers, this shift in management focus represents a tremendous challenge. However, successful third-party relationships have occurred because these logistics managers have changed the way they view their business and the roles they play in it. Many organizations have accepted the fact that logistics is not their area of expertise and have decided to turn over the management of this

STOP OFF

MERCEDES TAPS AVERITT

Mercedes-Benz U.S. International has tapped Averitt Express to handle the logistics honors at its new plant in Tuscaloosa County, Alabama Averitt Express is responsible for primary LTL, dedicated carriage and working with the carmaker to create a logistics plan that will meet production requirements.

Mercedes-Benz will make 270 vehicles a day of the M-Class All-Activity Vehicle at the Alabama plant when production reaches capacity. The first Daimler-Benz passenger vehicle manufacturing site in this country, the plant is a significant investment for Mercedes-Benz, which described it as "the most important project outside of Germany" in its 1996 annual report.

A sport utility vehicle, the M-Class is a new product line for Mercedes-Benz with production to begin in February. The company expects to employ between 1,200 and 1,500 people at the 1 million-square-foot facility. Averitt will place a logistics manager and support staff on-site.

"Our team had a list of criteria from which we based our decision and Averitt did very well," said Brent Lambiotte, logistics assistant manager for Mercedes-Benz. Based in Cookeville, Tenn., Averitt Express won the contract over 34 other bidders. Mercedes liked Averitt's plan for meeting the daily vehicle production schedule, Lambiotte said. "We were also impressed by their failure-mode effect analysis, designed to identify potential problems, including identification of counter measures to solve problems."

Averitt is working with Mercedes-Benz to review supplier locations, quantities shipped and daily delivery requirements, said Dan Singer, director of Averitt's logistics business unit. Once the plant is running, Averitt will be responsible for 150 daily loads from 10 suppliers. The suppliers are within 100 miles of the plant. Averitt also will deliver freight from about 25 parts suppliers outside that 100-mile radius. Besides handling parts delivery, Averitt will manage Mercedes' returnable containers.

The plant will use two types of ordering systems. One is ITAS, for "in time and sequence," where requested parts arrive in a specific sequence as the M-Class is made. ITAS carries no safety stock, relying instead on the carrier (Averitt) to keep deliveries on schedule. The second system is "materials release delivery" which allows Mercedes-Benz to order parts based on production planning as well as the actual ITAS schedule.

"Our job is to effectively coordinate freight movement between Mercedes and their suppliers," said Jim Barnett, Averitt's on-site manager at Mercedes-Benz. "We have to meet the set pick-up and delivery windows and monitor transit times to ensure we're moving freight into the plant in a manner that supports Mercedes' stringent inventory levels."

Mercedes-Benz Averitt is supporting more than the German automaker's supply line. It's also buttressing a new way of doing business within Mercedes-Benz. The manufacturer retooled its organizational structure this year, merging two major business units and giving its remaining 23 businesses more control over their purchasing and production decisions. In exchange, Mercedes-Benz is asking those units to show a return of 12 percent or more in the "medium range" future.

Fortunately for Mercedes-Benz and its suppliers in the United States, Americans in the market for a luxury car find it hard to resist a Mercedes. The automaker sold 90,800 passenger cars in this country in 1996, a jump of 18 percent over 1995, giving it 10 percent of the U.S. luxury car market.

Source: "Mercedes Taps Averitt," *Traffic World*, November 17, 1997. Reprinted with permission of *Traffic World*, the Logistics News Weekly.

process to organizations that possess that expertise. Logistics can never be totally eliminated from an organization; someone will always need to be present in the shipper organization to manage the relationship and assure that shipper financial and service goals are attained. However, the operations of logistics can be transferred to a third party. Doing this successfully and managing the resulting relationships can be problematic to some shippers because their organization structure and culture are not conducive to using third parties. However, successful third-party relationships are characterized by shippers that have recognized the need to change the way they do business and have begun the process to adapt both their organizations and culture.

Relationship Challenges

With an understanding of the characteristics inherent in a strong third-party relationship, it is possible to better understand the challenges faced by organizations as they decide to enter into a relationship with a third party. Suppliers and buyers alike need to develop new methods for managing the logistics process in these types of relationships. Too often, firms tend to continue utilizing traditional methods of doing business in a changing environment. The decision to use a third party is not necessarily an easy one. This section will discuss some of the challenges faced by buyers and suppliers of third-party services when entering into a relationship.[21]

Buyer Challenges

Buyers are often not sure what they are buying or why. In most organizations, logistics cuts across functional boundaries. The decision to transfer a logistics activity to a third party then must include all of the parties impacted. This can make the decision process long and complex. For example, the decision to transfer the operation of the inbound warehouse that services the plant would possibly involve materials management (responsible for the inbound warehouse) and manufacturing (responsible for the plant).

Another challenge faced by potential buyers can be caused by who in the organization makes the decision to use a third party. In some instances, these decisions are not made in the logistics group but in finance or information systems.[22] Financial decisions are usually made to reduce assets and/or costs in logistics. When this occurs, the logistics manager might not be convinced which logistics activity should be given to a third party and what implications it might have on logistics cost and service.

Buyers do not perceive synergies from single-sourcing logistics. When the use of third parties began with buyers using common and contract carriers, the strategy was to spread risk among many suppliers. In this way, no single third party had a significant portion of the shipper's business and could not exert influence over the shipper's decisions. Also, if a third party left, it could be easily replaced. This mentality exists today in many firms. Logistics executives are reluctant to allocate too much business with a single supplier. However, this strategy limits a third party's ability to efficiently consolidate shipments and effectively route its equipments to take advantage of continuous moves.

Buyers do not understand how to change boundary-spanning, internal processes. Many third-party decisions are made and implemented by **cross-functional teams** within buyer firms. Inexperience at managing the team concept makes this decision a lengthy one. Coupled with this can be the disagreement within the team concerning cost and service requirements from the third-party provider. Managing these two aspects of the decision is critical to providing the third party with a clear understanding of the scope of the relationship as well as what measurements will be used to measure the performance of the third party.

Sometimes what appears to be a lack of organization on the buyer's part in implementing the relationship is actually a reluctance to use a third party in the first place. If the logistics function is responsible for implementing the third-party relationship but was not part of the initial decision, there could be a reluctance on the part of logistics to make it work. Logistics could see the third party as a threat to job security. As such, the implementation will be difficult to complete. Successful implementations include the implementing department in the third-party decision.

Finally, transferring a logistics activity to a third party requires that the buyer maintain a level of expertise in that activity. A previous discussion mentioned that logistics executives manage assets and relationships. If the assets are outsourced, the need to manage relationships is strengthened. However, a knowledge of the activity given to a third party is necessary to communicate expectations to the third party, develop appropriate measurement systems, and continue to implement solutions to improve the activity. Also, this expertise is necessary in case the activity is brought back "in-house." For example, a food manufacturer recently transferred its private warehouse network to a third-party provider. To prevent losing warehousing expertise, the manufacturer retains managers in the warehouses as well as one of the third-party managers in the manufacturer's corporate logistics office. This is also extremely beneficial to communications between the two firms.

Supplier Challenges

Suppliers have not achieved a clarity of offer. Many third parties refer to themselves as "logistics companies" without having expanded their basic transportation service. Some have added broker services to justify the new title. These suppliers approach potential buyers offering logistics when, in fact, they still are transportation companies. Another mistake made by third parties is not clearly defining what services they provide. For example, one shipper explained that when it asked a third party, "What services do you provide?," the reply was, "What would you like us to provide?" This gives the impression that the third party is not sure what its core competencies are and is not sure what a third-party provider really is (refer to Figure 12.1, which addressed the concept of clearly defining the product offerings of a third-party supplier).

Suppliers have no proven method of marketing their services. Third parties traditionally approached either transportation or purchasing managers when marketing and selling their services. Since the single service being marketed was transportation, the point of contact in the buyer firm was relatively easy to determine. However, since the scope of services offered by true third parties has expanded and, in many cases, has crossed functional lines within the buyer firm, the contact point has become difficult to determine. In some instances, the contact person is in finance; in other instances, it is in logistics. Determining how to approach a firm is difficult without knowing who to contact. Traditional contacts in transportation or logistics might not be effective if they perceive third parties as a threat to job security.

Suppliers must compete against entrenched internal groups. A private fleet department within a buyer firm represents a formidable barrier to the success of a third party. This department has developed a reputation for service, a network of alliances with other departments, and an accepted methodology for costing and pricing their services. In these instances, the burden of proof is on the third party to prove its superiority to the internal group. This can pose a challenging problem for the third party because it needs to change the buyer firm's culture towards the internal group.

Suppliers have not proven long-term profitability. Third-party providers sometimes approach buyers with estimated "quick hit" cost reductions through asset elimination or non-union labor. Although this provides an immediate improvement in buyer profits, it disappears in a short period of time. Buyers also sometimes require continuous cost reductions from the third party. This can result in additional profits for the buyer but might result in reduced profits for the third party because of a necessity to lower price. Long-term profitability for a buyer and supplier in a third-party relationship might actually require additional investments by both parties. This "return on investment" mentality is superior to that of short-term improvements in profits. However, many third parties are either reluctant to or are not capable of communicating their efficiency to the buyer in financial terms.

Conclusion

Third-party providers will continue to successfully serve the logistics needs of the market. Many successful relationships have been implemented and continue to grow. However, caution must be used by both the buyers and sellers in this market to approach the relationship in a way that will guarantee its success. Poor planning on either part will result in failure. Relationship management by logistics executives will continue to be an important part of managing the logistics process.

The Negotiation Process

The previous discussion focused on the types of relationships that exist between buyers and sellers and how to manage third-party relationships in logistics and transportation. The next logical discussion is one describing how to establish relationships between shippers and third-party providers. One method used for establishing these relationships is negotiations. This technique can be used to eliminate or minimize differences between the requirements of the two parties. This section will attempt to provide an overview of the negotiation process and its role in third-party relationships. Appendix 12-A contains a detailed discussion of the negotiation process. Figure 12.2 provides a framework of the shipper/third-party negotiation process and will be used as the basis for discussion in this section. Market power, negotiating philosophy, and goals/objectives are part of what can be called environmental analysis and planning. These activities are crucial to the negotiation process because they allow each party an opportunity to develop a comprehensive plan to use as the basis for bargaining. Bargaining is where the parties attempt to close the gaps on any differences they might have on the issues. This is where the plan is put into place and modified when necessary. The last section is outcome. Two outcomes will be discussed: agreement and breakdown.

Market Power

Many firms operate from multiple plants and warehouses, which might be included within one operating division or across several operating divisions. Regardless, firms have discovered that volume can create leverage with third parties. Many firms have organized transportation councils, comprised of individuals representing the transportation function across several sites or operating divisions. These councils combine their freight to simplify the negotiation process with third parties as well as to attempt to lower freight costs. This **system-wide negotiation** has resulted in firms using fewer third parties and spending less on transportation.

Many other factors influence the market power that the buying firm might have in the negotiation process. These factors impact the third party's cost structure, and thereby influence prices. **Total dollars spent** by the buying firm represents the volume that is available to the third party from one firm or shipping location. As previously stated, the larger the volume or dollars spent, the more leverage the shipper has and the more volume the third party has over which to allocate its fixed costs. **Density and handling**, also used for freight classification, directly impact the third party's costs. Density influences the third party's ability to fully utilize weight and

FIGURE 12.2 Shipper/Third Party Negotiation Process

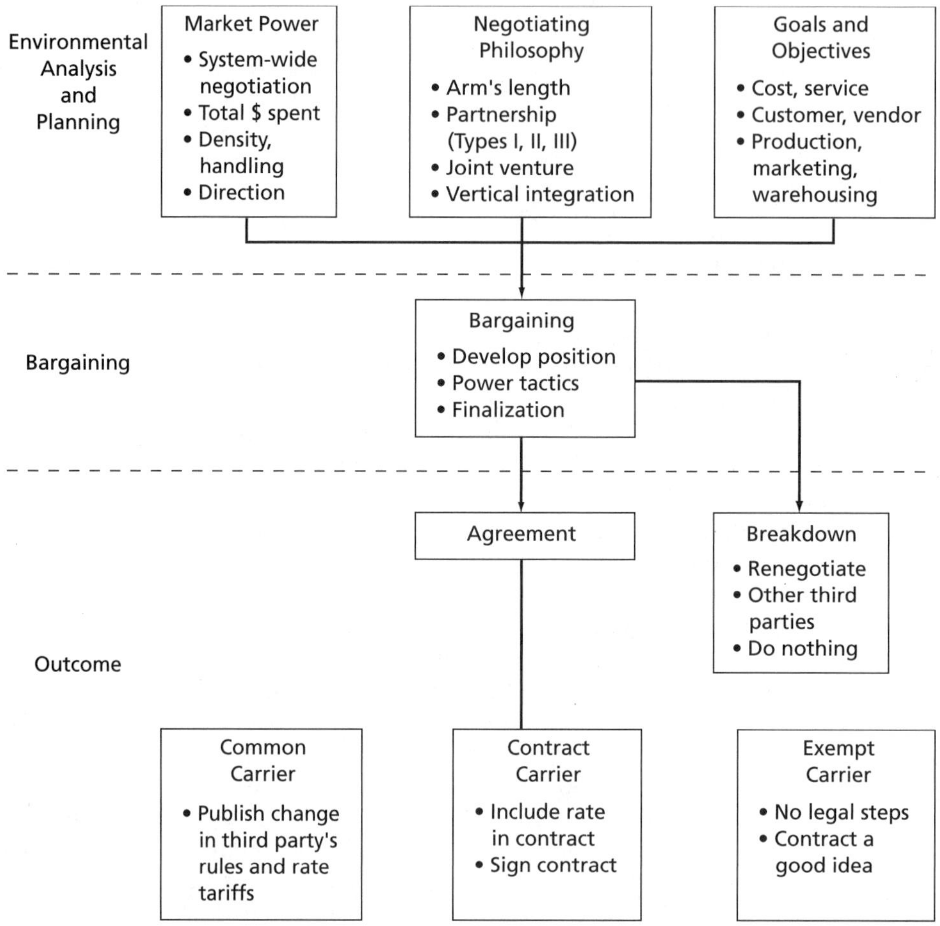

Source: Edward J. Bardi, 1997.

cube capacities of vehicles. The denser the freight, the more efficiently the equipment capacity is utilized. Handling is a variable cost that is passed on directly to the shipper in the freight price. The more often a product is handled by the third party, the more expensive it will be for the shipper. Pallets, consolidation programs, shipper load and count, and zone skipping are all methods to help reduce the number of times a third party needs to handle a product. These practices are discussed in more detail in Chapter 14, "Shipper/Carrier Network Strategies." Finally, direction can create a forward haul or fill an empty backhaul. A third party's price will include a portion to cover the costs of system-wide empty miles. If a shipper's freight flow parallels a third party's empty backhauls, a significant cost reduction and price reduction can occur for both parties. However, if the freight flow is in the direction of major headhauls (and where third-party capacity is scarce), the value of service pricing is sure to be used.

Negotiating Philosophy

As discussed earlier in this chapter, many types of relationships exist between shippers and third parties. In developing a negotiating strategy, the shipper must identify the type of relationship desired with the third party. This will influence how both parties approach the negotiation.

Goals and Objectives

In any type of buying situation, the buyer will establish a set of **desires** (cost) and **demands** (service) to be obtained from the seller.[23] Buyers of transportation will usually pre-screen a third-party base using service requirements. This can also include a third party's information technology capabilities, which will be discussed further in Chapter 13. Only those third parties that can meet a certain minimum service level will move on to the second phase of the selection process. In most cases, these service requirements, or demands, are not negotiable. The second phase, dealing with desires or cost, is where much of the negotiation will take place. Service and cost objectives are set based on the requirements of the customer group to be satisfied: vendors, production, marketing, or warehousing. This underscores the importance of including customers in the development of the cost and service objectives. The transportation negotiator will then translate the objectives into terms that are understandable to and attainable by the prospective third parties.

Bargaining

Bargaining is the step in the negotiation process where the third party and shipper meet to develop their position and determine how close or far the parties are from agreement. If the parties are totally in agreement with their initial positions, bargaining is not needed. Normally, however, there will be some inconsistencies between the positions of the parties and bargaining is necessary. During this process, **power tactics** can be used to change the position of the other party so compromise can be reached. Market power analysis, discussed previously, will determine which party has power and which type of power it has for the bargaining process. Once the parties have reached agreement or compromise, **finalization** is performed. In this step, both parties "agree to agree" on each item discussed during the negotiation process. In other words, each agreement is revisited to make sure that what was agreed upon was what was intended. This step is necessary for contractual purposes. Once the parties leave the negotiation process with an agreement, an oral contract is in effect. This oral contract is subsequently put into writing by one of the parties. These two contracts should be one and the same. Once the contract is signed, either party has 10 days to invalidate the written contract. After the 10-day period, the contract becomes the governing document, even if it conflicts with the initial oral contract. This 10-day limit is a criterion in the "Statute of Frauds" clause in the Uniform Commercial Code. Thus, it is important to revisit the terms of the oral contract before it is put into writing as well as to reexamine the written document to verify its accuracy.

Breakdown

If the initial positions of the parties are drastically different, bargaining might prove to be futile and breakdown might occur. Breakdown might also occur during bargaining when it becomes evident that one or both parties are no longer willing to compromise. Breakdown is also used as a power strategy. However, when breakdown occurs, three alternatives exist: renegotiate, explore other third parties, or do nothing. In many cases, a "cooling off" period is necessary for either one or both parties to rethink their positions. After this period, renegotiation is many times successful. However, agreement between the parties still might appear to be impossible. In this situation, it is appropriate that both parties "agree to disagree;" both realize that agreement is futile and that the negotiation process has ended. At this point, the shipper can either investigate negotiating with other third parties or do nothing. The "do nothing" option is rarely used because customer needs do not disappear because of an unsuccessful negotiation process.

Agreement

An important step in the negotiation process is capturing the results in some type of document recognized by a regulatory, state, or federal government agency. The Overcharge Claim situation faced by shippers in the late 1980s and early 1990s was a result of this step not being properly managed. Carriers and shippers were quick to agree on rate reductions as an effective way to improve their business relationships. However, neither party bothered to make sure that these lower rates were published in a legal document, making them the rates that governed the relationship. Three options exist for formalizing the agreement. If the relationship is with a common carrier, the changes should be published in the carrier's rules and rate tariffs (tariff-filing requirements were discussed in more detail in Chapter 2, "Transportation Regulation and Public Policy"). If the relationship is with a contract carrier, the agreement must be formalized in a valid contract. The concept of a "valid" contract will be discussed in a following section. Finally, relationships with exempt carriers require no formalized legal steps. However, it is prudent to establish a written contract to govern long term and/or large volume relationships with exempt carriers.

The Bidding Process

Negotiation is a process used when the services or costs requested by the shipper are not normal offerings made by third parties; in other words, a third party would have to alter its normal market offerings to satisfy the needs of the shipper. On the other hand, if the shipper only requires standard third-party services but desires a longer term relationship, the bidding process is appropriate. Government agencies have used bidding in many of its supplier relationships. Bidding and negotiation are not mutually exclusive. Both processes can be used simultaneously to reach an agreement with a third party. What bidding allows is a standardization of the shipper's service demands. Negotiation then allows compromise on the shipper's price/cost desires. Figure 12.3 presents the framework for the bidding process to be discussed.

Qualifying Third Parties

The first step in the bidding process is to qualify third parties. This step is used to include only those third parties in the potential bid base that meet certain legal, financial, or operating requirements. Shippers will many times request proof of operating authority, copies of financial statements, equipment lists (number, age, and ownership), operating scope, client references, and hazardous materials/safety

FIGURE 12.3 The Bidding Process

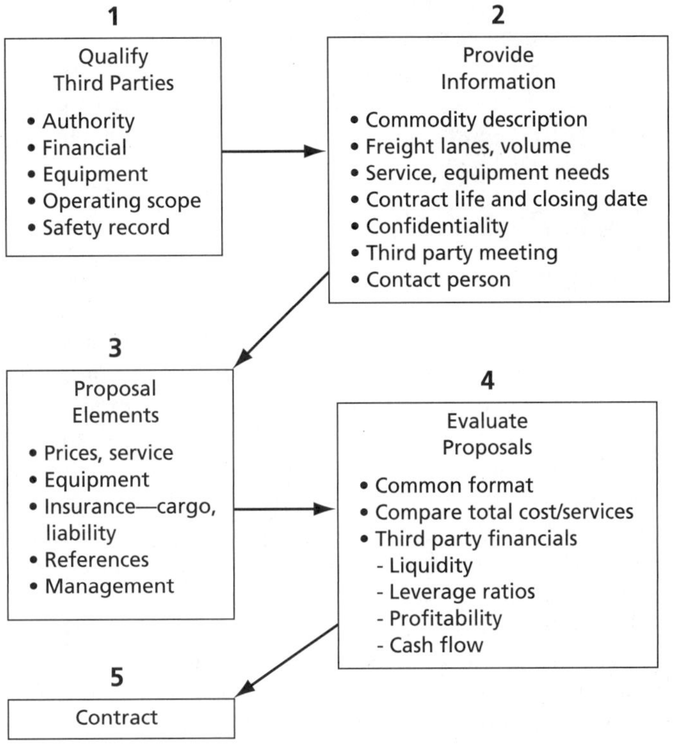

Source: Edward J. Bardi, 1997.

qualifications from the third parties. This helps identify those third parties that the shipper desires to do business with as well as alleviate any fears the shipper might have about the third party's ability to provide the service needed in a fiscally responsible manner.

Providing Information

The shipper must carefully identify and communicate to the third-party base all data needed to describe the shipper's business and service requirements. Much of this data, such as freight flows, can be contained in a spreadsheet to be given to the third parties for analysis. Data must be accurate, complete, and timely because third parties will base their proposals on them. In some instances, shippers discover that their freight information systems do not capture all of the necessary data needed to develop a valid bid package. This would require either manual data generation or an investment in information system improvement. Shippers that use third-party freight payment firms can many times gather all necessary bid data from the freight bill payment system. Other information provided to the third party would include contract length, delivery time requirements, payment/billing schedules, confidentiality clauses, and a requested third-party meeting.

Proposal Elements

To properly evaluate bids from several third parties, it is important that each contain the same type of data in the same format. Also important is that all data needs to be calculated in the same manner. This allows all bids to be directly compared to each other. The shipper then decides what elements should be contained in the proposal. Several types of proposal elements are identified in Figure 12.3. Unsolicited data from third parties should be avoided in the evaluation stage because this does not allow for unbiased analysis.

Evaluate Proposals

As previously mentioned, it is important that bids be presented in a common format. Many times bids will also be in spreadsheet format to facilitate shipper analysis. As in the negotiation process, shippers must identify cost and service guidelines for evaluation proposals. Lowest price is slowly disappearing as the single criterion for bid evaluation, while lowest total cost is being used more and more as the final metric for bid evaluation. Lowest cost includes both third-party price and service in the analysis. For example, Federal Express partnered with National Semiconductor to operate a newly consolidated warehouse and provide expedited transportation service on a worldwide basis. Although the resulting transportation price increased in this relationship, National Semiconductor experienced tremendous overall savings in warehousing, planning, order processing, and inventory costs, more than compensating for the increased transportation price.[24] Thus, the cost implications of the third party's service must be included with the cost implications of the third party's prices.

Prudent shippers will also evaluate the financial implications of the third party's prices on the third party's financial position. Pricing strategies used by third parties in the early 1980s to price below variable cost to increase volume proved disastrous to third party financial strength. Many third parties went out of business, leaving shippers without service and unpaid overcharge claims. If the relationship desired with third parties chosen with the bid process is to be long term, the shipper must assure that the third party's prices provide a suitable return to the third party to guarantee long-term financial success.

Contract

Like the negotiation process, a suitable outcome of the bidding process is a contractual relationship with the successful third party(s). The same logic applies to the bidding process, as it did to the negotiation process when it comes to establishing relationships with common carrier-based third parties, contract carrier-based third parties, or exempt carrier-based third parties.

Third-Party Contracts

Once a relationship between a shipper and a third party is established, it needs some type of document to make the arrangement legal and to be used as a guideline for implementation. The document that fills both roles is called a third-party contract. The Interstate Commerce Commission (ICC) initially identified guidelines to evaluate the validity of a third-party contract (it must be remembered here that the ICC formerly and the STB currently regulate only transportation; this chapter is using the generic term "third party" to represent both transportation carriers and firms offering expanded

FIGURE 12.4 Guidelines for Third-Party Contracts

Suggested Minimum Content Requirements for a Motor Carrier Contract:

1. It must identify the parties;
2. It must commit the shipper to tender and the carrier to transport a series of shipments (emphasis added);
3. It must contain the contract rate or rates for the transportation service to be or being provided;
4. It must state that it provides for the assignment of motor vehicles for a continuing period of time for a shipper, or state that it provides that the service is designed to meet the distinct needs of the shipper;
5. It shall be retained by the carrier while in effect and for a minimum period of 3 years thereafter.

Source: Negotiated Rates Act of 1993, Section 6.

logistics services). These specific guidelines were necessary to complement the general contract guidelines offered by the Uniform Commercial Code. ICC guidelines were instrumental in the resolution of overcharge claims between shipper and third-party bankruptcy trustees. The latest version of the contract guidelines were specified in the Negotiated Rates Act of 1993 (NRA 1993) and adopted by the Trucking Industry Regulatory Reform Act of 1994. The ICC Termination Act of 1995 did not include specific language regarding third-party contracts (Chapter 2 discussed these Acts in further detail). Figure 12.4 lists the requirements for third-party requirements, as found in the NRA 1993. Although specific language is not required by current legislation, these guidelines should be used to help supplement those specified by the UCC.

Although all transportation contracts are unique, several topics are commonly addressed. Figure 12.5 contains a list of clauses, or sections, commonly contained in a third-party contract. The following is a brief discussion of these common sections.

Disclosure of Goods

The shipper has the duty to inform the third party of the nature of the product. This might include special handling requirements, temperature requirements, nature of hazard (if any), and value. Failure to inform the third party of the special characteristics of the shipment could preempt the shipper's ability to collect on damage claims. The third party could use the "Act of the Shipper" defense as the exemption from the claim action.

If the shipment is hazardous, the shipper is required by law to inform the third party of the type of hazard the shipment could pose in transit (contract liability) as well as the hazard it could pose to individuals and/or the environment if it was mishandled (strict liability). The Code of Federal Regulations (CFR), Title 49, contains severe penalties for shippers that attempt to ship a hazardous product without proper documentation, marking, labeling, and notification of the third party.

FIGURE 12.5 Common Sections Found in Third-Party Contracts

- Disclosure of Goods
- Responsibility for Goods
- Routing, Mode, and Method of Operation
- Term, Termination, and Modification
- Volume Requirements
- Scope of Operation
- Performance Standards
- Operational Standards—Indemnification
- Force Majeure
- Billing and Payment
- Applicable Law
- Assignability
- Breach of Contract
- Dispute Resolution
- Confidentiality

Source: Joseph L. Cavinato, Department of Business Logistics, Penn State University, 1998.

Responsibility for Goods

With all relationships between third parties and shippers, the basis for product liability must be defined. Under a contractual agreement, the value of the goods and the liability for the goods are determined by the parties of the contract. CFR Title 49 defines how product value is to be calculated and which party bears the liability for the goods. The **claims** filing **process** should also be defined. Unless otherwise stated, the claims process in a contract will be handled through the Uniform Commercial Code (UCC). Because the UCC is written for the transaction of products, many remedies allow for the product's replacement. The UCC defines several types of warranties a manufacturer makes about its product. If a warranty is breached, the UCC provides for the manufacturer to reimburse the buyer with either a replacement product or a refund of the purchase price. Many of these warranties do not apply to third parties since they do not manufacture or own the products they transport (unless it is private). As such, the UCC claims process is adequate but not effective for transportation claims. CFR Title 49 contains a detailed process for the filing and disposition of transportation claims, including overcharges, late delivery, and product damage. The updated provisions regarding motor-carrier liability and claims filing can be found in Sections 14705 and 14706 of the ICC Termination Act of 1995. Many third-party contracts will reference the appropriate CFR sections for claims process governance.

Routing, Mode, and Method of Operation

The shipper and third party must agree on the equipment type and size to be used for the life of the contract. This is especially true for rail and motor carrier transportation because of the various types and sizes of rail cars and trailers available. This section would also address special routing requirements the shipper might have. The growth of intermodal TOFC/COFC has prompted shippers to require notice from the third party if it intends to put the trailer on a rail flatcar. Trailer loading and product damage has influenced this decision by shippers. Some contracts have clauses preventing rail carriers from using hump yards to process a shipper's car. Again, this is caused by car loading and product damage concerns.

Term, Termination, and Modification

Legal contracts have beginning and end dates. End dates, however, can be fluid if the parties agree to extend the contract automatically unless either party objects. In either case, a contract is a document with a specific lifespan. This section also must address early termination by either party. The early termination process must be described as well as who can initiate it and under what circumstances it can occur.

Contract modification is a very common practice. However, contracts normally do this process little justice. Items to be addressed include: 1) under what circumstances can and should the contract be modified? 2) who is responsible for contract modification? 3) can the contract be automatically modified under certain circumstances? 4) must every modification be handled as a renegotiation? Modification is especially important in longer-term contracts for transportation prices. Fuel price fluctuations, interest rate changes, and labor agreements can have dramatic impacts on a third party's operating costs. This section must identify if, when, and how a third party can increase as well as decrease prices. Special care must be taken when linking price changes to changes in an external index, such as the Consumer Price Index. The concern here is that the third party's cost change might have nothing to do with a change in the CPI. The resulting price changes then become random fluctuations without addressing the problem of the third party's cost changes. Since fuel and labor comprise the majority of every third party's variable costs, it might be prudent to develop an index (if one is to be used) based on these two cost drivers.

Volume Requirements

This is also called the **shipper's consideration** in a contractual relationship. Minimum volume commitments on the part of the shipper should be a requirement for a valid contract. In fact, CFR Title 49 was specific in requiring a "series of shipments" for a third party contract to be valid. Volume requirements can be stated in pounds, shipments, units, and so on. This volume requirement should be stated for a specific period of time, such as per week, month, or quarter.

This section can also be used to allow the third party to commit a minimum amount of capacity to the shipper's needs. Obviously, these capacity needs will be based on the shipper's volume commitment. This is especially helpful if the contract has a requirement for a drop lot at a shipper facility. For example, Schneider National and Corning Asahi (manufacturer of television picture tubes) have an agreement where Schneider maintains a minimum trailer pool at Corning Asahi's plant. This minimum trailer pool is based on minimum volume requirements and the trailer pool is increased based on volume fluctuations.

Scope of Operation

This section describes exactly what is and what is not the responsibility of the third party. This section needs to be as detailed as possible. Activities such as vehicle spotting, loading, and unloading should be assigned as a responsibility of one of the parties. In the case of hazardous shipments, this section would identify who provides placards and who secures them to the vehicle. If the services provided include more than transportation, such as consolidation, order management, or total transportation management, this section should address all aspects of the third party's duties.

Performance Standards

This is part of the **third party's consideration** in a contractual relationship. Specific performance measures related to transit time, pick-up/delivery reliability, damage rates, and billing accuracy are detailed in this section. In the case of expanded logistics services, KPI's (Key Performance Indicators) could be determined for each logistics activity performed by the third party. Care must be given to decide over what time period these measures are calculated. Are they to be weekly, monthly, or quarterly measures? For some of these measures, the third party might possess more accurate and timely data. This section must specify which party is responsible for collecting and compiling the data for measurement purposes.

Operational Standards—Indemnification

Many firms require certain indemnification clauses to be included with any contractual relationship with suppliers. The intent of these clauses is to protect the shipper from liability caused by the action or lack of action by the third party on issues not under the control of the shipper. For example, motor carriers are responsible to assure that their drivers are properly licensed to drive a particular class of vehicle. Assume that the shipper's goods are in a vehicle driven by an unlicensed driver and that vehicle is in an accident. An indemnification clause is designed to absolve the shipper of any liability for that accident or any damages it caused. These clauses are intended to define the liability each party has in the relationship, unrelated to liability for the product (defined in Responsibility for the Goods).

Force Majeure

Conditions outside the responsibility of either party can occur that prevent the implementation of the contract. For common carriage, these are many times referred to as Acts of God. For example, natural disasters that destroy a third party's vehicles or facility or a shipper's facilities would prevent the movement of product as required by the contract. However, natural disasters are mostly unpredictable and uncontrollable. As such, the party affected should not be held in breach of the contract for non-performance. This section should specify what occurrences are outside the responsibility of both parties that would prevent contract performance as well as the process used when such occurrences happen.

Billing and Payment

Most contracts are for large numbers of transactions across multiple facilities. Generating an invoice for each transaction can become tedious, confusing, and inefficient. In many cases, a third party will generate one invoice per week for a shipper across all shipping points, with appropriate detail for each shipment attached. The shipper needs only to generate one check to satisfy payment. This is a very common practice for large customers of small package delivery services, such as UPS, FedEx, and RPS. It is important to identify who is responsible for receiving and paying the invoice.

Credit terms and payment cycle are important elements in this section. Will the third party offer a discount for early payment? A penalty for a late payment? How much time does the shipper have to pay the bill? What happens if the shipper does not pay? This section can also include requirements for the billing and payment cycle to be handled electronically. If this is the case, EDI transaction requirements would need to be detailed in this section.

Applicable Law

A contract can specify which state law will have jurisdiction over contract implementation or contract disputes. In the case of a dispute, the court system of the state specified would be used. If a state is not specified, intrastate contracts are under the jurisdiction of the state involved; interstate contracts are under the jurisdiction of the federal court system.

Assignability

If a third party cannot meet its vehicle requirements in terms of capacity for a given shipper's operation, three options exist. First, the shipper will not be able to move all of its product because of the third party's inability to supply the proper number of pieces of equipment. Second, the third party can assign the loads to another third party. Third, the shipper can find another third party to move the product. The difference between the second and third option is whose responsibility it is to find another third party. Option number one is not appropriate over the long term because of stock-out situations for the shipper's customers. Options two and three are the most common occurrences. However, some shippers do not want to allow a third party to assign a load to another third party. Lack of control over third party quality is the single point of concern here. Some shippers do not have the capability on a short-term basis to find alternative third parties. Some contracts allow the contracted third party to assign missed loads to other third parties, but only if these alternative third parties are approved by the shipper. Many third parties operate brokerage services with other third parties in which a contract between the two parties is in effect. This allows for a better quality check on the assigned third party.

Breach of Contract

This section must specify what constitutes a breach for both parties. It must also describe the process used to rectify the breach and the process used to terminate the contract (this can be referred to in the Term, Termination, and Modification section). Also, any restitution to be paid by either party because of breach must be identified here.

Dispute Resolution

For product claims, CFR Title 49 can be used to describe the process to be used. However, this process does not recommend actions if and when the claim cannot be settled. In other words, if the claim is not resolved at the end of the process and a resolution is not imminent, Title 49 makes no recommendations on how to resolve the dispute. Other types of disagreements or disputes can occur in other areas of the contract. If not otherwise specified, these disputes are normally handled in the court system identified in Applicable Law. Although very effective, this method of resolution can be lengthy and expensive. An alternative method of dispute resolution is **arbitration.** Both parties must agree to arbitration since its decision is binding on both parties. If arbitration is chosen, then a decision needs to be made in this section as to how the arbitrator is to be chosen and paid.

Confidentiality

Almost every third party contract has a confidentiality clause. This clause protects proprietary data contained in the contract from reaching the public domain.

Contracting Hints

Contracts between third parties and shippers have, and will continue to be, effective mechanisms for managing relationships. Many of these contracts, however, are written to satisfy the legal requirements rather than the operating requirements of the relationship. Although these legal requirements are necessary, they should not obscure the operating characteristics. Some contracting hints will be offered in this section that will allow the contract to be used more for operating purposes, rather than for legal purposes.

Indemnification Clauses

Most shipper legal departments will require that it be held blameless for any action the third party takes that might cause someone harm. These clauses, called indemnification clauses, are necessary for a contract to be approved by the shipper's legal department. One suggestion would be to include these clauses at the end of the document, rather than in front. A contract which immediately defers all blame to the third party might set a negative tone for the entire relationship.

Penalty Clauses

Contracts revolve around service/price commitments from third parties and volume commitments from the shipper. This quid pro quo provides the basis for the relationship. However, situations occur (not including force majeure) where one or both parties might fail to meet their obligations. Many contracts only "punish" the third party for failure, while leaving the shipper whole when it fails. Because contracts involve numerous transactions, it is inevitable that one or both parties will fail (even a six sigma philosophy will experience two failures per one billion occurrences). As such, "incentives to improve or comply" could be used in place of penalty clauses. For example, a third party could be paid the agreed-upon price if it complies with a 96 percent service level, a lower price for a lower service, and a higher price for a higher service. Likewise, a shipper could be charged the agreed-upon price for meeting its agreed-upon volume commitments, a higher price for lower volume, and a lower price for a higher volume. The point of this philosophy is not to penalize either party for failure, but to include incentives for compliance and improvement.

Service Requirements

Special care must be taken to determine what the service requirements will be on the part of the third party and additional care must be taken in defining these requirements. For example, is on-time defined as when the vehicle enters the consignee's location or when unloading/loading begins? This section of the contract needs to be very explicit. Delivery "windows" need to be identified as well as who is to collect the data for service performance measurement. Because of the increasing sophistication of third-party technology, some shippers have agreed to allow the third party to collect service performance data. Another consideration is the reporting period: will it be weekly, monthly, or quarterly? Also, who is to receive these reports?

Finally, some contracts contain what is called a "balanced scorecard."[25] In a shipper/third-party environment, this would include various measures of service and financial performance on the part of the third party. Success is defined by the third party's achieving compliance with all measures, previously identified as KPI's, rather than achieving some and failing at others. These types of measurement systems provide incentive for the third party to reduce costs and provide exceptional service for the shipper. The incentive for the third party is in the form of higher financial compensation.

The "Living" Contract

Many contracts are written as very rigid documents; any changes negate the original document and require wholesale renegotiation. As a shipper/third-party relationship matures and grows, requirements will change. A "living" contract is written to allow these new requirements to be included effortlessly as part of the relationship. This type of contract will not work in every situation. However, in situations where both parties agree that the relationship will grow, it is quite appropriate. This is very evident in the movement from a "reliability" relationship to a "responsiveness" one, and on to an "innovation" relationship between the shipper and third party.

Prices

Always include the listing of prices and charges levied by the third party in the body of the contract. To refer to other documents or tariffs might not only be confusing but also might be illegal (refer to Chapter 2 for a discussion on this topic). This also allows the contract to become the comprehensive document governing the relationship.

Conclusion

The point of these contracting hints is to make the contract easy to understand, specific as to the duties of each party, and allow the contract to evolve into an operating document. Even though contracts are not necessary in Type III partnerships, the responsibilities of each party need to be defined in every relationship. Sometimes this definition is in writing, sometimes it is not. In either case, since success or failure by either party is assessed in the relationship, specific guidelines are needed to allow the relationship to grow and be successful.

SUMMARY

- Six different types of relationships are found to exist: arm's length, Type I, Type II, Type III, joint ventures, and vertical integration.
- Transportation and logistics are conducive to managing relationships because of their boundary-spanning responsibilities.
- Third-party organizations are used by shippers to provide not only transportation service, but also many other logistics services.
- The use of a third party to provide transportation and other logistics services has both risks and rewards. However, the risks can be minimized by incorporating certain concepts into the relationship.
- The negotiation process can be complex and time-consuming; it is most effective when used to establish relationships where the third party and shipper must alter their normal operating procedures to comply with each other's demands.

• The bidding process is also used to establish relationships; it is best used when the third party does not need to alter its basic service offerings to meet the demands of the shipper.

• Third-party contracts are documents that must meet both the legal and operating requirements of both parties.

• Third-party contracts can be written to elicit a positive working relationship between the third party and shipper while avoiding the negative connotations of "penalizing" failures.

Key Terms

arbitration pg. 369
core competency 350
claims process 366
cross functional teams 357
desires versus demands 361
density and handling 359
economies of scale 349
economies of scope 349
finalization 361
increased risk 345
joint planning 352
no formal endpoint 347
power tactics 361
private fleets 347
shipper considerations 367
short term 345
standard service 344
system-wide negotiation 359
third party's considerations 368
third party growth 348
total dollars spent 359

Study Questions

1. What are the six different types of relationships? How are they different? In what types of situations would each relationship be most appropriate?

2. Why are relationships with third parties so prevalent in transportation today?

3. What are the characteristics of a successful relationship? What would prevent parties in a relationship from achieving these characteristics?

4. Identify the risks associated with outsourcing from the perspectives of both the buyer and the supplier.

5. What are the different elements of the negotiation process? The bidding process? When should each be used?

6. What are the legal requirements for a valid transportation contract?

7. Identify any five topics addressed in a transportation contract and explain their importance to the contract.

8. How would you prepare for a bid package? What information should be included? What information would you seek from the carrier? If you are the third party, what information do you want from the shipper?

Notes

1. Gardner, John T., Martha C. Cooper, and Tom Noordewier, "Understanding Shipper-Carrier and Shipper-Warehouser Relationships: Partnerships Revisited," *Journal of Business Logistics,* Vol. 15, No. 2 (1994), p. 123.

2. Lambert, Douglas M., Margaret A. Emmelhainz, and John T. Gardner, "Developing and Implementing Supply Chain Partnerships," *The International Journal of Logistics Management,* Vol. 7, No. 2 (1996), pp. 1-17.

3. Gardner, Cooper, and Noordewier, op.cit.
4. Lambert, Emmelhainz, and Gardner, op. cit., p. 2.
5. The discussion of the three types of partnerships is based on the framework developed by Lambert, et.al.
6. Tompkins, James A., "Evaluating the Performance of Partnerships," *CLM Annual Conference Proceedings,* (1995), pp. 431-450.
7. Ellram, Lisa M., and Thomas E. Hendrick, "Partnering Characteristics: A Dyadic Perspective," *Journal of Business Logistics,* Vol. 16, No. 1 (1995), p. 41.
8. See, for example, the diagnostic tool developed by the research of Lambert, et.al., op. cit.
9. Maltz, Arnold B., and Robert C. Lieb, "The Third Party Logistics Industry: Evolution, Drivers, and Prospects," *Proceedings of the Twenty-Fourth Annual Transportation and Logistics Educators' Conference,* (Oak Brook, IL: Council of Logistics Management, 1995), pp. 45-75.
10. Delaney, Robert, *Contract Logistics Services: The Promises and the Pitfalls,* (St. Louis, MO: Cass Logistics, Inc., 1993).
11. Sink, Harry L. and C. John Langley, Jr., "A Managerial Framework for the Acquisition of Third Party Logistics Services," *Journal of Business Logistics,* Vol. 18, No. 2 (1997), pp. 163-189.
12. Ibid.
13. For a further discussion of the financial impacts of logistics on a firm's financial performance, see Thomas W. Speh and Robert A. Novack's "The Management of Financial Resources in Logistics," *The Journal of Business Logistics,* Vol. 16, No. 2 (1995), pp. 23-42.
14. Ibid.
15. Lambert, Emmelhainz, and Gardner, op.cit.
16. Novack, Robert A., C. John Langley, Jr., and Lloyd M. Rinehart, *Creating Logistics Value: Themes for the Future* (Chicago, IL: Council of Logistics Management, 1995), p. 197.
17. Lieb, Robert C., and Hugh L. Randall, "A Comparison of the Use of Third Party Logistics Services by Large American Manufacturers, 1991, 1994, and 1995," *Journal of Business Logistics,* Vol. 17, No. 1 (1996), pp. 305-320.
18. For example, see Lambert, et.al., op.cit.; Jakki Moore and Robert Spekman, "Characteristics of Partnership Success: Partnership Attributes, Communication Behavior, and Conflict Resolution Techniques," *Strategic Management Journal,* Vol. 15 (1994), pp. 135-152; Gardner, Cooper, and Noordewier, op.cit; Lisa. M. Ellram and Thomas E. Hendrick, "Partnering Characteristics: A Dyadic Perspective," *Journal of Business Logistics,* Vol. 16, No. 1 (1995), pp. 41-64.
19. This triangular concept was adapted from William C. Copacino's "Reliability is No Longer Enough," *Traffic Management* (August 1991), p. 65.
20. For a further discussion on the logistics product mix, see Robert A. Novack, C. John Langley, Jr., and Lloyd M. Rinehart's *Creating Logistics Value: Themes for the Future* (Oak Brook, IL: Council of Logistics Management, 1995), pp. 112-114.
21. This discussion is based on research conducted by Arnold B. Maltz and Robert C. Lieb, "The Third Party Logistics Industry: Evolution, Drivers, and Prospects," *Proceedings of the Twenty-Fourth Annual Transportation and Logistics Educators' Conference* (Oak Brook, IL: Council of Logistics Management, 1995), pp. 45-75.
22. Lieb and Randall, op.cit., p. 309.
23. Novack, Robert A. and Stephen W. Simco, "The Industrial Procurement Process: A Supply Chain Perspective," *Journal of Business Logistics,* Vol. 12, No. 1 (1991), pp. 145-168.
24. Novack, Langley, and Rinehart, op. cit., pp. 119-122.
25. Kaplan, Robert S. and David P. Norton, "The Balanced Scorecard—Measures that Drive Performance," *Harvard Business Review,* (January-February 1992), pp. 71-79.

Suggested Readings

Buxbaum, Peter, "Global Logistics: Setting Your Sites Overseas," *Inbound Logistics* (May 1998), pp. 41–46.

Ellram, Lisa M. and Daniel R. Krause, "Supplier Partnerships in Manufacturing Versus Non-Manufacturing Firms," *The International Journal of Logistics Management,* Vol. 5, No. 1 (1994), pp. 43–53.

Ellram, Lisa M. and Thomas E. Hendrick, "Partnering Characteristics: A Dyadic Perspective," *Journal of Business Logistics,* Vol. 16, No. 1 (1995), pp. 41–64.

Foster, Thomas A., "You Can't Manage What You Don't Measure," *Logistics* (May 1998), pp. 63–68.

Gardner, John T., Martha C. Cooper, and Tom Noordewier, "Understanding Shipper-Carrier and Shipper-Warehouser Relationships: Partnerships Revisited," *Journal of Business Logistics,* Vol. 15, No. 2 (1994), pp. 121–143.

Kaplan, Robert S. and David P. Norton, "The Balanced Scorecard—Measures That Drive Performance,"

Harvard Business Review (January-February 1992), pp. 71–79.

Lambert, Douglas M., Margaret A. Emmelhainz, and John T. Gardner, "Developing and Implementing Supply Chain Partnerships," *The International Journal of Logistics Management,* Vol. 7, No. 2 (1996), pp. 1–17.

Lieb, Robert C. and Hugh L. Randall, "A Comparison of the Use of Third Party Logistics Services by Large American Manufacturers, 1991, 1994, and 1995," *Journal of Business Logistics,* Vol. 17, No. 1 (1996), pp. 305–320.

Maltz, Arnold B. and Robert C. Lieb, "The Third Party Logistics Industry: Evolution, Drivers, and Prospects," *Proceedings of the Twenty-Fourth Annual Transportation and Logistics Educators' Conference,* (Oak Brook, IL: Council of Logistics Management, 1995), pp. 45–75.

Moore, Jakki and Robert Spekman, "Characteristics of Partnership Success: Partnership Attributes, Communication Behavior, and Conflict Resolution Techniques," *Strategic Management Journal,* Vol. 15 (1994), pp. 135–152.

Novack, Robert A. and Stephen W. Simco, "The Industrial Procurement Process: A Supply Chain Perspective," *Journal of Business Logistics,* Vol. 12, No. 1 (1991), pp. 145–168.

Sink, Harry L. and C. John Langley, Jr., "A Managerial Framework for the Acquisition of Third Party Logistics Services," *Journal of Business Logistics,* Vol. 18, No. 2 (1997), pp. 163–189.

Sparkman, David L., "Strategic Alliances: Glorious in Theory, Tenuous in Fact," *Transport Topics* (September 21, 1992), pp. 77–78.

Tompkins, James A., "Evaluating the Performance of Partnerships," *CLM Annual Conference Proceedings* (1995), pp. 431–450.

Walton, Lisa Williams, "Partnership Satisfaction: Using the Underlying Dimensions of Supply Chain Partnerships to Measure Current and Expected Levels of Satisfaction," *Journal of Business Logistics,* Vol. 17, No. 2 (1996), pp. 57–76.

CASE

CASE 12.1

Shipper—Carrier Negotiation Project

Shipper Situation

Boll Weevil Inc. of Harrisburg is one of eight firms in Pennsylvania that harvest and sell raw "cumulus cotton" to textile manufacturers in the United States. The company has had previous problems gaining a competitive advantage in the market because of poor arrangements for transportation of the commodity between Harrisburg and textile mills in Knoxville, Tennessee; Greensboro, North Carolina; Atlanta, Georgia; Union, South Carolina; Elberton, Georgia; Lincolnton, North Carolina; and Pikeville, Tennessee. The former traffic manager, who perceived his job to be very similar to that of the Maytag repairman has left you with the responsibility of arranging transportation for all future shipments of the commodity to these customers.

Cumulus cotton is a new product invention that allows the harvesting and transformation of clouds into a cotton type of product that can be used as a substitute for traditionally grown cotton. The characteristics of this product must be maintained at a temperature of between five degrees and 38 degrees Fahrenheit at all times while in its raw state. Second, poly-propho gas must be added to the product every three hours to allow the product to maintain its natural consistency. This gas is quite expensive ($5 for 20 pounds). Twenty pounds of gas will protect approximately 5,000 pounds of the cumulus cotton. Previous estimates of the density of the product indicate that 1,000 pounds of the cotton equals approximately 100 cubic feet of space.

Demand from these customers is anticipated to be a total of 10,500,000 pounds per year. Each individual customer's demand is expected to be as follows:

Knoxville	2,000,000 lbs.
Pikeville	250,000 lbs.
Atlanta	5,000,000 lbs.
Elberton	250,000 lbs.
Union	500,000 lbs.
Lincolnton	500,000 lbs.
Greensboro	2,000,000 lbs.

The demand from each of these customers is expected to be fairly constant over the course of the year. Your landed production cost at the plant's shipping dock is $3.00 per pound; you can sell cumulus cotton to your customers at $5.00 per pound.

Production capacity has been listed at 20,000,000 pounds, which is within the needs of the anticipated market demands for all customers of the company. However, this capacity is not consistent over the course of the year. The following list indicates anticipated production capacity per month.

January	3,000,000 lbs.
February	3,000,000 lbs.
March	3,000,000 lbs.
April	3,000,000 lbs.
May	2,000,000 lbs.
June	1,000,000 lbs.
July	0 lbs.
August	0 lbs.
September	1,000,000 lbs.
October	1,000,000 lbs.
November	1,000,000 lbs.
December	2,000,000 lbs.

Your boss, who is the owner of the firm and one of the individuals who perfected the harvesting process, has recently learned that alternative transportation arrangements through contracts can save the company substantial sums of money and increase the service level from the carrier. Your responsibility is to create this type of benefit for the company.

Carrier Situation

The Baahd Company is a total transportation company that has a 48-state motor-carrier operating authority to provide transportation service to shippers. A growing and highly competitive industry that requires transportation service is the "cumulus cotton" industry, which uses transportation service between points in Pennsylvania and southern markets that use the product in the manufacture of textile goods. Attached is a copy of the characteristics of this industry. The eight companies in this industry are identical in their characteristics and have similar points of origin.

Seven other transportation firms have also developed recent interest in this market and are pursuing business in this industry. All of these carriers have similar operating characteristics. For example, all pay their drivers $10 per hour. Fuel currently costs $1 per gallon and the equipment of all carriers averages five miles per gallon on line-haul movements. All firms have relatively new equipment and estimate that their maintenance costs average $.02 per mile. Administrative costs are anticipated to be 10 percent of the variable costs of the move.

Your boss, the marketing manager, has done some initial calculations that indicate you do not have the capacity to provide service to more than one of these shippers. However, she does want to establish your firm as a competitive transportation company in this market. You are therefore being saddled with the responsibility of securing business in this industry.

Destination Market	Miles from Harrisburg, PA
Knoxville, TN	455
Pikeville, TN	532
Atlanta, GA	564
Elberton, GA	564
Union, SC	320
Lincolnton, NC	400
Greensboro, NC	310

Your terminal in Harrisburg is located 15 miles from the shipper's location. Your terminal coverage in the Southeast allows each terminal to be located about 10 miles from each customer for his cotton.

Virgin Cumulus Cotton Industry

Eight firms in Pennsylvania harvest and sell raw "cumulus cotton" to textile manufacturers in the United States. The main markets for these firms are in Knoxville; Greensboro, NC; Atlanta; Union, SC; Elberton, GA; Lincolnton, NC; and Pikeville, TN.

As stated earlier, cumulus cotton is a new invention that can be used as a substitute for traditionally grown cotton. Total demand for virgin cumulus cotton production from each manufacturer in the southern markets is 10,500,000 pounds.

Appendix 12-A

The Negotiation Process

Negotiations are part of every manager's responsibilities. However, it can be very difficult to determine the proper manner in which to begin and manage the negotiation process. Although there is no secret formula, success can be a factor of how well the negotiation process is structured.

This appendix presents a conceptual model of negotiation for logistics managers as developed by Lloyd M. Rinehart of Michigan State University, and Ernest R. Cadotte and C. John Langley, Jr., both of the University of Tennessee. We gratefully appreciate receiving permission from Jean Clarkson, editor of the *International Journal of Physical Distribution and Logistics Management,* to reproduce this article in this appendix.

Shipper-Carrier Contract Negotiation*

Introduction

In the early 1980s deregulation forced logistics managers and carrier managers into a new operating environment[1–3]. One result of the regulatory changes was the increased necessity for shippers and carriers to negotiate contracts for transportation service, since changes in market structure resulting from deregulation have substantially increased the number of shippers and carriers. Thus, it becomes more important for shipper and carrier practitioners to learn as much as possible about the negotiation process to benefit from potential contractual relationships.

Marketing and purchasing scholars are also showing greater interest in the study of negotiation[4–6]. However, most of the work in logistics negotiation has looked at the characteristics of the contract resulting from the negotiations, rather than from the process itself[7–9]. From the literature it is apparent that little work has been done on integrating and synthesising negotiation concepts into a unified framework that can be applied across disciplines. Theoretical development would benefit from a unified framework of the subject, which should include a definition and identification of key concepts and their interrelationships[10].

This article serves two purposes. First, it provides a broad conceptual foundation to help managers understand the elements of the negotiation process between shippers and carriers and, second, it provides a framework which integrates prior research and guides future research efforts through the conceptual elements of the negotiation process.

Interorganisational Negotiation Defined

Proper assessment of the activities which comprise transportation contract negotiation requires a definition of the content and boundaries of negotiation. The following definition of interorganisational negotiation has been developed for application to this environment:

Negotiation is a management process involving the preparation for bargaining, the interaction of two or more parties in a bargaining situation, and the resolution or outcome of this interaction. Preparation includes the collection of information and its use on the formulation of interactive strategies designed to achieve the firm's objectives in a bargaining situation. Bargaining includes the execution of these strategies and the "give and take" over individual issues, which is

* A conceptual foundation for logistics managers by Lloyd M. Rinehart, Ernest R. Cadotte, and C. John Langley, Jr. Lloyd M. Rinehart is Associate Professor of Marketing and Logistics at Michigan State University. Ernest R. Cadotte is Professor of Marketing, and C. John Langley, Jr. is Professor of Marketing and Transportation, both at the University of Tennessee, Knoxville.

FIGURE A.1 A General Process of Negotiation

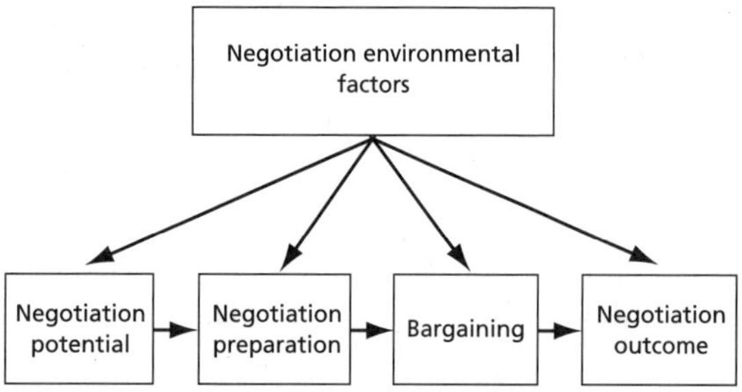

necessary to satisfy the parties. Outcome represents an agreement between the parties designed to accomplish mutual gain or the discontinuance of the negotiation process.

Using this definition as a basis, a conceptual model has been developed which represents the process of transportation service contract negotiations between shippers and motor carriers. Figure A.1 demonstrations the general form of the process model, which contains the five basic areas of interest. These areas include the environmental factors which influence negotiation activities, the nature of the relationship or potential for a relationship between the parties, the preparation for bargaining, the actual bargaining activities, and the outcome. Each of the following sections addresses the elements of the negotiation process as presented in Figure A.1.

Negotiation Environmental Factors

Negotiation activities are influenced by the characteristics of the macroenvironment, the organisations, and the participating individuals[11]. In addition, the negotiator must distinguish between influences from different elements *within* the firm and those from outside the firm. With the Webster and Wind model as a basis, the Negotiation Environmental Factors have been classified into four groups as represented in Figure A.2[12]:

External
General organisation
Participating department
Personal environments of the individual negotiators.

FIGURE A.2 Negotiation Environmental Factors

External Environment	Organizational Environment	Departmental Environment	Personal Environment
Competition Technological Political Economic Cultural	Organizational context Organizational structure Organizational climate	Department goals Department communication Participant responsibility	Personal characteristics Personality

External Environment

The macroenvironment involves variables over which the organisation has little control, such as competition, technology, legislation and political influences, the economy, and cultural factors. Competition influences the relationships between carriers and shippers. At the carrier level, there is direct competition between, for example, liner and steamship companies which compete in the same international markets. Competition also occurs between carriers or shippers with substantially different operating characteristics, such as railroads and motor carriers. The competition that shippers face in their markets further influences shipper-carrier negotiations. As competition increases in the shippers' markets, increases or decreases in demand influence their needs for transportation service. This in turn influences the arrangements necessary to provide transportation service to meet their market demand. These forms of competition influence the approaches which negotiators use in negotiating transportation service contracts.

Technology also significantly influences negotiation activities. Computer technology offers shippers immediate information pertaining to shipment tracing, the availability of equipment in various localities, and an improved ability to expedite shipments. Technological advances in equipment can also benefit shippers and carriers. For example, the availability of side-loading trailers can reduce loading and unloading time, while road-trailer applications reduce the equipment inventory by reducing the need for flat cars used in TOFC movements. Both applications produce potential increases in equipment utilisation for the shipper and carrier. However, the costs and benefits involved must be negotiated between the shipper and carrier to achieve the best mutual benefit.

Shippers and carriers now operate under the legal structure of deregulation. Two major implications have evolved. First, both parties must now observe antitrust regulation restrictions which are significantly different from the intent of the previous transportation regulatory structure. Thus, carriers and shippers alike are forced to consider their approaches to interaction with the other party. Both parties must also be aware that, although federal deregulation has become effective, many states still use economic regulation to control intrastate transportation movements. Therefore, they must consider the implications of legal constraints on each individual movement under one contractual agreement.

Economic factors also influence the approaches to negotiation of contracts, particularly those that allow for rate changes based on increased carrier costs through fuel and labour cost changes. Carriers frequently demand fuel increase allowances within the terms of the negotiated contracts in order to meet their increased costs while maintaining a continued relationship after expiration of the current contract.

Finally, each negotiator must understand the influence of the cultural factors which surround him and his organisation, as well as those which will influence the other party's positions and decisions. For example, cultural differences are especially acute in negotiations between firms from different countries. Steamship companies have faced the dilemma of differing attitudes towards negotiations when dealing with representatives from Asian countries. These Asian negotiators emphasise the cultural activities of their country during the carrier negotiators visit to their country, and hold off on discussions of the contract issues until the representative is scheduled to leave the country. This strategy combined with the expectation of agreement by the carrier organisation leaves the carrier negotiator in a dilemma as his departure draws near. These social and cultural elements can significantly influence the outcome of the negotiations.

Organisational Environment

The organisational environment comprises the context, structure, and climate of organisations which participate in the negotiation process[13]. The context includes a size (revenues and number of employees), resources (financial inputs, human inputs, and physical inputs), and ownership (public or private). Organisational structure includes the internal characteristics of the organisation, such as the configuration of its members, standardisation of the organisational processes, the authority structure (centralisation or decentralisation of decision making), and the formalisation of the communication structure within the firm. Organisational climate considers the perceptions of support by members, willingness of risk-taking by members, and the progressiveness of the organisation.

The structure and climate of the organisation influence the approaches negotiators use to prepare for bargaining activities. Negotiators must be able to assess the representative of the other party who has the decision-making authority for the terms of the contract. An inaccurate assessment may result in temporal delays such as excessive numbers of caucuses and outside discussions between members of the other party. Delays can also result in telephone conversations between the representative and his superiors over the issues of the contract. These issues can influence the strategies negotiators use to gain advantages over the other party.

Departmental Environment

The departmental environment is defined as the group of individuals within the organisation who perform the negotiating activities for transportation service contracts. The sales department or operations department for the motor carrier and the purchasing department or traffic department for the shipper are examples. This conceptual distinction is necessary so that we recognise that different departments of the organisation may have divergent goals, which in turn can create internal conflict, especially when the conflict involves issues contained in the contract for transportation service. Divergent goals are most notable between purchasing departments and traffic departments. Purchasing departments have traditionally emphasised procuring materials and services at the lowest possible price while traffic departments are concerned with using carriers who will provide specific service levels such as reduced transportation times or reduced variability in delivery times, at rate levels which may not be absolutely the lowest offered.

The carrier organisation is also influenced by the department representing its own interest in the negotiation situation. Sales representatives are more concerned with securing the shipper's business while being less aware of the resulting operational requirements necessary to provide the service. Operations, however, may be less aggressive in the pursuit of some business because of proposed contract requirements. Therefore, shipper and carrier representatives should be aware of their own roles as well as those of their opponents.

Personnel Environment

Characteristics of the personal environment can be classified as the personal and personality characteristics of the negotiators. Personal characteristics include age, sex, general physical condition, formal education level and performance, professional affiliations, and negotiation experience and knowledge[14]. The knowledge of the negotiator can be classified as three types: knowledge about the parties involved, knowledge about the interests involved, and knowledge about the facts involved. These characteristics may influence the perceptions of the relationship between the parties as well as the approaches to the preparation and the bargaining activities of the negotiation process itself. For example, experienced negotiators who have been previously represented shippers and carriers using contract motor carriage service may be more detailed in their approaches to preparing for negotiations than less experienced negotiators. Most active transportation contract negotiators today acknowledge the importance of personal characteristics and negotiator experience as being crucial factors in the negotiation process.

Personality variables also greatly influence the negotiation process. Personality characteristics have previously been tested using factors such as dominance, endurance, social recognition, empathy[15], the need for certainty, generalised self-confidence, and the need to achieve[16]. These characteristics can influence the perceptions and expectations of the shipper and carrier representatives, affect the approaches which negotiators use to develop strategies for negotiations, and determine each party's actions and reactions during bargaining.

Negotiation Potential

The ultimate benefit derived from the contract will be based on the nature of the power-dependence relationship between the two parties presented in Figure A.3. This relationship is assessed in two ways:

FIGURE A.3 Negotiation Potential

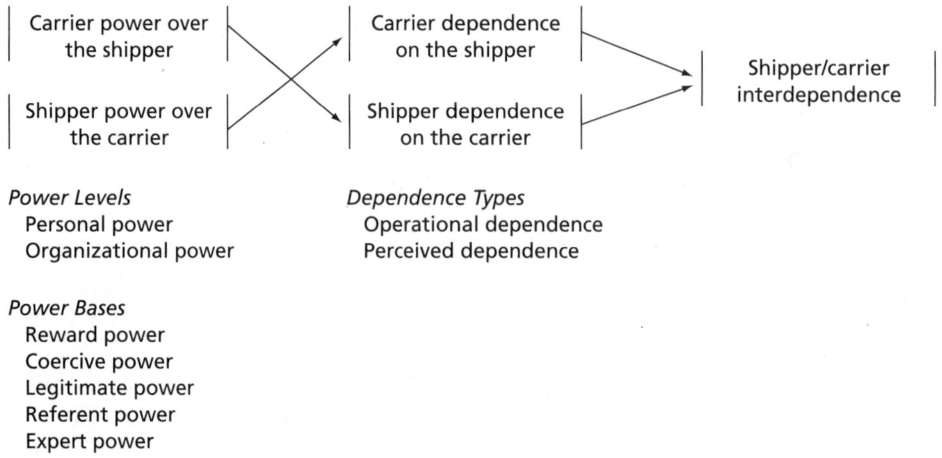

- By the perceptions of their positions by the two parties prior to and during the activities of the negotiation process;
- By the characteristics of the organisations and markets which produce actual relationship factors such as market share and the percentage of total business the agreement will comprise.

The perceptual assessments of their relative positions may significantly influence the negotiators' attitudes as they prepare for the bargaining sessions, bargain with the other party, and assess the quality of the final contract. Perceived power can also be assessed at two levels:

- Each organisation has power derived from current and past competitive positions in the industry;
- Each negotiator has personal power which can be used during bargaining to influence the other negotiator on a personal level.

As an example, a negotiator who perceives the other party to be a formidable opponent at the organisational level may spend more time preparing strategies to reduce his response time to the proposals submitted by the other party, thus allowing the negotiator to keep the other party on the defensive. On the other hand, the negotiator who perceives his opponent to possess considerable power from association with his organisation may prepare less and find himself unable to address specific issues introduced during bargaining sessions; this may in turn jeopardise the possible contractual agreement because of delays in the negotiation process. The relationship between the parties during both the preparation and bargaining phases demonstrates the importance of continual reassessment of the power-dependence relationship.

The business climate between shippers and carriers offers a second assessment of the power-dependence relationship, raising the consideration of the power-dependence relationship from the individual level to the organisational level. Therefore, market offerings, current business between the two parties, and service offerings can influence the negotiator's attitude towards the other party. For example, as the number of alternative carriers increases, the shipper becomes less dependent on any one carrier. In contrast, dependence may increase as the size of the shipper's freight bill increases for a single carrier. Similarly, a rail carrier with a substantial investment in siding track is dependent on its shippers to maximise the utilisation of that asset. The nature of the relationship between the parties provides the initial influence over the approaches used during preparation for the bargaining phase.

Negotiation Preparation

Initiation of the behavioural activities of the contract negotiation process are based on the perception of the obtainable benefits relative to the costs through the potential relationship. Each party must assess the other's relative needs and capabilities. Negotiation preparation allows the collection of information to help reach a level of "readiness"[17] for bargaining activities between parties.

Negotiation preparation requires detailed analysis of the situation, including the collection, organisation, and evaluation of information about the participants, organisations, and external environmental factors which influence the bargaining activities and the resulting contractual agreement. Negotiators use this information as a basis for developing goals and strategies to be implemented during the bargaining phase. The preparation elements of negotiation are presented in Figure A.4.

FIGURE A.4 Negotiation Preparation

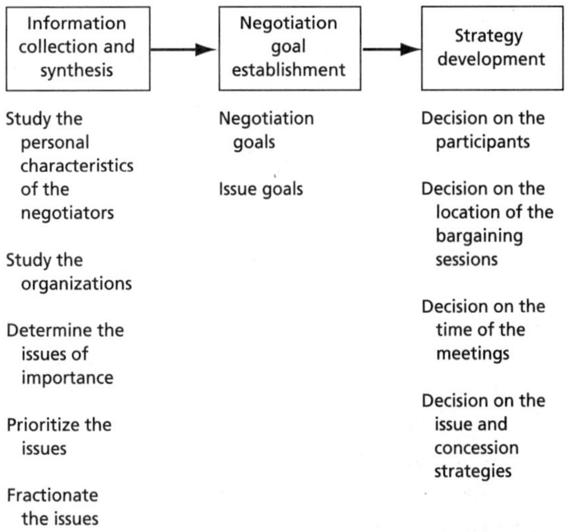

Negotiators may collect information throughout the term of the negotiations, implying that the negotiation process is a cyclical process in which the participants progress to a point of interaction, discuss proposals, and then adjourn to reassess their relative positions and develop new strategies appropriate for the environment. Therefore, participants are continually collecting and analysing pertinent information throughout the negotiation process, which may also include the time between several different meetings.

Information Collection and Synthesis

Information collection and synthesis is the process of collecting, organising, and evaluating the environmental information relevant to the contract negotiation situation between the shipper and carrier. The information can be classified into three basic categories:

(1) Information must be collected on specific contract issues of relevance to the two parties. This information includes the data used in most selections of mode and carrier decisions by shippers, such as the cost and rate structure of the goods movement, reliability of the parties, and the capabilities of the parties to fulfill the terms of the contract[18].

(2) Consideration must be given to the factors which influence the behavioural aspects of the negotiation situation. Negotiators should answer questions about *who* should participate in the preparations and discussions and *where* and *when* the discussions should take place.

(3) Lastly, the sources and types of information to be collected must be considered. A traffic lane analysis may be performed by the shipper using internal resources such as previous sales figures or sales forecasts by markets, previous distributor inventory levels, current carrier rates and service levels, and anticipated service levels provided to the distributors. Information is also collected from outside sources such as credit bureaus, rating agencies, and other experts who have knowledge of the activities of the other party. Internal and external information is beneficial to both parties as they prepare offensive strategies and assess their own weaknesses.

As issues evolve from the information collected, two analysis activities take place. First, negotiators assess the issues to determine their appropriate priority levels. Second, the issues are divided into individual segments to give the negotiator greater flexibility to create cumulative outcomes from the bargaining activities[19]. As the issues are fractionated, the negotiator must again establish priority levels for each alternative segment of each issue. This step allows the negotiator to introduce each issue in its smallest form and gives the parties greater flexibility in the give-and-take process.

Negotiation Goal Establishment

Development of goals for the negotiation process occur at two levels[20]. Goals established for general negotiation activities address the desired relationship between the negotiators and their organisations. The desire of each party concerning the duration of the contract and the power-dependence relation influences the goals each establishes for the negotiation process. For instance, a shipper with long-term transportation needs might negotiate a short-term contract with a carrier because of their lack of previous experience with that particular carrier.

The second group of goals is established for the relevant issues of a specific contract. Negotiators create bargaining strategies by determining those issues absolutely necessary for agreement and those seen as concessions to the other party. Shippers use this bargaining technique to minimise the cost of various levels of service. A shipper may stand firm on a specific low rate and push for increased levels of service from the carrier. When the two parties come close to the level of service desired through concessions made by the carrier, the negotiator for the shipper can concede a rate level higher than that previously demanded, thus achieving his goals while making the carrier believe he is being compensated for the increased service.

Establishment of negotiation goals also depends on the duration of the negotiations. During the cycle of the negotiation process, the goals of each organisation may alter, depending on the positions of the parties. Therefore, as the goals change, they can influence the development of strategies at different points in the negotiation process.

Strategy Development

Strategy development occurs when the parties develop proposals intended to present the relative position of their organisation on behavioural and contract issues. Behavioural issues can include the intent to influence the interactive phase by planning the time, location, and immediate physical setting of the interactive phase[21,22]. In addition, negotiators consider each party's willingness to co-operate during the bargaining phase[23]. Firms using a problem-solving strategy may find a more co-operative response than firms using a more self-centered approach[24,25]. The resulting strategy forces the negotiator to make decisions on the level of co-operation he will use during bargaining, the approach to honesty and accuracy of the information he presents, and the trade-off between long-term and short-term benefits for his organisation.

The general negotiation strategy consists of the selection of alternative issues which allow the firm to attain its negotiation objectives most easily[26]. Individual strategies developed for the contract issues are part of the entire negotiation strategy. These strategies are based on the issues classified and the goals developed during the preparation phase. As an example, a carrier may identify 10 different levels of service available to the shipper in 10 different price categories. As the discussions develop between the parties, the shipper may propose a particular level of service at a lower price with different equipment constraints. To prepare for this situation, the carrier must anticipate the proposals that the shipper might introduce. To achieve a solution to this dilemma, both parties might create a series of scenarios centered around general issue areas, which will allow each negotiator to determine the total benefits and costs derived from each individual set of alternative actions. This could be done by constructing a model decision tree to assess each set of issue outcomes.

Consideration of the behavioural and contract issues during the preparation phase of the negotiation process will help each participant to be completely prepared for the actual meetings.

FIGURE A.5 Bargaining

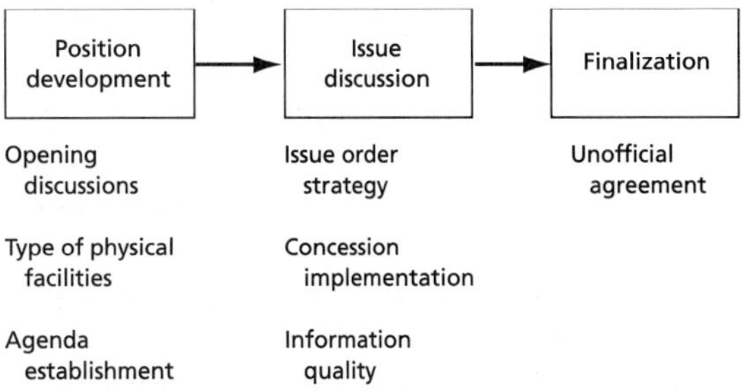

Bargaining

Bargaining activities involve the actual face-to-face meetings between the shipper and carrier. This phase, represented in Figure A.5, consists of three stages of discussion[27]. Position development comprises the initial period when the parties are trying to "set the stage" for the discussion of the contract issues. Issue discussion is the second phase of bargaining, which includes discussions over the majority of the contract issues. Finalisation includes the point at which discussions cease and negotiators reach an unofficial agreement. Recognising the importance of the discussion process will help one understand the implementation of the strategies developed during negotiation preparation.

Position Development

Position development considers factors within the negotiation environment:

- The arrangement of the room in which the bargaining activities will take place;
- The individuals who will be allowed to participate in the discussions;
- The individuals who will be allowed to observe the discussions;
- The agenda of contract issues.

The initial setting can substantially influence the attitudes of the negotiators during the issue discussion phase. Shippers and carriers can use the location as a way of influencing and controlling the availability of information to the negotiators. Shippers negotiators sometimes prefer to concede the advantage of meeting at their own offices and agree to meet at the location of the carrier. This concession, in turn, makes the carrier's information readily available to the shipper, thus reducing the opportunities for the carrier to stall the decision process. Consequently, the carrier will naturally have all the information available to introduce into the bargaining sessions, simultaneously providing the shipper with the opportunity to view the carrier's operations and to see the equipment that would be used under the terms of the contract. Carriers, on the other hand, may use the shipper's strategy to their own advantage because it provides them with control over the physical surroundings of the bargaining activities, which psychologically may allow them to use power ploys as manipulative tools.

As the bargaining sessions begin, the participants introduce their initial positions. The initial proceeding includes the agreement reached by the parties about which issues will be discussed and in what order. These positions provide a basis for future discussions and therefore influence the eventual outcome of the negotiations.

Issue Discussion

Issue discussion involves the relationship between priorities established for the contract issues and the order of the agenda. The order of the issues discussed can influence the importance of the contract issues. For example, if issues of minor importance are discussed and resolved first, the sum of their collected importance can total more than the priority importance of the remaining issues. This situation can influence the participants' approach to resolving high priority issues and yet maintain the previous issue agreements.

In addition, the initial position can influence the number of concessions made by negotiators. If a negotiator's initial position is very close to his perceived point of final acceptance, he will then be less likely to make concessions on the issues of interest. On the other hand, an initial position which obviously goes beyond acceptable terms might indicate that the negotiator, when pressed, will make significant concessions to achieve his objectives. Therefore, each negotiator develops a strategy based on the other's initial position and rate of concessions.

The strategies on the initial positions and the concession rates of the negotiators also influence the duration of the negotiations and the number of meetings necessary to reach agreement. As the length of time of the negotiations increases, additional information becomes available. The negotiator then repeatedly carries through the process from assessment of the relationship between the parties, through preparation, and back into discussions[28]. The length of time between bargaining sessions may be weeks or months, or merely the time between a lunch or coffee break. However, this cyclical process influences the perceived and actual quality of the information used by the negotiators. The perception of the honesty and accuracy of the information can affect the actions and reactions of each negotiator as the discussions conclude.

Finalisation

The last stage in the bargaining phase of the negotiation process addresses the perceptions and interpretations of the participants at the point when a verbal or tentative agreement is established. The finalisation stage occurs when the two parties finish the discussions and agree to the terms of the contract as perceived. In most negotiation situations, finalisation occurs prior to the drafting of an official or documented agreement between the shipper and the carrier. The perceptions derived by the parties influence the need for verification of the agreement when drafted in its final documented form. Finalisation is crucial, since one of the parties will be responsible for developing the final draft. Therefore, finalisation is represented in the opinions of the negotiators and crystallised in the notes which each party takes during the negotiation phase.

Negotiation Outcome

Negotiation outcome includes the elements which address the nature of the final agreement. The three elements considered at this stage of the process are verification, negotiation breakdown, and contract agreement, as presented in Figure A.6.

Verification which involves the specific characteristics of the contract is important in situations in which the party responsible for the preparation of the final document includes provisions not previously agreed. Therefore, negotiators must verify the contents of the contract according to the terms agreed to during finalisation. Verification will take

FIGURE A.6 Negotiation Outcome

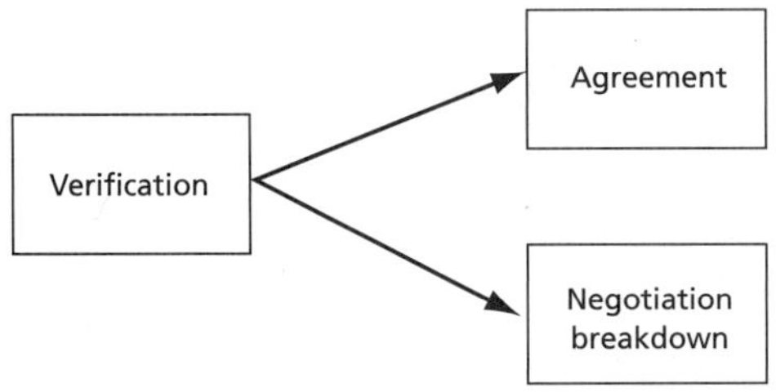

Verification
Documented agreement
Performance appraisal

Agreement
Win-win agreements
Win-lose agreements

Negotiation breakdown
Other business opportunities

one of two forms. Some negotiations might lead to verbal agreements between the shipper and carrier. Under these circumstances, verification will be in the form of performance appraisal measures, that is, the assessment of the performance by the parties under the perceived interpretation of the verbal contract. Verification might also take place prior to the signing of a written contract developed by one of the two parties. In situations where the formal written contract will represent the terms of the agreement, both parties must reach agreement based on their notes and interpretations of the bargaining sessions.

Breakdown of negotiations is another possible outcome. A breakdown results when the two parties fail to agree on the contract issues and decide that their mutual needs can be better satisfied by other sources.

When the shipper and carrier can agree on the terms of the final document, contract agreement may result in one of four outcomes:

- Both parties profit from the contract;
- Neither party profits from the contract;
- The shipper profits from the contract but the carrier does not;
- The carrier profits but the shipper does not[29].

The nature of the agreement reached by the parties will depend on the relative positions of the parties throughout the negotiation process, the amount of preparation, and the strategies used.

The information from the negotiation process which becomes part of the collection of negotiation environmental factors may be used in future negotiations between the two parties (for instance, the renewal of the contract or the development of a new agreement), or between one of the parties and another party in a new negotiation situation. The negotiation process allows negotiators to learn more about their own characteristics and those of the other party, but most important, it allows them to learn about their own performance for future negotiation situations.

Conclusion

The major conclusion drawn from this article is that negotiation is a process which can significantly influence the nature of the contract between the shipper and carrier. Its importance is crucial to both practitioners and scholars who study the process.

Practitioners must realise that negotiators who do not properly recognise the relationship between the parties, or who prepare inadequately for the bargaining sessions, can jeopardise their firms' position during the bargaining phase. The end result of this type of planning can lead them to sign a non-beneficial agreement. As managers of shipper and carrier organisations increasingly recognise the positive implications of transportation service contracts, they will need to place greater emphasis on the negotiation process used to achieve those contracts.

The academic community can use the framework presented here to research different logistics applications and to test potential theoretical relationships which may be represented through the conceptual process structure. Some of these practical and theoretical issues that may arise may be addressed in the following general research questions:

Negotiation environment questions:

- Do the elements of the negotiation process change when it is applied to motor carrier, railroad, or liner and steamship contracts?
- Is there a difference between the application of the negotiation process for truckload and less-than-truckload contracts?

• Do shippers and carriers who use bidding to initiate negotiations apply the process differently from those who do not?

Negotiation process questions:

• What effect does the level of perceived dependence by the participating organisation have over the amount of information collected during the preparation phase of the negotiation process by that organisation?

• What effect does the level of dependence of the party have on their influence over the number of concessions that are made during the bargaining sessions?

• What effect does the use of a bidding procedure have on the structure of the transportation contract achieved between the shipper and carrier?

• What effect does the size of the proposed contract, the frequency of negotiations, and the length of time that each party spends preparing for the bargaining sessions, have on the final price and service levels achieved in the contract?

These research questions introduce issues important to understanding how the negotiation process is applied by logistics practitioners. Further empirical testing of the variables and their relationships will help to formalise the conceptual framework presented and add to knowledge of the negotiation process. The answers to these questions and many others can help the logistics practitioner to implement the negotiation process in a manner which provides the maximum benefit to his organisation. However, the answers to these and other questions can be addressed only within a conceptual framework that encompasses the elements of negotiation and provides the opportunity for a range of applications by the practitioner.

NOTES

1. The Motor Carrier Act of 1980, Public Law 96–296, 1980.
2. The Staggers Rail Act of 1980, Public Law 96–448, 1980.
3. The Shipping Act of 1984, Public Law 98–237, 1984.
4. McFillen, J., Reck R. and Benton, W. C., "An Experiment in Purchasing Negotiations", *Journal of Purchasing and Materials Management,* Vol. 19 No. 2, Summer 1983, pp. 3–8.
5. McAlister, L. Brazerman, M. H. and Fader, P., "Power and Goal Setting in Channel Negotiations", *Journal of Marketing Research,* Vol. 23, August 1986, pp. 228–36.
6. Evans, K. and Beltramini, R., "A Theoretical Model of Consumer Negotiated Pricing: An Orientation Perspective", *Journal of Marketing,* Vol. 51, April 1987, pp. 58–73.
7. Atrogge, P., "Railroad Contracts and Competitive Conditions", *Transportation Journal,* Vol. 21 No. 2, Winter 1981, pp. 37–43.
8. Bagby, J., Evans, J., and Wood, W., "Contracting for Transportation", *Transportation Journal,* Vol. 22 No. 2, Winter 1982, pp. 63–73.
9. Cavinato, J., "Transportation Contracts: Pointers and Pitfalls for Buyers", *Journal of Purchasing and Materials Management,* Vol. 20 No. 1, Winter 1984, pp. 9–15.
10. Bartels, R., *Marketing Theory and Metatheory,* Richard D. Irwin, Homewood, Ill. 1970.
11. Frazier, G., "Interorganizational Exchange Behavior in Marketing Channels: A Broadened Perspective", *Journal of Marketing,* Vol. 47, Fall 1983, pp. 68–78.
12. Webster, F. and Wind, Y., "A General Model for Understanding Organizational Buying Behavior," *Journal of Marketing,* Vol. 36, April 1972, pp. 12–19.
13. Payne, R. and Pugh, D., "Organizational Structure and Climate", in Dunnett, M. (Ed.), *Handbook of Organizational Psychology,* Rand McNally, Chicago, 1976, pp. 1125–73.
14. Fisher, R., "Negotiating Power: Getting and Using Influence", *American Behavioral Scientist,* Vol. 27, November-December 1983, pp. 149–66.
15. Lamont, L. and Lundstrom, W., "Identifying Successful Industrial Salesmen by Personality and Personal Characteristics", *Journal of Marketing Research,* Vol. 14, November 1977, pp. 517–29.
16. Wilson, D., "Industrial Buyers' Decision-Making styles", *Journal of Marketing Research,* Vol. 8, November 1971, pp. 433–6.
17. Thompson, J. and Evans, W., "Behavioral Approach to Industrial Selling", *Harvard Business Review,* March-April 1969, pp. 137–51.
18. Souza, D., "Shipper-Carrier Negotiation: A New World for the Traffic Manager", *Traffic World,* 19 March 1984, pp. 34–38.
19. Whitney, G., "Before You Negotiate: Get Your Act Together", AMACOM: Periodicals Division, American Management Association, 1982, pp. 13–26.

20. Duckman, D., *Human Factors in International Negotiations,* Sage Publications, Beverly Hills, 1973, p. 11.

21. Morse, B., *How to Negotiate the Labor Agreement,* Trends Publishing Company, 1976.

22. Shaw, M. E., *Group Dynamics: The Psychology of Small Group Behavior,* McGraw-Hill, New York, 1976, pp. 131–53.

23. Rubin, J., "Negotiation: An Introduction to Some Issues and Themes", *American Behavioral Scientist,* Vol. 27, November-December 1983, pp. 135–48.

24. Pruitt, D., "Strategic Choice in Negotiation", *American Behavioral Scientist,* Vol. 27, November-December 1983, pp. 167–94.

25. Tracy L. and Petersen, R., "Tackling Problems Through Negotiation", *Human Resource Management,* Summer 1979, pp. 14–23.

26. Fisher, R. and Ury, W., *Getting to Yes,* R. R. Donnelley, Harrisonburg, VA, 1985, pp. 101–11.

27. Richardson, R., *Collective Bargaining by Objectives,* Prentice-Hall, Englewood Cliffs, NJ, 1977, pp. 65–105.

28. Cohen, H., *You Can Negotiate Anything,* Bantam Books, New York, 1980, pp. 91–100.

29. Dommermuth, W., "Profiting from Distribution Conflicts", *Business Horizons,* December 1976, pp. 4–13.

PART 4

Technology and Strategies

CHAPTER

13

INFORMATION MANAGEMENT AND TECHNOLOGY

The use of technology to collect and convey information is not new to the transportation industry. Railroads use microwave technology to manage and track train movement, airlines use sophisticated avionics to manage the flight of their aircraft, ocean vessels use on-board computers to navigate domestic and international waterways, motor carriers use on-board computers and satellite systems to efficiently manage their asset base, and pipelines use computer technology to manage pumping stations to ensure the smooth flow of their products. What is new is the integration of this technology among carriers, shippers, receivers, and third parties to efficiently and effectively manage the supply chain.

The adoption of information technology in the supply chain has exploded during the 1990s and its use will continue to grow well into the next century. What has caused this exponential growth in the use of information technology? Many companies have found that using information technology has allowed them to significantly reduce assets (inventories or equipment) and better manage information, product, and cash flows among all supply chain partners. The cost of information technology has also decreased significantly over the last ten years.

A related driver of the growth in information technology over the last several years is the Year 2000 problem. Rather than fix existing legacy information systems to accommodate the year 2000, many firms have opted to totally reengineer their information systems with new systems and technology. This chapter will examine information systems and technology from a supply chain perspective; it will look at both topics from the perspectives of the shipper, carrier, and receiver. This focus is important because of the need for carriers and their customers to be able to integrate the flow of information. To accomplish this goal, this chapter is divided into four major sections: 1) Information Systems, 2) Information Sources, 3) Information Technology, and, 4) Types of Information Technology. The authors would like to acknowledge the contributions to this chapter from Dr. William L. "Skip" Grenoble, Administrative Director of the Center for Logistics Research at Pennsylvania State University.

Information Systems

Before a discussion on technology can begin, the concept of information systems must be addressed. Logistics and transportation operations are sometimes overwhelmed with the vast amount of data available to them. Information systems are designed to use the available data to portray meaningful information to decision makers. Decisions are made at various organizational levels within carrier firms and their customers' firms. These decisions can be made at the transactional levels as well as at the strategic level. For example, a transactional carrier decision might be how to best dispatch a driver and vehicle to minimize empty miles and maximize revenue. A strategic carrier decision might address fleet sizing based on forecasted freight flows over the next five years. The transactional decision is influenced by the strategic decision and vice versa. Similar types of decisions are made by shippers and receivers. The point is that some type of information system integration is necessary to link all of the players in the supply chain. The diagram in Figure 13.1 can be used as a mechanism to help link the different types of information systems in a shipper or receiver organization.[1] The importance of this diagram is its ability to link data base files with transactional decisions and strategic decisions. This diagram also identifies the types of data necessary to make these decisions. Decisions regarding inventories, warehousing, manufacturing, and transportation are linked to a common

FIGURE 13.1 Integration of Logistics Information Systems on a Hierarchical and Make-to-Stock Basis

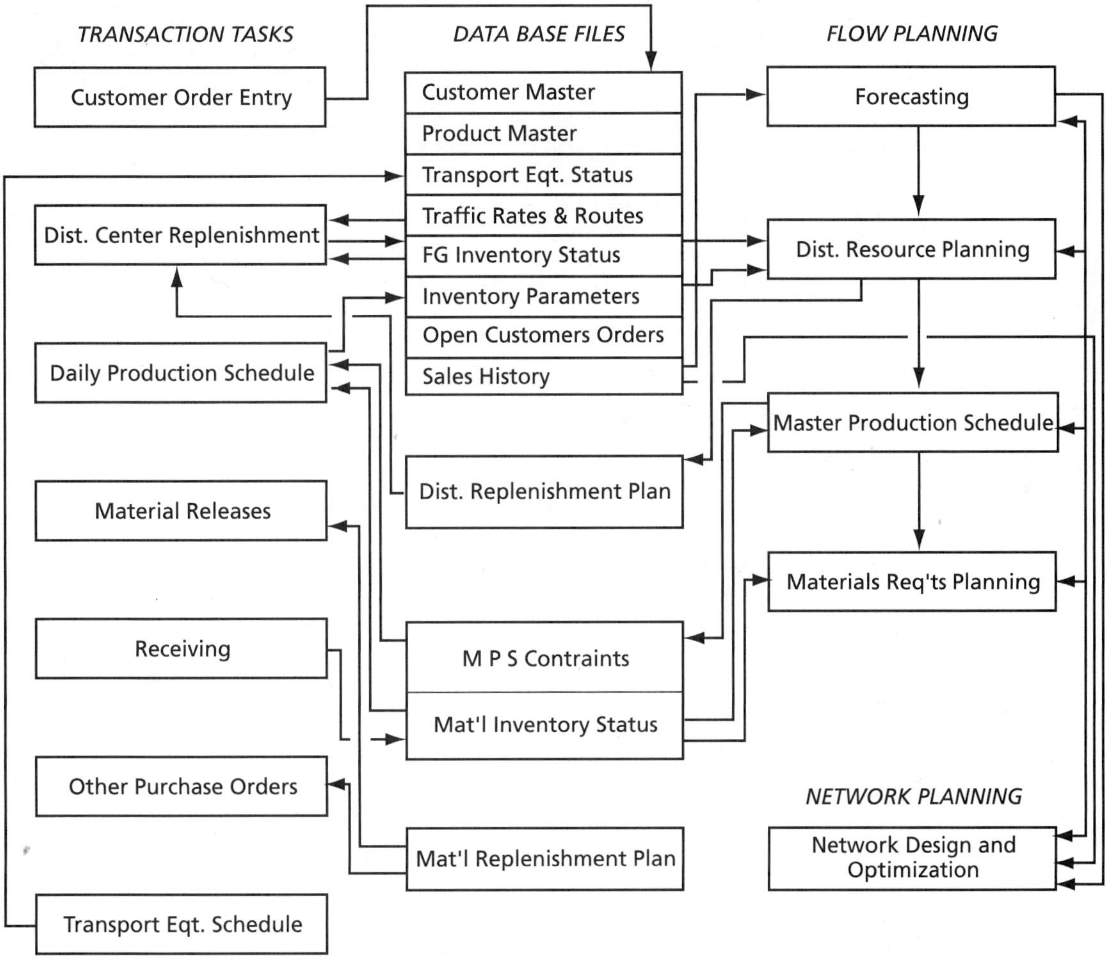

Source: Alan J. Stenger, Steven C. Dunn, and Richard R. Young, "Commercially Available Software for Integrated Logistics Management," *The International Journal of Logistics Management,* Vol. 4, No. 2, (1993), p. 63.

database. This is the basis for Enterprise Resource Planning (ERP) systems. The sources of data necessary to manage the transportation process will also be discussed in more detail later in this chapter.

Certain types of information are necessary to facilitate the transportation process between a shipper and a receiver. All of the elements in Figure 13.1 provide inputs to and receive outputs from transportation. More specifically, information required to make the transportation process work can be classified into pre-transaction, transaction, and post-transaction.[2] Pre-transaction information includes all information necessary to plan the carrier movement, transaction information includes all information necessary while the shipment is in motion with the carrier, and post-transaction information includes all information necessary after the shipment has been delivered.

TABLE 13.1 Information Needed to Manage the Transportation Process

Transportation Activity	Information User: Shipper	Carrier	Receiver
Pre-Transaction	P.O. Info Forecasts Equipment Availability	BOL Info Forecasts Pickup/Delivery Time	Advance Ship Notice Delivery time
Transaction	Shipment Status	Shipment Status	Shipment Status
Post-Transaction	Freight Bill Carrier Performance Proof of Delivery Claim Info	Payment Claim Info	Carrier Performance Proof of Delivery Claim info

Table 13.1 shows the requirements for all three types of information for the shipper, carrier, and receiver. Although it is not comprehensive, the table does show that information flows must be linked among all three parties to make the shipment arrive as promised. In the pre-transaction phase, the shipper needs purchase order information and possibly forecast and point of sale (POS) data to help plan carrier capacity and selection decisions. The shipper also needs information from the carrier as to equipment availability and scheduled pick-up time. Strategically, the carrier needs volume forecast data from the shipper to plan capacity appropriately. Transactionally, the carrier also needs bill of lading (BOL) information as well as desired pick-up and delivery times from the shipper. The receiver requires an advance shipment notice (ASN) from the shipper as well as a scheduled delivery time from the carrier (or from the shipper in the ASN).

The transaction phase requires that all three parties receive information regarding shipment status (such as, will it arrive as planned?). Many carriers manage shipment status through technologies such as satellite tracking, on-board computers, and bar coding. Normally, it is the carrier that generates shipment status information. Often this is handled on an exception basis where the shipper and/or receiver are notified of shipment status only if changes occur in delivery times or other shipment requirements.

Finally, the post-transaction phase requires a freight bill from the carrier if the shipment is free on-board (FOB) destination as well as a proof of delivery (POD) and other verification of carrier performance, such as damage or claims information. The carrier requires payment information (when and how much) from the shipper as well as claims information, if necessary, from the receiver. The receiver might require carrier performance information (on-time, damage free) from the carrier as well as POD from the shipper or carrier to initiate the payment process to the shipper for the product. These various types of information and their flows are captured in Figure 13.2.[3]

Again, a critical component of the transportation process is that all the information flows among the various parties are integrated, just as they are for the logistics process shown in Figure 13.1.

Information Sources

The previous section identified the various types of information needed to manage the transportation process. This section will identify the sources of this information. Traditionally, transportation information has come from what can be called "docu-

FIGURE 13.2 Examples of Information Flows

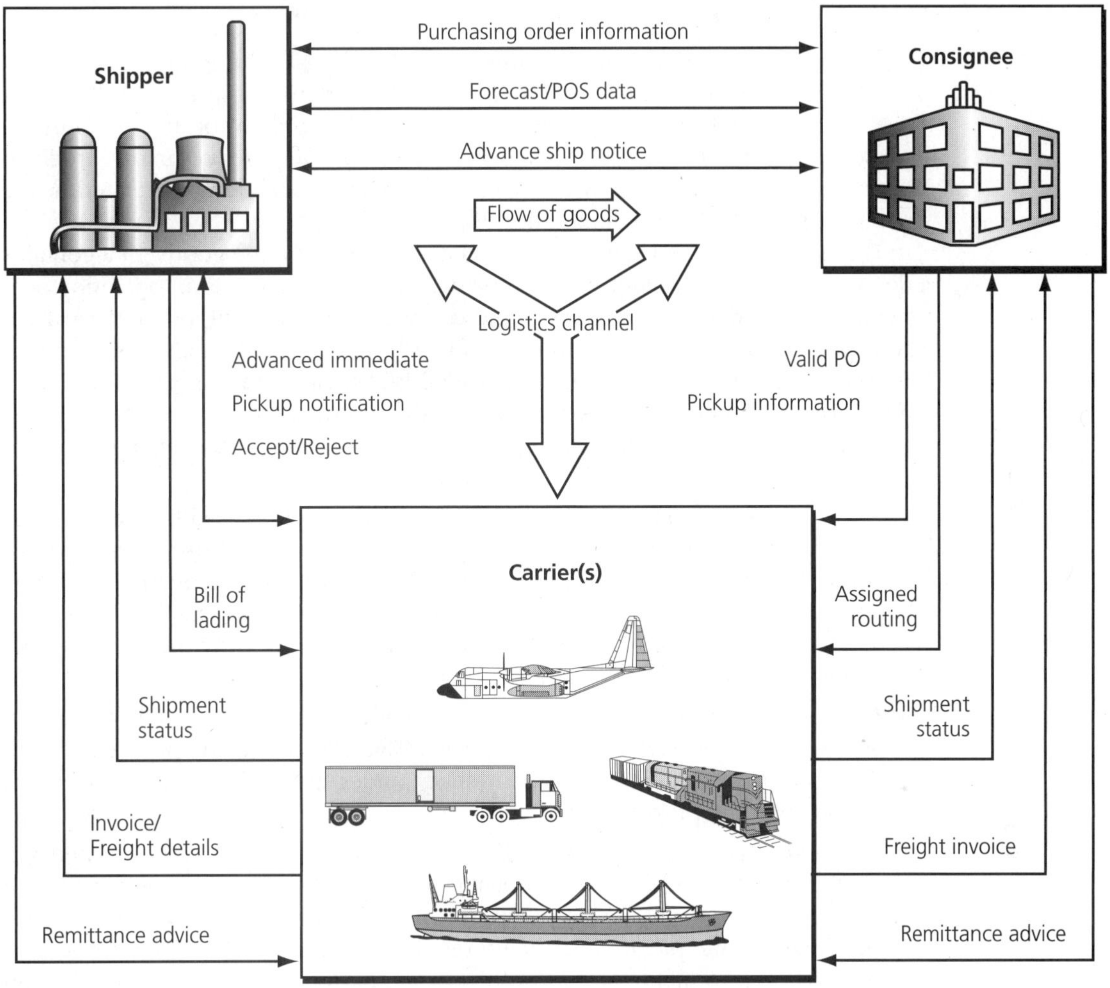

Source: Coyle, Bardi, and Langley, *The Management of Business Logistics,* Eighth Edition, (Minneapolis, MN: West, 1996), p.403.

mentation." This implied paperwork was generated by the shipper and carrier to initiate, perform, and terminate a shipment. The paperwork required to perform this service included bills of lading, waybills, manifests, and freight bills. In many cases, this paper trail was produced manually and caused many problems for the successful delivery of a shipment. Bills of lading and freight bills were required to be generated by the carrier with their requirements defined by the Surface Transportation Board (STB).

Today many of these transactions have become "paperless" through the use of Electronic Data Interchange (EDI) among carriers, shippers, and receivers. This has eliminated many of the problems associated with manually generated documents and has improved transportation service for shippers and receivers as well as cash flow for carriers. This discussion will not focus on the legal requirements of the various sources of transportation information, but will pay attention to the role of these various "documents" and the information they convey.

Bill of Lading

The Bill of Lading (BOL) is the document used to initiate the request for a transportation movement. This is probably the most important transportation document since it provides information necessary for the carrier to plan for and perform the transportation service. Although the federal government requires common carriers to generate a BOL for every shipment, most BOLs are customized and generated by the shipper. Figure 13.3 is an example of a BOL.

The BOL serves five legal purposes: 1) it is a receipt for the goods; 2) it contains a description of the shipment; 3) it can be evidence of title; 4) it is an operating document; and 5) it defines the terms of the contract between a shipper and a carrier. Although BOLs are usually customized to fit a shipper's needs, certain basic types of information are included at a minimum on all BOLs. Table 13.1 specified the information contained in the BOL as necessary in the pre-transaction phase of the transportation process. The following represents the minimum requirements for BOL information:

1. *Origin/destination of the shipment.* This information is used by the carrier to identify the freight lane that will be used for the shipment. It also allows the carrier to identify the availability of equipment and personnel to provide the transportation, or to begin to position capacity to move the shipment. This might not be the same as the billing location. This can also be used by the carrier to determine pick-up and delivery times.

2. *Carrier designation.* Shippers will generally integrate their BOL generation process with their carrier-routing process. This allows the shipping location to comply with its contracts and/or routing guides and helps identify the initial contact with the pickup carrier.

3. *Special operating instructions.* This information allows the carrier to perform the transportation service in compliance with the needs of the shipper. Special instructions might include temperature control, loading/unloading requirements, blocking/bracing, pickup or delivery requirements, and so on. The point of this information is to make the carrier fully aware of the nature of the shipment and what might be necessary, above and beyond normal transportation service, to deliver the shipment in compliance with the demands of the shipper.

4. *Shipment description.* This information includes not only a description of the commodity but also the quantity and weight of the commodity or commodities. The carrier will use this for equipment selection, pickup, and rating/billing decisions. This section can also alert the carrier of any hazardous materials that might be in the shipment.

5. *Billing instructions.* If not the same as the origin identified above, this provides the carrier the information concerning the identify of the party responsible for paying for the transportation service.

Two types of BOL exist: 1) straight, or non-negotiable; and 2) order, or negotiable. The title to the shipment cannot be transferred to another party using a straight BOL. An order BOL can be used to transfer the title to the goods. A sample order BOL can be seen in Figure 13.4. The order BOL actually becomes evidence of the title to a shipment and is very indicative of the product, cash, and information flows present in a supply chain. Figure 13.5 represents a schematic of how the order BOL works.

FIGURE 13.3 Bill of Lading Example

CARRIER

STRAIGHT BILL OF LADING-SHORT FORM-Original-Not Negotiable

SCAC NO. AGENT'S NO. 10

RECEIVED, subject to the classifications and lawfully filed tariff rates in effect on the date of the issue of this Bill of Lading. AT

DATE

the property desciribedbelow. in apparent good order. except as noted (contents and condition of contents of packages unknown) consigned. and detined as indicated below. which said carrier (the word carrier being understood throu contract as meaning any person or corporation in possession. the property desciribedbelow. in apparent good order. except as noted (contents and condition of contents of packknown). marded. consigned. and detined as indicated below. which said carrier (the word carrier being understood throntract as meaning any person or corporation in possession. the property desciribedbelow. in apparent good order. except as noted (contents and condition of contents of packages unkarded. consigned. and detined as indicated below. which said carrier (the word carrier being understood throughout this contract as meaning any corporation in possession. the property desciribedbelow. in apparent good order. except as
the property desciribedbelow. in apparent good order. except as noted (contents and condition of contents of packages unknown).consigned. detined as indicated below. which said carrier (the word carrier being understood throughout this contract as meaning any person or corporation in . the property desciribedbelow.

ORDER NO.	REQUESTED SHIP DATE	REQUESTED DELIVER DATE	BILL OF LADING NO.	CUSTOMER NO.	IF UNDELIVERABLE CALL CUSTOMER SERVICE AT	CARRIER MUST SHOW THIS SHIPPERS NO. ON ALL FREIGHT BILLS.

CONSIGNED TO

CAR/TRUCK INITIALS

CAR/TRUCK NO.

SEAL NO'S.

ROUTE

MAIL FREIGHT BILLS WITH THIS SHIPPER'S NUMBER TO NABISCO BRANDS. INC.

DELIVERING CARRIER

If charges are to be Prepaid, write or stamp here, "To Be Prepaid."

TO BE PREPAID

CUSTOMER ORDER NUMBERS

SHIPMENT ORIGINATED AT

DELIVERY / SPECIAL INSTRUCTIONS

Where the rate is dependent on value, shippers are required to state specifically in writing the agreed or dclared value of the property.

THE DESCRIPTIONS AND WEIGHT INDICATED ON THIS BILL OF LADING ARE CORRECT, SUBJECT TO VERIFICATION BY THE **CARRIER'S WEIGHING & INSPECTION BUREAUS** ACCORDING TO AGREEMENT

Subject to Section 7 of condition if this shipment is to be delivered to the consignee wihout recourse of the consignor, the consignor shall sign the following statement:
The caarrier shall not make delivery of this shipment without payment of freight and all other lawful charges

NABISCO BRANDS, INC.

(Signature of consignor)

"TENDERED IN SORTED OR SEGREGATED LOTS BY PRODUCT, SIZE, FLAVORS OR CODES."

UPC CODE MFG. CODE	UPC CODE ITEM NO.	QUANTITY	DESCRIPTIONS	GROSS WEIGHT SUBJECT TO CORRECTION	COMM. GROUP	

B/L PARTS OF	TOTAL QUANTITY		TEMPERATURE REQUIREMENTS MAINTAIN RANGE OF THRU	TOTAL GROSS WEIGHT		TOTAL CUBIC FEET	

NABISCO BRANDS, INC., Shipper

PER

PERMANENT ADDRESS OF SHIPPER EAST HANOVER, NJ 07936

APPT. TIME	TIME IN	PALLETS IN
	TIME OUT	PALLETS OUT

Agent

PER

FIGURE 13.4 A Sample Order Bill of Lading

UNIFORM ORDER BILL OF LADING
(ORIGINAL)

PAID
JUL 07 1993
TEXAS ... BANK
ARLINGTON

Shipper's No. 8952

Agent's No.

to: ST. PAUL, MN 55124 JUNE 29 19 93

from ARCTIC ENTERPRISES, INC.

Consigned to ORDER of ARCTIC ENTERPRISES, INC.

Destination ARLINGTON State of TX 76013 County of

Notify THE SLALOM SHOP 3644 W. PIONEER PARKWAY

At ARLINGTON State of TX 76013 County of

Route

Delivering Carrier Car Initial Car No.

No. Packages	Description of Articles, Special Marks and Exceptions	Weight (Subject to Correction)	Class or Rate	Check Column
6	SKIS, POWER—NOI in Boxes, Crates			
	Item #25255, Sub 1	2700	125	
	SERIAL NUMBERS: 12268			
	12274			
	12045			
	12260			
	12253			
	12264			
	FREIGHT COLLECT			
	NOTIFY: GARY COX AT SLALOM SHOP			
	817/469-3100			

Donald Churchill
(Signature of Consignor)

COLLECT

Received $

Charges Advanced

$

ARCTIC ENTERPRISES, INC. Shipper. Yellow Freight System, Inc. Agent

Per Donald Churchill Per Bob White 6/29/93

Permanent post-office address of shipper 702 FORDHAM RD., ST. PAUL, MN 55124

Source: Yellow Freight Systems, Inc. Reprinted by permission.

The BOL is signed by the carrier and is sent by the shipper to a bank indicating the shipment is in progress. The bank notifies the consignee that it has received the BOL and requests payment of the invoice. If the consignee forwards payment to the bank, the bank releases the BOL to the consignee as evidence of the title. Before the carrier can deliver the shipment to the consignee, the consignee must present the BOL to the carrier. Most cash and information flows using the order BOL are done electronically in today's environment.

FIGURE 13.5 The Process of Using an Order Bill of Lading

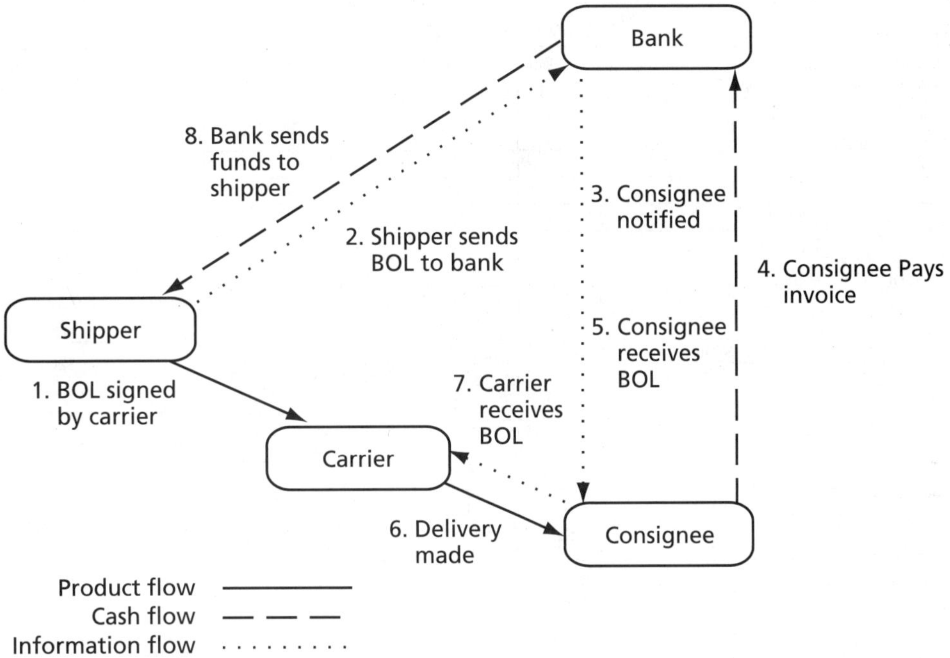

Source: John F. Tyworth, Joseph L. Cavinato, and C. John Langley, Jr., *Traffic Management*.

Waybill

What a BOL does for a shipment, a waybill does for a rail car. It is the operating document that governs the movement of the car as well as the descriptive document of the car's contents. The waybill assigns a car to a train, designates switching points, identifies routes, specifies trailer numbers for TOFC/COFC shipments, and contains billing information. Every rail car will be identified by a waybill. Today most railroads generate and transmit waybills electronically.

Manifest

A manifest is used as the operating and descriptive document for motor-carrier trailers. It has basically the same function as a waybill. A sample manifest can be seen in Figure 13.6. One specific difference is that the manifest documents the weight loaded in each quartile of the trailer. This is done specifically to address axle weight restrictions on the highway system.

Freight Bill

A freight bill is the carrier's invoice for transportation and related charges. A sample freight bill can be seen in Figure 13.7. The freight bill has some of the same information as the BOL, such as origin/destination and commodity description. The freight bill also serves the purpose of notifying the buyer of the charges and how they were assessed. It also can serve as proof of delivery. These two pieces of information are identified as important to the transportation process, as shown in Table 13.1.

FIGURE 13.6 A Freight Waybill

TRAILER MANIFEST
00 8 (Revised 3/86) YELLOW FREIGHTT SYSTEM, INC. DESTINATION COPY

PRELOADING INSPECTION (1)

TRAILER SWEPT ☑ DOORS OK ☑
HOLES PATCHED ☑ TARP OK ☐
NAILS PULLED ☑
APPROVAL SIGNATURE: *Bill Anderson*

DATE STARTED *2/23/87*
TIME STARTED (2) *1530*
SCH. CLOSE OUT TIME *2300*
DATE FINISHED *2/23/87*
TIME FINISHED *2315*

RELAY DISPATCH (3)

FROM	TO	TRACTOR	DATE	DRIVER

ORIGIN DISPATCH (4)

ORIG/DES *DEC/NSH*
TRAILER *50973*
DATE *2/23/87*
LTG *2315*
ADT *0300*
BILLS *38*
SEIGHT *27,493*
CUBE *98*
DOLLY
TRACTOR
DRIVER

LOCATION OF FOODSTUFFS (5)

ANY MATERIAL EDIBLE BY HUMANS OR ANIMALS MUST NOT BE LOADED WITH CLASS 'A' OR 'B' POISONS

POSITION	WEIGHT
N/A	

LOCATION OF HAZARDOUS MATERIALS (6)

00.74 MUST BE AFFIXED TO DD 8 IF HAZARDOUS MATERIAL IS ON TRAILER
00.74 A MUST ACCOMPANY ALL BILLS ON HAZARDOUS MATERIALS (SDFSDFKL;JFSF ☐)

CLASS	POSITION	WEIGHT
FLL	*10D*	*71*

PUP FIRST HALF / **PUP SECOND HALF**

A POS	46' FIRST QUARTER PIECES	WEIGHT	INITIALS	B POS	46' SECOND QUARTER PIECES	WEIGHT	INITIALS	C POS	46' THIRD QUARTER PIECES	WEIGHT	INITIALS	D POS	46' FOURTH QUARTER PIECES	WEIGHT	INITIALS
1	45	1,940	LL	1	1	3,000	DB	1	120	1,940	MH	1	2	693	MH
2	1	1,015	LL	2	2	1,000	DB	2	15	1,015	MH	2	7	350	DB
3	1	95	LL	3	1	10	DB	3	175	95	MH	3	3	110	TD
4	1	120	LL	4	2	60	DB	4				4	1	73	TD
5	2	815	LL	5	1	20	DB	5				5	10	193	TD
6	1	682	LL	6	1	10	DB	6				6	2	111	TD
7	2	220	LL	7	5	100	DB	7				7	5	425	TD
8	1	101	LL	8	5	150	DB	8				8	3	255	TD
9	1	875	LL	9	2	450	MH	9				9	7	1,062	TD
10	24	3,840	LL	10	10	100	MH	10				10	2	71	TD
11				11	60	600	DB	11				11			
12				12	21	307	DB	12				12			
13				13	200	1,400	DB	13				13			
14				14	100	700	MH	14				14			
15				15	19	40	MH	15				15			
16				16				16				16			
17				17				17				17			
18		(7)		18		(8)		18		(9)		18		(10)	
19				19				19				19			
20				20				20				20			
SECTION WGT		9,703				7,947				6,500				3,343	

SUPERVISOR'S SIGNATURE: *Bill Anderson* *Bill Anderson* SUPERVISOR'S SIGNATURE: *Bill Anderson* *Bill Anderson*

LOAD PROFILE (11)

CUBE *99* % CUBE *99* % CUBE *99* % CUBE *97* %

LOADED INSPECTOR (12)

CUBE OR WEIGHT MAXIMIZED? ☐ IS THIS A *NO*
FREIGHT PROPERLY STACKED? ☐ SHIPPER'S
BLOCKING WHERENEEDED? ☐ LOAD & COUNT?
IF TRAILER NOT FVC. WHY? *run for service*
APPROVAL SIGNATURE: *Bill Anderson*

(13)
1. *11,820* 3. *22,520* 5.
2. *26,140* 4. GROSS *60,480*

COMMENTS (14)

137-106475
Run on first driver

RECORD (15)

SEAL NO. APPLIED *90717* INT. *BA* SEAL NO. REMOVED INT.
SEAL NO. APPLIED INT. SEAL NO. REMOVED INT.

Source: Yellow Freight Systems, Inc. Reprinted by permission.

FIGURE 13.7 A Sample Freight Bill

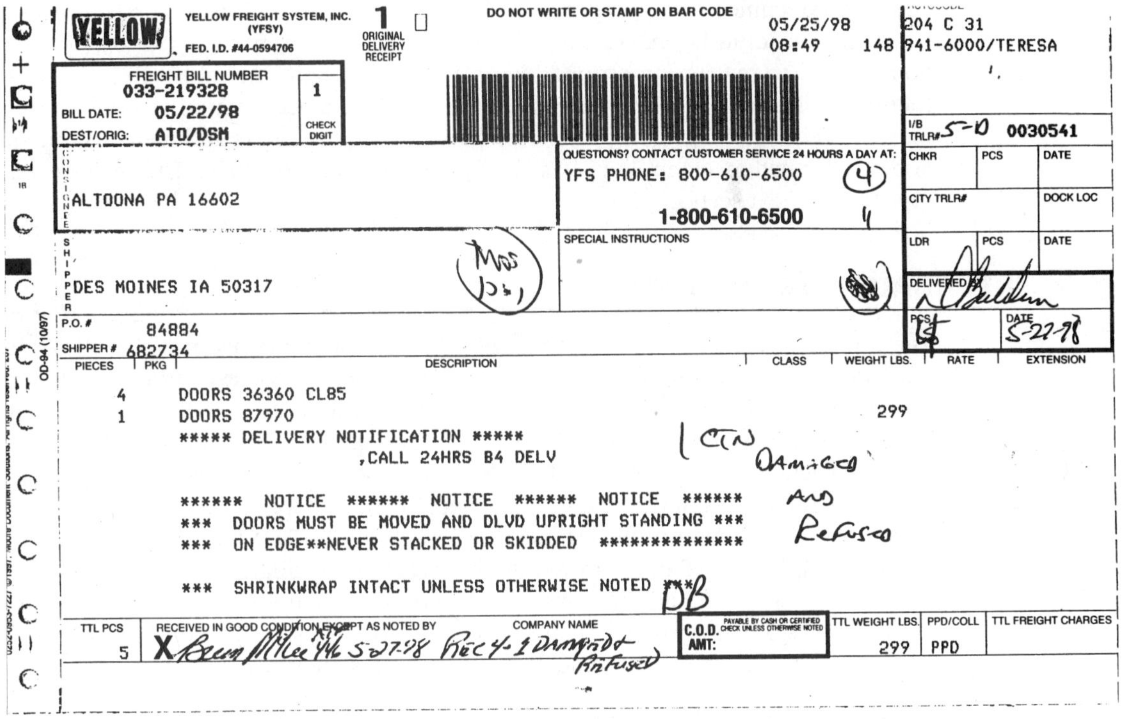

YELLOW FREIGHT SYSTEM, INC. (YFSY)
FED. I.D. #44-0594706
1 ORIGINAL DELIVERY RECEIPT
DO NOT WRITE OR STAMP ON BAR CODE
05/25/98 08:49 148
204 C 31
941-6000/TERESA

FREIGHT BILL NUMBER 033-219328
1 CHECK DIGIT
BILL DATE: 05/22/98
DEST/ORIG: ATO/DSM

I/B TRLR# 0030541

CHKR | PCS | DATE
CITY TRLR# | DOCK LOC
LDR | PCS | DATE
DELIVERED BY
PCS | DATE 5-27-98

QUESTIONS? CONTACT CUSTOMER SERVICE 24 HOURS A DAY AT:
YFS PHONE: 800-610-6500
1-800-610-6500

CONSIGNEE: ALTOONA PA 16602

SPECIAL INSTRUCTIONS

SHIPPER: DES MOINES IA 50317

P.O.# 84884
SHIPPER# 682734

PIECES	PKG	DESCRIPTION	CLASS	WEIGHT LBS.	RATE	EXTENSION
4		DOORS 36360 CL85				
1		DOORS 87970		299		
		***** DELIVERY NOTIFICATION ***** ,CALL 24HRS B4 DELV				
		****** NOTICE ****** NOTICE ****** NOTICE ******				
		*** DOORS MUST BE MOVED AND DLVD UPRIGHT STANDING ***				
		*** ON EDGE**NEVER STACKED OR SKIDDED **************				
		*** SHRINKWRAP INTACT UNLESS OTHERWISE NOTED ***				

1 CTN DAMAGED AND REFUSED

TTL PCS	RECEIVED IN GOOD CONDITION EXCEPT AS NOTED BY	COMPANY NAME	C.O.D. AMT: PAYABLE BY CASH OR CERTIFIED CHECK UNLESS OTHERWISE NOTED	TTL WEIGHT LBS.	PPD/COLL	TTL FREIGHT CHARGES
5	X			299	PPD	

OD-94 (10/97)

Source: Yellow Freight Systems, Inc. Reprinted by permission.

Many buyers will not begin the payment process until a proof of delivery (signed freight bill) is matched with a BOL, a packing list for the shipment, and possibly an ASN. Some carriers, like FedEx, use electronic signatures on their delivery receipts. When a shipment is delivered to a customer, the carrier will capture the receiver's signature electronically on a hand-held computer. This receiving information, along with time and date, is then stored in the carrier's data base and linked with the BOL. Proof of delivery can then be supplied electronically by the carrier. The generation of a hard copy proof of delivery using traditional methods can be a lengthy process and negatively impact the carrier's cash flow. However, electronic signature capture has reduced the time necessary to prove delivery by the carrier and has improved the carrier's ability to collect freight charges quickly.

The evaluated receipts process, used in the automobile industry with its suppliers, has also drastically reengineered the payment process between carriers and their customers. The charges for the transportation are agreed upon between the carrier and the customer; many times these charges are stated in contracts. When the shipment arrives, the ASN is checked against the packing slip and/or the BOL. If they match, the documents are sent to accounts payable and a check is not sent to the carrier or an electronic funds transfer is made to the carrier's bank. The carrier does not produce a freight bill and a separate proof of delivery document is used. This process, although not yet common in the transportation industry, has reduced the cost of the payment process for both the carrier and its customers as well as improved the carrier's cash flow.

Many other documents might be needed for a shipment depending upon the information needed to manage the transportation process. This is especially true for international shipments. Chapter 9, "International Transportation," addressed several additional documents necessary for international shipments. This discussion was by no means meant to be exhaustive. The intent was to identify the types of information needed to manage transportation and identify where the information is to be found. Traditionally, this information was generated and transmitted manually, complicating product, information, and cash flows between carriers and their customers. Today information technology has totally changed this practice. This will be the topic of the next section.

Information Technology

The adoption of information technology (IT) is a leading concern of logistics and transportation managers today. The push to be more competitive from a cost and service perspective has driven firms to take a hard look at how they traditionally provided logistics and transportation services. A recent survey conducted by KPMG Peat Marwick LLP concluded that IT was second only to cost control as a top logistics issue. The results of this study can be seen in Table 13.2.[4] An argument could be made that every issue on this list has an IT application. Two issues arise when deciding to implement IT in a transportation or logistics setting: 1) where to start, and 2) how to integrate the different systems. The purpose of this discussion is not to answer these two questions. The main purpose is to introduce the concept of IT and the various aspects of its implementation for carriers and their customers.

Areas of Application

In a recent study, information system executives were asked which areas of their firms' significant investments will be made in IT. The results of this study are shown in Table 13.3. The customer service area includes call center operations, a significant operation for most carriers. The areas of the most significant investment are those included in the supply chain.

Four reasons push this investment in the supply chain. First, information can be a substitute for supply-chain assets, costs, and even services. Making inventory visible through information allows firms in the supply chain to reduce or, in some cases,

TABLE 13.2 Top 10 Logistics Issues

1. Cost Control	22%
2. Information Technology	18%
3. Inventory Management	17%
4. Customer Service	13%
5. Transportation Cost	11%
6. Cycle Time	8%
7. Freight Management	5%
8. Fleet/Driver Management	5%
9. Quality	4%
10. Delivery Time	4%

Source: Stephen Barr, "Putting It All Together," *CFO* (July 1995), p. 62.

TABLE 13.3 Technology Application Areas: Where Will the Money Be Spent?

Customer Service	68%
Order Processing	52%
Systems Development	49%
Manufacturing	47%
Delivery/Logistics	45%
Marketing	34%
Accounting	33%
Sales	33%
Human Resources	21%
Engineering Time	9%

Source: Cleveland Consulting Survey of IS Executives.

eliminate safety stock inventories. This ultimately takes costs out of the supply chain, rather than pushing costs back to suppliers or carriers. For example, satellite technology for carriers has allowed them to know exactly where a shipment is and whether it will meet its scheduled delivery time. If a delay is expected, the receiver is notified so proper actions can be taken. This allows firms to reduce the uncertainty of late deliveries and the necessity of extra inventories. Second, the cost of information continues to fall. This trend has been accelerated by the decreasing cost of technology. For example, desktop personal computers today can be purchased for less than $1000; the same system cost five times that much 10 years ago. So as processing and storage technology declines in price, so will the cost of information. Third, demands for information from supply chain partners are rising. The availability and effectiveness of information regarding supply-chain operations are causing firms to need more information to manage their processes. Initiatives such as Collaborative Planning, Forecasting, and Replenishment (CPFR) in the retail industry are requiring not only more information but also the sharing of that information with all relevant supply-chain partners. Sharing demand forecasts with carriers allows them to better manage and position capacity. An important point to be made here is that the information shared must be relevant to the supply-chain partner. Firms are beginning to develop logistics data warehouses with storage capacities measured in terabytes. Sharing all information with all partners will result in data overload and be counterproductive. Finally, in supply chain management, managing information flows is as important as managing product and cash flows. Chapter 1, "Transportation, the Supply Chain, and the Economy," included all three flows in its description of the supply chain. These three flows are inseparable; one cannot work without the other two. An argument might even be made that managing information might be the most important because it can be used to manage product and cash flows. The point, however, is that information flows are critical in managing the relationships that exist among all members of a supply chain.

Types of Technology

The number and types of technology that exist to facilitate transportation and logistics operations continue to grow at a rapid pace. However, certain types of technology are critical to these processes. Table 13.4 is a listing of what can be considered the basics, emerging, and the future technologies to be applied to logistics and transportation. This section will present discussions on the most relevant of these technologies.

STOP OFF

Copacino on Strategy

The IT-enabled supply chain: Key to future success

In 1990, I wrote a column in this magazine that explained why information technology (IT) was critically important to logistics management and suggested that the importance of IT to logistics would increase. This prediction clearly has been realized, if not exceeded.

IT developments over the past eight years have enabled companies to achieve a quantum leap in their supplychain performance. Those that do not have robust "IT-enabled supplychain" capability, by contrast, simply can not compete effectively in today's business environment. An IT-enabled supply chain requires the following elements:

- *Enterprise Resource Planning (ERP) software,* which links functions such as finance, sales, distribution, materials management, and production planning in an integrated way with a common database. ERP is particularly valuable for linking global operations and providing a current and common view of a corporation's operational status, such as current sales by customer or geographic area, inventory status, and so forth.
- *Decision Support software,* including supplychain optimization and demand-planning software. These programs, which include such capabilities as forecasting, Distribution Resource Planning, manufacturing, scheduling, network analysis, operations planning/optimization, and transportation scheduling, often are very important for effective supplychain management. These capabilities are being integrated with ERP software as ERP vendors expand their software's functionality and conclude alliances and formal product-integration programs with decision-support software developers. This convergence is one of the most powerful developments affecting the potential of supplychain management.
- *Manufacturing and Logistics Execution software,* which manages shop-floor control, costs, documents, warehouse-management systems, transportation, etc. The integration of this software with the types of operating software mentioned above is contributing to enhanced supplychain performance. The emergence of real-time inventory-development software, moreover, provides companies with entirely new tools for logistics management.
- *Channel Integration software,* such as electronic data interchange (EDI) and new approaches such as collaborative planning, forecasting, and replenishment (CPFR) and other Internet-based applications. The emergence of these software packages is allowing companies to manage the extended supply chain more effectively and efficiently.

To develop distinctive supplychain capabilities, companies still will need to make the most of their supplychain infrastructure, operating processes, and organizational design in addition to fully using IT support. Nevertheless, with advances in application software, network linkages, and the ability to integrate more types of software, an IT-enabled supply chain will be at the core of differentiated supplychain strategies in the new millennium.

Source: William Copacino, *Logistics* (April 1998), p. 36.

The Basics—Comprehensive, Quality EDI

Electronic Data Interchange (EDI) is probably one of the oldest forms of technology used in logistics and transportation. It can be defined as the application-to-application exchange of standard format business transactions. Once thought to be a luxury, EDI today is becoming a requirement for doing business.

Many reasons exist for carriers and their customers to electronically transmit transactional data. First, EDI eliminates human intervention, which can help to reduce or eliminate human errors in transcription and interpretation. Second, EDI reduces the cost of the transaction because it eliminates much of the labor cost

Table 13.4 Information Technology for Transportation

➤ **The Basics**

- ✓ **Comprehensive, Quality EDI**
- ✓ **Automatic ID: Bar Coding**
- ✓ **Track and Trace**

➤ **Emerging**

- ✓ **Internet**
- ✓ **Transportation Planning**

➤ **The Future**

- ✓ **Internet-Intelligent Appls.**
- ✓ **Transparent EDI**
- ✓ **Data Warehousing**

Source: W. L. Grenoble, Center for Logistics Research, Penn State University (1998).

TABLE 13.5 Reasons Given for EDI Adoption (Cumulative Frequencies of the Number One and Two Ranked Reasons for EDI Adoption)

Statement	Customer	Carrier	Shipper/Supplier	Total
To stay competitive	20	37	60	117
To reduce costs	35	38	40	113
Influence for channel partner	10	64	39	113
To increase customer service	—	50	57	107
To decrease order cycle time	30	—	44	74
To free personnel	15	—	37	52
To reduce errors	22	—	—	22

Source: Lisa Williams Walton, "Electronic Data Interchange (EDI): A Study of Its Usage and Adoption Within Marketing and Logistics Channels," *Transportation Journal*, Vol. 34, No. 2 (Winter 1994), p.44.

associated with filling out a BOL, freight bill, manifest, waybill, or purchase order. Third, EDI improves customer service by automatically alerting customers of exceptions to their shipments, allowing them to reduce the cost of the exception. Fourth, EDI is used in many cases because customers demand it. Large customers, like manufacturers, demand that all suppliers use EDI to transmit operational as well as billing information.[5] This can cause significant investments on the part of the suppliers. However, this cost can be recouped through an increase in the number of transactions with that customer. Plus, once a supplier (such as a carrier) is "up" on EDI, adding other customers to the system adds only marginal costs. Table 13.5 shows that this last reason is actually the one most cited by carriers for adopting EDI. However, other reasons do exist, and carriers and their customers have found the use of EDI to be extremely beneficial to managing supply-chain relationships.

TABLE 13.6 Commonly Used ANSI ASC X12 Standards for Transportation EDI Transmissions

Standard	Description
104 SA	Air Shipment Information
110 IA	Air Freight Details and Invoice
125 MR	Multilevel Rail Car Load Details
204 SM	Motor Carrier Shipment Information
210 IM	Motor Carrier Freight Details and Invoice
213 MI	Motor Carrier Shipment Status Inquiry
214 QM	Transportation Carrier Shipment Status
217 FG	Motor Carrier Loading and Route Guide
218 FH	Motor Carrier Tariff Information
250 PV	Purchase Order Shipment Mgmt. Document
300 RO	Reservation (Booking Request)(Ocean)
301 RO	Confirmation (Ocean)
303 RO	Booking Cancellation (Ocean)
304 SO	Shipping Instructions (Ocean)
309 SO	U.S. Customs Manifest
310 IO	Freight Receipt and Invoice (Ocean)
312 IO	Arrival Notice (Ocean)
313 QO	Shipment Status Inquiry (Ocean)
315 QO	Status Details (Ocean)
317 SO	Delivery/Pickup Order
319 SO	Terminal Information
322 SO	Terminal Operations Activity (Ocean)
323 SO	Vessel Schedule and Itinerary (Ocean)
324 SO	Vessel Stow Plan (Ocean)
325 SO	Consolidation of Goods in Container
350 SO	U.S. Customs Release Information
352 SO	U.S. Customs Carrier General Order Status
353 SO	U.S. Customs Master In-Bond Arrival
361 SO	Carrier Interchange Agreement (Ocean)
404 SR	Rail Carrier Shipment Information
410 IR	Rail Carrier Freight Details and Invoice
414 CR	Rail Car Hire Settlements
417 WB	Rail Carrier Waybill Interchange
418 IC	Rail Advance Interchange Consist
419 SR	Advance Car Disposition
420 CH	Car-Handling Information
421 IS	Estimated Time of Arrival and Car Sched.
422 DM	Shipper's Car Order
423 RL	Rail Industrial Switch List
425 WT	Rail Waybill Request
426 SR	Rail Revenue Waybill
435 SF	Std. Transportation Commodity Code Master
440 WR	Shipment Weights
451 EV	Rail Event Report
452 PL	Rail Problem Log Inquiry or Advice
453 ST	Rail Service Commitment Advice
456 EI	Rail Equipment Inquiry or Advice
466 TP	Rate Request
468 TP	Rate Docket Journal Log
475 RF	Rail Route File Maintenance
485 TP	Rate-Making Action
490 TP	Rate Group Definition
492 TP	Miscellaneous Rates
494 TP	Scale Rate Table
601 SE	Shipper's Export Declaration

TABLE 13.6 (Cont.) Commonly Used ANSI ASC X12 Standards for Transportation EDI Transmissions

Standard	Description
602 TS	Transportation Services Tender
622 IP	Intermodal Ramp Activity
810 IN	Invoice
820 RA	Payment Order/Remittance Advice
830 PS	Planning Schedule with Release Capability
853 RI	Routing and Carrier Instruction
854 DD	Shipment Delivery Discrepancy Info.
856 SH	Ship Notice/Manifest
857 BS	Shipment and Billing Notice
858 SI	Shipment Information
859 FB	Freight Invoice
862 SS	Shipping Schedule
869 RS	Order Status Inquiry
870 RS	Order Status Report
920 GC	Loss/Damage Claim—General Comm.
925 GC	Claim Tracer
926 GC	Claim Status Report and Tracer Reply
940 OW	Warehouse Shipping Order
945 SW	Warehouse Shipping Advice
990 GF	Response to a Load Tender

Source: Reprinted courtesy of Penske Logistics, Reading, PA.

EDI transmissions between trading partners are based on standards. These might be universal standards developed through organizations like ANSI or they might be standards developed for use in a particular industry, such as the Automotive Industry Action Group (AIAG). A standard specifies the data to be transmitted, the order of the data, and the length of the field containing the data. Using standards, any two trading partners will know that an 856 transmission (advance shipment notice) will always be the same. This allows multiple trading partners to communicate electronically using only one translation protocol, rather than having proprietary translations for every trading partner. This discussion will not attempt to define what every standard is because there are too many. Table 13.6 shows a listing of the more common types of EDI transmissions utilized in the transportation process and their corresponding ANSI number. Figure 13.8 is an example of what some of these transmissions and their standard numbers might look like when they are used between members of an automobile supply chain.

The most popular use of EDI transactions is normally for receiving customer orders and for sending orders to suppliers. Table 13.7 is a summary of the current uses of EDI and the predicted use in three years. This also shows that advance shipment notices are very popular. There is also a growing use of invoicing and electronic funds transfer (EFT) transmissions between firms in the supply chain. Historically, firms were reluctant to apply EDI to the flow of cash between trading partners for fear of losing control over float and/or payment terms. However, EFT has proven to improve the control of float and significantly reduce the cost of invoicing and payment.

Implementing EDI, however, has its barriers within many firms.[6] These barriers include: hardware/software compatibility, consistent formats, security, investment, senior management support, and ownership (MIS department versus operational units).

FIGURE 13.8 MCS Corporation Logistics Information Flows ("Big 3" Model)

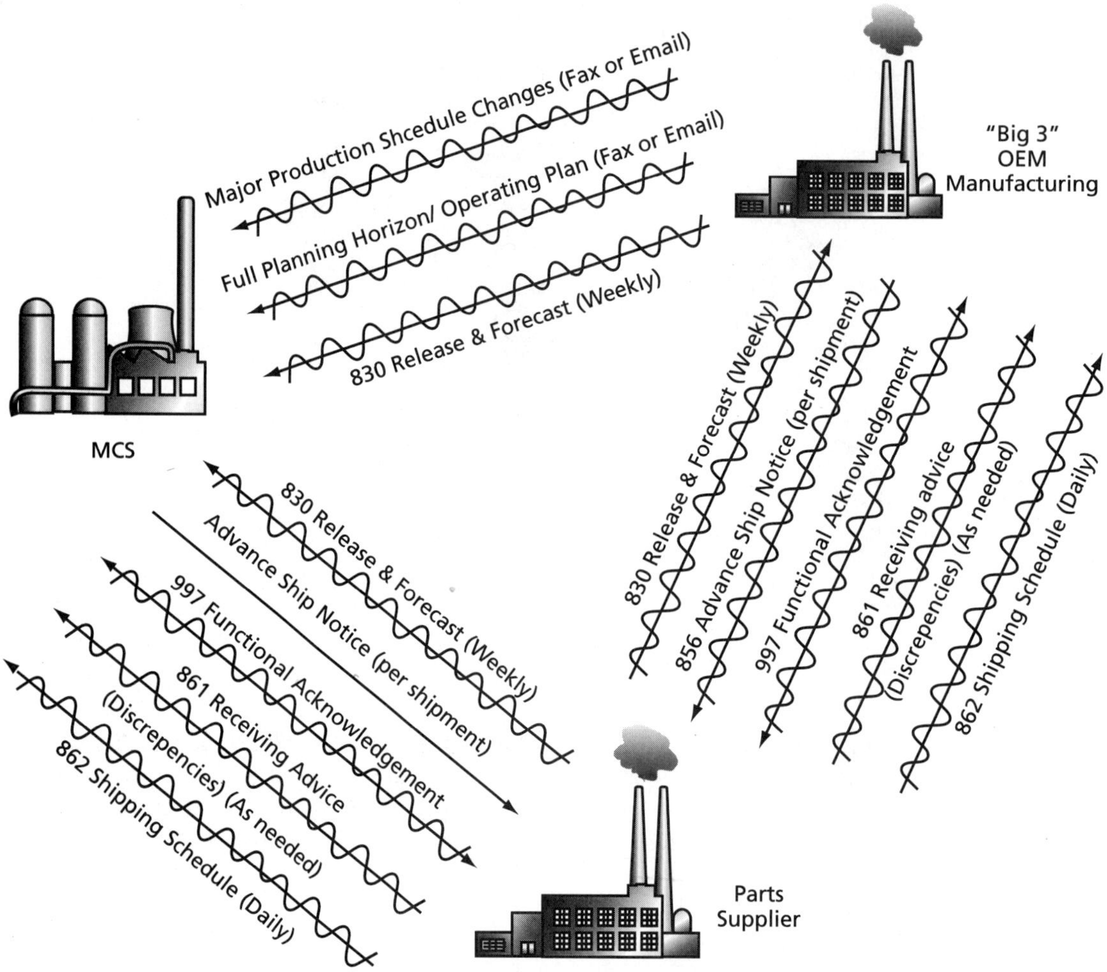

Source: Center for Logistics Research, Penn State University, 1998.

Many, if not all, of these barriers exist for the initial implementation of an EDI system. Like any technology installation, the first attempt requires the large investment and causes all of the challenges. However, the learning curve with EDI is very positive; each succeeding application should become easier. Economies of scale also exist with subsequent applications. Some firms decide to reduce implementation and operational costs as well as improve security by using third-party providers called Value Added Networks (VANs). These firms receive EDI transmissions from multiple firms that might have proprietary standards and translates these into standard formats, which are then transmitted to their trading partners. This process allows a transmitting firm to develop a single transmission network, rather than a dedicated transmission network for each customer. Many carriers use VANs for their EDI transmissions. For example, a motor carrier that uses satellite technology to monitor shipment

TABLE 13.7 EDI Company Utilization

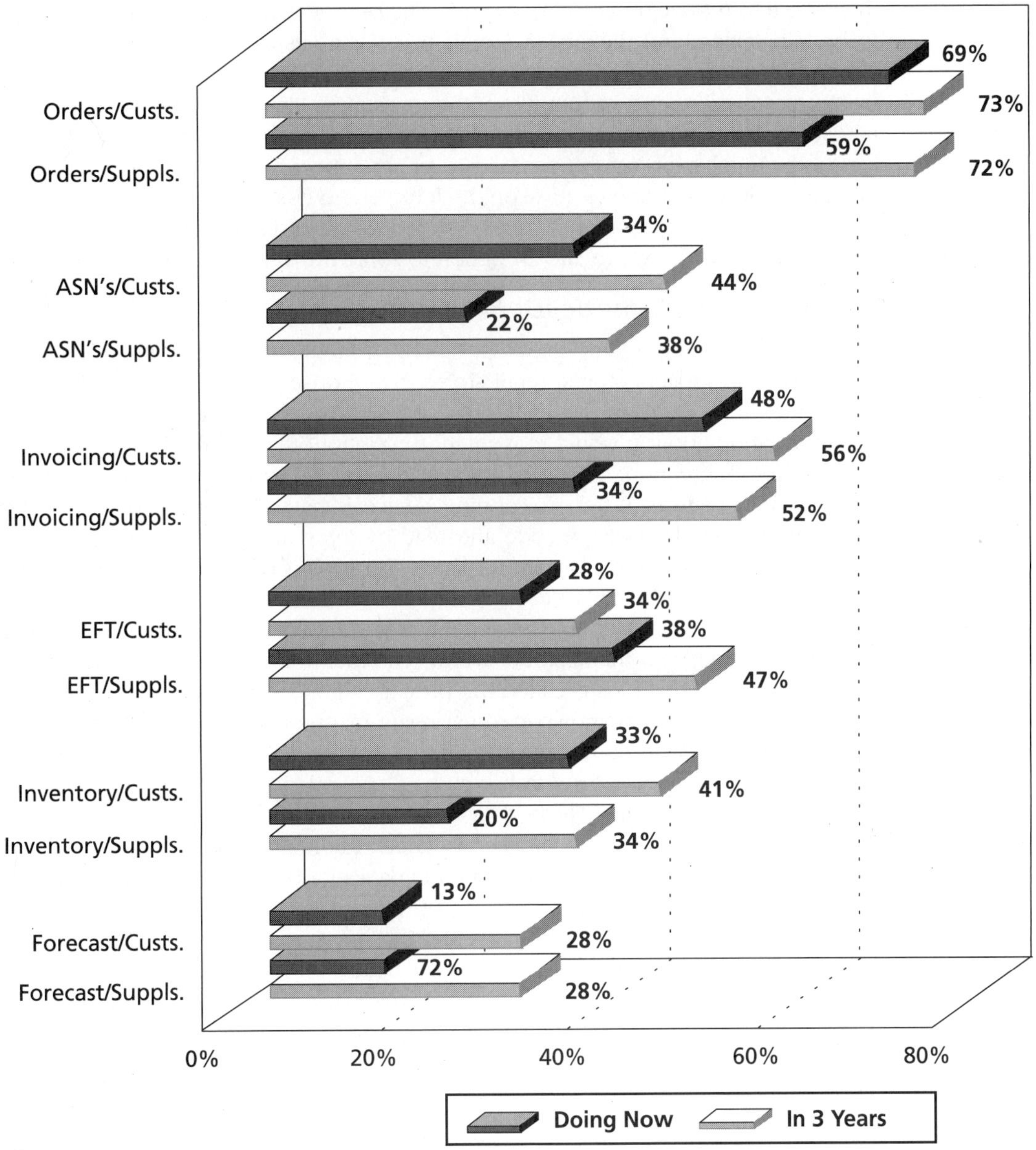

Source: Center for Logistics Research, Penn State University, 1978

status for all of its customers will transmit shipment status data to a VAN. The carrier's customers can then access the VAN, using a customer ID, to download status information on their shipments alone. If all of that customer's carriers also use the same VAN, the customer can also reduce its number of dedicated EDI connections. A VAN for EDI transactions can be compared to a wholesaler for product transactions.

What does the future hold for EDI? Speculation has grown concerning the use of the Internet to replace dedicated EDI networks. Internet sites currently exist that can be used to transmit EDI documents. Both the sender and receiver have to subscribe to the service to receive an account number. The sender specifies the type of document to be transmitted, and the screen automatically formats to the desired data requirements. Some feel that the Internet system will work for small firms that do not have many transmissions and cannot justify the investment. Some feel that since the Internet is "free," the investment in any type of dedicated network is not worth it, regardless of the number of transactions. However, an issue with the Internet is capacity. If EDI transactions continue to grow on the Internet, no guarantee could be given to the trading partners that capacity would be added to avoid delays in transmission. However, the Internet could provide an option to some firms for their EDI transactions.

The Basics—Automatic ID: Bar Coding

Bar coding is another technology that has been in use for quite a while. Bar codes can be seen in grocery stores, retail stores, warehouses, manufacturing plants, and carrier terminals. Coupled with EDI, bar codes provide a powerful tool for providing information about product movement throughout the supply chain.

Bar codes are rather simple in their design, consisting of spaces and bars arranged in a pattern. When a scanning device is passed over the bar code, light waves are reflected off of the code and read by the scanner. These waves are converted to a frequency and assigned a "0" or a "1" (this is called a binary code) based on whether light is reflected or absorbed by the code. A dark bar would absorb light; a light space would reflect light. The relative width of bars and spaces is important in basic bar codes, not the absolute width. The method used to assign these zeroes and ones to the reflections is called the primary algorithm. This algorithm describes the combinations of bars and spaces that result in a 0 or 1. For example, a wide bar and a narrow space in combination might be encoded as a 0. Once a series of zeroes and ones are created from a bar code, a secondary algorithm is used to translate it to meaningful data. These data might be used to access a product file in a grocery store so the price can be used to check out a customer.

Three variations can be used to encode data in a bar code. A "2 of 5" bar code measures bar-to-bar relationships; a "2 of 5 interleaved" is used to measure bar-to-bar and space-to-space relationships; and "MSI" measures bar-to-space relationships. The most common bar code in use today is called Code 39.[7] Figure 13.9 shows an example of a Code 39 bar code, which uses five bars and four spaces. In the figure, two bars and one space are wide (three wide) and the remaining six spaces and bars are narrow. The three wide elements out of the nine total is where the name Code 39 comes from.

Another common format for bar codes is Code 128. An example can be seen in Figure 13.10. This code consists of 11 total modules per character with each encoded character containing three bars and three spaces. This code can cover the full 128 ASCII character set, which gives this code its name.[8]

A relatively new development in bar codes is called 2-D, or two-dimensional. Several variations of the 2-D code exist. The first type is called a stacked bar code. Figure 13.11 shows an example of this code. An example of a stacked bar code is Code 49. Code 49 contains two to eight rows of fixed width bar codes stacked on top of one another. Each row has 49 possible values, giving this code its name.[9] An advantage of this 2-D code is its adaptability to conventional bar code scanners. Figure 13.12 is an example of Code 49.

FIGURE 13.9 Code 39 Bar Code

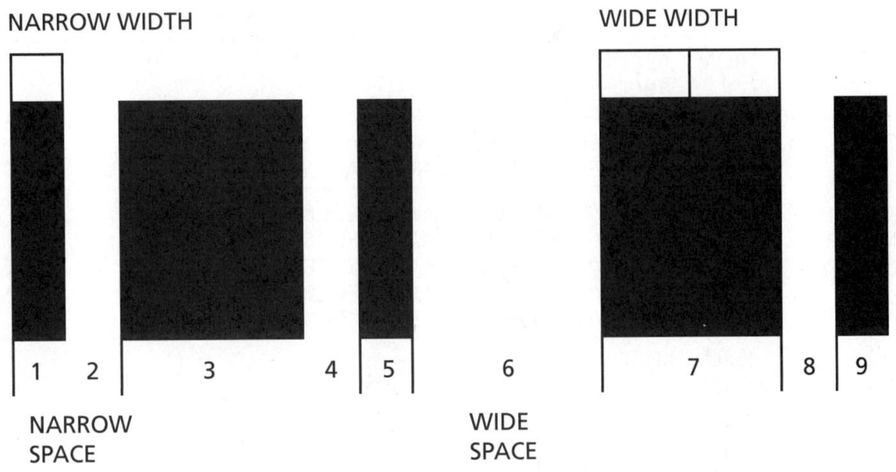

FIGURE 13.10 Code 128 Bar Code

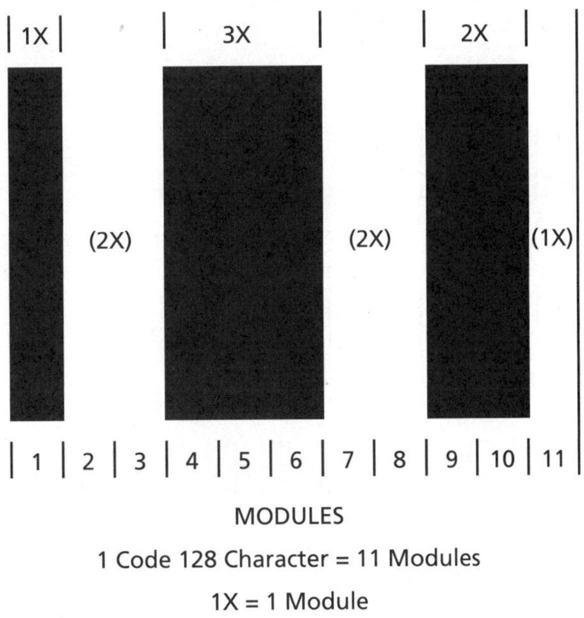

Finally, several types of matrix bar codes have been developed that have significantly increased the amount of data portrayed by the bar code. The matrix bar code resembles a checker board with the absence or presence of a black or white dot in a cell portraying the data. One of the earliest successful matrix bar codes was

FIGURE 13.11 Stacked Bar Code

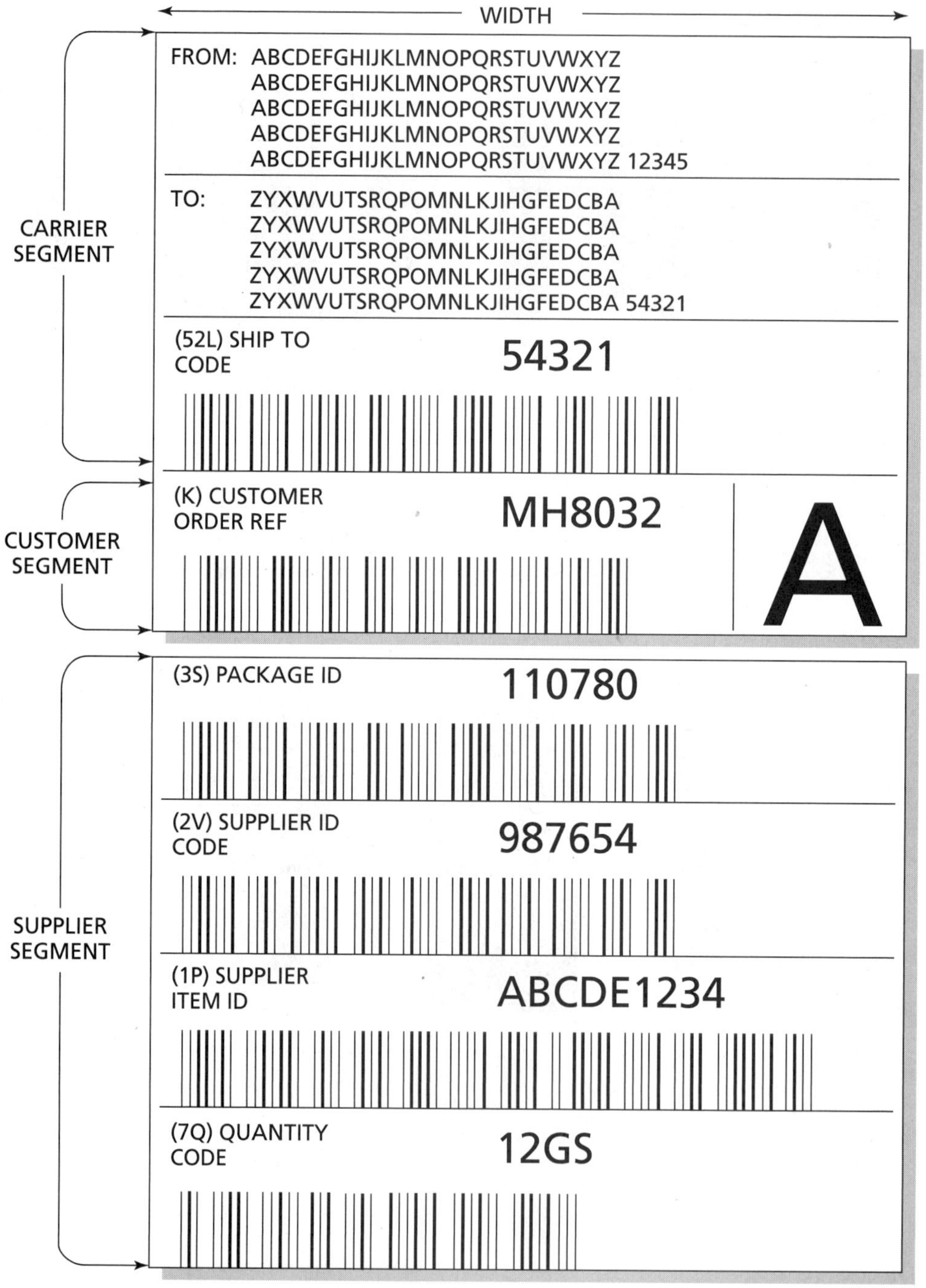

Source: *Transportation and Distribution* (October 1991), p. 26.

FIGURE 13.12 Code 49 Bar Code

developed by the United Parcel Service (UPS). It resembles a checkerboard pattern with a bull's eye in the middle. Figure 13.13 shows the UPS matrix code. This code is now in the public domain.

Another advancement in the development of bar codes is called the "license plate." This bar code, called SSCC-18, is used to identify and manage pallets, rather than traditional consumer or industrial packages.[10] When a pallet is created by the manufacturer, an SSCC-18 is applied and identifies the product, quantity, production lot, date of manufacture, hold status, and storage location.[11] Because these codes use Code 128 formats and are globally unique and context neutral, they can be used anywhere in the supply chain.[12] This allows shippers, carriers, and receivers alike to share common information about the movement of a pallet through their respective networks.

Bar codes were developed to allow for quick data capture as packages move through the supply chain. They require some type of reader and contain static information. A new technology developed by Texas Instruments, called the "tag-it", is a revolutionary way to identify packages and manage inventory.[13] Called a "smart tag", this new technology takes the place of a bar code and uses radio frequency to make it work. An advantage of the smart tag is the capability to update its information anywhere along the supply chain. The smart tag can be manufactured into ship-

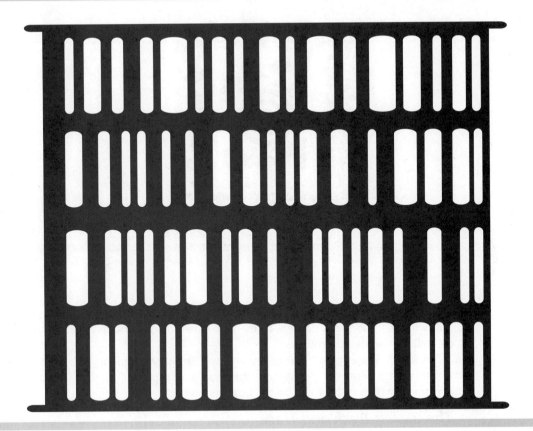

FIGURE 13.13 Matrix Bar Code

Source: United Parcel Service

ping labels or other types of documentation following a shipment. This technology will allow shippers and carriers to manage inventories through distribution centers as well a break-bulk terminals.

A key to the effective use of bar code technology is linking it to other types of technology to allow for inventory visibility. One of these technologies is called track and trace, which is the focus of the next section.

The Basics: Track and Trace

Full visibility of a shipment in the supply chain requires the ability to know where it is in a warehouse or terminal as well as knowing where it is in transit. Bar codes provide an important source of information to be able to provide both types of visibility. In a warehouse or carrier's terminal, bar codes can track a shipment from when it arrives until it leaves, providing status updates along the way. Normal bar code readers store data on product movements and then periodically download this data to a host computer. A new technology called radio frequency, or RF, can provide real-time data. When the bar code is scanned using an RF reader, the data are transmitted immediately using radio frequencies to the host computer. The smart tag mentioned above is another application where RF technology can be used.

Until recently, tracking a shipment inside a facility was relatively easy when compared to tracking it in transit. However, developments in tracking technology have allowed carriers to communicate with their vehicles in transit as well as determine their location. The major breakthrough in making this visibility a reality is the use of satellite technology. Motor carriers, such as Penske, Schneider, Chemical Leaman, and Prime have installed satellite transponders in the roofs of their tractors to interface with various satellite systems. Coupled with on-board computers, this satellite communication has allowed carriers to not only know the position of their vehicles and their freight, but also better manage their asset base. This two-way communication between driver/vehicle has actually allowed carriers to reduce their fleet size while improving utilization. One of the more popular satellite systems is provided by a company called Qualcomm. The Qualcomm system can update the position of a vehicle in transit as often as the user requires as well as provide a two-way communication between a driver and the dispatcher. These updates, along with RF data from warehouses and terminals, can help provide total supply chain visibility for freight.

Some satellite technology applications are used for one-way communications. These passive "transponders" can be applied to trailers or rail cars and are used to either transmit data or help determine vehicle position. A disadvantage of the satellite technology on motor-carrier tractors is the inability to track the freight in the trailer when the trailer is unhooked. For example, TOFC trailers can become "lost" in the rail system because their capability to transmit location data resides with the tractor. However, putting a transponder on the trailer allows the trailer to be live on the rail.

Another application for this technology is being tried in the refrigerated motor-carrier industry. Putting refrigerated trailers on a rail car has presented problems in the past with being able to monitor and control the temperature inside the trailer. However, some carriers are experimenting with these transponders to periodically transmit temperature data back to a central dispatch location. Although they cannot yet control the temperature, this technology allows the motor carrier dispatcher to alert the railroad if a temperature problem occurs.

Tracking and tracing has come a long way in the last 10 years. Shippers have demanded better ways to determine where their shipments are and if they will arrive on time. Carriers have also needed a better way to manage fleet utilization. However, not every firm has taken advantage of technology to provide full inventory visibility. Shippers will normally fall into one of three categories of tracking and tracing capability: lagging edge, mainstream, or leading edge. Table 13.8 summarizes the characteristics of each category. Leading edge firms can be described as reactive and using little or no technology to track and trace. They are very slow to respond to requests from customers on shipment location, and the track and trace process is completely manual.

There have been dramatic advances in this area in the last two years even though the original technology dates from the late 1980s. First, the current systems were enhanced to add features which allow a dispatcher to monitor the tractor's engine condition, the speed of travel and other related areas. Features were added to control refrigerator units remotely including monitoring the temperature and starting

TABLE 13.8 Tracking and Tracing Capability

	Degrees of Performance		
Attribute	**Lagging Edge**	**Mainstream**	**Leading Edge**
Responsiveness	Reactive, Phone based	Reactive, Systemitized	Proactive, Systemitized
Database	None	Uses carrier capability	Has own capability, SKU-entry
Connectivity	Phone	Terminal inquiry	EDI
Operations Mode	Batch Daily	Batch 3-4 times daily	Online Realtime
Shipment Location Specicifity	Which carrier/ company	Company and general location. ETA	Geographic specific satellite/radio links
Use of Info	React to customer request	React and maintain performance data	Automatic pass on to customers

Source: William L. Grenoble, Center for Logistics Research, Penn State University, 1998.

the refrigeration unit if required. The enhanced systems have more accurate location placement information and have incorporated geographic data to assist with vehicle placement. One system uses road net and mapping information to graphically depict where the vehicle is located on a specific highway.

The newest systems have overcome the problem of monitoring trailers when not hooked up to a tractor. Past systems relied on power from the tractor and once the trailer was dropped, that portion of the tracking no longer functioned.

The development of long lasting power supplies and additional technology now allows the trailer's location to be monitored regardless whether it is attached to a tractor. One system not only maintains the trailer location, it can determine whether the trailer is loaded or empty. This is accomplished by a sensor in the nose of the trailer which scans for light or the absence of light to determine if there is cargo on the trailer.

This technology will spread beyond the trucking industry as other modes adopt this control system. Railcars and containers are the next logical choice and shipper demand will no doubt push carriers to implement tracking technology as a competitive advantage.

Mainstream firms are reactive but use some technology, possibly the carrier's, to track and trace. Because the process is systematic, these firms are able to respond rather quickly to customer requests. Because the track and trace process of these firms uses terminal inquiry, some manual activities have been replaced with technology. Finally, leading-edge firms are proactive in their approach to track and trace. They utilize technologies such as EDI and satellite/RF to capture and transmit data automatically. These firms supply real-time shipment status information to their customers, eliminating the need for the customer to request a status update. These firms will sometimes proactively alert a customer if a shipment will be late. Very little, if any, manual interaction is necessary for track and trace for these firms because of the extensive use of technology.

Satellite and RF technologies have certainly helped both carriers and shippers achieve efficiency and profitability goals. Some track and trace systems are proprietary between a carrier and a shipper. Other carrier track and trace systems are in the public domain and are available from the Internet. UPS and Federal Express are two examples. The use of the Internet in transportation will be the focus of the next section.

The Internet Emerges

The Internet actually began in the 1960s as a network of networks linking government and university computers. Mostly used for research, this linkage allowed for participating institutions to share information. Because its members were volunteers, no formal ownership of the Internet ever existed. This is still true today. A major advantage of the Internet during the 1960s as well as today is that its use is free.

The three major uses of the Internet are for information resources, communications, and transactions. Companies develop Internet sites to provide potential customers with product and price information. Many carriers have developed Internet sites to allow customers to track their shipments. Once on a carrier's site, the customer enters a customer code and shipment identifier to find the status of a shipment. Federal Express can even provide a copy of the receiver's signature on the delivery receipt. Appendix A contains a short compilation of some carrier Internet sites.

The Internet can also be used to communicate between individuals as well as between companies. Companies can use the Internet for EDI transmissions well as for internal and external communications. Companies are beginning to use Internet-based systems to share demand and production forecasts. This concept, called Col-

STOP-OFF

The Internet
UPS Plans Document Delivery Over the Internet

UPS wants to go from ground to cyberspace delivery.

The Atlanta-based parcel and express giant announced last month that it planned to launch a new service, "UPS Document Exchange," that would provide secure electronic delivery of information across the Internet. UPS will be able to transmit over the Internet anything contained in a digital file, including documents, images, video, and software. The service, which UPS will provide in conjunction with NetDox of Deerfield, Ill., and Tumbleweed Software of Redwood City, Calif., will become available in the second quarter of this year.

UPS will offer two levels of service in the Document Exchange program. The first, UPS OnLine Dossier, will use encryption and digital certificates to authenticate senders and receivers. It also will provide tracking. Though this service requires both sender and receiver to load special software onto their computers, that software can be downloaded for free.

The second, UPS OnLine Courier, is designed for customers who want more open access to the 'Net because it will work with any computer processing a browser and e-mail. Customers will have security options, including password protection, and will be able to receive tracking and receipt confirmation. Software for that service also can be obtained for free.

UPS is betting that there will be a market for certified, encrypted e-mail in such industries as banking and insurance, which now require surface mail to be "certified" for legal purposes.

Source: *Logistics* (April 1998), pp. 29–30.

laborative Planning, Forecasting, and Replenishment (CPFR), was started by Wal-Mart as a way to communicate inventory data to its suppliers. Some shippers and carriers use the Internet in lieu of a broker. Available shipments are posted on an Internet site and interested carriers can respond with a price quote for the move. A shipper can then either accept or reject the offer. If the offer is accepted, a confirmation message is generated and the transaction is completed.

Finally, the use of the Internet for cash transactions is growing. Because of the increased security offered by firms to protect credit card numbers and bank account numbers on the Internet, buyers and sellers can consummate sales through an Internet site, with cash flow occurring through a credit card or a bank. Although this use is minimal today, it is expected to grow tremendously in the future.

The growth of Internet users has been phenomenal. In 1996, there were approximately 10 to 20 million users in the United States alone. By the year 2010, it has been projected that the numbers of users on a worldwide basis will reach one billion.

Some challenges still remain with the use of the Internet for transportation transactions. First is the issue of capacity. Since no single entity owns the Internet, capacity decisions are not the responsibility of a central organization. An analogy would be if the interstate highway system had no single entity responsible for it. As traffic increases and capacity is constrained, the decision to add highway miles or add technology to manage traffic flow would be no one's responsibility. As usage on the Internet goes up, response times can go down. This is a major consideration for companies who have time-sensitive transmissions.

Second is the issue of security. Although protection of confidential information on the Internet has improved, no guarantee can be given that information transmitted will not be available to the public domain. In fact, many Internet sites provide a warning message before a transmission alerting the sender that the data could be accessed by unauthorized individuals.

The future of the Internet holds many applications for carriers and their customers. Carriers will be able to use the Internet as a sales interface. Information such as service offerings, routing guides, fleet availability, and pricing schedules would be easily accessible and maintained through the Internet. As some carriers have already proven, the Internet is effective as a customer service utility. Basic requests such as shipment status and arrival times can be accessed through the Internet, allowing carriers to utilize human customer service personnel more effectively. More and more companies could use the Internet for EDI transmissions. As security improves and capacity increases, firms with no need for dedicated links with their customers could use the Internet to provide a viable alternative to EDI.

One of the latest developments involving the use of the Internet has been growth and development of load matching services. The firms serve the same purpose as a broker by linking the carrier and the shipper. One of the differences is that in some cases the shipper can post their loads and respond to offers by carriers directly without the use of a "middleman". Many of these firms charge a fee for their services while leaving the negotiation of the transportation details to the shipper and carrier. Shippers can post loads with options ranging from simple faxes which the operator will add to the site, up to sophisticated file transfer protocols. A few accept credit cards and some offer other services including truck stop directories, highway mileages, links to insurance companies and e-mail service. One site even offers links to news and weather forecasting service as well as stock quotes.

Finally, the Internet could facilitate the sharing of information between carriers and their customers. This could include information regarding planned shipments, production schedules, fleet availability, and so on. The types of information that could be shared through the Internet are limited only by the restrictions placed on them by the firms involved.

Emerging: Transportation Requirements Planning

Transportation Requirements Planning (TRP) systems allow shippers and carriers to share information regarding transportation movements and to improve the efficiency and effectiveness of freight flows. TRP systems can be stand-alone systems or they can be connected to Enterprise Resource Planning (ERP) systems. Figure 13.14 shows that the TRP system requires freight movement information from the shipper as well as capacity and pricing information from the carrier as inputs. Once this information is received, the TRP system can provide optimal shipment planning, allowing truckload consolidation for the shipper and continuous moves for the carrier. The system also allows for real-time status reporting, if the carrier and the shipper have the technology to capture real-time data. TRP systems can also provide performance reports as well as allow simulation analysis to answer "what if" types of questions.

A real-time application of a TRP system can be seen in Figure 13.15. This system, developed by Penske Logistics, is called a Logistics Management System (LMS). The LMS has interfaces with the warehouse, the carrier, and the customer. Electronic messages into and out of the system are shown with arrows. As customer orders are processed in the warehouse, the LMS is planning for the optimum shipment schedule, taking into consideration customer requirements as well as carrier equipment and driver requirements. Once the shipment schedule is made operational, the LMS communicates with the carriers via the Qualcomm network to update shipment status. After delivery, the LMS generates management reports as well as bills customers for the transportation service. As previously discussed, a system like this is success-

FIGURE 13.14 TRP Model

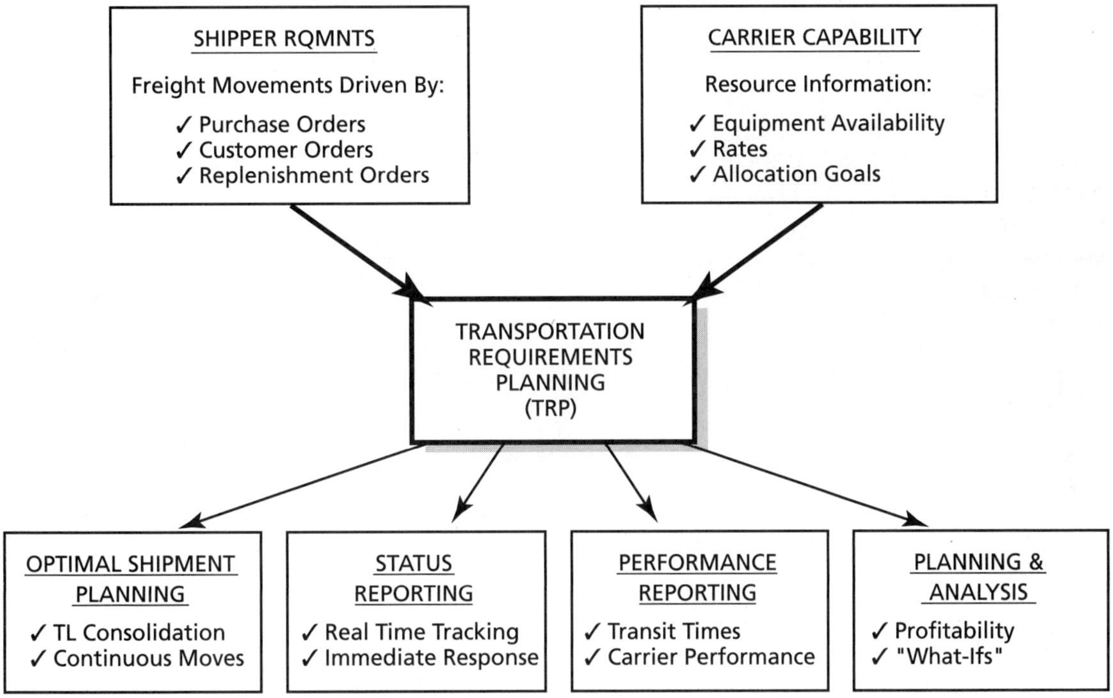

Source: W. L. Grenoble, Center for Logistics Research, Penn State University (1998).

ful only if the different systems and technologies can communicate with one another. Figure 13.15 shows how this communication takes place.

Figure 13.16 illustrates the types of information systems relationships in a TRP system. Notice that this type of system allows the shipper to connect to vendors, customers, and carriers. Again, this sharing of information is necessary to optimize freight movements. The TRP system also utilizes map and distance data (such as Rand McNally) as well as providing inputs to carrier freight payment systems. TRP systems are an application of managing the transportation process as shown in Figure 13.1.

Transportation management software development and implementation has become the focus of many software firms because of the growing use of ERP systems and the importance of transportation to the firm. Table 13.9 shows some of the firms involved in transportation software implementation. Many of these firms are also involved with ERP systems implementation as well as other types of logistics information system software. An important point to be made concerning emerging technologies is their flexibility and connectivity. Historically, information flowed vertically along functional lines within firms. These new technologies are allowing information flows to parallel the horizontal movements of product and cash. The management of these supply-chain flows is critical for being competitive in today's environment.

FIGURE 13.15 Logistics Management System

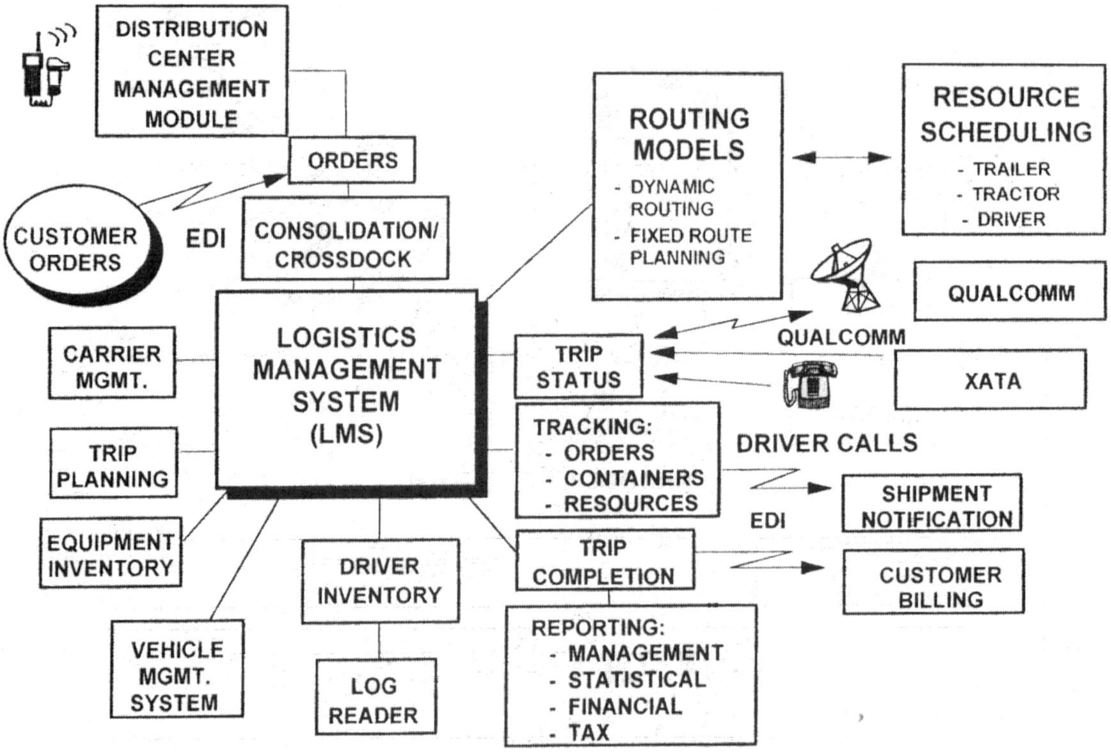

Source: Reprinted courtesy of Penske Logistics, Reading, PA.

TABLE 13.9 Third-Party Resources: Transportation Information Support

Company	Service	Type	Service/Software
ITLS	Venture	Transp. Mgmt.	Software
Schneider Logistics	SUMIT	Transp. Mgmt.	Service
Manugistics	MTP	Transp. Mgmt.	Software
CAPS Logistics	CAPS Toolkit	Transp. Mgmt.	Software
Metasys	MetaFreight	Transp. Mgmt.	Software
IBM	Trans Connect	Transp. Mgmt.	Software
Westinghouse	SureShipping	Transp. Mgmt.	Both
STI	POWERnet	Track/Trace	Service

Source: W. L. Grenoble, Center for Logistics Research, Penn State University (1998).

The Future: Internet Intelligent Applications

Information technology has developed so quickly over the last few years that it is difficult to speculate what the future holds. However, some developing technologies will be of interest to carriers and their customers. The first developing technology is

FIGURE 13.16 TRP Info Systems Relationships

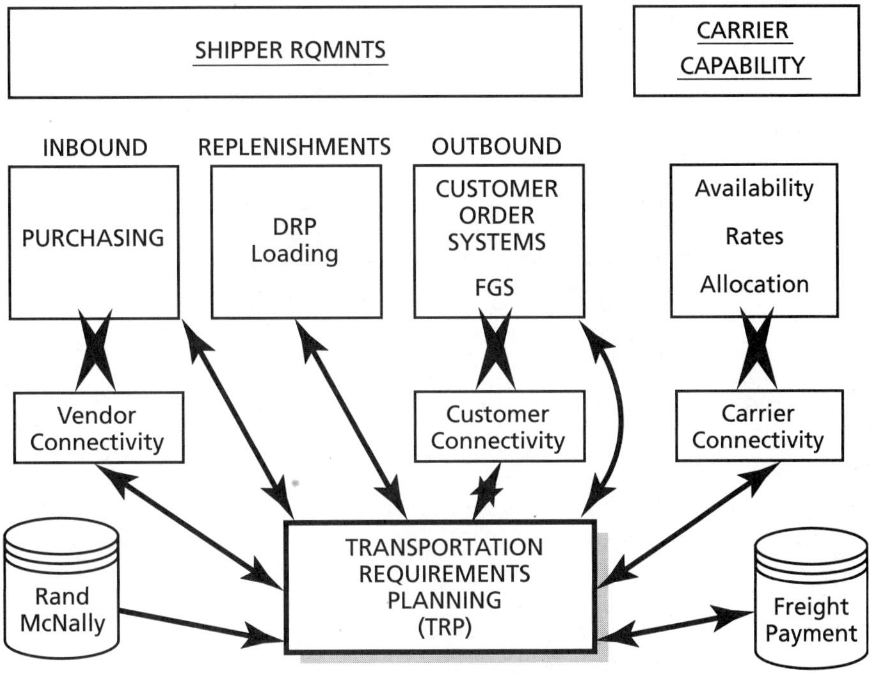

Source: W. L. Grenoble, Center for Logistics Research, Penn State University (1998).

called Internet Intelligent Applications. This technology would be very much like an Internet search engine. It could be programmed to search through the Internet until it finds what it needs, then it would initiate and consummate the transaction.

For example, a shipper using the Internet to post available loads today does so manually. The carrier also receives and analyzes these tenders and replies manually. The shipper then either accepts or rejects the carrier's offer manually. Internet Intelligent Applications would allow the carrier and shipper to eliminate most of the manual interaction in the transportation process by determining heuristics for a carrier's pricing options and a shipper's acceptance options. The application could also acknowledge acceptance of the carrier's offer as well as determine pickup times and so on.

The Future: Transparent EDI

A second developing technology can be called Transparent EDI. EDI transactions today are inflexible and require intensive set-up time because of the rigid standards necessary for both parties to communicate. Transparent EDI would make EDI transactions more use- friendly by allowing more flexibility in the standards and less investment in technology for firms to communicate. Radio frequency identification (RFID) could also be used in this application. RFID would allow the capture and transmission of data without the rigid standards and fixed infrastructure of traditional EDI networks.

STOP-OFF

Take a Load Off
10 Benefits of Load Planning Software

You can expect to reap the following benefits from your load planning software, according to Eric May, manager of business development, TransPack Software Systems.

1. Increase outbound load efficiency. For cargo that doesn't weigh out, a load planning system can often result in improvements in cubic efficiency of 10 percent or more, resulting in a substantial reduction in transportation costs.

2. Eliminate overweight and unbalanced loads. For cargo that does weigh out, a load planning system calculates arrangements that ensure compliance with bridge laws and meet load balancing requirements for overseas containers.

3. Increase inbound load efficiency. A load planning system can also be used to monitor the efficiency of inbound shipments, leading to better performance by your suppliers.

4. Increase sales. Sales personnel and customer service representatives can view load plans while an order is being placed, allowing customers to increase their order to fill unused vehicle space.

5. Reduce load time. 3-D load diagrams provide step-by-step instructions for optimal loading of vehicles, eliminating time-consuming trial-and-error loading.

6. Reduce unload time. Load diagrams speed up receiving by showing the exact location of every item in the vehicle.

7. Minimize delivery errors. For multi-stop shipments, load diagrams clearly indicate stop breaks to ensure the correct cargo is unloaded at each stop.

8. Eliminate time spent manually configuring loads. The time it takes to manually plan one shipment can be hours or even days. A load planning system will cut this time to seconds.

9. Standardize loading rules. Inconsistent loading leads to damaged cargo and inefficient loads. Load planning software provides a solid database of products linked with their specific loading rules to eliminate inconsistencies and errors in loading.

10. Improve customer service. The ability to confidently tell customers exactly what will be delivered greatly enhances customer service, which can lead to new or additional business.

Source: Deborah Catalano Ruriani, *Inbound Logistics* (April 1998), p. 38.

The Future: Data Warehousing

Finally, the concept of data warehousing is growing among firms, especially those that have implemented ERP systems. Traditionally, firms held functional data bases in computers that reflected the activities of a single functional activity, such as transportation. These databases were not relational; they were not connected, so communication among functional areas was not possible. Since ERP systems provide a common database, data warehouses are single- storage facilities for all functional data in a firm. Although sometimes very large, data warehouses allow a single access point for all data and all are connected by a common transaction base.

The advantage of a data warehouse is obvious: data connectivity. The disadvantage might not be as obvious. Data warehouses contain large amounts of data and require tremendous storage space. Because there is so much data, firms might become overwhelmed with trying to manage it. More data does not necessarily translate into more information. Carriers and their customers need to carefully examine their information needs to successfully manage the transportation process and access those data required to provide this information.

Conclusion

Information systems and information technology are critical to effectively manage the processes in the supply chain. Improvements in both of these areas over the last few years have allowed firms to significantly reduce assets and operating costs as well as improve over logistics service. However, information technology is a means, rather than an end, to effectively manage the supply chain. Applying technology to a poorly designed process only allows mistakes to be made faster and possibly cheaper. The transportation management process is one of these. Carriers and their customers need to integrate transportation process requirements among all supply-chain partners. Technology is then applied to make the process more visible and efficient. Using information to replace assets and inventories has become a very successful strategy for today's leading firms.

Summary

- The use of technology in transportation is not new. What is new is the integration of this technology and its information among carriers, shippers, and receivers.
- Decisions are made at the transactional as well as at the strategic levels within firms. Information systems must capture the appropriate data and report them meaningfully to support these decisions.
- The four basic sources of information to manage the transportation process are the bill of lading, waybill, manifest, and freight bill.
- Firms are making significant investments in information technology applications to manage the supply chain and reduce pipeline inventories.
- Basic information technologies in transportation include EDI, bar coding, and track and trace.
- Emerging information technologies in transportation include the Internet, Enterprise Resource Planning, and Transportation Requirements Planning.
- The future of information technology applications in transportation include Internet Intelligent Applications, transparent EDI, and data warehousing.

Study Questions

1. Three types of information are necessary to manage the transportation process. What are they? Give examples of the types of information classified in each.

2. What are the five purposes of a bill of lading?

3. What is the difference between a straight bill of lading and an order bill of lading?

4. What is the purpose of a waybill and a manifest? What information does each contain?

5. Describe how the freight payment process can be used to influence cash flows between a carrier and its customers.

6. What are the major reasons firms adopt EDI technology? What are some of the barriers to EDI implementation?

7. What is the difference between a Code 39 and Code 49 bar code?

8. What reasons have carriers used to rationalize their investments in satellite technology?

9. What are the advantages of using the Internet for transportation transactions? What are the disadvantages?

10. Discuss how a shipper's implementation of an TRP system will impact its carriers.

Notes

1. Stenger, Alan J., Steven C. Dunn, and Richard R. Young, "Commercially Available Software for Integrated Logistics Management," *The International Journal of Logistics Management,* Vol. 4, No. 2 (1993), p. 63.

2. This classification system is a modified version of one initially specified in Bernard J. LaLonde and Paul H. Zinszer's *Customer Service: Meaning and Measurement.* (Chicago, IL: The National Council of Logistics Management, 1976), p. 281.

3. Scheff, Stanley and David B. Livingston, *Computer Integrated Logistics: CIL Architecture in the Extended Enterprise* (Southbury, CT: IBM Corporation, U.S. Transportation Industry Marketing, 1991), p. 9.

4. Barr, Stephen, "Putting It All Together," *CFO* (July 1995), p. 62.

5. See Lisa R. Williams' "Understanding Distribution Channels: An Interorganizational Study of EDI Adoption," *Journal of Business Logistics,* Vol. 15, No. 2 (1994), pp. 173–204.

6. For a detailed discussion of these barriers, see Robert A. Millen's "Utilization of EDI by Motor Carrier Firms: A Status Report," *Transportation Journal,* Vol. 32, No. 2 (Winter 1992), pp. 5–13.

7. For a further detailed discussion of bar coding technology, see Richard C. Norris' "Bar Coding, Auto ID, and Data Carriers: Partners to EDI," *EDI Forum,* 1991.

8. Ibid.

9. Ibid.

10. Cummins, Chris, "Keeping On Track With Pallet 'License Plates'," *Food Logistics* (October/November 1997), pp. 68–71.

11. Ibid., p. 70.

12. Ibid, p. 71.

13. "Smart Labels: They're (Almost) Here," *Parcel Shipping and Distribution* (May/June 1998), pp. 12–13.

Suggested Readings

Aron, Laurie Joan, "Scanning Bar Code Options," *Inbound Logistics* (January 1994), pp. 42–47.

Bardi, Edward J., T.S. Raghunathan, and Prabir K. Bagchi, "Logistics Information Systems: The Strategic Role of Top Management," *Journal of Business Logistics,* Vol. 15, No. 1 (1994), pp. 71–85.

Binkow, Phil, "Electronic Freight Payables Processing Pays Off," *Parcel Shipping & Distribution* (May/June 1998), p. 28.

Bowersox, Donald J. and Patricia J. Daugherty, "Logistics Paradigms: The Impact of Information Technology," *Journal of Business Logistics,* Vol. 16, No. 1 (1995), pp. 65–80.

Closs, David J., "Positioning Information in Logistics," *The Logistics Handbook* (New York, NY: The Free Press, 1994), pp. 699–713.

Cooke, James Aaron, "Technology Ups the Ante in the Quality Game," *Traffic Management* (April 1994), pp. 64–68.

Critelli, Michael J., "Tilt," *Chief Executive* (July 1997), pp. 37–39.

Cummins, Chris, "Keeping On Track with Pallet 'License Plates'," *Food Logistics* (October/November 1997), pp. 68–71.

Daugherty, Patricia J., "Strategic Information Linkage," *The Logistics Handbook* (New York, NY: The Free Press, 1994), pp. 757–769.

Donovan, R. Michael, "ERP Can Deliver Quantum Leap in Performance," *Inbound Logistics* (April 1, 1998), pp. 18–19.

Duff, Mike, "Satellite Tracking Provides More than Just Location," *Food Logistics* (August/September 1997), pp. 56–57.

Emmelhainz, Margaret A., "Electronic Data Interchange in Logistics," *The Logistics Handbook* (New York, NY: The Free Press, 1994), pp. 737–756.

Fox, Thomas, "Logistics Information Systems Design," *The Logistics Handbook* (New York, NY: The Free Press, 1994), pp. 737–756.

Gentry, Connie, "Logistics IT: Keystone to Integration," *Inbound Logistics* (April 1998), pp. 20–26.

Gustin, Craig M., Patricia J. Daugherty, and Theodore P. Stank, "The Effects of Information Availability on Logistics Integration," *Journal of Business Logistics,* Vol. 16, No. 1 (1995), pp. 1–21.

Lewis, Ira, and Alexander Talalayevsky, "Logistics and Information Technology: A Coordination Perspective," *Journal of Business Logistics,* Vol. 18, No. 1 (1997), pp. 141–157.

Martin, Michael H., "Smart Managing," *Fortune* (February 2, 1998), pp. 149–151.

Ramaswami, Rama, "Internet Customer Service," *Operations & Fulfillment* (January/February 1998), pp. 10–19.

Ruriani, Deborah Catalano, "Planning Efficient Loads: Software that Makes Cents," *Inbound Logistics* (April 1998), pp. 37–40.

Schwartz, Beth M., "Tracking Down Need," *Transportation & Distribution* (October 1997), pp. 50–55.

"Smart Labels: They're (Almost) Here," *Parcel Shipping & Distribution* (May/June 1998), pp. 12–13.

Walton, Lisa Williams, "Electronic Data Interchange (EDI): A Study of It's Usage and Adoption Within Marketing and Logistics Channels," *Transportation Journal,* Vol. 34, No. 2 (Winter 1994), pp. 37–45.

Walton, Lisa Williams, "Moving Toward LIS Theory Development: A Framework of Technology Adoption Within Channels," *Journal of Business Logistics,* Vol. 16, No. 2 (1995), pp. 117–136.

Williams, Lisa, Auril Nibbs, Dimples Irby, and Terrence Finley, "Logistics Integration: The Effect of Information Technology, Team Composition, and Corporate Competitive Positioning," *Journal of Business Logistics,* Vol. 18, No. 2 (1997), pp. 31–42.

Williams, Lisa R. and Kant Rao, "Information Technology Adoption: Using Classical Adoption Models to Predict AEI Software Implementation," *Journal of Business Logistics,* Vol. 19, No. 1 (1998), pp. 5–16.

CASE

CASE 13.1

Braxton Stores, Inc.

Braxton Stores was established in 1924 as one of the first general merchandise retail establishments that offered a wide array of merchandise at prices attractive to the average consumer. Braxton started with one store in Emporia, Kansas and has grown today to over 1,500 locations. The original store started as a stand-alone location. Most of Braxton's stores today are located in enclosed malls as anchor stores. The strengths of Braxton's product line were in tools and appliances. Although these lines are still strong today, Braxton has attempted to establish a very strong presence in clothing and electronics, especially personal computers.

Braxton's original competitors were other types of stores that were similar in product line and location. However, new competition has quickly emerged from discount stores that is either stand-alone or acts as an anchor in strip malls. These new stores were quickly able to deteriorate Braxton's and their competitors' market shares by offering comparable quality goods at lower prices. This low-price strategy by the discount stores was enabled by the lower retail rents of their locations as well as by the efficiencies of their logistics operations.

Braxton was able to respond to this price pressure by initiating several new logistics initiatives. First, Braxton rationalized its warehouse network down to 15 from 35. This quickly reduced warehousing costs as well as inventory costs. Transportation to and from these larger warehouses was handled by truckload carriers, drastically reducing transportation costs. New materials handling procedures, especially for garments on hangers, were introduced in both the warehouses and trailers to further increase logistics efficiency as well as to increase product availability at the store level. With these initiatives, Braxton was able to become price-competitive with the discount chains while maintaining its reputation for high-quality merchandise.

At a meeting of the top executives at Braxton, Alex Johns, Vice President of Marketing, indicated that a new type of competitor was starting to erode Braxton's market share in its core product lines. These competitors used the Internet to post their catalogues on Web pages so consumers could shop in the comfort of their own homes. "These new competitors are beginning to eat us alive in both clothing and electronics," Alex complained. "They're able to custom-embroider clothing or custom-build personal computers for consumers and guarantee delivery to the home within days. They do this while maintaining very little finished goods inventory. Granted, their transportation costs to consumers are higher, but these are passed on to them and they don't seem to mind. Our format forces us to have higher inventories, but our transportation costs are lower. We need to consider putting our clothing and electronics lines on our Web page to allow consumers to order in smaller quantities so we can compete in this new market."

Judith Noe, Vice President of Logistics, was well aware of the new competition but was quite uneasy about changing how Braxton traditionally went to market with these items. "Alex, I understand your concerns but remember that we just streamlined our supply chain to gain volume efficiencies in our transportation network. Fewer warehouses and larger shipments made us competitive with the discount chains. Now you want to undo this and compete with the Internet firms. Taking these volumes out of our supply chain will increase the costs on the remaining product lines. Also, our warehouse-to-consumer shipments will need to be handled by small package carriers, driving our transportation costs through the roof. I don't see how we can compete in both markets. We will have to choose one market and stick with it."

Listening to this conversation was the CEO of Braxton, Samuel E. Braxton III. Having grown up in the retail business, Sam knew that competitors came and went and that Braxton was usually able to withstand new competition. However, Internet competitors were a totally new brand of retailer. "Consumers' buying habits and sophistication have changed since 1924," he stated. "Braxton has always been able to compete with brick and mortar retailers. We have always been able to find a way to compete in that channel. However, consumers are changing and telling us that brick and mortar stores are not always required in the purchase transaction. If we are trying to establish ourselves in the clothing and electronics lines, I see no alternative but to offer the Internet as an option for our consumers. Alex and Judith, I want both of you to develop a plan that will allow us, over the next two years, to be the leading retailer of clothing and electronics over the Internet."

Case Questions

1. What would be the strategy Braxton could use to introduce their retailing on the Internet? Would both product lines be introduced at once? Would items be home-delivered or would consumers be required to pick them up at the store?
2. How could you minimize the impacts on Braxton's supply-chain costs and service? What would the new transportation network look like? Are there shipper/carrier network strategies that Braxton could use to manage the transportation in this new supply chain?
3. What would be the next logical use of the Internet for Braxton?

Appendix 13-A

Transportation Sites on the Internet

Many organizations have found the use of the Internet to be extremely beneficial in promoting their businesses. Transportation firms are no exception. This appendix contains only a sample of the transportation firms that have developed a Web page for potential and current customers. Notice that many of the sites provide more than just information about the company. They allow customers to find rates as well as track shipments. The flexibility and opportunities the Internet offers to these firms and their customers are quite broad. This can be seen on the Web pages to follow.

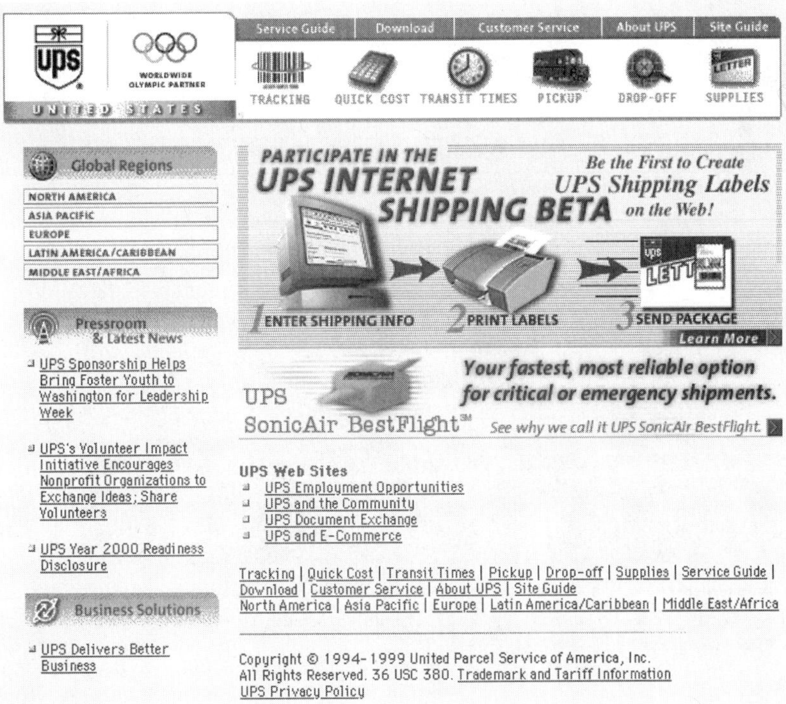

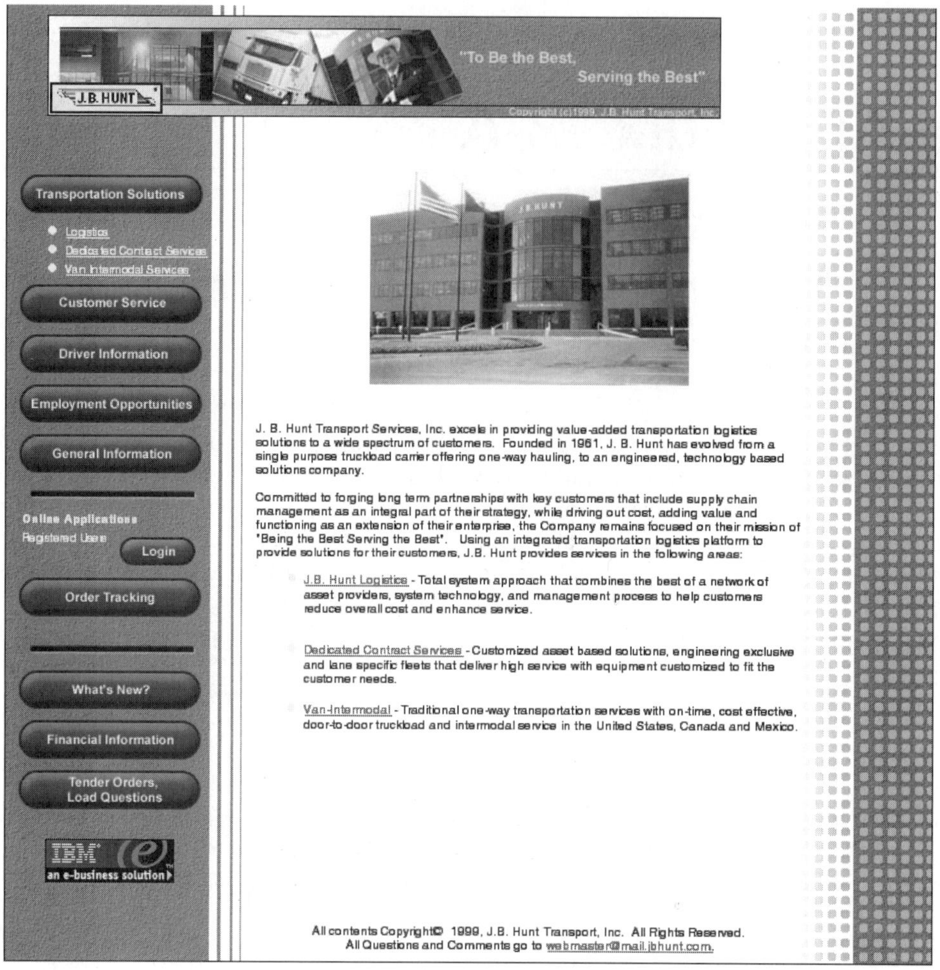
"To Be the Best,
Serving the Best"
J.B. HUNT
Copyright (c)1999, J.B. Hunt Transport, Inc.
Transportation Solutions
Logistics
Dedicated Contract Services
Van Intermodal Services
Customer Service
Driver Information
Employment Opportunities
General Information
Online Applications
Registered Users
Login
Order Tracking
What's New?
Financial Information
Tender Orders, Load Questions
IBM an e-business solution
J. B. Hunt Transport Services, Inc. excels in providing value-added transportation logistics solutions to a wide spectrum of customers. Founded in 1961, J. B. Hunt has evolved from a single purpose truckload carrier offering one-way hauling, to an engineered, technology based solutions company.
Committed to forging long term partnerships with key customers that include supply chain management as an integral part of their strategy, while driving out cost, adding value and functioning as an extension of their enterprise, the Company remains focused on their mission of "Being the Best Serving the Best". Using an integrated transportation logistics platform to provide solutions for their customers, J.B. Hunt provides services in the following areas:
J.B. Hunt Logistics - Total system approach that combines the best of a network of asset providers, system technology, and management process to help customers reduce overall cost and enhance service.
Dedicated Contract Services - Customized asset based solutions, engineering exclusive and lane specific fleets that deliver high service with equipment customized to fit the customer needs.
Van-Intermodal - Traditional one-way transportation services with on-time, cost effective, door-to-door truckload and intermodal service in the United States, Canada and Mexico.
All contents Copyright© 1999, J.B. Hunt Transport, Inc. All Rights Reserved.
All Questions and Comments go to webmaster@mail.jbhunt.com.

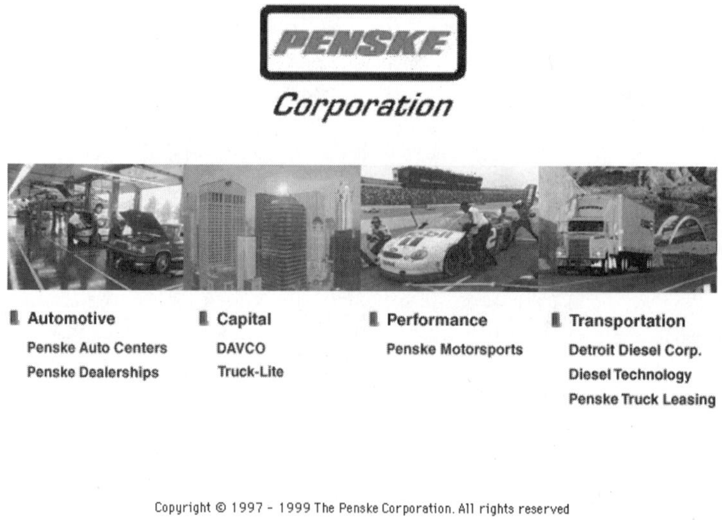
PENSKE
Corporation
Automotive
Penske Auto Centers
Penske Dealerships
Capital
DAVCO
Truck-Lite
Performance
Penske Motorsports
Transportation
Detroit Diesel Corp.
Diesel Technology
Penske Truck Leasing
Copyright © 1997 - 1999 The Penske Corporation. All rights reserved

TransportLink
Transportation Menu

The TransportLink Menu is a web site designed for the many facets of motor carrier transportation. Sponsored by Atlanta-based Southern Motor Carriers (SMC), the TransportLink Menu houses and links the home pages of motor carrier, third-party logistics and industry provider organizations in one convenient location. The goal is to connect traffic and other industry professionals with multiple field-related resources quickly and easily, providing a valuable networking agent for site visitors.

Motor Carrier Listings

Weekly Fuel Prices * **FHWA Phone Resources**
Transport Career Web * **Transport News Bytes**

Listings are provided as a free service to qualifying industry organizations, and are accessed by the linked images on the right. Should your company or business wish to request a listing within the TransportLink or change your existing link listing, please choose one of the two submission methods linked below. If your browser does not allow forms, please submit your listing using the email link.

Service Listings

Email Us! / **Add Your Link** / **Update Existing Links**

As of 12/1/98, the TransportLink offers banner advertisement options within this website. To find out more about advertising opportunities on the TransportLink, our advertising rates or which TransportLink pages accept ads, please go to the ad information page.

Logistics Listings

Guestbook

[Motor Carriers / Logistics / Services / Fuel Prices / FHWA Resources / Guestbook
News Bytes / Sponsor / Advertising / Add A Link / Edit A Link / Email]

Accessed 46495 since 9/16/96

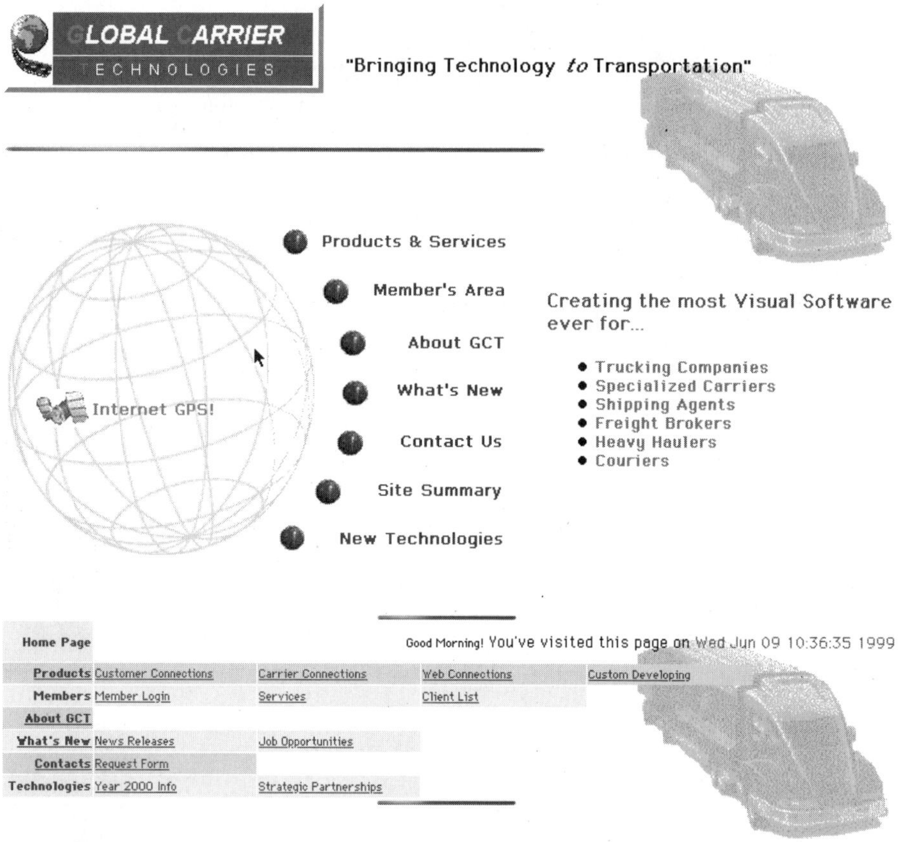

GLOBAL CARRIER TECHNOLOGIES
"Bringing Technology to Transportation"
Products & Services
Member's Area
About GCT
What's New
Contact Us
Site Summary
New Technologies
Internet GPS!
Creating the most Visual Software ever for...
Trucking Companies
Specialized Carriers
Shipping Agents
Freight Brokers
Heavy Haulers
Couriers
Home Page
Good Morning! You've visited this page on Wed Jun 09 10:36:35 1999
Products Customer Connections Carrier Connections Web Connections Custom Developing
Members Member Login Services Client List
About GCT
What's New News Releases Job Opportunities
Contacts Request Form
Technologies Year 2000 Info Strategic Partnerships

FedEx
United States
Welcome to fedex.com
Registration
Shipping
Tracking
Dropoff Locator
Rate Finder
Service Guide
eBusiness Tools
About FedEx
Index|Search
Contact Us
Global Home
FDX Companies
Enhanced FedEx Ship Software that's ready for the Year 2000 is available for downloading.
Ship Faster
Try the new and improved FedEx interNetShip® and expedite all your shipping needs.
FedEx International Document Assistance℠
New help features make online completion of export shipping forms even easier.
Add Tracking to your handheld device
Put the power of FedEx Tracking in the palm of your hand.
© 1995-1999. Federal Express Corporation.
This site is protected by copyright and trademark laws under U.S. and international law.
Review our privacy policy. All rights reserved.

CT GROUP

Specialized Transportation Services and Equipment

We are proud to introduce to you the **CT Group**, a supplier of quality, specialized transportation services and equipment.

Throughout the years, we have expanded to better serve the diverse needs of our customers. Since 1966, **Catawba Truck Rental** has provided rental and lease trucks, tractors and trailers. In 1982, another operation - **Cargo Transporters** - was established under authority of the Interstate Commerce Commission (ICC) transporting raw materials and finished goods under contract and as a general commodity carrier into and out of 48 states and Canada.

In 1991 - **Cargo Consolidation Services** - was created to serve furniture retailers in major markets throughout the United States. CCS provides professional handling, consolidation, and delivery of fine upholstery and casegoods merchandise from manufacturers in North Carolina, Southwest Virginia, and Eastern Tennessee.

CARGO TRANSPORTERS

Customer Service
Employment Opportunities
Equipment/Technology
Press Releases

CATAWBA TRUCK RENTAL

Equipment Rentals
Contract Maintenance
Full Service Leasing

CARGO CONSOLIDATION SERVICES

Consolidation Map

CARGO ONLINE

Shipment Tracking
Rate Request
Proof of Delivery Request

CT GROUP
North Oxford Street
P.O. Box 339
Claremont, NC 28610-0339

Phone: 828-459-3200
Fax: 828-459-3291

E-mail us with your questions or comments about this web site.

You are visitor number 005329 since October 25, 1997

M.R.S Freight Forwarding Services, Inc.

700 Armsway Blvd., P.O. Box 5340
Godfrey, IL 62035
PHONE 800-500-4915 FAX 618-466-9895

For free brochure & pricing information, call Susan Dearduff, Vice President of Pricing & Marketing or Larry Gold, Corporate Sales Manager:
USA 800-500-4915
CANADA 800-879-0115
MEXICO 95-800-010-1096
48 State LTL Pool Distribution Network, Multiple Distributors at All Major Locations

M.R.S. Freight Fowarding Services Offers:

- For our Customers - Activity Report updated daily.
- Full Coverage Cargo & Liability Insurance
- Over 6,000 Trucklines Under Contract
- Check our current Loads Available - Updated Many Times Daily
- Specializing in Retail and Grocery Vendor Merchandise Truckloads
- Intermodal Management Services
- Consolidation/Pool Distribution & Warehousing Services
- Multiple Stop Off Truckload Direct Store Delivery
- One Freight Bill For All Services

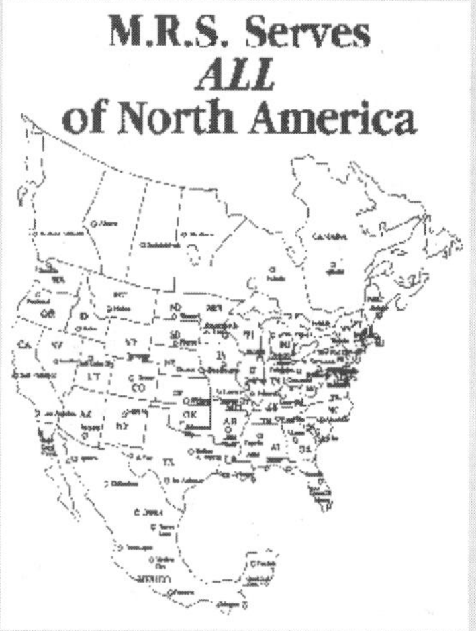
M.R.S. Serves
ALL
of North America

"M.R.S. has been handling retail chain store and grocery house traffic since 1985, it is not a side line with M.R.S., it is our core business."
Michael R. Solomon, President

You can e-mail M.R.S. Freight Forwarding at Mail Info OR Select Here to Download Company Information Package

M.R.S. Freight Forwarding Services, Inc., 700 Armsway Blvd., Godfrey, IL 62035 **FF-1250**
© 1996 The M.R.S. Companies Feb 29, 1996, Last Update May 14, 1998

Web Site design by Thorman Computer Solutions and Updated by the M.R.S. Companies

The Drapeau Transport Logistics Team

Drapeau Transport has provided trucking services from Toronto for over 25 years. We concentrate our fleet in the Greater Toronto area, Southern Ontario, Montreal and Northern and Eastern United States.

Commercial Warehousing Logistics provides storage, handling, distribution, re-routing, consolidation, and other value-added services to manufacturers and shippers.

Main Page	Drapeau	CW	HOGG
Safety	Information	Drivers Page	Links

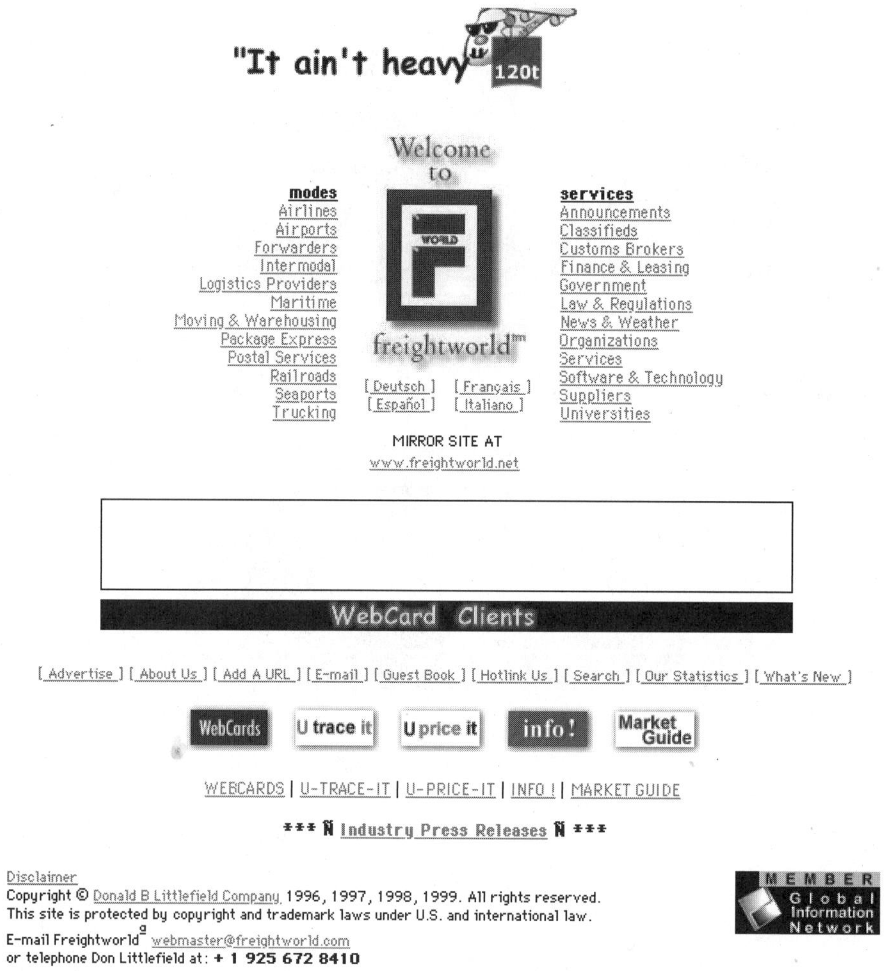
"It ain't heavy"
120t
Welcome to
freightworld™
modes
Airlines
Airports
Forwarders
Intermodal
Logistics Providers
Maritime
Moving & Warehousing
Package Express
Postal Services
Railroads
Seaports
Trucking
[Deutsch] [Français]
[Español] [Italiano]
services
Announcements
Classifieds
Customs Brokers
Finance & Leasing
Government
Law & Regulations
News & Weather
Organizations
Services
Software & Technology
Suppliers
Universities
MIRROR SITE AT
www.freightworld.net
WebCard Clients
[Advertise] [About Us] [Add A URL] [E-mail] [Guest Book] [Hotlink Us] [Search] [Our Statistics] [What's New]
WebCards
U trace it
U price it
info!
Market Guide
WEBCARDS | U-TRACE-IT | U-PRICE-IT | INFO ! | MARKET GUIDE
*** Ñ Industry Press Releases Ñ ***
Disclaimer
Copyright © Donald B Littlefield Company 1996, 1997, 1998, 1999. All rights reserved.
This site is protected by copyright and trademark laws under U.S. and international law.
E-mail Freightworld webmaster@freightworld.com
or telephone Don Littlefield at: + 1 925 672 8410
MEMBER
Global Information Network

CHAPTER 14

SHIPPER/CARRIER NETWORK STRATEGIES

Both shippers and carriers utilize strategies to manage their respective networks. The shipper strategy is focused on purchasing and managing transportation services to meet the needs of their external and internal customers. Carrier strategy is focused on the efficient use of resources to provide the economical and efficient service the shipping public desires. Carriers also try to maximize return on deployed assets.

In most shipper organizations, traffic/transportation management is the term used to describe the functional area dedicated to shipper network strategy. The traffic manager develops strategies to address the procurement of transportation in general as well as small, bulk, and inbound shipments. At the same time, **carrier management** is concerned with network strategies dealing with operations, equipment, technology, marketing, and terminals.

This chapter presents many of the techniques used by shippers and carriers to effectively manage their transportation networks. The first part of the chapter deals with shipper strategies and traffic management, while the latter part is concerned with the economic principles of successful carrier network management.

Shipper Transportation Strategy[1]

The transportation function is one element of the total logistics function. The strategies and operating decisions used in **transportation management** must support the strategies and objectives of the logistics function and those of the company. Transportation decisions must be made to benefit the total logistics function and the firm, not merely the transportation department.

Current management strategy focuses on optimization between the various elements within the logistics sector. Transportation is often one of the largest cost elements, and decisions in this area can favorably or negatively impact the total distribution performance. As an example, slow but low cost transportation can have an adverse impact on customer service and inventory levels. Although such methods may minimize transport cost, inventory levels may need to be much higher to accommodate longer transit times. These higher stocking levels, with the resultant increase in inventory carrying cost, may more than offset any saving in freight charges.

As Figure 14.1 indicates, transportation strategy is concerned with the purchase and control of transportation services. Transportation purchasing decisions include modal selection, consolidation, private trucking, intermediaries, and contracting. The resources, organization, and trade terms decisions are concerned with controlling transportation. The strategies in guiding the transportation decision maker are discussed below.

General Strategy

As Figure 14.1 indicates, transportation strategies have been separated into those strategies that apply to all types of shipments, including small and bulk shipments. Passage of the transportation deregulation acts dramatically changed general transportation management strategy. Before that time, transportation managers primarily were concerned with tariff rates and regulations.

Proactive Management

With the elimination of economic regulations to control transportation rates and services, the transportation manager is able to develop innovative approaches to a company's transportation problems. The "you cannot do that because of regulation" approach has given way to a proactive management philosophy that emphasizes

FIGURE 14.1 Transportation Strategy

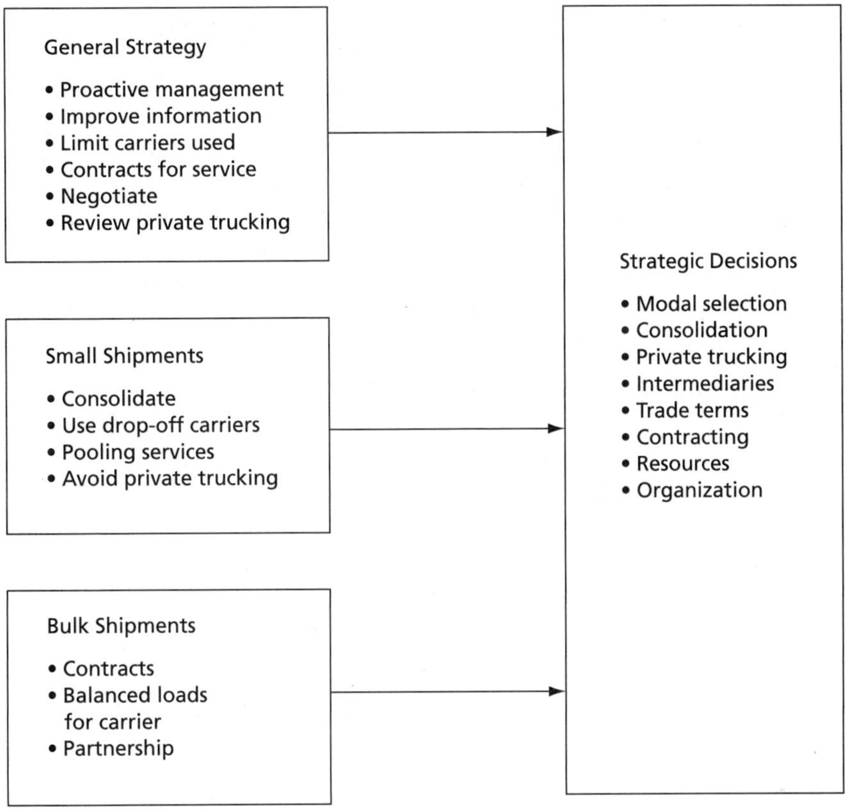

finding solutions to company transportation problems. The transportation manager relies on basic management techniques to seek innovative transportation systems that will provide the company with a competitive price or service advantage in the marketplace.

The thrust of the proactive management strategy is problem solving. Before deregulation, transportation management was concerned with developing expertise in regulatory manipulation to gain a competitive edge in the market. Today the transportation manager must rely on his or her ability and creativity to design a transportation system that permits product differentiation and a competitive advantage.

The current competitive environment requires that the transportation manager focus on customer service and competitive strategies. Successful logistics strategies are seen as a true competitive advantage, requiring transport support that can respond to ever increasing demands for smaller inventory levels combined with immediate delivery.[2]

Part of the success of a major discount store such as Wal-Mart has been attributed to its success in increasing inventory turns while reducing distribution costs. Often suppliers are expected to become "partners" with their customer, with transportation being one of the more critical elements. The ability of such techniques as "just in time" inventory and "efficient consumer response" rely on cost-efficient and sophisticated transportation methods.[3]

Improve Information

To effectively manage the transportation function, reliable and current information is a necessity. Without information, the manager is unable to plan and control the transportation activities or make sound decisions. Transportation costs, shipment volume, and carrier performance are the typical data collected. These data are essential to carrier negotiation, freight consolidation, contracting, and private trucking decisions.

A major source of transportation information is the bill of lading. The bill of lading indicates the customer or vendor, the shipment volume, origin and destination, date, and carrier. The carrier's freight bill (invoice) provides similar data as well as the transportation cost for the shipment. Other sources include the purchase order, order entry system, invoice, and internal studies. Some companies use a third-party provider, such as a bank or freight payment company, to pay freight bills, and most of these freight payment firms have the computer capabilities to provide transportation data reports in the format required by management.

Limit Number of Carriers Used

By reducing the number of carriers it uses, a shipper increases its market power and therefore its ability to effectively negotiate with its carriers. This strategy increases the shipper's importance to the carrier, thereby increasing its negotiating strength with the carrier. With increased negotiating strength, the shipper is able to secure desired rates and services.

It is quite common for a shipper to use fewer than 50 carriers to ship the majority of its freight, concentrating 75 to 80 percent of its total freight dollars with 25 or fewer motor carriers. Rail shippers commonly use just one or, at best, two carriers because usually only one rail carrier can provide service to the shipper's plant or warehouse.

A recent trend has been the move to **"core" carriers**. These firms are chosen from the existing carrier base, usually after an intensive bidding process. The "core" carriers usually divide the business and their share may be as much as 25 percent of the total. It is not unusual for a shipper to go from nearly 100 carriers to less than 10. The risk is that should one of the core carriers exit the business, the remaining carriers may not be able to handle the business. Replacement carriers may be difficult to obtain in times of tight equipment or high demand.

The disadvantage of limiting the number of carriers used is the increased dependency on the carriers that are used. If one of the major carriers ceases operation, the service disruption results in reduced customer service level, increased managerial costs, and greater transportation costs. The greater cost and lower customer service level exists until a replacement carrier is selected and is efficiently operating.

Carrier Negotiation

Negotiating with for-hire carriers is standard operating procedure today. Before deregulation, carrier negotiation was almost nonexistent, given the rate bureau influence in common carrier rate making. With the marketplace in control, all carrier rates and services are matters for negotiation.

Market power determines the shipper's ability to negotiate acceptable rates and services. To increase market power as discussed above, shippers use the strategy of limiting the number of carriers, thereby concentrating more of its economic power with a carrier and increasing the carrier's dependence on the shipper.

A shipper's market power and negotiating strength also are determined by the characteristics of its freight. Freight that has low density, is hard to handle, is easily damaged, and moves in small volumes irregularly is undesirable freight for the carrier. Conversely, products that have high density and high value, are difficult to damage, and move in large volumes regularly are more economical for the carrier to move. (For an in-depth discussion of carrier negotiations, refer to Chapter 12, "Relationship Management.")

Given the problems motor carriers have experienced in recruiting and retaining drivers, some firms have adopted new policies when responding to negotiation requests from shippers. Carriers are now seeking "driver-friendly" freight, which generally means that the driver does not have to assist with either the loading or unloading. One Fortune 500 shipper has responded by working with its retail customers to provide incentives for rapid unloading and relieving drivers of tasks other than driving. Finally, the shipper's negotiating position is improved if the freight moves in the direction of the carrier's empty backhaul.

Contracting

Deregulation has permitted increased contracting with for-hire carriers. The contracts allow the shipper to realize the lower rates and necessary service levels that are not attainable from a regulated carrier. During the term of the contract, the shipper is guaranteed the contracted rate and service (most contracts are for one year, but other time periods may apply). If properly written, the provisions of the contract take precedence over the bill of lading and transportation regulations. The transportation manager must take precautions to ensure that the contract provides desired terms such as rates, services, equipment, and liability.

Rail contracting is common today. Rail shippers usually have two or more rail contracts in effect to govern a given commodity move over a given origin-destination, and contracts generally are rate-oriented.

Motor carrier contracts usually cover one to three years with stipulations for tailored service. Other motor carrier contracts along with air and water carrier contracts emphasize the contract rate.

Review Private Trucking

The decision to use or discontinue the use of private trucking is a continual strategic issue for the transportation manager. In today's dynamic transportation market, competitive pressures have forced for-hire trucking rates below the cost of many private fleet operations. Through the use of contracting, the service level of for-hire carriers is equivalent to that provided by private trucking. With both the for-hire cost and service comparable to that of private trucking, the review of private trucking is a prevalent transportation strategy. A detailed discussion of private trucking was provided in Chapter 10, "Private Transportation."

Small Shipment Strategy

As Figure 14.1 indicates, the small shipment strategies consist of freight consolidation, using drop-off carriers and pooling services, and avoiding the use of private trucking. The strategic thrust for small shipments is to reduce the inherently high transportation costs associated with small-sized shipments. By increasing the size of the shipments, the shipper can take advantage of the carrier's low rates for heavier shipments. Rate discounts from 30 percent to 50 percent or more are possible for heavier loads.

A shipper consolidates its freight by using its order entry system. As customer orders arrive, a computer uses a three-digit zip code to match shipments going to the same general area. As discussed above, the need for information is critical to any freight consolidation program. The transportation manager must know the shipments that are shipped to a given area on a given date as well as delivery requirements.

TABLE 14.1 Freight Pooling Example

		Direct LTL		Pool Truck Service to Toledo			
Customer	**Shpmt. Wt.**	**Rate**	**Total Cost**	**Line-Haul**	**Handling**	**Local**	**Total**
Toledo	8,250	9.25	$763.13	$449.63	$61.88	$111.38	$622.88
Findlay	4,350	9.85	$428.48	$237.08	$32.63	$58.73	$328.43
Lima	3,600	9.95	$358.20	$196.20	$27.00	$48.60	$271.80
Sandusky	5,350	8.85	$473.48	$291.58	$40.13	$72.23	$403.93
Monroe	3,780	9.55	$360.99	$206.01	$28.35	$51.03	$285.39
Defiance	5,670	9.95	$564.17	$309.02	$42.53	$76.55	$428.09
Totals	31,000		**$2948.43**	$1,689.50	$232.50	$418.50	**$2,340.50**
				Saving with Pool Truck Service =			**$607.93**

Pooling Rates

Linehaul to Toledo	=	$5.45/cwt
Handling Cost	=	$0.75/cwt
Local Delivery Rate	=	$1.35/cwt
Total Rate	=	$7.55/cwt

If the consolidated load consists of many shipments going to different consignees in a general area, the shipper may use the **pooling** service offered by for-hire carriers. The pooling service charges the shipper the lower volume rate from one origin to one destination. Because the consolidated load contains shipments for many consignees at different destinations, a warehouse or drayage firm is used to separate and deliver the individual shipment, and an added cost is incurred for this additional break-bulk and delivery service.

Table 14.1 provides an example of the cost-saving potential from freight pooling. In this example, six small (LTL) shipments are destined for locales around Toledo, Ohio. The cost of shipping each shipment separately to the consignees is $2,948.43. (See the two columns labeled Direct LTL in Table 14.1.) By consolidating the six shipments into one 31,000 truckload shipment and shipping it to a warehouse in Toledo for reshipment to the individual consignee, the total cost is $2,340.50, a savings of $607.93 (20.6 percent). The pooled shipment rate of $7.55/cwt combines the line-haul rate to Toledo ($5.45) with the warehousing handling cost ($0.75) and local delivery rate ($1.35).

Another small shipment strategy is the use of **stopping-in-transit (SIT) service** provided by motor carriers. SIT permits the shipper to load a number of shipments on a vehicle and stop along the way to unload the individual shipments. Conversely, SIT can be used for inbound shipments by having the carrier stop along the way to load additional shipments and deliver a consolidated raw material shipment to the plant, warehouse, or retail store.

Figure 14.2 is an example of SIT. The shipper has two shipments departing from the origin (O), one destined for C_1 (10,000 pounds) and one for D (20,000 pounds). The cost to ship the two shipments without SIT is $745.00, compared with $615.00 with the SIT, a savings of $130.00 (17 percent). SIT rules require the shipper to use the highest truckload (TL) rate ($1.90/cwt) and the highest weight in the vehicle at any time (30,000 pounds) and to pay for the intermediate stop(s) ($45.00).

Finally, the use of private trucking for small shipments is normally not cost-effective. The small shipment size precludes full use of the private trucking equip-

FIGURE 14.2 Stopping-in-Transit Example

O ———— C_1 ———— D

		Rates			
Shipment Weight		LTL	TL	Min Wt.	
O–C_1	10,000	$2.25	$1.70	30,000	Stopoff Charge = $45.00/stop
O–D	20,000	2.60	1.90	30,000	
	30,000				

Cost with SIT

300 cwt @ $1.90	=	$570.00
Stopoff Charge	=	$45.00
Total	=	**$615.00**

Cost without SIT

O–C_1	100 cwt @ $2.25	=	$225.00
O–D	200 cwt @ $2.60	=	$520.00
	Total	=	**$745.00**

ment, with the result that costs are higher than the charges assessed by for-hire carriers. For-hire carriers are in a position to consolidate small shipments from many shippers to make the operation economical. One major exception to this strategy is the driver/salesperson operation in which the driver performs sales service functions (customer order filling and stock rotation, for example) in addition to driving.

Bulk Shipment Strategy

The primary strategy used in the transportation of bulk commodities is contracting. Most bulk raw materials are moved under long-term contracts with rail, water, and motor carriers. The large volume of product moved gives the shipper the requisite negotiating and market power to realize lower rates and guaranteed service levels.

The sheer volume of transportation involved has caused both shippers and carriers to realize their mutual dependency. If the carrier ceases operation, the shipper experiences serious disruptions in service, higher costs, and possibly a short-run closing of production because alternative transportation is not available. Likewise, the carrier is aware of the large percentage of its business that is accounted for by one shipper.

Given this mutual dependency, a shipper attempts to provide the carrier with a **balanced load,** that is, a load into the facility and one out of the facility. A balanced load eliminates the empty backhaul costs that the carrier must account for in the initial loaded move and enables the carrier to spread this round-trip cost over two commodity moves instead of one. To accomplish the balanced load strategy, cooperation is required between outbound and inbound (purchasing) transportation and may necessitate resourcing material purchases from areas where the carrier experiences empty backhauls. Recently, a major manufacturer contacted other shippers in an attempt to generate freight for its contract carrier to haul over an otherwise empty backhaul. This can be difficult if the commodity being transported requires dedicated or specialized trailers.

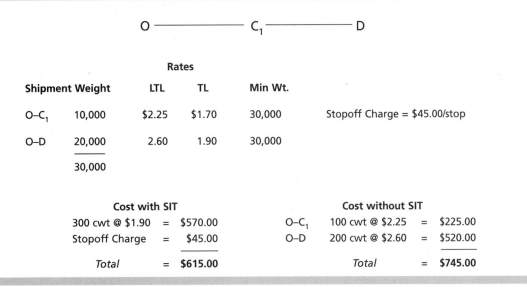

Inbound Transportation Strategy

Today companies are giving considerable attention to inbound logistics and inbound transportation. They are recognizing that the **terms of sale** used by purchasing do not provide them with sufficient control over inbound transportation costs. In the past, the purchase order items would stipulate "FOB, Delivered" or "ship the best way." These terms of sale give the vendor control over the purchaser's inbound transportation and assume that the vendor has the ability and desire to use the transportation carrier that minimizes the purchaser's costs.

By modifying the shipping terms to "FOB, Origin," the buyer takes on the inbound transportation responsibility and authority and can apply the transportation strategies identified above to achieve lower rates and improved service. Limiting the number of inbound carriers used builds market power, provides balanced loads to carriers, and results in lower inbound transportation costs.

Another approach is to use the "FOB, Delivered" term in the purchase order but demand that the vendor use one of the carriers from a list of carriers approved by the buyer. This strategy concentrates the purchaser's inbound freight into a limited number of carriers but permits the vendor to select an acceptable carrier from the approval list.

In addition to increased attention to inbound shipments, **reverse logistics** is a new area requiring significant transportation activity and, in some cases, extreme control. Reverse logistics can cover everything from the return of repairable items and parts for rebuilding to the recall of food or pharmaceuticals. In some cases, this is really a continuous cycle. An example would be the return of an expended copier toner cartridge after it is replaced with a new one. Often, such items come in packaging materials that allow the round trip. The packaging may even contain a preaddressed label and prepaid shipping cost. In another situation, pallets, totes, and baskets are returned from a retail store to the distribution for reuse or recycling.

Some carriers have formed divisions specifically to facilitate reverse logistics. CF Reverse Logistics, a division of Consolidated Freightways, formed a partnership with a major chemical company to return stainless steel totes from customers to its plants for reuse. Other firms, including a computer manufacturer and an consumer goods electronics firm, have put reverse logistics programs into place.[5]

The strategies discussed above provide the guidelines for the transportation manager to follow in carrying out the transportation function. The next section examines the traffic management functions.

Traffic Management

Traffic management is the traditional term for the task of obtaining and controlling transportation services for shippers or consignees or both. It is a term applied to a position or an entire department in almost any extractive, raw material, manufacturing, assembling, or distribution firm. The term *transportation management* is beginning to replace *traffic management,* but *traffic management* continues to be the favored term applied to the purchase and control of transportation services.

The job of traffic manager has traditionally been a low-status position in a firm. Since the 1950s, however, it has risen in corporate stature to a position that commands a large part of total corporate expenditures. In many firms, traffic management is the core of business logistics department. Transportation in the firm exists in close trade-off relationships with purchasing, warehousing, inventory control, packaging, production scheduling, and marketing. As such, traffic management requires close coordination with these other departments, with counterpart departments in other firms, and with carrier firms.

The effectiveness of transportation management necessarily depends on an understanding of how customers (shippers and receivers) perform their modal and carrier selection decisions.

What Is Traffic Management?

Traffic management is a special form of procurement that entails both line and staff activities. It is a field that has grown in both importance and corporate recognition. However, it is a field that is currently undergoing change as a result of the removal of the economic regulations applying to and affecting transportation.

Traffic Management as a Procurement Function

Traffic management is a special form of procurement and purchasing. **Procurement** is a term that applies to a wide range of activities that basically consists of obtaining goods and services for the firm. Procurement includes analysis and activities in the following areas: 1) quality, 2) pricing, 3) specifications, 4) supply source, 5) negotiations, 6) inspection and assurance of quality, 7) timing, 8) conducting value analysis of alternative methods and sources, 9) capital analysis, 10) make or buy decisions, 11) legal and regulatory constraints, and 12) general management. All of these factors provide the firm with a system to obtain the physical goods and special services it requires.

Traffic management performs all of these specific activities in its acquisition and control of transportation *services* for the firm. Traditionally, a minimum transportation cost goal was employed for this function. In most firms, this was replaced by a goal of minimum total logistics expense. Today many companies first establish a customer service goal, then evaluate traffic and logistics in terms of minimized total logistics costs while attaining the service goal. This, in a way, is similar to the balanced-value approach.

Part of this change is the manner by which the performance of the traffic manager is evaluated. Historically, the traffic manager was judged by their cost control efforts. They were required to spend as little as possible for transportation. Since they were evaluated on this criteria, the traffic manger would choose the lowest cost method consistent with the minimum service requirements. Under current management requirements, the traffic manager is evaluated by how well they participate in the overall optimization and achievement of the logistics goals. This may include using premium transportation or other more expense techniques, the cost of which is offset elsewhere in the logistics cycle.

Line and Staff Functions

Originally, traffic management was a clerical activity devoted to shipping or receiving the firm's goods. Today it entails a range of line functions that often are specialized and require communications and data systems. Traffic managers must observe field trends, evaluate potential procedural and system changes, plan for the implementation of appropriate changes, and propose some of these changes to top management. The full range of general management activities is now found in traffic departments.

Carrier Selection Process

Purchasing transportation service is one of the primary traffic manager functions. The traffic manager's decisions have a direct impact upon the company's total logistics costs and quality of service provided to the customer.

The transport selection decision is a two-part decision. The initial decision involves the selection of the mode and the second division relates to the selection of the specific carrier within the mode. That is, the traffic manager examines the cost and service characteristics of the different modes, including the combination of two or more modes (intermodal or multimodal service), and selects the mode that matches the company's cost and service goals. Next, the traffic manager examines the cost and service characteristics of the individual carriers within the selected mode and selects the specific carrier to provide the desired transport service.

The transport decision begins with an identification of the cost and the service goals of the transport service to be provided. From these goals the pertinent carrier performance measures are identified and examined in the selection of the carrier. The relevant carrier selection factors include transport cost, transit time, transit time reliability, accessibility, capability, and security. These factors impact the total logistics costs of movement and storage and are used in both the selection of the mode and specific carrier.

Transport Cost

The transport cost factor includes the rate charged by the potential carrier. In addition, this factor examines the charges assessed by the carrier for ancillary services such as residential delivery, controlled-temperature vehicles, and stops in transit. The transport cost varies from mode to mode because of the different cost structures of the modes, whereas the cost variation among carriers within a mode is less because the carriers have similar cost structures. Thus, transport cost is somewhat more important in the modal selection decision than in the specific carrier selection decision.

Transit Time and Transit Time Reliability

As noted earlier in this section, the total-cost implication of the carrier selection decision considers not only the direct transportation cost incurred but also the indirect costs associated with the quality of the service provided. **Transit time** and reliability of transit time are two transport service qualities that affect inventory costs and stockout costs. Transit time impacts the level of inventory held and the consequent inventory carrying costs. The longer the transit time, the higher the inventory levels and the higher the inventory carrying costs. Therefore, the total cost impact of using a carrier (mode) with a longer transit time is higher inventory carrying costs.

Likewise, the reliability of transit time affects the level of inventory required. Unreliable transit time requires an increase in the level of inventory to guard against stockout conditions and the resultant cost of lost profit or lost productivity associated with not having the product available to meet the demand. Viewed from a marketing perspective, reliable transit time affords the buyer the opportunity to reduce or control both inventory and stockout costs. Thus, using a carrier that provides reliable transit time provides the seller with a marketplace advantage.

Accessibility

The **accessibility** factor considers the ability of the carrier to provide the transport service between a specific origin and destination. The modes differ in their ability to provide direct service to specific locations. Physical limitations associated with roadways and terminals prohibit certain modes from providing direct services to a specific site. To overcome the accessibility of a mode, the services of another more accessible mode must be purchased. The additional expense to surmount a mode's inability to service a particular location is the accessibility cost.

For example, the motor carrier is the most accessible of the modes. It can go virtually anywhere there is a road. Conversely, water carriers are restrained to providing service to users located adjacent to waterways. Likewise, the railroads except for intermodal service have limited accessibility to shippers located along rail tracks with sidetracks, air carriers to freight shippers located at airports, and pipelines to servicing freight customers adjacent to the pipeline. Thus, the motor carrier is often used, at an additional transport (accessibility) expense, to enable users of the other modes to gain direct transport service to specific sites not adjacent to the mode's physical facilities.

Capability

The **capability** factor refers to the ability of the carrier (mode) to provide the unique transport services and equipment required by the user. The traffic manager will use the carrier that has the ability to provide the unique services or equipment required. Examples of special equipment requirements include controlled-temperature vehicles for the movement of frozen foods, high cube capacity vehicles for the movement of low-density products (plastic bottles, for example), and tank vehicles for the movement of bulk liquids. Unique transport service needs include specified pickup or delivery times, carrier information systems to locate and expedite shipments, and electronic data interchange capabilities.

Security

The final factor, security, considers the indirect transport service cost if the shipment is damaged or lost in transit. A damaged shipment has the same impact on inventory costs and stockout costs as unreliable transit time. A product damaged or lost in transit is not available for use when demanded and the user incurs the cost of processing a damage claim or legal action against the carrier to secure reimbursement, incurs the loss if reimbursement is not received from the carrier, or pays for insurance to provide protection against the in-transit damage.

In practice, each of these carrier selection factors are broken down into a number of more specific measures of the cost and service characteristics. Table 14.2 shows an expanded list of carrier selection factors and the relative importance of each in selecting motor carriers. Reliability of transit time is the most important carrier selection factor, followed by transportation rate, total transit time, willingness to negotiate, and financial stability of the carrier. Less important selection factors may include special equipment, quality of carrier salesmanship, claims processing, and line-haul services.

TABLE 14.2 Importance of Motor Carrier Selection Factors

Transit time reliability or consistency	Shipment expediting
Door-to-door transportation rates or costs	Quality of operating personnel
Total door-to-door transit time	Shipment tracing
Willingness of carrier to negotiate rate changes	Willingness of carrier to negotiate service changes
Financial stability of the carrier	Scheduling flexibility
Equipment availability	Line-haul services
Frequency of service	Claims processing
Pickup and delivery service	Quality of carrier salesmanship
Freight loss and damage	Special equipment

Source: Adapted from Edward J. Bardi, Prabir Bagchi, and T. S. Raghunathan, "Motor Carrier Selection in a Deregulated Environment," *Transportation Journal*, Vol. 29, No. 1 (Fall 1989), pp. 4—11.

Line Aspects of Traffic Management

The daily activities of traffic management are numerous. Although the management of individual traffic officers may vary, the typical traffic management process is as follows:

- Shipment planning
- Carrier selection
- Ordering service
- Expediting/tracing
- Preauditing/rating
- Auditing/paying the freight bill
- Detention/demurrage processes
- Claims, if any
- Other—private car or truck fleet management, transportation budget management

Shipment Planning

Traffic management continually monitors inbound and outbound shipping schedules, which should be coordinated with purchasing and distribution or production. A continuous flow of product should be maintained, unhindered by the unavailability of transportation (no equipment or service). Further, physical loading and unloading must be planned according to the efficient use of docks and labor. Management must ensure that transportation is not scheduled too early or in excess of actual needs because dock and track congestion and equipment detention and demurrage charges will result.

Carrier Selection

This task involves selecting the actual carrier that will move the shipment. In rail contexts this might be largely confined to the carrier that has a siding into the plant. But even here, the traffic manager may have some latitude in route selection through use of intermediate or alternative route carriers. In connection with motor carriers, traffic managers often will give shipment preference to the firm's own private carriage vehicles or use a contract carrier before considering common carriers. Within both rail or motor selection, traffic managers evaluate a number of factors, as discussed in the preceding section.

Ordering Service

To order transportation service, the traffic manager may contact a railroad car distributor who will arrange empty car delivery or call a trucking firm's local **dispatcher**. Electronic methods are becoming more common and the use of the Internet is accelerating this trend. In other cases, long-term arrangements for equipment supply include trailer pools and scheduled rotation. The traffic manager needs to inform the carrier personnel of the shipper's name and pickup point, weight, commodity, destination, and sometimes the cube measurement of the shipment. Upon vehicle arrival, the equipment is loaded according to plans established in the first step (shipment planning). They include crew assignment, loading arrangement, bracing, dunnage, documentation, and any other special needs.

Expediting/Tracing

The traffic manager keeps track of shipment progress and alerts the carrier of any en-route changes that might be necessary. Some shippers have direct computer links with carrier shipment systems. These provide daily position reports of all the shipper's railcars or shipments. Some carriers provide tracing services via the Internet. Other carriers place information in a secure Web site that only particular shipper can access. This information is updated on a scheduled basis. Expediting/tracing is a valuable control tool for the shipper and consignee because they can plan production and assembly around shipment progress or problems.

Preauditing/Rating

Preauditing is the process of determining what the proper freight charges for a shipment should be. Often shippers preaudit shipments before billing by the carrier so that freight bill overcharges and undercharges can be reduced or avoided. Computer rating systems have greatly assisted with this task.

Auditing/Paying the Freight Bill

Auditing entails checking the accuracy of the freight bill after it is presented by the carrier or after it has been paid. Some firms do this in-house, whereas others hire outside consultants to perform this job after the bill has actually been paid. The traffic department generally confirms the freight bill and passes it along to the office responsible for payment.

Deregulation has largely been responsible for price simplification. Contract rates and services, the diminished importance of rate bureaus and their complex tariffs, and the growth of computers enable preauditing and postauditing to take place with fewer resources than in the past. Many carriers offer their rates on computer floppy disks or will update a shipper's file via an EDI link automatically. Rate checking and auditing can also be performed by many computer-based firms such as Cass Information Systems.

Detention/Demurrage Processes

Detention is a charge assessed by a motor carrier against a shipper or consignee for keeping equipment for loading or unloading beyond a specified period. **Demurrage** is the same concept in the rail industry. The traffic manager is usually responsible for monitoring, managing, and paying for detention and demurrage obligations. The manager must trade off the loading, unloading, and personnel costs against the cost of holding carrier equipment.

Claims

Loss and damage sometimes occur to shipments while in the possession of carriers. Traffic managers will then file **claims** to recoup part or all of these damaged amounts. They also handle overcharges on the freight bills.

Commercial trucking companies and railroads are liable for all loss, damage, and delay to a shipment with limited exceptions as provided under the Carmack Amendment. These exceptions include the following:

- An act of God—an unavoidable catastrophe
- An act of a public enemy—armed aggression against our country
- An act of public authority—through due process of law, a government agency causes damage, loss, or delay
- An act of the shipper—actions by the shipper contribute to the damage, such as improper packaging
- The inherent nature of the goods—natural deterioration

To recover damages from a regulated motor carrier or railroad, the shipper must file a claim in writing within nine months of the date of shipment. The carrier must acknowledge the receipt of the claim within 30 days and must inform the claimant within 120 days whether it will pay or refuse to pay the claim. If the carrier does not dispose of the claim within 120 days, the carrier must inform the claimant of the claim's status every 60 days. If the carrier refuses to pay the claim, the claimant has two years from the date of disallowance to bring legal action against the carrier.

The carrier is normally liable for the full value of the product at destination. However, carriers, especially a motor carrier, can limit its liability by use of the released value rate. In return for a lower rate, the shipper agrees to hold the carrier liability to something less than the full value of the product. Some carriers have inserted automatic released value rules in their tariffs and terms of sale. The automatic released value rules reduce the value of the product to that stipulated in the tariff unless the shipper states otherwise on the bill of lading at the time of shipment.

For other carriers (air and exempt trucking), liability for loss and damage is based on negligence. That is, the carrier is held liable if it did not provide the ordinary care a reasonable person would provide in protecting his or her goods. This is the standard to which a warehouse is held.

Private Car and Truck Fleet Management

In some firms, the traffic manager is also responsible for private railcar and truck fleet management. This entails coordination and control tasks with the goal of minimizing fleet costs and providing quality service. Private transportation was discussed in greater detail in Chapter 10.

Transportation Budget Management

The transportation budget is the major overriding financial control in all these tasks. The traffic manager must keep track of current and future activities and expenditures and relate them to the original plan. Cost escalators, such as fuel and insurance, have created major problems for most traffic managers who attempt to operate within planned budgets. Escalation will no doubt continue to be a complicating cost and budget problem in the future.

Staff and Administrative Aspects of Traffic Management

Traffic management has grown over the years to become more than a mere line activity. Many planning tasks or staff activities have developed as support functions. These other activities increase the cost efficiency or customer service capability of the line activities.

Mode Selection

The traffic manager selects the mode for specific classes of shipments or products, market areas, or each plant or warehouse. Each mode offers specific inherent service and cost advantages. Usually, the selection is made infrequently so that routing and carrier selection personnel can operate within the modal choice.

Monitoring Service Quality

The quality of the transportation provided can differentiate a company's product, thereby providing a competitive advantage in the marketplace. If the traffic manager can get the products to the customer in a timely, consistent, and undamaged basis, the buyer's inventory and stockout costs are lowered, making it advantageous for the buyer to do business with the seller.

The key to monitoring transportation service quality is information. The traffic manager must have information regarding the customer's demands for transportation service and the service level provided by current carriers. This information is critical to making rational modal and carrier selection decisions and to meeting corporate service and cost goals.

Figure 14.3 is a sample **carrier evaluation** report. Usually on a quarterly basis, the traffic manager evaluates the current carriers based on actual performance versus targeted goals. The carrier evaluation report is used to assure that carriers are providing the service quality that is demanded by the customers or specified by agreement. Carriers not providing the expected level of service are asked to take corrective actions or the traffic manager will replace the carrier.

Examination of Figure 14.3 reveals the criteria used to evaluate carrier performance, which are the same as those used to select the carrier. Typically, the most important evaluation criteria are meeting pickup and delivery schedules and transit time. Normal transportation documentation—bill of lading, freight bill, and so on—does not contain this information. The traffic manager must obtain these data directly from the shipping and receiving areas.

Service/Supply Assurance

During the late 1990s, strikes in the trucking industry caused several periods of carrier supply disruption. As a reaction to those events, many firms have prepared for such future occurrences by planning for alternative and backup forms of transportation. This is a contingency type of management that heretofore was not necessary, nor was it employed until recently.

Negotiations

This activity is increasing in importance because of 1980s regulatory changes and the ICC Termination Act of 1995, which allow great price flexibility. Rate negotiations are now a commonplace activity. Negotiations require a large degree of preparation, analysis, and proper approach and conduct. A negotiation that attains a rate that the carrier eventually finds unremunerative and incapable of serving effectively is to be avoided. In this instance, both the shipper and carrier lose.

Rail and motor contract services are increasing in use, and many negotiations take place for specific services, rather than lower rates. These include specific car supply or transit time performance. Here, too, a sound analysis and approach is necessary.

Regulatory Matters

Traffic managers and staffs traditionally had been involved in routine regulatory processes before federal and state agencies. These regulatory processes included rate protests, rail abandonment petitions, or carrier merger applications. Deregulation has almost eliminated the traffic manager's attention to regulatory matters. Safety issues such as hazardous materials transportation require expertise and skill to avoid serious problems.

Policy Matters

Traffic managers often will become involved in presenting their firms' policy positions in proposed legislative or regulatory proceedings. These policy areas relate to carrier credit regulations, rail rate regulation standards, exempt transportation, or any

FIGURE 14.3 Carrier Evaluation Report

CARRIER:______________________________ TIME PERIOD:____________

MAXIMUM SCORE	EVALUATION CRITERIA	CARRIER SCORE		COMMENTS
13	Meets Pick-up Schedules	13		
13	Meets Delivery	10		
9	Transit Time	9		
10	Transit Time Consistency	7		
7	Rates	5		
3	Accessoral Charges	1		High residential delivery
5	Operating Ratio	3		96.5%, rising
4	Profitability	3		
3	Claims Frequency	3		
3	Claims Settlement	3		
10	Billing Errors	7		
9	Tracing Capabilities	7		
11	Equipment Availability	1		No flatbeds
100	TOTAL SCORE	72		

Evaluator: ______________________________ Date: ____________________

Best Score = 100; Worst Score = 0

Procedure:
1. Assign maximum score for each evaluation criteria; total maximum score = 100
2. Give carrier score for each criteria, up to maximum score for criteria
3. Add all criteria scores for carrier
4. Carrier with highest score is "best"

other proposed change in the field. When involved in these areas, the traffic manager will conduct analyses, prepare position statements, be active in industry associations representing the firm, and often submit testimony on the firm's behalf.

Planning Annual Transportation Requirements

Another staff-related task is interpreting the firm's purchasing, production, and marketing plans for future periods and translating the plans into specific shipping needs. This list represents the specific type of equipment needed and the quantities and timing of its use. Automobile manufacturers often must work with railroads several years in advance so that railcars exist when new automobile models of specific sizes and shapes roll off assembly lines. In shorter-term contexts, this planning often entails leasing rail equipment, arranging for contract carriage, or merely determining whether the existing carriers will be capable of handling the forecasted shipments.

Budgeting

Traffic managers play the key role in establishing transportation budgets for future periods. The budget usually integrates volumes, expected modal mixes, specific shipping patterns, and expected inflationary impacts. Capital budgets are prepared for analyzing the technical and financial feasibility of proposed major asset acquisitions such as private fleets, railcars, new docks, expanded rail sidings, computer systems, or warehouse and dock space. The activity brings the traffic manager into contact with engineering and finance personnel, as well as top management.

Information Systems

The astute traffic manager will always seek ways to attain and report information relating to the carrier's services and individual manager performance. Many firms monitor and report cost and transit time performance for all movements, including the private fleet. They also may record cost recoveries and claims progress. In all, performance reevaluation and decision-making information systems are a prime necessity. The traffic manager can make recommendations about the design of these systems.

Systems Analysis

The combinations of transportation services and rates offered by carriers number in the hundreds. There is no one best way of always transporting a firm's goods. Where motor might be a proper choice in normal periods, air freight might be necessary occasionally. What is a good choice one day might be a poor one the next. Within traffic management, continuous analyses must be conducted to put together the best service and total cost configuration.

Traffic management must be integrated within the overall materials management and distribution scheme of the firm. In this context, traffic management often is forced to make less than optimal decisions in light of overriding system factors for the total cost and service pattern of the firm.

Management and Executive Development

Traffic and transportation are changing at a fast pace in a manner not experienced in the past. It is imperative that all personnel keep track of changes in the field, analyze them, and provide for positive action by the firm. They also must update their personal technical knowledge and management skills by reading about all aspects of transportation and management, keeping in contact with others through professional associations, taking advantage of educational opportunities, and keeping a perspective on how a present task and position fit into an overall business strategy scheme.

Traffic Department Human Resources Management

Another major area of managerial analysis with which traffic managers are concerned is the use of human resources within the department. Typically, a key area

STOP OFF

A Support System to Boot

Successful logistics relies heavily on information technology to see it through. Seattle-based fine paper and wood pulp manufacturer, Simpson Paper has a logistics program that is no exception. The company's Coated and Specialty Group moves more than a half-million tons per year by a variety of modes.

In 1995, the company realized it was time for a change. It decided to outsource all traffic management and freight bill payment, in effect downsizing a 30-person department to two while improving customer service and implementing cost-saving structures. The business unit fully incorporated Schneider Logistics' SUMIT(System (Schneider Utility for Managing Integrated Transportation) in December 1995, after an eight-month phase-in period that implemented the program in seven mills/DCs—one at a time.

The system manages all inbound and outbound freight, including dedicated carriage, continuous move opportunities, freight payment, audit, carrier negotiations, rate quotations, and trailer pools. In addition, Simpson is able to track and trace all transportation modes, including rail shipments, as well as file and resolve all freight loss and damage claims. In-house, two people staff the department, while Schneider supplies personnel to administer the system at the mills.

Finding the right solution was neither quick nor simple, says Ted Farmer, Customer Service and Logistics Manager for the group. In the end, Simpson chose Schneider because "the SUMIT System seemed to be more powerful and flexible. It was able to provide us with the information we needed to meet what we think are pretty unique customer service requirements," recalls Farmer. "We had been in the process of implementing some strategic supply chain initiatives that went well beyond vendor-managed inventory. The program worked well with our supply chain vision."

SOURCE: Jodi E. Melbin, "A Support System to Boot," *Distribution,* December 1997, p. 51. Reprint permission granted by *Logistics* (formerly *Distribution*) Magazine.

of discretion for the traffic manager is in assigning rate and analytical personnel either to preaudit and postaudit freight bills or to create analytical projects that seek varied transportation and distribution methods. These decisions are being forced in many firms because many departments are required to show a profit or return to the company from employee wage dollars spent. In this regard, traffic managers often must determine whether human resource hours will return more for the firm if allocated to auditing freight bills or to analyzing new transportation processes. Because freight bills can be audited by outside auditing firms (the fees of which are based upon a percentage of the overcharges recovered), these human resource hours can often more productively be applied to transportation analysis.

In the next section, carrier network strategies, operations, and terminals are discussed.

Carrier Strategies

Transportation firms experience the same laws of economics that production entities experience, but in transportation these guiding principles often manifest themselves in different ways. The transportation industry faces and manages its particular set of economic rules in its own way.

Transportation is a service, not a production activity. Except for pure pleasure cruise travel and some auto travel, transportation faces a derived demand and not a primary demand for its services. Further, transportation is a service that cannot be stored; it is unlike a physical product that can be produced according to certain logistical efficiencies and then held until the market demands it. Transportation managers must seek efficient management approaches through various efficiency techniques and through responsive management structures.

This section presents many of the techniques of transportation efficiency that are inherent to sound economic principles and that have been used by successful carrier managements. It also covers the role of the terminal, which is a basic element of a transportation network.

Operations

The **rule of efficiency** states that it is most efficient to move in a continuous, straight line whenever possible. This rule describes the most efficient movement for goods and people. It calls for little or no circuitry and minimized stopping and restarting. Sporadic movement means energy loss, chances for delay and damage, and an overall increase in costs.

This general rule can be observed in practice in many areas. Unit trains such as coal or grain avoid intermediate classification yards between the shipper and receiver. Truck firms attempt to consolidate long-haul loads so that a single through run, with no intermediate handling, is made and the goods can be sorted for final local delivery at the ultimate destination. The airline industry strives to maximize long-haul nonstop flights because major fuel and engine-wear costs are incurred in take-offs. Further, the costs of maintaining a transportation vehicle in constant motion are small in relation to the energy and effort expended to get a vehicle from rest to a constant cruise speed.

Intermediate handlings should be minimized. This rule of thumb bears special attention when different transportation firms meet as part of a through move. Railroads often use run-through trains with the engines and cars remain intact in interline moves to minimize interchange time loss. Pre-blocked cars are another example of this technique in which interlined cars are handled in groups rather than singly. Truck firms interline trailer loads. Freight is moved from interior points in the United States to Europe inside containers via rail, truck, and ship without the individual goods being handled.

The full capacity of the transportation vehicle should be maximized on each run. Transportation costs of trucks, trains, ships, and planes are similar in that the costs of personnel, depreciation, licenses, and taxes are relatively fixed costs that are incurred for each run. The variable amount of goods or people in the run will affect fuel costs, some servicing costs, and loading and unloading costs. On the whole, the firm experiences less per-unit cost as more passengers or freight are added to a run. Therefore, most transportation managers seek to fill the capacity of the vehicle before dispatching it. In the railroad and trucking industries, managers often will delay runs so that more freight can be accumulated for the long haul. The driver or engine crew is paid the same regardless of the weight in the truck or the cars on the train. Airline marketing and pricing managers use low-cost excursion fares to entice vacationers to fill what normally would be empty seats.

Consolidation and break-bulk activities should be used for long-haul advantages. One means of attaining full equipment use is to use a pickup and delivery network to accumulate freight for the line-haul efficiency. Trucking firms do this with city vehicles that bring different shipments to a terminal for sorting, accumulation, and shipping in bulk to the destination city terminal. This system avoids the prohibitive use of many small trucks and shipments by using large, efficient single units on 400 to 500 mile runs. Railroads perform this task in much the same way. Many airlines have adopted hub-and-spoke route strategies around such cities as Atlanta,

Denver, St. Louis, Pittsburgh, and Chicago. Here smaller planes bring passengers from less populated, outlying cities to the hub where the larger, more efficient planes can be used for the long haul. At the destination, the process is reversed: Goods or people are distributed outwardly from the large destination terminal.

Empty mileage should be minimized. The cost of moving an empty vehicle is almost that of moving a loaded one without the offset of revenue. Energy is a major cost in transportation systems. In very few instances can a firm afford one-way loaded movements with empty return hauls. Each mile traveled requires the use of energy, and often the payload in freight or passengers represents only a small part of the total energy consumed in the move. That is, the movement of the vehicle itself can often be responsible for a large part of the fuel consumed. For this reason, transportation route strategies, carrier marketing and pricing personnel, and dispatchers strive to arrange two-way or three-way moves with almost all miles bearing revenue payloads. Empty miles represent wasted fuel, labor, capital costs, and lost revenue. Motor carriers strive to maintain empty miles at 10 percent or less of total miles.

Movements should be scheduled and dispatched so as to fully use labor and equipment in line with the market. Transportation service cannot be stored. Because the service must be in place for the market, this rule calls for the optimal equipment levels to be in place with the required personnel. Neither the equipment nor the required labor should delay the move. In some rail and trucking firms, power units accumulate at one end of the system while there is a need for them elsewhere, but no crews are available to move them back. Likewise, a waste occurs when crews arrive for work and there is no equipment available for the trip or little freight to be handled that day. Some motor carrier firms avoid this problem through the use of online shipment record systems that indicate to terminal managers how much freight will be arriving inbound during future shift periods. Thus, crews of optimal size can then be called for particular shifts of work.

Technology and Equipment

The more expensive the long-haul vehicle, the greater the required investment in fast load/unload and other support equipment. Transportation vehicles represent capital investments. The economies of high capital investment call for high utilization of the equipment throughout the day, week, month, or year. Because these expensive investments are only earning revenue when they are running, firms strive to operate with a minimum of down time or loading and unloading time. This principle can be seen at airports where aircraft costing \$110 million each arrive and depart within as little as one hour. Instead of being hand-loaded onto planes, food, luggage, and freight are loaded by mechanized equipment into expensive containers that are later unloaded by crew members while the plane is enroute. The basic financial principle here is that the cost of ground support equipment is less than the lost revenue that would result from not having the large vehicle itself in operation.

Generally, the larger the vehicle, or the more freight or passengers that can be moved in it, the less each unit will cost to move. Economies of scale suggest that railroad operating managers generally prefer to operate one long train per day than two shorter trains every 12 hours. This can be counterproductive in terms of service, so the trade-offs must be examined. With most transportation vehicles, the larger they are, the lower the ton-mile or seat-mile cost will be—for several reasons. One reason is that the manufacturing cost of most forms of propulsion engines makes larger horsepower or thrust engines cost less per horsepower than smaller units.

FIGURE 14.4 Fuel Consumption in Relation to Speed

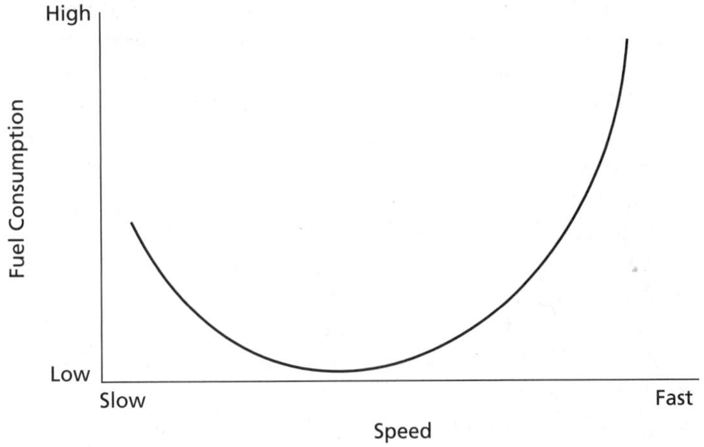

A second reason is that larger planes, trains, trucks, and so on can carry more payload without a proportionate increase in crew requirements. Simply illustrated, both a 10-passenger van and a 60-passenger bus are operated by one driver. Tankers capable of carrying 100,000 deadweight tons of oil require a 42- to 45-member crew. In addition, there are a multitude of other efficiencies in having fewer but larger vehicles in the fleet (in maintenance, training, and spare parts inventories). Overall, this principle of the larger the vehicle, the less each unit will cost to move is reflected in the trucking industry's efforts to get larger highway vehicle length and weight limits as well as barge industry efforts to get larger locks and dams for larger tows.

The fastest possible speed is not always the most efficient for economical operations. The cost of fuel consumption in relation to speed for most transportation vehicles is shown in Figure 14.4. As shown, the cost of fast speeds is very high. In the water carrier industry, this is often expressed as follows: As the speed of a vehicle doubles, the fuel consumption and horsepower requirements are squared. On the other hand, even with very low speeds, fuel consumption can be costly. For every form of vehicle (including planes and ships), a rough *J* curve represents fuel consumption in which the most fuel-efficient speeds are somewhat less than the vehicle's maximum possible speed.

Vehicle weight should be minimized in relation to **gross weight.** Transportation propulsion equipment as well as wings, hulls, rails, and highway pavements and bridges are designed for certain fixed gross weights (weight of the vehicle and the payload in freight or passengers). Therefore, the less the vehicle itself weighs, the more it can carry in the form of freight or passengers. Similarly, when a BTU of energy is burned, it is better for it to be spent on revenue-producing weight than on moving the vehicle itself. This is the reason why lighter metals and plastics are designed for use in motor-carrier tractors and in aircraft. Several airlines are changing their aircraft color schemes to show bare metal on the main body fuselage. Paint represents several hundred pounds of weight, even on a DC-9, that can be more effectively used for more freight or passenger carriage. Many motor carriers buy tractors that utilize fiberglass and plastic in the body of the vehicle.

Equipment should be standardized as much as possible. Standardized equipment simplifies planning, purchasing, crew training, maintenance, and spare parts inventories. When equipment is standardized among firms, efficient equipment interchange can take place. Standardization came early to the railroad industry in the form of the standard track width of four feet, eight and a half inches. This allowed cars from most railroads to move over other lines and to avoid rehandling of freight. Truck trailer hitch systems now are made so that almost total interchange can take place between any two power units and trailers. Even the airline industry's computerized reservation systems are designed so that other airlines can key in and make joint reservation and ticketing arrangements.

Equipment should be adapted to special market and commodity requirements. Many shipping firms require specialized equipment for the economical movement of particular commodities. During the 1960s, grain shippers desired the larger, more economical covered hopper cars in place of the traditional small boxcar. Airlines use the smaller DC-9 to serve shorter-distance, smaller cities; B-727s are used in longer-range markets; and jumbo planes are used in transcontinental long hauls. Each plane is designed for economical operation on certain routes. Transportation managers, however, must take care in adapting equipment. On one hand, there is the need to adapt equipment to special markets, and on the other hand, there is the need to recognize the advantages of standardization. Given the high capital cost and long life of transportation equipment, only long-range market planning and sound engineering and financial analysis can provide an optimum balance in this area.

The transportation industry is also characterized by extremely sophisticated communications technology. The railroads, for example, have utilized microwave communications for many years in the operation of trains. In fact, the communication network developed by the Southern Pacific Railroad was later sold and became what is known today as SPRINT. Nearly all truckload carriers such as Schneider National and J.B. Hunt have installed satellite technology and computers on their tractors to be able to communicate in real time with drivers. Aircraft, of course, employ sophisticated avionics in the cockpit to not only keep in touch with air traffic control but also to help maneuver the aircraft. Communications technology continues to be an important asset to carriers in their attempt to maximize the efficiency of their operations.

The Hub-and-Spoke Route System

Many motor carriers in the 1970s and airlines in the 1970s and 1980s realigned route structures to the **hub-and-spoke system**. Figure 14.5 illustrates how this is applied. In the former point-to-point system, carriers attempted to use routes with stops that would maximize passenger or freight revenue. For example, a run might have been set up for A-G-C-F, another for E-B-A, and still another for E-C-G-D. Because too many stops resulted in loss of business to and from far points, demand was limited to nonstop and one-stop routes. Many times the carrier served two points between which passengers seldom traveled. Some routes were densely traveled, whereas others were sparse.

The hub-and-spoke system concentrates the flow of passengers and freight along a fewer number of routes with a main mixing point (hub) at a center. All flights or runs meet at this hub where passengers or freight can be switched to runs to any other point in the system. Thus, passengers from point A can quickly reach B, C, D, E, F, and G all within a few hours. It expands the number of points the carrier can offer travelers with good schedules, and it concentrates more business

FIGURE 14.5 Point-to-Point System Versus Hub-and-Spoke System

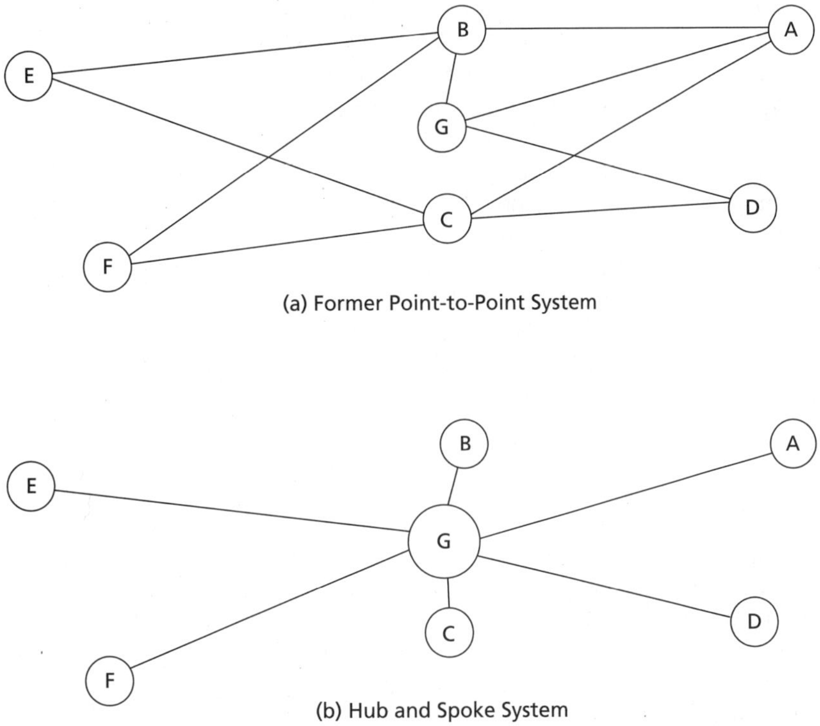

into a fewer number of runs. The motor-carrier industry employs this structure using break-bulk terminals that consolidate freight to faraway points with a minimum of intermediate handling.

A type of intermediate terminal is more common in the air industry. Called **hub terminals,** they serve as connection points for passengers departing from feeder, short-, and intermediate-haul flights from smaller cities and catching outbound spoke flights on long-haul jumbo planes. Northwest employs this concept at Detroit, American at Dallas-Fort Worth, United at Chicago, and Delta at Atlanta. At these cities, a major proportion of enplaning passengers is not originating from the hub city itself. This concept allows economical use of commuter lines and allows company DC-9s and B-727s to feed longer-haul L-1011, DC-10, and B-747 jumbos.

Marketing

In a manufacturing firm, customer services complement the tangible output. In a service firm, customer service *is* the output. The intangibility of a service makes it more difficult to both sell and purchase. Transportation firms are faced with the challenge of developing and marketing something that cannot be felt, inventoried, or tested. This makes the marketing of carrier services extremely important to the profitability of the firm, and a knowledge of marketing concepts is critical to this success.

Service marketing is different from product marketing because of the differences between products and services. First, services are intangible. The inability to see, feel, and try a service before it is produced makes it more difficult to sell and more difficult for buyers to make purchase decisions. Second, there is a focus on the service provider. For example, the satisfaction an airline traveler feels toward a flight can be greatly influenced by the service provided by cabin attendants and ticket agents. Likewise, truck drivers who make customer deliveries can reinforce the positive image of a carrier or change a customer's perception of that image. Third, service providers are usually highly labor-intensive. This can make service quality subject to more variability. Although carriers have high investments in equipment, people actually provide the service. In fact, for most modes, labor is the largest cost category. Fourth, there is a simultaneous production and consumption of services; that is, there is no inventory. Transportation services cannot be produced before demand occurs to take advantage of production economies. Equipment, in the form of capacity, can be put into place in anticipation of demand, but production of transportation service occurs at the same time as demand. Finally, services are perishable. A move by rail has no shelf life. Likewise, empty seats on an airplane are lost forever immediately after take-off.

These characteristics of services make the application of marketing concepts challenging, but not impossible. In fact, some transportation firms, such as Federal Express, are quite adept at marketing their offerings to the public. This was not always the case. Before the deregulation of the transportation industry, most carriers had an operational focus, rather than a marketing focus. This occurred because regulation, it has been argued, removed the incentive and opportunity for carriers to differentiate themselves in their markets. Pricing was controlled so service became the competitive factor.

Today, however, many carriers have adopted a marketing focus because of the freedoms given them by deregulation. Carriers that stress operations are more likely to optimize their existing system at the expense of customer satisfaction. These carriers see themselves as separate entities, rather than as a part of a buyer or receiver's logistics system. They tend to be inflexible and are very inwardly focused. On the contrary, marketing-oriented carriers stress customer satisfaction by tailoring their system and services to meet customer needs. These carriers are outwardly focused, are very flexible, and perceive themselves to be supportive of a buyer or receiver's logistics and business needs. More and more carriers are making the transition to a marketing orientation because of the demands of the market for this way of conducting business. In some cases, carriers have expanded to include tasks once performed by the shipper or consignee. An example is a carrier which hauls garments on hangers, adding labels and price tags prior to delivery.

Coordination

Marketing and operations should be coordinated. Many transportation firms operate with a loose coordination between marketing and operations. While sales personnel strive to attract more business and revenue, operating personnel strive to reduce total costs, which means minimized runs, trains, and so on. The two departments often come into conflict over daily decisions and long-term planning. A hallmark of successful carrier firms is that a close coordination exists between the two departments. A close link ensures that marketing efforts are conducted with operational costs in mind and that an operating department does not allow marketing efforts to be wasted on poor service.

Accountability for profit should begin in the lowest-level divisions of the firm. It is often difficult for every person in the firm to relate each of his or her actions to overall profitability. When no accountability system exists, it is difficult to measure good performance. Good accountability systems attempt to measure and present profitability by shipment, traffic lane, terminal, or another responsibility area. A good accountability system should also measure operating performance against selected standards so that minimizing total cost through slow or unreliable service is not always the operating department rule. The accountability system should relate company profit to operating and marketing performance within the realm of the company's market opportunities and needs.

Consistent, reliable service is often more desirable than the fastest possible service. Many surveys of traffic managers and travelers indicate that a later but reliable arrival time is generally preferred to a faster time that is less reliable. Many successful carriers set transit time standards that are attainable 95 percent of the time. This system is often preferred by shippers over promises of faster delivery that are only attainable 50 percent of the time. Because both early and late arrivals usually incur cost penalties, shippers often will select carriers that might take a day longer but that are more reliable in deliveries. Discounting the occasional need for fast, emergency shipment service, the cost of reliable but extra time in transit often is perceived as less than that of shorter but unreliable time service. Airlines adapt to normal delays by padding schedules.

These efficiency approaches have evolved over time and are cited by firms as part of the reason for their success. The list is by no means exhaustive; more guidelines exist in the pricing area. Changes in the business environment, markets, and transportation technology might cause these rules to change as we move into the twenty-first century. The key is that planners and managers should always observe the economies of the firms they operate within and should steer their companies to the above-mentioned long-standing approaches or implement new or altered approaches as the conditions change.

Challenges Affecting Carrier Management

Transportation companies face some conditions that are not always present in manufacturing firms. These conditions, combined with the available ways in which carriers attempt to work around and with them, mean that there is no *one* ideal form of carrier management.

Transportation firms are geographically dispersed. By their very nature, carrier operations take place over vast distances. Unlike some manufacturing firms where all operations and management are often under one roof, transportation firms typically operate across oceans, through difficult mountain terrain, and in different countries. This causes carriers to rely upon tight controls, often with decentralized structures and close communications. The dispersion problem is compounded by the fact that the firm's product availability is constantly in motion.

The carrier employee who came in contact with the customer traditionally had been given relatively low status and training within the carrier organization. Today's carriers, however, have realized the importance these customer contact personnel play in shaping customer perceptions concerning service quality. Examples of such personnel would include truck drivers, ticket agents, cabin attendants, and city dispatchers. More and more firms are investing in training for these individuals in an attempt to elevate their status within the organization and to prepare them to deal with the many problems that can occur in a service delivery operation. The driver shortage in the trucking industry and attempts to deal with this problem are an example of the trend. It is also important, however, that these trained individuals have access to upper or middle management to express ideas or to make suggestions concerning service improvements. In some cases, carrier organizations have used the concept of "empowerment" to allow customer contact personnel to solve problems and make decisions concerning dissatisfied customers immediately. Problems can result if the employee is not trained on how to use empowerment or does not "buy into" the concept.

Transportation operating employees are often minimally supervised. Operating personnel in trucks, trains, barges, and so on are often out of reach of minute-by-minute management supervision. Unlike production crews that are under close supervision, carrier crews often come into contact with their supervisors for only minutes per day and often only by phone or radio. Motor-carrier managers know that one of the key productivity problem areas is in local pickup and delivery operations. Without supervision, a driver has the potential opportunity for low performance and little accountability to the terminal managers. This has caused many carriers to implement strong communication and performance measurement systems.

The task of efficiently operating the transportation technology of the firm can create "monolithic" management structures. Every mode of transportation operates with vehicles and equipment requiring large investments and numbers of people. Coupled with the problem of geographic dispersion, carrier managements traditionally have attempted to organize along lines of skill specialization. This phenomenon is largely solidified by union labor contract job classifications in this industry. As a result, many carrier structures have evolved into very strong vertical hierarchies consisting of operations, finance, marketing, and many other disciplines. Modern systems management theory shows that a vertical management organization is flexible, resistant to change, a hindrance to cross-communications at low and middle management levels, and often inconsistent with overall corporate goals and missions. This specialization phenomenon often is cited as the reason that larger, mature firms sometimes tend to be unresponsive to the market and business environment, whereas smaller growing firms in the same mode display growth and vitality. The rise of regional airlines in the late 1970s is partial evidence of this phenomenon.

Single accountability for the transportation service "product" is often minimal. Because of the geographic dispersion factor, carriers often divide the operating department into distinct districts, regions, or divisions. A shipment often will pass through the responsibility sphere of several top operating managers. In interline movements, this situation is further complicated because the transportation "production function" is carried out by several carriers between the shipper and consignee. Without specific service performance systems measuring their tasks, individual operating personnel can lose sight of the need to maintain the company service standard or the assurances made to the customer by the salesperson. In manufacturing settings, the production manager can easily be held responsible for the quality of factory output. Although transportation service standards can be established, without effective discipline and accountability, reliable service is difficult to maintain.

It is often very difficult to determine the exact cost of transportation. Transportation is an activity in which the total cost consists of large amounts of fixed, overhead, and joint costs. These costs, presented in Chapter 11, "Costing and Pricing in Transportation," complicate the task of determining the cost of moving a passenger or package of freight. Specific production costs can easily be determined in most manufacturing activities, but in transportation, costs can be affected by season, direction of traffic, volume of other goods in the same movement, the equipment being used, and the relative amounts of business in other parts of the firm.

All of these factors represent management challenges and conditions under which transportation managers function. Some of the factors appear to make transportation different from manufacturing, but the same principles of economics are at play here as in any other business entity. The difference lies in the extent of the challenges and how transportation firms handle them.

The Terminal: The Basic Transportation System Component

The physical flows of carrier equipment and personnel are linked to the location and activities of terminal networks. Terminals are the nodes in a carrier system and perform various duties to facilitate the movement of their passengers or freight. All modes of transportation use terminals in one context or another. This discussion will address the terminals of all modes, but additional discussions will be presented on LTL carrier hub-and-spoke networks.

General Nature of Terminals

A terminal is any point in a carrier's network where the movement of freight or passengers is stopped so some type of value-adding activity can be performed. Important here is the concept of "value-adding." One of the basic tenets of logistics is to keep an item moving at a constant speed through the system. Once this item is stopped, costs are incurred, so a delay at a terminal must add more value than it incurs costs.

Terminals provide various **value-adding** activities in their role in a carrier's network. One of the more common activities is called concentration or **consolidation**. This activity takes small shipments or groups of passengers and combines them to make larger units. For example, the airlines use commuter operators from small communities to feed their major hubs where larger aircraft are dispatched to the next larger hub. Consolidation can offer the benefit of operating efficiencies for carriers because vehicle capacity is more fully utilized. However, consolidation can also affect service because shipments or passengers might be delayed until a vehicle is full. On the other hand, a fully consolidated vehicle (with similar destinations) in an LTL network might enjoy better service because its freight will not need to be handled at each intermediate terminal on the way to its final destination.

A second terminal value-adding activity is called *dispersion* or **break-bulk**. The opposite of consolidation, this activity involves separating larger units of freight or passengers into smaller units, normally for delivery to final destination. Consolidation and dispersion are usually performed simultaneously at most types of terminals.

Shipment services are also performed at terminals. These involve the storage of freight or accommodating passengers in transit, the protection of freight or passengers from the elements, and routing and billing (or ticketing). Passengers waiting in an airline terminal for the next flight are actually being warehoused. They are moved, segregated at their proper gate, and stored in the waiting area until their flight is ready to depart.

Many types of terminals are used to provide vehicle services, which could include equipment maintenance and the storage of equipment until it is needed. In LTL networks, break-bulks serve as major maintenance facilities for line-haul equipment and also temporarily store equipment that is not needed during periods of slow business.

Finally, terminals can provide weighing services, customs inspections, claims processing, and interchange operations. All of these terminal activities are performed in an attempt to add value to either freight or passengers. These represent part of the carrier's "service package" offering to the customer and are critical to the successful delivery of the shipment or passenger.

Terminal Ownership

Terminals can represent a high level of fixed investment within a carrier's network. As discussed in Chapter 11, these costs will have a definite impact on a carrier's pricing structures and competitive stance within its markets, so how these costs are allocated to a carrier is important to its cost structure.

If the terminal is owned by the carrier, it will incur fixed costs, such as interest, depreciation, and taxes that will not vary in total with the volume of freight. As volume increases through these terminals, however, the fixed cost allocation per unit will decrease, which can be an indicator of economies of scale. Railroads, motor carriers, and pipelines almost exclusively own their terminals. Air freight and some port terminals also fall under private ownership.

The other method of terminal financing is through government ownership. In this case, the government (state, local, or federal) owns the terminal facility and charges carriers a user fee based on their activity level at the facility. This still results in the burden of high fixed costs. However, the government bears this burden and passes it along to users as a variable cost. This variable cost can affect the carrier's cost structure and, ultimately, its pricing structure. For example, passenger airlines pay a landing fee at airports and pay rent for ticketing and other space within the facility. Many port facilities are also provided by the government, with charges assessed for loading and unloading ships at these facilities.

Types of Terminals

Carriers utilize different types of terminals within their networks. This section will briefly describe these different types and specifically discuss the types of terminals used in an LTL motor-carrier network

Rail

The most common form of rail terminal is called a **hump** or marshalling **yard.** Freight cars go through these yards and are then reclassified into new trains according to their destination or are sent to their final destination via a switching operation. Trains enter the receiving yard, where the road locomotives are removed and a yard engine is attached to the rear car. From here, the cars are moved to an inspection area where running gear is inspected for defects. The cars are then moved to the hump, which is an artificial hill that uses gravity to direct the car to a new train on another track. The speed of the cars going down the hump is controlled by retarders; these retarders also control car speed on the tracks so the humped car does not bang into the other cars. These new trains are held on classification tracks, also called *bowls.* From here, the trains move to the departure and forwarding yard where they receive road motive power, where appropriate.

The railroad industry also uses what can be called **transloading terminals,** where TOFC and COFC units are moved by road tractors to and from rail flat cars. These intermodal terminals operate in a similar manner to LTL terminals, consolidating and dispersing trailer and container units. In some cases, this is how interchange between railroads is handled.

Water

Water terminals consist of a harbor and a port. The harbor provides the water portion for the staging, loading, and unloading activities of ships, while the port is the land area that provides space for freight and the loading and unloading of equipment. Harbors are either natural (such as bays) or constructed (such as a seacoast).

The port area of a water terminal includes pilotage and towage facilities for ships not able to use their own power to enter the port. Also included here are the mechanical aids used in the loading and unloading of the ships, such as overhead cranes, conveyors, and fork trucks. The port area also provides warehouse space, both open and closed, for the storage of goods and the holding of freight until it is cleared by customs. Several types of ancillary services are also performed at the port area. These would include ship repairs, bunkering or refueling, victualling (supplying the ship with food, drink, and other provisions), customs, security services, and medical services.

Air

Freight and passenger terminals perform the same activities but do them in a somewhat different manner. Freight terminals include an area for staging the aircraft during the loading and unloading process and for staging before departure and after landing. Another area in the terminal itself is used for the consolidation and dispersion activities and the readying of air freight containers for the next portion of their journey. Also in the terminal area is storage space used for intermodal containers and oversize freight.

Passenger terminals also perform the consolidation and dispersion activities. However, because these are done using people, the terminal is designed to meet their needs. Gate areas are staging areas for individuals before departure. The walkways in the terminal allow for the movement of people to their proper destination, facilitating the consolidation and dispersion processes. Baggage-handling facilities allow passengers to match up with their luggage after arrival and prepare luggage for departing flights.

Because individuals are the units being handled in a passenger airport, various ancillary services are offered in the terminal. The more common types are restaurant, medical, and small shopping areas for people to utilize before departure. Various types of land transportation are also offered at these terminals. Pittsburgh's new airport has expanded on these ideas by developing a "mall" atmosphere within the terminal that includes numerous shops and eating establishments. This was done not only to service airport customers but to cater to the general public, so passenger terminals are unlike freight terminals in ambiance but like them in their operations.

Pipeline

Pipeline terminals consist of storage facilities, gathering lines, trunk lines, and pumping stations. These facilities provide temporary storage for a commodity (such as oil), provide movement of the commodity from gathering lines to trunk lines, and allow movement of the commodity to customers. Much of the operation at a pipeline terminal is automated, requiring very little intervention by personnel. These terminals provide consolidation and dispersion activities, much like terminals in other modes.

Motor Carrier (Truckload)

Truckload movements consist of one shipment between one consignor and one or more consignees. As such, these movements do not require intermediate handlings, nor do they require consolidation and dispersion activities. Truckload terminals, thus, do not generally offer freight handling services. Rather, these facilities normally provide dispatching, maintenance, and fuel and maintenance services. Some carriers, such as Schneider National, are expanding the services offered by their terminal facilities. These carriers are adding restaurant and hotel services to give their drivers an alternative to truckstops. These terminals are designed primarily to accommodate drivers and equipment, but not freight, and provide the nucleus for the operation of the truckload network.

Motor Carrier (Less Than Truckload)

The terminal is a key facility in the operation of a less than truckload (LTL) hub-and-spoke system. This section will present an expanded discussion of the types and roles of the terminal in this system.

The most common type of terminal found in the LTL system is the pickup and delivery (PUD) terminal. These are also called *satellite* or *end-of-the-line (EOL)* terminals. The PUD terminal serves a local area and provides direct contact with both shippers and receivers. The basic transportation service provided at this terminal is the pickup and/or delivery of freight on peddle runs. A **peddle run** is a route that is driven daily out of the PUD terminal for the purposes of collecting freight for outbound moves or delivering freight from inbound moves. A PUD terminal will have several peddle runs in its customer operating area. Figure 14.6 gives an example of how a peddle run is designed. The PUD terminal is located in Altoona, Pennsylvania. Attached to it are four peddle runs, one each to Tyrone, State College, Lewistown, and Huntington. Every Monday through Friday morning, a driver will depart the Altoona terminal and deliver freight to customers located on that driver's assigned peddle. During and after the deliveries, freight will be picked up from customers and returned with the driver to the Altoona terminal at the end of the day. When all the drivers return at the end of their shifts, the Altoona terminal will have

FIGURE 14.6 Terminal Peddle Run

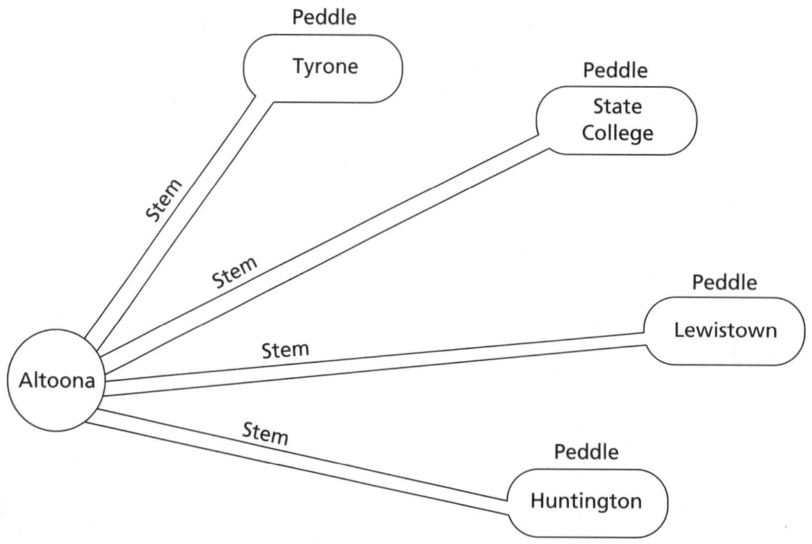

freight to be consolidated and moved outbound from customers in Tyrone, State College, Lewiston, and Huntington to customers in other areas of the country.

Note that there are two elements of a peddle run, one called **stem time** and the other called peddle time. Stem time is the time that elapses from when the driver leaves the terminal until the driver makes the first pickup or delivery; it is also the time that elapses from when the driver makes the last pickup or delivery until returning to the terminal. This is nonrevenue-producing time because no shipments are handled. A carrier would want to locate PUD terminals in such a way that this nonrevenue-producing travel time is minimized. (This aspect of LTL service will be discussed later in this chapter.) The other type of time is peddle time. This is the time during which the driver is actively involved in the pickup and delivery of freight. This is revenue-producing time because it occurs when shipments are handled. Obviously, carriers would want to maximize the amount of time a driver spent performing these activities.

The basic terminal services performed at these facilities are consolidation and dispersion. For example, freight moving inbound to Altoona from other terminals (passing through a break-bulk) will be "broken" into individual deliveries by peddle run to be handled by the driver during that particular shift. Freight that is brought back by the peddle drivers for movement inbound from Altoona will be consolidated into line-haul trailers for subsequent movement to the appropriate break-bulk. This is a basic cross-dock type of operation with the direction of freight flow across the dock that changes depending on whether the move is inbound or outbound.

The dispatch operation provided at the PUD terminal is critical to the operating efficiency of the peddle runs. Freight can be picked up on peddle runs in one of two ways. First, a customer on a peddle run might have a standing order for a pickup every day at 10 A.M. The PUD driver is aware of this, so the customer has no need to notify the carrier in advance for the pickup. Second, a customer might call the local PUD terminal to order service for a pickup. This is where the local dispatcher becomes involved. The dispatcher records the nature of the shipment and required time of pickup and assigns that shipment to the driver on the appropriate peddle run. The PUD driver will periodically call in to the dispatcher to determine the order and frequencies of new pickup requests. Obviously, the dispatcher needs to be familiar with the geography of the peddle runs and the capacity of the PUD drivers and trailers to efficiently route freight with the appropriate vehicle.

Other services that are provided at the PUD terminal may include tracing, rating and billing, sales, and claims. However, some carriers are beginning to centralize these functions at break-bulks or other locations by taking advantage of telecommunications technology. For example, some LTL carriers use the Internet for tracing purposes. When the customer accesses the carrier's Web site, the shipper keys in the pro number or waybill number and the system provides the current status of the shipment.

Another type of terminal found in an LTL hub-and-spoke system is called a break-bulk. This facility performs both consolidation and dispersion (or break-bulk) services. Customers will rarely have contact with the operations at the break-bulk facility. The main purpose of this terminal is to provide an intermediate point where freight with common destinations from the PUD terminals is combined in a single trailer for movement to the delivering PUD terminal. Break-bulks will have many PUD terminals assigned to them as primary loading points. For example, assume that a shipper in Toledo, Ohio wanted to send an LTL shipment to a customer in Pottstown, Pennsylvania. The Toledo PUD terminal is attached to the Cleveland, Ohio break-bulk, and the Philadelphia PUD terminal, which handles the Pottstown peddle, is attached to the Lancaster, Pennsylvania break-bulk. At the completion of the peddle run, the Toledo driver brings the shipment back to the Toledo PUD terminal. There it is sorted and combined with other shipments going to the Lancaster break-bulk service area (this could include all PUD terminals covering significant portions of Pennsylvania, New York, New Jersey, and parts of Maryland). These shipments are consolidated into one trailer that will be dispatched to the Lancaster break-bulk.

Once the trailer arrives in Lancaster, it will be unloaded, and all of the freight destined to Philadelphia and its peddle runs will be loaded into an outbound trailer. This trailer will be dispatched from the break-bulk and arrive at the Philadelphia terminal to be unloaded in the early morning so the freight can be segregated into peddle delivery vehicles for an early morning delivery schedule. So, just as with the airline hub-and-spoke system, the LTL system utilizes the full capacity of its vehicles in the line-haul operation.

Break-bulk facilities also serve as driver domiciles. City drivers located at a PUD terminal will always remain in their local area during their shift and will be able to return home when it is over. Line-haul drivers, however, might or might not be able to return home after a trip, depending on the length of haul they are assigned. For example, a turn means that a line-haul driver is assigned a load to be taken from the break-bulk (domicile) to a PUD terminal that is no more than five hours away. Because of DOT-mandated driving limits of 10 hours, that line-haul driver can make the trip, drop the trailer, and pick up another shipment destined back to the break-bulk within the 10-hour limit. However, a movement that requires more than five hours driving time in one direction will require a "layover"; that is, when the driver reaches the destination, an eight-hour rest period is required before that driver will be able to take a return load back to the break-bulk and return to the domicile. So at the maximum, a driver facing a 10-hour run with an eight-hour layover and a 10-hour return trip will return to the domicile within 28 hours of the original departure. Sometimes, however, a return load is not immediately available, which will delay the driver's return.

LTL networks utilize what is called a **relay terminal.** A relay provides a layover point between break-bulks that are more than 10 hours apart. Relays do not handle freight; they are service facilities for drivers and equipment. For example, a line-haul run between Kansas City and Seattle might require a layover somewhere in Wyoming. If a break-bulk is not located in Wyoming, a relay is established. A shipment from Kansas City to Seattle will be dispatched in a vehicle with a Kansas City-domiciled driver. That driver will run to the relay in Wyoming, where the driver must be off duty for eight hours. It is hoped that when that driver reaches the relay, there will be a Seattle-domiciled driver finishing the eight-hour rest period who can get into the vehicle, continue it on its journey to Seattle, and return to the Seattle domicile.

LTL hub-and-spoke networks are sophisticated operations requiring hundreds of different types of terminals and thousands of pieces of equipment. Even within types of terminals, there are different sizes and terminals that are more "inbound" or "outbound" than others. This makes the management of such a system very complex and requires that certain management decisions be made to make it operate efficiently and effectively. These decisions are the focus of the next section.

Terminal Management Decisions

Many types of operating decisions need to be made when utilizing terminals in a carrier's network. Along with making these decisions, carrier management must also consider their strategic implications. This section will address a few of these types of decisions.

THOMSON LEARNING
DISTRIBUTION CENTER
7625 EMPIRE DRIVE
FLORENCE, KY 41042

The enclosed materials are sent to you for your review by
HIGHER EDUCATION GSF 800 590-9951

SALES SUPPORT

Date	Account	Contact
07/14/00	643338	19

SHIP TO: Pat McInturff
CA St U San Bernardino
Dept of Management
5500 University Parkway
JB-461
San Bernardino CA 924077500

WAREHOUSE INSTRUCTIONS

SLA: 7 BOX: Staple

LOCATION	QTY	ISBN	AUTHOR/TITLE
K-20C-002-14	1	0-538-88180-1	COYLE/BARDI/NOVACK TRANSPORTATION 5E

INV# 27076525SM
PO# 17484126
DATE: / /
CARTON: 1 of 1
ID# 6894574

PRIME-INDUCT
-SLSB

VIA: UP

PAGE 1 OF 1

BATCH: 0971309
004/011

Number of Terminals

In many modes, this is a relatively simple decision. For example, passenger airline terminals will be located close to major population centers. This decision, however, usually does not belong to the carrier but to some local government agency. Railroads must also make this decision but are limited by geography and track locations for terminal sites. Railroads will not normally have many terminals in their networks. The mode with probably the most difficult decision in this area is LTL motor carriage, primarily because of the vast numbers of terminals in these systems and the relatively small investment needed to develop a terminal site.

The obvious question for an LTL motor carrier is "How many terminals should we have?" The obvious answer is "It depends." First, the degree of market penetration and customer service desired by the carrier will help determine the number of terminals to establish. In theory, the more terminals, the closer to the customer, the better the service. This also has proven to be true in practice. Realistically, at some point additional terminals will result in no incremental increase in service and might even detract from service.

Second, the dilemma of small-terminal-versus-long-peddle must be addressed. Figure 14.7 represents this situation. In Example 1, assume that a carrier's market is the state of Pennsylvania with one terminal located in Harrisburg with peddle runs to Erie, Scranton, Pittsburgh, and Philadelphia. This network utilizes only one terminal but has extremely long and expensive stem times for its peddle runs. The terminal must also be large to accommodate the volume of freight that will come from these four peddles. Example 2 shows a network that utilizes two terminals, each having two peddle runs with significantly shorter stem times. Each terminal in this scenario is smaller than the one terminal in Example 1. Thus, Example 2 has doubled the number of terminals but decreased stem times for customer PUD. The small-terminal-versus-long-peddle decision would be made based on the service implications of establishing terminals closer to customers versus the cost of adding another terminal.

Many times in distribution system decisions for shippers, an assumption is made that manufacturing facilities are fixed and warehouse decisions must be made based on this fixed network. This assumption is also part of the terminal decision process for LTL motor carriers, except their "manufacturing facilities" are break-bulk terminals. Whether or not another terminal can be added to a break-bulk's operating region might simply be a question of available capacity at that break-bulk. Normally, each PUD terminal is assigned at least one door at a break-bulk. To add another PUD terminal means eliminating an existing terminal, physically adding another door to the break-bulk, or improving the productivity at the break-bulk to turn trailers in doors more than once per shift.

Locations of Terminals

Closely related to the decision of how many terminals to establish is the decision of *where* to establish them. As previously mentioned, for airlines and railroads, this decision can be relatively simple because of geographic, government, and demand variables. LTL carriers, however, must consider some other variables. First, the Department of Transportation (DOT) limits the amount of time a driver can continuously operate a vehicle before a rest period is required. Currently, this limit is 10 hours, so optimally, PUD terminals should be located no more than 10 hours away from a break-bulk. This would allow a driver to complete the run without having to lay down or use team drivers. Second, PUD terminals should be located to minimize the distance freight would need to be backhauled to the break-bulk. The assumption here is that freight flows form east to west and north to south in the United

FIGURE 14.7 Small Terminal Versus Long Peddle

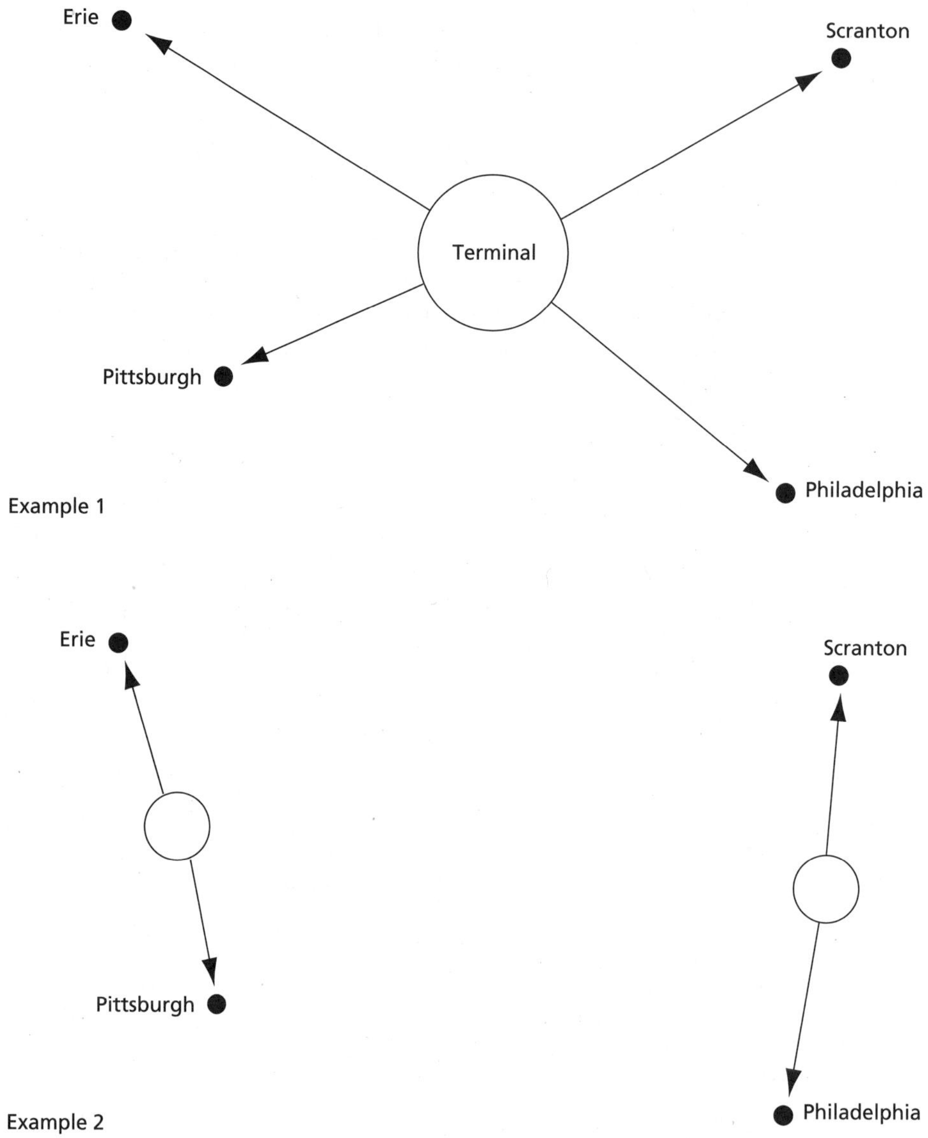

States. When a shipment is picked up, the idea is to send in that freight in one of these directions as soon as possible. For example, given that a carrier has two breakbulks, one in Lancaster, Pennsylvania and the other in Columbus, Ohio, where would a PUD terminal based in Pittsburgh send its freight? Based on the assumption made earlier about freight flows, Pittsburgh would send its freight to Columbus; that is, a shipment picked up by a Pittsburgh peddle driver would begin its east-west journey more productively by being sent to Columbus because if it were sent to Lancaster, it would conceptually duplicate this distance when it began its journey from Lancaster to the west (actually passing right by Columbus). Finally, market penetration and potential will help determine terminal location. As mentioned in the decision process for determining the number of terminals, getting closer to the customer can many times improve the level of service given to that customer.

Recent trends in the LTL sector have seen significant reductions in the number of terminals as these carriers strive to provide overnight and second-day delivery to more and more customers. In order to do this, many inter-terminal runs have been realigned with the resultant elimination of intermediate handling. This has resulted in increased load factors and reduce transit times. Less handling has also improved the claims experience for the LTL carriers. The long haul LTL carriers will still favor the hub and spoke operation, while the regional carriers will still look towards fewer terminals with more direct runs.

Yellow Fright reduced its number of terminals from 350 from 650, while Roadway Express has shrunk from more than 600 facilities to less than 435. This trend will continue as the competition in the 500 to 1,200 mile lanes increases. The regional LTL carriers are challenging the national carriers in these lanes so that each must find more efficient handling methods to stay competitive from both a cost and service standpoint.[6]

Equipment Selection and Development

In most cases, equipment represents the largest operating asset that a carrier maintains. With all of the different types and locations of equipment, positioning becomes critical to successful operations. Seasonal influences such as holidays or harvest times must also be considered, as this can drastically alter demand. Airlines must decide which type of aircraft to dedicate to a specific flight, depending on length of flight and passenger demand. The longer the flight, the more efficient a larger aircraft will be.

Truckload and LTL carriers need to make two types of decisions: what type of tractor (power) and what type of trailer. In a TL operation, equipment positioning at terminals is not as important as it is in an LTL operation. However, power must be specified to be able to handle the size and length of the load along with the terrain over which it travels. Many different specifications for tractors can be used, including single axle and twin axle with different engine and drive train combinations. Decisions regarding trailers include length (45 feet, 48 feet, 57 feet) and trailer type (dry van, refrigerated, ragtop, container, flatbed). These decisions will be made in light of market demands and the type of carrier operation.

LTL carriers must make the same types of equipment decisions as a TL carrier, along with deciding where to deploy this equipment. Similar to an airline equipment decision, LTL carriers need to position certain types of equipment at certain terminals. For example, city delivery vehicles and tractor/trailer combinations (either 28-foot or 40-foot trailers) will be positioned at PUD terminals, while line-haul trailers (usually 45 or 48 feet) and line-haul tractors (single or twin axle) will be assigned to break-bulks. Compounding the LTL decision is the inclusion of 28-foot trailers (also called *pups, twins,* or *double bottoms*) in the equipment decision. Having the right mix of power and trailers at a particular terminal location determines its ability to efficiently serve its customers.

Rail equipment decisions can become increasingly difficult because of the numerous types of cars utilized in a rail operation. Different types of cars can be assigned to specific customers depending on the type of commodity moved. This means that the empties have to be repositioned to the customer's location at the proper time for loading. Railroad operations include hopper cars, gondola cars, boxcars, dry bulk cars, and tank cars. Also, decisions concerning motive power must be made. The length and weight of trains along with the type of terrain will determine the proper mix of motive power. For example, engines that operate in some western states are equipped with snow plows on the front to help clear a snowy track. In other operations, unmanned helpers (engines without human operators controlled by radio from the front engine) are used over hilly terrain.

Water carriers normally have fixed types of ships; for example, they will operate a container ship or a tanker. Of concern here, especially for container ships and general cargo ships, is having the right mix and type of containers or other freight-storage devices in the correct position. Many shipping lines have their own containers and also participate in common container pools with other ship lines. Because ocean containers normally come in two lengths—20 feet and 40 feet—it is important to have the right container in place to be loaded with freight. Since containers need chassis for road transportation, this must also be factored in the equipment mix. Also, ships are often configured for a certain mix of container lengths (although they can be changed to accommodate a different mix). Finally, pipelines must also make equipment decisions. Although one might not think that pipelines operate "equipment," their pipes represent their rolling stock. Decisions concerning pipe diameter (affected by distance, type of commodity, and speed), pipe length, and type of pipe are made when pipelines are constructed. Unlike the other modes, pipeline decisions are usually made only once because of the large fixed investment involved.

Equipment decisions are important to all modes of transportation. Equipment represents the rolling stock of the carrier and provides the actual movement of freight between modes. Carriers have significant investments made in their equipment and utilize sophisticated maintenance programs to keep their investment roadworthy. These decisions, then, are critical to successful terminal management.

Summary

- Transportation strategy is a key element of total logistics strategy and is used to guide the purchase and management of transportation services including bulk shipments and small shipments.
- When selecting a transportation carrier, the traffic/transportation manager will evaluate specific service characteristics, such as transit time, reliability, safety, capability, and accessibility in addition to the transportation rate.
- Traffic management in today's deregulated environment can be looked on as a special form of procurement emphasizing the purchase of transportation services.
- The scope of the traffic management function includes both line and staff responsibilities.
- The basic transportation efficiency techniques include moving in a straight line, minimizing handlings, utilizing full vehicle capacity, minimizing empty miles, and effective scheduling.
- The hub-and-spoke carrier network allows for the efficient use of carrier capacity through hub and PUD-type terminals.
- The marketing of transportation services is different than that for products because of the intangibility of the service.
- The terminal is the basic component of carrier operating networks. Various types of terminals exist, and each has its own role in successful carrier operations.
- Carrier management terminal decisions include the number of terminals, the location of terminals, and equipment selection and deployment.

KEY TERMS

accessibility pg. 442
auditing 445
balanced load 439
breakbulk 459
capability 443
carrier evaluation 447
carrier management 434
claims 445
consolidation 459
core carriers 436
demurrage 445
detention 445
dispatch 444
gross weight 453
hub-and-spoke system 454
hub terminals 455
hump yard 460
market power 436
peddle run 462
pooling 438
procurement 441
relay terminal 464
reverse logistics 440
rule of efficiency 451
stem time 463
stopping-in-transit service 438
terms of sale 440
traffic management 440
transit time 442
transportation management 434
transloading terminal 460
value-adding 459

STUDY QUESTIONS

1. When a traffic/transportation manager evaluates potential carriers, what factors are taken into consideration in making a final decision?

2. Discuss the general strategies used by transportation managers for small shipments versus bulk shipments. Why are they different?

3. Traffic management is typically referred to as a special type of purchasing or procurement function. Why?

4. Describe the process used to monitor carrier service quality.

5. Distinguish between line and staff traffic management responsibilities.

6. Cite the techniques of efficiency and the underlying economic principle(s) in the following transportation practices:

a. Lower airline passenger rate for a Saturday stayover

b. Replacing 48 feet trailers with 57 feet trailers

c. Railroad and motor carrier contract rates

7. Explain the economic rationale for having an efficient communication system in today's transportation company.

8. Describe the value-added role of the carrier's terminal.

9. Discuss the economic strategy for the different types of terminals used in an LTL carrier operation.

10. Describe the hub-and-spoke system. What purpose does it serve in carrier operations?

NOTES

1. Michael S. Galardi, "Transportation Strategies: A Review and Forecast," *Proceedings of the Council of Logistics Management,* Vol. 1 (1986), pp. 36–50.

2. Jeff Holmes, "Hot Spots of Supply Chain Management," *Inbound Logistics,* October 1997, pp. 40–44.

3. Helen Richardson, "Make Time an Ally," *Transportation & Distribution,* July 1995, pp. 46–50.

4. David Sparkman, "How to Be a Partner," *Transport Topics,* April 29, 1996, pp. 8–9.

5. Toby Gooley, "There and Back Again," *Logistics Management,* April 1999, pp. 57–62.

6. Peter Bradley, "In It For the Long Haul," *Logistics Management,* January 1997, pp. 47–50.

Suggested Readings

Bardi, Edward J., Prabir K. Bagchi, and T. S. Raghunathan, "Motor Carrier Selection in a Deregulated Environment," *Transportation Journal,* Vol. 29, No. 1, Fall 1989, pp. 4–11.

Bergin, Sara. "Ports Are Challenged by the Future," *Transportation & Distribution,* November 1996, pp. 35–40.

Bradley, Peter. "Fleets Change with the Times," *Logistics Management,* May 1996, pp. 35–43.

Con, Larry A. "Establishing Effective Transportation Controls in a Decentralized Company," *Council of Logistics Management Annual Conference Proceedings,* 1995, pp. 391–398.

"The Giants of Shipping," *Logistics Management,* September 1997, pp. 48–52.

Greenfield, Mark. "Railroads Engineer Capacity Improvements," *Progressive Railroading,* March 1996, pp. 51–57.

Hastings, Larry. "Transportation Carriers Use Internet to EDI Solution," *EDI Forum,* Vol. 9, No. 3, pp. 53–58.

Kent, John L., Mary Collins Holcomb, Karl B. Manrodt, and Edward L. Oldham. "Profile: The Fifth Annual Survey of the To-U.S. Purchasers of Transportation Services," *Council of Logistics Management Annual Conference Proceedings,* 1996, pp. 173–183.

Kling, James A., and Ken A. Smith. "Identifying Strategic Groups in the U.S. Airline Industry: An Application of the Porter Model," *Transportation Journal,* Vol. 35, No. 2, Winter 1995, pp. 26–34.

Liberatore, Matthew J., and Ian Miller. "A Decision Support Approach for Transport Carrier and Mode Selection," *Journal of Business Logistics,* Vol. 16, No. 2, 1995, pp. 85–116.

Murphy, Paul R., and Patricia K. Hall. "The Relative Importance of Cost and Service in Freight Transportation Choice Before and After Deregulation: An Update," *Transportation Journal,* Vol. 35, No. 1, Fall 1995, pp. 30–38.

Taylor, G. Don, Santhanam Sarit, John R. English, and Gary Whicker. "Hub-and-Spoke Networks in Truckload Trucking: Configuration, Testing, and Operations," *The Logistics and Transportation Review,* Vol. 31, No. 3, September 1995, pp. 209–248.

Cases

Case 14.1

Shiner International Transportation Company

Shiner has been a truckload carrier for the past 20 years and is currently the largest carrier of its type in North America. It has been able to establish its leadership in its industry through aggressive marketing, intermodal agreements, and leading-edge communications technology. However, Shiner sees its growth as being limited in its current markets and continuously faces new competitors in the truckload business.

Top management at Shiner has agreed that growth could come with entry into a relatively oligopolistic industry—LTL trucking. Because Shiner is a truckload operation, it has a relatively low debt load and could absorb an initial high investment in terminal facilities. Shiner also sees that entry into this market could offer its already stable customer base a larger service package over a wider range of shipment sizes. Shiner feels that its experience in the truckload transportation business will position it favorably for entry into the LTL business.

Shiner is also aware that this entry into a free market-based segment of the transportation industry will not go unchallenged. Current carriers in the LTL industry have established terminal networks, have gained economies of scale and of scope, and have very loyal customer bases. These existing carriers could certainly start a price war or develop special services that would make survival difficult for Shiner in the LTL market. However, Shiner's management feels that the time is right for new competition in this segment of the market and have prepared a public stock offering to get equity capital for terminal facility investments. Success for Shiner rests with its ability to generate customer interest and demand and not only meet existing competitor service levels but exceed them on new and innovative services.

Case Questions

1. Perform an environmental analysis of the LTL industry and of Shiner to determine its strengths, weaknesses, opportunities, and threats.

2. Develop a marketing plan to help guide Shiner in its entrance into the LTL industry.

CASE 14.2

Southern Products, Inc.

"Amy, these will not do. We can't use these. The job descriptions are 10 years out of date," said Jim Smyth, Vice President of Traffic and Transportation. Amy Freemont, the new personnel representative of Southern Specialty Chemicals' traffic and transportation department, was mildly shocked. Jim quickly went on, "I'm sorry that we didn't warn you about this. It's something that none of us thought of until we took a look at them just now. It's not your fault. But before we go forth with some of our reorganization, I'd like some skills analysis and position descriptions from you."

This was Amy Freemont's first meeting at the end of the first day on assignment in the traffic and transportation department. Amy was hired from the personnel department of Cotton State Insurance Company. She had extensive experience in human resource administration at Cotton State, and her specialty was doing developmental work in new and specific job functions. The position she now held at Southern Specialty Chemicals was newly created in response to the rapid changes taking place in the overall logistics functions in the company.

That night Amy took home the old files that were the subject of discussion at the afternoon meeting. They were job descriptions written in the middle 1970s, and they covered each of the 30 positions that then existed in the traffic and transportation department. She also took home the performance evaluation files of each of the 30 professional people in the department. She noticed that the activities and accomplishments mentioned in the periodically updated personal performance evaluations showed great differences with the descriptions in the first set of files. She began to notice that what people were doing today was vastly different than what was done a decade ago.

Southern Specialty Chemical had four plants from Virginia to Louisiana and the corporate headquarters were in Greensboro, North Carolina. Traffic and transportation was centralized in Greensboro, but there were some local traffic functions taking place at the plants. The company had a small private fleet, and this involved four professional people. Where the company used to maintain a large common carrier tariff library, today's shipping was performed mostly under contract with both less-than-truckload and truckload carriers. Most of these rates were reduced to contract and/or were in computer form.

Amy looked over the information before her and made out a checklist. The list consisted of organizational changes, process changes, job function changes, and manpower requirements. She started to gather what information she could. She contacted many people in the department, including you.

Case Question

What would be your input for each of these four areas?

Appendix A

Equipment of Domestic Freight Transportation

It is often difficult to visualize transportation, which is a service and not a physical, tangible product. It is helpful to ask: What is the transportation product? It is a service to the user. It has basic characteristics that make obtaining this service similar to buying goods.

One aspect of transportation service consists of the *movement service*. This includes the speed, whether it is door-to-door or terminal-to-terminal, and the frequency of transportation. Another factor is the *equipment* used, which is a major consideration in both passenger and freight service. The equipment relates to passenger comfort, whereas in freight service it is a major factor in shipment preparation, size, and loading and unloading costs. This appendix presents an overview of the type of transportation equipment available to the user.

Rail

Categories of Rail Equipment

The rail mode has many forms of equipment available for use. Freight cars have distinct movement characteristics for different commodities, shipments, or services.

Two broad categories of rail equipment exist: standard or specially equipped. Standard equipment consists of basic box, gondola, flat, and hopper cars that are provided for shipments on a nondiscriminatory basis. Special equipment consists of similar cars that have extra features that are more costly to provide and are usually more desirable for shippers to use. Specially equipped cars technically need not be made available for use by the entire shipping public. Because of their extraordinary investment costs, railroads often will not provide such equipment to particular shippers of specific low-rated commodities. Instead, the railroads will control these cars and offer them in a variety of ways. One is to treat them as "freerunners," which are controlled and made available for loading whenever compatible high-rated shipments are requested. Another control approach is to assign a group of specially equipped cars to a specific shipper for its exclusive use. These are often called "shipper pools." An example is rail cars for automobile parts; these cars have internal features usable only by one auto firm. A final major group of rail cars is shipper-supplied cars. These are cars that are either leased or purchased by shippers and are used only by them or other firms that sublease the cars. This is a practice employed by large shippers when they require a particular type of car and seek an assured supply of that type of rail equipment.

Specific Types

Descriptions of specific forms of rail equipment are presented below

Standard Boxcars

These are, in essence, enclosed boxes that provide sealed protection for shipments. These cars have no internal features other than a floor and walls into which nails can be driven when bracing shipments. Standard boxcars are used for packaged goods and some bulk commodities, such as specialty ores and grain, which require protection from the elements. Standard boxcars typically are 40 feet long (4,000 cubic feet) and 50 feet long (4,900 cubic feet) and have payload capacities of 100,000 pounds or 50 tons. The smaller car is useful for commodities of 28 pounds per cubic foot or more, whereas the 50-foot car will fully "weigh out" at 100,000 pounds. The full visible capacity of the car will be loaded if the goods reach about 22 pounds per cubic foot. Some railroads have standard 60-foot boxcars as well. The trend is for more 50-foot and 60-foot cars and fewer 40-foot cars. Boxcars of 89 feet are used by shippers of light and/or bulky material such as car doors or hoods.

Standard Flatcars

These open platform-like cars are useful for moving large machinery such as lumber construction and farm equipment. The flatcar can be end, top, or side loaded in ways the boxcar will not permit.

Standard Hopper Cars

These are open-top cars that also allow for unloading by bottom chutes. These are the primary bulk commodity movers for commodities that can withstand exposure to the elements. Coal, some ores, sand, gravel, and stone are moved in these cars. In periods of high grain movements when insufficient covered hopper cars are available, some railroads provide temporary plastic covers for these cars so that bulk grain can be shipped while being protected from the elements.

Standard hopper cars come in two basic sizes: large and regular. The regular cars haul fairly dense goods such as coal; their cubic and weight capacities are designed for that traffic. Bulk wood chip movements are made by paper companies, but service is not economical in a regular plain hopper because wood chips are extremely light and bulky. Several railroads have provided jumbo open-top hoppers for this traffic.

Special Boxcars

Specially equipped boxcars provide internal bulkheads and special cushioning devices that reduce shipper bracing expenses. These cars come in 40-foot, 50-foot, 60-foot, and 86-foot sizes. Some are insulated to protect ladings from heat and cold, and others have refrigeration equipment built into them. These cars and all those following are assigned to shipper pools, are owned or leased by shippers, or are distributed by railroads according to shipment profitability.

Covered Hopper Cars

These are basically hopper cars that have permanent tops with hatches that allow for top loading as well as sealed protection. These come in four basic cubic sizes, all of which typically hold 70 or 100 tons. The 1,900-cubic-foot covered hopper is ideal for very dense commodities, such as lime, in the 70-pounds-per-cubic-foot range. The 3,2000- to 3,500-cubic-foot range car is good for fertilizers and flour having 50 to 60 pounds per cubic-foot density. The 4,700-cubic-foot covered hopper is cubed and weighted out on such goods as oats, corn, and wheat, which are in the 42- to 45-pound-per-cubic-foot range. The 5,700-cubic-foot jumbo covered hopper is useful for light plastic pellets and some bulk-free shipments. Covered hopper cars allow for bottom-latch or vacuum unloading.

Equipped Flatcars

These cars are equipped with special tie-down equipment for securing trucks, autos, trailers, and frames. The auto flats come in two- and three-tier configurations. Some have bulkheads on the ends so that cut pulp wood or large packaged lumber can be moved. Some railroads have drop-frame flatcars for moving extremely heavy goods such as utility boilers and turbines.

Equipped Gondolas

These are covered gondolas or cars equipped with troughs for coiled steel movement, or both. They eliminate much shipper bracing and cover protection.

Tank Cars

These haul bulk-liquid or gas commodities such as chlorine, alcohol, corn syrup, or propane. Due to cleaning and contamination problems, the railroad industry has not provided this type of equipment. Instead it has only been available by leasing from the shipper or purchasing it from car builders.

Piggyback/Container Equipment

Piggyback shipments consist of highway trailers on special tie-down equipped flatcars. Container "boxes" are moved in this manner as well. These containers come in sizes of eight feet by eight feet, 12 feet, 20 feet, 35 feet, and 40 feet, and they are generally compatible for rail, highway, and container movement. Some containers are equipped with refrigeration, and others have enclosed tanks for bulk chemical, wine, or liquor movements.

Special Types

Railcars have generally evolved from the demands of special commodities. Though special cars exist or can be designed and constructed, the basic rail network of the United States (bridges, rail loads, and so on) has the capacity to accept cars weighing a total of 263,000 pounds. Because most cars weigh about 30 tons, the normal freight payload limit (unless the car is built for smaller loads) is 100 tons. Generally, if additional payloads are desired, the car weight itself will have to be reduced so that the 263,000-pound limit is not exceeded. Some research has been conducted into using lighter aluminum in car construction, but the extra material cost is generally regarded as not worth the small weight and revenue gain.

Some specially designed heavy payload flatcars can carry up to 200-ton loads, and in one instance, 400-ton loads. These cars, however, are limited to a few heavy-capacity lines.

Motor-Carrier Equipment

Basic Types

Motor-carrier equipment comes in five basic types, all of which are somewhat similar to the types of rail equipment.

Vans

A van is a basic box having little interior bracing equipment, though it can be equipped with such. Vans come in all sizes, from a single truck of 40 feet to 55-foot-long trailers. Some have open tops for overhead crane loading and canvas covers affixed for weather protection. Other trailers are insulated and refrigerated.

Flatbed Trailers

These are designed for flexible loading and unloading from tops, sides, and the rear. Sometimes large construction equipment is seen on heavy-capacity drop-frame trailers. This is a form of equipment generally available through contract carriers or the special commodity divisions of common carriers.

Racks

These are special trailers that have racks affixed for carrying automobiles.

Bulk Trailers

Bulk trailers are special trailers designed for commodities such as dry chemicals, flour, cement, and fertilizers. The open-top version of this trailer is often referred to as a dump truck.

Tanks

These are designed for bulk-liquid movements.

Size and Weight Restrictions

The overall limitations of highway transportation are seen in federal and state size and weight restrictions. The highest federal interstate highway weight limitation is 80,000 pounds, which means about 40,000 to 42,000 pounds maximum can typically be hauled in the form of goods. Weight limitations are also present in the form of weight per axle. Length limitations are generally state imposed; 55 feet or 75 feet in overall length is allowed, with trailers being 45 feet and 55 feet, respectively. Width limitations are typically eight feet with a minimum of 8.5 feet on an interstate highway. Generally, this does not vary except in special permit situations. The motor-carrier industry continually strives for increased length and weight limitations because this is one of the few readily available productivity gains the industry can seek. States allow a single tractor to haul two trailers and some allow three trailers, which brings labor cost savings in over-the-road operations and intermediate break-bulk handling.

Domestic Barge Capabilities

Basic Types

The domestic barge industry offers five basic barges for commodity movement.

Open-top Standard Barges

The current standard barge is 35 feet by 195 feet in overall dimensions and can carry up to 1,500 tons. Most carriers assess a minimum charge of

600 tons if the barge itself is not loaded with that weight. This standard size allows uniform tow makeup and traversing in combinations of six or nine barges in 600-foot-long locks, or 15 barges in 1,200-foot-long locks.

Covered Hoppers

These are standard hoppers with removable hatches that protect lading from the weather. Lumber, some steel, and specialty coal are moved via this equipment. The barge firms sometimes are reluctant to invest in this extra feature because it is prone to handling damage.

Bulk-Liquid Barges

Some barges are designed as tank barges, which are used for gasoline, oil, and chemicals.

Integrated Tow Barges

This is a series of barges with a tow designed to operate together as one unit. In individual barge form, they vary in design and shape. They are usually constructed for bulk-chemical carriage.

LASH Barges

These special Lighter Aboard Ship (LASH) covered barges are found in the inland waterway system. They are loaded and towed to New Orleans, where they are physically loaded onto a ship and carried overseas intact. Lykes Steamship Company is a major operator of several LASH ships between the Gulf of Mexico and Europe. The advantage of this system is that it avoids physical handling of the goods at the interfacing port.

Air Freight Movement

Basic Types

The air mode permits freight to be moved in three basic forms.

Packaged Freight

This form of movement consists of hand-loaded packages that are carried in the belly of aircraft. It is the least efficient form of loading and unloading because the airplane could otherwise be in flight during this dead time.

Igloos

These are pallets onto which packages or whole shipments are loaded and held in place by a net, cover, or blanket. This system makes for fast loading and unloading. The igloo shape of the shipment fits the internal wall contorts of a narrow-body airplane.

Containers

These are metal or fiberglass boxes into which freight is loaded for fast loading and unloading to and from the airplane. Containers come in all sizes and are usually designed with a specific airplane in mind. Containers are used for belly and main-floor loading.

Primary Services

Two primary services are also considered in air freight movements.

Wide-Body Service

The movement of freight in any of the above forms is often sought on what is called "wide-body service." This means movement on B-747, DC-10, and L-1011 aircraft. Shippers seek this service for particularly large payloads.

Air-Freight Service

Many airlines offer all-freight plane service. The advantage of this is that palletized and large container shipments can be shipped on these flights. Otherwise, shipments would have to be broken up into sizes that would fit into the bellies of passenger aircraft.

Pipelines

This mode of service is only available for bulk carriage of liquid commodities or those commodities that can be made into liquid form by the addition of water in what is then called a "slurry." This mode of service is used for the movement of coal.

Appendix B

Transportation Sites on the Internet

AIR RELATED SITES

America West Airlines:
http://www.americawest.com

Air Transport Association:
http://www.airtransport.org

Continental Airlines:
http://www.flycontinental.com

Delta Air Lines Home Page:
http://www.deltaair.com

Federal Aviation Agency Safety Home Page:
http://nasdac.faa.gov

Frontier Airlines Page:
http://www.frontierairlines.com

FedEx:
http://www.fedex.com

Skyway Air Freight:
http://www.skyway.com

United Airlines:
http://www.ual.com

GOVERNMENT RELATED SITES

U.S. Department of Transportation:
http://www.dot.gov

Office of Highway Policy Information Home Page:
http://www.fhwa.dot.gov/ohim

Code of Federal Regulations on GPO Access:
http://www.access.gpo.gov/nara/cfr/cfrtablesearch.html

Federal Highway Administration Home Page:
http://www.fhwa.dot.gov

Hazardous Management Information System:
http://www.dlis.dla.mil/hmis.htm

Office of Highway Policy Information Home Page:
http://www.fhwa.dot.gov/ohim

INTERMODAL AND SPECIAL CARRIERS

Hub Group, Inc.:
http://www.hubgroup.com

Intermodal Association of North America:
http://www.intermodal.org

RPS Homepage:
http://www.shiprps.com

Transportation Intermediaries Association:
http://www.tianet.org

UPS Home Page:
http://www.ups.com

United States Postal Service:
http://www.usps.gov

LOGISTICS SITES

Activitybased Costing: The ABC Authority:
http://www.abctech.com

Caliber System Companies:
http://www.calibersys.com

Cat Logistics Services:
http://www.CatLogistics.com

Cass Information Systems:
http://www.cassinfo.com

Council of Logistics Management:
http://www.clm1.org

DSI Home Page:
http://www.dsii.com

Freight Management Specialists:
http://www.fmsnet.com

Freightworld freight, transportation, logistics, cargo, shipping:
http://users.ccnet.com/~ltlfield

LOGcity transportation, logistics, cargo, shipping resources.:
http://www.logcity.com

National Industrial Transportation League:
http://www.nitl.org

PENSKE Logistics:
http://www.penske.com

LOGISTICS - SOFTWARE

CSI Freight Management Services:
http://www.freightware.com

i2 Technologies:
http://www.i2.com

Interchain, Software for Logistics Service Providers:
http://www.interchain.nl

J.D.Edwards Company:
http://www.jdedwards.com

McHugh Software International:
http://www.mchugh.com/data/products.htm

Manugistics, Inc:
http://www.manugistics.com

SAP America, Inc.:
http://www.sap.com/usa

Logility:
http://www.logility.com

Traffic World Magazine's Software Tech Center:
http://www.trafficworld.com/techcenter

MAGAZINES AND PERIODICALS

Business Trucking Magazine:
http://www.nptc.org/privmag/carrier.html

Journal of Commerce:
http://www.joc.com

Logistics Management Magazine:
http://www.manufacturing.net/magazine/logistic

LogisticsWorld The Worldwide Directory of Transportation and Logistics:
http://www.logisticsworld.com

Traffic World Magazine:
http://www.trafficworld.com

Transportation Law Journal:
http://www.du.edu/~transplj

Transport News:
http://www.transportnews.com

Transport Topics Online:
http://www.ttnews.com

Transportation & Distribution Magazine:
http://www.newspage.com

The WorldWide Web Virtual Library: Logistics:
http://www.logisticsworld.com/logistics /

MISCELLANEOUS SITES

American Society of Transportation & Logistics:
http://www.astl.org

Bureau of Transportation Statistics, US DOT:
http://www.bts.gov

Delta Nu Alpha Transportation Fraternity:
http://www.wmgt.org/deltanualpha/aboutdna.htm

Eno Transportation Foundation:
http://www.enotrans.com/index.htm

Freightworld A Guide to World Freight Transportation and Logistics:
http://www.ccnet.com/~ltlfield

Global Freight Market:
http://www.freightmarket.com

Insurance Institute for Highway Safety:
http://www.hwysafety.org

National Assoc. of Truck Stop Operators:
http://www.natsofoundation.org

BTS Products National Transportation Statistics:
http://www.bts.gov/btsprod/nts/chp1v.html

NAFTAnet Trade Law:
http://www.nafta.net/tradelaw

National Transportation Data Archive:
http://www.bts.gov/ntda

Transportation Law Center:
http://www.transportlaw.com

TransportLink:
http://www.transportlink.com

TransportWorld The Official Freight and Transport Index:
http://www.transportworld.com

Transportation Research Forum:
http://www.utexas.edu/depts/ctr/trf

MOTOR CARRIER RELATED SITES

ABF Freight System, Inc. Welcome Page:
http://www.abfs.com

American Trucking Associations:
http://www.truckline.com

Central Freight:
http://www.centralfreight.com

ConWay Transportation Services:
http://www.conway.com

Consolidated Freightways:
http://www.cfwy.com

CRST International:
http://www.crst.com

J. B. Hunt Home Page:
http://www.jbhunt.com

Motor Cargo:
http://www.motorcargo.com

National Private Truck Council Home Page:
http://www.nptc.org

Intrenet Trucking:
http://www.intrenetinc.com

Roadway Express:
http://www.roadway.com

Ryder System, Inc.:
http://www.ryder.com

Schneider National:
http://www.schneider.com

Yellow Freight System:
http://www.yellowfreight.com

PIPELINE RELATED SITES

American Pipeline Association:
http://www.api.org/industry/pipelines/pbasic.htm

Interstate Natural Gas Association of America:
http://www.ingaa.org

Office of Pipeline Safety:
http://ops.dot.gov

Pipe Line & Gas Industry:
http://www.pipeline.com

RAILROAD RELATED SITES

Association of American Railroads:
http://www.aar.org

Amtrak:
http://www.amtrak.com

BNSF Burlington Northern Santa Fe Railway:
http://www.bnsf.com

Canadian National:
http://www.cn.ca

Canadian Pacific Railway:
http://www.cpr.ca

CSX Corp.:
http://www.csx.com

High Speed Ground Transportation:
http://www.bts.gov/hsgt

Kansas City Southern:
http://www.kcsi.com

Norfolk Southern Corporation:
http://www.nscorp.com

OmniTRAX Inc.:
http://www.omnitrax.com

RoadRailer:
http://www.roadrailer.de/index_e.html

Union Pacific Railroad:
http://www.uprr.com

Wisconsin Central Transportation:
http://www.wclx.com

Wabash National Corporation:
http://www.wncwabash.com

TRUCK BROKERAGE SITES

DAT Services:
http://www.dat.com

Internet Truckstop:
http://www.truckstop.com

LTL Route Guide:
http://www.routeguide.com

M.R.S. Companies Home Page:
http://www.mrsco.com

NetTrans Login:
http://www.nettrans.com

TIE Services:
http://www.tieservices.com

TON Services:
http://www.tonservices.com

TranServ:
http://www.transerv.com

WATER CARRIER RELATED SITES

American Association of Port Authorities:
http://www.aapaports.org

American Waterways Association:
http://www.americanwaterways.com

American President Lines:
http://www.apl.com

Atlantic Container Line:
http://www.aclcargo.com

Maersk Line:
http://www.maerskline.com

SeaLand Service:
http://www.sealand.com

Appendix C

Selected Transportation Publications

Air Cargo World
6151 Powers Ferry Road
Atlanta, GA 30339

American Mover
1611 Duke Road
Alexandria, Virginia 22314
Telephone 703-683-7410
Fax 703-683-7527

American Shipper
33 S. Hagen St.
Jacksonville, FL 32201
Telephone 904-355-2601
Fax 904-791-8836
E-mail AmShpJx@aol.com

Business Week
1221 Avenue of the Americas
New York, NY 10020
Telephone 212-512-2511

Canadian Trans & Logistic
1450 Don Mills Road
Don Mills, Ontario M3B2X7
Telephone 416-445-6641
Fax 416-442-2214

Commercial Carrier Journal
Chilton Way
Radnor, PA 19089
Telephone 610-964-4514
Fax 610-964-4512

Defense Transportation Journal
50 South Pickett Street
Alexandria, VA 22304
Telephone 703-751-5011
Fax 703-823-8761

EDI Forum
1818 H Street
Washington, DC 20433
Telephone 202-473-6349
E-mail edipub@worldbank.org

Fleet Owner
McGraw-Hill
1221 Avenue of the Americas
New York, NY 10016

Global Sites & Logistics
P.O. Box 4127
Merrifield, VA 22116
Telephone 703-560-7779
Fax 703-560-9304

Grocery Distribution
625 North Michigan Avenue
Chicago, IL 60611
Telephone 312-654-2330
Fax 312-654-2323

Heavy Duty Trucking
1800 East Deere Avenue
Santa Ana, CA 92705
Telephone 949-261-1636
Fax 949-261-2904

Inbound Logistics
Five Penn Plaza
New York, NY 10001
Telephone 212-629-1563
Fax 212-629-1565
E-mail Ileditor@aol.com

Industrial Distribution
275 Washington Street
Newton, MA 02158
Telephone 617-964-3030
Fax 617-558-4327

Industry Week
1100 Superior
Cleveland, OH 44114
Telephone 216-696-7000
Fax 216-696-7670

International Journal of Physical Distribution and Logistics Management
MCB University Press
P.O. Box 10812
Birmingham, AL 35201

Journal of Commerce
2 World Trade Center, 27th Floor
New York, NY 10048
Telephone 212-837-7000
Fax 212-837-7005

Logistics Management & Distribution Report
275 Washington Street
Newton, MA 02158
Telephone 617-558-4473
Fax 617-558-4327
E-mail lm@cahners.com

Modern Bulk Transporter
4200 S. Shepard, Suite 200
Houston, TX 77098

Motor Truck
1450 Don Mills Road
Don Mills, Ontario M3B2X7
Telephone 416-442-2000
Fax 416-442-2213
E-mail Lsmyrlis@southam.ca

NAPM Insights
2055 Centennial Circle
Tempe, AZ 85285
Telephone 602-752-6276
Fax 602-752-7890

Nation's Business
1615 H Street N.W.
Washington, DC 20062
Telephone 202-463-5650
Fax 202-887-3437

Operations & Fulfillment
535 Connecticut Avenue
Norwalk, CT 06854
Telephone 203-857-5656
Fax 203-854-2956

Parcel Shipping & Distribution
2424 American Lane
Madison, WI 53704-3102
Telephone 608-241-8777
E-mail editor@itis.com

Private Carrier
66 Canal Center Plaza, Suite 600
Alexandria, VA 22314
Telephone 703-683-1300
Fax 703-683-1217

Progressive Railroading
2100 Florist
Milwaukee, WI 53209
Telephone 414-228-7701
Fax 414-228-1134
E-mail pat.foran@tradepress.com

Purchasing Magazine
Cahners Building
275 Washington Street
Newton, MA 02158
Telephone 617-558-4359
Fax 617-558-4327

Railway Age
345 Hudson Street, 17th Floor
New York, NY 10014
Telephone 212-620-7233
Fax 212-633-1165

Refrigerated Transporter
4200 S. Shepherd Drive
Houston, TX 77090
Telephone 713-467-6519
Fax 713-523-8384

Traffic World
741 National Press
Washington, DC 20045
Telephone 202-383-6140
Fax 202-661-3383
E-mail editor@trafficworld.com

Transport Topics
2200 Mill Road
Alexandria, VA 22314
Telephone 703-838-1770
Fax 703-548-3662
E-mail ttnews@ttnews.com

Transportation & Distribution
1100 Superior Avenue
Cleveland, OH 44114
Telephone 216-931-9274
Fax 216-696-2737

Transportation Journal
320 East Water Street
Lock Haven, PA 17745-1419
E-mail info@astl.org

U.S. Distribution Journal
233 Park Avenue South
New York, NY 10003
Telephone 212-979-4811
Fax 212-228-3142

Appendix D

Transportation-Related Associations

Air Transport Association of America

Type: A trade association in which airlines hold membership.

Purpose/objective: The Air Transport Association of America is the trade and service organization of the largest airlines of the United States.

Air Transport Association of America
1301 Pennsylvania Avenue, NW
Washington, DC 20004
202-626-4000
http://www.airtransport.org

American Society of Transportation & Logistics, Inc. (AST & L)

Type: A professional organization in which individuals hold membership.

Purpose/objective: To establish, promote, and maintain high standards of knowledge and professional training; to formulate a code of ethics for the profession; to advance the professional interest of members of the organization; to serve as a source of information and guidance for the fields of traffic, transportation, logistics, and physical distribution management; and to serve the industry as a whole by fostering professional accomplishments.

American Society of Transportation and Logistics, Inc.
320 East Water Street
Lockhaven, PA 17745
717-748-8515
http://www.astl.org

American Trucking Associations, Inc. (ATA)

Type: A trade organization representing the interests of the trucking industry.

Purpose/objective: The American Trucking Associations, Inc., is the national trade association of the trucking industry. The ATA Federation includes the ATA national headquarters, 50 affiliated state trucking associations, and 14 affiliated national conferences and independent organizations. The mission of ATA is to serve the united interests of the trucking industry; enhance the trucking industry's image, efficiency, productivity, and competitiveness; promote highway workplace safety and environmental responsibility; provide educational programs; and work for a healthy business environment.

American Trucking Associations, Inc.
2200 Mill Road
Alexandria, VA 22314
703-838-1700
http://www.truckline.com

Association of American Railroads

Type: A trade association of railroad companies.

Purpose/objective: The Association of American Railroads serves two major purposes for its members. It provides industry support on matters that require cooperative handling to better enable railroads to operate as a national system in the areas of operation, maintenance, safety, research, economics, finance, accounting, data system, and public information. It also provides leadership for the industry, working with committees made up of representatives of member railroads on matters affecting the progress of the industry as a whole.

Association of American Railroads
50 F Street, NW
Washington, DC 20001
202-639-2100
http://www.aar.org

Canadian Industrial Transportation League (CITL)

Type: A trade association in which corporations hold membership.

Purpose/objective: To develop a thorough understanding of the transportation and distribution requirements of industry, and to promote, conserve, and protect commercial transportation interests.

Canadian Industrial Transportation League
1090 Don Mills Road
Don Mills, ON, Canada M3C 3R6
416-447-7766

Council of Logistics Management (CLM)

Type: A professional organization in which individuals hold membership.

Purpose/objective: The mission of the Council of Logistics Management is to provide:

- Leadership in developing, defining, understanding, and enhancing the logistics process on a worldwide basis.
- A form for logistics professionals to exchange concepts and best practices.
- Research that advances knowledge and leads to enhanced customer value and supply-chain performance.
- Education and career development programs that enhance career opportunities in logistics management.

The Council of Logistics Management is an open organization that offers individual membership to persons in all industries, types of businesses, and job functions involved in the logistics process. In recognition of diversity, the Council of Logistics Management will give priority to actively involving individuals from currently underrepresented populations in its activities. The Council of Logistics Management will operate on a not-for-profit, self-supporting basis, with emphasis on quality and in a cooperative manner with other organizations and institutions.

Council of Logistics Management
2805 Butterfield Road, Suite 200
Oak Brook, IL 60523
630-574-0985
http://www.clm1.org

Delta Nu Alpha

Type: A professional organization in which individuals hold membership.

Purpose/objective: To be a service organization providing educational opportunities to those having a professional interest in transportation, logistics, and related fields, and to serve as a sustaining resource for future needs of the industry.

Delta Nu Alpha
530 Church Street, Suite 300
Nashville, TN 37219
605-251-0933
http://www.wmgt.org

Eno Transportation Foundation, Inc.

Type: Private operating foundation endowed in 1921 by William Phelps Eno (not a grant or charitable organization).

Purpose/objective: Pursuant to Mr. Eno's mandate, the Foundation provides a responsive and credible institution and resource for transportation betterment facilitated through safe, efficient, and environmentally sound systems and services. In support of its role, the Foundation 1) monitors transportation trends, developments, and related problem areas, with counsel from its board of advisors; 2) maintains effective lines of communication with transportation leaders and their trade and professional organizations; 3) develops information for dissemination to all modal interests, the media, and the general public; 4) undertakes and manages selected research projects, studies, and seminars; and 5) works to advance the development of transportation leadership.

Eno Transportation Foundation, Inc.
44211 Statestone Court
Landsdowne, VA 22075
703-729-7200
http://www.enotrans.com/index.htm

National Customs Brokers and Forwarders of America, Inc. (NCBFA)

Type: A trade association in which corporations hold membership.

Purpose/objective: National Customs Brokers and Forwarders Association of America, Inc., is the trade association representing the licensed customs brokers, international freight forwarders, and international air cargo agents located throughout the United States.

National Customs Brokers and Forwarders of America, Inc.
1200 18th Street, NW #901
Washington, DC 20036
202-466-0222

National Defense Transportation Association (NDTA)

Type: A nonprofit educational association.

Purpose/objective: The National Defense Transportation Association is an educational, nonprofit, worldwide organization that combines the transportation industry's human resources and skills with the expertise of those in government and the military to achieve the mutual objective of a strong and responsive transportation capability. NDTA membership represents the transportation operators, users, mode carriers, manufacturers, traffic managers, and related industries and military and government interests.

National Defense Transportation Association
50 South Pickett Street, Suite 220
Alexandria, VA 22304-3008
703-751-5011

The National Industrial Transportation League (NITL)

Type: The NITL is the oldest and largest broad-based shippers' organization in the United States. Carriers and other service providers are eligible for associate status.

Number of members: 1,600.

Dues: Membership dues and associate fees are based on gross sales.

Purpose/objective: The League represents shippers in the legislative, judicial, and regulatory arenas. Among its specific benefits are designing and implementing transportation policy, fighting legal battles on behalf of shippers, providing networking opportunities, offering educational seminars, as well as holding a domestic and international meeting and trade show and producing informative publications.

The National Industrial Transportation League
1700 N. Moore Street, Suite 1900
Arlington, VA 22209-1904
703-524-5011
http://www.nitl.org

National Private Truck Council (NPTC)

Type: A trade association in which corporations that operate their own truck fleets as an extension of their primary business enterprises hold membership.

Purpose/objective: The purpose of the National Private Truck Council is to represent the interest of the private trucking industry before legislative, administrative, regulatory, or judicial branches of government; to collect and disseminate information concerning matters of interest to private fleet operators; to provide fleets; and to foster and promote greater public understanding and appreciation of the private trucking industry. In addition, NPTC publishes a monthly management journal, *The Private Carrier,* and a monthly newsletter, *The Private Line.*

National Private Truck Council
66 Canal Center Plaza, 6th Floor
Alexandria, VA 22314
703-683-1300
http://www.nptc.org

National Small Shipments Traffic Conference (NASSTRAC)

Type: An organization in which regular membership is extended to shippers on both an individual and a corporate basis. Associate membership is done on both an individual and corporate basis.

Purpose/objective: The purpose of NASSTRAC is to:

- Assist members in identifying new and innovative ways to save money on LTL distribution of goods
- Provide an educational program for professional development of executives
- Provide a vehicle for professional interchanges and an introduction to experienced LTL distribution officials who can provide guidance as needed
- Keep members up to date on developments in LTL distribution techniques and on regulatory and rate matters
- Provide legal representation for appropriate litigation and basic legal guidance
- Provide a platform for professional interchange with carriers
- Provide legal representation in regulatory matters with federal and state regulatory agencies in the courts

National Small Shipments Traffic Conference
1750 Pennsylvania Avenue, NW, Suite 1111
Washington, DC 20006
202-393-5505

Transportation Consumer Protection Council, Inc.

Type: A trade association in which corporations hold membership.

Purpose/objective: The Transportation Consumer Protection Council, Inc., is an educational institution developing the latest teaching tools and techniques on carrier liability and claims administration through seminars and publications. Its objective is to develop a greater degree of professionalism in claims management.

Transportation Consumer Protection Council, Inc.
120 Main Street
Huntington, NY 11743
516-549-8984

Transportation Intermediaries Association (TIA)

Type: A professional and trade association in which corporations hold membership.

Purpose/objective: The TIA is the professional association for licensed general commodity freight brokers in the United States. Created in 1978, TIA is a not-for-profit corporation whose sole purpose is to serve the needs and represent the interests of transportation intermediaries. The TIA seeks to promote professionalism in the brokerage industry, maintain high ethical standards, provide continuing education opportunities, represent brokers' interests to the ICC and other government agencies, and promote the benefits of professional brokerage to the public and other segments of the transportation industry.

Transportation Intermediaries Association (TIA)
3601 Eisenhower Avenue, Suite 110
Alexandria, VA 22304
703-329-1894
http://www.tianet.org

Transportation Research Board (TRB)

Type: An organization in which membership is extended on both an individual and/or corporate basis.

Purpose/objective: To advance knowledge concerning the nature and performance of transportation systems by stimulating research and disseminating the information derived therefrom.

Transportation Research Board
2100 Constitution Avenue, NW
Washington, DC 20418
202-334-2934

Glossary

Accessibility The ability of the carrier to provide service between the origin and destination. It also refers to the carrier's ability to serve the shipper or consignee's place of business. For example, in order to ship and receive a railcar, both the origin and destination must have a side track.

Agency Tariff A publication by a rate bureau that contains rates for many carriers. This publication is also call a "bureau tariff."

Aggregate Demand The total effective demand for the nation's output of goods and services. This can also refer to the sum of individual demands for a mode's or carrier's services.

Air carrier A transportation firm that operates aircraft for the transportation of passengers or freight as a "common carrier."

Air Traffic Control System The method by which aircraft traffic is controlled in the air so that planes are separated by altitude and distance for safety. This system is administered by the Federal Aviation Agency.

Balance load This occurs when the shipper provides the carrier with round trip loads to avoid an empty backhaul.

Bareboat charter A long-term lease or charter where the lessee provides the crew, fuel, and supplies and operates the ship. The lessor provides only the ship.

Bill of Lading A transportation document that is the contract of carriage between the shipper and the carrier; it provides a receipt for the goods tendered to the carrier, the "terms and conditions of sale" between the carrier and shipper, and the evidence of who has title to the goods while in transit.

Breakbulk Ocean cargo that is not containerized but must be handled manually into and out of a ship.

Broker An intermediary or "third party" who represents either the shipper or the carrier and seeks to match freight with empty trucks. The broker's fee can be included in the freight charges or collected separately. A broker is not considered a carrier for legal purposes.

Bundle of Services A grouping of services offered by a carrier that may be integrated into a total package. An example would be a carrier that offers line haul, sorting, and segregating with local delivery to specific customers.

Capability The ability of a carrier to provide service or multiple services to the shipper to meet the specific requirements of that customer.

Cargo Preference A federal law requiring that at least 50 percent of certain U.S. government-owned or sponsored cargo move on U.S. flag registered vessels.

Carload A full weight or size shipment placed into or on a railcar. This term also refers to rates that apply to a specific minimum weight for railcar shipments.

Carmack Act A law that defines the carrier's legal obligations to the owner of goods if they are lost or damaged while in the possession of a carrier. Recovery under the Carmack Act is subject to the terms contained in the Bill of Lading contract.

Carriage and Insurance paid to This term of sale defines the seller's obligations to pay transportation and insurance for a shipment to a specific location. At that location, the responsibility passes to the buyer.

Carriage paid to This term of sale defines the seller's obligations to pay transportation for a shipment to a specific location. At that location, the responsibility passes to the buyer.

Carrying Capacity The capability of a transport vehicle to carry or transport shipments of a particular weight or size in relation to the shipper's requirements. As an example, a 53-foot trailer could carry 48,000 pounds or a shipment of 3,392 cubic feet.

Cash flow Funds or money as it passes from buyer to seller during a commercial transaction and is sometimes measured in a time relationship.

Certificate of Origin A legal document that verifies the country where a particular product originated. This certificate must often accompany the shipment so the importing country can determine if it complies with that country's laws.

Claim A demand for payment made to a carrier for loss or damage to a shipment or the refund of alleged overpayment of freight charges.

Class I Carrier A railroad with an annual income over $256 million or a motor carrier with an annual income over $10 million.

Class II Carrier A railroad with an annual income less than $256 million but more than $20.5 million or a motor carrier with an annual income less than $10 million but more than $3 million.

Class III Carrier A motor carrier with an annual income less than $3 million.

Clayton Act A law that strengthened the Sherman Anti-Trust Act and specifically described some business practices as violations of the law. This was done to counter some practices that were used to avoid the Sherman Anti-Trust Act.

Coast Guard A military unit attached to the Department of Transportation. The Coast Guard is charged with certain law enforcement tasks related to protecting the shores of the U.S. and the usage of waters both domestically and along the shores of the U.S. The Coast Guard is also tasked with safety standards for commercial users, search and rescue missions on inland and coastal waters, and small boat safety programs.

COFC (Container On Flat Car) A type of rail shipment where only the container or "box" is loaded on the flat car. The chassis with the wheels and landing gear is only used to carry the container to and from the railroad.

Commercial Invoice A specifically prepared invoice for the merchandise contained in a shipment. The document is often required for international shipments.

Common Carrier A transportation company that provides freight and/or passenger service to any who seek its services.

Common Law A legal system based on court decisions and precedents that recognizes past decisions when deciding current legal questions. The legal system of the U.S. is based on this along with civil or statuary law.

Consular Invoice A specifically prepared invoice that is prescribed by the importing country for the merchandise contained in a shipment. The invoice will be written in the language of the importing country and may be required to be signed by an employee of the government of the nation to which the shipment is destined.

Container A specific type of "box" into which freight is loaded before the shipment is given to the carrier. The container can be rectangular such as those used for rail and ocean shipments or can be shaped to fit the transport vehicle, such as an aircraft. The container avoids the need for the carrier to handle individual parts of the shipment.

Container Rate A rate that applies only when the shipment is placed into a container prior to tendering the shipment to the carrier. This rate recognizes that the shipment is much more easily handled by the carrier.

Cooperative Association A group of individuals or companies who band together to purchase goods or services jointly and achieve price incentive based on the combined purchasing power of the members. Typically, cooperatives are chartered as not-for profit and require that the participant be members.

Cost and Freight A term of sale indicating that the price includes both the cost of the goods and the freight expense necessary to transport it to the buyer.

Cost, Insurance, and Freight A term of sale indicating that the price includes the cost of the goods, insurance premiums necessary to protect the cargo, and the freight expense necessary to transport it to the buyer.

Cost of Lost Sales The income that is lost when a customer chooses to purchase a product or service from another firm. This could be due to the product not being available when and where needed or the service did not meet the requirements of the buyer.

Cost of Service Pricing A method used by carriers when they seek to only cover the actual expense of providing that specific service. Such pricing does not usually cover shared or overhead costs.

Customer Attitude The customer's perception of the service or product provider.

Customer Filter The perception of the customer of the quality of the service that is "filtered" or influenced by more factors than just the quality of the specific offering.

Customer Perception The way in which the customer views or perceives the service offering that will influence their decision to buy or use the service. This view could be based on judgment or past experience.

Demand Elasticity The amount that the demand for a product or service will change by the changes in price and the availability of substitutes.

Delivered at Frontier A term of sale that indicates the title will pass from the buyer and seller. It also indicates to what extent freight and other expenses will be paid by the seller.

Delivered Ex Ship A term of sale that indicates shipment will be delivered to the buyer at the seller's expense alongside the ship. The seller will pay all expenses to that point, including any cost associated with unloading the consignment from the ship.

Delivered Ex Quay A term of sale that indicates shipment will be delivered to the buyer at the seller's expense on the "quay" or pier alongside the ship. The seller will pay all expenses to that point including any cost associated with unloading the consignment from the ship.

Delivered Duty Unpaid A term of sale that indicates that the seller will not pay any import duties or taxes.

Delivered Duty Paid A term of sale that indicates that the seller will pay any import duties or taxes levied by the importer's home country.

Department of Transportation The cabinet level branch of the U.S. Government responsible for various aspects of transportation policy, safety, and, in some cases, economic regulation for all carriers and modes.

Draft A type of bank transaction that insures payment for goods. It is a written order for a sum of money to be paid by the buyer to the seller upon presentation of the document to the buyer's bank.

Economic Deregulation The removal of governmentally enforced price and entry controls in the transportation industry. The "free market" will provide the necessary competition to insure competitive prices and services.

Existence Fee A basic charge or fee that must be paid to engage in business or be granted a certain right or privilege.

Extent of Market This relates to the extent of the size of a market that a firm may serve on a competitive basis. Cost of the product and freight will determine how far from its base a firm may compete effectively.

Federal Energy Regulatory Commission The federal agency that oversees rates and practices of pipeline operators and is part of the Department of Energy.

Federal Highway Administration The federal agency that oversees motor carrier safety including hours of services, driver qualifications, and vehicle size and weight, as well as overall operation and development of the national highway system. This agency is part of the Department of Transportation.

Federal Highway Trust Fund A fund that receives federally collected fuel taxes used for highway construction and upkeep.

Federal Railroad Administration The federal agency that oversees railroad safety by establishing and enforcing rules and regulations. This agency is part of the Department of Transportation.

Federal Trade Commission The federal agency that administers the Sherman Anti-Trust

Act and the Clayton Act. This agency does not have direct control over transportation.

Free Alongside Ship A term of sale that indicates that the buyer will pay all freight and insurance charges necessary to bring the consignment to the side of ship but will not cover the cost of loading.

Freight All Kinds A pricing method where the carrier establishes a rate that will apply on any cargo loaded in the carrier's vehicle regardless of the nature of the freight.

Freight Flows The geographic direction in which freight "flows" or moves from producing locations to areas of consumption.

Freight Transportation The movement of goods or products from the producer or manufacturer to the user or customer.

Front Haul The first half of a round trip move from origin to destination. The opposite is "back haul," which is the return of the equipment to its origin point.

General Cargo Rate A pricing method where the carrier establishes a rate that will apply on any cargo loaded in the carrier's ship, regardless of the nature of the freight.

Globalization Recognition that commercial activity now spans the world and that many firms buy and sell throughout the world.

Head Haul The first half of a round-trip move from origin to destination. The opposite is "back haul," which is the return of the equipment to its origin point.

Home-flag Airline An airline owned by or sponsored by the government of the country in which the carrier is based. Typically, only "home flag" airlines are allowed to operate between airports within that country. This prevents foreign carriers from serving domestic locations.

Hump Yard A railroad yard that uses an artificial hill or "hump" to assist in switching and classifying railcars. The cars are pushed up the hill by a switch engine and at the top of the hill the railcar or group of railcars is uncoupled and rolls down hill to the correct track.

Information Flow The flow or movement of information or data between trading partners or companies that facilitates commerce or business.

Integration The act of mixing various elements into a single group. An example would to combine transportation and warehousing to allow trade-offs between the two functions for the maximum benefit.

Intermodal The combination of various modes to form a transportation movement. An example would be a truck picking up a trailer and taking it to a railyard for movement by train to the destination city where another truck would take the trailer to the receiver's location. This term may also refer to competition between modes such as truck and rail.

Intramodel Movement within a modal- or carrier-type category. This could refer to shipments moved with more than one truck line. This term may also refer to competition within a mode, such as between trucking firms.

Landed Cost The cost of the product at the source combined with the cost of transportation to the destination.

Landed Cost Advantage The advantage one supplier has over another based on the lower transportation cost due to favorable proximity to the market.

Lardner's Law A finding by transportation economist Dionysius Larder that when transportation cost is reduced, the area where the producer can compete is increased in a directly proportional basis.

Letter of Credit A document issued by the buyer's bank that guarantees payment to the seller if certain terms and conditions are met.

Lighter-Aboard Ship A type of vessel which is capable of carrying barges or "lighters" onboard. This method of transportation allows a barge to be loaded on an inland waterway, transported to shipside, taken to a harbor nearest destination and the barge can then taken to the destination by an inland waterway without having to rehandle any of the cargo.

Loss and Damage The risk to which goods are subjected during the transportation cycle. The shipment may be separated from its documentation and misdirected. Handling by the carrier as well in-transit incidents can cause damage to or destruction of the shipment. This is a factor in mode and carrier selection as well as packaging and handling techniques. This risk factor also enters into the carrier's pricing decisions.

Maquiladora The name for a manufacturing facility established inside Mexico within close distance of the U.S. border. Materials are shipped from the U.S., processed in the maquiladora plant, and returned to the U.S. No customs duties or fees are accessed.

Marketing Mix This consists of the four basic elements of marketing: product, price, place, and promotion. This is also known the "four P's" of marketing.

Mileage Rate A rate or price based on the total mileage between the origin and destinationm including stop-offs, if any.

Micro-bridge A technique where ocean containers are transported to an interior destination, such as Chicago or St. Louis, on a through bill of lading and the cost of the inland move is included in the total price.

Mini-bridge A technique where rail transportation is substituted for a portion of ocean transportation. As an example, a shipment from Japan to New York could move via the Panama Canal. The mini-bridge substitutes rail from a West Coast port to New York for the Panama Canal portion.

Minimum Level of Safety A base requirement for all aspects of safe operation by a transportation firm, as prescribed by a government agency.

Mobility The ease or difficulty with which people or goods are moved by the transportation network.

Modal Demand The request or demand made by users for service provided by a particular type of carrier or method of transport.

Monopolistic The ability of very few suppliers to set a price well above cost by restricting supply or by limiting competition.

Monopoly A market segment where there is only one supplier, such as public utilities such as electricity of transit systems.

National Highway Traffic Safety Administration This branch of the U.S. Department of Transportation is responsible for motor vehicle safety. In this role, NHSTA oversees design features, sets performance-related safety standards, and oversees governmental fuel economy standards.

National Transportation Safety Board This agency is responsible for investigating transportation-related accidents, regardless of whether or not the incident involved the private sector or a public carrier. They are responsible for recommending preventative measures to avoid future accidents.

Not-for-hire A carrier who does not hold itself to the general public to provide transportation service but rather transports for the owner firm exclusively.

Oligopoly A shared monopoly where there are few suppliers and, in the case of transportation, entry barriers and cost are significant. Examples would be railroads and airlines.

Operating Expense The cost of providing a service by a carrier. This can include such factors as taxes, interest, and deprecation but not necessarily profit.

Peddle Run A truck operation where many pickups or deliveries are made while the vehicle travels over a pre-set route.

Peddle Time This is the time that the driver is actively involved in either pick up or delivery.

Penetration Price A pricing strategy that sets a price designed to allow the supplier to enter a market where is already established competition by slightly underpricing the existing firms.

Per se Violations A violation of the law that is, on its own, deemed to be harmful, regardless of its effect on the market or competitors.

Pickup and Delivery The act of collecting freight from shippers or delivering freight to consignees.

Price Elasticity The measurement factor by which the change in demand for a product or service is affected by the price.

Price Inelasticity An economic condition where the change or increase in the price of a product or service does not produce a proportional change in demand.

Price-Sensitive The measures the relationship between prices and the demand for products or services.

Primary Trip Markets The geographical area of interest where a carrier focuses its sales and operational effort.

Procurement Another term for purchasing that represents more than just the buying of a product or service.

Product Flows The course where goods move between the point of origin to the point of consumption.

Pro-Forma A document issued by the seller to acquaint the importer/buyer and the importing country's government authorities with the details of the shipment.

Pure Competition A condition in which there is a large number of sellers, the product or service is standardized and interchangeable, and no one seller can control the price or output. An example would be the LTL sector.

Quality Gap The difference in perception of a product or service between the buyer and seller.

Rate Basis Number This number is an expression of the relative distance between an origin and destination. The number may be given in miles or another factor and will form one of the required inputs to develop a rate between the two points.

Rule of Reason An alleged violation of an anti-trust law where economic harm to competitors must be proved.

Regional Rail Reorganization Act of 1973 A law passed by Congress in response to the bankruptcies of the Penn Central and other railroads. Conrail, which has since been purchased the Norfolk Southern Railroad and CSX, was created from this law to operate the lines of six northeastern U.S. railroads.

Relative Use A fee placed on the users of a service or facility to cover the cost of providing that service or facility.

Return on Investment The amount of money realized or generated on an investment that flows back to the lenders. This is often used to gauge the worthiness of an investment by measuring the potential profits and the source of the capital.

Roll-On Roll-Off Ship A type of vessel that has ramps upon which vehicles can be driven directly into the hold of the ship. This type of vessel is often used to transport busses, trucks, construction machinery on wheels, and other types of wheeled shipments.

Rule of Efficiency The "Rule" refers to the fact that the most efficient transportation is in a continuous, straight line. There should be little circuitry or out-of-route operations with as few stops and starts as possible.

Security The actions of a carrier to protect the goods entrusted to their care from loss or damage.

Service The furnishing of an operation that fulfills the needs of the customer. This could be transporting a product or person to the desired location.

Service Elasticity Assuming no significant price differential, the mode or carrier providing the best level of service as perceived by the user will be the first choice.

Service Inelasticity Price, rather than service, is the controlling factor. The customer's choice of supplier will be made on price, assuming the service offered also meets the requirements as perceived by the user.

Sherman Anti-Trust Act A body of law that restricts businesses the ability to dominate a market by engaging in certain practices. This includes price fixing and other free-market-constricting activities.

Shipper's Export Declaration A document filed by the shipper/exporter or its agent with the government of the country in which the shipper/exporter resides. This form supplies the government with information about the shipment for statistical and control purposes.

Shipping Act of 1984 A body of law that governs the pricing and services of ocean carriers operating between the U.S. and foreign countries.

Side-by-Side Merger A merger of railroads whose lines operate in proximity of each other, rather than end to end.

Skimming Price A price set by a provider who seeks to attract a market that is more interested in quality, uniqueness, or status and is relatively unconcerned with price.

Technology The systematic knowledge of a particular discipline or science.

Tenders An offer to provide a minimum shipment size or volume in exchange for a price proposal from the carrier. This may also represent the minimum volume a carrier will accept or the least amount of money the carrier will accept for transportation of a specific shipment.

Third-Degree Price Discrimination A situation where a seller sets two or more different prices for separate groups of buyers of essentially the same commodity.

Time Charter A rental or long-term lease that includes both the vessel and crew and is for a specific length of time.

Time Value of Money This relates to the value of money over the lifetime of a project. As inflation reduces the value or purchasing capability of a dollar over the life of a project, this must be taken into consideration when establishing an interest or discount rate for the borrowed funds.

TOFC (Trailer On Flat Car) A method where a highway trailer complete with wheels and chassis is loaded on a railroad flatcar for long-haul movement.

Statutory Law This is based on the Roman legal system and refers to a body of law passed by legislative bodies.

Stem time The time consumed by a truck to reach its first delivery after leaving the terminal and the time consumed by truck to return to the terminal after making its last pickup.

Stowability and Handling The ease or difficulty experienced in loading, handling, and unloading freight. This factor influences the carrier's cost of providing a service and will be reflected in the price charged for the shipment. This is also two of the four factors considered when classifying freight.

Sunk costs Costs that cannot be easily retrieved or may not be retrieved at all when liquidating a business. This includes investments in specific machinery or buildings.

Surface Transportation Board The agency created under the Interstate Commerce Commission Termination (ICC) to replace the ICC and exercise economic jurisdiction of the modes of transportation.

Tank Farm A large group of storage tanks, usually at the end of a pipeline where liquid products are stored pending transfer to a tank truck or tankcars for further shipment.

Transaction Specific A perception by the customer of the satisfaction derived from each business exchange on an exchange-by-exchange basis.

Transloading Facility A facility where shipments can be transferred from one mode to another or within the same mode between carriers. This may be a rail-to-truck transfer or a situation where larger shipments are broken down for delivery to individual stores or consignees.

Transportation The act of moving goods or people from an origin to a required destination. It also includes the creation of time and place utilities.

Transportation Interaction The relationship and business exchanges between the three primary groups involved in this area: the users, the providers, and the government.

Unit Volume Pricing This is a technique whereby the carrier sets its prices to utilize its capacity to the fullest. Multiple pickup discounts in the LTL area and multiple car rates in the railroad sector would be two examples.

User Charges Costs or fees that the user of a service or facility must pay to the party furnishing this service or facility. An example would be the landing fee an airline pays to an airport when one of its aircraft lands or takes off.

Utility Creation This refers to a form utility that results from production, time, and place utilities created by logistics.

Value Added The value added to the product or service through the utility created by the logistics function.

Value Creation Value is created when the performance quality meets or exceeds customer perceptions of logistics service.

Vehicle Standards The requirements imposed by the National Highway Transportation Safety Administration for the design and manufacture of motor vehicles.

Voyage Charter A rental or term lease that includes both the vessel and crew and is for a specific trip.

Author Index

I

J

K

L

M

N

O

P

R

S

T

Subject Index

D

E

F

I

N

Q

R

S

T

U